D1108042

American Women Stage Directors of the Twentieth Century

American Women
Stage Directors
of the Twentieth Century

Anne Fliotsos
and Wendy Vierow

University of Illinois Press

Urbana and Chicago

© 2008 by Anne Fliotsos and Wendy Vierow
All rights reserved
Manufactured in the United States of America
C 5 4 3 2 1
∞ This book is printed on acid-free paper.

Library of Congress Cataloging-in-Publication Data
Fliotsos, Anne L., 1964–
American women stage directors of the twentieth
century / Anne Fliotsos and Wendy Vierow.
p.   cm.
Includes bibliographical references and index.
ISBN-13: 978-0-252-03226-4 (cloth : alk. paper)
ISBN-10: 0-252-03226-8 (cloth : alk. paper)
1. Women theatrical producers and directors—
United States—Biography.
I. Vierow, Wendy. II. Title.
PN2286.8.F55   2007
792.02'33092273—dc22 [B]   2007023277

Contents

Illustrations follow page 202

Acknowledgments

Our heartfelt gratitude goes to the directors, their families, and their colleagues who gave their time to be interviewed and sent materials to us. We were delighted to find sources who were happy to tell us about their careers and who also expressed their gratitude for our work in putting this study together. Our thanks, too, to the theatre staff members who sent us headshots and resumes, making the book more complete and visually appealing. The librarians at the Billy Rose Theatre Collection in the New York Public Library for Performing Arts at Lincoln Center deserve our acknowledgment for their helpfulness as well.

Anne Fliotsos wishes to thank the Dean of the College of Liberal Arts at Purdue University for several Dean's Incentive Grants, the Purdue Research Foundation for a Summer Faculty Grant, and the Purdue Library for their Library Scholar's Grant, all of which provided financial support to conduct this research. Wendy Vierow would like to thank Brooks McNamara, May Joseph, Carol Martin, John Bell, and most importantly, Richard Schechner, for their guidance on her dissertation, which served as a source for this book.

Our thanks goes to the support and enthusiasm of our editor, Joan Catapano, at the University of Illinois Press, who believed this was an important study, and to the many support staff who helped put this book into print. Their editing and consultations have made this a stronger volume, as have the comments from our outside evaluators.

We thank our colleagues who have given us valuable feedback, including Rich Rand, Suzanne Bennett, Susan Jonas, Cheryl Black, and Jeannie Woods.

Finally, we thank our spouses, Eric Felix and Chris Whitaker, and our families for their support, encouragement, and patience on this journey of discovery.

Introduction

Although women directors came into the spotlight in 1998 when Garry Hynes and Julie Taymor became the first women ever to receive Tony Awards for Best Director and Best Director of a Musical, women directors still struggle for recognition and steady work. On Broadway, where salaries and recognition are the highest, the percentage of women directors is even lower. At the end of the twentieth century, the percentage of women directors on Broadway remained at approximately 8 percent, while the percentage of women directors Off Broadway increased to approximately 20 percent (Jonas 1998, 2, 11). By the beginning of the twenty-first century, women directed approximately 16 percent of productions in Theatre Communications Group theatres, which include nonprofit theatres in New York City and regional theatres across the country (Jonas and Bennett 2002, 3). Although there are fewer women than men working in the field of directing, these statistics do not reflect the corresponding percentages in union membership.[1]

Considering the 1998 benchmark event of Taymor and Hynes winning Tony Awards for directing, the time is ripe to look back to those who have paved the way throughout the twentieth century. Many women directors want to be studied based not on their gender but on their artistic talent and achievements. We understand their position but also realize that women have not been equally represented in this profession, nor have their accomplishments been well chronicled. In addition to presenting a historical and contextual overview of women in directing, this book profiles fifty women who have made significant contributions in professional directing, mainly through directing on and Off Broadway but also through their work in regional theatres and stock theatres across the United States.

Literature on Women Directors

Although women's careers in theatre have received recent attention, the tale of women's battles and victories as stage directors has been largely ignored by scholars. In conducting our own research, we discovered that it was difficult to find material on women directors. Interviews and articles are scattered when they exist at all, and often women directors make up only a small percentage of entries in reference books. The study of directors is particularly challenging, for their work is ephemeral. Production reviews, articles, and published interviews cannot completely do justice in describing a director's work or aesthetic approach. Furthermore, interviews capture only one point in the span of a director's career, providing a snapshot of her current methods and ideas. Despite these obstacles, several authors have fought to chronicle the works of these impresarios of the theatre. Our goal is to provide both information about each of the women directors and sources to consult for further study.

Although no other volume focuses on the careers of women directors in the United States over the course of the twentieth century, several books about great directors deserve mention for their relationship to this topic. *The Director's Voice* (1988), by Arthur Bartow; *The Great Stage Directors: 100 Distinguished Careers of the Theater* (1994), by Samuel Leiter; *Theatrical Directors: A Biographical Dictionary* (1994), edited by John W. Frick and Stephen M. Vallillo; and *Fifty Key Theatre Directors* (2005), edited by Shomit Mitter and Maria Shevtosova, all contribute greatly to our knowledge of directors and their methods. However, the percentage of women included in these books is small. Books addressing women in theatre, such as *Notable Women in the American Theatre: A Biographical Dictionary* (1989), edited by Alice M. Robinson, Vera Mowry Roberts, and Milly S. Barranger, or *Women in American Theatre* (2006), edited by Helen Krich Chinoy and Linda Walsh Jenkins, must split coverage to include actors, playwrights, directors, artistic directors, producers, and designers. Consequently, little attention is paid to women directors in particular, though the contribution to the study of women in theatre is exceptional. Three books specifically about women directors are excellent sources of information but with particular focal points: Helen Manfull's *In Other Words: Women Directors Speak* (1997) examines only British directors; Rebecca Daniels's *Women Stage Directors Speak: Exploring the Influence of Gender on Their Work* (1996) provides a gender study of women directors in the United States; and Ellen Donkin and Susan Clement's edited volume, *Upstaging Big Daddy: Directing Theatre as if Gender and Race Matter* (1993) analyzes feminist directors and their application of feminist theory to performance.

Scope, Arrangement, and Limitations

American Women Stage Directors of the Twentieth Century provides an excellent starting point for anyone researching women directors and their careers. Entries are alphabetical for easy access, with a chronological list of women directors in Appendix A. A list of sources appears after each entry, and a general bibliography on women and directing is included for those wishing to do further investigation into the field.

The selection of women to be included in this book was a difficult task, for many artistic directors, actors, choreographers, and playwrights also direct. We searched for women who had a significant impact as directors and for whom professional stage directing composed a significant portion, usually the primary portion, of their careers. Our criteria for selection were based on the criteria used in *Notable Women in the American Theatre:*

1. The individual should have been born in the United States or have had the major portion of her career in the United States;
2. The individual's achievements should have been important and significant in the American theatre;
3. The individual should have been influential in her own lifetime in the American theatre; and
4. A pioneering or innovative quality should have characterized the individual's contributions. (Robinson, Roberts, and Barranger 1989, xiv)

Secondarily, commercial success, such as breaking the glass ceiling on Broadway, was considered to be as important as artistic innovations in lesser-known theatres. Directing awards, grants, and other honors were taken into consideration, and we also strived to include ethnic and geographic diversity and to represent women over the entire course of the century. The resulting list of women includes a diverse mix of artists who deserve our attention.

Each entry includes brief biographical material, a chronology of the woman's career in directing, excerpts from reviews, a description of the director's approach to casting and rehearsal (when available), and a summary of the director's legacy or contributions, including directing awards or professional achievements. "Representative Directing Credits," found at the end of each entry, include plays, dance-theatre, performance art, musicals, and operettas. Directing credits are divided by types of venue: Broadway, Off and Off-Off Broadway, regional theatre (and stock, when required), tours, international theatre, and other.[2] Opera, community theatre, educational theatre, and other non-professional theatre credits are excluded from the list of credits but may be referred to in the entries themselves.

There are several limitations to this study. As noted, the act of directing is ephemeral, and research data often are extremely limited, particularly for early directors. Newspaper reviews from the early twentieth century often bypassed the director's contributions, focusing instead on the script and the acting. In addition, the terminology was in flux. The terms *director* and *producer* were sometimes used interchangeably. In cases where women directors were also company managers, the word *director* could easily apply to a woman's work as a company (or managing) director rather than as the stage director of a particular production. In some cases the names of women directors emerged from historical accounts, but little or nothing was recorded about their work as stage directors. In such cases, these women have been included only in the historical overview here, not as separate entries in the book. Although we are keenly aware of the problems of balancing a personal life while building a career, biographical material is limited to that which is considered most pertinent to the women's careers; as a rule, marriages, divorces, and births are noted only when the women brought them up in interviews or these events were judged to have an immediate influence on their careers. We have also limited the list of "Representative Directing Credits" at the end of each entry to represent the directors' careers over time. With some women directing hundreds of productions, not every credit could be included.

Historical Overview: Western Precedents to the Modern Director

The concept of a theatrical director is a modern phenomenon that most historians trace to the mid-nineteenth century and the work of Georg II, Duke of Saxe-Meiningen. Despite the fairly recent appearance of the stage director in theatrical history, actors, managers, playwrights, and others have performed many of the functions of the modern director in the past.[3] In ancient Greece, playwrights assumed various directorial functions, such as casting and working with actors to interpret the script. In some cases a separate *didaskalos*, or teacher, was hired to coach the chorus. In Roman theatre, an actor-manager, or *dominus*, organized rehearsals and performances, made arrangements for costumes, hired musicians, bought plays, and kept track of financial transactions. The managerial figure of the Middle Ages, sometimes called the ordinal, prompted the amateur actors during performance and coordinated the stage machinery and special effects that dominated the spectacular cycle plays of the High Middle Ages. During the Renaissance, many responsibilities of the director were divided among the stage manager, the leading actor, the company manager, and the playwright. Likewise in the seventeenth and eighteenth centuries, there were numerous playwright-managers and actor-managers who coached actors and took responsibility for basic staging. One such figure was Molière (Jean Baptiste Poquelin), who provided evidence of his rehearsal technique in *The Rehearsal at Versailles,* in which he played himself and coached his actors' characterization, line delivery, blocking, and physical business.

For centuries a string of men dominated as leaders of theatrical production work. For example, Conrad Ekhof, an eighteenth-century German, took on numerous directorial functions for the Court Theatre. Another German, playwright Johann Wolfgang Goethe, took responsibility for casting and coaching actors in the early nineteenth century, stating that he "explained to every actor his one part . . . and talked with the actors as to any improvements that might be made" (Goethe 1874, 426). In a similar vein, French playwright Victor Hugo gained a reputation for his staging techniques, which broke with tradition and caused rioting. Many others paved the way before Germany's Duke of Saxe-Meiningen solidified the new trend toward creating an illusion of reality in scenery and costumes as well as acting. Meiningen became known for his attention to detail and, more importantly, for the unification of all of the production elements—costumes, scenery, properties, and lifelike acting—to form a whole, coherent picture on stage. Unlike his predecessors, who shared the tasks of directing with those of playwriting, stage managing, or acting, he specialized in creating a world of illusion and dynamic action on stage. His touring productions inspired others, such as Constantin Stanislavski and André Antoine, to start their own explorations with realism and naturalism. By the late nineteenth century, theatre had changed sufficiently to create a need for such a person—for one director to coordinate the increasingly complex technical aspects and orchestrate realistic detail.[4]

Women Managers

The precursors to the modern director of Western theatre have been almost exclusively men, for historically women were relegated to positions as performers or occasionally playwrights, if allowed to participate in theatricals at all. Though women are commonly excluded in the history of directing, Rosamond Gilder highlights early women director-managers and actor-managers in her book *Enter the Actress,* published in 1931. Eighteenth- and nineteenth-century European women such as Carolina Neuber, Marguerite Brunet (known as La Montansier), and Madame Vestris helped to pave the way for the women managers and directors who followed.

Born Friederike Carolina Weissenborn (1697–1760), Carolina Neuber and her husband, Johann, formed an acting troupe in Germany that toured Europe from 1725 to 1750. Decrying the lamentable state of German theatre, Neuber created managerial rules for the troupe and is most famous for her collaboration with critic Johann Gottsched, for together they worked to improve the state and status of German theatre through a number of reforms. Part of Neuber's quest was to refine the German acting style by emulating the French troupes of the period. Gottsched pressed for emulation of French neoclassical plays as well, arguing that French scripts be translated into German until native playwrights could match their literary value. Neuber's contributions extended to the rehearsal hall, where she staged her company's plays. She insisted on carefully memorized lines in rehearsals, with attention to rhythm and meter. Gilder writes, "For the first time in the history of the German theatre, stage business was worked out in detail. Neuber was as much interested in the movement and grouping of her actors as in their individual performance. She had the true director's sense for mass effects and was the first woman to earn a reputation for the way she handled her crowds" (1931, 214). Neuber was fond of scenic devices and effects, and though her theatre company traveled, she endeavored to bring as much splendor to her productions as possible.

Marguerite Brunet (1730–1820), known as La Montansier, was a manager, theatre owner, "directress," and key figure of the cultural life of eighteenth-century France (Gilder 1931, 227). By the time of her death at age ninety, Montansier had owned and managed a number of French theatres, including several provincial theatres, the Théâtre Montansier in the Palais Royal in Paris, and a theatre at Versailles that was popular with the royal court. At one point in her career, she schemed to create a monopoly to own all the theatres in France, but she was unsuccessful. The entrepreneur was of simple birth and led a colorful life, which led to her imprisonment on more than one occasion. Despite her questionable social status, Marie Antoinette frequented La Montansier's theatres, keeping the theatre proprietor in the limelight during the monarchy but making her suspect during the French Revolution. Gilder calls La Montansier "the first business manager and directress of the European theatre" but provides little information about her actual work with actors or the physical staging of productions. One of the few descriptions, a critique of Dubuisson's operetta *Le Roi Théodore à Venise* in 1787, reflects very well on La Montansier's staging: "The execution of the grand finale of the second act was perfection . . . not only on account of the precision and excellence of the *ensemble,* but also and more especially because of the way the whole scene has been conceived, the continuous movement of the actors, carried out without confusion and without distracting attention from the scene." Along with Neuber, Gilder calls Montansier "one of the first directors to understand and make use of crowd effects" (1931, 239). Notably, Montansier did not come to the profession as an actor, in the tradition of actor-managers. Instead, her sole intent was theatre ownership and production, and she was a true pioneer as a woman in those fields.

Madame Vestris (Lucia Elizabetta Bartolozzi, 1797–1856) was a well-known actor in burlesques, extravaganzas, and comedies but is best remembered for her pioneering role as the proprietor of the Olympic Theatre in London and later as the manager of London's Covent Garden and Lyceum theatres. Although other women had managed theatres in England, none had the success and lasting power of Vestris. She began as an actor and became a popular performer in her own right, but Vestris was not content with merely treading the boards. Gilder suggests that her brief experience at the Haymarket Theatre as an assistant stage manager fueled her pursuit of theatre management and staging. Perhaps it was Vestris's experience performing with the famous classical actor Talma in Paris that set her artistic inclinations toward more realistic productions than England had known. In France she was exposed to a new school of acting that Talma had introduced and was shocked at his dedication to historical accuracy when he donned a toga, sans breeches, to play Horace, a practice unheard of at the time. Later, in her own theatres, Vestris was known for bringing similar innovations in costume and scenic design to the English stage, a practice that delighted her audience and added to her popularity. Vestris worked diligently with the actors and unified the production through close attention to details of the set, costumes, and props. Gilder writes, "No manager had as yet attempted anything as revolutionary as Vestris did in inaugurating the custom of rehearsals. She was careful of every detail of her productions, and when she was not on the stage herself, she would watch the play from a box, checking up on any slovenly performance and assuring herself that the stage effects were as fresh and successful on the last as on the first night" (1931, 275). As a further measure of her desire for realistic staging, she introduced the box set, complete with ceilings, to England in 1832. Like Neuber before her, Vestris is remembered not only as a pioneering woman in management but as a reformer whose ideas and practices changed the world of theatre around her.

In the United States, Laura Keene (1826–1873) was the most famous woman to pave the way in theatre management and staging in the nineteenth century, though there were others, such as Anne Brunton Merry, Charlotte Cushman, Catherine Sinclair, Louise Lane Drew, and Matilda Viney Wood. Born Mary Moss in England, Keene briefly acted for Vestris's company at the Lyceum before launching her acting career in the United States. She undertook management of the Charles Street Theatre in Baltimore for several months in 1853 before traveling to California to both act and manage. In 1855 she leased the Metropolitan Theatre in New York and opened Laura Keene's Varieties, facing strong opposition from the male managers of New York's commercial theatres. In the face of vandalism, libelous newspaper reports, and the loss of her lease, Keene built a new building, the Laura Keene Theatre, which she managed until 1863. After her adventures as a theatre proprietor in New York, Keene formed and managed a touring company and later managed the Chestnut Street Theatre in Philadelphia, albeit briefly. Despite her virtues as a stage actor, her tenacity in the face of opposition, and her ability to make her theatres both profitable and popular, Keene is most remembered for her role in bringing *Our American Cousin* to Ford's Theatre the night President Lincoln was assassinated. Keene's nickname, The Duchess, reflects her unrelenting discipline in rehearsal and production. She was a stickler for detail, and her extravaganzas and burlesques were lavish in their sets and costumes, attracting an appreciative audience.

Women Directors in the American Theatre

By the late nineteenth and early twentieth centuries, the role of the modern director was being defined and developed. European theorists and practitioners such as Edward Gordon Craig and André Antoine struggled to define both the artistic and managerial aspects that characterized this position of authority. More women were directing during this pivotal period of growth and exploration, though their contributions are largely invisible in the annals of history, for many of their efforts were not on the commercial stage but in private homes, educational institutions, little theatres, and other amateur ventures across the nation. Most often, women directors came from the ranks of playwrights, actors, and managers. Two actresses, **Minnie Maddern Fiske** and **Jessie Bonstelle**, made the jump to producing and directing their own theatres early in the twentieth century.[5] In addition, playwright–director **Rachel Crothers** probably made her directing debut on Broadway in 1908, with her play *Myself Bettina*.

During this early phase of the era of the modern director, Nina Moise and Ida Rauh deserve special attention as directors for Provincetown Players, an early art theatre that launched careers of such notable playwrights as Eugene O'Neill and Susan Glaspell. Moise was the most prolific director of Provincetown Players, directing seventeen productions and co-directing three from January 1917 to May 1918, including four plays by O'Neill and five by Glaspell. Provincetown historian Cheryl Black named Moise the most influential director of the group, "largely responsible for the shift in the company's directing methods from collectivism to specialization." Moise's artistry and leadership earned the trust of O'Neill, who confessed to her, "You know my work and understand the spirit underlying it as few people do—I have complete confidence in your direction" (Black 2002, 99). Moise left the company abruptly in 1918 but continued in her career as director, manager, and coach. In 1921 she became the company director of the Santa Barbara Community Arts Players, where she staged at least nine plays, and in the 1930s Moise became a dialogue director for Paramount and assistant director to Cecil B. DeMille.

In contrast to Moise, who came to Provincetown Players specifically to direct, Ida Rauh was Provincetown Players' leading actress, and she directed five productions for the group. In 1919 she directed O'Neill's *The Dreamy Kid,* for which she recruited African American performers from Harlem rather than bending to the custom of blackface. Rauh later organized and directed the Santa Fe Players and co-founded the Workers Drama League in 1926. She continued with her primary career as an actor as well, and in 1937 Rauh became one of the few women to direct on Broadway, with *Murder Sails at Midnight.* Other women from Provincetown Players jumped into the fray as directors as well, though not with such frequency or lasting effect as Moise and Rauh.

In the 1910s women directed less than five percent of the plays on Broadway, and the majority of those women also wrote the plays they directed (Housely 1993, 107). By the 1920s and 1930s, however, women directors showed a stronger presence. Some of the earliest pioneering directors included **Agnes Morgan, Antoinette Perry,** and **Eva Le Gallienne,** all of whom had directed on Broadway by 1930. Several African American women were producing directors of theatre companies during this era, including Anita Bush, who founded the Lafayette Players (originally the Anita Bush Stock Company) in Harlem; Ida Anderson, whose company toured major U.S. cities; and Abbie Mitchell, who staged productions in Harlem for the Frederick Douglass Players as well as her own company (Black, correspondence, 2007).

Many women who directed in the first half of the twentieth century received little critical recognition because they directed for colleges, little theatres, or other amateur theatricals. For example, Margaret Anglin, an actress-manager and director from the turn of the century, staged many Greek tragedies in the 1910s and 1920s, starting at the University of California, Berkeley, though she remains fairly unknown. Constance D'Arcy Mackay was a famous writer of children's pageants in the 1910s and 1920s and directed her own plays, though her work received little attention until Brook Davis's dissertation, "Constance D'Arcy Mackay: Playwright, Director, and Educator," in 1999. Winifred Ward co-founded Illinois's Children's Theatre of Evanston in 1925, where she also directed and wrote plays, though her career as producer and playwright was more prominent. In a similar vein, sisters Alice and Irene Lewisohn founded New York's Neighborhood Playhouse in 1915 and sometimes directed, though their work as producers was primary. Clearly, women were directing, though their directing work was not always at the forefront of their careers.

Hallie Flanagan's name has earned a place in the annals of theatre history as a producer and head of the Federal Theatre Project from 1935 to its dissolution in 1939. Her stage directing at Vassar College deserves further recognition, for she was one of the early proponents of experimentation based on the work of Russian artists Constantin Stanislavski, Alexander Tairov, and Vsevelod Meyerhold. Scholar Fran Hassencahl writes, "The Vassar theatre under Flanagan in the years 1925 to 1942 gained a reputation as one of America's leading experimental theatres. Broadway critics journeyed up from New York for major productions, theatre leaders abroad were impressed, and Vassar students devoted enthusiastic energy to their director. . . . Most innovative were the productions of Shakespeare's *Antony and Cleopatra* in 1934, Chekhov's *The Marriage Proposal* in 1933—first seen as a realistic drama, then as an expressionistic and constructivist drama all in the same evening—and *Can You Hear Their Voices* in 1931" (Robinson, Roberts, and Barranger 1989, 291). Flanagan chronicles these fertile years in her book *Dynamo,* published in 1943.

Another producer who directed in this period was Cheryl Crawford, one of three directors of the Group Theatre from its founding in 1931 to her resignation in 1937. Crawford primarily took charge of many of the financial and managerial duties of the Group and somewhat reluctantly directed three productions: Dawn Powell's *Big Night* in 1933, Clifford Odets's *Till the Day I Die* in 1935, and Nelisse Childs's *Weep for the Virgins,* also in 1935. She went on to an illustrious career as a producer on Broadway and elsewhere. She also co-founded the American Repertory Theatre in 1946, the Actors Studio in 1947, and served in a managerial and producing capacity for both.

In addition to the aforementioned women, several women were making their marks first as actors or playwrights, then as directors in this first wave of pioneering women directors.[6] **Osceola Archer, Mary Hunter,** and **Margaret Webster** all followed the path from acting to directing. In addition, although little is known of actor Rose McClendon's direction, she was a director for the Negro Experimental Theatre (also known as the Harlem Experimental Theatre) in the late 1920s. Actor Evelyn Ellis directed a children's play, Dorothy Hailparn's *Horse Play,* for the Negro Theatre Unit of the Federal Theatre Project in 1937 and later directed and performed in the Broadway revival of Jack Kirkland's *Tobacco Road* in 1950, making her one of the first African American women to direct on Broadway.[7] Playwright and novelist Rose Dorothy Lewin Franken sometimes directed her own work, including her Broadway hit *Claudia* in 1941, and subsequent Broadway productions of *Outrageous Fortune* and *Soldier's Wife.*

Several women were at the forefront of the regional theatre movement in the first half of the century, serving as both producers and directors. **Margo Jones** founded the Dallas Civic Theatre in Dallas, Texas; **Nina Vance** founded the Alley Theatre in Houston, Texas; and **Zelda Fichandler** co-founded the

Arena Stage in Washington, D.C. All three were frequent directors at their theatres and set a precedent for the many women to follow in their footsteps in the later half of the century. On a similar note, **Dorothy Raedler** started an Equity company in New York City, The American Savoyards, who specialized in the operettas of Gilbert and Sullivan.

Although women had directed plays on Broadway, they had much more difficulty getting hired for Broadway's cash cow: the musical. During the golden age of musical theatre, roughly from the 1940s to mid-1960s, women found themselves confronted with a prejudice from producers: they were rarely trusted to handle the big budgets, large casts, and enormous design demands of a Broadway musical.[8] In addition, shifting cultural attitudes during the postwar years led to a decline of women in the workplace. Once men occupied their former positions in the workforce, women were relegated to the home, as housewives and mothers. Historian Helen Housely's statistics attest to the decline of women directing on Broadway at mid-century: from 1945 to 1950 women directed an average of 11.6 percent of Broadway productions, but from 1951 to 1961 the average plummeted to 2 percent (1993, 112).

Several British women were breaking the Broadway barrier by directing in the late 1940s and 1950s and deserve mention here, though their careers in the United States were fleeting. Anna Bethnell and Eleanor Evans directed Gilbert and Sullivan operettas with the touring D'Oyly Carte Opera Company in the 1947–48 and 1950–51 seasons, respectively. Bethnell directed seven productions in repertory and Evans four, all on Broadway stages. In addition, Vida Hope directed Sandy Wilson's *The Boy Friend* in London, then on Broadway in the 1954–55 season, though the producers barred Hope and Wilson from rehearsals shortly before opening, citing artistic differences. Hope did not press charges but did retain credit for the direction of the musical.

The 1960s brought substantial societal changes, particularly for women and people of color. It is not surprising that the next wave of pioneering directors includes a number of African American women making their voices heard. **Vinnette Carroll, Shauneille Perry, Barbara Ann Teer,** and **Glenda Dickerson** all made their marks as African American women directors in the 1960s and beyond. Carroll, Teer, and Dickerson often directed performances they created themselves, drawing from African ritual and other cultural traditions. In addition, women of various cultural and ethnic backgrounds stepped forward to add their directorial voices in the 1960s and 1970s, then into the 1980s. **Maria Irene Fornes** immigrated from Cuba and quickly became associated with both feminist theatre and Hispanic theatre; **Margarita Galban,** also from Cuba, became co-founder and artistic director of Los Angeles's Bilingual Foundation of the Arts. **Muriel Miguel,** a Native American, became co-founder of Spiderwoman Theater, a women's theatre steeped in Native

American traditions. **Graciela Daniele,** born in Argentina, became a celebrated director–choreographer on Broadway. In addition, **Tisa Chang** formed New York's Pan Asian Repertory Theatre, where she is artistic director.

The cultural revolution and questioning of tradition in the 1960s also spurred women to direct experimental productions. Two early leaders in the movement were **Judith Malina,** co-founder of The Living Theatre, and **JoAnne Akalaitis,** one of the founders of Mabou Mines. Several experimentalists were also involved in the feminist theatre movement. **Martha Boesing** was a founding member of the women's collective, At the Foot of the Mountain, in Minneapolis, where she directed. Working primarily in New York, Roberta Sklar helped establish the Off-Off Broadway movement, directing at Café Cino and La MaMa ETC (Experimental Theatre Club), founded by **Ellen Stewart,** who later went on to direct productions at her venue and abroad. Sklar also co-directed with Joseph Chaikin at the Open Theatre before helping to create the Womanrite Theatre Ensemble and Women's Experimental Theatre. Later in the century, experimental women directors such as **Meredith Monk, Martha Clarke,** and **Elizabeth LeCompte** blended different genres and media to create performance art pieces. A more recent wave of experimentalists includes such director–auteurs as **Anne Bogart, Julie Taymor,** and **Mary Zimmerman.**[9]

Many other women have made a name for themselves primarily through freelance directing across the country. One of the trailblazers, **Sue Lawless,** was among the first women to direct at many of the nation's finest stock and regional theatres. Other freelance directors of excellent repute include **Roberta Levitow, Pamela Berlin, Liz Diamond, Gloria Muzio,** and **Tina Landau,** as well as Melia Bensussen, Pamela Hunt, Amy Saltz, Seret Scott, and Evan Yionoulis, to name a few. In addition, many women started as freelance directors and either founded their own theatres or otherwise ascended into the administrative capacity of artistic directors at some of the nation's top regional theatres, where they continue to direct. In the 1980s there were only a handful, but now the list is long: **Libby Appel,** former artistic director at the Indiana Repertory Theatre and at the Oregon Shakespeare Festival; **Tina Packer,** founder and artistic director of Shakespeare & Company; **Lynne Meadow,** artistic director of the Manhattan Theatre Club; **Josephine Abady,** former artistic director for the Berkshire Theatre Festival, the Cleveland Play House, and New York City's Circle in the Square; **Carole Rothman,** co-founder and artistic director of Second Stage Theatre; **Sharon Ott,** former artistic director of the Berkeley Repertory Theatre and the Seattle Repertory Theatre; **Emily Mann,** artistic director at the McCarter Theatre; **Mary B. Robinson,** former artistic director of the Philadelphia Drama Guild; and **Carey Perloff,** artistic director of the American Conservatory Theatre (A.C.T.) and former artistic director of Classic Stage Company. The list is far from complete and continues to grow.[10]

After a period of almost no women directing Broadway musicals in the 1950s and early 1960s, a few American women pioneers began directing musicals on Broadway, including **Julianne Boyd** and **Susan H. Schulman,** both of whom have sustained successful directing careers. A more recent trend for women directing Broadway musicals has been the growing list of well-known director–choreographers. Following **Graciela Daniele's** lead, choreographer Lynne Taylor-Corbett made her debut directing (and choreographing) the dance musical *Swing* in 1999, which won a Tony as Best Musical and earned her a Tony nomination as Best Director. **Susan Stroman*** made her directorial debut on Broadway in 2000 with *The Music Man* and *Contact,* both of which earned her nominations for Tony Awards in directing and choreography, then won a Tony Award as Best Director for *The Producers* the next year. In their footsteps, choreographer Kathleen Marshall took on the directing mantle for the Broadway revivals of *Wonderful Town* in 2003, *The Pajama Game* in 2006, and *Grease* in 2007. She earned nominations for Tony Awards for Best Director of a Musical for *Wonderful Town* and *The Pajama Game,* and won Tony Awards for Best Choreography for both productions.

Gender Issues: An Overview

Although some women directors dislike being categorized according to their gender, many included in this book have experienced problems in their careers based on gender. Because many of the problems that women directors experience are similar, common issues are examined here rather than detailed in individual entries.

From the beginning of the twentieth century, women directors have struggled to obtain work and recognition. Before her marriage to newspaper editor Harrison Fiske, Minnie Maddern Fiske received her own directing credits. After their marriage, Harrison Fiske participated in his wife's career and shared directing credits with her. Often, Harrison Fiske received a directing credit at the top of a theatre program whereas Maddern Fiske received one, in small print, at the bottom, lessening the perception of her contribution as a director.

Near the end of the century, Taymor and Hynes were the first women to win Tony Awards for Direction of a Musical and Direction of a Play, creating the illusion that women directors were finally on equal footing with men. However, these awards are misleading. From the beginning of the Tony Awards in 1947 to 2007 only nine women were nominated for Best Direction of a Play (two of whom won) and eighteen women for Best Direction of a Musical (two of whom won) (see Appendix B, pp. 450–51). In 2000, a record three women were nominated for Best Direction of a Musical. However, the sole man,

Michael Blakemore, won the award for *Kiss Me Kate*—ironically a musical based on a play about taming the spirit of an independent woman.

The Tony Award nominations indicate a better acceptance of women as director–choreographers than strictly as directors. Rothman notes that women have made great strides in moving from the position of choreographer, where women have been traditionally accepted, to director–choreographer, a field previously dominated by men such as Bob Fosse and Michael Bennett. She explains that women director–choreographers "have a lot of power in the theatre right now, and have had for a while. So I think that there's been a lot more acceptance of women, and there are many, many more that are working. I don't know how many more [women] are directing plays on Broadway— that's still tough" (Interview, 2004).

Society and Communication

Like many American women in positions of authority, women directors face obstacles stemming from differences in the ways men and women communicate in society. In the 1990s, a number of women directors, who were also artistic directors, were dismissed from their theatres. The problems that these women experienced with each theatre's board of directors are similar to problems that most women directors in the commercial theatre face when confronted by a team of mostly male producers.

Bogart, who was dismissed from Rhode Island's Trinity Repertory Company in 1990 after only one year, believes that her democratic management style was problematic for the theatre's mostly male board. She explains, "They weren't used to it. The organizations they worked for—banks or law firms—weren't run that way." In addition, she says, "Women are trusted less, in general. People are not used to having women in positions of power. If I were a man, I would not have been thrown out after a year. I would have been given a chance to do another season" (Dace 1994, 20).

Scholar and writer Deborah Tannen conducted studies on gender communication that gives insight into the discrepancies between male and female patterns of interaction. In a study of children, she found that boys tend to be openly competitive within a hierarchical organization and strive for status and a place from which to give orders that others follow. In contrast, girls, who value intimacy, are not as comfortable in a hierarchical structure (Tannen 1990, 46–47). Tannen explains, "Appearing better than others is a violation of the girls' organization ethic: People are supposed to stress connections and similarity" (217).

Akalaitis, who served as artistic director of the New York Shakespeare Festival from August 1991 until her dismissal in March 1993, sees communication style as a problem for women. She explains, "When I would go to meetings with producers, if there were myself and two men, one man would address the other man. His body language would be geared toward the man. I noticed it all the time. In a meeting, the people who were talked to were the men and not the women. It was probably unconscious. . . . But somehow the culture empowers men to turn their bodies away from women because women are erasable" (Dace 1994, 21).

Abady, who was artistic director of Ohio's Cleveland Play House from 1988 until 1994, discusses her dismissal, saying, "People cut men more of a break. Boards—mostly male businessmen, especially the executive boards—feel more comfortable with men in the job than with women. They're more forgiving of the difficulties that men encounter than those women do. My predecessor at Cleveland was there for 30 years; he had some good years and some bad. At the end of his tenure his work wasn't terrific, but the board kept him on despite their dissatisfaction. After six years, when times got a little tough, the board let the girl go" (Dace 1994, 23).

Acting as an authoritative figure can have negative consequences for women directors no matter how they choose to handle a situation. If women wield authority in a different style from men, it is seen as abnormal. A democratic management style may seem alien and weak to those who are used to ruling by fiat. However, when women wield authority in the same way that men do, it is also seen as abnormal. Tannen discusses how our society associates authority with masculine qualities and what happens when women attempt to take on positions of authority. She explains, "Ways of talking associated with masculinity [speaking louder, longer, with more assertion] are also associated with leadership and authority. But ways of talking that are feminine are not. Whatever a man does to enhance his authority also enhances his masculinity. But if a woman adapts her style to a position of authority . . . she risks compromising her femininity in the eyes of others. . . . If a man appears forceful, logical, direct, masterful, and powerful he enhances his value as a man. If a woman [does this] . . . she risks undercutting her value as a woman" (1990, 240–41).

A woman dealing primarily with men in the commercial theatre may need to adapt a different mode of communication, which can be stressful and put her at a disadvantage. Tannen believes that when women participate in mixed gender groups, they often adjust their communication style and interact according to men's norms (1990, 235).

Sometimes women directors have problems asserting their authority, a necessary requirement for the job. Bogart explains, "I think it's harder for me to go to a regional theatre and demand a higher budget, my own designers, actors of my choice. I find that men are forgiven more for throwing tantrums and making demands. This is not an original thought by any means, but the minute a woman makes a demand, which directors tend to do, they're seen as temperamental. So I'm very self-effacing, and I think that has to do with conditioning" (Daniels 1996, 83–84).

A double standard in temperament is an issue for women directors as well. Taymor notes that a poor temperament is accepted as part of the creative spirit in men but frowned upon when occurring in women. She explains, "I've wondered about—why an 'enfant terrible' is a male-dominated sort of identity. . . . When a woman has that kind of temperament it's usually said she's a bitch as a director. It's very acceptable for men to have the kind of personalities where it doesn't matter if you like them as directors. They're such geniuses, they're so brilliant that people do what they say because of the prestige of being in this man's production" (Daniels 1996, 77).

Labels such as "dragon lady" or "bitch," are at times applied to strong women directors. Chang notes, "I have a reputation for being a dragon lady, or overly strong" (Daniels 1996, 74). Ott acknowledges the problem of labels, saying, "When a woman gets mad, it's perceived in a different way . . . often that she's being bitchy; when a man gets angry, it's not usually given that sort of adjective. It's the crucial issue. If you can't exert strength, how can you be in a powerful position?" (75).

Women may also have issues of low self-esteem that inhibit their sense of authority. Perloff explains, "I see that we have both made radical strides and are carrying around this internal voice that tells us we are not worthy of being at the center of our story. . . . How do we rewrite that to see ourselves at the center of a narrative? Because until we do, we will always be marginalized" (Women's Project 1997, 55).

Levitow says that even though her mother raised her to be a strong woman, she still finds herself struggling when it comes to dealing with conflict. She says, "I have, and I've seen others hesitate to follow through, which is really demeaning to our work. But we sense intuitively that if we're gonna go to the end choice on this, which we need to do as artists, we're gonna have to cross a line of comfort to a zone of discomfort and conflict. And then we're going to have to get through that conflict. We're going to have to get onto the other side of it and have it be okay. And I find that very hard" (Interview, 2004).

Working with Men

Some women have difficulties working with men who are technicians or actors. In the first part of the twentieth century, Antoinette Perry had difficulty directing older men. She said, "I was never a bossy woman . . . and it was really the most difficult thing for me to tell a man how he should behave under certain circumstances. But now that I am old and frumpy, they seem to have more respect for me and I can tell them whatever I please" (Crowther 1937, n.p.). As the century progressed, women continued to have problems directing men. Akalaitis notes, "[S]ome middle-aged male actors have a very hard time working with women directors" (Daniels 1996, 68). Chang observes that white male actors have tested her the most (74). Fornes has found that in some instances, she has "had to get into battle and prove that I know what I'm doing" (72).

Performers who are men have reacted to Mary Robinson's gender and her youth, making inappropriate comments. She says, "I can remember walking into a rehearsal when I was twenty-two years old, directing a play, a Shakespeare play, and having an actor say to me, 'Well, that's the way a woman would think, but this is a scene with men.' Or having somebody say to me early when I was directing *Of Mice and Men,* which is a very male play, 'You're going to learn a lot about men in this process.' You know, comments like that. They wouldn't say that to a man. I remember once walking into rehearsal and a man whom I had cast . . . but had not met face to face said, 'My god, you're young enough to be my daughter.' I bet he wouldn't have said, 'You're young enough to be my son'" (Daniels 1996, 68).

Gender and Play Selection

Gender stereotyping also seems to play a role in plays women are hired to direct, thereby affecting the breadth of their careers. Muzio says that before she directed Off Broadway's *Other People's Money,* by Jerry Sterner, she was often offered sentimental plays and plays specifically about women's relationships. Muzio believes that *Other People's Money,* which had a strong leading male character and was about money and business, helped to change her career. Because the play was a hit, she was subsequently offered a greater variety of plays to direct.

Women directors who are also artistic directors have more control over the plays they direct. As artistic director of the McCarter Theatre, Mann presents a diverse selection of plays that include women and people of color, whereas the previous management had presented primarily the work of white European males. Mann discusses the problem women have with producers, saying, "You only produce that which deeply affects you, and if you are separated from the work by gender and race, then you truly have a slim chance of choosing to see the work produced. . . . White male producers present some of the hardest problems. The easiest play for a woman to place with a producer like that is romantic comedy" (Dace 1993, 23–24).

As an artistic director, Perloff has been criticized by critics for having a feminist agenda because she selected plays that dealt with issues in women's lives (Women's Project 1997, 54–55). Perloff discusses the power she has as an artistic director to select plays that she wants to direct. She says, "That's the greatest thing about having your own theatre. You think, 'I don't have to do this play . . . the play with the two brilliant men and the muse.' . . . And that is such a relief. . . . I'm so fascinated and thrilled by . . . women's stories, and how women navigate things. . . . It's only when you really go look, and you realize how hard it is to find them. . . . People will say to me, 'Why have you done so little Shakespeare?' And I think, 'I love Shakespeare but . . . I don't want to spend my time in a room in rehearsal with thirty men and two women.' . . . So you do Racine . . . or Greek tragedy—and those [protagonists] are all women. So I've tended to gravitate to classical literature. . . . [T]hose are the plays I've chosen. And it is conscious" (Interview, 2004).

As playwright, director, and artistic director for At the Foot of the Mountain, a women's collective theatre in Minneapolis, Martha Boesing had the unique opportunity to create performances drawing on her actors' life experiences. Having their own feminist theatre group meant that Boesing had the freedom to direct with political and social messages in an environment in which mainstream criticism was not of the utmost concern. Their theater was by, about, and for women. "I want desperately to hear the stories of these women knowing that then I will love them," Boesing wrote in her journal in 1976 (1996, 1012).

Getting and Keeping Work

Getting work is especially difficult for freelance women directors. Because white men still occupy most of the positions of power, they maintain financial control and make many of the decisions about hiring and firing. Statistics show that teams with only men producers are less likely to produce plays directed by women than teams that include women (Vierow 1997, 103–4). Women directors, such as Rothman, have been denied jobs because a woman wrote the play they hoped to direct, and producers felt that a team with a woman writer and director might spell financial doom (Rothman, interview, 1995).

Some women have chosen to run theatres as artistic directors in order to find steady employment as a director for themselves. Rothman explains, "I think that a lot of women run theatres and find that's a good way to start their work because they're going to be in a supportive atmosphere" (Interview, 1995). Of freelance directors, Rothman says, "If you do well, and you're successful, and you make a lot of money for somebody, then they'll continue to hire you. . . . I think that when it gets to Broadway, it's still a tough deal" (Interview, 2004).

Levitow notes how male directors seem to be able to better recover from failures than women. She calls this phenomenon "buoyancy," explaining, "I have seen a lot of my male colleagues be very buoyant after a failure. I've got to say I have seen very few women bounce back. I'm not sure what that is. . . . Is that the networking process? Or somebody's already committed to four jobs so when they get this miserable, horrible, humiliating review in *The New York Times* so what? . . . I see women who really never bounce back. And I don't think it's the women. I think we would bounce back. But I think somehow we're not given a second chance or a third chance . . . It's taken me some time to learn how to be a player, and not shrink, not overcompensate . . . when I've been hit. I think maybe I don't come back as easily as a man who knows that's the gig. . . . You have to be the bouncer backer. Nobody's going to come over to you and say, 'Come on little lady! Can I help you up?'" (Interview, 2004).

Broadway's Glass Ceiling

While women directors have made strides in regional theatre and Off-Off Broadway, their participation in Off Broadway and Broadway remains marginal. Although many women directors do not aspire to Broadway, there is a glass ceiling in the industry for those who do. Broadway offers directors a chance at national and international recognition and the highest salaries.

Women may be excluded from Broadway because it is where huge budgets and high salaries exist. Likewise, women are practically excluded from work in large-budget films and television, where, according to the Directors Guild of America, women directed only 12 percent of primetime television episodes in 2004–05 season ("DGA," 2006). Mann once made the connection that the reason women have been able to move into regional theatre is because the men left for Hollywood, where the money was better (Daniels 1996, 196). In addition, women who take positions as artistic directors often find that their male predecessors have left them with failing organizations. They inherit serious financial problems along with the opportunity to choose plays they want to direct and the chance to shape theatre in their communities. According to journalist Misha Berson, "The new wave of women (and men) replacing the old guard often walk into landmine situations" (1994, 19).

The New York State Council on the Arts Theatre Program's "Report on the Status of Women: A Limited Engagement?" in 2002 found a relationship between high budgets and a scarcity of women. The report noted, "Women, for a variety of reasons, fare better in the non-commercial arena, where resources, compensation, and status are lower. But even within the non-profit theatre landscape, the representation of women playwrights and directors is inversely related to budget. . . . And women are plentiful when resources are scant. . . . Furthermore, when women are present at theatres with significant resources, they are frequently relegated to readings, workshops, the 'second' stage, or to children's theatre" (Jonas and Bennett 2002, 3).

Muzio analyzes the gap between high budgets and jobs, stating, "Where you see the disparity is when it has to do with money. That somehow producers don't risk a million-dollar budget with a woman. You risk it with a man" (Interview, 2004). Perloff noted the relationship, stating, "Women directors rarely get the Shakespeare slot because that's the one that costs the most money in a season" (Winn 1991, E1). Fichandler discusses prejudices about money that exist on Broadway. She explains that historically Broadway "was a money medium . . . and men controlled the money, so men hired people that could protect the money which is mostly other men. . . . It's a type casting that men handle money better than women" (Hennigan 1983, 106). This can lead to a "Catch 22" situation in which women are not hired because they lack experience raising money for producers, and are unable to gain that experience through work. Lawless, who had only one opportunity to direct on Broadway, recalls, "I have had firsthand experiences that producers trying to raise money had trouble if it was [raised] for an 'unknown,' which, of course, pretty much said it all for a woman director. . . . They [producers] could legitimately claim that I had no history of making money for producers, but then again, I never had the chance" (Correspondence, 2000).

In addition to budget, other factors are at work, which limit job opportunities. Diamond explains, "It takes a woman longer to be trusted with a big production than a man. Unquestionably. . . . These are very deep unconscious impulses operating. Big play, big director. Kings, a lot of sword fights, you need to get a man" (Daniels 1996, 189). Perloff sums up the problem, explaining, "What I discovered at A.C.T. [American Conservatory Theatre] . . . is that we are all allowed to play in our sandboxes as long as they are relatively marginal. When it is a big sandbox, then it's a whole different thing" (Women's Project 1997, 53).

Lawless has her own idea of why Broadway was not attainable for her after one short-lived production: "There were many mitigating circumstances. The press wasn't as open about covering everything; they didn't hype directors; there was not interest in women as directors; there were not many awards or recognition for anybody. You just got jobs and worked, if you were lucky . . . [but] the one big chance never came. Could be said about a lot of people" (Correspondence, 2000). Despite her acceptance of not making it on Broadway, the idea that discrimination may have played a part still bothers her. Lawless states, "I never thought much about being prejudiced against, because I did get some chances. In a lot of cases it was to replace a man that they had already tried. But they were mostly losing propositions from the start and luck wasn't with me. It was only as I got older and had more credits that I wondered why

I was not given *more* chances. When I interviewed against men as opposed to having come with the project for whatever reason, the men always got the important jobs. . . . That I was a woman was, I have to believe, a large part, but there were other reasons. I never did get the chance or didn't have what it took to 'make it big.' I'll never know" (Correspondence, 2003).

One way for women to bypass the budget problem is to develop plays at their own theatres and then transfer them to Broadway. Women directors whose Broadway plays originated at their own theatres include Abady, Carroll, LeCompte, Le Gallienne, Mann, Meadow, Rothman, Webster, and Hunter. Although Zimmerman is not an artistic director, her affiliation with Chicago's Lookingglass Theatre and Goodman Theatre helped with the development of *Metamorphoses,* which she directed on Broadway in 2002. Rothman believes that transferring a play from your own theatre is the easiest way for a woman director to get to Broadway. She explains, "It's not so hard to get a play transferred to Broadway when you get great reviews in the *New York Times* and article after article about it" (Interview, 1995).

Some women directors get to Broadway via nonprofit theatres. The three plays that Muzio directed on Broadway were presented at the Roundabout, a not-for-profit theatre with a Broadway house. Muzio explains, "The major difference is that when you're doing a commercial Broadway play you're really dealing with a corporation. You're dealing with businessmen and investors, and it's a lot more money. It's much, much more money, and there's a lot of personal money at stake. . . . In not-for-profit you . . . have an audience subscription. It's not like the theatre is going to lose its supporters if you do a show that their audience doesn't like. The producers, however, have their careers . . . that's . . . their weight in getting investors. . . . Now if they produce a play that's not a success, they're not going to continue to work (Interview, 1995).

Critical Reviews

The paucity of women critics affects how women directors are perceived. As of 2007, Linda Winer was the only first-string woman theatre reviewer on a major New York daily newspaper, *Newsday* (Silverstein 2007). In the New York commercial theatre, critics can influence the life or death of a show. Rothman says, "The critics are male and they're not particularly interested in what women have to say. . . . Everything's perceived through their eyes, and we're told what's successful and what's not successful—how those male eyes view it. . . . You know, sometimes issues that women may ask about over and over again in our daily lives that don't go away seem trite and stale to a male critic" (Interview, 1995).

Julia Miles of the Women's Project, a theatre in New York City, believes the press is especially judgmental when it comes to women. She discusses Akalaitis's dismissal from New York City's Public Theater saying, "I don't think, if she had been a man, the press would have been so harsh on her. They didn't say anything about her great achievements, her unique vision, her influence on younger artists. Somehow people feel that either women are so strong that they can take it better than men, or they don't care and they just feel they can get away with not being as well mannered towards women as they are towards men" (Daniels 1996, 76).

Because women directors are so few, most critics and audience members are aware that they are viewing a play directed by a woman. Viewers may watch productions expecting to see a woman's point of view in a play directed by a woman. In contrast, viewers do not expect to see a man's point of view when seeing a play directed by a man. Critical reviews of women's work reflect society's attitudes. A 1935 article in the *New York Sun* explained how Antoinette Perry received unfair criticism of her directing from the press, stating, "One minor point in the acting of 'Ceiling Zero' had been pilloried by several critics on the grounds that it had been done by a woman director, and Miss Perry was so gleeful when she found the same bit of action in another Broadway play which was done entirely by a man that she took a tumble" ("Theater," 1935, n.p.).

Sometimes criticism from reviewers comes in the form of backhanded compliments. Muzio discusses a "compliment" that she received from *New York Times* Critic Mel Gussow about her direction of *Other People's Money*. Muzio says, "He [Gussow] said, 'If you were to see *Other People's Money*, there's no way you would even guess that it was directed by a woman.' And I thought, 'What does that mean?' . . . Does that mean it was so good you couldn't tell it was directed by a woman? Does that mean it wasn't weepy?" (Interview, 1995). Gussow's comment shows that he was aware of the director's gender and had expectations of what he might see. It also indicates that a play directed by a man is perceived as the model way to direct.

Mann also received a backhanded compliment. Of her play *Execution of Justice* she says, "One of the funniest statements ever said to me was by a rather eminent man of the theatre down in Louisville when *Execution of Justice* opened. He said, 'I love this play. You think like a man.' Now where do you begin with a statement like that? I remember being just dumbfounded. What do you say? Thank you? No words came" (Daniels 1996, 38).

Personal Life and Career

Balancing a family and a career is difficult for women directors, especially freelance directors who need to travel to obtain work. Some women, such as Boyd, Fichandler, Rothman, Perloff, and Mann, became artistic directors, which enables them to direct consistently in one location so that they could raise children without uprooting them repeatedly. As artistic director of A.C.T., Perloff says, "It's why we all did it. I never had any aspiration to run a theatre. But, you know, if you actually want to do the work you want to do and be in one town, it's the only way to go. It's the only solution" (Interview, 2004). As artistic directors, women must juggle managing, directing, and parenting, which is very time-consuming. Fichandler talks about balancing her theatrical career and family, stating, "What is hard is to have the energy and psychic attention for both those domains [children and theatre]. It's hard to tune in sensitively and creatively to that many people in one day. That takes a lot out of you, and there are things you give up" (Interview, 1988). Rothman explains why she turned down many opportunities that could have advanced her career commercially. "I turned down a lot . . . that was supposed to go to Broadway. I had to because I just personally made other choices in my life, in my career. . . . I turned things down because I had a family. I turned things down because I run a theatre and that was more important to me. . . . I just think it's a constant battle that women have, but that might change. . . . You can't put in the hours. . . . I'd be perfectly happy to direct on Broadway, but am I able to go out of town for three months with a show? Nope" (Interview, 1995).

Perloff helps women work around their families at A.C.T. She says, "It's a field that's very hard for women with children, particularly freelance women with children. So, I try to really make it possible for people to bring their kids here. But the women I started out with . . . my generation of women, I look at them and think they should be at the top of the field now. They're incredibly talented; they're really smart. Why aren't they? Because they had children. And it's a very, very hard thing to juggle" (Interview, 2004).

Finding theatres that will accommodate children is rare. Akalaitis, who had young children at the time, created a schedule to work around her children. Actress Joan MacIntosh explains the rehearsal schedule of *Request Concert*, an Off-Off Broadway play in which she performed, directed by Akalaitis in the early 1980s. "Working with JoAnne was extraordinary. We both had children. . . . We rehearsed the play for a little over three weeks for very few hours a day. We worked the entire rehearsal schedule around our children, which was the only time in my life that's been able to happen" (Hill 1993, 36).

Race

Although this book is focused primarily on an examination of gender, race is a factor that must be further addressed and studied. Some of the issues that women directors face in theatre apply to people of color as well. For example, producers in positions of power often are white men, whose background influences the aesthetics of what they choose to produce and whom they choose to hire. Therefore, not only are they less likely to hire a woman, but they are even less likely to hire a woman who isn't white. These white producers may also choose to mentor people who remind them of themselves at a younger age: other white men. In addition, any prejudices that white male producers may hold against women are compounded by prejudices that they have against people from cultures that are different from their own. Thus, a director who is both a woman and a person of color faces an exceptionally hard battle.

Women directors such as Chang, Galban, and Miguel have fought prejudices by creating their own theatres, where they could present work specific to their cultures that was not being presented elsewhere. African American directors, such as Carroll, Dickerson, and Teer, also created their own theatres, where they could present works that would not be produced by white producers. Mann believes that although women still face obstacles in theatre, especially on Broadway, race is a larger problem than gender in the theatre today (Interview, 2004). As one way of combating this, Mann has tried to present multicultural productions at the McCarter Theatre.

Although some directors who are women of color have created their own theatres, they face the problem of audience reception. White audiences are less apt to attend productions that they believe do not apply to them and may also avoid theatres that specialize in work by people of different cultural backgrounds. The education of audiences and conscious acceptance of artists of color into the mainstream by those in positions of power would help to create more opportunities for women and lessen racism in the theatre.

Solutions

The New York State Council on the Arts Theatre Program's "Report on the Status of Women: A Limited Engagement?" suggests seven solutions to the problems women directors face: research to evaluate gender bias; education of gender bias; preservation of women's work and lives in theatre history; creation of high-quality productions; advocacy to valorize women's work through awards, critical attention, and documentation; alliances using strategies such as networking and mentorship to increase opportunities; and a forum to continue discussion of diversity (Jonas and Bennett 2002, 7).

Early women directors understood the importance of networking. Crothers noted, "[F]or a woman, it is best to look to women for help; women are more daring, they are glad to take the most extraordinary chances. . . . I think I should have been longer about my destiny if I had to battle with men alone (Barnes 1931, 18).

Role models are important for aspiring women directors. Miguel did not think of herself as a role model until she was approached by three young Native American girls, who had never seen a Native American theatre director before (Interview, 2004). Fichandler, who teaches at New York University (N.Y.U.) notes, "Before I went to N.Y.U., I didn't fully understand the influence and force of role models. It's important not only to teach but to stand for something, to have an artistic value system that can be revealed in the work" (Interview, 1988, 125).

Mentors are also an important part of the solution. When aspiring directors have mentors who are women, they can also see how to deal with problems involving sexist attitudes. Playwright Caryl Churchill believes that it is very difficult for women directors to break into the field of directing because men dominate it. She says, "[E]stablished men tend to take a young male director under their wing, and seem to feel more uncomfortable with a woman director because they can't quite see where she is, because they weren't like that at her age" (Betsko and Koenig 1987, 61).

In her 1983 dissertation "The Woman Director in the Contemporary, Professional Theatre," Shirlee Hennigan notes that one obstacle for women is the lack of role models at the college and university level. This problem continues. Toward the end of the twentieth century, a survey performed by the Higher Education Arts Data Services for the National Association of Schools of Theatre showed that men still make up the majority of theatre faculties.

Just as Title IX required schools to provide equal opportunities for girls in 1972 to alleviate discrimination, producers need to consciously think about hiring women in order to instigate change. Artistic directors such as Perloff and Rothman consciously hire women to help create opportunities for them. Robinson does the same but calls the choice instinctive rather than conscious. Until women directors gain equality with men, they will continue to be seen as separate and to be judged differently. Boyd sums up the problem, saying, "One woman's failure is a failure for all women, and one woman's success is her own success until more women succeed" (Daniels 1996, 65).

Notes

1. Near the century's end, membership for women in the Society of Stage Directors and Choreographers (SSDC) was 22 percent at full membership (directors

under an SSDC contract), 44 percent at associate membership (early career and college directors), and 17 percent nonmembership (occasional work in an LORT theatre and dinner theatre) (Jonas 1998, 8).

2. In most cases, credits are listed alphabetically by year. In addition, the names of co-directors are included when available. For cases in which Off Broadway theatres are also regional (LORT contract) theatres, credits appear in the Off and Off-Off Broadway category.

3. A more thorough overview of men's contributions to directing is found in Helen Krich Chinoy's "The Emergence of the Director," in *Directors on Directing,* edited by Toby Cole and Helen Krich Chinoy.

4. No doubt the emphasis on realistic and historical authenticity came into vogue (at least in part) through the influence of photography, an artistic and technical innovation in itself.

5. Bold text indicates one of the fifty women profiled in this book.

6. A number of other actors have followed suit, exploring their talents as directors. For example, June Havoc began directing summer tours in the early 1950s and in the 1960s was nominated for Tony Awards for Best Play and Best Director for her play *Marathon '33.* Between 1969 and 1971 she became the artistic director of the New Orleans Repertory Theatre, where she also acted and directed. Havoc starred in and directed touring productions in the 1970s, including *The Effect of Gamma Rays on Man-in-the-Moon Marigolds* and *The Gingerbread Lady.* In a similar vein, Elaine May is known as a comedian and comic writer but also directed several films and her stage play, *Adaptation* (1969), which won her an Outer Critics Circle Award for directing and writing.

7. Ellis's all–African American production of *Tobacco Road* received mixed and poor reviews and played only seven performances, although it made Ellis one of the first African American women (if not the first) to direct on Broadway. We acknowledge the research of Professor Cheryl Black, who brought Ellis's career to our attention.

8. For a much more detailed discussion of women directors of musicals, see Anne L. Fliotsos' chapter "Open a New Window, Open a New Door: Women Directors Take the Stage" in Bud Coleman and Judith Sebesta's book *Women in American Musical Theatre.*

9. See also Nancy Putnam Smithner's 2002 dissertation from New York University, "Directing the Acting Ensemble: Meredith Monk, Elizabeth LeCompte, and Anne Bogart."

10. Other directors deserving attention include Eve Adamson, founder and former artistic director of New York City's Jean Cocteau Repertory Theatre; Irene Lewis, artistic director of Baltimore's Center Stage; Molly Smith, artistic director of Washington, D.C.'s Arena Stage; Timothy Near, artistic director of the San Jose Repertory Theatre; Patricia Anne McIlrath, founder and first artistic director of the Missouri Repertory Theatre; Penny Metropulos, associate artistic director of the Oregon Shakespeare Festival; Margaret Booker, former artistic director of Florida's Asolo Theatre, Connecticut's Hartman Theatre, and Seattle's

Intiman Theatre; Miriam Colòn, artistic director of the Puerto Rican Traveling Theatre; Elizabeth Huddle, former artistic director of Portland Center Stage and Seattle's Intiman Theatre; Mame Hunt, former artistic director of San Francisco's Magic Theatre; Susan V. Booth, artistic director of Atlanta's Alliance Theatre; Kyle Donnelly, former associate artistic director at Arena Stage; Loretta Greco, former producing artistic director of Women's Project in New York City; Karin Coonrod, founding director of Off-Broadway's Arden Party; and Marcy Arlin, founder and artistic director of New York's Immigrants' Theatre Project (ITP). Despite its length, this list is not exhaustive.

Sources

Barnes, Djuna. 1931. "The Tireless Rachel Crothers." *Theatre Guild* 8 (May): 18.

Bartow, Arthur. 1988. *The Director's Voice: Twenty-One Interviews.* New York: Theatre Communications Group.

Berson, Misha. 1994. "Women at the Helm." *American Theatre* 11 (May/June): 14–21, 66.

Betsko, Kathleen, and Rachel Koenig. 1987. *Interviews with Contemporary Women Playwrights.* New York: Beech Tree Books.

Black, Cheryl. 1995. "Technique and Tact: Nina Moise Directs the Provincetown Players." *Theatre Survey* 36 (May): 55–64.

———. 2002. *The Women of Provincetown: 1915–1922.* Tuscaloosa: University of Alabama Press.

———. 2007. Correspondence with Anne Fliotsos. 11 June.

Boesing, Martha. 1996. "Rushing Headlong into the Fire At the Foot of the Mountain." *Signs: Journal of Women in Culture and Society* 21 (4): 1011–23.

Chinoy, Helen Krich and Linda Walsh Jenkins, eds. 2006. *Women in American Theatre.* 3rd ed. New York: Theatre Communications Group.

Cole, Toby and Helen Krich Chinoy, eds. 1963. *Directors on Directing: A Source Book of the Modern Theatre.* New York: Macmillan.

Crowther, Bosely. 1937. "The Lady in the Case." *New York Times,* 14 Mar., n.p. Billy Rose Theatre Collection, scrapbook. New York Public Library for the Performing Arts.

Dace, Tish. 1993. "Sexism in the Theatre." *Back Stage,* 5 Mar., 1, 20–25, 27.

———. 1994. "Women's Work: Six Directors on Their Lives in the Theatre." *Back Stage,* 4 Mar., 1, 20–24.

Daniels, Rebecca. 1996. *Women Stage Directors Speak: Exploring the Influence of Gender on Their Work.* Jefferson, N.C.: McFarland.

"DGA Report Shows Top 40 Primetime TV Lacks Diversity in Directing." 2006. *DGA Monthly* 3 (4) (April). http://www.dga.org/news/dgamontly-0406/news_diversity-406.php3 (accessed 5 June 2007).

Donkin, Ellen and Susan Clement. 1993. *Upstaging Big Daddy: Directing Theatre as if Gender and Race Matter.* Ann Arbor: University of Michigan Press.

Fichandler, Zelda. 1988. Interview with Arthur Bartow. In *The Director's Voice:*

Twenty-One Interviews, by Arthur Bartow, 108–27. New York: Theatre Communications Group.

Flanagan, Hallie. 1943. *Dynamo.* New York: Duell, Sloan and Pearce.

Fliotsos, Anne L. 1997. "Teaching the Unteachable: Directing Pedagogy in Colleges and Universities of the United States: 1920–1990." Ph.D. diss., University of Maryland, College Park.

———. 2008. "Open a New Window, Open a New Door: Women Directors Take the Stage." In *Women in American Musical Theatre: Composers, Lyricists, Librettists, Arrangers, Choreographers, Designers, Directors, Producers, and Performance Artists,* ed. Bud Coleman and Judith Sebesta. Jefferson, N.C.: McFarland.

Gilder, Rosamond. 1931. *Enter the Actress.* Boston: Houghton Mifflin.

Goethe. 1874. *Conversations of Goethe with Eckermann and Soret.* London: George Bell and Sons. Quoted in *Source Book in Theatrical History,* by A. M. Nagler, 425–27. New York: Dover, 1959.

Hennigan, Shirlee. 1983. "The Woman Director in the Contemporary, Professional Theatre." Ph.D. diss., Washington State University.

Higher Education Arts Data Services. 1996. "Theatre Data Summaries, 1995–96." Reston, Va.: Higher Education Arts Data Services.

Hill, Holly. 1993. *Actors' Lives: On and Off the American Stage: Interviews by Holly Hill.* New York: Theatre Communications Group.

Housely, Helen. M. 1993. "The Female Director's Odyssey: The Broadway Sisterhood." From *Women and Society,* proceedings of the 2nd Annual Seminar on Women, Marist College, Poughkeepsie, N.Y.

Jonas, Susan, with preparation by Celia Braxton. 1998. "Report on the Status of Women Directors and Playwrights in the New York City Theater." 21 Sept. New York: New York State Council on the Arts.

Jonas, Susan and Suzanne Bennett. 2002. "Report on the Status of Women: A Limited Engagement?" Executive Summary. New York: New York State Council on the Arts Theatre Program.

Lawless, Sue. 2000. Correspondence with Anne Fliotsos. 18 Oct.

———. 2003. Correspondence with Anne Fliotsos. 16 Sept.

Levitow, Roberta. 2004. Telephone interview with Wendy Vierow. 16 July.

Mann, Emily. 2004. Interview with Wendy Vierow. Princeton, N.J. 24 May.

Miguel, Muriel. 2004. Interview with Wendy Vierow. New York City. 9 June.

Muzio, Gloria. 1995. Telephone interview with Wendy Vierow. 12 Oct.

———. 2004. Interview with Wendy Vierow. New York City. 19 July.

Native American Women Playwrights Archive. n.d. "Spiderwoman Theater: Origins." http://staff.lib.muohio.edu/nawpa/origins.html (accessed 9 Aug. 2004).

Perloff, Carey. 2004. Telephone interview with Wendy Vierow. 4 Aug.

Robinson, Alice M., Vera Mowry Roberts, and Milly S. Barranger. 1989. *Notable Women in the American Theatre: A Biographical Dictionary.* New York: Greenwood.

Rothman, Carole. 1995. Telephone interview with Wendy Vierow. 13 Nov.
——. 2004. Telephone interview with Wendy Vierow. 14 July.
Silverstein, Melissa. 2007. "Women's Voices Missing from the Theatre—Does Anyone Care?" Women's Media Center, 7 Feb. http://222.womensmediacenter .com/ex/020707.html (accessed 5 June 2007).
Smithner, Nancy Putnam. 2002. "Directing the Acting Ensemble: Meredith Monk, Elizabeth LeCompte, and Anne Bogart." Ph.D. diss., New York University.
Tannen, Deborah. 1990. *You Just Don't Understand: Women and Men in Conversation*. New York: Ballantine.
"Theater Credo of Miss Perry." 1935. *New York Sun,* 1 May, n.p. Billy Rose Theatre Collection, clippings. New York Public Library for the Performing Arts.
Vierow, Wendy. 1997. "Women on Broadway: 1980–1995." Ph.D. diss., New York University.
Winn, Steven. 1991. "New Artistic Director at ACT." *San Francisco Chronicle,* 20 Nov., E1.
Women's Project & Productions. In conjunction with the New School for Social Research. 1997. "Sources for Support." *Women in Theatre: Mapping the Sources of Power.* Conference journal, New York City, 7–8 Nov.

Abady, Josephine

Born August 21, 1949 in Richmond, Virginia, Josephine R. Abady became a director before launching a career as artistic director of the Berkshire Theatre Festival, the Cleveland Play House, and the Circle in the Square. Although her tumultuous career as an artistic director is well documented, her legacy as a director is harder to trace.

Abady earned a B.S. degree, cum laude, from Syracuse University in 1971. She was the only woman in her class pursuing the M.F.A. in directing, a degree she received from Florida State University in 1973. In an interview for the *Christian Science Monitor,* she revealed, "When I came out of school and I said I wanted to be a director, everyone said to me, 'Well, why don't you be an actress?' And it was very hard for me to get work of any kind except as an assistant in an office, stage management, those kinds of jobs" (Mason 1992, Arts 10). Despite her employment at menial jobs, she found work freelancing as a director at the Ensemble Theatre in Tampa, Florida; the Roundhouse Theatre in Manchester, Vermont; and the Paul Arts Center in Durham, New Hampshire. In 1976 she was appointed to be a director and visiting professor of theatre at Hampshire College in Bennington, Massachusetts, where she stayed until 1979. Before she turned thirty, Abady got her first job as an artistic director at Berkshire Theatre Festival in Stockbridge, Massachusetts. After she accepted the job, she realized that she was offered the job because no one else wanted it. She had inherited a bankrupt theatre with a slew of problems, but she stayed from 1979 to 1988, specializing in producing revivals of American classics, many of which she directed herself (Eaker 2000, 7). While at Bennington and Berkshire she continued to freelance as a director as well, working at the New York Theatre Ensemble in New York City; the Cincinnati Playhouse in the Park; the Charles Playhouse in Boston; the

Merrimack Regional Theatre in Lowell, Massachusetts; the American Place Theatre in New York City; the Syracuse Stage in Syracuse, New York; the Alley Theatre in Houston; the Long Wharf in New Haven, Connecticut; and the Carter Theatre Group in Los Angeles.

One of her first productions to receive critical acclaim in New York City was *The Boys Next Door*, produced Off Broadway at the Lamb's Theatre in 1987, where it ran for 168 performances and 16 previews. She was nominated for an Outer Critics Circle Award for directing and directed the play again in 1989 at the Cleveland Play House. The plot follows four roommates who are mentally and socially challenged as they try to make their way in the world. The *New York Times* gave Abady a very favorable review, praising the detailed characterizations and stating, "As skillfully directed by Josephine R. Abady, the play follows the men through their daily routine while revealing their anxieties, limitations, enthusiasms, and identifying traits" (Gussow 1987, C20).

Also in 1987 Abady directed Dorothy McGuire in a national tour of the play *I Never Sang for My Father*. Robert Anderson's play about a father and son who cannot communicate got mixed reviews, based in part on an uneven performance. The *Akron Beacon Journal* declared, "Director Josephine R. Abady might be credited with the fashioning of the characters, which has been done with some degree of sensitivity. But she must also be faulted with an unevenness in some of the scenes, a sense that there are some moments that are out of tune with the play" (Mastrolanni 1987). The twentieth-anniversary tour played large touring houses despite its intimate tone, a problem many of the reviewers acknowledged.

In January 1988 immediately after the tour, Abady took the helm at the Cleveland Play House, where she stayed as artistic director until 1994. Although she made a controversial move by bringing in New York City actors, she was credited with increasing ticket sales, attracting an African American audience, creating a venue for new plays, producing more plays by women, and beginning an international exchange with the Soviet Union. Richard Hahn, board president and chairman at the time of Abady's tenure, recalls, "The Abady years, from an artistic point of view, were the best the Play House has had in the past several decades. . . . She engendered excitement on the stage and in the building" (Brown 2002, E1).

Her first directing assignment for the Cleveland Play House was *Born Yesterday,* starring Ed Asner and Madeline Kahn, which went on national tour before moving to Broadway in 1989. Playwright Garson Kanin called Abady's "the definitive production," high praise from a man who had been withholding Broadway revival rights for more than forty years. Set in the mid-1940s, the comedy revolves around scoundrel Harry Block, who wants to buy off a Washington senator. Block decides that his ditzy blond mistress, Billie Dawn, needs some polish to be accepted in Washington circles. As Billie becomes educated, in the manner of Eliza Doolittle of *Pygmalion,* she sees Block for what he really is. Of the original Cleveland production, one critic wrote, "Miss Abady's direction properly allows the exploration of the side roads that run off the play's main highway. And with Miss Kahn, she has an actress who can handle the nuances that suggest an inner awakening" (Mastrolanni 1988). Once the play hit Broadway, a critic noted that although Abady directed the production, director John Tillinger stepped in as production supervisor once the play left Cleveland. "So it's impossible to say which of them is responsible for some of the overemphatic comedic bits that occasionally make one think of lesser regional theaters" (Collins 1989). However, critics overall praised the production and the run was successful, playing for six months on Broadway.

In addition to *Born Yesterday,* Abady directed a number of productions during her tenure in Cleveland, including *On the Waterfront* (a world premiere), *The Boys Next Door, The Cemetery Club,* and *The House of Blue Leaves.* One of her greatest accomplishments was a 1991 theatre exchange with Cleveland's sister city, Volgograd, in Russia (then the USSR). Abady was the first American woman to direct a Russian theatre company and as such faced a number of obstacles (Abady 1994, 27). While working through a Russian translator to direct *A Streetcar Named Desire,* she found that the Soviet actors would not ask questions or look her in the eye. Abady complained, "Now, the only way you can direct theatre, if you can't speak the language, is to make eye contact. . . . [Y]ou must look at me so that we can learn about each other through our eyes, through our body language, through the timbre of our voices. It took me almost three weeks to have anyone look at me. I was constantly having to touch people's faces and hold them to have them talk to me. And that kind of physicalization was something with which they were very uncomfortable" (26). In addition, she found that her gender led to resistance because none of the actors had worked with a woman director. She quickly found a solution to this problem as well: "I solved this by teaching all the men in the company to play poker for the poker scene in *Streetcar.* Then we played for money and I won! I didn't have any more problems" (26). On opening night, one thousand people showed up for seven hundred seats, and the second day saw sixty thousand ticket sales. Abady reflected, "I must say, in spite of the hardships, never in this country have I ever felt as celebrated as an artist" (26).

Despite an upturn in ticket sales and a rise in national prestige, the board of the regional theatre decided not to renew her contract in 1994, sparking outrage and accusations in the Cleveland area and the theatrical community at large. Regardless of the turmoil, Abady landed on her feet as the co–artistic director of the troubled Circle in the Square in New York City in 1994, until their bankruptcy in 1996. During her last year there, she directed a production of *Bus Stop,* starring Mary-Louise Parker, Ron Perlman, and Billy Crudup. Abady refused to think of it as a revival, considering it "a different piece . . . [about] life, love, work, loneliness. I think it has new meaning for this age in which we're living by computers, Internet, email" (Tallmer 1996, 17). William Inge's now-classic play tells of a bus stranded at a small town during a blizzard. The audience is introduced to the passengers, particularly a cowboy named Bo who is falling head over heels for a runaway chanteuse, Cherie. Theatre critic Marianne Evett raved, "[D]irector Josephine Abady serves 'Bus Stop' with a masterful hand" and with "amazing immediacy. . . . Abady turns the difficulties of arena staging into assets. While two characters talk, the others are also in the diner, going about their lives. They do not distract you from the focus of the scene, but give the feeling that all this is really happening" (Evett 1996, 10I). Critic Vincent Canby agreed that the staging was fluid but found the acting forced, particularly the dialect work, commenting, "[P]rincipal performances appear to have been shaped in desperation" (1996, C1).

In 1996 Abady also directed *The Philadelphia Story* at the Royal Exchange Theatre in Manchester, England. Made famous by the movie version with Katharine Hepburn, Philip Barry's play tells the tale of a socialite who finds romance with a fast-talking reporter. The critic from the *Independent* newspaper praised the play as "a stylish, witty, confident production" (Wainright 1996, Arts 6), and the critic from the *Financial Times* drew comparisons to Noel Coward. Of the directing, he wrote, "She succeeds in obtaining performances . . . which avoid loading the play with either more poise or more angst than it was meant to bear. Some English directors might have been tempted to go at full speed down Noel Coward Avenue, but such an approach would have resulted in an overwrought production. This is cheesecake, not meringue—and in this version, it is cheesecake like Mama used to make" ("Philadelphia," 1996).

It was at about this time that Abady became public about her fight with cancer. She continued to freelance as a director and to teach at universities until her untimely death in 2002, at the age of 52. Abady's last productions included the musical *Abyssinia* in Dallas, Texas; the Pulitzer Prize–winning cancer play *Wit* in her hometown of Richmond, Virginia; and *The Tale of the Allergist's Wife* at the Asolo Theatre in Sarasota, Florida. Although her doctor objected to this strenuous travel and activity, Abady's passion for directing prevailed. She wanted to be defined not as a patient but as a director (Brown 2002, E1).

As a director and producer, Abady took great pride in nurturing talent. In one article, she states, "Of course, the most rewarding aspect of the job is giving young talent an opportunity and then watching them go on. I gave Holly Hunter one of her very first jobs" (Dace 1994, 22–23).

Pat McCorkle, of McCorkle Casting, was a close friend and colleague and first met Abady at the Berkshire Theatre Festival in 1979. Since that time, she cast more than 125 productions with Abady. McCorkle and Abady quickly found they had similar tastes. Once their casting partnership became established, Abady trusted McCorkle to make casting decisions for last-minute replacements (McCorkle, interview, 2003). McCorkle described Abady as a woman with Southern charm and a tremendous drive, which was sometimes misinterpreted. She explained that Abady's controversial move to bring in New York actors at the Cleveland Play House was not correctly represented in the press. Although reports made it sound as if Abady were "cleaning house" and ridding the theatre of the resident company, she merely wanted to improve casting options, both for the productions she directed and for other directors at the theatre. Instead of guaranteeing the resident company an annual contract (a method abandoned by most regional theatres at the time), Abady authorized auditions for each production, opening auditions to actors in Cleveland and elsewhere. She hoped to bring in some new talent, not oust the company actors. Her move was misinterpreted, but as McCorkle said, she did it for the right reasons: to improve the quality of the productions (Interview, 2003).

Actor and friend Peggy Cosgrave worked on numerous productions with Abady, including the Broadway run of *Born Yesterday*. Of Abady's work she said, "Her great gift was casting. She could get stars to work for 325 dollars a week and do very difficult roles. She could get wonderful actors, and they also were good people. . . . They were always a wonderful group of people that worked well together. And that included the entire team—all the top people. They didn't work for her because they wanted to go to Cleveland at Christmas time. They worked because it was always artistically high quality and it was always a wonderful experience that was fun to do" (Interview, 2003).

One of the obstacles Abady faced was directing while producing, in essence wearing two hats simultaneously. Former stage manager Don Walters, who worked on more than twenty productions with Abady, including *Born Yesterday* and *I Never Sang for My Father*, remembers that she would come to rehearsal as director at ten in the morning after working the phones in the office for two hours, wearing her producer hat. He recalls, "We were at summer stock at the Berkshires, we were getting ready to start rehearsal, and she came in barking orders to the stage managing staff. And I said, 'Now Josie, go outside the door of rehearsal, come in, and let's start the day with a 'Good Morning!' And she reluctantly walked out and she reentered and said, 'Good Morning! How are you?' She hated doing that" (Interview, 2003). Cosgrave also found that running the theatre left Abady little time in the studio for rehearsals, yet despite the time constraints Cosgrave never felt pressured because their limited studio time was quality time and outside time was used to work on lines. In terms of Abady's work with actors, Cosgrave commented,

"She wasn't someone who told you what to do" (Interview, 2003). Walters agreed: "Josie's directing style was to let the actors go, let them create" (Interview, 2003). Especially in a stock situation with only two weeks to rehearse, Abady would set the blocking, let the actors have discovery time, then rein them back in to create one vision. In addition, Walters notes that she never lost her temper with the actors, although she might do so with the designers or stage managers, but was always quick to apologize. He also commented that she would "give you the shirt off her back" and was always available for an actor in crisis (Interview, 2003).

Abady left a legacy not only as a strong leader who could build up failing theatres but as a director of American classics and as an educator. During her impressive career she found time to teach at a variety of colleges and universities, including the aforementioned Hampshire College, Bennington College, and Ohio University. She served as a guest artist at New York University, the University of Washington, and Smith College. She also received a variety of awards and nominations, including an Obie nomination and Outer Critics Circle Award nomination for directing *The Boys Next Door* at the Lamb's Theatre Off Broadway in 1987. In 1980 she was appointed by President Carter to the President's Commission on Scholarship in the Arts, and she was a recipient of the Sawyer Falk Memorial Award. In 2005 the League of Professional Theatre Women instated an award in Abady's name to go to an emerging director or producer who is inclusive of women of color.

Although a chronicle of her work speaks volumes, her demeanor while performing that work is also remembered. Ben Cameron, who was executive director of the Theatre Communications Group at the time of her death in 2002, remembers her strong leadership at several of the finest not-for-profit theatres in the United States. "She is known for the sharpness of her mind, her ability for working with actors, her caustic humor and her generous heart" (Brown 2002, E1).

Sources

Abady, Josephine. 1994. "The New Experimental Theatre, Volgograd: The Truth About Blanche." *Journal for Stage Directors and Choreographers* 8 (1) (Spring/Summer): 25–27.

Brown, Tony. 2002. "Josie; Former Director of Play House Shows Spirit in Cancer Battle." (*Cleveland*) *Plain Dealer*, 22 May, E1.

Canby, Vincent. 1996. Rev. of *Bus Stop*, by William Inge. *New York Times*, 23 Feb., C1.

Collins, William R. 1989. "A New Life for 'Born Yesterday.'" Rev. of *Born Yesterday*, by Garson Kanin. *Philadelphia Inquirer*, 31 Jan. In NewsBank, Performing Arts, fiche 36, grid G5.

Cosgrave, Peggy. 2003. Telephone interview with Anne Fliotsos. 15 Dec.

Dace, Tish. 1994. "Women's Work: Six Directors on Their Lives in the Theatre." *Back Stage*, 4 Mar., 1, 20–24.

Eaker, Sherry. 2000. "Women in Theatre: Stay True to Your View." *Back Stage*, 21 Jan., 7.

Evett, Marrianne. 1996. "Abady Recaptures Inge Insight." *(Cleveland) Plain Dealer*, 3 Mar., 10I.

Gussow, Mel. 1987. "Learning for All." Rev. of *The Boys Next Door*, by Tom Griffin. *New York Times*, 25 Nov., C20.

Mason, M.S. 1992. "Cleveland Play House Holds Its Stride." *Christian Science Monitor*, 21 Apr., Arts 10.

Mastrolanni, Tony. 1987. "'I Never Sang' Has Moments, but Lacks Subtlety." Rev. of *I Never Sang for My Father*, by Robert Anderson. *Akron Beacon Journal*, 2 Oct. In NewsBank, Performing Arts, fiche 54, grid G1.

———. 1988. "'Born Yesterday' Shines as Play House Opener." Rev. of *Born Yesterday*, by Garson Kanin. *Akron Beacon Journal*, 12 Sept. In NewsBank, Performing Arts, fiche 201, grid D5.

McCorkle, Pat. 2003. Telephone interview with Anne Fliotsos. 5 Dec.

"The Philadelphia Story." 1996. Rev. of *The Philadelphia Story*, by Philip Barry. *Financial Times*. http://www.cix.co.uk/~shutters/reviews/96058.htm (accessed 10 Nov. 2003).

Tallmer, Jerry. 1996. "Josephine's Travels: Abady's 'Bus Stop' on Broadway." *Back Stage*, 23 Feb., 17, 23.

Wainright, Jeffery. 1996. Rev. of *The Philadelphia Story*, by Philip Barry. *Independent* (London), 19 July, Arts 6.

Walters, Don. 2003. Telephone interview with Anne Fliotsos. 23 Dec.

Representative Directing Credits

Broadway:

Born Yesterday (1989), *Bus Stop* (1996)

Off and Off-Off Broadway:

Kings (1979), *Territorial Rites* (1982, 1983), *The Boys Next Door* (1987), *The March on Russia* (1990), *Bus Stop* (1996)

Regional and Stock Theatre:

Private Lives (1973), *A Thurber Carnival* (1974, 1978), *Private Ear, Public Eye* (1974), *The Owl and the Pussycat* (1974), *Just So Stories* (1974), *Hay Fever* (1975), *West Side Story* (1976), *The Petrified Forest* (1979), *Sexual Perversity in Chicago* (1979), *The Little Foxes* (1980), *The Palace of Amateurs* (1980), *The Glass Menagerie* (1980), *A Coupla White Chicks Sitting Around Talking* (1981), *A View from the Bridge* (1981), *A Safe Place* (1981), *The Dresser* (1982), *Talley's Folly* (1982), *Sunrise at Campobello* (1982), *A Thousand Clowns* (1982), *The Big Knife* (1983), *Fanny* (1983), *A Loss of Roses* (1984),

Sabrina Fair (1984), *A Lesson from Aloes* (1985), *Caught* (1985), *Painting Churches* (1986), *Duse Died in Pittsburgh* (1987), *I Never Sang for My Father* (1987), *Born Yesterday* (1988), *On the Waterfront* (1988), *New Music* (1989), *The Boys Next Door* (1989), *The Cemetery Club* (1989), *A Streetcar Named Desire* (1991), *Abyssinia* (1991, 2001), *David's Mother* (1992), *The House of Blue Leaves* (1993), *Bus Stop* (1996), *Wit* (2001 or 2002), *The Tale of the Allergist's Wife* (2002)

Tours:
I Never Sang for My Father (1987), *Born Yesterday* (1989)

International Theatre:
A Streetcar Named Desire (1991), *The House of Blue Leaves* (1993), *The Philadelphia Story* (1996)

 # Akalaitis, JoAnne

Born on June 29, 1937, in Cicero, Illinois, JoAnne Akalaitis has been a director, writer, performer, designer, and artistic director. She is known for her experimental and visual style of directing that emphasizes physicality and combines text, movement, sound, and design. Productions under Akalaitis's direction have won five Obie Awards and have drawn both critical acclaim and controversy.

As a child, Akalaitis acted in school pageants. She recalls three events that made an impression on her, explaining, "First, when my parents took me to see 'South Pacific' at the Shubert Theatre, and I saw a woman wash her hair on stage. And second when I saw Jean Cocteau's 'The Blood of a Poet' at a Doc Films program at the University of Chicago. I wasn't exactly sure what it was, but I knew it was art. A few years later, I saw 'Citizen Kane' at the Museum of Modern Art in New York, and I knew that was art, too" (Christiansen 1990, 8).

Akalaitis attended the University of Chicago with plans to become a doctor but changed paths and graduated in 1960 with a B.A. in philosophy. She continued to graduate school, studying philosophy at Stanford University in California. While there, she became active in the theatre department and left Stanford to become a performer. She worked as a technician at San Francisco's Actors' Workshop, where she met director Lee Breuer and performers Ruth Maleczech and Bill Raymond, all of whom later became members of the avant-garde theatre group Mabou Mines with Akalaitis. While in San Francisco, Akalaitis also worked at the San Francisco Mime Troupe and San Francisco's Tape Music Center, where she met many avant-garde artists.

In 1962 Akalaitis moved to New York City, where she performed and studied acting with teachers including Herbert Berghof and Gene Frankel. She left New York in 1965, moving to Paris with her husband, the avant-garde musician Philip Glass. In Europe, Akalaitis performed with Maleczech and David Warrilow in Samuel Beckett's *Play*, directed by Breuer. With music composed by Glass, Beckett's play about a romantic triangle opened in 1967 at Paris's American Cultural Center. Akalaitis returned to the United States that year but went back to Europe in 1968 to study with Polish director Jerzy Grotowski. Influenced by Grotowski, Akalaitis came to view the actor as an active participant in the creative process of a production rather than just an interpreter. She also embraced Grotowski's emphasis on physicality in acting. The next year she studied again with Grotowski when his Polish Lab Theatre came to New York City.

In 1969 Akalaitis, Glass, Breuer, Maleczech, and Warrilow formed a collaborative theatre group and created *The Red Horse Animation*. They first performed the piece at the Guggenheim Museum in 1970, the same year that the group named itself Mabou Mines. Inspired by people such as choreographer Yvonne Rainer and painter Robert Rauschenberg, Mabou Mines created productions that combined movement, music, text, and design. Because the group's work was highly collaborative, some pieces took years to create. While they developed material for Mabou Mines, members also worked on projects outside the group.

Akalaitis made her directing debut in 1975 with the Mabou Mines production of Beckett's *Cascando* and was rewarded with an Obie Award for her direction. First presented at New York City's Ontological-Hysteric Theater, *Cascando* went on a European tour and then opened in 1976 at the New York Shakespeare Festival's Public Theater in New York City. Akalaitis expanded the two-character radio play into a visually rich production featuring eight performers and music by Glass. Michael Feingold of the *Village Voice* wrote, "[I]mages, like the zombie drone of the five overlapping voices, carry the conviction of quietitude [sic]. . . . We are down at the bottom of Beckett's well" (Saivetz 2000, 23).

After *Cascando*, Akalaitis began to create her own pieces, adding multimedia, such as film and slides into the mix. In 1977 Akalaitis created, directed, designed, and performed in the Mabou Mines production of *Dressed Like an Egg*. The original idea and the scenery for the piece were inspired by a photograph of the French author Colette in a gymnasium (Akalaitis, interview, 1988, 3). Opening at the Public Theater's Old Prop Shop Theater in New York City, the production presented images of Colette portrayed by different performers in a variety of settings. Mel Gussow of the *New York Times* wrote, "Miss Akalaitis has created visual counterpoint to spoken words.... Repeatedly, the show takes us by surprise with its stage pictures: a hip-deep bathtub is filled with steaming water from a kettle, the smoke swirling into rhythmic patterns; a single beam of light as thin as a crack, strikes the stage as if the sun had just entered a jet-black cave; an actress moves off stage, but her costume remains in place, a stiff-backed object like a Claes [sic] Oldenberg sculpture" (1977, 27). *Dressed Like an Egg* received an Obie Award for Distinguished Production that year.

In 1979 Akalaitis created and directed the Mabou Mines production of *Southern Exposure* at New York City's Performing Garage. Inspiration for the piece came to Akalaitis from a *New York Times* book review of a biography about Antarctic explorer Robert Scott. Gussow described the production's two performers, writing, "Representing various explorers, the two are glimpsed in a flashing series of tableaux. They are captured as if in frozen frames, or as if they are mounted on exhibition behind glass at the Museum of Natural History. In this and other sequences we feel the timelessness and the endlessness of the icy expeditions" (1979, C19). The multimedia production won a Special Citation Obie Award for Akalaitis and its performers, Ellen McElduff and Warrilow.

The next year, Akalaitis created and directed the Mabou Mines production *Dead End Kids* at the Public Theater. The production included numerous playing areas that presented tableaux and scenes with a variety of characters such as medieval alchemists, Faust, a nightclub comedian, and scientists Madame Curie and J. Robert Openheimer. In his review of the multimedia collage, Frank Rich of the *New York Times* wrote, "Through it all, the pace accelerates. Actors fly in and out of doors along the theater's back wall. Blistering lights pop on and off. Laboratory garments and apparatus float in and out of the action like hallucinatory visions. By the time Miss Akalaitis unleashes her heaviest arsenal—percolating Geiger counters, toy bombs, seat-shaking rumbles—we've already been made half-crazy. It's not just the fear of death that gets to us, but also the show's slapstick portrait of an America gone berserk" (1980, C34). Akalaitis and Mabou Mines won a Special Citation Obie Award for the production. The play was made into a film in 1986.

Akalaitis next turned to Franz Xaver Kroetz's *Request Concert,* a wordless one-woman play that explored the isolation of a middle-aged, middle-class woman who commits suicide. Working independently of Mabou Mines, Akalaitis directed the production in 1981 at New York City's Women's Interart Center to excellent reviews. Akalaitis also directed two other plays by Kroetz for Mabou Mines. In 1984 she directed Kroetz's *Through the Leaves* at Women's Interart Center and won an Obie Award for her direction. Like

Request Concert, the play focused on a lonely woman, a butcher who listens to the radio. Then in 1986 Akalaitis directed Kroetz's play about unemployment, *Help Wanted,* at New York City's Theatre for a New City.

Controversy arose from Akalaitis's direction of Beckett's *Endgame* at Boston's American Repertory Theatre (A.R.T.) in 1984. Akalaitis set the play in an abandoned subway station, included music by Glass, and cast two African Americans in the show. Beckett objected to these alterations with legal threats but agreed to let the production run with the addition of statements in the program, including one by him that read, "A complete parody of the play. Anybody who cares for the work couldn't fail to be disgusted" (Gontarski 1991, 142). Despite Beckett's negative comments, critics gave the play positive reviews. William K. Gale of the *Providence Journal* wrote, "In this setting . . . Beckett's Endgame, becomes no less than a brilliant, clearly defined view of the end of individual worlds. . . . Surely, if Beckett took up ART's offer to come from his home in Paris and see the show at the theater's expense, he might be persuaded to drop his objections" (1984, A14). Kevin Kelly of the *Boston Globe* also discussed the contrast, noting, "What has been lost, it seems to me, is some of the tantalizing, allusive power of Beckett's play, the layered ambiguity. . . . And yet . . . the Akalaitis/ ART production is pretty compelling. . . . When ART's 'Endgame' moves into its final section, the chill that coils down the set's subway walls is suddenly like the threat of history settling over us (inescapably, forever) and with a power perhaps not even fully imagined by Beckett himself" (1984, 68).

Akalaitis continued to direct innovative productions Off Broadway and in regional theatres. In 1989 she had one of the greatest critical successes of her career with her direction of Jean Genet's *The Screens* at Minneapolis's Guthrie Theatre. Jack Kroll of *Newsweek* called the production "one of the major events of the decade in American regional theater" and added that it was "the best work this gifted and often controversial director has ever done" (1989, 76). The play dealt with the Algerian revolution but had a contemporary resonance with the Palestinian intifada. It contained seventeen scenes that alternated in time and place—as well as between the living and dead. Jennifer Wicke of *The Nation* described the play as "a landmark in American theater." She wrote, "[T]he actors swarm in the aisles, stream past as they gird for combat, sit nonchalantly among the audience as colonial spectators or rush to escape from the intolerable events onstage, threading the ennui and the rage of each side of the conflict through the permeable, and thus complicit, rows of theatergoers." Wicke praised Akalaitis's effective use of scenery through the use of screens, which were "used to articulate changes or scene, to call attention to the theatricality of the play's events, as when the burning of the colonists' orange trees and roses is drawn on the screens by the actors playing Algerians, and also to create the boundary between the worlds of the living and the dead: The realm of the dead is entered as characters burst through white paper screens. In the Guthrie production this realm is literally overhead. The actors penetrate the screens to walk on a netting suspended above the stage, where they bounce about softly like trapeze artists or trampolinists, occupying the ceiling space as theatrical territory" (1990, 464).

An admirer of Genet, Akalaitis directed two more plays by him: *The Balcony* at A.R.T. in 1986 and *Prisoner of Love* at the New York Theater Workshop in New York City in 1995.

In addition to her work at the Public Theater with Mabou Mines, Akalaitis worked there as a freelance director. In 1989 her controversial production of Shakespeare's *Cymbeline* was applauded by some critics and criticized by others. Impressed for many years by Akalaitis's aesthetics and commitment to theatre, New York Shakespeare founder and artistic director Joseph Papp appointed her as his artistic associate in the spring of 1990. Akalaitis resigned as co-artistic director of Mabou Mines that summer to focus on her new appointment. That autumn, she directed a critically acclaimed revival of *Through the Leaves*. In the spring of 1991 she directed Shakespeare's *Henry IV, Part I* and *Henry IV, Part II*. That summer Joseph Papp appointed her artistic director when he resigned from the position.

While artistic director, Akalaitis restaged her previously produced production of John Ford's *'Tis Pity She's a Whore* at the Public Theater in 1992. The play, which focused on incest and chaos, struck a chord with the audience. Michael Kuchwara of the *Chicago Tribune* wrote that the play seemed "remarkably pertinent to our own equally violent times" and called it "one of the most effective revivals seen at the New York Shakespeare Festival in a long time" (1992, 18). Originally staged by Akalaitis in 1990 at Chicago's Goodman Theatre, Akalaitis set the play in Mussolini's Fascist Italy and included visually rich scenes inspired by surrealist art, with strong lighting and electronic music.

In January of 1992 at the Public Theater, Akalaitis received mixed reviews with her direction of Georg Buchner's *Woyzeck*. Just two months later, the New York Shakespeare Festival's Board of Directors unexpectedly fired Akalaitis. Although some critics attributed the dismissal to a transitional phase of a theatre under financial duress, others believed that if Akalaitis had been a man, she would have been given more time to settle into her position. The board replaced Akalaitis with George C. Wolfe, who had a more commercial view of theatre.

Akalaitis's one venture on Broadway met with mixed reviews when she directed Jane Bowles's *In the Summer House* at Lincoln Center in 1993. Many reviewers criticized the casting and performances in the play, which focused on mothers and daughters. Although he agreed that the casting was a problem,

Edwin Wilson of the *Wall Street Journal* found Akalaitis's collage-like approach ideal for the play, writing, "Ms. Akalaitis understands that because of its offbeat, unpredictable quality, a form of surrealism is the best lens through which to view 'In the Summer House'" (1993, A9).

Akalaitis continued to work at many regional theatres and in 1997 began to direct primarily at Chicago's Court Theatre. Her direction of *The Iphigenia Cycle* that year included Euripides' *Iphigenia at Aulis* and *Iphigenia in Taurus*. The two plays focused on the effects of war and death on one family. Andrew Patner of the *Chicago Sun-Times* described how Akalaitis was able to make the play contemporary with a "chorus of six teeny-boppers who look like they're on a SoHo shopping outing," "speeches . . . given at standing microphones," and Athena's "closing ode to victory that recalls Aretha Franklin, complete with the chorus as her backup singers" (1997, 56). The production was presented in 1999 Off Broadway to less enthusiastic reviews.

Continuing with her exploration of Euripides, Akalaitis directed *The Trojan Women* at Washington, D.C.'s Shakespeare Theatre in 1999. She discusses her attraction to Euripides, explaining, "In all his work, he has a tremendous sense of irony. That, of course, is one of the reason [sic] people find Euripides so contemporary. Because he deals with psychology, he deals with humor, he deals with states we're hyper-aware of . . . like vanity, for example. Also his plays have very powerful women characters" (Sacasa 1999). Lloyd Rose of the *Washington Post* drew parallels between the Trojan War and other wars of the century, including those in Kosovo and Bosnia. In her review of the play, she described the production, writing, "Greek drama is stylized anyway, and Akalaitis makes sure that the production never mimics the psychological realism of modern plays. The shaved-head chorus sings its lines and performs ritualized movement" (1999, C01).

In 1999 Akalaitis returned to the Court Theatre to direct Pedro Calderón de la Barca's *Life's a Dream,* which examines the concept of reality. Her association with the Court Theatre continued with her direction the next year of Glass's opera *In the Penal Colony,* with a libretto by Rudolph Wurlitzer. John von Rhein of the *Chicago Tribune* called the production a "must-see show" (2000, 1). Based on Franz Kafka's story about an execution that occurs in front of a penal colony, Akalaitis added Kafka as a character and created lines for him using his diaries. During the production, Kafka controlled the action as he wrote the story on the stage floor. In his review of the New York City production, directed by Akalaitis at the Classic Stage Company the next year, Ben Brantley of the *New York Times* wrote about its impact, observing that the play's "images give off a taint of shame and outrage that eventually creeps into the audience" (2001, E1).

Akalaitis's next project was the direction of Friedrich Schiller's *Mary Stuart* at the Court Theatre in 2001. Hedy Weiss of the *Chicago Sun-Times* called the production "Akalaitis' most thrilling and engaging work to date" (2001, 52). The play, which focused on the struggle between Mary Queen of Scots and Queen Elizabeth I, included postmodern touches such as freeze frame poses and the sound of opening Diet Coke cans by the characters. The following year at the Court Theatre, Akalaitis directed Jean Racine's *Phèdre*, a retelling of the ancient Greek story in which a queen lusts after her stepson. Akalaitis set the production in a seaside resort and directed characters to use ritualized gestures and dramatic poses. Jack Helbig of Chicago's *Daily Herald* called the production "flawless" (2002, 27).

In 2004 Akalaitis directed Harold Pinter's *The Birthday Party* at A.R.T. Jon Lehman of the *Patriot Ledger* praised the direction and performances, writing, "This is a production not to be missed" (2004, 16). The play is about a birthday party that turns into an interrogation and had contemporary parallels to the interrogations of prisoners in Guantanamo Bay, Cuba, and elsewhere in the world. Akalaitis discussed her collaboration with set designer Paul Steinberg to create an effective solution for the production's surrealism, explaining, "We talked a lot about the sea, and how this play is set near the sea. Originally, I had wanted to use a scrim that would allow us to see outside, but our budget prevented it. It often turns out, however, that when you can't afford a specific design, you come up with something better. So we created this room with a surreal painting of a green sea on the walls. Many of Pinter's plays are about a room—and what happens outside is unknown, dangerous, and perilous" (Interview, 2004).

Back at the Court Theatre the next year, Akalaitis directed Heiner Müller's *Quartet,* which was based on the French novel *Les Liaisons Dangereuses* by Choderlos de Laclos. In *Quartet* the play's two characters play a game of seduction and destruction. Instead of using Müller's setting, which began in an eighteenth-century French parlor and ended in a futuristic war bunker, Akalaitis set the play in what looked like a low-budget motel room. She also reversed Müller's time sequence by setting the play in the present and traveling backward in time through the device of costume changes. Critic Michael Phillips of the *Chicago Tribune* wrote, "[T]his Court Theatre production is eerily beautiful in ways you can't always pinpoint. It represents theatrical design of the highest order, the sort that can only happen under a director who has never stopped asking questions" (2005, 5).

Throughout the course of her varied career, Akalaitis has relied on her ability to first visualize a piece before staging it, whether she creates the piece from scratch or selects one to stage. When writing an original piece, Akalaitis says, "[I]deas come from deep, subconscious events and bleed from one project to the next. Being in the creative process causes you to dream creatively. I think these events are triggered by things from the real world like a song or a picture or something from a magazine" (Interview, 1988, 3). When selecting pieces written by others, Akalaitis notes, "[I]f I don't have a visual picture of something, then I shouldn't do the play. It doesn't mean that the play is good or bad; it means that I shouldn't be doing it" (Pressley 1999, C01). To clarify her vision, Akalaitis often works on a play for months before beginning rehearsals by reading and traveling to research settings. She explains, "I read a lot about the writer and I read all of the writer's plays. I read whatever I can. It's like being a graduate student. It's also important to be reading philosophy when you're directing a play. We should always be reading philosophy" (Interview, 2004).

Akalaitis often uses nontraditional casting for both race and gender in her productions. For her play *Green Card,* which she directed at Los Angeles's Mark Taper Forum in 1986, she cast Asian and Hispanic performers to play Jews in the production. The play presented a collage of the immigrant experience. Akalaitis said of the production, "It's exciting to confront the audience with that, the conflict of images. What are the cliches of the Asian, the Jew, the Hispanic, of California? We take all those characterizations, those cliches—and explode them" (Arkatov 1986, 1).

Despite careful research and casting, Akalaitis consciously goes into a rehearsal without a fixed understanding of the piece. She explains, "I really embrace the idea of finding one's way through a piece. . . . I do not stand in front of the cast and say, 'this is what this play is about.' Because I really don't know. You find out when you do it" (Interview, 1988, 13). During rehearsal, Akalaitis admits when she doesn't know or understand something. "I find meaning in space, in music, in language, through the body and what the actors bring to it," she says. "Meaning keeps changing right up until we open. The structure and shape emerge well into the rehearsal process" (Steele 1987, 01G).

Influenced by Grotowski, Akalaitis begins rehearsals with physical exercises. She explains, "I don't sit around a table much. I'm too impatient for that. I want to get the play up on its feet as soon as possible and I want the actors to start working deep inside their bodies. A lot of people don't know how to do that, but it's very important in establishing working relationships and in forming a group of people into a company" (Christiansen 1990, 8). During rehearsals, Akalaitis often asks performers to dance to music that is somehow related to the production. She states, "I do movement exercises that help develop a company—exercises that help the actors learn to talk to each other with their bodies. I would never do a show without these exercises. It's very hard for me to go into rehearsal and just start working—I need the actors to do something first. The actors lead me to exploration, I don't lead them" (Interview, 2004). In addition to physical exercises, Akalaitis may have actors write their own character histories. She also tries to incorporate Genet's advice that each scene be treated as if it were a play in itself (Christiansen 1990, 8).

Akalaitis admits that "[T]here is no such thing as a totally open collaborative situation, and at some point . . . you're in a position where something needs to happen that cannot happen by direct appeal" (Interview, 1988, 9). She tries to create a community with the cast and to treat performers sensitively. She says, "The whole business of giving notes is so delicate and serious that it's about what the actors can take at a certain moment. If there are very serious, hard notes, can they take them? Should they get them? . . . I tend to be very compulsive about detail. But at some moment in the process, I have to say, 'I've got to let this go'" (11–12).

Earlier in her career, Akalaitis often blocked rehearsals to create an outline for the performance and changed the blocking as rehearsals progressed (Interview, 1988, 8). However, she no longer blocks plays. She states, "[T]he actors do it better than I can. Eventually, of course, it's all very choreographed, very seriously blocked. But I just stopped blocking. And it's a lot of fun to let that go. The actors are amazing. So I let them sort of wander around the stage, and they figure it out. And sometimes what they figure out is very complicated" (Interview, 2000, 186).

Akalaitis also uses a technique of director Joe Chaikin called "worlds." She explains, "The idea is that there is a world onstage and sometimes it's the world of the person who is speaking the lines of the script, but not necessarily. It could be the world of the guy standing upstage holding the coffee cup. It is the business of everyone onstage to know what the world is and to enter that world in his or her own particular, idiosyncratic, special way using body and voice" (Interview, 1988, 15).

Combining the new and the old, Akalaitis borrows movements and ideas from her previous productions to incorporate into new ones. She notes, "[W]e all borrow, we all keep doing the same thing in some way. But I do not rely on a system. I reinvent the gestures and movements for every show, and it is always a very collaborative process. I also work with the gestures the actors bring to the process" (Interview, 2003, 261). In her productions, Akalaitis often uses formalized gestures called *mudras,* which are based on the Indian Kathakali theatre. Frequently performed in slow motion, Akalaitis hopes these movements "hit the audience in a nonintellectual, almost Jungian way. . . . When you slow down, your perceptions become enlarged, clarified, heady" (Interview, 1988, 6).

Over the years, the rehearsal process has changed for Akalaitis. She explains, "I used to feel I had to rehearse all the time. Now I feel I can walk into the room and say, 'We're going to be here from noon to five,' and we can do a good day's work" (Interview, 2000, 195).

Akalaitis gives a place of prominence to the design in each of her productions. Her designs are contemporary, and she believes performers and plays should always be contemporary, even if the play was written long ago (Steele 1987, 01G). She discusses how journalists perceive sets, stating, "There's an anti-visual bias in the American theater . . . from the point of view that the set is the background for the unfolding of events that the playwright has written." She adds that journalists believe "if there's some kind of 'look' onstage it denies the playwright" (Interview, 1990, 132).

In addition to her renowned work in the theatre, Akalaitis directed the 1983 *Stop Making Sense* tour for the band Talking Heads. She has also directed operas, including Gottfried von Einem's *The Visit of the Old Lady* at New York City Opera in 1997 and Leos Janácek's *Katya Kabanova* at the Opera Theater of St. Louis in 1998.

Along with her previously mentioned awards, Akalaitis received an Obie Award for Sustained Achievement in 1993 as well as Obie Awards as a member of Mabou Mines for General Excellence in 1975 and Sustained Achievement in 1986. She is a winner of the Edwin Booth Award for Theatrical Achievement in New York, the National Endowment for the Arts Award for Artistic Achievement, and the Rosamund Gilder Award for Outstanding Achievement in Theatre. She was awarded the Guggenheim Fellowship for experimental theatre, a National Endowment for the Arts grant, a Rockefeller Foundation grant, and a Pew Charitable Trusts National Theatre Artist Residency Program grant. She was an artist in residence at the Court Theatre, the Andrew Mellon co-chair of the Directing Program at Julliard School and the Wallace Benjamin Flint and L. May Hawver Flint Professor of Theater at Bard College in New York's Hudson Valley.

Reflecting on her career, Akalaitis says, "I've never considered anything I've done to be a failure, but I've had disappointing experiences. But isn't that true for everyone, isn't that what life is suppose to be about?" (McKeough 2002, 2).

Sources

Akalaitis, JoAnne. 1988. Interview with Arthur Bartow. In *The Director's Voice: Twenty-One Interviews,* by Arthur Bartow, 3–19. New York: Theatre Communications Group.

———. 1990. Interview with Deborah Saivetz. In *An Event in Space: JoAnne Akalaitis in Rehearsal,* by Deborah Saivetz, 129–44. Hanover, N.H.: Smith and Kraus, 2000.

———. 2000. Interview with Deborah Saivetz. In *An Event in Space: JoAnne Akalaitis in Rehearsal,* by Deborah Saivetz, 185–99. Hanover, N.H.: Smith and Kraus, 2000.

———. 2003. Interview with Martin Puchner. *Germanic Review* 78 (3) (Summer): 261.

———. 2004. Interview with Ryan McKittrick. "Party Politics." *ARTicles Online* 2 (3) (Mar.). http://www.amrep.org/articles/2_3b/party.html (accessed 16 Aug. 2004).

Arkatov, Janice. 1986. "'Green Card': Drawing Ethnic Parallels." *Los Angeles Times,* 21 May, 1.

Brantley, Ben. 2001. "Kafka's Pen? A Branding Iron." Rev. of *In the Penal Colony,* by Philip Glass. *New York Times,* 15 Jun., E1.

Christiansen, Richard. 1990. "Setting 'Pity' JoAnne Akalaitis Lights the Fuse on a 1633 Drama." *Chicago Tribune,* 11 Mar., 8.

Cole, Susan Letzler. 1992. "JoAnne Akalaitis Directs The Voyage of the Beagle." In *Directors in Rehearsal: A Hidden World,* 75–88. New York: Routledge.

Daniels, Rebecca. 1996. *Women Stage Directors Speak: Exploring the Influence of Gender on Their Work.* Jefferson, N.C.: McFarland.

Fiscella, Laurie Lassiter. 1989. "Mabou Mines, 1959–1989: A Theatre Chronicle." Ph.D. diss., New York University.

Gale, William K. 1984. "Endgame Offers Message of Hope Amid Darkness." Rev. of *Endgame,* by Samuel Beckett. *Providence Journal,* 15 Dec., A14.

Gontarski, S.E. 1991. "Lee Breuer and Mabou Mines." In *Contemporary American Theatre,* ed. Bruce King, 135–48. New York: St. Martin's.

Gussow, Mel. 1977. "'Dressed Like an Egg,' From Mabou Mines, Is Visual Counterpoint to Words of Colette." Rev. of *Dressed Like an Egg,* by JoAnne Akalaitis. *New York Times,* 17 May, 27.

———. 1979. "Downtown Setting for Antarctic Adventure." Rev. of *Southern Exposure,* by JoAnne Akalaitis. *New York Times,* 28 Feb., C19.

Helbig, Jack. 2002. "Court Theatre's 'Phèdre' Shines With Terrific Cast." Rev. of *Phèdre,* by Jean Racine. *(Chicago) Daily Herald,* 20 Sept., 27.

Kelly, Kevin. 1984. "American Rep's 'Endgame' Takes Its Compelling Course." Rev. of *Endgame,* by Samuel Beckett. *The Boston Globe,* 13 Dec., 68.

Kenvin, Roger. 1989. "Akalaitis, JoAnne." In *Notable Women in the American Theatre: A Biographical Dictionary,* ed. Alice M. Robinson, Vera Mowry Roberts, and Milly S. Barranger, 8–11. Westport, Conn.: Greenwood.

Kroll, Jack. 1989. "Major Doings in Minneapolis." Rev. of *The Screens,* by Jean Genet. *Newsweek,* 20 Nov., 76.

Kuchwara, Michael. 1992. "Director Akalaitis Makes Her Mark with Powerful, Unnerving 'Pity'." Rev. of *'Tis Pity She's a Whore,* by John Ford. *Chicago Tribune,* 7 Apr., 18.

Lehman, Jon. 2004. "This 'Birthday Party' Is Worth Celebrating." Rev. of *The Birthday Party,* by Harold Pinter. *(Boston) Patriot Ledger,* 15 Mar., 16.

Leiter, Samuel L. 1994. "JoAnne Akalaitis." In *The Great Stage Directors: 100 Distinguished Careers of the Theater,* 4–7; New York: Facts on File.

McKeough, Kevin. 2002. "Her Story Is Behind the Scenes." *Chicago Tribune,* 25 Sept., 2.

Nouryeh, Andrea J. 1994. "JoAnne Akalaitis." In *Theatrical Directors: A Biographical Dictionary,* ed. John W. Frick and Stephen M. Vallillo, 4–6. Westport, Conn.: Greenwood.

Patner, Andrew. 1997. "'The Iphigenia Cycle'." Rev. of *The Iphigenia Cycle,* by Euripides. *Chicago Sun-Times,* 17 Sept., 56.

Phillips, Michael. 2005. "Akalaitis' 'Quartet' Views Liaisons Dangerously." *Chicago Tribune,* 13 Feb., 5.

Pressley, Nelson. 1999. "Director Bearing Greek Gifts; JoAnne Akalaitis Puts a New Face on the Classics." *Washington Post,* 27 Mar., C01.

Rich, Frank. 1980. "Mabou Mines 'Dead End Kids'." Rev. of *Dead End Kids,* by JoAnne Akalaitis. *New York Times,* 19 Nov., C34.

Rose, Lloyd. 1999. "'Trojan Women'" A Tragedy for Our Times." Rev. of *The Trojan Women,* by Euripides. *Washington Post,* 30 Mar., C01.

Sacasa, Roberto Aquirre. 1999. "Fire from Heaven." *Asides.* http://www.shakespearedc.org/pastprod/troplayy.html (accessed 17 Oct. 2004).

Saivetz, Deborah. 1993. "The Architecture of Chaos: Actor, Image, and the Dynamics of Space in the Directing Process of JoAnne Akalaitis." Ph.D. diss., Northwestern University.

———. 1998. "An Event in Space: The Integration of Acting and Design in the Theatre of JoAnne Akalaitis." *TDR/The Drama Review* 42 (2) (T158) (Summer): 132–56.

———. 2000. *An Event in Space: JoAnne Akalaitis in Rehearsal.* Hanover, N.H.: Smith and Kraus.

Steele, Mike. 1987. "'Leon and Lena (and Lenz)' Should Be Vintage Akalaitis." *(Minneapolis-St. Paul) Star Tribune,* 18 Oct., 01G.

von Rhein, John. 2000. "Kafka in Song: Philip Glass Work Does Justice to the Master of Existential Horror." Rev. of *In the Penal Colony,* by Philip Glass. *Chicago Tribune,* 13 Nov., 1.

Weiss, Hedy. 2001. "Mary Stuart." Rev. of *Mary Stuart,* by Friedrich Schiller. *Chicago Sun-Times,* 17 Sept., 52.

Wicke, Jennifer. 1990. Rev. of *The Screens,* by Jean Genet. *The Nation* 250 (13) (2 Apr.): 464–66.

Wilson, Edwin. 1993. "Akalaitis's New Approach to a '50s Play." Rev. of *In the Summer House,* by Jane Bowles. *Wall Street Journal,* 6 Aug., eastern edition, A9.

Representative Directing Credits

Broadway:
   In the Summer House (1993)

Off and Off-Off Broadway:
   Cascando (1975, 1976), *Dressed Like an Egg* (1977), *Southern Exposure* (1979), *Dead End Kids* (1980), *Request Concert* (1981), *Red and Blue* (1982), *The Photographer/Far from the Truth* (1983), *Through the Leaves* (1984,

1990), *Green Card* (1986), *Help Wanted* (1986), *American Notes* (1988), *Cymbeline* (1989), *Henry IV, Part I* (1991), *Henry IV, Part II* (1991), *'Tis Pity She's a Whore* (1992), *Woyzeck* (1992), *Prisoner of Love* (1995), *The Iphigenia Cycle* (1999), *In the Penal Colony* (2001), *When the Bulbul Stopped Singing* (2006), *Beckett Shorts* (2007), *The Bacchae* (2007)

Regional Theatre:
   Endgame (1984), *The Photographer/Far from the Truth* (1984), *Through the Leaves* (1984), *The Balcony* (1986), *Green Card* (1986), *Leon and Lena (and Lenz)* (1987), *The Voyage of the Beagle* (1987), *The Screens* (1989), *The Mormon Project* (1990), *'Tis Pity She's a Whore* (1990), *The Rover* (1994), *Suddenly Last Summer* (1994), *Dance of Death* (1996), *The Iphigenia Cycle* (1997), *Ti Jean Blues* (1998), *Life's a Dream* (1999), *The Trojan Women* (1999), *In the Penal Colony* (2000), *Mary Stuart* (2001), *Phèdre* (2002), *The Birthday Party* (2004), *Quartet* (2005), *Thyestes* (2007), *When the Bulbul Stopped Singing* (2007)

International Theatre:
   Cascando (1976)

 # Appel, Libby

Born May 14, 1937 in New York City, Libby Appel's career in theatre has taken her across the United States as an educator, a prolific freelance director, and the artistic director of two theatres: Indiana Repertory Theatre in Indianapolis and the Oregon Shakespeare Festival in Ashland.

Appel was smitten with theatre at the age of five or six, when her parents took her to see George Bernard Shaw's play *Pygmalion*. At that point she resolved that she would be an actor. She spent her teenage years in Queens and ventured to Manhattan on her own to attend musicals and the plays of Tennessee Williams and Arthur Miller. In high school she was introduced to Anton Chekhov and Eugene O'Neill, fueling her passion for dramatic literature. She studied acting at the University of Michigan, where she graduated Phi Beta Kappa with a B.A. degree in 1959. While there, she attended classes taught by Claribel Halstead, who inspired her study of dramatic literature, eventually leading Appel from acting to directing. "I began to be far more interested in the play as a whole and the action of all the actors on stage than I was in my own performance," Appel explains. "While I continued to act, I started my study of dramatic literature from a director's point of view" (1993, n.p.).

After graduation, she followed in the footsteps of her peers by marrying and staying home with her children until they reached school age. It was Appel's mother who led Appel from a life of domesticity back to one of theatre. Near death after suffering a heart attack, Appel's mother gazed up at her and asked, "Well, Libby, when are you getting on with it?" Appel interpreted, "She recognized that my other talents and inner-world creativity needed to be expressed" (Appel 1993, n.p.). Yet it took Appel two additional years to take action. At the age of thirty, she enrolled at Northwestern University in Evanston, Illinois, and reaffirmed the central role that theatre had in her life. After graduating with an M.A. in directing from Northwestern University in 1969, Appel felt at a loss, as if everyone directing professionally were ten years younger. She began her own commedia dell'arte theatre group in Chicago, called I Commedianti. When her husband decided to attend graduate school, Appel took a job teaching acting in Chicago at the Goodman School of Drama, where she taught from 1970 to 1976. She also directed at the Goodman and area theatres, such as Chicago's Court Theatre.

Although many directors have also taught, Appel has had more academic experience than most. She entered the academic realm as the head of the acting program at California State University at Long Beach, where she taught from 1976 to 1981. During this time she also worked at the California Shakespeare Festival, serving as associate director in 1980 and 1981. She was named dean and artistic director of the School of Theatre at the California Institute of the Arts, Valencia, in 1981. While in her academic mode, she published three books and created and produced a videotape on acting and mask work.

During her academic appointments, Appel found freelance directing jobs during the summers. She comments, "I started free-lancing [during the school year] in 1988 and I really had great luck and got a lot of jobs, but I was always hired as the 'woman director' to do the 'women's plays'—you know, *Steel Magnolias* and things like that that I had no interest in whatsoever. So I really felt like a token. But that's all changed now. I don't feel like a token any more" (Brock 1999). When she directed Pirandello's *Enrico IV (The Emperor)* at the Oregon Shakespeare Festival in 1988, Appel came to a sudden realization: "I knew my life had changed absolutely, and I wouldn't be able to go backwards. There was no turning back for me. I had finished my academic career. . . . I had really done what I could offer in that area, and I knew there was a new path for me" (Newman, interview, 2004). She gave notice at her job but continued freelancing and working as dean until her institution could replace her in the 1989–90 academic year.

Working as a freelance director from 1989 to 1992, Appel directed as many as seven productions a year across the United States, including Beckett's *Happy Days* at the Seattle Repertory Theatre in 1989, Shakespeare's *The Merchant of Venice* at the Oregon Shakespeare Festival in 1991, and Robert Bolt's *A Man for All Seasons* at the Alliance Theatre in Atlanta in 1991.

Appel accepted her first position as an artistic director at the Indiana Repertory Theatre (IRT) in Indianapolis, where she directed as many as four productions a year from 1992 to 1995. In her first year at IRT she ran the theatre with two other women and recalls that the female administration was unusual in the conservative city. Her mission there was to "bring diversity to every aspect of the theatre, reinvigorate the theatre's approach to the classics, increase dialogue with the community . . . expand the theatre's commitment to young people, and increase the commissioning of new projects" (Langworthy 1994, 15). The result was that Appel directed a wide variety of productions, ranging from Shakespeare and Chekhov to contemporary works and even musical reviews, such as Fats Waller's *Ain't Misbehavin'*. Appel cites one of the most meaningful productions that she directed at IRT as *Dancing at Lughnasa,* which she directed in 1995 and had directed a year earlier for Atlanta's Alliance Theatre. Brian Friel's character-driven play is about five sisters and a brother who grew up in the Irish village of Ballybeg. Critic Jay Harvey of the *Indianapolis Star* congratulated Appel for her fine casting, the sense of intimacy, and the brilliant character work she attained. Harvey reflected, "The Mundy sisters are vividly characterized, reveling in their individuality even as they create a believable picture of a close-knit household" (1995, D5).

Her excellence as a director and artistic director built Appel a solid reputation, and in 1995 she accepted a position as artistic director of the Oregon Shakespeare Festival (OSF), the very theatre that inspired her to seek a professional directing career. From 1995 to 2007, when she retired from OSF, Appel directed one or two productions a year there while leading the nation's largest theatre company, consisting of some 70 actors and 350 production and administrative personnel.

Although Appel does not seek controversy, many of the productions she has directed at OSF and elsewhere have stirred passionate and disparate responses from critics and audiences. "I feel strongly that there's no point in having a theatre experience if it's not going to be vibrant and alive. . . . Boldness and freshness in interpretation is a crucial part of what we do, and therefore we're taking risks all the time. Because when you're not doing museum theatre, you're taking risks," she explains (Newman 2004).

In 1991 before Appel began her tenure as artistic director at OSF, she directed one of her riskiest productions there as a freelance director, *The Merchant of Venice.* Shakespeare's portrayal of Shylock, a greedy, calculating merchant, is often considered anti-Semitic to modern audiences. As a Jew herself, Appel decided to attack the disturbing play head-on, arguing that of all of Shakespeare's plays it was most in sync with modern culture as a play about materialistic, xenophobic people who are "on a collision course with disaster" (Knickerbocker 1991, Arts 11). Her interpretation blended Armani-clad Wall Street tycoons with the world of Venice, a juxtaposition that one journalist likened to the comingling of sexual and monetary power in Tom Wolfe's *Bonfire of the Vanities*. Appel knew she would disturb the audience but welcomed that opportunity. In a newspaper article, she challenged the audience: "The purpose of theater is to reach people's lives. . . . I think it's important to make you aware that our society moving toward greed and materialism will bring us all to ruin and disaster. . . . I wanted you to be aware that what we do to one another is pretty ugly, ladies and gentlemen, and we've got to get a hold of that and examine that in our lives, and not let greed push us so far that we lose our values" (Arts 11).

In her first production as artistic director at OSF, Appel directed another of Shakespeare's challenging plays: *King Lear*. Critics responded to her stunning visual imagery, but some found the play missed the human connection. Misha Berson of the *Seattle Times* wrote, "The disappointment of this skillfully composed, verbally cogent interpretation is that it seduces the eye and stirs the intellect, while only grazing the heart. That's largely because the production's psychological conceptions tend to be broader and less developed or interlinked than its visual ideas" (1997, M1). Robert Hurwitt of the *San Francisco Examiner* had an opposite reaction, finding the production "a triumph." He gave credit to Appel's talent at cutting the script, her "savvy casting," her attention to sharply drawn characters, and her conceptual vision. Hurwitt wrote, "Appel's *Lear* traces a sharply etched, compelling trajectory from Edwardian formality to harrowing, almost hopeless Beckettian endgame. . . . But it is Appel's staging that makes the most memorable impact. The opening scene alone . . . is a stunner. . . . All are sitting stiffly, facing the audience, dressed in tuxes and formal gowns, as if posing for an Edwardian formal portrait. The starched artifice of the opening lends an artful authenticity to Lear's demands and a genuine horrific shudder to the tantrum with which, scattering the chairs and shattering the tense decorum, he banishes the pitifully distraught Cordelia" (1997).

Appel scored excellent critical reception and national attention with her staging of Lillian Groag's comic drama, *The Magic Fire* in 1997. She first staged the production at OSF, with the aid of a grant from the Kennedy Center's Fund for New American Plays, then directed it at the Kennedy Center in Washington, D.C., in 1998. The memory play centers on Groag's childhood in Buenos Aires, Argentina, under the heavy-handed rule of Juan Perón. As Perón's politics interfere with family life, they turn up their opera recordings to drown out the world around them. Appel, who attended Northwestern with the playwright, found she connected to the work in very personal ways. "The play has brought out things for me that may not have come out. The whole sense of heroic journey, of peoples moving from native homelands into new worlds—that's very personal, since my family came over from Russia" (Preston 1999, 1F). Based on Appel's production at the Kennedy Center, *Time* magazine named *The Magic Fire* one of the best theatrical productions of 1998.

Appel's direction of *Hamlet* in 2000 earned her positive reviews and additional applause for her dramaturgical ingenuity. True to her nature as a risk taker, Appel reversed the order of the first two scenes, providing provocative results. Steve Winn of the *San Francisco Chronicle* reported, "In an unorthodox opening to what turns out to be a pretty blunt account of Shakespeare's febrile tragedy, the audience is plunged immediately into 'Hamlet's' corrupted court at Elsinore. By reversing the play's first two scenes, director Libby Appel delays the first visitations by the ghost of Hamlet's father. In fact, with Barry Kraft doing potent voice-over duty in the role, the murdered king is never visible at all. That's an intriguing idea, one of several in Appel's staging" (2000, B1).

Despite these positive reviews, critics have often taken issue with Appel's choices. Part of the controversy stems from her casting. Long before it became politically correct to engage in cross-gendered or racially blind casting, Appel followed her instincts to cast in a way that would challenge the audience and their perceptions of the play "to unfold the language and ideas of the play in a refreshing and bold way" (Interview, 2004). She has also taken classic works and drastically reduced the number of cast members, casting few actors in multiple parts. Her casting choices inform her interpretation of the play, but they also keep her resident company healthy by exploring the actors' range, often resulting in offbeat casting. When casting for a season, Appel must make choices for seventy actors in eleven plays. "The casting is really about the health of the company," Appel observes. "And I've never done it for political reasons; it's always about what it's done for the literature" (Interview, 2004).

In approaching a classic script, Appel balks at treating the play like a museum piece. "When you see a Shakespeare play, I want you to pulsate with what these images, and these ideas, and these characters are saying about your life. Not about somebody who died 400 years ago" (Newman 2004). *Macbeth,* part of OSF's 2002 season, was one of her recent productions to stir critical response. Appel condensed the play to 110 minutes and cast six actors, playing multiple roles. Winn found the production had arresting moments but ultimately did not work. "Appel's intentions are unmistakably earnest. She means to strip *Macbeth* to its psychological and bone-deep emotional essence. This is meant to be an excavation of a murderer's addled mind. But neither the actors, who work with the added difficulty of playing in the round, nor the gravely self-conscious staging, serves that risky end" (2002, D3). Evidence of Appel's intent to bring the classics alive and support new works is also found in the 2004 season, which included two premiere adaptations based on *Henry VI*, Parts One, Two, and Three, which Appel co-directed with the adapter, Scott Kaiser.

Despite her propensity for re-imagining classics, Appel always begins with a healthy respect for the script, ferreting out the essence of meaning before interpreting that with bold visuals for the audience. Her productions often begin with striking images that make the world of the play abundantly clear. She also leans toward abstract and minimalist imagery. Appel explains, "I try to set the vocabulary from which the audience can understand how to perceive this play. So there will often be a large theatrical gesture that will speak to how abstract this production is going to be—not just the period, but a sense of style" (Interview, 2004). She gives an example from her 2003 production of *Richard II*. During her script analysis, she found Richard was "informed by extravagance," which eventually proved to be his downfall. "So I opened the play with this HUGE gesture of the entire cast—over twenty—coming out in exquisite silk robes with Richard's insignia on the back chanting medieval church music, all in homage toward him. He came out on the highest height in our theatre, and he was surrounded by this apotheosis of kingship—a big sun—and over a loudspeaker came the divine right of kings speech from *Richard II,* then in came this chorus all singing to him. That gesture told everybody who this guy was and what his problem was" (Interview, 2004). Such bold, startling images have become a trademark of Appel's directing style.

Appel describes her work in production as highly collaborative. Playwright Octavio Solis agrees but notes that she is decisive as well: "She encourages people's opinions and ideas, and when they're good she'll go for them. But ultimately she always asserts her own authority. She's not wishy-washy at all" (Newman 2004).

Appel likes to conduct significant research before rehearsals, then "let it go" in the rehearsal room, choosing instead to depart on a new journey with the actors "because I'm completely interested in what the actor is going to bring to the situation" (Interview, 2004). She does not pre-block her productions but spends one to two weeks working on text, then rough blocks with the actors to get a sense of the entire arc of the play. Appel explains, "I need to see the whole thing, and I think actors do too—so that they know the large shape that they're going to be specifically filling in—every single gesture, idea, and thought" (Interview, 2004). She next works on specifics, polishing the production over the last three or four times through the play. Appel's work with masks has influenced the way she explores character development. "I believe characters are built through layers. . . . [T]hat's actually the basis of my mask work. It's not 'quick take' with a mask, to develop a commedia dell'arte character, but rather a deepening through a myriad of exercises, to discover the next layer, the next layer, the next layer. I believe that's how human beings are built" (Interview, 2004). Ultimately, she aims for clarity of the dramatic action.

Appel has a special love for the design process and enjoys working with the same pool of designers, those who know her style and methods. She states, "I work very strongly from abstract images. For example, I'll bring in a painting from Franz Kline, or other abstract expressionists, or George de La Tour, a sixteenth century French artist. It's to give a sense of the light, the feel, the dynamism of the play. Francis Bacon's contemporary paintings and Franz Kline's paintings were the inspiration for my *King Lear*. . . . We work through the play image by image, scene by scene, just to talk about it. To really find out what it is that we want to communicate and how" (Interview, 2004).

Over the course of her career, Appel has directed at more than twenty of the nation's regional theatres as well as at the theatres for which she has been artistic director. She has been recognized for her achievement in directing, winning the Drama-Logue Award for *Enrico IV (The Emperor)* at the OSF in 1988 and Drama-Logue and Robbie Awards for *The Philadelphia Story* at South Coast Repertory, in Costa Mesa, California, in 1991. She was also awarded Back Stage West Garland Awards for *The Magic Fire* and *King Lear* in 1997 and *Uncle Vanya* and *Measure for Measure* in 1998.

When asked what she would be remembered for, Appel first cited the obvious: running the largest theatre company in the country, which used to be "a man's profession" (Interview, 2004). But she also reacted to her legacy as a director. She hopes to be remembered for making large theatrical gestures and exploring the humanity of the characters. More importantly, she is concerned with the larger message communicated to the audience. Her risk taking as a director may partially explain the vitality and popularity that OSF has enjoyed.

Sources

Appel, Libby. 1993. "Still Star Struck." *Theatre at Michigan. The University of Michigan Department of Theatre and Drama Newsletter,* Fall/Winter, n.p. Billy Rose Theatre Collection, "Appel, Libby" file. New York Public Library for the Performing Arts.

———. 2004. Telephone interview with Anne Fliotsos. 9 Jan.

Berson, Misha. 1994. "Women at the Helm." *American Theatre* 11 (May/June): 14–21, 66.

———. 1997. "Appel's Ashland—Oregon Shakespeare Festival Weathers the Storms to Open Its New Season." Rev. of *King Lear,* by William Shakespeare. *Seattle Times,* 9 Mar., M1.

Brock, Lisa A. 1999. *Newspaper of the Minnesota Women's Press,* 20 Jan. http://www.womenspress.com/newspaper/1999/14–22%20articles/14–22garrett-groag.html (accessed 7 Jan. 2004).

Harvey, Jay. 1995. "IRT's *Dancing at Lughnasa* Easy to Connect With." Rev. of *Dancing at Lughnasa*, by Brian Friel. *Indianapolis Star,* 18 Mar., D5.

Hulbert, Dan. 1997. "Turning Tragedy into Success." Rev. of *King Lear,* by William Shakespeare. *San Francisco Examiner,* 3 Mar., C.

Hurwitt, Robert. 1997. "Turning Tragedy into Success." Rev. of *King Lear,* by William Shakespeare. *San Francisco Examiner,* 3 Mar. http://sfgate.com/cgibin/article.cgi?f=/e/a/1997/03/03/STYLE2814.dtl&hw=turning+tragedy+into+success&sn=001&sc=1000 (accessed 26 June 2007).

Knickerbocker, Brad. 1991. "Highly Charged Topics in Shakespeare Play Raise Modern Hackles." *Christian Science Monitor,* 23 Jul., Arts 11.

Langworthy, Douglas. 1994. "Libby Appel: A Natural Seque." *American Theatre* 11 (5) (May/June): 15.

"Libby E(ve Sundel) Appel." 2001. *Contemporary Authors*. In Gale Literary Databases. http://www.galenet.com (accessed 8 Jan. 2004).

Newman, Bruce. 2004. "The Oregon Shakespeare Festival Keeps Reaching Beyond the Bard Thanks to One Tenacious Woman." *Via Online*, Jan. http://www.viamagazine.com/top_stories/articles/libby_appel04.asp (accessed 8 Jan. 2004).

Preston, Rohan. 1999. "Outrunning 'Fire.'" *(Minneapolis) Star Tribune,* 17 Jan., 1F.

Winn, Steven. 2000. "Ashland's *Hamlet* Pulls out All the Stops." Rev. of *Hamlet,* by William Shakespeare. *San Francisco Chronicle,* 19 June, B1.

———. 2002. "Spare *Macbeth* Too Self-Conscious." Rev. of *Macbeth,* by William Shakespeare. *San Francisco Chronicle,* 4 Mar., D3.

Representative Directing Credits

Regional Theatre:

Antony and Cleopatra (1985), *Enrico IV (The Emperor)* (1988), *Happy Days* (1989), *Breaking the Silence* (1989), *The Seagull* (1989), *The Winter's Tale* (1990, 2006), *The Merchant of Venice* (1991), *A Man for All Seasons* (1991), *The Philadelphia Story* (1992), *Yerma* (1992), *Miss Evers' Boys* (1993), *Hamlet* (1993), *The Cherry Orchard* (1993, 2007), *Dancing at Lughnasa* (1994, 1995), *Much Ado About Nothing* (1994), *A Raisin in the Sun* (1994), *Holiday Memories* (1994), *Ain't Misbehavin'* (1995), *Broadway Bound* (1995), *The Tempest* (1996, 2007), *Angel Street* (1996), *King Lear* (1997), *The Magic Fire* (1997, 1999), *Uncle Vanya* (1998), *Measure for Measure* (1998, 2000), *Henry VI, Part Two* (1999), *Molly Sweeney* (2000), *Henry V* (2000), *Hamlet* (2000), *The Trip to Bountiful* (2001), *The Three Sisters* (2001), *Macbeth* (2002), *Richard II* (2003), *Henry VI, Part One: Talbot and Joan* (co-directed, 2004), *Henry VI, Parts Two & Three: Henry and Margaret* (co-directed, 2004), *Richard III* (2005), *Bus Stop* (2006)

Other:

The Magic Fire (1998)

Archer, Osceola

Born June 13, 1890, in Albany, Georgia, Osceola Marie Macarthy (also spelled MacCarthy) Archer became a pioneer as one of the first African American women to direct professionally. She directed primarily at the American Negro Theatre in New York City and at the Putnam County Playhouse in Mahopac, New York, where she directed summer stock. Although mainly remembered for her acting career on and off of Broadway and in radio, television, and film, Archer's early foray in directing deserves recognition, though very few records exist to chronicle her work as a director.

After studying at Albany Normal School and Fisk University in Nashville, Tennessee, Archer earned a bachelor's degree in 1913 from Howard University in Washington, D.C. There she was a member of Howard Players and made her stage debut as Pauline in Edward Bulwer Lytton's play *The Lady of Lyons* in 1913. While at Howard, Archer co-founded the Delta Sigma Theta sorority, now one of the largest African American sororities in the United States. Soon after, in 1915, she married Numa P. G. Adams, a chemistry professor at Howard who became the first dean of Howard's medical school. The Adamses lived in Chicago from 1919 to 1929, where they raised a son. While her husband was in medical school, Archer studied at the Master School of Design and worked as a dress designer, but once their son finished high school, Adams encouraged his wife to pursue a master's degree. She graduated from New York University in 1936 with a master's degree in drama and took the stage name Osceola Archer. Impressively, she made her Broadway debut as an actor in Elmer Rice's *Between Two Worlds* in 1934, while still in graduate school. Throughout the years, she continued her professional training at the Repertory Playhouse Associates from 1932 to 1934, the Equity Library Theatre (no date available), the American Theatre Wing in 1955, the Robert Lewis Workshop in 1960, and the Actors Studio in 1965. During her subsequent acting career, she appeared on Broadway four times and became known for her work with modern classics.

Archer was of African, European, and Indian decent, which created problems with getting cast. In a 1968 story in the *New York Times*, she reported that she had been turned down for African American parts because her skin was too light or her speech too perfect (Lewis 1997, 55). Rather than deter her, racial discrimination fueled her determination to fight the barriers she encountered. Although she had performed at the National Theatre in Washington, D.C., she had to disguise herself as a white woman to gain admittance as an audience member (News Services 1983, B6). Eventually, Actors' Equity boycotted the National Theatre, causing them to change their policy, and the trend continued in other segregated theatres. She helped to fight discriminatory practices in part by serving on the Actors' Equity Committee for Minority Affairs and the Actors' Equity Council.

After initiating a theatrical career as an actor, Archer ventured into the areas of theatre educator and stage director. At her husband's suggestion, Archer taught dramatic arts and directed from 1937 to 1939 at Bennett College in Greensboro, North Carolina, but her professional theatre career remained of utmost importance to her. While she was touring in a production of *The Emperor Jones* in 1940 her husband died, and Archer relocated to New York City to concentrate on adding to her professional credits.

Throughout the 1940s Archer taught and directed at the American Negro Theatre (ANT), a permanent acting company dedicated to the presentation of artistic productions that were vital to the Harlem community. Although artistic director Abram Hill and a host of guest artists directed the majority of ANT productions, Archer directed as well. Unfortunately, the records of her directing credits are conflicting. Scholar Ethel Pitts Walker reports Archer directed only Katherine Garrison Chapin's *Sojourner Truth* in 1948 (1980, 56), whereas Walter Rigdon's *Notable Names in the American Theatre* reports that Archer also directed Thornton Wilder's *Our Town* in 1944, John Silvera and Abram Hill's *On Strivers' Row* in 1945, and *Days of Our Youth* in 1946 (1976, 519).

Sojourner Truth follows the career of Truth from her days as a slave in a tavern near Kingston, New York, to her freedom in that state, where she became a spiritual leader before the Civil War. Brooks Atkinson of the *New York Times* was complimentary about Muriel Smith's performance in the title role, citing the "dignity, power and magnificence" of her acting (1948, 35). He was less impressed with other aspects, calling the playwriting unskilled and the cast uneven and finding no firm directorial hand to pull it all together (35). The cast included a then-unknown actor billed as Harold G. Belafonte in the role of Peter.

When ANT started its own school of drama, the Studio Theatre, Hill invited Archer to head the program. According to an interview with Archer, "[T]he A.N.T. Studio Theatre became the first Black theatre institution to be incorporated by the New York State Board of Education" (Walker 1980, 58). The Studio Theatre maintained a separate production schedule, and several sources credit Archer with both directing and teaching famous Studio Theatre Alumni such as Sidney Poitier, Ozzie Davis, and Harry Belafonte.

ANT may have launched Archer's career as a director, but the Putnam County Playhouse in Mahopac, New York, solidified it. She directed in their summer seasons annually from 1946 to 1954 and in 1958, for a total of twenty-four productions. Carl Harms, who created a company scrapbook and acted for the stock company, wrote several notes by hand on the pages of the book. One reads, "To my knowledge she was the first director who was black to work in summer stock. She also acted in many of the theatre productions" (1946–49, n.p.).

The first season for the Putnam County Playhouse, 1946, featured a resident company of paid actors. Jill Miller, the general manager of the playhouse, also directed, sometimes alongside Archer as a co-director. Very few newspaper clippings mention Archer's directorial work, but the few that do seem to center on her well-received production of Tennessee Williams's *The Glass Menagerie* in 1948. Chris Beels of the *Villager* called it "the best play in the Putnam County Playhouse's summer season thus far," featuring a cast that was "superb in every respect" (Harms 1946–49, n.p.). Robert Lewis, an actor, Broadway director, and drama teacher, deemed it "the best summer stock" he had seen, writing, "The play as a whole went over better than the New York performance" (n.p.). Archer again received praise for her direction of Henrik Ibsen's *A Doll's House* at the Putnam County Playhouse. Thomas Dash wrote that the actors deserved accolades and that "Osceola Archer has directed the Ibsen masterpiece with intelligence" (n.p.). The implications of these scant reviews are that Archer was well respected for her talents as a director, perhaps most particularly for her coaching of the actors.

Archer pursued directing venues in New York City as well, including the Equity Library Theatre, where she directed *Soledara* (author unknown) in 1950, and at the Long Beach Theatre, where she directed Maxwell Anderson's *The Bad Seed* in 1956. She was artistic coordinator of Greenwich Mews Theatre from 1953 to 1954, and she taught acting for the American Theatre Wing from 1953 to 1955. In her 70s, she continued to pursue her professional acting career but found time to direct on occasion, including productions of Lorraine Hansberry's *A Raisin in the Sun* at Prospect Park in 1965, Philip Hayes Dean's *This Bird of Dawning Singeth All Night* at the Chelsea Theatre in 1967, and John Galsworthy's *The Silver Box* at the Harlem School of the Arts Community Theatre in 1971. That same year, at the age of eighty-one, she appeared Off Broadway in Jean Genet's *The Screens*.

Unfortunately, no information is available about Archer's directing style or her casting and rehearsal techniques. What we can glean from the little written about her career is that Archer is remembered as an "elegant and eloquent woman" who fought hard against racial barriers in her profession and forged new paths for African American directors who followed (Lewis 1997, 57). Her life's work was recognized in 1974, when the mayor of Detroit issued a proclamation honoring her contributions to theatre (Rigdon 1976, 519) and again in 1978, when she won the AUDELCO Outstanding Pioneer Award. She served her profession through committee work for Actors' Equity, on the Ethnic Minorities Committee and the Actors' Equity Council, and through her membership on the Executive Committee of the Stage Door Canteen during World War II. Although she is remembered primarily for her acting career, her career as a pioneering director deserves renewed attention.

Osceola Archer died at home in New York City on November 20, 1983, at the age of ninety-three.

Sources

Afrolumens Project. 2004. "Numa P. G. Adams." http://www.afrolumens.org/ century%20of%20change/ adamsnpg.html (accessed 2 Feb., 2004).

Atkinson, Brooks. 1948. Rev. of *Sojourner Truth*, by Katherine Garrison Chapin. *New York Times*, 22 Apr., 35.

Fraser, C. Gerald. 1983. "Osceola Adams, Actress, Dies." *New York Times*, 24 Nov., B16.

Harms, Carl. 1946–49. *Putnam County Playhouse Scrapbook*. Billy Rose Theatre Collection. New York Public Library for the Performing Arts.

Lewis, Barbara. 1997. "Archer, Osceola." In *Facts on File Encyclopedia of Black Women in America*, ed. Darlene Clark Hine, 55–57. New York: Facts on File.

Mapp, Edward, ed. 1990. *Directory of Blacks in the Performing Arts*. 2nd ed. New York: Scarecrow.

News Services. 1983. "Osceola Adams, Noted Actress, Dies at Age 93." *Washington Post*, 25 Nov., B6.

Rigdon, Walter, ed., 1976. *Notable Names in the American Theatre*. Clifton, N.J.: J.T. White, 516.

Walker, Ethel Pitts. 1980. "The American Negro Theatre." In *The Theatre of Black Americans*, vol. 2, ed. Errol Hill, 49–62. Englewood Cliffs, N.J.: Prentice Hall.

Representative Directing Credits

Off and Off-Off Broadway[1]:
> *Our Town* (1944), *On Strivers' Row* (1945), *Days of Our Youth* (1946), *Sojourner Truth* (1948), *Soledara* (1950), *The Bad Seed* (1956), *A Raisin in the Sun* (1965), *This Bird of Dawning Singeth All Night* (1967), *The Silver Box* (1971)

Regional and Stock Theatre:
> *The Octoroon* (1946), *Hedda Gabler* (1947), *Lady Precious Stream* (1947), *The Glass Menagerie* (1948), *The New York Idea* (1948), *For Love or Money* (1948), *A Doll's House* (1949), *Dear Brutus* (1949), *The Two Mrs. Carrolls*

(1950), *Amphitryon 38* (1951), *A Streetcar Named Desire* (1951), *Angel Street* (1951), *The Rose Tattoo* (1952), *Clutterbuck* (1952), *The Lady's Not for Burning* (1952), *The Children's Hour* (1952), *Bell, Book, and Candle* (1953), *The Member of the Wedding* (1954), *My Three Angels* (1954), *The Country Girl* (1954), *The Diary of Anne Frank* (1958), *Time of Storm* (1958), *The Seven Year Itch* (1958), *The Loud Red Patrick* (1958)

Notes

1. As noted in the text, Archer's direction of *Our Town, On Striver's Row,* and *Days of Our Youth* cannot be verified because of conflicting records.

 # Berlin, Pamela

Born December 13, 1952, in Newport News, Virginia, Pamela Berlin became one of the few women to direct on Broadway, with her premiere of *The Cemetery Club* in 1990. Berlin has directed many new plays, including two of her best-known Off Broadway premieres: *Crossing Delancey* in 1986 and *Steel Magnolias* in 1987. Her work has been seen in New York City theatres such as the Manhattan Theatre Club, the Works Progress Administration (WPA) Theatre, Second Stage Theatre, and the Ensemble Studio Theatre, among others, and her career extends to theatres across the United States, from the Kennedy Center in Washington, D.C., to the Pasadena Playhouse in California. She has also directed operas in New York City, Utah, Kansas City, and Vancouver.

Berlin grew up in southern Virginia, occasionally attending productions in New York City as a child. She had an early interest in music and studied violin. When her older sister started to participate in musicals, Berlin joined in. Despite her early interest and participation, she never considered theatre as a career. Instead, she enrolled at Radcliffe College at Harvard, intending to enter a service profession such as medicine or clinical psychology. After settling on a major in American history and literature, Berlin found herself participating in the many extracurricular arts events, playing in the orchestra and performing in theatrical productions. By her sophomore year she had found an affinity for directing, and she continued to direct in her junior and senior years, at the same time working with the Experimental Theatre Lab in Boston.

Berlin obtained a bachelor of arts degree in 1974 and started working in a clinic in Cambridge, Massachusetts, only to discover that she had a desire to pursue directing. The following year she entered the directing program at Southern Methodist University (SMU), where she obtained a master of fine arts degree in 1977. Although she realized that she learned from her classes at SMU, Berlin discovered the true value of her undergraduate experience, which encouraged entrepreneurship, risk taking, and artistic freedom.

After graduation, Berlin joined friends at a fledgling company in St. Louis, a valuable learning experience where "everyone did everything" (Interview, 2004). Although she enjoyed opportunities to stage manage, act, and work on advertising, Berlin had little opportunity to direct, save for some children's theatre productions. She left after one year, determined to work her way up the ladder in New York City. Arriving in Manhattan in 1979, her first step was to join Actor's Equity as a stage manager and work under a variety of directors, which she considers one of the best ways to observe and learn the craft of directing. She stage managed in the summer at a theatre in Colorado and directed some stock as well.

In the early 1980s Berlin found her first real theatrical home when she joined the Ensemble Studio Theatre (EST) on West 52nd Street, first as an assistant to the director, then as a stage manager, and finally as a literary manager. Working full time under artistic director Kurt Dempster, Berlin grew in her abilities to read and study new plays, which later came to be her passion as well as her bread and butter as a director.

Berlin's professional directing career began in earnest when she left her position as a literary manager to pursue freelance work as a director. While at EST, she benefited from networking with new playwrights, which later paid off in directing work. She had a connection with playwright Michael Brady and in 1984 directed his play *To Gillian on Her 37th Birthday* at EST, which later transferred to Circle in the Square Downtown. Set on a New England island on the anniversary of Gillian's premature death, Brady's play mixes comedy and drama as Gillian's husband, daughter, and aunt come to terms with their loss. Berlin's work with the actors received brief praise from critic John Beaufort of the *Christian Science Monitor,* who commented, "*To Gillian* . . . is acted with appealing sensitivity under Pamela Berlin's direction" (1984, 21). With a solid beginning and positive press, Berlin soon got other offers and worked at both small regional theatres and New York City theatres for the next several years.

In 1985 Berlin directed another successful new play, *Crossing Delancey.* Susan Sandler's comedy, produced by the Jewish Repertory Theater, relays the story of Izzie, a young woman searching for love in the wrong places. Led on by a trendy poet, then rejected, Izzie gradually learns to accept her grandmother's old-fashioned matchmaking. In reviews, Berlin was again praised for drawing out sensitive, well-drawn characters, a talent for which she was quickly gaining a reputation.

Berlin's biggest hit was her production of Robert Harling's *Steel Magnolias,* which opened at the WPA Theatre in 1987, then transferred Off Broadway to the Lucielle Lortel Theatre, where it ran for 1,126 performances. The play went on a long-running tour and subsequently became popular with both community and theatre groups across the country, cresting in popularity with a star-studded movie version in 1989. Harling's comedy tells of the troubles and celebrations of an intergenerational group of regulars at Truvy's beauty salon in a small Louisiana town. Berlin found herself in a perfect setting, suited to her strengths of creating unique, well-defined characters who drive both the humor and pathos of the play. Though reviews dwelt on the accomplishments of the playwright and actors, they reflected well on Berlin's attention to detail, pacing, and characterization. She also deserves credit for forming an ensemble play while the script was still being reworked. "The first version of the script felt a bit like the M'Lynn and Shelby show with four other characters," she explained. "So we knew some of the focus needed to change. With the exception of one scene, all the people are on stage all the time. It's a function and a theme of the play itself, how these people are a shoulder and a support" (Kaufman 1987, sec. 2, 5).

The same year, 1987, brought the birth of Berlin's daughter soon after the opening of *Steel Magnolias.* Although she took her infant daughter on the road to rehearsals for the first eighteen months, Berlin curtailed her regional work and focused more on working near her home in New York.

By the time her daughter was five, Berlin was directing her first Broadway play, Ivan Menchell's *The Cemetery Club.* Menchell's plot revolves around the routine monthly meeting of three widows who visit their husbands' graves, but their routine is disrupted when a widower shows up and tests their bonds of friendship. Berlin was immediately taken with the play, which was first produced at Yale. "It's very funny, and it has a tremendous amount of heart, which is something I, personally, as a director, always look for. . . . It's also a play about people who have the opportunity, even in their later years to make other lives for themselves, if they so choose. I found that very appealing" (Brown 1990, N15). Berlin's production, starring Eileen Heckart, Elizabeth Franz, Doris Belack, and Lee Wallace, received a warm reception from the press. John Beaufort of the *Christian Science Monitor* wrote, "*The Cemetery Club* delights in the material of its milieu: gossipy small talk, reminiscence, Jewish-American coinage, and plenty of wisecracks for Miss Heckart to deliver with her patented brand of crackle and snap. . . . The comedy has been staged by Pamela Berlin with due regard for its primary purpose: to keep the customers amused" (1990, Arts 11). The *Boston Globe* concurred: "Pamela Berlin has directed *The Cemetery Club* proficiently. . . . The play is wonderfully paced, with expert timing between the run-on humor and the gentle heartbreak" (Kelly 1990, 86).

In 1994 Berlin made a trip to the Seattle Repertory Theatre to direct *Dancing at Lughnasa,* another play focusing on women's camaraderie, this time among five Irish sisters. Berlin's research was jump-started in an unanticipated way when she visited playwright Brian Friel in Ireland in 1982. She fell in love with the land and the people, stating, "Ever since my trip there I've developed this abiding love of Irish theatre and Ireland itself. . . . The place is so desolate and beautiful, it just got into my blood. There's a great soulfulness—in the land and the people" (Berson 1994, G12). Berlin felt an affinity for the play, which mixes humor and sadness with a dose of "volcanic emotions." She explained, "The heart of this play is the relationships between these women. . . . It's a valentine to their incredible spirit and loyalty" (Interview, 2004).

Berlin continued to direct a steady stream of plays through the next decade, and added opera to her repertoire, which provided her with a different set of opportunities. One of the liberties she has in opera is directing classic works, something she has not often experienced in the theatre world. "First of all," she comments, "it's a huge canvas: big cast shows, big stages, big houses. So, there's that appeal as well as an inherent kind of theatricality to a number of pieces I've worked on. Not to mention getting really inside the music" (Interview, 2004).

Whether directing opera or theatre, Berlin has certain priorities with her cast and design team. When casting, Berlin looks for actors who are compelling and charismatic and "will engage with other people—[actors] who, in addition to being proactive, are listeners" (Interview, 2004). She tries to put actors at ease and get past the artificial quality they invariably bring to auditions, encouraging them to ask questions. "Even if I'm absolutely 'wowed' in an audition I will ask them to make some sort of adjustment," Berlin explains. "Number one, just to see if they're capable of doing that, but also, it begins to forge, on an almost gossamer kind of level, a relationship" (Interview, 2004).

In articulating her rehearsal process, Berlin is aware of her "hermetic" quality as a director—not knowing how others conduct rehearsals but acting on impulse and instinct, uncertain of her own style. In keeping with her goal for true collaboration, she asks the actors many open-ended questions designed to provoke thought and discussion. She feels her best work occurs when she's most collaborative, including her work with designers. "I look for designers who like to have lots of meetings, because I need that, and I find that ultimately that's how we arrive at something that's the most exciting, the most organic, the most unique," Berlin observes. "And that is what I encourage [with actors] in the rehearsal hall as well" (Interview, 2004).

Perhaps due to her background as a literary manager and her long-standing work with new plays, Berlin likes to spend as much time as possible with table work, though it depends on the project and the actors involved. She does not take one approach to coaching actors but works according to each actor's approach as much as possible, and she resorts to improvisation in rehearsal only once the actions and the parameters of the scene have been set.

Though she would like to explore more theatrical styles, Berlin's work thus far has been mainly in realistic drama and comedy. "In addition to Strindberg and Ibsen, the canon of those plays that I'm very interested in, I also find I'm increasingly drawn to less naturalist or realistic material," she explains (Interview, 2004). Her directing style varies with each play, though she sees her primary directorial emphasis on establishing relationships. "Ultimately, I think that the material that touches me the most—whatever it is—speaks to the human condition, is about relationships. That's what interests me in life, that's what interests me in the theatre," she states (Interview, 2004).

It is partly coincidence that many of the plays she has directed focus on women, such as *Crossing Delancey, Steel Magnolias,* and *The Cemetery Club.* Although she has not sought out such productions, she clearly relates to the stories and relationships within them. In a rehearsal for *Steel Magnolias,* Berlin's experience as a woman aided her at a time when her all-female cast was flagging. "I remember we were in rehearsal at the WPA and I had only told a handful of people that I was pregnant. I was a little over two months. We were rehearsing the scene where the character [Shelby] tells everyone in the beauty parlor that she's pregnant, and it was feeling pretty anemic—both her telling and their responses. So I just stood up and said, 'Alright everybody. Guess what? This is the truth: I'm pregnant!' And everyone screamed. I said, 'That's it!' I'll never forget that day" (Interview, 2004).

Over the course of her career, Berlin's goal has been simply to work, a goal she has accomplished. She looks forward to the next phase in her career, once her daughter goes to college and she is free to take on more jobs away from home. Until that time, Berlin remains a busy freelance director, working both in New York City and across the country. She has taught and directed at several universities and studios, including Sarah Lawrence College, New York University, Boston University Theater Institute, and numerous studios in New York City. True to her instinct in college to work in a service profession, Berlin has chosen to give back to the profession through her service and leadership, first on the board of the Society of Stage Directors and Choreographers and as its president, from 2001 to 2004.

Sources

Beaufort, John. 1984. "*Gillian* Explores Family Tragedy with Care and Compassion." Rev. of *To Gillian on Her 37th Birthday*, by Michael Brady. *Christian Science Monitor*, 29 Mar., 21.

———. 1990. Rev. of *The Cemetery Club*, by Ivan Menchell. *Christian Science Monitor*, Arts: 11.

Berlin, Pamela. 2004. Interview with Anne Fliotsos. 31 June. New York City.

Berson, Misha. 1994. "Dancing at the Rep—New York Director Brings Some Irish Spirit to Seattle." *Seattle Times*, 30 Dec., G12.

Brown, Joe. 1990. "Berlin: Bound for Broadway." *Washington Post*, 6 Apr., N15.

Kaufman, David. 1987. "Six *Steel Magnolias* Are Blooming Onstage." *New York Times*, 13 Sept., sec. 2, 5.

Kelly, Kevin. 1990. "Slick *Cemetery Club* Has Humor, Warmth." Rev. of *The Cemetery Club*, by Ivan Menchell. *Boston Globe*, 26 Apr., 86.

Representative Directing Credits

Broadway:
>   *The Cemetery Club* (1990)

Off and Off-Off Broadway:
>   *The Self-Begotten* (1982), *Ord-way Ames Gay* (1982), *To Gillian on Her 37th Birthday* (1984), *Elm Circle* (1984), *Crossing Delancey* (1985), *Mama Drama* (1987), *Steel Magnolias* (1987), *Early One Evening at the Rainbow Bar and Grille* (1989), *Club Soda* (1991), *Peacetime* (1992), *The Family Of Mann* (1993), *Pretty Fire* (1993), *Joined at the Head* (1994), *Black Ink* (1995), *Three in the Back, Two in the Head* (1996), *Wallflowering* (1996), *The Adjustment* (1997), *The Red Address* (1997), *'Til the Rapture Comes* (1998), *Anonymous* (2000), *Endpapers* (2002)

Regional Theatre:
>   *The Plough and the Stars* (1985), *On the Verge* (1986), *Dancing at Lughnasa* (1994), *Ruler of My Destiny* (1999), *South Pacific* (1999), *Tea* (2001), *Driving Miss Daisy* (2002), *Copenhagen* (2003), *According to Goldman* (2004)

Boesing, Martha

Born Martha Gross on January 24, 1936, in Providence, Rhode Island, Boesing is best known as the artistic director and a founding member of At the Foot of the Mountain (AFOM) in Minneapolis from 1974 to 1984. Boesing has worn many hats in the theatre, from performer, to technician, to publicist, to playwright and director. As a productive feminist artist, Boesing has worked all her life to obtain one goal: "to expose the oppressive limits of society" (Greeley 1995, 161).

Boesing (then known as Gross) grew up with theatre and music and clearly remembers her early exposure to professional theatre, such as attending *A Member of the Wedding* on Broadway and seeing the masterworks of Rodgers and Hammerstein on Broadway with her father, who lived in New York. She attended boarding school at the Abbot Academy in Andover, Massachusetts, and took part in singing and theatricals, doing summer stock during her vacation time. She earned her bachelor's degree in English in 1957 at Connecticut College for Women, where she wrote her first play her junior year and also directed class plays. She then earned a master's degree in English literature from the University of Wisconsin in 1958. Soon after, she moved to New York City, married her first husband, and lived in Cambridge, Massachusetts, before the couple moved to Minneapolis, where they were both enrolled at the University of Minnesota. Boesing (whose married name was Gross Pierce) started doctoral work in theatre but very quickly dropped out to work with the Minneapolis Repertory Theatre from 1960 to 1962. She both acted and directed there, directing *Under Milk Wood* and a Christmas show of her own creation. In 1961, while still in Minneapolis, she co-founded the Fifth Street Players and the Moppet Players, the latter of which became the prestigious Minneapolis Children's Theatre. She directed productions for her two new theatres before taking time off to have her first child in 1962.

The most influential period of Boesing's theatrical development was the time she spent as a company member at the Firehouse Theatre in Minneapolis, from 1963 to 1969. The Firehouse had a connection with the Open Theatre, and she was greatly influenced by the work of Joseph Chaikin and other New York City experimental groups. "We [The Firehouse Theatre] were involved in everything the sixties offered us, from politics to drugs, from burning draft cards to running around nude on stage," she states (Boesing 1987, 321). According to Boesing, the Firehouse Theatre was a seminal experience and ultimately changed not just her view of theatre but her view of life: "We were aggressive and brave and willing to experiment with our own hearts and psyches to create our art. Resistance amounted to cowardice and we faced each other with an unspoken challenge to make each act more outrageous than the last" (321). The Firehouse Theatre "pushed the envelope of consciousness" in the same way as the Living Theatre, the Open Theatre, and The Performance Group, ultimately resulting in transformational theatre (Boesing, interview, 2004). Boesing explains, "One actor often played many roles; characters transformed mid-scene into alter-egos, animals, even trees. We questioned the notion of a single or static personality as we began to notice that each of us is really made up of many different images, feelings, attitudes and styles that are constantly changing depending on who we are with and what is expected of us" (Boesing 1987, 322). These ideas would soon resurface in Boesing's role as creator and director with AFOM.

During the Firehouse years Boesing was divorced, married to her second husband, Paul Boesing, and gave birth to two daughters. Together, she and her husband wrote several music-theatre pieces and toured around the United States for a time as a folk-singing duo. When the family moved to Atlanta in 1972, Boesing wrote plays for the Academy Theatre, where she became playwright in residence. In 1974 Boesing and four actors from Atlanta took her play *Pimp* to Minneapolis. This group, which included men, formed the nucleus for the founding of AFOM in 1974, which reorganized and became a women's collective in 1976.

While directing and serving as artistic director of AFOM until 1984, Boesing was a prolific playwright, writing at least two plays a year (Greeley 1995, 161). Although her legacy has been primarily as a playwright, Boesing's theatrical training is diverse. "I was trained in the theatre as an actor, technician, director; and hence to this day I passionately see theatre as a nonliterary art form—a collaborative performance art which takes place in *time*, not in space (as on the page or canvas). Sometimes I call myself an architect of the theatre rather than a playwright" (Leavitt 1989, 73). Boesing's plays often are developed collectively, around women's rituals of different magnitudes—from the everyday to the ceremonial. As a layering of rituals, her feminist works are episodic rather than linear, trying not to produce a final outcome but to raise issues and questions that will provoke the audience socially and politically. Her form and style derive from her passion to honor women's feelings and nurture their values through a theatre of protest and celebration, all part of the mission of AFOM (Boesing 1996, 1011).

Boesing cites many highlights of her directing career at AFOM, most of which stirred controversy. In 1975 Boesing's play *River Journal* took Minneapolis by storm, creating lines around the block at the box office. The play centered on an Everywoman character and expounded on the essence of women's lives. Brechtian aspects included "realistic scenes, readings, songs and characters so stripped down they are most like one aspect of a single personality" (Leavitt 1980, 76). Boesing experimented extensively with the production from night to night. Although the lines and blocking were set, the actors were free to try out emotional subtexts that were radically different from the lines. "A scene which was filled with rage one night might be played sweetly and deliciously, or etched in fear, the next," she explained (Boesing 1987, 322). The process invigorated the actors and effectively stimulated the audience as well. One audience member reflected, "Much of the play's ability to elicit a response is due to the fine ensemble work of the cast, sensitively directed by Boesing" (Leavitt 1980, 77).

Boesing wrote and directed *Raped: A Woman's Look at Bertolt Brecht's "Exception to the Rule,"* which struck a disturbing chord with the audience when it opened in 1976. The piece explored "the economic base of permissible violence against women," whether physical or psychological (Boesing 1987, 323). Critic Arthur Sainer found Boesing's creation had a profound effect, writing, "As a male, what the play brought home to me more starkly than ever before is the sense that women must feel they are living in an armed camp. . . . It is one thing for a male to feel pained at the sight of a woman being ogled as she walks down the street; it is quite another to be that woman 24 hours a day—on the street, in subways, on the job, in her home" (Leavitt 1980, 77). *Raped* became a powerful piece for the group, and they toured it for several years. One night Boesing invited the all-female audience members to stand and yell "stop" at any point in the performance and add their own experiences of rape. "The room was electrified by suspense," Boesing recalled. The testimonials provided a bridge to the community and evidence that "real change was happening" in their midst (Boesing 1987, 323).

In 1978, Boesing created and directed *The Story of a Mother,* again experimenting with audience involvement and working to elicit a response. The performers invited the audience on the journey into their mothers' lives through a meditative state. Boesing explains that the audience would "enter into the inner lives of their own mothers and then share in certain litanies" (1987, 324). By the end of the play the audience joined with the cast, reciting a litany of their matriarchal lineage. When she directed the play again in 1987 for AFOM, Boesing found that the 1978 version, which was based on the mother–daughter experiences of her all-white company, had to be completely rewritten for her new, multiracial cast. Boesing found a new common ground from which to draw: "[A]ll their [the performers'] mothers were immigrants and experienced a lot of pain and suffering coming into a culture that was alien to them" (Collins 1998, 33). Where the first version asked the audience to stand and testify, the second version found "a more conventional form blending seemingly disparate stories into a single interconnected pattern" (33). The production played to excellent reviews but took its toll on the company members, who spent an abundance of time and energy reshaping the script and rehearsing it.

In 1981 Boesing created and directed AFOM's production of *Junkie!*, about addictions in women's lives. As with many other collaborative works, the stories of addiction were developed from the performers' lives. Boesing in turn shaped them into a script and added a clown character, Esther, "serving as a dramatic device to both lighten the dialogue and integrate the stories through her ability to interact with others who are disconnected from each other because of their addictions" (Greeley 1995, 173). Lynne Greeley studied Boesing's dramaturgy and describes her powerful, symbolic imagery as a director, including a visual depiction of the family being psychologically torn apart. Greeley writes, "Lorraine [the mother] is pulled in the position of a crucifix, with her 'husband' pulling one arm and her 'mother,' the other; the children are at her knees like mourning women. With her head dropped backwards, Lorraine sustains an expression of anguish throughout" (175–76).

In 1982 Boesing wrote and directed AFOM's production of *Ashes, Ashes, We All Fall Down,* a play about nuclear war. Again, she used imagery to convey the tone and emotional content of the piece. In one scene "the actors slowly take off their clothes and, in dimmed lights with their hands above their heads, line up before a dark door frame" (Greeley 1995, 178). One woman recalls the audience's reaction as they realized that the scene represented Auschwitz: "Oh, they're going to take off their clothes—they're taking off their clothes—oh, God, look what it is!" (178).

In 1984 Boesing won a $20,000 Bush Foundation Fellowship, allowing her to leave AFOM and explore other opportunities as an artist. One of her first projects was to start the Environmental Action Theatre Project in Minneapolis and collectively create a performance piece that she directed in 1990, called *Standing on Fishes.* Boesing asked each member of the group to bring in an animal that could give humans a lesson to learn. She directed the performance with the masked performers portraying the animals, giving their messages to humankind in a manner that was both poetic and immediate. In 1991 the group toured the play east of Minneapolis all the way to Maine, performing in communities that had ecological and environmental problems.

Boesing has continued to direct for a variety of theatres, both traditional and experimental. Her direction of a play in 1986 at the Actors Theatre in St. Paul required her to go back into the constructs of what she calls "traditional" theatre, where she went in as an authority figure with ideas for blocking and interpretation and got little questioning in return. Because she was accustomed to the performers collectively creating a piece of theatre, she found herself inviting the actors to contribute. She was again in a non-traditional setting in 2004, both directing and creating "Street Retreats" for the Faithful Fools Street Ministry, in San Francisco's Tenderloin district. Combining her love of theatre and activism, Boesing's "Street Retreats" aid in the theatre's mission to "address the existence of poverty in the midst of material wealth." The Faithful Fools Web site explains Boesing's objective: "Ms. Boesing has found that combining potential actors from the street with professionals serves as an inspiration and a model, giving permission to everyone to play more freely and to go more deeply into the substance of our lives. The improv performances will be created out of the stories, poems, dreams, fantasies, and visions of the company of actors, informed by their shared experiences of living on the street" (Faithful Fools Web site).

To understand Boesing as a director is to understand how her leadership is inextricably linked to the highly collaborative process of creating theatre. Casting, in its traditional sense, was not conducted at AFOM because at any given time there were only between five and seven performers, and pieces often were shaped by the performers' personal experiences or input. Rather than leaving personal problems at the door, as many actors are requested to do at rehearsals, the AFOM actors considered exploring those problems as part of their work—part of their preparation. Boesing agreed with second-wave feminists, who sought to make the personal political. She wanted to bring the personal experiences of her own group to the social problems at hand. She explains, "[A]fter choosing the major issue of the piece (rape, madness, prostitution, nuclear war, addiction, etc.), we began the work on all of our plays with ourselves" (Boesing 1996, 1012). The cast shared feelings and stories about their relationships to the subject at hand, and the preliminary psychological exploration prepared the cast to become physical. "We forgave ourselves much," writes Boesing, "by seeing all of our own character defects in the context of our oppression, as well as our particular ethnic and class backgrounds. We got up on our feet and searched for the essential, primal center of these experiences and gave image to them in movement, language, and song" (1012). Boesing explains the rational and challenges of this particular approach to performance:

> We believed that in order to create fully realized characters, we had to become awake to what was really going on inside of us. Coming from a lifetime of suppression meant that we had to become practiced at really knowing and being able to articulate what we were feeling at any given moment (the "condition") and what it was we wanted (the "action"). . . . [W]e learned to tell the truth about ourselves and to use this skill in our performances. Sometimes we would create a sound or a movement image

from the inner life about which we were reporting. Other times we would take the actual feelings we were having and put them into the improvisation or scene we were working on as a kind of subtext, regardless of what the text itself seemed to call for. It gave a strange undercurrent of life to the acting style for which we became known, an acting style that did not look like acting, that looked more like a documentary or kind of gripping realism. . . . [M]any of the women who worked with At the Foot of the Mountain were indeed very highly skilled and trained actors who had to work hard to drop much of their training facade to move into the deeper presence of this work. (Boesing 1996, 1016–17)

Committing to this non-hierarchical approach to rehearsal was both exhilarating and amazingly difficult for Boesing and for the performers. In one of Boesing's journal entries from 1977 she writes, "The rehearsals are enormously exciting. We are learning new ways to get down to the essence, the emblem of a scene or a moment and then to extend into wonderfully theatrical gestures of sound and movement that seem to say it all in a moment. But the learning is slow . . . the incredible concentration, staying constantly in the condition without falter is difficult. It is also exhausting" (1996, 1016). In addition, the collective focused on process rather than product. In a journal entry from 1976, Boesing admits, "I want to postpone the opening, work without endgaining . . . find our own voice and style before we open a show" (1017). Despite AFOM's collaborative style, Boesing was still clearly a leader in the creative process, taking the performers through the process and facilitating discussions, then having final say on the forms, images, movements, and text evoked from the group.

Pondering how her directing has changed over the decades, Boesing states, "I never studied directing, or anything like that. I've certainly moved from not knowing what I was doing to being a very confident director. I feel very comfortable working with actors. I like working with actors. I like pushing the envelope a little, inviting actors to look at other possible ways of approaching a work . . . to get away from consistency. . . . I feel very, very grateful for the opportunities I've had and for the companies of actors I've worked with. I feel very, very lucky" (Interview, 2004).

Over the course of her four decades in the theatre, Boesing has won numerous awards, grants, and honors, including a National Endowment for the Arts Individual Artist Grant in 1987, the Theatre Communications Group Pew Residency Director's Grant in 1996, and a McKnight Theatre Artist Award in 2001. In addition to AFOM and the Firehouse Theatre, Boesing has directed at the Playwright's Center, In the Heart of the Beast Puppet and Mask Theater, the Environmental Theater Project, and Actors for Change. She has directed in San Francisco with A Traveling Jewish Theater and the Faithful Fools Street

Ministry. In addition to her published plays, Boesing published an article about her experiences with AFOM and is working on an autobiography that highlights her experiences as a radical during revolutionary movements such as the civil rights movement and the women's movement. As her career continues, she is focusing more on her directing than her playwriting but still continues her quest to expose oppression in society. Always the activist, Boesing states, "Art should move us. From one place to another—psychically, physically. Its work is to turn us around, to re-volve us, re-turn us to our roots, to home. It is re-volutionary by definition if it's any good—especially in a culture which has lost its way" (1996, 1022).

Sources

Boesing, Martha. 1987. "Process and Problems." In *Women in American Theatre,* ed. Helen Krich Chinoy and Linda Walsh Jenkins, 321–25. New York: Theatre Communications Group.

———. 1996. "Rushing Headlong into the Fire At the Foot of the Mountain." *Signs: Journal of Women in Culture and Society* 21 (4): 1011–23.

———. 2004. Telephone interview with Anne Fliotsos. 20 July.

Collins, Robert. 1998. "A Feminist Theatre in Transition." *American Theatre* 4 (2) (Feb.): 32–34.

Faithful Fools Web site. www.faithfulfools.org/_unused/projtheater.htm (accessed 21 June 2004).

Flynn, Meredith. 1986. "The Feeling Circle, Company Collaboration, and Ritual Drama: Three Conventions Developed by the Women's Theatre, At the Foot of the Mountain." Ph.D. diss., Bowling Green State University.

Greeley, Lynne. 1988. "Spirals from the Matrix: The Feminist Plays of Martha Boesing, an Analysis." Ph.D. diss., University of Maryland, College Park.

———. 1989. "Martha Boesing: Playwright of Performance." *Text and Performance Quarterly* 9 (3): 207–15.

———. 1995. "Making Familiar: Martha Boesing and Feminist Dramatic Structure." In *Theatre and Feminist Aesthetics,* ed. Karen Laughlin and Catherine Schuler, 160–81. Madison: Farleigh Dickinson University Press.

Leavitt, Dinah Luise. 1980. *Feminist Theatre Groups.* Jefferson, N.C.: McFarland.

———. 1989. "Boesing, Martha Gross." In *Notable Women in the American Theatre: A Biographical Dictionary,* ed. Alice M. Robinson, Vera Mowry Roberts, and Milly S. Barranger, 71–74. New York: Greenwood.

Stephens, Judith L. 1989. "Subverting the Demon-Angel Dichotomy." *Text and Performance Quarterly* 9 (1): 53–64.

Representative Directing Credits

Regional Theatre:
> *Under Milk Wood* (1962), *Oh Dad, Poor Dad, Mama's Hung You in the Closet and I'm Feeling So Sad* (1964), *River Journal* (1975), *Raped: A Woman's Look at Brecht's "Exception to the Rule"* (1976), *The Moon Tree* (1977), *The Life* (1980), *Junkie!* (1981), *Ashes, Ashes, We All Fall Down* (1982), *Antigone Too* (1983), *Las Gringas* (1984), *The Nightingale* (1985, 2002), *Home at Seven* (1985), *Photograph* (1986), *The Story of a Mother* (1987), *Snake Talk* (1988), *Heart of the World* (1989), *The Reaper's Tale* (1989), *The Cicada Journals* (1995), *Like a Mother Bear* (1996), *Old, Jewish & Queer* (1997), *The Witness* (2002)

Tours:
> *Standing on Fishes* (1991)

 # Bogart, Anne

Born September 25, 1951, in Newport, Rhode Island, Anne Bogart is one of the most influential directors in the American theatre. Her productions have been staged in numerous theatres in New York City, across the United States, and overseas in such countries as Germany, Switzerland, Czechoslovakia, Poland, Japan, the United Kingdom, the Georgian Republic, and France. Her postmodern approaches to both new performance texts and American classics have caused controversy and created enormous interest in her directorial methods. Over the years Bogart has worked with new plays, classics, operas, and her own performance pieces, usually through collaboration with the Saratoga International Theatre Institute (SITI) company. Critic Mel Gussow states, "She has often been involved in controversy, splitting audiences as well as critics. Depending on the point of view, she is either an innovator or a provocateur assaulting a text" (1994, sec. 1, 11).

Bogart's postmodern emphasis on fragmentation is not surprising, given that she grew up in the post–World War II society of the 1950s and 1960s. She reflects, "The moments of my life are discontinuous and jump" (2001, 8). As the child of a naval officer she was often uprooted and moved around the United States and the world, where she was exposed to diverse cultures and perspectives. Early on, she learned that removing herself from the United

States helped her gain a new perspective of American culture and identity, an issue she would return to as a director.

At fifteen years of age, Bogart attended a kabuki-style production of *Macbeth*, directed by Adrian Hall of Trinity Repertory Theatre. She walked out thinking, "I have no idea what happened, but I [thought] that's what I want to do with the rest of my life" (Nevius 2004, E4). She attended four colleges before graduating from Bard College in 1974, then earned an M.A. in theatre history at New York University (NYU) in 1977. While in graduate school she directed three New York City productions: *Macbeth, Two Portraits,* and *RD1, The Waves,* an adaptation of Virginia Woolf's *The Waves* ("Bogart," 1999, 78). In 1979 NYU invited her to teach for the Experimental Theatre Wing, furthering her work with unorthodox approaches to performance. A primary influence was Mary Overlie, with whom she collaborated on a dance/theatre piece called *Artourist* in 1980. It was Overlie's modern dance techniques that helped launch Bogart's investigation of the Viewpoints, linking the actor's physical movement with psychological action.

At about this time Bogart also became enamored of German theatre and expressionism. She studied the language and started incorporating ideas she derived from German films and publications. Eventually, the German magazine *Theatre Heute* published a story about her work, which in turn brought invitations to direct in Germany, Austria, and Switzerland. A devastating experience directing in West Berlin forever changed Bogart's outlook as a director. She had resolved to direct like a German, speaking to the cast only in German. "I was sure Americans were superficial, and I wanted more than anything to be European," she confessed (Bogart 2001, 14). The result of such thinking was a disastrous production in West Berlin, which provoked the audience to hurl insults at the actors on stage. Reflecting on her failure provided Bogart with new perspective. She writes, "It was in a pension in the Dolomite mountains in northern Italy after the Berlin failure that I had a big personal revelation that saved me. I realized with profound conclusiveness that I was an American; I had an American sense of humor, and American sense of structure, rhythm, and logic. I thought like an American. I moved like an American. And, all at once, it was clear to me that the right American tradition of history and people exists to tap into and own. Suddenly, I was free. All the rest of my work in Europe and, in fact, since that moment in the pension in Italy, has been lighter and more joyful" (14).

Transformed by this new awareness of her heritage, Bogart began an exploration of American culture through several means: the reinterpretation of classic American plays, the creation of new works about cultural phenomena, and the creation of performance pieces about the lives and works of famous Americans, such as Gertrude Stein, Orson Welles, and Robert Wilson. She explains, "I'm interested in remembering and celebrating American spirit in all its difficult, ambiguous, and distorted glory" (Bogart 2001, 15). The key word is *distortion*, for Bogart is not guided by linear continuity but, as a postmodernist, is interested in creating "a collage of repetitive gestures, patterns of speech and dialogue, and tableaux vivants which evoke mood and create meaning through associative images" (Malnig 1994, 42). In *A Director Prepares*, Bogart writes that she wants to produce an artistic explosion, explaining, "I am researching new approaches to acting for the stage that combine vaudeville, operetta, Martha Graham and postmodern dance. I want to find resonant shapes for our present ambiguities. I want to contribute to a field that will engender moments onstage that broaden the definitions of what it is to be human" (2001, 39).

Early in her career Bogart earned a reputation for ruthlessly deconstructing beloved American classics, a technique that brought her controversy, notoriety, and ultimately acclaim. In 1982 she adapted Tennessee Williams's *A Streetcar Named Desire* and cast her production with eight Blanches and twelve Stanleys. Two years later she returned to Tisch School of the Arts at NYU to direct a deconstructed version of *South Pacific*. Rather than setting the 1949 Rodgers and Hammerstein musical in the balmy Pacific islands, Bogart set it in a clinic for shell-shocked war veterans. Removing the romanticized backdrop of the original helped Bogart "probe issues aroused in the original work, including the nature of patriotism, racism, and the relationship of the individual to authority" (Malnig 1994, 41). Although controversial, her creative vision won her a New York Dance and Performance (Bessie) Award.

In the mid- to late 1980s, Bogart directed several new plays in New York City, including Mac Wellman's *Cleveland* and Gillian Richard's *In His Eighteenth Year*. She co-wrote a play with Wellman in 1986 called *1951*. After its initial production at the New York Theatre Workshop, it toured in California and to Paris, France. Her most memorable production of the 1980s won her an Obie Award for direction. In *No Plays, No Poetry, but Philosophical Reflections, Practical Instructions, Provocative Prescriptions, Opinions, and Pointers from a Noted Critic and Playwright,* Bogart created what critic Stephen Holden of the *New York Times* described as "an avant-garde carnival that carries the audience from scene to scene in a choreographed comic pageant that sends up the theoretical writings of Bertolt Brecht" (1988, C32). Created as a collaborative performance piece by three experimental theatre groups, including Bogart's recently formed Via Theatre, the content is telling of Bogart's love for theatre history. She explained, "It is a letter to the theatre community in the form of a play. . . . The letter addresses theatre issues through the eyes of Brecht and his funny theories in which he contradicted himself all the time. Around 97 percent of the words are from Brecht himself" (C32). The next year she staged the production at the Trinity Repertory Theatre in Providence, Rhode Island, as the season opener during her single year as artistic director there.

Bogart's brief post at Trinity Repertory highlights her problem of pleasing a mass audience at a regional theatre, an audience that she says has come to expect entertainment above theatre. She explains,

> There are two ways of thinking about the audience. The first is to want everybody in the room to feel the same thing. I tend to think of that as what Spielberg did in *E.T.* You cry at all the right places, but everybody else is crying at those places, too, and at the end you feel like a manipulated rag. It's actually easy to make a whole audience feel one thing. It's also called fascism.
>
> The second way is to create a moment onstage that triggers *different* associations in everybody in the audience. It's much harder to do that. I try to set up contradictions on the stage. In between those contradictions lives something very bright. I try to think of the audience as detectives; I'm leaving clues for them. The older I get, the more I try to do the least I possibly can onstage, so that the most happens in the audience's head. (Diamond 2001, 34)

Although her season at Trinity Rep was artistically acclaimed, the box office ticket sales fell 20 percent (De Vries 1990, sec. 2, 5). The problems with the company were complex, but in the end Bogart refused the budget cuts handed down by the board, which the board translated into a resignation. Looking back, Bogart mused that if she had been a man, she would have gotten a second chance to improve the situation the next season (Gussow 1994, sec. 1, 11).

After her experience in Providence, Bogart returned to freelance directing and won her second Obie Award with the premiere production of Paula Vogel's *Baltimore Waltz* in 1992 at the Circle Repertory Company in New York City. The nonlinear plot revolves around Anna, who discovers she has Acquired Toilet Disease, or ATD, and takes an imaginary trip to Europe with her brother, Carl. By the end of the play, the audience understands that it is actually the brother who is sick and dying, presumably from AIDS, and that Anna has constructed a fantasy to keep his spirit alive and cope with her loss. Critics were fascinated both by the metaphorical story and the theatricality of the play. In a backhanded compliment, Frank Rich of the *New York Times* wrote, "the supple production . . . finds the director Anne Bogart treating a new script with a becoming delicacy and polish she does not always lavish upon the classics" (1992, C15). Bogart directed another premiere of a Vogel play, *Hot 'n Throbbin'*, two years later.

Also in 1992, Bogart and Tadashi Suzuki co-founded the Saratoga International Theatre Institute (SITI), which has since become the creative birthplace for the majority of Bogart's conceptual performance pieces. The company strives to create innovative theatre and train young performers through a combination of the Viewpoints—based on the actors' physical manifestation of tempo, duration, kinesthetic response, repetition, shape, gesture, architecture, spatial relationship, and topography—and the "Suzuki Method," a physical performance technique designed by Suzuki. SITI seeks to "incorporate artists from around the world and learn from the resulting cross-cultural exchange of dance, music, art, and performance experiences" (Sarasota 2004). Bogart's prolific record of creation and direction through SITI includes *bobrauschen-bergamerica*, *ROOM*, *War of the Worlds*, *Cabin Pressure*, *Culture of Desire*, *Bob*, *Private Lives*, *Miss Julie*, *Alice's Adventures*, *Small Lives/Big Dreams*, *The Medium*, *Songs and Stories from Moby Dick*, *Gertrude and Alice*, and *The Seven Deadly Sins*. Her SITI productions routinely tour or are invited to regional theatres across the country, greatly expanding her audience.

In the 1990s Bogart continued on her quest to understand the American identity through a postmodern lens. At Hartford Stage in Connecticut, she staged the American classic *The Women*, a play she had directed at Bennington College in the mid-1980s. Clare Booth Luce's comedy, set in 1936, depicts the catty relationships of a group of Park Avenue socialites. Although traditionally presented in a realistic setting, Bogart's production was minimalist, with very little furniture. Instead, she created her *mise-en-scène* through the movement and composition of bodies on stage. Characters who were supposed to exit the stage were directed to cross behind a giant glass wall upstage, posing, parading, and observing the action. She interpolated songs into the text as well, and rather than emphasizing face-to-face conversation, she had actors turn to the audience or to thin air. Critic David Richards of the *New York Times* mused, "Such directorial inventions are head turners, all right. The question is, what do they do for Luce's play? And the answer is, not a whole lot. . . . The director has such an idiosyncratic vision of the script that Luce's contribution seems altogether secondary" (1994, C13). Bogart admits that the audience for the production, later performed at the San Diego Repertory Theatre, was totally dead. Disheartened, she again asked herself why her work in regional theatre was not resonating with the audience. She concluded, "I was looking at this thing the wrong way. It's not the audience that I'm talking to . . . but that I'm trying to reach a part of them, a part that can hear what I'm saying. And sometimes that part won't be there and won't listen. The question is not 'Who is my audience?' but 'What part of any audience am I working for?'" (Dixon and Smith 1995, 118).

Her thirst to investigate memories of American culture continued with a trilogy she created in the 1990s: *American Vaudeville* (1992), *Marathon Dancing* (1994), and *American Silents* (1997). The first piece premiered at the Alley Theatre in Houston and was Bogart's exploration of vaudeville performance through a medium that proved to be both educational and entertaining. Authentic vaudeville songs, sketches, and routines were interspersed with performers' discussions about their craft. *Marathon Dancing* opened in New York City, produced by En Garde Arts at the site-specific Masonic Hall. Set in the Great Depression during a dance marathon, the piece investigated human fate in light of the collective despair of the Depression. *American Silents,* a reflection of the silent film industry, premiered at the Raw Space in New York City. The actors portrayed real people from the film industry, including Claire Booth Luce, Mary Pickford, and D. W. Griffith. The innovative script incorporated the language of these historical figures, from interviews and memoirs ("Bogart" 1999, 80).

Bogart explored a living American master in her 1998 Off Broadway production *Bob,* a one-man show based on the work of postmodern director and designer Robert Wilson. *New York Times* critic Peter Marks reflected that *Bob* was difficult to grasp for average theatre-goers:

> Because *Bob* is stingy with the facts, the production is impenetrable for quite some time. But despite its exotic tendencies, it eventually evolves into a fairly straightforward dissection of how an artist develops an esthetic, and of the influences emotional, intellectual and environmental that help to shape his creations. . . . The relationship between artist and audience is one of Ms. Bogart's recurring themes in *Bob;* another is the conflict between the power of the visual versus the verbal, an issue that comes up frequently in discussions of the work of imagists like Ms. Bogart, whose essentially cold creations reveal a greater comfort with pictures than with words. (1998, E16)

Several high-profile productions brought Bogart into the new millennium, including her collaboration with musician and performance artist Laurie Anderson on *Moby Dick* in 1999, a transformation of Orson Welles's American classic *War of the Worlds* in 2000, and a study of artist Robert Rauschenberg, *bobrauschenbergamerica,* in 2001. The latter was presented at the Actors Theatre of Louisville, Bogart's home away from SITI, where she has directed fairly regularly. The *New York Times* raved that Charles L. Mee's *bobrauschenbergamerica* was the best piece in the 25th Humana Festival. Critic Bruce Weber wrote, "On the one hand, in its jumble of realistic and abstract imagery and its quirkily inquisitive spirit, the play is meant to emulate the style of Mr. Rauschenberg's well-known assemblages. On the other, it is also a kind of history lesson, tying the evolution of our culture in the 20th century to the education of the artist" (2001, B7).

Among other projects in the early twenty-first century, Bogart took on Shakespeare's *A Midsummer Night's Dream* at San Diego Repertory Theatre, the first time she had directed a play by the Bard. In collaboration with the SITI company, Bogart continues her prolific work without reserve. She reflects, "I decided long ago that I would only do a play because of interest in it. I would never take an assignment just for the money. That sort of compromise is the way to kill creative spirit. And ever since I made that decision, I've never had any problem finding the work I wanted" (Evans 1992, 14).

Bogart's directing process begins with a deep plumbing of the script or subject at hand, always with an eye toward cultural history. Critic Mel Gussow of the *New York Times* writes, "Even as she diversifies, she plans to continue to scrutinize plays from America's recent theatrical past. These are, she says, 'memory capsules of who we are.' Repeatedly, she asks herself how she can capture the original energy of a play, and concludes, 'The more cultural baggage a play carries, the more I have to go through the back door'" (1994, sec. 1, 11). Because she sees scripts through a historical, cultural lens, Bogart dislikes the labels "experimental" or "avant garde." Director Robert Woodruff comments, "I find her to be one of the most articulate theatre creators around. Her approach is not a front-door examination, but a deep exploration of a work, and the way the text is then brought to light, through the collaboration of her company, is extraordinary" (Byrne 2003, SCE, So5).

Not surprisingly, Bogart looks for risk takers who are somewhat like herself in their willingness to jump into the unknown and explore. She finds the casting process highly personal and complex but reveals that in auditions she is influenced by "level of talent, taste, eroticism, surprise. You're always attracted to something that you'd like to be," she explains, "so you see that in another person" (Daniels 1996, 157).

Her starting point with actors and designers is source-work: the research into the world of the play, including associative material (e.g., music, photographs, paintings), that the collaborators collect, study, and share before rehearsals begin. In addition, she asks questions of the actors, drawing on their personal associations. Playwright and collaborator Tina Landau explains, "When I visited Anne in rehearsal for *Strindberg Sonata* (a piece she made about Strindberg's world at the University of California San Diego) . . . she had asked the actors to fill in the blanks: 'When I think of Strindberg, I see ____, I hear ____, I smell ___,' etc. . . . The first things that came up were the most obvious, but Anne encouraged the actors to lean into the clichés and stereotypes rather than try to ignore them. By going through them, she explained, they would come out the other side with something that used, but transformed them. Most importantly for me, the lists had served to waken the imaginations of the actors and to start creating the vocabulary for their 'play-world'" (1995, 19).

Since her work with the SITI company, Bogart's rehearsals have begun with physical work based in both the Suzuki Method and the Viewpoints. One of the questions she continually asks, writes Porter Anderson, is "What do you do with the meat?" Although it is a seemingly obscure question, SITI company members understand Bogart's intended meaning: "What do you do with your body?" (Dixon and Smith 1995, 107–8). The actors must explore a myriad of physical relationships in order to help Bogart divine the answer to the question.

Journalist Terry Byrne observed her rehearsals and wrote,

> The exercises, which take up the first half-hour of every rehearsal, demand focus and an awareness of the space the actors occupy and how they connect to each other. "Rather than trying to be clever," Bogart says, "the actors' natural sense of humor emerges from the Viewpoint."
>
> Watching a rehearsal, the actors' intense focus, even on walking, is impressive. Then the air develops a kind of thickness of its own as the actors move through the Viewpoints. The focus, SITI actor Will Bond tells the group, is on the energy that comes from within each actor.
>
> "I discovered that directing has nothing to do with intelligence," Bogart says. "It's about manipulating time and space. The art form of theater is about creating movement for words, not simply illustrating words." (2003, SCE, S05)

Bogart works very collaboratively, giving actors the freedom to explore, then cutting and shaping the pieces that work. She explains that she does not always have a predetermined idea of what she wants because she starts with questions. She writes, "If you already have the answers, then what's the point of being in rehearsal? But you certainly need to know what you are looking for." When things go wrong, she looks for the impetus of the energy in the situation and tries to use that to her advantage. Bogart advises directors to "walk a tightrope between control and chaos" (2001, 132). Eelka Lampe sees a Taoist influence in Bogart's directorial style, particularly her ability to delegate creative responsibility to her performers. She writes, "Such allowing of forces other than one's own mind to determine the aesthetics of a piece partakes in taoist [sic] ideas: to be grounded in a stillness which allows for a deep responsiveness to the world around oneself" (Dixon and Smith 1995, 155).

Bogart explains that she creates an environment that allows the actors to emote, rather than focusing on the creation of emotion in and of itself. She explains, "I try to create an environment in which many-colored emotions might occur. I find that if I try to *make* emotions happen, the environment is cheapened. So I try to create the circumstances in which emotions can be free. Now what I find is, in rehearsal, if you concentrate on detail, things start happening. The trick is to keep working on *something*. And eventually the emotions that need to happen—the arc of the scene—emerges, not because you're trying to make it happen, but because you're taking care of things around it" (Diamond 2001, 34). She is an outspoken critic of Method-based training of actors in the United States, a system that Bogart regards as a warped, misguided interpretation of Stanislavski's early work in psychological realism. Her visual and aural aesthetic emphasizes spatial and physical events "both inside an actor's body and between actors' bodies—rather than psychological plumbing" (Singer 2003, N9).

Bogart's openly collaborative style is popular with actors, as it allows for ample creative exploration on their part. SITI member Will Bond comments that she galvanizes actors, "unlocking the actors as clowns and dancers." He adds, "In 22 years, I've never had such a freeing experience; she makes you feel safe to make a fool of yourself" (Singer 2003, N9). Actor Ellen Lauren, also of the SITI company, explains that Bogart does not want actors to mime the scene. "What Anne is asking is that you build with your fellow players a physical life unrelated to the text; choreography with perhaps ten stops or moments that in and of themselves speak of a relationship. Not relationship as in lovers or enemies, rather a relationship to time, the surrounding architecture, physical shape" (Dixon and Smith 1995, 67).

Controversy and dismissal are not new to Bogart. She not only accepts these factors but embraces them, for they reflect her fearlessness as a risk taker. For Bogart, to create "safe" theatre is to create theatre without life or vitality. She explains, "Every creative act involves a leap into the void. The leap has to occur at the right moment and yet the time for the leap is never prescribed. In the midst of a leap, there are no guarantees. To leap can often cause acute embarrassment. Embarrassment is a partner in the creative act—a key collaborator. If your work does not sufficiently embarrass you, then very likely no one will be touched by it" (Bogart 2001, 113).

Her unique approach to performance has catapulted Bogart to distinction in her field. Her list of awards and honors is considerable: The 1980 Villager Award for Best Direction for *Out of Sync,* the 1984 Bessie Award for her direction of *South Pacific,* a 1987–88 Artistic Associate Grant from the National Endowment for the Arts in association with Music-Theatre Group, a 1988 Obie Award for Best Direction of *No Plays, No Poetry . . . ,* a 1992 Obie Award for Best Direction of *The Baltimore Waltz,* a designated Modern Master for Modern Masters Festival at Actors Theatre of Louisville in 1995, the 1999 Association for Theatre in Higher Education (ATHE) Achievement in Professional Theatre Award, a Guggenheim Fellowship in 2000–2001, the 2001 Kellogg Award from Bard College, and the Elliot Norton Award for outstanding direction in 2003. In the midst of her active directing career, Bogart oversaw the Graduate Directing Program at Columbia University, where she also taught as a professor. In the past she has taught at numerous universities and at Playwrights Horizons, Trinity Repertory Conservatory, the School for Movement Research, and other organizations. She has served her profession as a member of various committees and as a past president of the Theatre Communications Group from 1991 to 1993.

Distilling such a varied body of work into few words can be treacherous and misleading. As journalist Everett Evans of the *Houston Chronicle* points out, "Bogart is not readily identified by a trademark style or principle. Though fascinated by popular culture, she also believes that great art has elitist elements. Yet she finds it ironic that she has been described as an avant-garde experimenter when so much of her work is rooted in tradition and cultural study" (1992, ZEST 14). Study of Bogart's own books, *A Director Prepares* (2001), *The Viewpoints Book: A Practical Guide to Viewpoints and Composition* (2005, co-author Tina Landau), and *And Then You Act: Making Art in an Unpredictable World* (2007) provides a greater opportunity for insights into the world of Bogart's art.

Sources

"Bogart, Anne." 1999. *Current Biography Yearbook.* New York: Wilson, 77–82.

Bogart, Anne. 2001. *A Director Prepares: Seven Essays on Art and Theatre.* New York: Routledge.

———. 2007. *And Then You Act: Making Art in an Unpredictable World.* New York: Routledge.

Bogart, Anne and Tina Landau. 2005. *The Viewpoints Book: A Practical Guide to Viewpoint and Composition.* New York: Theatre Communications Group.

Byrne, Terry. 2003. "Engaging Return: Anne Bogart Brings Her Creativity Back to Hub." *Boston Herald,* 31 Jan., SCE, S05.

Cummings, Scott T. 2006. *Remaking American Theater: Charles Mee, Anne Bogart and the SITI Company.* Cambridge Studies in American Theatre and Drama. New York: Cambridge University Press.

Daniels, Rebecca. 1996. *Women Stage Directors Speak.* Jefferson, N.C.: McFarland.

De Vries, Hilary. 1990. "How a Real-Life Drama Came to an Unhappy End." *New York Times,* 15 Jul., sec. 2, 5.

Diamond, David. 2001. "Balancing Acts." *American Theatre* 18 (Jan.): 30–34, 104–6.

Dixon, Michael Bigelow and Joel A. Smith, eds. 1995. *Anne Bogart: Viewpoints.* Foreword by Jon Jory. Lyme, N.H.: Smith and Kraus.

Evans, Everett. 1992. "Exploring, Learning and Educating." *Houston Chronicle,* 29 Mar., ZEST 14.

Gussow, Mel. 1994. "Iconoclastic and Busy Director: An Innovator or a Provocateur?" *New York Times,* 12 Mar., sec. 1, 11.

Herrington, Joan. 2000. "Directing with the Viewpoints." *Theatre Topics* 10 (Sept.): 155–68.

Holden, Stephen. 1988. "Brechtian Collaboration in Experimental Theater." Rev. of *No Plays, No Poetry . . .*, a collective theatre piece by Otrabanda, the Talking Band, and Via Theater. *New York Times*, 18 Mar., C32.

Lampe, Eelka. 1992. "From the Battle to the Gift: The Directing of Anne Bogart." *TDR/ The Drama Review* 36 (1) (T133) (Spring): 14–47.

Landau, Tina. 1995. "Source-Work, the Viewpoints and Composition: What Are They?" In *Anne Bogart: Viewpoints*, ed. Michael Bigelow Dixon and Joel A. Smith, 13–30. Lyme, N.H.: Smith and Kraus.

Malnig, Julie. 1994. "Anne Bogart." In *Theatrical Directors: A Biographical Dictionary*, ed. John W. Frick and Stephen M. Vallillo, 41–42. Westport, Conn.: Greenwood.

Marks, Peter. 1998. "Portrait of an Imagist by a Like-Minded Artist." Rev. of *Bob*, conceived by Anne Bogart and created with Will Bond. *New York Times*, 8 May, E16.

Nevius, C. W. 2004. "Shakespeare or Steinbeck? You Be the Judge." *San Francisco Chronicle*, 29 Jan., E4.

Rich, Frank. 1992. "Play About AIDS Uses Fantasy World to Try to Remake the World." Rev. of *The Baltimore Waltz*, by Paula Vogel. *New York Times*, 12 Feb., C15.

Richards, David. 1994. "Unorthodox View of Luce Classic." Rev. of *The Women*, by Claire Booth Luce. *New York Times*, 13 Jan., C13.

Saari, Kevin Phillip. 1999. *The Work of Anne Bogart and the Saratoga International Theatre Institute: A New Model for Actor Training*. Ph.D. diss., University of Kansas.

Sarasota International Theatre Institute (SITI). 2004. Homepage. http://www.siti .org (accessed 3 Jul. 2004).

Shteir, Rachel. 1998. "Dispensing with Dogma in the Education of Actors." *New York Times*, 2 Aug., sec. 2, 4.

Singer, Thea. 2003. "Theatre Movers and Shakers." *Boston Globe*, 2 Feb., N9.

Weber, Bruce. 2001. "A Festival of Images, via Rauschenberg and Others." *New York Times*, 7 Apr., B7.

Representative Directing Credits

Off and Off-Off Broadway:

Macbeth (adaptation) (1976), *RD1*, *The Waves* (1977), *Women and Men, A Big Dance* (1982), *Inge: How They Got There* (1984), *1951* (1986), *No Plays, No Poetry but Philosophical Reflections Practical Instructions Provocative Prescriptions Opinions and Pointers from a Noted Critic and Playwright* (1988), *In the Jungle of the Cities* (1991), *The Baltimore Waltz* (1992), *Behavior in Public Places* (1993), *Hot 'n Throbbing* (1993), *Escape from Paradise* (1994), *Marathon Dancing* (1994), *Birth of a Nation* (1994), *American Vaudeville*

(1994), *The Medium* (1994), *Small Lives/Big Dreams* (1995), *American Silents* (1997), *Bob* (1998), *Culture of Desire* (1998), *Gertrude and Alice: A Likeness to Loving* (1999), *Moby Dick* (1999), *War of the Worlds* (2000), *Songs from an Unmade Bed* (2005)

Regional Theatre:

Sehnsucht (1982), *Small Lives/Big Dreams* (1982, 1995), *The Making of Americans* (1985), *Between Wind* (1986), *Cinderella in a Mirror* (1987), *Katchen von Heilbronn* (1988), *Once in a Lifetime* (1988, 1990), *Life Is a Dream* (1989), *No Plays, No Poetry, but Philosophical Reflections, Practical Instructions, Provocative Prescriptions, Opinions, and Pointers from a Noted Critic and Playwright* (1989), *Summerfolk* (1989), *On the Town* (1990), *In the Eye of the Hurricane* (1990), *Baltimore Waltz* (1992), *American Vaudeville* (1992), *Picnic* (1992), *The Women* (1992, 1994), *Hot 'n Throbbing* (1994), *Escape from Paradise* (1994), *The Medium* (1995), *The Adding Machine* (1995), *Going, Going, Gone* (1996), *Miss Julie* (1997), *Private Lives* (1998), *Cabin Pressure* (1999), *War of the Worlds* (2000), *bobrauschenbergamerica* (2001), *Hay Fever* (2002), *La Dispute* (2003), *A Midsummer Night's Dream* (2004), *Death and the Ploughman* (2004), *Intimations for Saxophone* (2005)

Tours:

1951 (1986–87), *The Medium* (1994–96), *Small Lives/Big Dreams* (1994–97), *Culture of Desire* (1997–98), *Alice's Adventures* (1998–99), *Bob* (1998–99), *Cabin Pressure* (2000), *War of the Worlds (Radio Play)* (2000–02), *War of the Worlds* (2001), *ROOM* (2001), *Score* (2005), *bobrauschenbergamerica* (2005), *Death and the Ploughman* (2005)

International Theatre:

Leb Oder Tot (1981), *Between the Delicate* (1982), *Die Gier Nach Banalem* (1982), *Grid* (1983), *Sommer Nachts Traum/Lost and Found* (1983), *Babel* (1987), *Orestes* (1992), *The Medium* (1993, 1995), *Small Lives/Big Dreams* (1994), *Going, Going, Gone* (1996), *Culture of Desire* (1998), *Bob* (1998, 1999, 2000, 2001), *War of the Worlds* (2000), *War of the Worlds (Radio Play)* (2000), *Cabin Pressure* (2000), *Death and the Ploughman* (2005)

Bonstelle, Jessie

Laura Justine Bonesteele (later Bonstelle) was born on November 19, in or around 1870[1] on a farm in Greece, New York, near Rochester. By the time of her death in 1932 she had earned a national reputation as a producer and manager, earning her the nickname "The Maker of Stars" or "The Star Lady." Spotting and training young talent was only one of Bonstelle's many accomplishments, however. In addition to her work as a producer, she took the mantle of actor, director, and teacher and founded the Detroit Civic Theatre, one of the nation's first community theatres. Although critics were harsh to Bonstelle's directing on Broadway, she maintained a popular following as a director in her stock theatres and deserves attention as one of the early pioneers in the profession.

According to Bonstelle's own account, her mother longed to be an actress and instilled the passion in Bonstelle from a young age. Initially her mother home-schooled Bonstelle in recitations, songs, dances, and Shakespeare and took her to the theatre in Rochester. At the age of about ten Bonstelle auditioned for the *Buffalo Express* theatre critic Thomas Keane, who encouraged her to go on stage. Accompanied by her mother, Bonstelle performed in a touring production while still a minor and upon her return home attended the Nazareth Academy in Rochester, where "she wrote and staged a series of little plays which won the approval of the teachers and the students alike" (Stark, "Little," n.d.). For five years the young Bonstelle was under the management of a newspaper publisher and opera house owner named Edward D. Stair. In 1886 she toured in his production of *Little Trixie,* which Stair wrote for her.

When her parents both died in 1890, Bonstelle went to New York City to further her acting career. She worked with German star Fanny Janauschek, whom she called "the greatest living actress," and subsequently worked for the infamous theatrical director Augustin Daly, a strict disciplinarian who modeled an autocratic style for the director-to-be (Bennett, Sept. 1928, 16). In 1893 she married the leading man in Janauschek's company, Alexander Hamilton Stuart, many years her senior. She and her husband joined the Forepaugh Stock Company in Philadelphia. Bonstelle played for other theatres as well, cast in leading roles such as Juliet and Camille. In the 1898–99 season she was the leading lady of Philadelphia's Standard Stock Company.

Bonstelle reports that her managing and directing career started with an offer from producer Jacob J. Shubert to manage a stock company in Rochester, an offer she accepted at the age of nineteen (Bennett, Oct. 1928, 24). However, historian William L. Deam reports otherwise. He reasons, "If the year of this event was 1900 [and it seems most unlikely that it could be earlier, since the Shuberts did not begin theatrical management before then], Miss Bonstelle was thirty instead of nineteen" (1954, 55). Bonstelle continued to manage and direct from this point forward while still maintaining her acting career. Beginning in 1906, Bonstelle managed both the Shubert's Star Theatre in Buffalo, and, beginning in 1910, the Garrick Theatre in Detroit, shuttling back and forth weekly to direct, produce, and often star in their productions. She reports that she played and managed summer companies in Rochester, Buffalo, Providence, Northampton, and Detroit and played or directed in New York City in winters (Bennett, Oct. 1928, 25). At about this same point in her career, she worked to found a women's national theatre but failed to raise the million dollars needed to fund the project.

Part of Bonstelle's new-found dedication as a producer came from her reflection of Janauschek's death in 1904. Bonstelle reasoned that although the actress was dead, the theatre lived and was bettered by Janauschek's dedication to her art. Bonstelle vowed, "[I]f I, Jessie Bonstelle, *lived for the theater* what I did *would last;* it mattered little what became of me. . . . I became humbler and more analytical" (Bennett, Oct. 1928, 25).

The most popular production Bonstelle directed toured nationally for a year before earning its place on Broadway in 1912, and later in London: Louisa May Alcott's *Little Women.* Bursting with entrepreneurial vigor, Bonstelle conceived and researched the project herself. She traveled to Boston, where members of the Alcott family placed records, letters, and diaries at her disposal. She also visited the old Alcott house and talked with friends of Alcott (Bennett, Oct. 1928, 97). At Bonstelle's request, Marian de Forest, drama critic at the *Buffalo Express,* wrote the adaptation and William A. Brady produced it. Bonstelle wore many hats to get her project off the ground. She reports, "I began at once hunting a cast, directing the painting for the scenery, getting the props and shopping for the materials for costumes." She continued, "I never would have been able to get *Little Women* to the point of triumphant production within four weeks if it had not been for Bertram Harrison [a Broadway actor who was beginning to produce and direct]. Bert helped me in directing the play, designing scenery and doing anything that helped" (98, 101). Bonstelle's passion for the material paid off when *Little Women* opened in 1911. She writes, "What can I tell you of *Little Women?* Of our triumphant progress up and down and across the whole land? Of the four companies I rehearsed and sent out at the same time so as to reach all the cities and towns; that East and West and North and South cried out for the play?" (101). The Broadway run in 1912 enjoyed a successful and lengthy run, and after World

War I, it opened in London starring Katharine Cornell, one of Bonstelle's many protégées (Clark 1989, 79). Amid the turbulent creation, staging, and success of Bonstelle's *Little Women* in 1911 her husband passed away. She never remarried but continued with her relentless pursuit to make a lasting impression on American theatre.

Bonstelle's record of actual stage direction is sketchy, particularly the plays she directed while managing her stock companies, for there is little data to distinguish which shows she directed and which she produced but did not stage. The problem is exacerbated by the terminology of the day, which did not always distinguish between director and producer or used the terms interchangeably. In addition, at times the word *director* appears to apply to her work as a company (or managing) director rather than the stage director of a particular production. Deam reports of her stock work, "She was primarily a Producer rather than a Director, even though during her stock producing days she did direct as well as star in her own productions" (1954, 87). In light of the paucity of information about her direction in stock, it is particularly significant that *The New York Times Theatre Reviews* reveals five productions she directed on Broadway: *The Lady from Oklahoma* in 1913, *Heaven* in 1920, *Leah Kleschna* in 1924, *That Awful Mrs. Eaton!* in 1924, and *Now-a-Days* in 1929.

Unfortunately, reviews of the early 1900s mentioned the direction of a play only in passing, if at all. Bonstelle both acted in and produced *The Lady from Oklahoma*, performed at the Forty-Eighth Street Theatre. Though no director is credited, it is almost certain she fulfilled that role as well. An anonymous *New York Times* critic called the formulaic play by Elizabeth Jordan "a little stale" but one that "provides plenty of opportunities for laughter" ("Oklahoma" 1913, 9). The trite plot revolved around a plain woman who receives a makeover, in part to fight for the love of her husband, a senator. The critic commented both on Bonstelle's performance and the heavy-handed feeling of the overall acting style, writing, "Miss Bonstelle's method is hard, overwrought, and unsympathetic. . . . Her method is that of popular stock, where it is deemed necessary to 'pound home' all the points. And the sort of insistent over-emphasis and underlying in which she indulges are frequently apparent in the acting of the others" (9).

Bonstelle fared little better in the assessment of *Leah Kleschna*, a play by C. M. S. McLellan, performed at the Lyric Theatre. It was described as a "sterling melodrama" twenty years old, and John Corbin of the *New York Times* found the performance to be "ragged, even in the matter of forgotten lines." He added, "Last night through long stretches the action slackened and suspense sagged . . . but the essence of the thing is there" (Corbin 1924, 19).

That same year, Bonstelle and Brady co-directed *The Awful Mrs. Eaton!*

in Detroit before Brady produced it at the Morosco Theatre on Broadway under Bonstelle's direction. The *Detroit Free Press* gave the romantic historical drama a mixed review but lauded the direction, stating, "The staging was such as stock patrons seldom encounter, historically fitting, and providing pictures of rare excellence" (Deam 1954, 121). However, Stark Young of the *New York Times* found the New York City performance, billed as *That Awful Mrs. Eaton!*, "literary rather than theatrical," writing, "The scenes and the writing have a fictional appeal, if you will; but there is very little of the projection, the accent, or the heightening through which writing becomes not literature but theatre" (Young 1924, 27). Although Young did not write about the stage direction per se, he did comment that the audience gave the play a warm reception.

It was five years before another review appeared in the *New York Times* for a play that Bonstelle directed. In 1929 Brooks Atkinson remarked on Bonstelle's reputation when he wrote his review of Arthur F. Brash's play *Now-a-Days,* performed at the Forrest Theatre. "As directed by Jessie Bonstelle, whose industry in the theatre is famous throughout Eastern America, the acting is sufficient to the occasion." Although "sufficient" acting is far from praise, at another point in the review he admits the play is "acted with disquieting conviction" (Atkinson 1929, 29). It seems Bonstelle's reputation drew kudos, yet her worth as a director was left unrecognized by most Broadway critics.

Despite these mediocre and poor reviews, Bonstelle managed to direct or assistant direct in New York City numerous times, thanks to her association with producers Shubert and Brady. Deam asserts, "As a director, she was excellent and was trusted by Shubert, Brady, and others with their best 'stars'" (1954, n.p.). Her "excellence" as a director remains in question, as Deam himself admits later when writing about the Detroit drama critics, who lavished praise on Bonstelle. "Too great a reliance on the Detroit drama critics for an analysis of Miss Bonstelle's productions and their level of professionalism would lead to the conclusion that she had no parallel and that frequently her productions surpassed the Broadway versions of the same plays. Investigation reveals all the 'critics' except one or two as employees of Stair or as friends of Miss Bonstelle. It is frequently difficult to separate personal admiration for her from a real evaluation of her productions." He also adds, "Very few of the one hundred and sixty-five plays that Miss Bonstelle produced were given critical reviews" (106).

Casting in a stock company was normally by type, but Bonstelle claimed her novice actors were assigned a wide range of roles, perhaps playing an ingénue one week and an elderly woman the next. She was well known for spotting and hiring young actors, then coaching them to stardom. She chose actors for their innate talent and their ability to work as part of a team. Wrote

Margaret Storey, "With a carefully chosen group, a steady routine of work on quickly changing material under sincere, intelligent direction, it is no wonder that the stock company furnished the main-spring of training for the young novice actors, extras, and bit players [who] were later to become leaders in the entertainment profession" (1940, 2–3).

Bonstelle's demeanor in the rehearsal hall is recorded through her actors and colleagues, who reacted to her perfectionism. With a new play presented each week, she had one play in rehearsal while another was in performance, making for extremely long, grueling days. Actors were given only sides—partial scripts with their characters' lines—rather than full scripts, and general blocking was dictated to them, though business and character bits were up to the actors. Recalling the grueling rehearsals, actor Sylvia Field called Bonstelle a "slave driver" but also showed respect for her work as a director. Deam summarizes from his interview with Field:

> Miss Bonstelle's changing of bills every week meant that on Monday the parts for the next week's production were handed out. Rehearsals were held morning and afternoons of the days in which there were no matinees. A show every night, with three matinees during the week, made a total of ten performances, including Sundays. . . . Thursday morning was the only time off, but during that time actors were expected to do all their shopping for costumes which they were required to supply for themselves, unless, of course, the play was a period piece and the costumes were rented from New York.
>
> She [Field] said that there were many times she felt like "wringing Miss Bonstelle's neck," and that Miss Bonstelle could make her feel furious. She could make her feel like a helpless and completely untalented actress. She could be harsh and cruel and make her cry. Miss Bonstelle could make her want to run away, but Miss Field added that it was never a personal feeling, it being generally realized that her treatment was motivated by her conceptions of the part played rather than of the person playing the part. (1954, 88–89)

Actor Walter Young concurred with Field, recalling a final rehearsal that began at 10:00 A.M. and ended at 8:15 P.M. He recalled, "An actor cooperated with Bonnie [Bonstelle]. If not, the actor did not operate for Bonnie very long. Bonnie was all the Niagara Falls, Boulder Dam, et al dynamos, for driving effort—for as near perfection as possible, rolled into one not too large body" (Deam 1954, 91). Young also found Bonstelle willing to help an actor at any time if he or she was struggling with a part. "[A]ll they had to do was to go to Bonnie after rehearsals and she would put out the emery wheel and the polishing stunt would be activated—but pronto" (91).

Although these descriptions conjure an image of a cruel tyrant, Field also commented that Bonstelle "always drove herself as much as or more than she drove any of the actors and that she was never satisfied with anything less than perfection in both herself and them" (Deam 1954, 91). Although her actors feared her, they also had tremendous respect and gratitude for her passion and drive, which in turn drove them to achieve their best results. Many of Bonstelle's protégées went on to become stars and thanked Bonstelle for her inspiration and training. Katharine Cornell wrote that Bonstelle was driven by high hopes and hard work. As a passionate theatre practitioner, Bonstelle instilled an enthusiasm for her art that made her actors willing to dedicate their lives to it as well (Storey 1940, foreword). Cornell was also much more complimentary of Bonstelle's directorial demeanor, which she considered straightforward, not fueled by temper but a critical eye. Cornell comments, "For example, when I was in London in *Little Women* she would come into the dressing room night after night and sit down and 'go at me,' but the process was always a quiet and careful one. . . . Her approach was essentially intellectual rather than emotional" (14).

Directors who worked with Bonstelle had similar sentiments about her perfectionism in the rehearsal hall. Josephine Hull was impressed with her constant quest for new talent, stating that "she never refused an interview with anyone and was willing to spend time with one discussing theatre" (Deam 1954, 90). Hull remarked on Bonstelle's "excellent sense of theatre, her fairness, and her high standards for productions," which she deemed "distinctly Broadway." Other colleagues noted that Bonstelle could not "keep her finger out of the pie," even for productions she was producing but not directing. Deam surmised, "Though she never openly disagreed with her director it is more than suppositional that she was constantly requiring that a scene be repeated time and again until she was satisfied." Of her need to drill her actors to perfection he concluded, "Miss Bonstelle had an ability, as a director, to bring out the best in an actor" (91–92).

Bonstelle's experience in theatre management eventually led to her legacy as founder of the Bonstelle Players in 1925, which became the Detroit Civic Theatre in 1928, one of the first civic theatres in America. Deam makes a case that the absence of Bonstelle's leadership and artistry as a director were clear through the productions at Detroit, writing, "As Miss Bonstelle was forced to devote more time to business matters and less to directing and acting the reviewers pointed out that in their opinion the main quality lacking in the Civic Theatre productions was intelligent directing" (1954, 187).

Although most often remembered for her accomplishments as a theatre administrator and "star maker," Bonstelle should not be overlooked as one of the pioneering women stage directors in the early twentieth century. Though her Broadway reviews were less than stellar, she directed on Broadway numerous times in addition to directing regularly in the stock companies she managed. By her performers' accounts, her work as a director was that of a perfectionist, requiring the highest standards from all members of the collaborative team. Despite failing health in her sixties, she never let her drive or passion for theatre die. In 1932 Bonstelle traveled to Hollywood, though reports of her objective for the trip vary: to explore opportunities in film directing, to scout territory for a new stock company (Clark 1989, 81), or to establish a school of acting for young performers (Deam 1954, 188). She became ill and returned to Detroit but did not allow her entrepreneurial spirit to weaken. The day before she died, Bonstelle was reportedly planning her next production (Stark, "Jessie," n.d.). She passed away in Detroit on October 14, 1932.

Sources

Atkinson, J. Brooks. 1929. Rev. of *Now-a-Days,* by Arthur F. Brash. *New York Times,* 6 Aug., 29.

Bennett, Helen Christine. 1928–1929. "The Star Lady." *McCall's.* Sept., 16–17, 106, 109, 110; Oct., 24–25, 96, 98, 101; Nov., 26–27, 125, 126, 147; Dec., 28, 72, 75, 76; Jan., 31; Feb., 35.

"The Bonstelle Players." n.d. Billy Rose Theatre Collection, clippings. New York Public Library for the Performing Arts.

Callaway, Gladys. 1926. "Preserving the Ideals of the Stage." *Dearborn (Mich.) Independent,* 4 Dec., 24–25.

Clark, Constance with additions by Mari Kathleen Fielder. 1989. "Bonstelle, Jessie." In *Notable Women in the American Theatre: A Biographical Dictionary,* ed. Alice M. Robinson, Vera Mowry Roberts, and Milly S. Barranger, 77–82. New York: Greenwood.

Corbin, John. 1924. Rev. of *Leah Kleschna,* by C. M. S. McLelland, revised by William A. Brady. *New York Times,* 22 Apr., 19.

Deam, William L. 1954. "A Biographical Study of Miss Laura Justine Bonstelle-Stuart Together with an Evaluation of Her Contributions to the Modern Theatre World." Ph.D. diss., University of Michigan.

"Oklahoma Lady Lacks Fresh Theme." 1913. Rev. of *The Oklahoma Lady,* by Elizabeth Jordan. *New York Times,* 3 Apr., 9.

Stark, George W. n.d. "We Old Timers . . .: Jessie Bonstelle." Billy Rose Theatre Collection, clippings. New York Public Library for the Performing Arts.

———. n.d. "We Old Timers . . .: Little Trixie." Billy Rose Theatre Collection, clippings. New York Public Library for the Performing Arts.

Storey, Margaret and Hugh Gillis. 1940. "Player's Nursery." Typewritten manuscript. Stanford University: Dramatists' Alliance. Billy Rose Theatre Collection. New York Public Library for the Performing Arts.

Young, Stark. 1924. Rev. of *That Awful Mrs. Eaton!,* by John Farrar and Stephen Vincent Benet. *New York Times,* 30 Sept., 27.

Representative Directing Credits

Broadway:
>   *The Lady from Oklahoma* (1913), *Heaven* (1920), *Leah Kleschna* (1924), *That Awful Mrs. Eaton!* (1924), *Now-a-Days* (1929)

Off and Off-Off Broadway:
>   *The Second Mrs. Tanqueray* (1923)

Regional and Stock Theatre:
[Direction mainly unrecorded]
>   *Hamlet* (1916), *Six Cylinder Love* (1923), *Sauce for the Gander* (1923), *The Awful Mrs. Eaton!* (1924)

Notes

   1. The exact year of Bonstelle's birth is unknown, and she would not give her age. It is estimated to be between 1869 and 1871.

 # Boyd, Julianne

Born December 22, 1944, in Easton, Pennsylvania, Julianne Boyd became one of the few women to direct a musical on Broadway in the 1970s. She went on to serve her profession by becoming the first woman president of the Society of Stage Directors and Choreographers (SSDC). She also helped create and direct several groundbreaking feminist musicals, including *A . . . My Name Is Alice,* and she researched gender inequity for women directors and designers. Eventually, Boyd started her own theatre company, the Barrington Stage Company, where her directing has won critical acclaim.

   Boyd attended Beaver College, where she received a B.A. in 1966, then earned her M.A. at Adelphi University in 1968. She always wanted to direct but knew of no other women directors, so she studied acting and eventually directed Off-Off Broadway for no pay. She decided to attend graduate school, but by that time she was married and living in New York City with two children. She realized that it was not feasible to move her family in order to attend Yale University (Columbia and New York University did not offer directing programs at the time), so she pursued a Ph.D. at the City University of New York in hopes of later teaching and directing for a university. While working toward her doctorate in classical Japanese theatre, Boyd was a script reader for the Manhattan Theatre Club and a director and producer of a new play series for the Classic Stage Company Repertory Theatre. There she directed a critically acclaimed production of Strindberg's *Miss Julie*. In the 1970s she directed more than a dozen productions Off-Off Broadway, including two musical revues, *Happy with the Blues: The Music of Harold Arlen* and *Lyrical and Satirical: The Music of Harold Rome*.

Given her entrepreneurial spirit and her familiarity with musical revues, it is fitting that Boyd's first commercial break was a musical revue she both conceived and directed. She stumbled upon an archival recording of Eubie Blake's *Shuffle Along* (produced in 1921), the first musical with an all-black cast to go from Harlem to Broadway, and fell in love with Blake's music. Although she knew the book was racist, she decided that it could be re-packaged as a musical revue. When she contacted Blake's wife, Marian, to obtain the rights, Marian supported her project but commented, "You sound like you're white." Undeterred by her racial difference, Boyd replied, "Well, I am, and I'm a woman too" (Boyd, interview, 2000). After querying a number of theatres, Boyd found that the sixty-seat Theatre Off Park in Manhattan was interested in a production for Black History Month. The revue, still titled *Shuffle Along* at that point, opened on Blake's ninety-fifth birthday on February 7, 1978. Boyd recalls that when the lights came down, Blake said to her, "Now we're all the same color" (Interview, 2000).

Once the papers reviewed the production, Boyd was flooded with offers from twelve producers. She immediately sought a lawyer and obtained the rights for "a first class production of all of Eubie's music" (Interview, 2003). A mere seven months later, *Eubie!* opened on Broadway, and by Christmas the producer, Ashton Springer, launched a national tour. Critics found the Broadway production energetic, fun, and filled with talented performers, including Gregory and Maurice Hines. Of Boyd's direction, Bob Lape of WABC-TV commented, "Creator-director Julianne Boyd has pumped in so much verve and style, you don't much notice some pretty dusty songs are being propped up with sex and splash" (1978, 219). Another critic found her direction of the comedy "obviously staged and obviously performed" (Cunningham 1978, 219), with one critic calling it "a case of the 'cutsies'" (Wilson 1978, 216), but both found the show entertaining overall and recommended it.

As Boyd worked as a director in commercial theatre, she learned that gender made a difference in how she was perceived. For example, her producer seemed to lack confidence in her as a younger woman and asked her whether she could "handle the stage hands." She was also encouraged to cut her hair in order to appear older (Chinoy 1987, 359). Further bumps in the road included stories in the newspapers about litigation the backers brought against the producer of *Eubie!* and a sensationalistic story about choreographer Billy

Wilson challenging the status of his billing after a Philadelphia tryout. Despite these negative aspects, Boyd recalls the sweetness of her first Broadway success, in part because she had accomplished so much at the age of thirty-three, with two small children at home.

Boyd's subsequent project on Broadway, a feminist musical titled *Onward Victoria!*, was not a success. In his review for the *New York Times*, Frank Rich ravaged the production, calling the book and lyrics witless, the set "threadbare," and the choreography and direction "lame" (1980, C15). The production closed quickly, and Boyd began searching for new projects.

Ironically, it was another feminist musical, *A . . . My Name Is Alice,* that brought her critical acclaim once more, winning the Outer Critics Circle Award as Best Musical in 1983. The impetus for *Alice* began while she was working on a benefit for the National Abortion Rights Action League with Joan Micklin Silver. They sent out requests to friends for songs about women's experiences, looking for something new. To their dismay, they received songs of abuse and neglect. Boyd reasoned that those negative perceptions were what women were used to writing, "that's what sold." She explained, "Things about women hadn't been funny things, where women could make fun of themselves. Up until *Alice* all of the women's stuff was like, 'He beat me, he left me, and I'm miserable.' It was all negative" (Interview, 2000). Silver and Boyd then opened the door for men to submit songs as well, reasoning, "We'll get anyone who has a good opinion of women" (Interview, 2003). Through the help of the Women's Project at the American Place Theatre, they produced a workshop of a revue-style production called *A . . . My Name Is Alice,* which went on to an extended run at the Top of the Gate in Greenwich Village. Their production was hailed a groundbreaking celebration of women's experiences as mothers, daughters, sisters, wives, and, quite simply, people. It also stirred critical controversy concerning "what a musical about women should be and do" (Chinoy 1987, 360). For example, Erika Munk of the *Village Voice* wrote that the "women's situation in 1984 deserves a bit of bite, a snarl of satire" (1984, n.p.). Benedict Nightengale of the *New York Times* had a more positive spin on its feminism, stating that the production "described itself as 'a feminist way to relax,' a claim that some would see as sheer self-contradiction. But neither is its feminism the grim, baleful sort, nor does it seek to relax you by lulling your mind with theatrical Valium. This is a sane, witty show, with time neither for macho swinishness nor broomstick paranoia" (1984, sec. 2, 5). *New York Times* critic Frank Rich also found their brand of feminism agreeable. As a backhanded compliment, he wrote, "[T]he show's feminism is worn lightly. If anything, women are as likely to be satirical targets as men" (1984, C14). Clearly, the production reached women without offending the mostly male critics. The success of *Alice* ultimately spurred two further collaborative works:

A . . . My Name Is Still Alice and, in the entrepreneurial spirit of combining the "best of" previous hits, *A . . . My Name Will Always Be Alice.*

After the success of *Alice,* Boyd spent several years directing in regional theatres, including the Pennsylvania Stage Company, the La Jolla Playhouse in California, and the Old Globe Theatre in San Diego. After two years as artistic director of the Berkshire Theatre Festival in Stockbridge, Massachusetts, Boyd left to co-found the nearby Barrington Stage Company in 1995. As the artistic director of her own theatre, Boyd staged numerous productions, including a world premiere of *On the Twentieth Century, Ciao!, A Little Night Music, A View from the Roof, Room Service, A . . . My Name Will Always Be Alice, Mack and Mabel, Cabaret, Company, South Pacific, Blanche and Her Joy Boys, Funny Girl,* a world premiere of *The Game* (a musical version of *Les Liaisons Dangereuses*), *Cyrano de Bergerac,* and *Follies.*

When casting, Boyd looks for actors who are truthful performers and are willing to take risks. She seeks actors who make very definite choices but have a sense of playfulness and creativity that allows them to try new ideas. When casting for most roles in musical comedy, she looks for what she calls "a high huggable quotient"—actors who have no walls and have an immediacy to their performance. Boyd explains, "You need to have that emotional relationship between the actor and the audience. . . . Sometimes I say, 'Does that person twinkle? Is there something very ALIVE about that performer?'" The actors she chooses are open and "really give something out without pushing" (Interview, 2003).

In working with designers, Boyd looks for collaborators who value the process and who are not exclusively result-oriented. She likes to take the time to meet with designers several times a week to "bat around ideas. . . . It's about having enough time to enjoy the process of developing the physical production" (Interview, 2003). She enjoys working with collaborative, easygoing team members who will entertain a wide canvas of ideas before closing in on one choice. By bringing their ideas together, Boyd finds it helps her "see more of the play" before going into rehearsal.

Having worked through the physical production with designers, Boyd comes into rehearsal with a concept to anchor the actors. Within the framework she provides, she leaves enough leeway for ideas and interpretation from the actors. She begins the rehearsal process by talking about why they are doing the play, how it fits into its historical and social milieu, and the playwright's intent. Next she proceeds to table work, breaking down the script and beginning character analysis as a group. "Then when we get on our feet," Boyd explains. "The actors are able to just move. They understand where they are. They understand the relationships with the characters" (Interview, 2003). Her job as a director is to "edit and elucidate" what the actors bring to the play and to have ideas for change when things are not working. She also ensures that the entire cast's ideas and approaches are "on the same page." Boyd explains, "I think when I was younger, I thought that my responsibility was to see that they had everything worked out ahead of time. I think as I have gotten more comfortable with the process, it's so joyful. It is so exciting. I find rehearsal totally exhilarating now, because it's a group of people totally creating something together based on an outline that the playwright and I have created, along with the designers" (Interview, 2003).

Boyd works from both the interior and exterior approaches to acting and characterization, depending on the actors' needs and needs of the scene. She notes that thirty years ago, when she started directing, "Good directors were considered clever blockers, who moved people well and had a lovely visual picture. But, I think the combination of the physical movement and what the actor is bringing forth and how it reaches the audiences is how the art is evolved and why it's so exciting. . . . [I]t's why I'm so exhilarated in rehearsal, and why I hope performers are as well" (Interview, 2003). Boyd sees her job as both intellectually analyzing the script and nurturing the actors' journey of discovery, through rehearsal.

Boyd does not subscribe to concepts that are superimposed on the script but looks for the core of the story to build upon, stripping away interpretations from previous productions and defining her own interpretation. In her award-winning production of John Kander and Fred Ebb's *Cabaret* in 1997, she decided that the character Sally Bowles was selling her soul to the devil. Boyd noted that the script called for one of the men in the cabaret to be a puppeteer and explained her vision for the production: "My concept was that the M.C. loved puppets. So at one point when he's singing a song, the puppet is sitting on the table with him, and it looks like a Charlie McCarthy/Edgar Bergen thing, which was very popular at the time. And at the end, when Sally's tumbling down, spiraling down, he's watching her. By the end, she's his puppet. Now was that meant [in the script]? No. Does it work within the context of the play? Yes" (Interview, 2000). The crowds and the critics agreed that it worked, for Boyd won the Boston Outer Critics Circle Award for Best Director and Best Production for *Cabaret*. Ed Siegel of the *Boston Globe* glowed, "Julianne Boyd's revelatory reworking . . . stripped much of the Fosse–Minnelli–Grey glitz from *Cabaret,* making it hair-raising as well as show-stopping" (1997b, E1). In a separate review, he wrote, "It's the most insightful, and ultimately most rewarding, version you're likely to see. . . . Together they [the characters] represent the twin towers of Germanic horror, evil and indifference (1997a, C10).

Boyd received similar acclaim for her interpretation of the often-hackneyed musical *South Pacific* in 2002. Once again, Siegel gave her credit for creatively stripping the show of its former trademarks and finding a fresh approach.

> Julianne Boyd at Barrington Stage Company in Sheffield knows how to get to the emotional and, when applicable, political center of a musical as well as any Broadway or West End director. Here she strips *South Pacific* down to its basics—two pianos, an assortment of gorgeous voices, small ensembles—and the result is a production that is about, oh, a million times better than the one in Boston last year.
>
> By casting first for vocal ability and second for stage presence, and by not making the singers compete with a full orchestra, Boyd has constructed a *South Pacific* that is full of surprises: This may be the first and last time that the sexiest woman onstage is the Tonkinese trader Bloody Mary. . . . The honesty of the emotions that Boyd puts onstage, with secondary characters as well as primary, makes the racial attitudes seem tragically contemporary. It's easy to produce Rodgers and Hammerstein musicals that wring the emotions. But, as she has so often in the past, Boyd has produced a musical that touches the soul. (2002, F1)

As her interpretations of *Cabaret* and *South Pacific* indicate, Boyd claims her most important function as a director is to tell the story, and that story must have an emotional basis. She explains, "What interests me in a play is strong emotional content. . . . If I transmit these emotions to the audience, then I've done my job. With musicals, emotional content is squared. Characters break into song when they can't talk anymore" (Pfeifer 2000, D1). Boyd states her priorities from the audience's point of view as well: "I want to be affected by the theatre. I want to be emotionally drawn in, and I want those actors on the stage and that audience to be one," she explains. One of her prime objectives with actors is to "carve out the role so that it's meaningful and something active that can reach the audience" (Interview, 2000). An emphasis on emotional connection should not be interpreted as an overall bias toward Realism, however. Studying classical Japanese theatre for her dissertation and visiting Japan helped Boyd embrace a theatrical style and affected her sense of color choice as well. "I'm not afraid to be presentational," she states (Interview, 2000).

In addition to setting an example for other women entrepreneurs, Boyd has been a voice for directors' rights. As the first woman president of SSDC from 1992 to 1998, Boyd championed improved working conditions and better contracts for directors. She also helped lead a study on women's careers as professional directors and designers in 1983, at a time when the glass ceiling of Broadway was a glaring reality. Boyd explained their findings: "One woman's success is her own success; one woman's failure is every woman's failure. So my success was, 'Oh great! She did a show. Wasn't that nice.' Had it been a flop, it would have been, 'That's why you don't hire a woman'" (Interview, 2000). However discouraging that message may be, she is heartened by the change over the last two decades of the twentieth century. At the time she directed *Eubie!*, a woman director on Broadway was an anomaly, but she has a different point of view about the climate at the turn of the twenty-first century. "Nowadays if you opened a show on Broadway it would open a lot of doors, because people are used to women in those positions," Boyd reasons (Interview, 2000). Boyd has been recognized for her efforts, winning the Outstanding Young Entrepreneur Award from Citicorp in 1980 and two Outstanding Alumni Awards from Beaver College and the City University of New York.

Sources

"Boyd, Julianne." Billy Rose Theatre Collection, clippings. New York Public Library for the Performing Arts.

Boyd, Julianne. 2000. Interview with Anne Fliotsos. 14 Mar. New York City.

———. 2003. Telephone interview with Anne Fliotsos. 14 Nov.

Boyd, Julianne, and Kay Carney. 1983. "Directors and Designers Report on Sex Discrimination in the Theatre." League of Professional Theatre Women. 8 Mar.

Chinoy, Helen Krich. 1987. "Women Backstage and Out Front." In *Women in American Theatre*, ed. Helen Krich Chinoy and Linda Walsh Jenkins, 353–73. New York: Theatre Communications Group.

Cunningham, Dennis. 1978. Rev. of *Eubie!*, conceived by Julianne Boyd, music by Eubie Blake. WCBS-TV, 20 Sept. Rpt. *New York Theatre Critics' Reviews.* 39 (15) (16 Oct.): 219.

Lape, Bob. 1978. Rev. of *Eubie!*, conceived by Julianne Boyd, music by Eubie Blake. WABC-TV, 21 Sept. Rpt. *New York Theatre Critics' Reviews.* 39 (15) (16 Oct.): 219.

Munk, Erika. 1984. Rev. of *A . . . My Name Is Alice*, by Julianne Boyd and Joan Micklin Silver. *Village Voice*, 6 Mar., n.p.

Nightengale, Benedict. 1984. "Stage View." Rev. of *A . . . My Name Is Alice*, by Julianne Boyd and Joan Micklin Silver. *New York Times*, 11 Mar., sec. 2, 5.

Pfeifer, Ellen. 2000. "Julianne Boyd's Theater Is Always Being Reinvented." *Boston Globe*, 20 Oct., 3rd edition, D1.

Rich, Frank. 1980. "Musical: 'Onward Victoria' A Woman's Freedom Fight." Rev. of *Onward Victoria*, book and lyrics by Charlotte Anker and Irene Rosenberg. *New York Times*, 15 Dec., C15.

———. 1984. "*A . . . My Name Is Alice* at American Place." Rev. of *A . . . My Name Is Alice*, by Julianne Boyd and Joan Micklin Silver. *New York Times*, 27 Feb., C14.

Siegel, Ed. 1997a. Rev. of *Cabaret*, book by Joe Maseroff, based on stories by

Christopher Isherwood and the play *I Am a Camera*, music by John Kander, lyrics by Fred Ebb. *Boston Globe*, 2nd edition, 7 July, C10.

————. 1997b. "A Menacing and Seductive *Cabaret*." Rev. of *Cabaret*, book by Joe Maseroff, based on stories by Christopher Isherwood and the play *I Am a Camera*, music by John Kander, lyrics by Fred Ebb. *Boston Globe*, 16 Oct., 3rd edition, E1.

————. 2002. "Stage Reviews." Rev. of *South Pacific*, book by Joshua Logan and Oscar Hammerstein II, based on *Tales of the South Pacific* by James A. Michener, music by Richard Rodgers, lyrics by Oscar Hammerstein II. *Boston Globe*, 26 June, 3rd edition, F1.

Wilson, Edwin. 1978. "Season Openers: Broadway Turns to Legends. . . ." Rev. of *Eubie!*, conceived by Julianne Boyd, music by Eubie Blake. *Wall Street Journal*, 22 Sept. Rpt. *New York Theatre Critics' Reviews* 39 (15) (16 Oct.): 216.

Representative Directing Credits

Broadway:
  Eubie! (1978), *Onward Victoria!* (1980)

Off and Off-Off Broadway:
  Stop the Parade (1973), *The Voice of the Turtle* (1976), *The Well* (1976), *Lyrical & Satirical: The Music of Harold Rome* (1977), *Mocking Bird* (1977), *Mary Hamilton* (1977), *Happy with the Blues: The Music of Harold Arlen* (1978), *Onward Victoria!* (1979), *The Collyer Brothers at Home* and *Period Piece* (1981), *A . . . My Name Is Alice* (1983, 1984), *Just So* (1985), *Maggie Magalita* (1986), *Tea* (1986), *Niedecker* (1989), *Maggie and Misha* (1991), *A . . . My Name Is Still Alice* (1992), *Brimstone* (1994)

Regional and Stock Theatre:
  I Do! I Do! (1984), *Just So* (1985), *Tea* (1988, 1989), *Legal Tender* (1990), *As You Like It* (1991), *The Country Wife* (1991), *Necessities* (1991), *A . . . My Name Is Still Alice* (1992), *Sweet & Hot: The Songs of Harold Arlen* (1992, 1993), *Brimstone* (1994), *Alice Revisited* (1995), *Room Service* (1996), *Cabaret* (1997), *A Little Night Music* (1998), *A View from the Roof* (1998), *Mack and Mabel* (1999), *Tea* (1999), *Company* (2000), *A . . . My Name Will Always Be Alice* (2000), *On the Twentieth Century* (2001), *Ciao!* (2001), *South Pacific* (2002), *Funny Girl* (2003), *The Game* (2003), *Blanche and Her Joy Boys* (2003), *Cyrano de Bergerac* (2004), *Follies* (2005), *The Human Comedy* (2006), *Ring Round the World* (2006), *West Side Story* (2007), *Uncle Vanya* (2007)

Tours:
  Eubie! (1979)

Carroll, Vinnette

Born March 11, 1922, in New York City, Vinnette Carroll never aspired to be one of the first African American women to direct on Broadway,[1] but that distinction has become part of her legacy. She has found a place in several "Who's Who" books for earning an Emmy and an Obie for her acting and winning numerous awards and Tony nominations for her directing and writing. A woman of many theatrical talents, Carroll is associated with the gospel-inspired song-plays she created and directed on Broadway and off of Broadway, and in national tours, such as *But Never Jam Today, Don't Bother Me, I Can't Cope,* and *Your Arms Too Short to Box with God.* The style of her work has been of particular note to critics and audiences alike. With it, she injected a unique African American aesthetic, previously foreign to the musical theatre of the 1960s and 1970s. Her work inspired imitators as well, with gospel-style musicals such as *Momma, I Want to Sing* and *Don't Get God Started* (Anderson 1994, 71).

Although born in New York City, Carroll spent her early childhood in Jamaica with her grandparents while her father finished dental school. When she and her sister returned to New York City in the 1930s, her mother immersed the children in cultural activities, taking them to the opera and concerts. As a college student, Carroll studied psychology at Long Island University, earning a B.A. in 1944, then an M.A. at New York University in 1946. She completed her doctoral work at Columbia University before turning her attention to the stage. She began her theatrical career by studying acting and won a scholarship to Erwin Piscator's New School of Social Research in New York City, which strongly influenced her directing style thereafter. Carroll toured in a one-woman show she created, then went on to teach drama at New York City's High School for Performing Arts for eleven years. Although she enjoyed success as an actor, she turned to directing in part because she "felt directing was the most fulfilling kind of work." Carroll explains, "As you get older, you begin to want to see the whole picture and to collaborate with the playwright. It's a much greater joy to watch young people act" (Interview, 1999).

Carroll's roles as a director and a creator of theatre are inextricably linked, both stemming from her goals to create African American theatre with positive role models that also reflect the values of the community. Hers was a theatre drawing from ritual, music, and dance, infused with a strong sense of spirituality. She proclaimed, "I want to show Black people that there's dignity and beauty in our art. That's my goal" (George 1977, D9). Part of her preparation came from childhood visits with renowned poet and author Langston Hughes, who came to the family home for dinner and discussed his poetry. More importantly, he invited her to visit various African American churches with him. Because of her Anglican upbringing in Jamaica, the call-and-response format and the gospel singing were foreign to her. Carroll recalled the thrill of those early visits, exclaiming, "When I went with Langston, boy—that would be great! That made a big difference, and I began to love, love, love that music. I thought, 'This is so theatrical and should be in theatre.' I fell in love with gospel music and met so many people" (Interview, 1999). She took more than the musical style from those journeys to the church. She also took ideas about movement and staging, such as bringing actors onto the stage down the aisles of the theatre singing, as a church choir would.

Carroll's first job as a director was for Howard Richardson and William Berney's *Dark of the Moon* at the Harlem YMCA in 1958, a production she remounted for the Equity Library Theatre Off Broadway in 1960. With energetic staging by Carroll and dazzling choreography by Alvin Ailey, the production went on to commercial success in Canada and helped secure a Ford Foundation Grant for Carroll for directing. Carroll's subsequent productions for the Equity Library Theatre included *Ondine* in 1961 and *Disenchanted* in 1962. But it was Hughes who provided Carroll with material that would launch her professional directing career: a 1961 Off-Off Broadway production of his play *Black Nativity*, a gospel-based telling of the nativity produced at the Forty-First Street Theatre.

Although Hughes is often credited with introducing the song-play genre with *Black Nativity*, Vinnette Carroll's collaborative contributions in staging the play were crucial to its development. Biographer Calvin A. McClinton writes, "Hughes may have coined the term 'gospel song-play' but it was Carroll who developed the style and paved the way for a distinct Black American Musical. The song-play is a 'tapestry of interaction woven together using poetry, dance and music whereas the weight and color of that tapestry changes with the energy of the moment'" (2000, 75). With her training in Epic theatre, Carroll brought nonlinear staging to the production, creating mosaics or collages rather than causal plots. Jerry Campbell, a longtime collaborator, called her unique style of staging the juxtaposition of opposites. McClinton explained, "Carroll was thrilled in working with a play when all of a sudden things would shift 180 degrees because of placement. The juxtaposition of opposites increased the value of a moment or emotion just because it was right next door to something totally different than itself" (76). Carroll considered her song-plays and their staging to be based on Greek theatre, complete with a chorus that moved rhythmically and sang. In *Black Nativity* and subsequent song-plays, Carroll wove her tapestry of song, text, dance, and mime in a way that celebrated life and evoked a soaring spirituality. Most critics agreed that *Black Nativity* was a joyous celebration, but a few questioned whether it was a play or an act of worship, and one critic found the poetry and lyrics of *Black Nativity* "banal" (80). With mostly positive reviews and an enthusiastic audience, the production toured both Europe and the United States.

Carroll continued to hone her skills by directing Hughes's 1965 Off-Broadway production of *The Prodigal Son,* another gospel song-play based on the well-known biblical parable. She replaced a previous director at Hughes's request, and she made it her own by cutting chunks of dialogue and replacing actors with her own breed of performers who could act, sing, and dance (McClinton 2000, 90). Carroll's dynamic staging did not go unnoticed. The critics, mainly Caucasian and Jewish men, tried to grapple with an unfamiliar aesthetic, that of African Americans joyously singing and moving to a type of music that was unexpected on commercial stages. Howard Taubman of the *New York Times* hailed the unique style of gospel-theatre, writing, "Vinnette Carroll's staging captures the spirit of naivete that was once the exclusive fashion in presentations of Negroes by Negroes. We know now that there are many other aspects to the Negro, and we tend to be sensitive about oversimplified displays of his talents. But if we remember that this is only one side of his nature and potentialities, we can share in his gift for rapturously innocent song and dance" (1965, 19). Despite his condescending rhetoric, Taubman's sense of enjoyment and wonder was evident in his review. *The Prodigal Son* ran for 141 performances at the Greenwich Mews, then went on to a successful European tour.

After a brief stint in 1967 directing at the Inner City Repertory Company in Watts, Los Angeles, Carroll's career took an important turn. With support of the New York State Council on the Arts in 1968, she helped found the Urban Arts Corps, which was designed "to train young Puerto Ricans and blacks as performers and to develop opportunities for professionals using materials by black playwrights and composers" (Tanner 1989, 112). As artistic director at the Urban Arts Corps, she fostered the crucial training ground for minority theatre artists who were developing their fledgling works. Carroll herself often conceived and directed the plays for classes and projects by drawing on folktales, literature, and the Bible. *But Never Jam Today,* created and directed by Carroll, was one of the group's first public successes. It was based on Lewis Carroll's *Alice in Wonderland* and *Through the Looking Glass,* and the Urban Arts Corps performed the production for the New York City Center's Black Expo week in 1969. Richard F. Shepard of the *New York Times* related it to what he knew from the Jewish theatre, marveling that the audience reacted "with the wholesome ingenuousness reminiscent of Yiddish theatre fans of years ago." Although he found their response somewhat puzzling, he concluded that by adding "soul" to the story of *Alice in Wonderland*, Carroll had created a piece that was "original and entertaining" (1969, 40). The critics' acceptance of her alternative style helped cement her legacy for introducing a foreign yet welcome deviation from mainstream theatre. Ten years later, in 1979, Carroll reworked the production and took it to Broadway, but it endured for only a brief run.

It was at the Urban Arts Corps that Carroll first met composer and future collaborator Micki Grant. Carroll recalled, "Micki came in here and sang her songs, and I knew it was right. . . . It's chemistry. I heard those lyrics and knew she was special; I didn't need Bernstein, or a panel of experts to tell me" (Fallon 1972, 48). When Grant gave Carroll a collection of songs with no book or concept, Carroll conceived a vision for a theatre piece, culminating in *Don't Bother Me, I Can't Cope,* which was developed at the Urban Arts Corps in 1970 before playing Ford's Theatre in Washington, D.C., then moving Off Broadway and earning the Outer Critics Circle Award in 1971. She earned a 1973 Tony nomination as Best Director of a musical for the revised and expanded Broadway production, which ran for more than 1,000 performances.

Don't Bother Me, I Can't Cope did not tell a story but provided a musical exploration of the human condition in a stress-filled world. With songs by Grant, the spirited revue captured the essence of how humanity is linked, regardless of race, and promoted the life-affirming messages that Carroll so often sought to put on stage. Although critics found the production to be different, they welcomed both the variety of music (gospel, rock, blues, jazz) and the new voice it propelled into a commercial venue. Mel Gussow of the *New York Times* was infected by the high spirits of the production, calling it "hand-clapping, foot-tapping, sky-reaching . . . [and] body-swaying" (1970, 60). Douglas Watt of the *Daily News* called the production "slickly professional," adding, "It has been staged with style and vigor by Vinnette Carroll. . . . Each number is smartly presented and the changes of pace are marvelously apt so that one piece slips effortlessly into the next. This is musical staging of a high degree" (1972, 304). *Time* magazine summed it up with "All heaven breaks loose on the stage" (Kalem 1972, 306).

Carroll's next production to gain "hit" status was the spirited *Your Arms Too Short to Box with God,* commissioned by the Italian government for the 1975 Festival of Two Worlds in Spoleto, Italy ("Carroll," 1983, 57). The songplay was developed at the Urban Arts Corps and conceived by Carroll, with music and lyrics by Alex Bradford and Micki Grant. Based on the Gospel of Saint Matthew, it told the story of Christ from birth through the celebration of the resurrection, staged through musical tableaux. Upon returning to the United States, *Your Arms Too Short to Box with God* played at Ford's Theatre before moving to the Lyceum Theatre on Broadway in 1976 and running for nearly 500 performances. Critics' responses were mainly positive, hailing the joyous staging and outstanding performances. A few felt it lacked narrative and "reverted back to a style of Black musicals that was less sophisticated and more stereotypical" (McClinton 2000, 117). James Lardner's review in the *Washington Post* sounded both notes: "The story of the crucifixion, obviously, has strong dramatic possibilities. Perhaps Carroll's decision to make Jesus an all-dancing, nonspeaking character is what robs this particular rendering of most of its potential force." He also admitted, "If church were always like this, we'd all go eight times a week" (1979, D19). The Broadway production showed its strength, earning three Tony nominations, including one for Carroll as Best Director. Carroll revised the show at the Urban Arts Corps before sending out a national tour. It opened on Broadway again in 1980, then a second national tour was launched in 1982, returning to New York City with a production at the Alvin Theatre. She staged a last revival that went on tour in 1996, then played the Beacon Theatre in New York City.

By 1980 Carroll had created and directed a string of plays and musicals for the Urban Arts Corps, mainly through her collaboration with Grant. Approaching sixty years of age, she was ready for semi-retirement and moved to Fort Lauderdale, Florida. At the request of the county arts council, she established a theatre group there in 1982, which became her own Vinnette Carroll Repertory Company two years later (McClinton 2000, 121). She directed numerous productions there until 1992, when her health and theatre politics forced her to slow down. When she suffered a stroke in 2000 and was unable to continue her work at the theatre, the company was renamed the Metropolitan Diversity Theatre at her request.

Casting a production could be difficult for Carroll because she was a perfectionist and demanded actors who could accomplish her vision. Carroll was up-front with her expectations and would replace actors who did not live up to her standards, who were unprofessional, or who showed a negative attitude. She tried to cast actors who understood her style of staging and leadership. "If all things are equal, really equal, and I have a choice between somebody I'm close to and somebody I'm not, I'll cast the person I'm close to," she explained (McClinton 2000, 57). Overall, she sought actors who were risk takers and exhibited creative freedom in their approach to a role.

Throughout rehearsal she was tough and warned the actors that it would be a "living hell" (McClinton 2000, 64). She did not give breaks and forbade eating and smoking at rehearsal. Despite her harsh reputation as a taskmaster, actors and others who have worked with Carroll describe her as nurturing, strong, and dynamic. One actor called her mercurial, saying, "She's spontaneous and she erupts. She's Vesuvius all over again. But she's one of the nicest people you'll ever meet when you get to the real person (McClinton 2000, 64). Throughout her career Carroll has helped a number of African American actors launch their careers, including such stars as Sherman Helmsley (Tanner 1989, 113), Phylicia Rashad, Ben Vereen, Jennifer Holliday, and Debbie Allen (Anderson 1994, 71).

One of Carroll's goals was to create a unified ensemble of open and truthful actors in rehearsal. Both individual and group spirituality were important to Carroll and tied to an African tradition. McClinton explains, "Carroll wanted the performers to have a sense of freedom, both spiritual and physical, that allowed the instrument to speak with clarity; one that was not burdened with lies. This kind of preparation was linked to a spiritual ancestral African American tie that went back to the African tradition of preparing the space and community and pulling all participants into the same spirit" (2000, 61). Rather than starting rehearsals with warm-ups, she began with a nondenominational prayer and ended the same way in order to create an ensemble ritual.

Carroll's own training as an actor proved influential in her later work as a director. In a contradictory mix, she trained both with Piscator, known for the theatrical, nonrealistic staging of Epic productions, and with Stella Adler, who adhered to a psychological approach to roles based on Stanislavski's Method. Therefore, evidence of her approach to directing is from two camps: an internal, psychological approach and an external, theatrical approach. Director and colleague Marc Primus summarizes her approach to directing actors as external: "She wants people who have certain artistic skills, real talent for movement and dance and mimicry but not that deep psychological examination of a character" (McClinton 2000, 52). She worked side by side with actors, physically showing them what she was after in her vision and asking them not to imitate her but to find that movement and spirit within themselves. McClinton observed her rehearsals of the 1996 production of *Your Arms Too Short to Box with God* and wrote, "Carroll and the actors together would move through the blocking on stage. She would paint, through movement and sound, very specific images for the actors to absorb" (53). In contrast, Carroll said that she loved working one on one with actors and used psychological approaches to character. She described using sense memory for her work on a production of *Medea* as one example (Interview, 1999). Evidently Carroll used either technique, depending on what was called for in rehearsal. She asked herself, "What system, what thing, can conjure up that feeling from her [the actor]? It has to come from the artist—it can't come from me or anybody else in the room" (Interview, 1999). Actor James Earl Jones explains, "She isn't theatrical to the extent that you lose the sense of credibility and reality of the characters. She tries to achieve both credibility and understanding—as well as the excitement of a role. That's the hardest job of all" (n.d., 2).

In terms of the visual style of her productions, Carroll said, "I know there's a style, a design to my work. The stage is very Brechtian, very simple and stark" (Dolan 1999, 18). As with the actors, Carroll sought designers who were on her wavelength and would support her vision. She was adamant that directing was not a democracy and that designers follow her aesthetic. In addition, she sought designers she could relate to personally, stating, "All personalities have to be right. It's important that the rhythm's right, so that's what I look for" (McClinton 2000, 66). Her focused work resulted in productions of very high quality, gaining her a reputation for professionalism.

Carroll earned a number of directing awards during her distinguished career, many of which were related to her productions of *Don't Bother Me, I Can't Cope:* the New York Outer Critics Circle Award in 1971, the Los Angeles Drama Critics Circle Award for Distinguished Director in 1972, the National Association for the Advancement of Colored People's (NAACP) Image Award for Distinguished Direction in 1972, and a Tony nomination for Best Director of a Musical in 1973. She also received a Tony nomination in 1977 for Best Director of a Musical and Best Book of a Musical for *Your Arms Too Short to Box with God.*

Although Carroll's accomplishments are many and her place in history as one of the first African American women to direct on Broadway is assured, her focus was not as much on commercial success as on the work itself. By her own admission, her joy has come from working with people she loves and pursuing the ideas in her head and heart. The actual business of theatre, however, was "enormously difficult and enormously painful" to her at times (Carroll, interview, 1999). Despite her accomplishments, Carroll regretted that she was not allowed to direct more classics. People knew her for her gospel work and were afraid she would be out of her element, in spite of her early training with Piscator and her love for classical theatre. She explained her painful experiences as a director, stating, "There are so many problems a black artist has to face. Yet you can't let it dominate your work, because it's so immobilizing. When I said I wanted to direct, I was told I'd have to take a third off the show's budget because I'm black, and a third off because I'm a woman. And I said, 'I'm gonna do a helluva lot with that other third'" (Dolan 1999, 17). Her spirit of determination and her grounded individualism helped her survive the business and bring a more diverse aesthetic to Broadway and beyond.

Vinnette Carroll died in Florida on November 3, 2002, at the age of 80.

Sources

Anderson, Addell Austin. 1994. "Vinnette Carroll." In *Theatrical Directors: A Biographical Dictionary*, ed. John W. Frick and Stephen M. Vallillo, 70–71. Westport, Conn.: Greenwood.

Carroll, Vinnette. 1999. "One-on-One: Vinnette Carroll." Interview with David Diamond. 9 Nov. Stage Directors and Choreographers Foundation, New York City. Tape recording.

"Carroll, Vinnette." 1983. *Current Biography Yearbook*, 54–58. 1983. New York: H. W. Wilson.

Dolan, Christine. 1999. "Vinnette Carroll: Looking at the Whole Picture." *Journal for Stage Directors and Choreographers* 18: 2 (Fall/Winter): 15–19.

Fallon, Beth. 1972. "Women Who Run Show Make Big Raves." *(New York) Daily News*, 6 June, 48.

George, Nelson. 1977. "Ms. Carroll Brings Black Richness to the Stage." *New York Amsterdam News*, 5 Mar., D9.

Gussow, Mel. 1970. Rev. of *Don't Bother Me, I Can't Cope*, conceived by Vinnette Carroll, book, lyrics, and music by Micki Grant. *New York Times*, 8 Oct., 60.

Jones, James Earl. n.d. "Vinnette Carroll: 'Like a Breath of Really Sweet Fresh Air.'" Press release. Billy Rose Theatre Collection, clippings. New York Public Library for the Performing Arts.

Kalem, T. E. 1972. "Jubilation." Rev. of *Don't Bother Me, I Can't Cope*, conceived by Vinnette Carroll, music and lyrics by Micki Grant. *Daily News*, 8 May. In *New York Theatre Critics' Reviews*, 33 (11): 306.

Lardner, James. 1979. "Gospel Glory." Rev. of *Your Arms Too Short to Box with God*, conceived by Vinnette Carroll, music and lyrics by Alex Bradford and Micki Grant. *Washington Post*, 13 Sept., final edition, D19.

McClinton, Calvin A. 2000. *The Work of Vinnette Carroll: An African American Theatre Artist*. Studies in Theatre Arts, vol. 8. Lampeter, Wales: Edwin Mellen.

Patterson, S. n.d. "Blacks' 'Alice': Lewis Carroll via Vinnette, Broadway Bound Sensation." Billy Rose Theatre Collection, clippings. New York Public Library for the Performing Arts.

Shepard, Richard F. 1969. "'But Never Jam Today' Follows Recipe." Rev. of *But Never Jam Today*, conceived by Vinnette Carroll, adapted from *Alice in Wonderland* and *Through the Looking Glass* by Lewis Carroll, music by Gershon Kingsley, additional music and lyrics by Robert Lorimer. *New York Times*, 24 Apr., 40.

Tanner, Jo A. 1989. "Carroll, Vinnette." In *Notable Women in the American Theatre: A Biographical Dictionary*, ed. Alice M. Robinson, Vera Mowry Roberts, and Milly S. Barranger, 111–14. New York: Greenwood.

Taubman, Howard. 1965. Rev. of *The Prodigal Son*, by Langston Hughes. *New York Times*, 21 May, 19.

Watt, Douglas. 1972. "*Don't Bother Me* Slick, Spirited Song & Dance." Rev. of *Don't Bother Me, I Can't Cope*, conceived by Vinnette Carroll, music and lyrics by Micki Grant. *Daily News*, 21 Apr. In *New York Theatre Critics' Reviews*, 33 (11): 304.

Representative Directing Credits

Broadway:
> *Don't Bother Me, I Can't Cope* (1972), *Your Arms Too Short to Box with God* (1976, 1980, 1982), *But Never Jam Today* (1979)

Off and Off-Off Broadway:
> *Dark of the Moon* (1960), *Ondine* (1961), *Black Nativity* (1961), *Disenchanted* (1962), *Trumpets of the Lord* (1963), *The Prodigal Son* (1965), *But Never Jam Today* (1969), *Don't Bother Me, I Can't Cope* (1971), *Step Lively, Boy* (1972), *The Ups and Downs of Theophilus Maitland* (1974), *The Flies* (1974), *When Hell Freezes Over, I'll Skate* (1979), *Boogie Woogie Rumble of a Dream Deferred* (1982), *Your Arms Too Short to Box with God* (1996)

Tours:
> *Don't Bother Me, I Can't Cope* (1975–76, 1976–77), *Your Arms Too Short to Box with God* (1979)

Regional Theatre:
> *The Flies* (1966, 1967), *Slow Dance on the Killing Ground* (1968, 1988), *Don't Bother Me, I Can't Cope* (1971, 1972, 1973, 1990), *Lost in the Stars* (1980), *When Hell Freezes Over, I'll Skate* (1983, 1984, 1991), *Medea* (1986), *Next Time I'll Rain Fire* (1986), *The Green Bay Tree* (1986), *What You Gonna Name that Pretty Little Baby* (1987), *At Our Age We Don't Buy Green Bananas* (1987), *I'm Laughin' But I Ain't Tickled* (1988), *Baby* (1988), *Dark of the Moon* (1989), *All the King's Men* (1991), *Witness for the Prosecution* (1992), *A Musical Taste of Things to Come* (1992), *What You Need and Nothing More* (1992), *Journey from There to Me* (1992), *On Any Street* (1992), *A Soulful Celebration: Christmas and Kwanza* (1992)

International Theatre:
> *Black Nativity* (1962, 1963, 1964), *Your Arms Too Short to Box with God* (1975, 1983)

Notes

1. Although Carroll is the first African American woman to receive critical acclaim on Broadway, she is preceded by Evelyn Ellis, who directed a short-lived revival of *Tobacco Road* on Broadway in 1950. (See the Introduction.)

Chang, Tisa

Tisa Chang was born April 5, 1941, in Chungking, China, and was educated in New York City where she attended the High School of Performing Arts, Barnard College, City College, and the Martha Graham School of the Dance. After beginning her theatre career as an actor and dancer on and off of Broadway, Chang turned her attention to directing, establishing the Chinese Theatre Group at the experimental theatre, La MaMa, in New York City in 1973. She honed her directing skills there, directing ten productions, many of which were performed in both Chinese and English. In 1977 she founded the Pan Asian Repertory Theatre, where she directs and serves as artistic director.

As a child, Chang exhibited the spirit of an activist. "When I was nine I told my father I wanted to be the Chinese 'Joan of Arc' and save my people," Chang recalls (Siegal 1992, 69). Chang's mission became the creation and sustenance of Asian American theatre in New York City. Her goal as a director and artistic director is to express Asian American consciousness, a difficult endeavor considering the many differences in the Asian American population. Chang endeavors to represent a wide variety of cultures, including Korean, Vietnamese, Chinese, Japanese, and Indian as well as cross-cultural people, such as Japanese Cambodian. She adds, "Asian American theatre must above all promote a certain kind of thinking and attitude. It must reflect truthfully . . . some of these experiences, whether they are struggles or joys" ("Asian" 1982, 47). She believes that examining the changing attitudes of several generations is key as well.

Blending traditions of classical Asian theatre, such as Peking Opera and Kabuki, with those of contemporary Western theatre quickly became a hallmark of Chang's work as a director and producer. The first production she directed in 1973 at La MaMa in New York City was an adaptation of the Peking Opera's *Return of the Phoenix,* a story she remembered from her childhood. She made changes, combining folk songs with contemporary songs of China. "In a way, it was quite a radical direction, and the Chinese traditionalists of Peking Opera were very upset. However, it was a way of introducing a rather alien form to American audiences," Chang reflects (Interview, 2002).

Chang directed the majority of the productions at the Pan Asian Repertory Theatre for the first several years, but by the 1980s she devoted more time to her position as artistic director, directing only once every year or two. One innovative production she directed in 1983, her bilingual *A Midsummer*

Night's Dream, was performed by a cast of twelve speaking in both Mandarin and English. Set in the city of Changan during the Chou dynasty (circa 1,000 B.C.), Chang's ancient China paralleled Shakespeare's ancient Greek setting, though the characters retained their Greek names. Mel Gussow of the *New York Times* called her production a "breezy, bilingual cameo version" and noted that the use of both languages caused some sacrifice for the English-speaking audience members, "though the evening does have its own modest virtues" (1983, C26).

After taking a break from directing from 1989 to 1991, Chang returned with a highly charged political production, *Cambodia Agonistes,* an original music-theatre epic about a Cambodian woman in New York who confronts the atrocities she witnessed during the Pol Pot years in her native land. At the time, Chang considered this to be Pan Asian's most ambitious production. It was written by company member Ernest Abuba, with music by Louis Stewart, and Pan Asian developed the production for three years. Chang asserts, "We wanted to rise to the challenge of trying to stage and theatricalize the unspeakable" (Spaid 1994, Arts 14). The play incorporated Cambodian dance, ritual, song, and masks and included Brechtian elements such as the identification of songs by title. Gussow wrote, "As skillfully directed by Tisa Chang, the play swirls in and out of the dancer's consciousness and through recent Cambodian history. The approach is more symbolic than sequential as the indictment against the dictatorship mounts" (1992, C3). *Newsday* critic Jan Stuart interpreted, "Beauty and horror bleed together with such unnerving fluidity in *Cambodia Agonistes,* it becomes difficult to distinguish where one ends and the other begins. . . . Its effectiveness can be delineated almost as neatly as its scored and spoken passages: When it talks, it often trips; when it sings, it soars" (1992, sec. 2, 51). In 1994 Chang took the production on tour to South Africa, shortly after Nelson Mandela became president. She found the touring experience particularly rewarding because it struck a political chord with the audience of white Afrikaners and diverse black Africans. "To hear the comments after the performance was just absolutely worth all the hardship of the technical grief," she commented (Interview, 2002).

Chang's passion for directing was refueled when she returned to her first love, musical theatre, directing *Shanghai Lil's* in 1997. Performed Off Broadway at the St. Clement's Theatre, the original musical by Lilah Kan and Louis Stewart was set at a restaurant in San Francisco's Chinatown, shortly before Pearl Harbor. When the restaurant's owner starts a Chinese amateur night, it leads to a transformation of the sleepy business to a thriving nightclub. Romantic subplots surface, as do melancholy moments about the sense of alienation the Chinese Americans feel in their new country. *Newsday* praised the New

York City production and singled out Chang's direction and choreography as "amazingly inventive," though the *San Francisco Chronicle* panned it the following year, on tour (Jacobson 1997, sec. 2, B5).

Both Chang's background as a dancer and her Asian aesthetic lead her to create pieces that are deceptively simple yet elegant in style. Her production of Susan Kim's stage adaptation of Amy Tan's novel *The Joy Luck Club* in 1999 and gave Chang the challenge of seamlessly melding the stories of four Chinese mothers and their American-born daughters. Her connection to the cultural specificity of the piece was very real. Chang explains, "My mother was born in 1918. She really was in America in the 1950s, with mahjong parties, and some of her friends were wives of diplomats. One had bound feet" (Interview, 2002). The play was a cumbersome eighteen scenes, and Chang's challenge was to ensure that the stories flowed and connected like "tendrils of a vine" (Interview, 2002). In addition to staging seamless transitions whenever possible, Chang looked for metaphors to use on stage. Where the script made reference to a boat ride, she broke up the language-heavy, expository problems of the script by inserting the illusion of a "boat ride with the mind and one long ribbon," which "really helped anchor it" (Interview, 2002). *Newsday* reviewer Aileen Jacobson wrote, "[W]e are seeing this work about digging back to one's roots to find renewal in the season devoted to rebirth. In many ways, this graceful production, fluently directed and choreographed by the Pan Asian Rep's artistic director, Tisa Chang, feels perfectly in synch with its material. . . . [T]he many roles are beautifully played in a touching production that reaches far beyond its Asian roots" (1999, sec. 2, B09). The *New York Times* found the play less successful but noted the "impressive efforts by director Tisa Chang" to keep the play cohesive (Bruckner 1999, E3).

Chang's illusionistic staging was also evident in her direction of Fay and Michael Kanin's stage adaptation of *Rashomon*, a play set 1,000 years ago in Kyoto, Japan, in which a bandit sets upon a samurai and his wife. She directed the play in 2001 at the West End Theatre Off Broadway and brought it back for a second appearance in 2002. Chang calls *Rashomon* an "elemental production . . . more evocative than realistic" (Interview, 2002). Rather than using a soundtrack, she had two musicians create a soundscape using instruments such as acoustic gourds, Japanese drums, and wood blocks, a choice that *New York Times* critic Wilborn Hampton found "successfully evoke[s] the haunting mood of the play." He wrote, "Under the taut direction of Tisa Chang, the Pan Asian Repertory has mounted a commendable revival that is all the more striking for its simplicity" (2001, E5). Chang focused on fluidic movement in *Rashomon,* both in terms of evoking the effect of water and light in an empty pit, representing a pool of water, and in terms of moving the actors seamlessly on and off stage. The set designer aided her with two rows of bamboo, which shifted to accommodate actors entering or leaving the space. "I think it's well-done, from my days of sleight-of-hand as a magician's assistant," Chang explains (Interview, 2002).

When casting, Chang must confront the issue of ethnicity for each role. Asked if she sought to cast only Chinese actors in Chinese parts or if she ignored country of origin, Chang replied, "I think it's acting ability first, but the important thing about ethnicity is the cultural resonance or cultural specificity. How much does he understand the character within a certain world: the movement, the vocal patterns, and the emotional connection, maybe that mystical connection?" (Interview, 2002).

On a larger scale, racial bias in casting is an issue Chang speaks adamantly against. Chang and others rebutted the casting of Caucasian actor Jonathan Pryce in the role of the Eurasian pimp in the 1990 Broadway musical *Miss Saigon*. According to Chang, the casting director stated that there were no Asian American actors qualified to perform the role, an excuse Chang found to be blatantly false. She wrote an article in *USA Today*, explaining the humiliation of yellowface, the practice of portraying Asian characters with Caucasian actors in exaggerated makeup. She asserted, "We are sensitive to the economic impact of a successful Broadway show, but it cannot be at the expense of perpetuating discriminatory practices and images" (1990).

As a firm believer in deep concentration and chi, a mystical life force, Chang brings an Eastern aesthetic into her rehearsals. She asks her actors to stay in character throughout the rehearsal process and respect the sanctity of the rehearsal space by keeping noise to a minimum. She chooses not to teach acting, citing that she has no patience and expects professional actors to come into rehearsals equipped with the tools to handle analysis on their own. She explains, "I love directing, meaning orchestrating many things happening. I like to see the larger picture and I know what I want in terms of details, but I don't like to spend a lot of time on exegesis, like spending two hours talking about a character" (Sun 1994, 67).

In order to bring cultural specificity into the rehearsal process, Chang asks that set and costume pieces be introduced into rehearsals as soon as possible, enabling actors to inhabit their movement through their costume and environment.

In terms of style, the theatricality and illusion of Asian theatre play heavily into her choices as a director and adapter. "I'm very interested in theater works that draw on indigenous forms of music, movement, oral history and puppetry. . . . I'm less interested in writers writing in the Western fashion," she reports (Gussow 1997, C16). "To me theatre must represent magic. It has to appear and it has to disappear. It has to tease the audience" (Sun 1994, 66). In order to achieve such magic, Chang relies heavily on designers to evoke the physical world of the play. "I need gestation time," she justifies (Interview, 2002). With Ruth Wolff's *The Empress of China,* produced at the West End Theatre in March 2003, Chang began working with a model of the set nine months ahead, trying to visualize the movement and physicality of that world.

In addition to her reputation as a creative director, Chang's leadership skills and service to her profession have made her a high-profile figure. Under her directorship, the Pan Asian Repertory Theatre has become the largest Asian American theatre in the United States. She has served her profession by sitting on executive boards of the League of Professional Theatre Women and the Society for Stage Directors and Choreographers. She has won several awards, including the Theatre Artists Award in 1980 from the Chinese American Arts Council, the Special Theatre World Award in 1988, a Barnard College Medal of Distinction in 1991, a NYC Cultural Pioneer Tribute in 1993, and the Lee Reynolds Award in 2001 from the League of Professional Theatre Women. Although she may not be the "Chinese Joan of Arc" she dreamed of as a child, Tisa Chang has clearly had a positive impact on Asian American artists and people's perception of them in the United States.

Sources

"Asian Americans in Theatre—East and West Coast." 1982. *East Wind* 1 (Spring/ Summer): 44, 47–48.

Bruckner, D. J. R. 1999. "For These Bonded Souls, Some Luck, but Little Joy." Rev. of *The Joy Luck Club,* by Susan Kim, based on the novel by Amy Tan. *New York Times,* 27 Apr., E3.

Chang, Tisa. 1990. "Race Is Crucial in Some Stage Roles." *USA Today,* 17 Apr. In Lexis Nexis Academic Database, www.LexisNexis.com (accessed 10 Sept. 2002).

———. 2002. Interview with Anne Fliotsos. 5 Oct. New York City.

Fliotsos, Anne. 2003. "Tisa Chang: In Praise of Illusion." *American Theatre* 20 (3) (Mar.): 36–39.

Gussow, Mel. 1983. "A 'Dream' Set in China." Rev. of *A Midsummer Night's Dream,* by William Shakespeare. *New York Times,* 20 Apr., C26.

———. 1992. "Destroying Its People, A Nation Loses Its Soul." Rev. of *Cambodia Agonistes,* book and lyrics by Ernest Abuba, music by Louis Stewart. *New York Times,* 13 Nov., C3.

———. 1997. "A Stage for All the World of Asian-Americans." *New York Times,* 22 Apr., C16.

Hampton, Wilborn. 2001. "Any Way You Look at It, the Story Is Not Pleasant." Rev. of *Rashomon,* by Fay and Michael Kanin. *New York Times,* 5 Mar., E5.

Jacobson, Aileen. 1997. "Engaging Shanghai: A Lively Asian-American Musical."
Rev. of *Shanghai Lil's,* book and lyrics by Lilah Kan, music by Louis Stewart.
Newsday, 26 Apr., sec. 2, B5.

———. 1999. "Mothers Nurture Roots of Renewal/Generations." Rev. of *The
Joy Luck Club,* by Susan Kim, based on the novel by Amy Tan. *Newsday,* 27
Apr., sec. 2, B09.

Rodriguez, Maria. 1989. "Chang, Tisa." In *Notable Women in the American Theatre: A Biographical Dictionary,* ed. Alice M. Robinson, Vera Mowry Roberts,
and Milly S. Barranger, 119–21. New York: Greenwood.

Siegal, F. 1992. "Pan Asian Repertory Theatre's Tisa Chang." *Ms,* Mar./Apr., 69.

Spaid, Elizabeth Levitan. 1994. "Cambodia's Tragic Past Haunts Today's Audience." Rev. of *Cambodia Agonistes,* book and lyrics by Ernest Abuba, music
by Louis Stewart. *Christian Science Monitor,* 25 Feb., Arts 14.

Stuart, Jan. 1992. "Music Born of Cambodia Nightmare." Rev. of *Cambodia Agonistes,* book and lyrics by Ernest Abuba, music by Louis Stewart. *Newsday,*
10 Nov., sec. 2, 51.

Sun, William H. 1994. "Sustaining the Project." *TDR/The Drama Review* 38 (2)
(T142) (Summer): 64–71.

Wolf, Stacy. 1994. "Tisa Chang." In *Theatrical Directors: A Biographical Dictionary,* ed. John W. Frick and Stephen M. Vallillo, 75–76. Westport, Conn.:
Greenwood.

Representative Directing Credits

Off and Off-Off Broadway:
Ghosts and Goddesses (1973), *Return of the Phoenix* (1973), *A Midsummer
Night's Dream* (1974, 1983), *Hotel Paradiso* (1975), *The Pursuit of Happiness*
(1975), *The Legend of Wu Chang* (1977), *Thunderstorm* (1978), *The Servant
of Two Masters* (1978), *And The Soul Shall Dance* (1979), *Monkey Music*
(1980), *An American Story* (1980), *Flowers and Household Gods* (1981),
Bullet Headed Birds (1981), *Station J* (1982), *Teahouse* (1982), *Empress of
China* (1984, 2003), *Ghashiram Katwai* (1985), *Wha . . . I, Whai, a Long
Long Time Ago* (1987), *Boutique Living & Disposable Icons* (1987, 1988),
Cambodia Agonistes (1992, 2005), *Shanghai Lil's* (1997), *The Joy Luck Club*
(1999, 2007), *Rashomon* (2001, 2002), *Kwatz! The Tibetan Project: The Sound
of a Hammer Hitting the Head* (2004)

Regional Theatre:
The Legend of Wu Chang (1975), *And the Soul Shall Dance* (1990)

Tours:
Return of the Phoenix (1973), *And the Soul Shall Dance* (1991), *Cambodia
Agonistes* (1994), *Shanghai Lil's* (1998)

Other:
The Fan Tan King (2006)

Clarke, Martha

Born on June 3, 1944, in Baltimore, Maryland, Martha Clarke is known for her visually expressive productions, which combine elements of movement, text, and music. As a choreographer and a director, Clarke works with writers and designers to create pieces that straddle the line between dance and theatre.

The daughter of two musicians, Clarke began studying dance at the age of six. She studied at Colorado's Perry-Mansfield School of Theater and Dance and took summer sessions at the American Dance Festival at Connecticut College School of Dance with artists including Alvin Ailey and José Límon. Clarke graduated with an B.F.A. in dance in 1965 from New York City's Juilliard School, where she studied with choreographers Anthony Tutor and Louis Horst, and practiced Martha Graham technique. She also studied painting at the Art Students League in New York City.

After graduating from the Juilliard School, Clarke began her career as a dancer in the modern dance company of Anna Sokolow, whose work she found inspiring and whom she had seen at the American Dance Festival. After a few years in Sokolow's company, Clarke retired and moved to Europe with her husband. After her return to the United States, she came out of retirement and in 1972 became one of the first female members of Pilobolus, an acrobatic dance theatre group. With Pilobolus, Clarke performed solos and duets with dancer Robert Morgan Barnett and co-choreographed a number of dances. Over time, Clarke became frustrated with the creative process in Pilobolus, which involved six people. Working outside Pilobolus in 1977, she directed the Music-Theatre Group's production of *Portraits* at the Lenox Art Center in Massachusetts. Clarke thus began what would become a long association with New York City's Music-Theatre Group, an organization dedicated to new work that combines music and theatre in a variety of genres ranging from performance art to opera.

At the suggestion of Charles Reinhart, director of the American Dance Festival, Clarke started her own company, Crowsnest, in 1978 with Barnett and French choreographer Felix Blaska. Her pieces in Crowsnest combined dance, theatre, and music with images. The company premiered at the American Dance Festival, now at Durham, North Carolina, in 1979—the same year that Clarke left Pilobolus. Among the Crowsnest pieces performed at the American Dance Festival was a solo choreographed by Clarke called *Fallen Angel*, in which she danced to a Gregorian chant wearing an evening gown and a bird's mask. Clarke's eye for visual impact and theatricality were clear in the performance. In her review of the piece, Anna Kisselgoff of the *New York Times* wrote that Clarke had "a great pictorial sense. She has in fact, a tendency toward making pictures come alive" (1979, C15).

With encouragement by Lyn Austin, producer of the Music-Theatre Group, Clarke began to focus more on directing. In addition to support by Austin, who produced many of Clarke's pieces, Clarke also received encouragement from Joseph Papp, producer of Manhattan's New York Shakespeare Festival. Clarke's early ventures in directing with the Music-Theatre Group included Massachusetts productions of Maria Irene Fornes's *Cabbages* and *Dr. Kheal* in 1979 and George W. S. Trow's *Elizabeth Dead* at New York City's Cubiculo Theatre in 1980.

In 1982 Clarke gained the public's attention by winning an Obie Award for Best New American Play with *A Metamorphosis in Miniature,* which opened at the Cubiculo Theatre. Created and directed by Clarke, the Music-Theatre Group production was based on Franz Kafka's *Metamorphosis* and chronicled the transformation of a man into an insect. Mel Gussow of the *New York Times* wrote, "The performance is the most persuasive metamorphosis of a man into a beast since Zero Mostel turned into Eugene Ionesco's 'Rhinoceros'" (1982, C13). With this piece, Clarke began what would become a lifelong collaboration with Paul Gallo, who designed lighting for the production.

Clarke continued to win critical recognition in 1984 with *The Garden of Earthly Delights,* based on a triptych painting by Hieronymus Bosch. Premiering Off-Off Broadway at New York City's St. Clement's Church, the Music-Theatre Group production created and directed by Clarke dramatized an apocalyptic vision of Bosch's painting in four parts: "Eden," "The Garden," "The Seven Sins," and "Hell." The production's seven performers, which included Clarke, played the painting's characters, animals, and objects. They were sometimes suspended in the air by wires. Although the piece did not contain text, it incorporated music and included its three musicians in the action. Clarke worked with composer Richard Peaslee on the production, adding him as a long-term collaborator with Gallo, the production's lighting designer. Because *The Garden of Earthly Delights* crossed genres, it was reviewed by theatre, dance, and music critics. In his review, Gussow wrote, "Whether one approaches it as theater, dance or music—or, more aptly, as a blending of the performing and visual arts—it is a work of exhilarating beauty" (1984, C3). The critically acclaimed production won several awards and toured the United States and abroad. It was revived Off Broadway in 1987.

In 1986 the Music-Theatre Group produced Clarke's new work *Vienna: Lusthaus,* which Clarke created and directed at St. Clement's Church. Based on *Fromage Dangereuse,* an earlier piece by Clarke that was presented the previous year at the Lenox Arts Center, *Vienna: Lusthaus* presented images and music from fin-de-siècle Vienna that touched contemporary chords with audiences. The production included lighting by Gallo, music by Peaslee, and text by Charles L. Mee Jr. that consisted of a collage of dialogue and writings culled from numerous sources, including composer Arnold Schoenberg, psychologist Sigmund Freud, and Mee's own dreams. Mee describes the production, saying, "I see civilization sleepwalking to the edge of doom, then and now. . . . Those people were unconscious of where they were headed in the same way that we seem to be unconscious of where we're headed, and both they and we are enormously resourceful at finding ways of avoiding reality—of insulating and isolating ourselves from ugliness, and anesthetizing ourselves to the harshness of the world" (Bennetts 1986, C15). Clarke used artist Egon Schiele's watercolors as a starting point for the work. The production's assemblage of images grew and alluded to figures including Freud, Schiele, artist Gustave Klimt, writer Arthur Schnitzler, and Adolf Hitler. All were displayed in a simple set composed of a white room with tilted walls and a scrim, designed by Robert Israel, who also became a frequent collaborator with Clarke. In his review of the production, Frank Rich of the *New York Times* wrote, "Miss Clarke seeks to evoke that cataclysmic historical and cultural turning point in a mere 60 minutes of hallucinations sculpted with dance, words, music and light. She has succeeded beyond one's wildest dreams—perhaps because she has tapped into everyone's wildest dreams." He added that Clarke "has distilled both the beauty and the ominous chaos of a vanished Vienna into a shape that seems completely contiguous with the modern world" (1986, C13).

Vienna: Lusthaus won Clarke an Obie Award for Playwriting in 1986. It transferred Off Broadway that year to the New York Shakespeare Festival's Public Theater and was performed in numerous regional theatres, including the John F. Kennedy Center for the Performing Arts in Washington, D.C., and toured internationally. The production was later revised as *Vienna: Lusthaus (Revisited)* and presented in 2002 at the New York Theatre Workshop in New York City, where its original themes still seemed relevant. Bruce Weber of the *New York Times* wrote, "The titillating eeriness of impending doom is exploited so gorgeously . . . that you can understand how civilizations become complicit in their own demise" (2002, B126).

Returning to Kafka with her collaborators Gallo, Israel, and Peaslee, Clarke conceived and directed *The Hunger Artist*. With text by Richard Greenberg, the production followed a variety of Kafka's storylines and focused on emotional and physical hunger. For inspiration for the piece, Clarke studied photographs, Fellini films, and the paintings of Chagall and Goya. First presented in 1987 by the Music-Theatre Group and the John F. Kennedy Center at St.

Clement's Church, the production was not as critically successful as Clarke's earlier pieces. Rich wrote in his review that "the director does at times open a door on the murky psychological landscape where Kafka's anguished figures reside. . . . It's also to Ms. Clarke's credit that she has avoided most of the banalities of depicting Kafkaesque evil" (1987, C3).

Working once again with Gallo, Israel, Peaslee, and the New York Shakespeare Festival, Clarke created and directed *Miracolo d'Amore* in 1988. The production caused controversy when members of the audience at South Carolina's Spoleto Festival left because of male nudity and sexual images. The piece was inspired by folktales of the Grimm brothers and Italo Calvino but contained no narrative. Examining male violence toward women, the production included sounds from nature, pidgin Italian songs, and music with lyrics of Petrarch and Dante. Like other works by Clarke, it was also inspired by paintings—in this case the work of Venetian painter Tiepolo and the illustrations of J. J. Grandville. Stage images used in the production came from Darwin's *The Expression of the Emotions in Man and Animals* and from improvisations in rehearsal. Visually, the piece mimicked the deep perspective of paintings of the Renaissance. In his review of the piece, later presented at the New York Shakespeare Festival, Rich wrote, "It's a beautifully achieved, spare-no-expense spectacle in which a director's boundless visual imagination and a melodic pastiche of a score dress up some punishingly anti-erotic cliches about sex and death" (1988, C17).

In 1990 Clarke directed her new work, *Endangered Species,* at Off Broadway's Brooklyn Academy of Music. Collaborating with Gallo, Israel, and Peaslee, the Music-Theatre Group production included performers, musicians, and animals such as an elephant and horses. The text was adapted by Robert Coe and included poems by Walt Whitman. The sound by Peaslee and Stanley Walden contained prerecorded music ranging from Stephen Sondheim to old opera recordings, jungle sounds, and Hitler speeches. Israel's set was circular with a back wall painted like the sky that contained a large double door through which animals appeared. This time Clarke was inspired visually by artist Henri de Toulouse-Lautrec's pastels. Despite all this effort, the piece received poor reviews and closed early. Explaining the meaning of the production, Clarke clarified, "What the piece is about . . . is all our connections, specifically our connection to animals; the frailty of the human condition, the frailty of the animal world. Indirectly, of course, it's about the Holocaust. . . . It's also about our Civil War, brutality, repression" (Kelly 1990, B27).

After the critical failure of *Endangered Species,* Clarke spent most of the 1990s directing opera and choreographing smaller pieces for dance theatre. In the early 1990s she directed Wolfgang Amadeus Mozart's *Cosi Fan Tutti* and Mozart's *The Magic Flute* at the Glimmerglass Opera House in Cooperstown,

New York, both to positive reviews. Clarke also directed Tan Dun's *Marco Polo*, which had its United States premiere by the New York City Opera at the New York State Theater in 1997 after productions in Munich, Amsterdam, and Hong Kong. Her direction of Polo's alleged journey incorporated balletic movement and visuals based in part on Chinese paintings from the ninth to fifteenth centuries.

During this period, Clarke also worked with the Nederlands Dans Theater III, a group of dancers who are all over forty years of age. Working with the older cast, Clarke created and directed *Dammerung,* an examination of fear and death. Visual overtones of artist René Magritte were combined with music by Alban Berg, and the production made its American debut in 1993 at the American Dance Festival. Expanding on *Dammerung,* Clarke directed *An Uncertain Hour,* which she co-created with Nederlands Dans Theater III. Inspired by Thomas Mann's novel *Magic Mountain,* the sparse piece showed dancers moving slowly up and down a mountain, to the accompaniment of German lieder. The piece, which was Clarke's first long work since *Endangered Species,* previewed in 1995 at the American Dance Festival, and then moved to New York City's John Jay Theatre. Clarke also created and directed a meditation on aging with Nederlands Dans Theater III called *Nocturne,* presented in 1994 at Jacob's Pillow Dance Festival in Massachusetts.

Venturing back to larger works, Clarke created and directed *Vers la Flamme.* Based on five short stories by Anton Chekhov, the piece was named after a composition by Alexander Scriabin and included the music of Scriabin and Sergei Rachmaninoff. Clarke explains the title saying, "The Chekhov characters always seemed to be hovering near a flame. They singe their wings but they don't get burnt" (Gussow 1999, sec. 2, 17). *Vers la Flamme,* which focused on people's mistakes and their desire for escape, contained only one word of dialogue: the word "Olga," spoken by a husband abandoned by his wife. Clarke's production premiered in 1999 at the American Dance Festival before moving to New York City's Lincoln Center and the Kennedy Center. Sarah Kaufman of the *Washington Post* wrote of Clarke's direction, "It's quiet, subdued and often comes to a complete halt. But in those moments of stillness, with the torrent of tension unleashed in a gaze, lies more potent drama than in many bigger, busier shows" (1999, C02). *Vers la Flamme* was a turning point for Clarke, who had considered herself a choreographer–director until then. After *Vers la Flamme,* Clarke told dance critic Deborah Jowitt, "I've taken away the word *choreographer,* because I feel I approach my work as a director now. And there's a difference, because I'm not looking for a lot of inventive movement" (Jowitt 1999, 75).

In 2000 Clarke directed Sebastian Barry's *Hans Christian Andersen,* based on the 1952 film *Hans Christian Andersen.* With music by Frank Loesser, the production was a visual spectacle with mermaids, gliding skaters, flying fairies, and other images. Presented at San Francisco's American Conservatory Theater (A.C.T.), the play received mixed reviews and did not proceed to Broadway as planned.

Clarke directed her first play by a nonliving author with William Shakespeare's *A Midsummer Night's Dream* in 2004 at the American Repertory Theatre in Massachusetts. Designed by Israel, the set included a dirt-covered stage with four pits. Of her visual inspiration, Clarke commented, "The set came partly from the rough spareness of Anselm Kiefer and the surrealist photographer Robert Parke-Harrison. The costumes evolved from Picasso's Rose period and Goya's *Caprichos*" (Lester 2003). Accompanied by sound from Peaslee, a goblin-like Puck and flying fairies graced the stage.

Later that year, Clarke directed her work *Belle Epoque,* with text by Mee, at Lincoln Center. Like *Endangered Species*, the production was influenced by the paintings of Toulouse-Lautrec. The world of the painter in late-nineteenth-century Paris was presented on a set that included two dark, tilted mirrors by Israel. Although he found the text a problem, Charles Isherwood of the *New York Times* wrote, "Ms. Clarke's staging, which incorporates the expected variations of the cancan and the quadrille, has a bustling freedom that is a fine theatrical metaphor for the restless speed of Toulouse-Lautrec's acute eye, forever settling on unexpected moments and awkward poses" (2004, E5).

Clarke's next project was inspired by the Italian writer Luigi Pirandello. More specifically, it was based on a 1984 Italian television film called *Kaos* by Paolo and Vittorio Taviani. Clarke also named her piece *KAOS* and directed it in 2006 at the New York Theater Workshop. Choosing to use only the Italian language, the production included projections of supertiles that translated the Italian dialogue for the audience. In his favorable review of the production, *New York Times* critic John Rockwell described the piece, writing, "In place of the dusty, stony Sicilian terrain, we have a mostly bare stage, which works almost as well. The black-clad performers articulate the text with seeming authenticity as to language. . . . Her choreography consists mostly of allusions to folk dance, especially snaking and circling of dancers. The music, drawn from historically accurate sources, is played and sung live and sensitively reinforces the whole" (2006, E3).

When preparing for a piece, Clarke picks a subject, reads about it, and looks at paintings, photographs, and films relevant to her idea. Many of her pieces begin with images. At times, specific images from art work end up in her pieces, but at other times, they serve as a springboard for new images.

Clarke doesn't usually audition performers but selects them through recommendations from friends. Clarke has to personally like the performer, and she chooses the look and personality of a performer over his or her technical ability. She explains, "My company is made up of actors who want to dance and dancers who want to act. I like working with a nucleus of familiar faces who have survived at least one piece. I also like to work with new faces because that keeps me from getting in a rut and repeating myself" (Interview, 1988, 59). She explains further, "I generally look for, if not older, more mature dancers—they're grown-ups. They have a real balance in their lives, between life and work. . . . I need excellent dancers, but I ask them to leave technique, as such, at the door with their shows. I'm working in that funny space between theater and dance" (Kriegsman 1988, F01). For example, in *Belle Epoque,* the performers varied in age, size, and training. Clarke describes the casting, saying, "[T]he theatrical backgrounds are so different. . . . There's a real sense of discovery and excitement in them sharing a stage" (Vincentelli 2004, 175).

Clarke's rehearsal process is collaborative. She describes rehearsals for *Belle Epoque,* saying, "We came into the first rehearsal with only the name Toulouse-Lautrec and some books of pictures. . . . We had no locations, no scenes. And at first, [Mee's] little monologues didn't even have [assigned] characters. They were just pages with text, with no scenes, no order. In rehearsals, we swapped around who was saying what until things landed. And then, through a kind of process—part play, part therapy—something emerged. . . . I look at pictures and movies, I pick up scraps, and then I collaborate very closely with the company" (Vincentelli 2004, 175).

Clarke often asks her performers—who include dancers, actors, and sometimes musicians—to improvise, and then selects parts of their improvisations. She takes suggestions from actors about how to shape the text of the piece. From dancers, Clarke says she takes movement to "create things which I shape and edit" (Giuliano 1999). While developing a piece, Clarke takes notes during rehearsals and later organizes material, such as by collating imagery of similar themes—for example, religious ideas (Shank 1991, 224). She also brings in period clothing for the dancers to wear early in rehearsal because clothing can affect their movement.

Like her performance pieces, Clarke's rehearsals are not linear. Rather than focusing on causal links, she explains, "The quality I enjoy creating the most is the atmosphere" (Giuliano 1999). Clarke notes that many of her performers who are actors become frustrated with her rehearsals because she comes from a dance background that deals more in abstraction than motivation. She explains her rehearsal process, saying, "If you watched a rehearsal of mine, you would see that nine tenths of it is in such disarray. . . . I'm foggy a lot of the time. And the actors and dancers have to search as much as I do. . . . The day-by-day process couldn't be more collaborative. It's really a workshop. . . .

During the last tenth of the process I get very decisive. Then I want precision. All those finishing elements—lights, costumes and sets are very important to me" (Interview, 1988, 58–59).

Rehearsals of her original pieces are a collaborative and lengthy process, taking anywhere from six months to two years. For rehearsals of others' works, Clarke may not have the luxury of time, although she still works collaboratively. She says, "I like to keep the atmosphere very, very playful until the third week, when you've got to be serious. Then I begin to make a gridwork that they [the performers] can rely on" (Foster 2004, N1).

Most of her own pieces are short—often about an hour long—because, according to Clarke, "I cut and cut and cut—I love editing" (Kriegsman 1988, F01). She frequently revises her pieces right up until the premieres, which are often referred to as "work in progress." As part of the ongoing process, Clarke expects members of the audience to work out their own meaning of the piece. She explains, "I'm used to being controversial. The best audience for me is one that's not afraid of being confused. People have to be willing to bring their own interpretation to a piece. Everybody brings their own and takes out what it means to them" (Giuliano 1999).

Among Clarke's many accomplishments are grants from the National Endowment for the Arts and the Guggenheim Foundation. She also received a MacArthur Foundation Fellowship in 1990 and a Doris Duke Award for New Work in 1999. In addition to her work with the Nederlands Dans Theater, Clarke has worked as a choreographer with the American Ballet Theatre, the Joffrey Ballet, London's Rambert Dance Company, and the White Oak Dance Project. In addition to those previously mentioned, Clarke's work in opera has taken her to such companies as the Canadian Opera Company and the English National Opera. She has also taught at the Juilliard School.

With a versatile background in dance and theatre, Clarke's work might be categorized as performance art today. Whatever the category, Clarke aims to create meaningful works. She explains, "I want to be altered when I go to the theatre, to be changed. I want to feel something strong, and I want to create work that achieves that" (Interview, 1988, 66).

Sources

Bennetts, Leslie. 1986. "Dream Imagery of 'Vienna: Lusthaus'." *New York Times*, 23 April, C15.

Clarke, Martha. 1988. Interview with Arthur Bartow. In *The Director's Voice: Twenty-One Interviews*, by Arthur Bartow, 51–66. New York: Theatre Communications Group.

Foster, Catherine. 2004. "Martha Clarke Puts Accent on Movement in ART's 'Midsummer.'" *Boston Globe*, 11 Jan., N1.

Giuliano, Mike. 1999. "Martha Clarke Turns to Chekhov in Dance/Theatre Work *Vers la Flamme* to Be Performed at Kennedy Center." *Johns Hopkins Peabody News Online,* Sept./Oct. http://www.peabody.jhu.edu/concerts-and-events/pn/sept99/clarke.html (accessed 5 Feb. 2002).

Gussow, Mel. 1982. "'Metamorphosis in Miniature.'" Rev. of *A Metamorphosis in Miniature,* adapted from Kafka's *The Metamorphosis,* conceived by Martha Clarke. *New York Times,* 8 Feb., C13.

———. 1984. "At St. Clement's New 'Earthly Delights.'" Rev. of *The Garden of Earthly Delights,* based on Hieronymus Bosch's painting, conceived by Martha Clarke. *New York Times,* 23 Nov., C3.

———. 1999. "Chekhov Without the Words." *New York Times,* 12 Sept., sec. 2, 17.

Isherwood, Charles. 2004. "Nightclub in Daylight Shows Corroded Underside." Rev. of *Belle Epoque,* by Martha Clarke and Charles L. Mee. *New York Times,* 22 Nov., E5.

Jowitt, Deborah. 1999. "Climb Toward the Flame." *Village Voice,* 14 Sept., 75.

Kaufman, Sarah. 1999. "'Vers la Flamme': A Good Match; Clarke Meets Chekhov at the Kennedy Center." Rev. of *Vers la Flamme,* based on stories by Chekhov, conceived by Martha Clarke. *Washington Post,* 22 Oct., C02.

Kelly, Colleen. 1994. "Martha Clarke." In *Theatrical Directors: A Biographical Dictionary,* ed. John W. Frick and Stephen M. Vallillo, 81–82. Westport, Conn.: Greenwood.

Kelly, Kevin. 1990. "From a Genius, a Circus-in-the-Works; MacArthur Grant Winner Martha Clarke and her Avant-Garde." *Boston Globe,* 5 Aug., B27.

Kisselgoff, Anna. 1979. "Martha Clarke Presents Her Crowsnest Trio at Durham." *New York Times,* 18 July, C15.

Kriegsman, Alan M. 1988. "Martha Clarke, Tending to Her 'Garden'; Creator of 'Vienna: Lusthaus' Restages a Seminal Piece." *Washington Post,* 31 Jan., F01.

Leiter, Samuel L. 1994. "Martha Clark." In *The Great Stage Directors: 100 Distinguished Careers of the Theater,* 68–71. New York: Facts on File.

Lester, Gideon. 2003. "Dreams of a Wood Sprite." *American Repertory Theatre Articles Online* 2 (1) (Dec.). http://www.amrep.org/articles/2_3a/sprite.html (accessed 6 Aug. 2004).

Martin, Kathryn Sarell. 1993. "The Performance Works of Meredith Monk and Martha Clarke: A Postmodern Feminist Perspective." Ph.D. diss., University of Colorado at Boulder.

Rich, Frank. 1986. "'Vienna,' From Martha Clarke." Rev. of *Vienna: Lusthaus,* conceived by Martha Clarke. *New York Times,* 21 Apr., C13.

———. 1987. "'Hunger Artist,' Kafka in Life and Work." Rev. of *The Hunger Artist,* based on the writings by Franz Kafka, conceived by Martha Clarke. *New York Times,* 27 Feb., C3.

———. 1988. "Martha Clarke Explores the Clash of the Sexes." Rev. of *Miracolo d'Amore,* conceived by Martha Clarke. *New York Times,* 30 June, C17.

Rockwell, John. 2006. "Dance and Theater Lead the Way in the Stark Landscape of Pirandello's Sicily." Rev. of *KAOS,* based on the stories of Luigi Pirandello and the film *Kaos,* by Paolo and Vittorio Taviani; conceived by Martha Clarke, text adapted by Frank Pugliese, dramaturgy by Giovanni Papotto. *New York Times,* 5 Dec., E3.

Shank, Theodore. 1991. "Contemporary American Dance Theatre: Clarke, Goode, and Mann." In *Contemporary American Theatre,* ed. Bruce King, 205–25. New York: St. Martin's.

Vincentelli, Elisabeth. 2004. "Absinthe Minded." *Time Out New York,* 18–25, Nov., 175.

Weber, Bruce. 2002. "Doom Chases Lust, but with Loveliness." Rev. of *Vienna: Lusthaus,* conceived by Martha Clarke. *New York Times,* 11 May, B15.

Representative Directing Credits[1]

Off and Off-Off Broadway:

Elizabeth Dead (1980), *Metamorphosis in Miniature* (1982), *The Garden of Earthly Delights* (1984, 1987), *Vienna: Lusthaus* (1986), *The Hunger Artist* (1987), *Miracolo d'Amore* (1988), *Endangered Species* (1990), *An Uncertain Hour* (1995), *Marco Polo* (1997), *Vers la Flamme* (1999), *Vienna: Lusthaus (Revisited)* (2002), *Belle Epoque* (2004), *KAOS* (2006)

Regional Theatre:

Portraits (1977), *Cabbages* (1979), *Dr. Kheal* (1979), *Fromage Dangereuse* (1985), *Vienna: Lusthaus* (1986), *The Garden of Earthly Delights* (1985, 1986, 1987, 1988, 1989), *Miracolo d'Amore* (1988), *Endangered Species* (1990), *An Uncertain Hour* (1995), *Vers la Flamme* (1999), *Hans Christian Andersen* (2000), *Vienna: Lusthaus (Revisited)* (2003, 2004), *A Midsummer Night's Dream* (2004)

International Theatre:

The Garden of Earthly Delights (1985), *Vienna: Lusthaus* (1988)

Notes

1. These works include those reviewed by dance and theatre critics. Examples of shorter works, which are reviewed primarily by dance critics, that straddle dance and theatre include *The Garden of Villandry* (choreographed by Clarke, Robert Barnett, and Felix Blaska in 1979, 1980, and 1988), *Dammerung (Twilight)* (1992, 1993, 1994), and *Nocturne* (1991, 1994).

Crothers, Rachel

Born on December 12 in the 1870s[1] in Bloomington, Illinois, to two physicians, Rachel Crothers was among the first women directors on Broadway. She was also a playwright, performer, and producer, known for her feminist point of view and plays that focused on women's lives. Her career on Broadway was prolific, spanning more than thirty-five years.

As a child, Crothers began writing and performing in plays. She went to Illinois State Normal School (now Illinois State University) in Normal, Illinois, graduating in 1891. She then attended and graduated from the New England School of Dramatic Instruction the following year. Crothers made her New York acting debut with E. H. Sothern's company in 1897. The same year she attended the Stanhope-Wheatcroft School of Acting in New York City, where she was a student for a term. Crothers cited Mrs. Wheatcroft, who asked Crothers to be a coach, as an important influence in her life (Barnes 1931, 18). While teaching at Stanhope-Wheatcroft, Crothers began to write and direct one-acts that featured her students as performers. She also designed costumes, props, and sets. Crothers believed her time at the school was "an experience of inestimable value because the doors of the theatre are very tightly closed to women in the work of directing and staging plays" ("National," 1939, 429).

Crothers's viewpoints about men and women were influenced by her mother, who faced much opposition as a female doctor. Similarly, most of Crothers's plays focused on issues about women's independence and conflicts between career and home life. Crothers believed that the evolution of women was "the most important thing in modern life" ("Miss," 1912, 38). She considered herself "the most ardent of feminists" and said, "The world is so old and the New Freedom for women is so new, so painfully young, groping. The modern woman who would lead her own life as a man does has but cracked the shell" (Ashton 1980, D3). Although the women characters in Crothers's plays often resorted to traditional roles, Crothers's life was atypical of most women at the time: she chose a career over marriage and family life.

Many of Crothers's one-act plays were produced in New York City from 1899 onward. In 1906 Crothers's first full-length Broadway play, *The Three of Us,* opened to excellent reviews. It centered on a sister, her two younger brothers, and their struggle to survive. The play, which was staged on Broadway by George Foster Platt, transferred to London the following year, with Crothers supervising the production (Gottlieb 1979, 24).

Crothers probably directed her first professional American production in 1908 in Chicago with her play *Myself-Bettina*. The play focused on a young, independent woman returning from Europe to the United States and her struggle to understand herself and others. Maxine Elliot, who produced and starred in the play, suggested that Crothers direct it. An article in the *New York Times* devotes an entire paragraph to the phenomenon, saying, "It will be one of the first times in which a woman author has been permitted to stage her own work" ("Maxine," 1908, 9). The word "permitted" in the article reveals obstacles that women faced with male producers at that time. Crothers wrote that Elliot had, "such an admiration for and faith in the work of women, that she was delighted to find a woman who could shoulder the entire responsibility" (1911, 14). She explained, "For a woman, it is best to look to women for help; women are more daring, they are glad to take the most extraordinary chances. . . . I think I should have been longer about my destiny if I had to battle with men alone" (Barnes 1931, 18). The play received negative reviews when it opened on Broadway later that year.

Shortly afterward, Crothers began to direct her own plays on Broadway. She caused a stir in 1910 when she directed her Broadway comedy *A Man's World,* which looked at the double standards applied to women. One playwright, Augustus Thomas, was so angered by Crothers's portrayal of men that he wrote his own play *As a Man Thinks,* which was produced on Broadway in 1911 to good reviews. Crothers continued to examine double standards with her play *Ourselves,* which she co-directed with J. C. Huffman on Broadway two years later.

In 1916 Crothers directed her play *Old Lady 31* on Broadway. The play was based on the novel about prostitution by Louise Forsslund. Crothers discussed the staging of *Old Lady 31* in a *New York Times* article that she wrote titled "The Future of the American Stage Depends on Directors." In the article she stated, "The critics have made much of the fact that a rocking chair is placed with its back to the audience, and that the character sits in it, of course, with her back to the audience. Now, this is not done for the sake of modernity. I will not say that it is even dramatically important that the characters should sit in that position, but it is natural that she should do so, and nothing is lost theatrically because her back is seen instead of her face" (Interview, 1916, SM13). The play, which had a successful Broadway run, was later made into a film called *The Captain Is a Lady.*

A prolific writer, Crothers staged two more of her plays on Broadway in 1918. Her play *Once Upon a Time,* which first opened the previous year at the National Theatre in Washington, D.C., revolved around an Irishman and his family. The production was basically a star vehicle for the actor Chauncey Olcoot. Her other play, *A Little Journey,* was set in a railroad sleeping car and required most of the characters to be on the stage at the same time. Crothers discussed the importance of making each actor's performance in the production permanent, writing, "Whether in the spoken scene or a background or undercurrent of it, each actor is doing something to help the scene which is being played at the moment. Because of the peculiarly intimate proximity of these people, the action is so tightly interwoven that the slightest deviation in one part upsets all the others and destroys the intricate network of the whole. The small bits of everyday life, which seem so impulsive and spontaneous as they are played, are in reality solidly and scientifically woven together" (1919, 40). The play had a very successful run on Broadway.

In 1919 Crothers wrote and directed a portrayal of life in a New York City boardinghouse called 39 East, which played on Broadway to favorable reviews. Two years later Crothers directed two more of her plays on Broadway. Nice People, which featured three flappers and examined the value of money and society's focus on youth, resulted in a successful Broadway run of 120 performances. Everyday, which focused on a young American woman's changed perspective after time abroad, ran for only half as long.

In 1924 Crothers wrote, produced, and directed another successful Broadway play—Expressing Willie. The play poked fun of Freudian therapy and ridiculed the idea that total expression of self is always beneficial. The next year, Crothers directed her play examining sexual freedom and virtue titled A Lady's Virtue. The production had a successful Broadway run and was reviewed in the New York Times as "enjoyable theatre, cleverly and adeptly assembled by Rachel Crothers and smoothly and gracefully acted" ("Ladies," 1925, 28).

Although she directed most of her own plays, Crothers also directed the works of others. Crothers discussed why a writer might choose to use an outside director, explaining, "Sometimes a play is tremendously helped by the director. . . . He can remold the play in such a way that he does for the author's idea what the author himself could not do, that is, make it logical, coherent, and clear" (Interview, 1916, SM13). Despite her reasoning, Crothers's direction and production of Broadway plays written by others was not very successful. Most often, Crothers overextended herself and staged another writer's play in the same year that she staged one of her own. The same year that she directed A Lady's Virtue, Crothers produced and directed John Kirkpatrick's The Book of Charm, a failure on Broadway. When Crothers directed Zoe Akins's Thou Desperate Pilot in addition to her play Venus on Broadway in 1927, both plays received negative reviews. J. Brooks Atkinson of the New York Times expressed his disappointment in the play about two aviators who found an egalitarian society on Venus when he wrote, "Just before the final curtain the two young aviators are summoned by telephone to Venus for a second visit. Directing this brief scene, Miss Crothers has expressed the magic and wonder of such an adventure. If the play were all in that key, how strange and exhilarating it might be!" (1927, 26). However, Crothers was moderately successful in staging Caroline Francke's *Exceeding Small* on Broadway in 1928. Her success may have been because Crothers could better focus on the play as she had no play of her own on Broadway that year.

The next year, Crothers had her biggest success on Broadway with the direction of her play *Let Us Be Gay*. The play was produced by John Golden, who continued to produce every play that Crothers directed until the end of her Broadway career in 1940. *Let Us Be Gay*, which focused on a woman who divorces her unfaithful husband, ran for an impressive 353 performances. Atkinson wrote that the parts were "well cast and directed" and noted, "What she achieves by way of humor and conclusion has a deliberation that might be disenchanting if Miss Crothers had not directed the performance so well" (1929, 19).

Crothers wrote and directed her next Broadway play, *As Husbands Go*, in 1931. The play examined women's sexual freedom and expectations for self-fulfillment and ran for 148 performances. Atkinson wrote, "Miss Crothers is quite as able a director as she is a playwright. She has cast her drama imaginatively and directed it brilliantly, giving every actor the chance to do his best work" (1931, 26).

Another successful Broadway production directed, written, and produced by Crothers was *When Ladies Meet*. The play, produced in 1932, focused on women's expectations of love and marriage versus reality. Atkinson wrote, "When she stages one of her own comedies and translates players into actors you are in good hands. . . . As the director she squeezes and coaxes the best out of [the actors]" (1932, 19). The Theater Club cited *When Ladies Meet* as the most outstanding play of the season. The play also won the Megrue Prize for best comedy. It was revived in 1933 under Crothers's direction on Broadway, but soon closed because of disputes over the size of the stage crew.

In 1937 Crothers directed her Broadway play *Susan and God*, which had the second-longest run of any of her plays at 288 performances. The play focused on an unhappy wife and mother, who takes up religion. Atkinson wrote, "Under Miss Crothers' personal direction the casting, the acting, and the costuming add to the fullness of the story" and noted, "By planning a play deliberately she knows how to draw her theme out of her characters, not forgetting to keep her story entertaining" (1937, 26). The Theatre Club gave the production its gold medal for the most outstanding play.

The last Broadway play that Crothers directed was Paul Vincent Carroll's *The Old Foolishness* in 1940. In preparing to direct the play, Crothers corresponded with Carroll in Ireland to gain an understanding of the play and its characters (Hughes 1940, 147). The production, set in Ireland, was a failure and closed after one performance. However, Burns Mantle of New York's *Daily News* did not blame Crothers. He wrote, "Rachel Crothers had directed it hopefully, realizing, I suspect, that what is needed isn't there" (1940, 182).

An examination of her directing record indicates that Crothers may have found it easier to prepare for her own plays. She spoke of her dual role of author and director, explaining, "If the author knows the theatre and understands directing he naturally gets more out of his play than any one else can, for the production of a play is the reflection of the mind of the director, and the more intimately and intelligently this person knows the characters of the play—their natures and background—the more illumination he gives to the actors playing these characters" (Interview, 1916, SM13).

Crothers's approach to casting is revealed in the way she cast *The Old Foolishness,* when she auditioned hundreds of candidates and selected a cast without stars. Charlotte Hughes of the *New York Times* described Crothers's casting process, writing, "She is more impressed with personality than with reputation. Interviewing, she has discarded the old formula of thrusting lines to be read at quailing actors. Instead she talks informally with them and tries to get a sense of their personalities" (1940, 147).

Crothers seems to have hired performers on trial when possible. She noted, "I think the best plan is for the director to engage the actors on trial, explaining to them that everything depends not on their general theatrical qualifications, but on their ability to do the particular thing that is demanded of them in this play. They should understand that the fact that they are on trial is no reflection of their ability, but is the result of merely an attempt to select the cast most appropriate for this play" (Interview, 1916, SM13).

Before the first reading, Crothers made sure she could visualize the play in its entirety. In rehearsal, Hughes wrote that Crothers focused on trying "to engender the spirit and the emotion, and let the mechanics take care of themselves. She never draws stage diagrams, or works out much business in advance" (1940, 147). Crothers spoke of how all elements, including costumes, props, and scenery were important in the expression of a production. She believed that a director should have both practical and creative ability, stating, "[T]he successful director, in addition to originality, tact, and technical knowledge, must have imagination. . . . Directing is orchestration, and the greatest violinist on earth, if he be a member of an orchestra, must be directed" (Interview, 1916, SM13).

A *New York Times* reporter who observed Crothers in rehearsal wrote of her "unrelaxing vigilance, her close attention to every inflection, every gesture, every breath, it seemed, of the actors, and her custom—not common among directors—of explaining carefully to every actor just why it was advisable for him to take three steps back at this point in the action, and to raise or to lower his voice at the end of that question" (Crothers, interview, 1916, SM13).

Crothers preferred realism in both staging and acting. She explained, "The stage is the most definite, telling, and effective reflection of the hour in which we live" (Interview, 1916, SM13). When working with performers, Crothers strove for performances that were naturalistic and not declamatory. She said,

> [D]irecting means not only the mental understanding of characters, but the dramatic and theatrical knowledge necessary to convey this understanding to the actor, and above all, the power to awaken the best in the actor, to stir latent fire he himself may not have known he possessed, to use his individuality to the best advantage, calling up on all he has to give to the characterization both temperamentally and physically, and modeling him into the living being which he must become for the play.
>
> This modeling process means not dwarfing the mentality and sympathy, sometimes severity and uncompromising firmness, but always tact and kindness, and the one undying intention to get the best out of the actor and the deep respect for his ability and the realization that upon that ability the play and its illumination depend. (Interview, 1916, SM13)

Working carefully with performers was an important concern for Crothers. She explained, "The importance of direction can't be overestimated. The acting instinct is delicate and sensitive and easily hurt or wrongly impressed. Each individual must be handled in a different way. Sometimes an actor can be helped to give a performance with qualities which he didn't know he possessed" (Hughes 1940, 147).

In general, Crothers believed that actors in the United States needed more training. She stated, "[T]here is a great need of a small school of acting for young people, connected with a stock theatre. There the highest standards of speech would be taught, and the culture of the body, and these things would be in preparation for character work. How we need this training for character work! So many of our actors use merely their own personalities—can play nothing but themselves" (Interview, 1916, SM13).

Once a performance was set, Crothers did not encourage actors to experiment because she believed that one performer's changes would affect the entire production. She thought that audiences could heighten inspiration in performers, but wrote, "[T]o change a performance after it has been 'born' is bad art, bad business, and bad workmanship" (1919, 40). Crothers discouraged flamboyant acting and wrote, "The naturalness which is coming more into the stage makes all acting more closely woven together, more interdependent than in the more artificial methods of yesterday" (1919, 40).

In order to keep her long-run plays fresh, Crothers called rehearsals periodically during the play's run. Crothers thought, "The greatest crime in the theatre is that its work is done too fast, and under the financial pressure of tryouts and other heavy overhead expenses" (Hutchens 1931, 111). Crothers admired repertory Theatre's approach with longer rehearsal periods, such as the Laboratory Theatre, also called the Russian School of Acting (1925, X2).

Among Crothers's many honors are inclusion as one of the "50 Foremost Women of the United States" by Ida Tarbell in 1930, honors by the Town Hall Club for distinguished achievement in 1937, a Chi Omega National Achievement Award that was presented to her by Eleanor Roosevelt in 1939, and the Drama Study Club's Clare M. Senie award for outstanding personality and contributor to theatre in 1941. Crothers also worked for many theatrical philanthropic causes and helped to found the Stage Women's War Relief in 1917 to help support the war effort for World War I. This organization later became the American Theatre Wing, which now focuses on theatre education and celebrating theatrical excellence through the Tony Awards.

Crothers died on July 5, 1958, in Danbury, Connecticut. Although she is best remembered for her role as a playwright, Crothers was a significant director who understood the value of stage direction. She said, "The future of the American stage does not depend on the playwrights. Nor does it depend on the actors. It depends on the directors" (Interview, 1916, SM13).

Sources

Ashton, Jean. 1980. "The Neil Simon of Her Day—And an Ardent Feminist." *New York Times*, 25 May, D3.

Atkinson, J. Brooks. 1927. "Towards Millennium." Rev. of *Venus*, by Rachel Crothers. *New York Times*, 26 Dec., 26.

———. 1929. "Two Bites at a Cherry." Rev. of *Let Us Be Gay*, by Rachel Crothers. *New York Times*, 22 Feb., 19.

———. 1931. Rev. of *As Husbands Go*, by Rachel Crothers. *New York Times*, 6 Mar., 26.

———. 1932. Rev. of *When Ladies Meet*, by Rachel Crothers. *New York Times*, 7 Oct., 19.

———. 1937. Rev. of *Susan and God*, by Rachel Crothers. *New York Times*, 8 Oct., 26.

Barnes, Djuna. 1931. "The Tireless Rachel Crothers," *Theatre Guild*, 8 (May): 18.

Chinoy, Helen Krich and Linda Walsh Jenkins, eds. 1987. *Women in American Theatre*. New York: Theatre Communications Group.

Crothers, Rachel. 1911. "Troubles of a Playwright." *Harper's Bazaar*, Jan., 14, 46.

————. 1916. Interview. "The Future of the American Stage Depends on Directors." *New York Times Magazine*, 3 Dec., SM13.

————. 1918. "The Producing Playwright." *Theater* 27 (Jan.): 34.

————. 1919. "The Arts of the Theatre." *New York Times*, 2 Feb., 40.

————. 1925. "In the Dramatic Mail Bag: To the Dramatic Editor." *New York Times*, 3 May, X2.

Fugate, Liz. 1989. "Crothers, Rachel." In *Notable Women in the American Theatre: A Biographical Dictionary*, ed. Alice M. Robinson, Vera Mowry Roberts, and Milly S. Barranger, 180–85. Westport, Conn.: Greenwood.

Gottlieb, Lois C. 1979. *Rachel Crothers*. Boston: Twayne.

Hughes, Charlotte. 1940. "Directed by Rachel Crothers." *New York Times*, 15 Dec., 147.

Hutchens, John. 1931. "That Times Square Veteran, Rachel Crothers." *New York Times*, 15 Mar., 111.

"'A Ladies Virtue' Is a Pleasing Drama." 1925. Rev. of *A Ladies Virtue*, by Rachel Crothers. *New York Times*, 24 Nov., 28.

Lindroth, Colette with James Lindroth. 1995. *Rachel Crothers: A Research and Production Sourcebook*. Modern Dramatists Research and Production Sourcebooks No. 8. Westport, Conn.: Greenwood.

Mantle, Burns. 1940. "'The Old Foolishness' Goes Back to Love on the Heights." Rev. of *The Old Foolishness*, by Paul Vincent Carrol. *(New York) Daily News*, 21 Dec. Rpt. *Critics' Theatre Reviews* 1 (18) (23 Dec.): 182.

"Maxine Elliot to Try a New Play." 1908. *New York Times*, 17 Jan., 9.

"Miss Crothers Talks Before the Drama League." 1912. *Boston Evening Transcript*, 14 Feb., 38.

"The National Achievement Award Is Presented to Rachel Crothers." 1939. *The Eleusis of Chi Omega* 41 (Sept.): 425–32.

"Rachel Crothers, Dramatist, Dead." 1958. *New York Times*, 6 July, 57.

Representative Directing Credits

Broadway:
  Myself-Bettina (1908), *A Man's World* (1910), *Ourselves* (co-directed with J.C. Huffman—1913), *Old Lady 31* (1916), *A Little Journey* (1918), *Once Upon a Time* (1918), *39 East* (1919), *Everyday* (1921), *Nice People* (1921), *Expressing Willie* (1924), *The Book of Charm* (1925), *A Lady's Virtue* (1925), *Thou Desperate Pilot* (1927), *Venus* (1927), *Exceeding Small* (1928), *Let Us Be Gay* (1929), *When in Rome* (1929), *As Husbands Go* (1931, 1933), *Caught Wet* (1931), *When Ladies Meet* (1932, 1933), *Susan and God* (1937), *The Old Foolishness* (1940)

Regional Theatre:
  Myself-Bettina (1908), *Once Upon a Time* (1917)

Tours:[2]
International Theatre:
    The Three of Us (1906), *Mary the Third* (1930)

Notes

1. Crothers was either born in 1870, 1871, or 1878 according to different sources.

2. Articles and clippings state that many of her Broadway plays went on tour before or after opening, but no further information is available as to whether she was the director. Productions that went on tour include *Myself-Bettina, Let Us Be Gay, Little Journey, 39 East, When Ladies Meet,* and *Susan and God.*

 # Daniele, Graciela

Born on December 8, 1939, in Buenos Aires, Argentina, Graciela Daniele has made her career as a director and choreographer in the United States, garnering numerous Tony and Drama Desk Nominations. In the 1990s she directed four musical theatre productions on Broadway, more than any other woman director before her. Throughout her career as a director, Graciela Daniele has celebrated the union of dance and drama; as one journalist keenly surmised, "Directing has allowed her to realize her vision of the world as constant motion" (Churnin 1992, F1).

Daniele began dancing at age seven and started a professional ballet career at age fifteen, leaving her native Argentina to tour Europe. A European tour of *West Side Story,* with choreography by Jerome Robbins, literally changed her life. Daniele explains, "[T]he fact that he used dance . . . to advance the story meant a lot to me, because that's what I yearned for. . . . So in a way, from far away, he was a mentor. He was an idol, a hero of mine" (Interview, 2000). Thus inspired, she moved to New York City and within two weeks was cast as a dancer on Broadway. Daniele worked consistently on Broadway and assisted master director–choreographers Bob Fosse and Michael Bennett before beginning her own career as a choreographer. This early apprenticeship was Daniele's education as a choreographer and director as she had no formal training in schools or conservatories.

It was the modeling of her mentors and serendipity that lead Daniele to try directing. While teaching a seminar in musical theatre at INTAR Hispanic

American Arts Center in New York City, the artistic director offered Daniele the opportunity to create and direct a piece of her own. Although not in need of a project, she replied with gusto, "Why not? Let's just jump in the lake and swim!" (Interview, 2000). Her project was *Tango Apasionado,* a piece she adapted herself based on Argentinean short stories and accompanied by music of Astor Piazzolla. After a workshop production in 1987, AT&T supported a transfer to the WestBeth Theatre Center Off Broadway. Once her colleagues found she could direct, she reports that offers came pouring in.

Daniele's first job directing and choreographing on Broadway came just two years later, in 1989, but *Dangerous Games* closed quickly after scathing reviews. The failure undermined Daniele's confidence, and when she was offered to direct and choreograph Lynn Ahrens and Stephen Flaherty's musical *Once on This Island,* she nearly did not accept, explaining, "My first concern was to the author and lyricist of *Once on This Island.* This was a big opportunity for them, and they were putting it on the lap of someone who was being run out of town [by critics]" (Churnin 1992, F1). The creators believed in her abilities and signed her anyway. *Once on This Island* opened Off Broadway to critical acclaim in 1990 at Playwrights Horizons, transferring to Broadway the following year and earning Daniele Tony Award nominations as both director and choreographer.

Based loosely on Rosa Guy's novel, *My Love, My Love,* and the play, *Once on This Island,* is the story of a poor island girl in the French Antilles and her ill-fated love with an affluent man of a different racial background. Critics gave Daniele credit for making the ninety-minute production sparkle. Reviewing the Broadway production, *Boston Globe* critic Kevin Kelly found the story a "feeble fable," but wrote that "under the swift direction of Graciela Daniele, who also did the knock-'em-dead choreography, the acting is high, wide, and handsome" (1991, 52). Michael Kuchwara of the Associated Press credits Daniele's hand in shaping the design as well as the pace of the earlier Off-Broadway production: "It never stops, thanks to Daniele's exuberant direction and nearly continuous use of song and dance. . . . The dances swirl throughout *Once on This Island,* turning the stage into a tropical never-never land that won't disappear from memory even after the curtain has fallen" (1990, n.p.).

As with *Once on This Island,* a lack of self-confidence almost derailed Daniele's direction of William Finn's *March of the Falsettos/Falsettoland* for Connecticut's Hartford Stage in 1991. Originally written as two one-acts, Hartford Stage produced the musicals in tandem for the first time, taking a risk on an unconventional musical about a Jewish man who leaves his family for a male lover and later confronts AIDS. Artistic director Mark Lamos invited Daniele to direct. Her reaction was, "I was the wrong person! I'm a woman, I'm Latin, I'm heterosexual, I'm not urban. I love the country, and I don't even speak English very well" (Interview, 2000). Fortunately, other members of the creative and producing teams convinced her otherwise. The production received overwhelmingly positive reviews with much of the success attributed to Daniele's direction.

Frank Rich of the *New York Times,* who had written a horrific review of her direction of *Dangerous Games* two years earlier, wrote, "[S]he has brought off an inspired, beautifully cast double bill that is true to its gay and Jewish characters . . . even as it presents the evening's densely interwoven familial and romantic relationships through perspectives that perhaps only a woman and a choreographer could provide" (1991, C13). Rich applauded her fresh perspective of Trina, the wife and mother left behind. No longer restricted to the role of comedic relief, under Daniele's direction Trina became more three dimensional: "a rueful figure who is allowed genuine as well as comic anger at all the 'happy men who rule the world'" (C13). He also congratulated Daniele on her use of space, for the Hartford Stage provided dimensions previously unavailable in New York City productions of the one-acts, which were directed by James Lapine. Her choreographic sense aided in the composition, balance, and movement of the piece. Rich raved, "Daniele exploits the spatial dimensions at her disposal with an overwhelming coup de theatre . . . that further reduces an audience to sobs and then raises it to its feet." On an uncluttered stage, she provides "the constantly changing configuration of Marvin's family in bouncy, lightly drawn geometric dance terms" (C13). The musical went on to play on Broadway and tour nationally under the combined title *Falsettos;* however, Daniele was no longer at the helm. The arrangements for the Hartford production to transfer to Lincoln Center fell through, and when composer and book writer William Finn took the prospect to Broadway, producers Barry and Fran Weissler immediately arranged for Lapine, the original director and a collaborator on *Falsettoland,* to direct (Marks 1992, 69).

In the 1990s Daniele started working as a resident director for New York City's Lincoln Center, directing and choreographing another Finn premiere in 1998, *A New Brain,* as well as New York City premieres of two musicals by Michael John LaChiusa: *Hello Again* in 1994 and *Marie Christine* in 1999. *Hello Again,* based on Arthur Schnitzler's play *La Ronde,* is set in twentieth-century America rather than Schnitzler's turn-of-the-century Vienna. It presents a string of sexual trysts in an episodic fashion, exploring the role of sex, love, and loneliness in America. *Hello Again* received mixed reviews, though *USA Today* critic David Patrick Stearns was delighted and praised Daniele, writing, "The brilliance of the score is matched by Graciela Daniele's direction and choreography. One astonishing turn after another illuminates the story's deeper currents. Without nudity, it never flinches from the sexual gymnastics that are part of the story" (1994, Life, 4D). LaChiusa's next premiere, *Marie Christine*, provided a voodoo rendition of *Medea*, set in the mulatto society of New Orleans and Chicago in the 1890s. Although reviews were mixed, Fintan O'Toole of the *Daily News* wrote, "[T]here is a fiercely uncompromising fusion of story and song. Everything about Graciela Daniele's fluid, elegant production is in harmony with this basic intention. Her choreography moves the cast with a stately formality appropriate to the ritual enactment of a tragic fate" ("Marie's," 1999, 80).

Also in the 1990s Daniele directed a production that transferred from Lincoln Center to the Plymouth Theatre on Broadway. She conceived, choreographed, and helped adapt from Gabriel Garcia Marquez's novel, *Chronicle of a Death Foretold*. With a Latin base in magical realism, Daniele had success with the visual and choreographic aspects of the production, but critical reception was mixed and the production closed after only one month in the summer of 1995.

Daniele proved her box office power on Broadway, directing a hit revival of Irving Berlin's *Annie Get Your Gun* in 1999, which played for two and a half years. Daniele's production of Annie Oakley's story highlighted the Wild West Shows that made Oakley famous and focused attention to Oakley's relationship with sharp-shooter Frank Butler. O'Toole of the *Daily News* praised Daniele's talents, writing that her contributions to the revival "allow both the audience and the performers to enter into the spirit of the story without doubts or reservations. [Bernadette] Peters and Tom Wopat, who plays Butler, can go for pure, unapologetic entertainment" ("Peters," 1999, 58).

At the start of the new millennium, Daniele felt a need to take a sabbatical from her hectic career for a time and enjoy a more relaxed lifestyle. She wanted to miss the work before returning to it, but even in her sabbatical she was reading scripts, knowing she would soon return to creating new works. By 2003 she was back in the director's chair at Off Broadway's Second Stage Theatre, staging LaChiusa's new musical, *Little Fish*.

Movement is clearly Daniele's forte and a hallmark of her productions. Even when directing a straight play, Daniele first and foremost ferrets out the rhythm and tempo of the play and finds its music. Journalist Nancy Churnin writes, "In a typical Daniele play, everything is choreographed. *Once on This Island* was described by one critic as 'wall-to-wall movement.' In *Captains Courageous*, she said she is choreographing 'the ropes and rigging and sails—every single moment'" (1992, F1).

Daniele views her progression from dancer to choreographer to director as a natural one because she considers a choreographer in the musical theatre tantamount to a co-director. In essence, as a musical is staged, choreographers are generally in charge of "anything that moves with music, even the set"

(Daniele, interview, 2000). Her conception of the bond between directing and choreography is so tight that the division between the two fields seems artificial to her, in part because she trained with director–choreographers who approached both aspects holistically. Daniele explains, "I personally feel that there shouldn't be any difference. Yes, there is a tendency sometimes in choreographers (not all of them, but some) to look at the piece from the point of view of motion, movement. And of course when you're doing a concert ballet, you're an autocrat. You're doing everything through yourself and through your body. But I believe that the work of the director is the play. What is the play about? What does the play need? So it's text, research, and most of all working with the author, if it's an original piece. . . . It's about getting inside the mind of the author to understand it. . . . But then again, I did that when I was a choreographer, too" (Interview, 2000).

According to Daniele, directors love working with her as a choreographer because she thinks like a director, probing deeply into the script, characters, and period. Their work together becomes seamless, as if conceived by one mind. She admits, "I find it easier to do both, to tell you the truth. It's much more work, of course, but I find it is much harder to get into the mind of somebody else, to see what they're talking about, or what they see, or what their perception is" (Interview, 2000). For Daniele, choreography starts not with the number of minutes to fill or the type of music, but with the whole of the play. "I go deep into the script and into the music—that is the heart of the musical theatre. . . . The text is the brain, the words are the ideas and the music is the soul of the piece" (Cooper 1992, N31).

Daniele prides herself in working closely with the actors to establish character kinesthetically, explaining, "Dance and movement are really another language to express a character, a feeling, a thought, but it all comes down to the root of who that character is" ("1998," 1998). In auditions, Daniele looks for actors with whom she has an immediate rapport. As with dancers, she expects actors to know their craft, but there must be something more than that in the audition. Daniele explains the concept of casting as her mentor, Wilford Leech, explained it to her: "It's just like two dogs meeting for the first time and smelling each other" (Interview, 2000). While it sounded crazy at first, she soon realized he was right. She looks for someone she can "romp around with for the next three months," who is "opening up, or interesting, or quirky" (Interview, 2000).

With the exception of the hit revival of *Annie Get Your Gun*, which ran from 1989 to 2001, Daniele's biggest successes, both commercially and artistically, have been with new musicals such as *Once on This Island, March of the Falsettos/Falsettoland, A New Brain,* and *Marie Christine.* She is passionate about working on new plays and musicals, particularly in a non-profit environment such as Lincoln Center. She favors large, sparsely furnished spaces that offer plenty of opportunity for her to work with movement, so that in essence, she is designing much of the visual style of the production. Daniele explains, "There is something about the design on stage with bodies that has an emotion all itself. You can create lines and groupings that have feeling; without even knowing it, they [the bodies in space] are telling you something that is important" (Interview, 2000).

As she reminisces about her career in theatre, she uses metaphors of running a house or raising children. Directing a play, Daniele muses, "is like having a nice dinner for six at home. Very elegant, very quiet, with Mozart playing. . . . Directing a musical is like going for a picnic in the summer at the beach in Italy—with the cousins, and the aunts, and the children, and the sausages, and the wine—everybody's talking at the same time. It's maddening!" (Interview, 2000). Her productions are her "children," and she dares not put one ahead of the other. "It doesn't matter if it's successful or not. It's a child of your own, and therefore, you're proud of your child. . . . Hopefully, you love them all" (Interview, 2000).

Throughout her career, Daniele has been in the commercial spotlight and her name has gained fame through many awards and nominations. As of 2007, in addition to her Tony Award nomination for the direction of *Once on This Island* in 1991, Daniele has earned eight Tony nominations for choreography, five Drama Desk nominations for choreography, and three more for direction: *Hello Again* (1994), *Chronicle of a Death Foretold* (1996), and *A New Brain* (1999). In 1998 she was presented with the Mr. Abbot Award for achievement in directing and choreography. Daniele clearly has shown her "children" off to their best advantage, creating compelling stage pictures in a world of constant motion.

Sources

Churnin, Nancy. 1992. "Back in the Saddle: Director Riding High Again." *Los Angeles Times*, 18 Aug., San Diego County edition, F1.

Cooper, Jeanne. 1992. "New Ford in 'Captains' Stream." *Washington Post*, 23 Oct., N31.

Daniele, Graciela. 2000. Telephone interview with Anne Fliotsos. 25 Mar.

Kelly, Kevin. 1991. "Calypso Whimsy is Cover for a Feeble Fable." Rev. of *Once on This Island*, book and lyrics by Lynn Ahrens, music by Stephen Flaherty. *Boston Globe*, 26 Feb., 52.

Kuchwara, Michael. 1990. "*Once on This Island*, A New Musical, Opens Off-Broadway." Rev. of *Once on This Island*, book and lyrics by Lynn Ahrens, music by Stephen Flaherty. Associated Press, 8 May, n.p. In LexisNexis Academic Database, www.lexisnexis.com.

Marks, Peter. 1992. "'Falsettos' Packages Two Cult Musicals Together. Will the Gamble Pay Off?" *(Long Island, N.Y.) Newsday,* 24 Apr., 69.

"1998 'Mr. Abbott' Award." 1998. Program. New York: Society of Stage Directors and Choreographers.

O'Toole, Fintan. 1999. "*Marie's* a Medea Sensation." Rev. of *Marie Christine,* by Michael John LaChiusa. *(New York) Daily News,* 3 Dec., 80.

———. 1999. "Peters Scores Bull's-Eye with *Annie.*" Rev. of *Annie Get Your Gun,* book by Herbert and Dorothy Fields, music and lyrics by Irving Berlin. *(New York) Daily News,* 5 Mar., 58.

Pogrebin, Robin. 1999. "Sending a New Musical into the World." *New York Times,* 5 Nov., E1.

Rich, Frank. 1991. "The 'Falsetto' Musicals United at Hartford Stage." Rev. of *March of the Falsettos,* book, music, and lyrics by William Finn. *New York Times,* 15 Oct., C13.

Stearns, David Patrick. 1994. "*Hello Again* to a Good Musical Comedy." Rev. of *Hello Again,* by Michael John LaChiusa. *USA Today,* 31 Jan., Life, 4D.

Representative Directing Credits

Broadway:
> *Dangerous Games* (1989), *Once on This Island* (1990), *Chronicle of a Death Foretold* (1995), *Marie Christine* (1999), *Annie Get Your Gun* (1999), *Chita Rivera: A Dancer's Life* (2005)

Off and Off-Off Broadway:
> *Tango Apasionado* (1987), *In a Pig's Valise* (1989), *Once on This Island* (1990), *Hello Again* (1994), *Dancing on Her Knees* (1996), *A New Brain* (1998), *Little Fish* (2003), *Dessa Rose* (2005), *Bernarda Alba* (2006)

Regional Theatre:
> *March of the Falsettos/Falsettoland* (1991), *Captains Courageous* (1992), *Little Mermaid* (1992), *Herringbone* (1993), *Chita Rivera: A Dancer's Life* (2005), *The Glorious Ones* (2007)

Tours:
> *Once on This Island* (1992)

Diamond, Liz

Born February 18, 1954, in Cambridge, Massachusetts, and raised in Reading, near Boston, Liz Diamond has been directing Off and Off-Off Broadway and regionally since the mid-1980s. Diamond has won national attention, in part through her direction of several premieres of Suzan-Lori Parks's plays, which fit Diamond's penchant for rich metaphor and layered, poetic language. She has taught at several universities in the United States and abroad and since 1992 has served as resident director at Yale Repertory Theatre.

Diamond's first memory of theatre was as a five-year-old attending a Boston production of *My Fair Lady*, starring Rex Harrison and Julie Andrews. She grew up with music and theatre as part of her life but did not foresee a career in the arts for herself. Her interest in politics led her to major in political science and history at Wellesley College in Wellesley, Massachusetts. Throughout college, she participated in productions as an actor, primarily in modern and contemporary experimental plays.

After graduating from Wellesley with a B.A. in 1976, she joined the Peace Corps and served in Burkina Faso, West Africa, from 1977 to 1980. She became involved in a project to start a national theatre and joined the debates among local theatre artists about the relationship of culture to the development of the country. With her African colleagues, Diamond developed an idea for a national rural theatre project which would create plays in local languages using traditional African performance forms to address issues faced by contemporary villagers. Through the Ministry of Culture Diamond drafted and won a Ford Foundation Grant for $15,000 to create the project. With Burkinabe theatre director Prosper Kompaore and a company of fifteen actors, she spent three years touring West Africa with the Rural Theatre Project, collecting stories from villagers and transforming them into theatre events that combined performance with community-wide conversations.

Upon her return to the United States, Diamond enrolled in the M.F.A. directing program at New York City's Columbia University, which she described as "a fledgling and very funky directing program" (Kelly 1994, 45). While still in graduate school she sought opportunities in the theatres of New York City. She served as an assistant to director Geraldine Fitzgerald for the 1981 Broadway production of *Mass Appeal*, by Bill C. Davis, and she served as an interpreter and assistant director to French playwright–director Simone Benmussa for the 1982 Manhattan Theatre Club production of Benmussa's

The Singular Life of Albert Nobbs. Diamond looked up to Benmussa as a model of fearlessness and rigor and was impressed with Benmussa's "highly evolved, formal imagination" (Interview, 2004).

Diamond's directing career began in earnest after graduation in 1983, when she directed at P.S. 122, the Women's Project, Vineyard Theatre, La MaMa, New York Theatre Workshop, and other experimental theatres in downtown Manhattan. One of her first opportunities in New York was entrepreneurial: she teamed up with a colleague and got permission to adapt, direct, and produce Samuel Beckett's *Fizzles* at P.S. 122. Funded in part by her own money, the tiny production got good press from the *New York Times* when critic Mel Gussow attended a dress rehearsal. A second crucial opportunity came when Diamond was selected as one of four directors for the New Director's Project, sponsored by the New York Theatre Workshop.

Diamond has playwright Mac Wellman to thank for her introduction to playwright Suzan-Lori Parks, a meeting that spurred a number of noteworthy collaborations. At the time of their meeting, Parks was twenty-six years old and had self-produced her first play. Diamond's reputation grew with her direction of Parks's *Imperceptible Mutabilities in the Third Kingdom,* produced in 1989 at BACA Downtown in Brooklyn. The play evoked the struggles of African Americans from slavery to the present, through four scenes. Diamond staged scenes one and four, then she and Parks pooled $4,000 of their own money to produce the entire play, which won Diamond an Obie Award for Direction in 1990 and earned Parks an Obie Award for Best New American Play. Mel Gussow of the *New York Times* described the play as "[a] double-edged comedy, mocking stereotypes while leaving us with a bitter message about the pitfalls of assimilation" (1989, C24). His description of one section provides a sense of the "myth and metaphor" he found in the performance: "'Open House' is a symbolic case of open-heart surgery, an exploration into the life and mind of a former slave who is dying. In a collage of nightmarish images, she relives events from her plantation past, including her disparagement at the hands of the white girls whom she raised for her master." Gussow congratulated Diamond for a "striking production" that showed both excellent performances and the full employment of the designers' imaginations (C24).

In 1989 Diamond directed two plays by Anthol Fugard at Maine's Portland Stage Company: *Sizwe Banzi Is Dead* and *The Island.* She followed up with Bertolt Brecht's *A Man's Man* at the same stage in 1990. Diamond next traveled to the opposite coast to direct her second production of Parks's *Imperceptible Mutabilities in the Third Kingdom* for the New City Theatre in Seattle in 1991.

Diamond continued to direct Off Broadway as well as at New York City's prestigious Julliard School, where she directed Brecht's *The Good Woman of*

Sechuan in 1991. She also took on two more works by Parks: *Betting on the Dust Commander* at New York City's Theatre Row in 1991 and *The Death of the Last Black Man in the Whole Entire World* at the Yale Repertory Theatre in New Haven, Connecticut, in 1992. Diamond had already discovered with *Imperceptible Mutabilities* that Parks's plays "do not function as linear stories as such, but they are stories nonetheless, told in jazzy riffs that circle back even as they move forward, great spirals of text, image, and sound" (Interview, 2004). *The Death of the Last Black Man* illuminated Parks's fascination of using the past as prologue. Through her multiple collaborations with Parks, Diamond earned a tremendous respect for her work, calling Parks "the most important writer of my generation, breathtakingly original" (Kelly 1994, 45).

Diamond's collaboration with Yale Repertory Theatre, which began with *The Death of the Last Black Man,* grew in the 1990s. She became resident director in 1992 and joined the Yale faculty, where she gained the position of full professor and chair of the Directing Program in 2003. Also in 1992 at Yale Repertory Theatre, Diamond met a mentor in Paul Schmidt, who came to work on a new translation of Brecht's *Saint Joan of the Stockyards.* Diamond explains, "He really was one of the most important influences on my life, artistically. As an exemplary artist, as a man of enormous integrity, imagination, and curiosity. He loved theatrical poetry, but he wanted theater to be completely, emotionally hot and immediate. He was an aesthete with a political conscience. . . . He would push me, and challenge me, and was totally supportive" (Interview, 2004). Schmidt and Diamond's collaboration drew results, for she won a Connecticut Critics Circle Award for Outstanding Direction for *Saint Joan of the Stockyards.*

Although Diamond has continued to direct outside of Yale, her productions there are noteworthy. Records for 1994 alone reveal four productions of very different types: Parks's *The America Play,* Moliere's *School for Wives,* Janusz Glowacki's *Antigone in New York,* and Charles Ludlam's *Le Bourgeois Avant Garde.* Her eclectic resume highlights Diamond's love of poetic language as well as her passion to explore the human condition through a variety of writing styles.

One of Diamond's most well-known productions, Parks's *The America Play,* started at Yale Repertory Theatre and transferred to the Joseph Papp Public Theatre in Manhattan, where it played for forty performances in 1994. Parks's mutability of meaning is pronounced in this play, which explores history through an African American man's impersonation of Abraham Lincoln in repeated versions of Lincoln's assassination. The repetitions and revisions of this act create various meanings, a postmodern construct that Diamond embraced as an invigorating challenge. "All I'm offering the world is my own very partial perspective on this amazingly rich play," she explains. "Meaning is now understood to be a highly contingent artifact of the process of reading as opposed to something that exists in the text. . . . There's gotta be a more flexible, plastic way of thinking about 'meaning' that allows it to be as contingent, permeable, ever-changing as possible in the theatre" (Drukman 1995, 60–62). Diamond credits Parks's plays with teaching her about the nature of poetry, an understanding that has influenced her subsequent interpretations when directing. She states, "It's in discovering the ways in which a text is a three-dimensional thing, in terms of its reverberating meanings and my desire to find ways to make the stage space reverberate in a similarly complicated way that has really been, for me, the most exciting part of the collaboration" (59).

Diamond's work at Yale Repertory Theatre has drawn high praise from the press. In 1996 Alvin Klein of the *New York Times* lauded Diamond's "illuminating staging" of George Bernard Shaw's play, *Mrs. Warren's Profession*. He highlighted the bold physicality of her cast in "a slew of sudden entrances and furious exits" and congratulated Diamond for taking a "dated and pedantic play" and staging a production, which instead "exudes living ideas in a stimulating exchange" (13CN, 10).

More extensive press was given to Diamond's 1998 production of Jean Racine's *Phaedra* at Yale Repertory Theatre, which was thereafter staged at the American Repertory Theatre (A.R.T.) in Cambridge, Massachusetts. Much like her work with Parks, Diamond was drawn to the poetry of the piece as well as to the exploration of the human condition. "It's thrilling to direct a play where the titanic struggle is a female's struggle, where the battlefield is a woman's soul," she told the *Boston Globe* (Anderman 1998, N1). In a separate interview, she discussed her vision for the world of the play via the set design. "What I kept returning to in the play is the image of the labyrinth, of the prison. I wanted to create a maddeningly logical, rational interior where Phaedra will be trapped. The interior needs to be monolithic, endless, relentless, airless. There is no place in the social world of the court for what Phaedra desires, which is an anarchic, passionate, taboo-blasting sexuality. So, with Riccardo Hernandez, the set designer (with whom I've enjoyed some of my happiest collaborations, precisely in terms of visual poetry), I spoke of wanting Phaedra's fleshy, earthly sensuality and violent passion to crash against the walls, so to speak" (Kiger 1998). She reacted passionately to the model of the massive set for the production, depicting movable copper-colored walls that reached nearly 30 feet. "It so much does what I wanted it to do," she confessed. "It's unbalanced, modern, and totally disturbing" (Anderman 1998, N1). The *Boston Herald* singled out A.R.T.'s production of *Phaedra* as one of the year's best, giving credit not only to the brilliant set design, but also to Diamond, who "guided her cast through measured and meaningful moves that made the internal anguish of Racine's play as fascinating as any action scenes" (Byrne and Fanger 1998, S05).

In 2001 Diamond took on John Steinbeck's masterpiece, *Of Mice and Men,* at Arena Stage in Washington, D.C. The saga of George and his mentally challenged brother, Lenny, struggling against the odds of the 1930s depression suited Diamond's zest for addressing the challenges of the human soul. The *Washington Post* gave the production a fairly positive review, agreeing with Diamond's goals, but not sure that they were always carried out successfully: "Director Liz Diamond means to deliver a lean, hard production of John Steinbeck's classic novel-turned-play, and most of the elements line up accordingly, from Ilona Somogyi's dirt-brown costumes to the distant train whistles in Timothy M. Thompson's sound design. If the acting were as stark, this show would be dynamite" (Pressley 2001, C01).

Over the last ten years Diamond has reflected on her art and her own understanding of her work as an artist. She states,

> The plays I've loved working on share one common element: language that is dense, layered, and complicated, however simple the surface may appear. The metaphors unfold like onion skin; the wordplay and imageplay seem to go forever. The plays of Suzan-Lori Parks, Molière, Brecht, Beckett, Sophocles, and Heaney all have this in common. I want a play on stage to operate like a poem—to have a sense of form carrying meaning, image giving way to image. But I am certainly not just interested in form from an aesthetic point of view. For me, the principal challenge and pleasure of directing, and sometimes the agony, is to try and make every plastic element in the production—clothes, gesture, movement, space, light, and sound—embody the emotions contained in the text. It's fantastic when you sit watching and listening in the theatre and suddenly you witness the alchemical transubstantiation spoken of by Artaud, where the invisible is made visible, where the abstract is made concrete, and you feel you have understood something viscerally for the first time. (Kiger 1998)

When casting, Diamond admits she has a bias "toward actors who have developed a highly physical imagination." They must have emotional as well as physical life and show a "formal imagination" (Robinson 1995, 29). In addition, she looks for charisma or what she calls "muchness." She explains, "There's something a bit much about them. Their mouths are too big. Their eyes are too big. There's a muchness to their physical life. There has to be something really kind of odd" (29). Based in part on her work with JoAnne Akalaitis in 1987 as part of a National Endowment for the Arts (NEA) Fellowship, she has come to prize actors who can cultivate a crucial gesture in the play, similar to Brecht's idea of *gestus,* or what Akalaitis called *mudra,* "an

Indian word meaning 'the gesture that means more'" (30). When casting, she seeks "to be arrested by someone" in terms of their physiognomy, their energy, their crafted performance, their life force, their scale, and their charisma. In addition, she seeks a "generosity of the spirit," which manifests itself in intellectual curiosity, in risk-taking and in a readiness to play. Lastly, she looks for an actor's ability to handle language through an expressive voice, clarity, and a connection between sound and meaning (Diamond, interview, 2004).

Diamond's rehearsal process is a highly collaborative discovery of meanings, which she then shapes into a final form. She explains, "I resist the temptation to impose one meaning on an event, a moment, a figure in the play. What I hope is happening in the course of the production is that the field of meanings that the play makes possible . . . are offered up by the particular way that figure's been cast, moves, speaks, etc.; that there will be a kind of wavelike effect so that one possible reading will be in the next instant contradicted by another and that all kinds of reverberating and clashing ideas will come up because that's very much the nature of this poetry" (Drukman 1995, 60).

As with most directors, Diamond spends considerable time with the script itself before subjecting her actors to the text in rehearsal. With Parks's new scripts, the two women work together initially. "We'll begin to do readings together and sometimes Suzan-Lori will read it out loud for me and I'll ask questions. We'll get images and ideas that pop up in the course of those oral readings and any rewrites and preliminary production ideas really take off from those first encounters, with the text in front of us, together" (Drukman 1995, 58). Parks's scripts are filled with hyphens, ellipses, and dashes, all of which Diamond considers "part of the musical score" which requires the deciphering of a rhythmic structure. She states, "Discovering exactly what the rhythmic share of that space [on the page] should be is what makes rehearsal so much fun, because you're just discovering what those musical, aural dynamics are, that are going to make it . . . pop. . . . You can only do that when everybody is up on their feet and their bodies are moving in space and you've got somebody 15 feet away from somebody else. It's fascinating with these plays to see that" (69–70). Diamond also reiterates her emphasis on action in language, "The hell with subtext. . . . The action that's on the language and in the language, the way it operates in your body and on your tongue, tells you how to play it. I think it's why I'm so drawn to poetic writing . . . because the language is the action. It's the fact that people either withhold and don't speak, or that they speak, that causes all the [things] to happen" (Anderman 1998, N1).

Over the years, Diamond finds she has gotten quieter as a director. She focuses on *doing* in rehearsal as opposed to talking. She gives her actors as much time on their feet as possible to probe their choices and live in the world of the play. Journalist Joan Anderman of the *Boston Globe* observed a rehearsal and made the following observations of Diamond's collaborative process:

> Diamond's fascination with the fundamental human process infuses her own work process; watching her in rehearsal, it quickly becomes clear that her reputation for coaxing stellar performances from actors by cultivating an open, nurturing ambience is well deserved. She listens attentively to long, ardent speeches from actors struggling to grasp the psychology of their characters. They discuss endless blocking possibilities, endeavoring to translate motivation into body language, emotion into motion. Diamond never seems to impose her will, but rather allows a remarkably fluid, collaborative interplay to unfold. When, after much experimentation, she finally does arrive at a blocking solution, Diamond explains it in an intimate whisper, or with a grand, theatrical gesture, as if the meaning itself had just that moment chosen to reveal itself. (1998, N1)

According to Diamond, when a professor in the school of management came to study her leadership style in rehearsal, he declared to her, "You deploy a method of thick description. You use a whole variety of ways to direct. You use your body, you use words." Diamond interprets, "I think what he was trying to say is you throw a lot of tomatoes at the wall and you see what sticks" (Interview, 2004).

Much like director Anne Bogart, who embraces chaos and the unknown as part of the rehearsal process, Diamond relies on fear and "happy accidents" as part of the equation in production. When approaching the script for *Phaedra*, she was terrified of Phaedra's frustrated passion and appalled by Theseus's murderous rage, but stated, "[W]hat frightens me is also precisely what draws me to the play" (Kiger 1998). When queried about her fears going into rehearsal for *Phaedra*, Diamond was straightforward: "Fears? They're always the same. Death by theatre for us and the audience. Blind alleys. Lame ideas. Other than those, none. [Laughter]" (Kiger 1998).

Trying to summarize her individual theatrical style, Diamond states that when a play is well directed, "there's a way in which the production reveals the poetry." She explains, "They're strongly visual, but the action yields up the story. Rhythm is an important characteristic. Clarity of story. I'm interested in metaphor: gestural, visual. Visually, if there's an aesthetic it's stark, it's spare—going for the essentials. I want the whole stage to signify: the movement, the gestures, the objects, the space, the choreography. . . . At the end of the day I want the theatre to be immediate and visceral. I want to be moved" (Interview, 2004).

As an award-winning director who is eager to work with both non-traditional and classical scripts, Diamond has opened avenues of exploration through her art and her teaching. Her stance toward the profession, and particularly toward women entering the profession of directing, is one of raising challenging questions to provoke thought. As a panelist for "Women Shaping the Theatre for the Future" at a conference sponsored by the Women's Project & Productions in 1997, Diamond questioned whether the next generation of women directors would still be working on breaking the glass ceiling of commercial theatre or, instead, transforming the world. "As a feminist, that's the question that interests me most. It's a question that leads directly to the question of form: what are the new theatrical forms that are evolving and what are the social and political forces giving rise to them? More concretely, what do we want the theatre of the future to look, sound, and feel like? And to whom do we want it to speak?" Perhaps her personal philosophy is best summed up by her last question: "Just how far do we want to go and how much are we willing to risk to make it happen?" (Women's Project 1997, 77).

Sources

Anderman, Joan. 1998. "Her Battlefield is a Woman's Soul." *Boston Globe*, 22 Nov., N1.

Byrne, Terry and Iris Fanger. 1998. "Direct Results: Not All of This Year's Stars Were on Stage." *Boston Herald*, 18 Dec., S05.

Contemporary Theatre, Film, and Television. 2000. Vol. 26. Detroit: Gale Group, 113–14.

Daniels, Rebecca. 1997. *Women Stage Directors Speak.* Jefferson, N.C.: McFarland.

Diamond, Liz. 2004. Telephone interview with Anne Fliotsos. 15 July.

Drukman, Steven. 1995. "Suzan-Lori Parks and Liz Diamond: Doo-a-dittly-dit-dit." *TDR/The Drama Review* 39 (3) (T147) (Fall): 56–75.

Gussow, Mel. 1989. "Identity Loss in 'Imperceptible Mutabilities.'" Rev. of *Imperceptible Mutabilities in the Third Kingdom,* by Suzan-Lori Parks. *New York Times,* 20 Sept., C24.

Kelly, Kevin. 1994. "Diamond Sparkles in the Director's Chair." *Boston Globe,* 28 Jan., 45.

Kiger, Jennifer. 1998. "Facing the Monster." *American Repertory Theatre,* http://www.amrep.org/people/diamond.html (accessed 28 May 2004).

Klein, Alvin. 1996. "Enterprising Women in Shaw's Style." Rev. of *Mrs. Warren's Profession,* by George Bernard Shaw. *New York Times,* 28 Jan., 13CN, 10.

Pressley, Nelson. 2001. "Sanitized Steinbeck." Rev. of *Of Mice and Men,* by John Steinbeck. *Washington Post,* 21 Nov., C01.

Robinson, Marc. 1995. "Liz Diamond." *Bomb* 51 (Spring): 26–31.

Women's Project & Productions. 1997. "Women Shaping the Theatre for the Future." *Women in Theatre: Mapping the Sources of Power.* Conference journal. New York City, 7–8 Nov.

Representative Directing Credits

Off and Off-Off Broadway:

War on the Third Floor (1984), *Breaking the Prairie Wolf Code* (1985), *Fizzles* (1985), *How to Say Goodbye* (1986), *Angel Face* (1987), *The Hypothesis* (1987), *The Dispute* (1988), *The Cezanne Syndrome* (1989), *Imperceptible Mutabilities in the Third Kingdom* (1989), *Hamlet's Ghosts Perform Hamlet* (1989), *Betting on the Dust Commander* (1991), *Dream of a Common Language* (1992), *The America Play* (1994), *Rice Boy* (2000), *Fighting Words* (2004)

Regional Theatre:

Sizwe Banzi Is Dead (1989), *The Island* (1989), *A Man's Man* (1990), *Imperceptible Mutabilities in the Third Kingdom* (1991), *The Death of the Last Black Man in the Whole Entire World* (1992), *Julius Caesar* (1992), *Saint Joan of the Stockyards* (1993), *The America Play* (1994), *School for Wives* (1994), *Antigone in New York* (1994), *Le Bourgeois Avant Garde* (1995), *The Sandalwood Box* (1995), *Mrs. Warren's Profession* (1996), *The Skin of Our Teeth* (1997), *Phaedra* (1998), *Brandon* (1998), *The Cure at Troy* (1998), *Betrayal* (1999), *The Trojan Women* (2000), *Of Mice and Men* (2001), *Gibraltar* (2005), *dance of the holy ghosts: a play on memory* [sic] (2006), *Distracted* (2007)

 # Dickerson, Glenda

Born February 9, 1945, in a small town near Houston, Texas, Glenda Dickerson became an important force in the Black Theatre movement in the 1960s and 1970s. She worked in New York City, where she formed the TOBA (Tough on Black Actors) Players, and in Washington, D.C., where she continued her work exploring new forms of theatre that incorporate poetry, African American heritage, and drama. She has directed on and Off Broadway, in regional theatres, and in universities. As a playwright, actor, director, folklorist, and educator, Dickerson has shown a pioneering spirit by celebrating African American culture through ritualistic theatre, most often through her own creations and adaptations.

As a child, Dickerson traveled to Europe, Asia, and around the United States due to her father's post as a military officer. The first play she remembers seeing was a Broadway tour of Lorraine Hansberry's *A Raisin in the Sun,* which changed her life. From that point on she participated in oratory contests at school and did extremely well, especially when performing a scene from *A*

Raisin in the Sun. Dickerson's grandmother also had an influence on her theatrical future. Dickerson writes, "My grandmother was the first director I knew. She played the piano for her Spanish classes and clubs and orchestrated and choreographed little plays for them. Her voice was the first one I remember hearing that could move groups of people around, telling them what to do and where to go and bringing order out of chaos" (1993, 154).

In 1966 Dickerson earned a B.F.A. in theatre arts from Howard University in Washington, D.C., where she studied under Owen Dodson, a poet, director, and playwright of the Harlem Renaissance. Dodson made a significant impact on his students, teaching them the value of their theatrical heritage. He also taught them to make connections between their African heritage and ancient Greece, sparking the idea of adapting classical texts into modern, African American contexts. After leaving Howard, Dickerson proceeded to Adelphi University in Garden City, New Jersey, where she earned an M.A. in speech and theatre arts in 1969. She also studied one summer in London, where she participated in a workshop with renowned British director Peter Brook.

Although Dickerson came into the professional theatre world primarily as a performer, she quickly became disenchanted with the impersonal mentality of the business. Armed with her passion to explore theatrical forms, Dickerson started her own theatre group in New York City, TOBA. In 1967 and 1968 TOBA worked to fuse poetry, choreography, and visual imagery into theatrical presentation, a form similar to a "choreopoem," a term later coined by playwright Ntozake Shange (Boston and Katz 1983, 22). Dickerson writes, "My vision as a creative artist was firmly rooted in the oral traditions of African slaves, of the masking miming ritual spied on the plantations in the knowledge that in African art the audience is chorus. My vision could not be contained in a bedroom, a kitchen. I wanted to lead the choral dance of misplaced people— the flying Africans—and thus experience ecstasy" (1993, 156).

Dickerson continued her exploration of theatrical form through African American heritage in Washington, D.C., where she became the artistic director of the Black American Theatre and directed productions from 1969 to 1972. During that period she returned to Howard University as assistant professor of speech and acting. These were incredibly fertile years in the Black Power movement, and Dickerson was among the leaders of black theatre in Washington, D.C. Her colleagues at Howard University, Taquiena Boston and Vera J. Katz, wrote, "She transformed the stage into a forum for the collective expression of the aspirations and mourning of black people. She preserved the cultural heritage found in the written and oral literature of Afro-Americans. Through theatre, she documented the historical past and black people's contributions, and she created new black forms that were suitable to addressing the issues and concerns of the community" (1983, 22). Productions Dickerson directed in Washington, D.C., from 1969 to 1976 include *Unfinished Song* at Howard University, *Jesus Christ, Lawd Today* for the Black American Theatre Company, *Trojan Women* at Howard, *El Hajj Malik* at Howard and at the Black American Theatre Company, *Torture of Mothers* for the Back Alley Theater, *Jump at the Sun* at the Theater Lobby, and *Owen's Song,* first at the D.C. Black Repertory Theatre, then transferring to the Kennedy Center.

Dickerson adapted or created her own works as well as directing them. For example, *Jump at the Sun* was her adaptation of Zora Neale Hurston's book *Their Eyes Were Watching God. Unfinished Song,* an original work, was "a love song to black people's pain, pride, and power" and "connected Afro-American poetry, heritage, and drama" (Boston and Katz 1983, 26). Together with Mike Malone, her creation, direction, and choreography of *Owen's Song* was a tribute to Owen Dodson and interpolated his poetry and plays in with dance. The *New York Times* critic Clive Barnes called the performance "a masque of our day, lyrical, succinct and meaningful." He was impressed not only with the professionalism, but the seamless simplicity and beauty of the staging, writing, "There is an infectious joyousness to the piece, a visual beauty and a swiftly poetic message. . . . This is a seamless masque and it is quite impossible to see where choreography starts or drama ends. It has the essence of poetry to it, with a grandeur of concept and a simplicity of effort. It has a style all its own" (1974, 28).

By the late 1970s Dickerson returned to directing in New York City. In 1978, she directed Alexis De Veaux's *A Season to Unravel* and Judi-Ann Mason's *Daughters of the Mock,* both for the Negro Ensemble Company, where she was a resident director from 1978 to 1980. She also staged Larry Neal's *The Glorious Monster in the Bell of the Horn* for the New Federal Theatre in New York City in 1979. Neal's play was an exploration of the anguish of life set on the day of the attacks on Hiroshima, beginning with a wedding sequence and progressing into the downward spiral as the bride and groom struggle with their own demons. The *New York Times* critic Richard Eder found much to compliment, including superb acting, the simple but beautiful set, and "above all, Glenda Dickerson's intelligent direction" (1979, C17).

In 1980 Dickerson became one of the few African American women to direct on Broadway, with the musical *Reggae.* Conceived by Michael Butler, with Dickerson as co-lyricist, *Reggae* featured Jamaican rhythms and a variety of story lines. Despite the high-energy performance, *New York Times* critic Mel Gussow found the musical confusing, fast, and ultimately unsuccessful, though he conceded there were joyous moments (1980, sec 3, 3). Regardless of the prestige of being one of the few African American women to direct on Broadway, Dickerson had a negative experience. She explains, "I'd never do it again. It was never a particular goal. In those days a woman director, black or white, was somewhat of an anomaly. I never really charted a career path for myself; I wouldn't even know how to do that. I was always very ensemble-oriented, trying to pull together a group of people to work with on ideas that we had. . . . The commercial theatre was never satisfying. I never got a production that I think really matched my skills and interests" (Interview, 2004).

The following year, Dickerson turned her back on commercial theatre to pursue a project that reflected her goals as an artist. She writes, "I longed to become a competent and complete personality in the 1980s, capable of reflecting a whole and holy vision in the works I brought to the stage, particularly from nondramatic sources" (1993, 156). Dickerson and poet–playwright De Veaux sorted through De Veaux's works and created a performance piece called *No!* by interweaving poems, stories, and a short play into a tapestry. Dickerson recalls, "Alexis was adamant that we have represented the spectrum of Africanamerican [sic] women, thereby defining Africanamerican beauty for ourselves through our choices. We wanted to say something about ourselves that had never been said before, and we wanted to say it in our own voices, in our own way" (159). The women took it upon themselves to produce the work, retaining the power of their vision. Dickerson directed the production, which premiered at the WOW (Women's One World) Festival at St. Mark's Place in New York City in 1981. Her directorial voice broke with many male traditions. She writes, "The sound and sensibility of each Diva's [performer's] voice dictated the material I assigned her. There was lots of trial and error. I blocked the play on the women, not from a prompt book of preconceived notions. There was no separation between us. I never sat down. I was right up onstage with them as I told them where to go. . . . Gone was the pompous director's gaze, absent the royal director's chair" (161).

No! caught the interest of Woodie King Jr., who produced the play at his New Federal Theatre in New York City in 1981. The production received excellent reviews, with Gussow writing, "Black roots and black rage are at the heart of Alexis De Vearux's *No!* This tapestry of stories, poems, music and motion has been given a stylish production by Glenda Dickerson. As adapter and director, she unifies a company linked with their author in a community of shared commitment" (1981, 14). Gussow was entranced by the contemporary folk tales of Act 1, in which black women recognize and embrace their individualism, as well as the political and social reflections of Act 2, sometimes resulting in the anguish of violence. He noted that Dickerson staged the actors to remain on stage at all times, watching the action when not performing and ultimately contributing to the "natural fluidity" of the play (14).

In 1983 Dickerson founded the Owen Dodson Lyric Theatre based in New York City. Her purpose was to create, direct, and produce the kind of plays she wanted to do: adaptations of African American novels and adaptations of classic plays. Her primary interest was to explore African American history and culture in a non-traditional way, based on ensemble-created works. She continued directing professionally through the 1980s and into the early 1990s, but gradually abandoned her professional stage career to focus on teaching and directing in a university setting, which still allowed her to produce her own adaptations and creations.

In the mid-1980s Dickerson was teaching at the State University of New York (SUNY), Stony Brook, and heard about an African American community in Long Island that predated the Revolutionary War. She started a community-based theatre project by collecting oral histories of the people and researching the community's past. After two years, she presented *Eel Catching in Setauket,* a performance event that began with an on-site historical tour of the Christian Avenue community, followed by a bus ride to SUNY Stony Brook for a performance of oral histories. The production was surrounded by an exhibit of artifacts from people's homes. Dickerson explains the interconnectivity of the events and artifacts: "Each evening during the walking tour, I picked flowers from Lucy Keyes's garden. When we returned to the black box to see the performance, I presented the flowers to Linda Gravatt [actor] who stood in a canoe holding a real eel spear . . . frozen in tableau. . . . At that moment the painting came to life and addressed the audience. At that moment, the Christian Avenue community dwellers, past and present, sprang into visibility" (1996, 121).

Dickerson continued delving into the past and into cultural consciousness in 1995 with the creation of *Zora and Lorraine & Their Signifying Tongues* at Spelman College in Atlanta, where she served as chair of the Department of Drama and Dance. Influenced by writer–anthropologist Zora Neale Hurston and playwright Lorraine Hansberry, Dickerson sought to create an imaginary literary battle between the two as they examined the African American experience (Williams 1995, Extra, 6D). Dickerson directed performers to deliver their lines as if from a sermon, adding song and dance as if in the midst of a gospel celebration. She states, "Zora said it best when she said, 'The Caucasian sees the world in words; the African sees the world in hieroglyphs'" (6D). This philosophy provides the underpinnings of Dickerson's highly visual and musical work.

Dickerson has continued her creative amalgamation of history and culture into new theatrical forms. She writes, "In creating these performance events I strive to liberate the uppity Black woman from the shroud of invisibility, take her off the auction block; make for her a Blackreality space, a space to talk out her life, a sassy space to witness the act" (1996, 109). At the University of Michigan she took leadership on a related project sponsored by the Ford

Foundation: *The Project for Transforming Thru Performing: Re/placing Black Womanly Images,* which "proposes to enter the black woman's performing voice into the scholarly discussion surrounding gendered identity as metaphor for all women and oppressed peoples, using 'witness' texts" (Dickerson, "The Project," 2004). She also continues to teach her Emancipation Theatre Techniques, which she developed in the mid-1990s. In lieu of the Aristotelian male tragic hero revealing his tragic flaw through a linear plot, Dickerson seeks a female protagonist revealed through what she calls an emancipatory narrative. "Eleanor Traylor says that an emancipatory narrative kills the slave and gives birth to the free woman," she explains. The rising action, in this case, leads to a cataclysmic event: the act of the celebrant [protagonist] "coming to voice" (Interview, 2004). In classes and workshops, participants take slave narratives, letters, autobiographies, and other artifacts and chart the events that lead to the celebrant's coming to voice. "You can teach it like an acting class, which I do, because it opens them up," she states. "But basically we're trying to think about how a dramatic journey can be thought about differently" (Interview, 2004).

Because her performance pieces are so unique, Dickerson has unique casting requirements as well. In 2004 Dickerson was working solely with women, many of whom were working, professional actors. The women she works with she calls Prayerful Performers. She explains what she requires of a Prayerful Performer, which informs her casting, stating,

> Because we're speaking the words of real women, the Prayerful Performer has to be willing to approach that woman's words with a particular kind of honor and respect, and a particular kind of humility, and a particular kind of willingness to do research, so that when we say a woman's words we're not just quoting them as we would a character in a play, but we're supporting those words with the proper historic perspective. If we quote, let's just say, a Pakistani woman, we're not just quoting the words we read in the newspaper, but we're understanding the complete historic context out of which those words arose. And everybody can't do that . . . particularly those who are more traditionally trained. So there's a spiritual element to the work that we do. . . . Those are the kinds of things I look for: a flexibility and being able to support the spoken word in a different, more holistic way, a patience to do the required research, and an ease with spirituality, in addition to a very highly refined physical instrument; the physical instrument has to be exceedingly flexible because we're playing a lot of different characters in a little bit of time. (Interview, 2004)

Balance in the ensemble is particularly important, and bringing new performers into an existing ensemble is often quite difficult because they have not come through the process together.

Much like Barbara Ann Teer's philosophy of liberating actors so that they may in turn liberate the audience, Dickerson leads her actors to truth and freedom through her Emancipation Theatre techniques. "Directing means plumbing down to those depths where truth lives and releasing it," she explains. "Working directly with the actor, you keep on plumbing until you touch something. It's so magical when it happens, it's frightening. The light goes off in an actor's eyes and it's almost always accompanied by tears. . . . To have something in your head and see it come back to you, there's nothing like that feeling. I live for it" (Boyd 1993, N2). The connection to spirit and soul is vital in African ritual and is therefore stressed in Dickerson's work. Actors are not just actors in the western sense, but testifiers, celebrators, and dreamers. Boston and Katz describe her early work with actors in Washington, D.C., in the 1970s, writing, "Everyone devoted long and strenuous hours to the creative process that has been described as sometimes being painful. The actors were not preened for a particular production in the style of the one-shot try on Broadway. They were trained for the construction of a company, an ensemble in the style of the Moscow Art Theatre, where long hours of preparation and weeks of rehearsal were invested in a production. The actors lived togetherness, and the cohesiveness of the ensemble communicated a philosophy about the art and politics of black people—namely, that they should be transformational" (1983, 25).

Dickerson sometimes directs in environmental spaces rather than in traditional theatres. Even when in theatre spaces, she likes to break or eliminate the barrier between the actor and audience, transgressing the fourth wall. She has staged productions in a wide variety of spaces and geographical locations, including an amphitheatre in Istanbul, Turkey. Although she misses the opportunity for dramatic lighting in some of these spaces, Dickerson notes, "This kind of work is so raw, it's so immediate and it's so transformatory, that the spaces are not really a challenge, the way they might be" (Interview, 2004).

Dickerson describes work with actors as that of a questioner. She listens and values what her Prayerful Performers bring into rehearsals. They spend a significant amount of time at the table with research, giving reactions and responses. "But then, at some point, all these papers, all these ideas, all these responses, all these reactions have to be shaped into something. And that's where my director's hand comes in" (Dickerson, interview, 2004). She functions as part dramaturg and part director as she shapes and edits the text as well as the performance, making a cohesive dramatic scene that "builds to something that is coherent" (Interview, 2004).

Through the course of her career, Dickerson has directed across the United States with the Seattle Repertory Theatre, the St. Louis Black Repertory, the Crossroads Theatre in New Jersey, the John F. Kennedy Center for the Performing Arts in Washington, D.C., and the Woman's Interart Theatre in New York City, in addition to the theatres previously mentioned. Dickerson has won two AUDELCO Awards for her stage work, one for directing *Magic and Lions*, in 1980, and a Special Award for Excellence for the Owen Dodson Lyric Theatre, in 1982, as well as awards for television work and teaching. She has taught at several highly regarded universities and is a professor of Theatre and Drama and the director of the Center for World Performance Studies at the University of Michigan in Ann Arbor.

Dickerson's legacy incorporates her work as a director, playwright, educator, and celebrant of cultural heritage. "My most fervent desire," she states, "is to raise women warriors who can transform the world through performance" (Interview, 2004).

Sources

Addell, Austin. 1994. "Glenda Dickerson." In *Theatrical Directors: A Biographical Dictionary*, ed. John W. Frick and Stephen M. Vallillo, 108–10. Westport, Conn.: Greenwood.

Barnes, Clive. 1974. Rev. of *Owen's Song*, conceived by Glenda Dickerson and Mike Malone. *New York Times*, 1 Nov., 28.

Boston, Taquiena and Vera J. Katz. 1983. "Witness to a Possibility: The Black Theatre Movement in Washington, D.C., 1968–1976." *Black American Literature Forum* 17 (Spring): 22–26.

Boyd, Valerie. 1993. "Inside the Arts; People in the Arts: Glenda Dickerson Makes Dramatic Entrance." *Atlanta Journal and Constitution*, 11 Apr., N2.

Dickerson, Glenda. 1993. "Wearing Red: When a Rowdy Band of Charismatics Learned to Say 'NO!'" In *Upstaging Big Daddy: Directing Theatre as if Gender and Race Matter*, edited by Ellen Donkin and Susan Clement, 153–176. Ann Arbor: University of Michigan Press.

———. 1996. "Festivities and Jubilations on the Graves of the Dead: Sanctifying Sullies Space." In *Performance and Cultural Politics*, ed. Elin Diamond, 108–27. London: Routledge.

———. 2004. "The Project for Transforming thru Performing: Re/placing Black Womanly Images." University of Michigan International Institute, Center for World Performance Studies. http://www.umich.edu/~iinet/cwps/transform.htm (accessed 27 July 2004).

———. 2004. Telephone interview with Anne Fliotsos. 21 July.

Eder, Richard. 1979. Rev. of *The Glorious Monster in the Bell of the Horn*, by Larry Neal. *New York Times*, 11 Jul., C17.

Gussow, Mel. 1980. Rev. of *Reggae*, conceived by Michael Butler. *New York Times*, 28 Mar., sec. 3, 3.

———. 1981. Rev. of *No!*, by Alexis De Veaux. *New York Times*, 6 Jun., 14.

Peterson, Bernard L. 1988. *Contemporary Black American Playwrights and Their Plays.* Westport, Conn.: Greenwood.

White, Richard E. T. 1997. "Dickerson, Glenda." In *Facts on File: Encyclopedia of Black Women in America,* ed. Darlene Clark, 91–92. New York: Facts on File.

Williams, Mara Rose. 1995. "Weaving Her Own Dramatic Reality; Playwright Believes 'in Having the Courage to Be Yourself.'" *Atlanta Journal and Constitution,* 19 Oct., Extra, 6D.

Representative Directing Credits

Broadway:
  Reggae (1980)

Off and Off-Off Broadway:
  Winti Train (1977), *Magic and Lions* (1977), *Daughters of the Mock* (1978), *A Season to Unravel* (1978), *The Glorious Monster in the Bell of the Horn* (1979), *Bones* (1979), *No!* (1981), *Ma Lou's Daughter* (1983), *Praise Singer* (1985), *Black Girl* (1986), *Tale of Madame Zora* (1986)

Regional Theatre:
  The Unfinished Song (1970), *Jesus Christ, Lawd Today* (1972), *Jump at the Sun* (1972, 1983, 1984), *Torture of Mothers* (1973), *Owen's Song* (1974, 1978), *Boesman and Lena* (1979), *Roshomon* (1982), *The Hatian Medea* (1982), *Gris Gris* (1987), *Wet Carpets* (1988), *Long Time Since Yesterday* (1988), *Shakin' the Mess Outta Misery* (1988, 1989, 1991), *Ana Bel's Brush* (1992)

International Theatre:
  The Golden Stool (1981), *Spreading Lies* (1985)

Other:
  Re/membering Aunt Jemima, A Menstrual Show (1992, 1994), *Talkstory of Style & Substance* (1996)

Fichandler, Zelda

Born Zelda Diamond on September 18, 1924, in Boston, Massachusetts, Zelda Fichandler is both a producer and director. As a co-founder of Arena Stage in Washington, D.C., Fichandler is a pioneer in the American regional theatre movement. The theatre gained national prominence under Fichandler's leadership when its 1967 production of Howard Sackler's *The Great White Hope,* directed by Ed Sherin, became the first play from a regional theatre to transfer to Broadway. Fichandler directed nearly fifty different plays in her forty years at Arena Stage.

From the age of four, Fichandler and her family lived in Washington, D.C., where she attended Rose Robinson Cowen's Studio for Children's Theatre. There she performed as Helga in *Helga in the White Peacock* and acted in other plays. At the age of eleven Fichandler won a dollar for an essay that she wrote about why she wanted to be an actor, which was later published in the *Washington Star.* In high school, she was influenced by a teacher who taught her about Shakespeare.

Despite her early interest in theatre, Fichandler did not intend to pursue it as a profession. With an interest in chemistry, Fichandler first attended college in Washington, D.C., but transferred to Cornell University in Ithaca, New York, where she graduated Phi Beta Kappa in 1945 with a B.A. in Russian language and literature. The next year she married economist Thomas C. Fichandler. She continued her studies at George Washington University in Washington, D.C., with plans to become a psychoanalyst, but switched majors and graduated in 1950 with an M.A. in theatre arts. During her last year at George Washington University, she began to work with her professor, Edward Mangum, to create a professional regional theatre. Mangum, who had seen director Margo Jones's theatre in Dallas, Texas, suggested an arena stage, and they converted an old movie house in Washington, D.C., into a theatre with 247 seats. After Mangum left in 1952 to pursue other interests, Jones encouraged Fichandler to continue at Arena Stage. Fichandler became the theatre's producing director, and her husband became its business manager. In 1956 the theatre moved to the 500-seat Old Vat, which had once been a brewery. The Arena Stage opened in its present location in Washington, D.C., in 1961.

Fichandler is contradictory when explaining what drove her to direct. Although she says, "I started wanting to have a theatre to fulfill my directing impulse" (Interview, 1988, 110), she also states, "I directed plays because someone had to, because one person couldn't do them all" (Interview, 1999, 22). Fichandler learned much about directing as she ran her theatre. She says, "I learned by watching directors I had hired at my theatre. Gradually over the years, I evolved my own way of working. What astounded me as I watched myself learn was that at the beginning I was a very choreographic director—I had everything written down and choreographed. It was very programmed and movement-oriented. And then as I found the way that I wanted to work, it became psychological and improvisational and very actor-oriented" (22). Fichandler often hired director Alan Schneider to direct at Arena Stage, and she cites him as an influence. She elaborates, "With Alan, I took his notes while he was directing and I observed his methods of rehearsal. . . . And I think he was my primary teacher. I don't direct the way he did anymore. . . . But he is a hero to me. His introduction of Beckett to the country and his productions of Beckett taught me so much. His way of combining reality and the imaginative world of style, his sensitive use of all of the tools of the theatre, light, sound, design, costuming and so forth. And I had to learn rapidly" (Transcript, 2003, 17).

Most of the plays that Fichandler has directed have been produced at Arena Stage. She acknowledges, "I think it would have been better for me to have gone to direct in another theatre—for me. And maybe better for the institution in the long run. But it always seemed to me that I needed to be there. . . . For twenty years of my time at Arena, I was raising a family, too. And it seemed very unimportant for me to go away for two months to do something" (Interview, 1999, 23).

In 1973 the United States State Department invited Arena Stage to tour the Soviet Union with their productions of Jerome Lawrence and Robert E. Lee's *Inherit the Wind* and Thorton Wilder's *Our Town*, making Arena Stage the first American theatre company to tour behind the Iron Curtain. Fichandler directed *Inherit the Wind*, first in Washington, D.C., at Catholic University's Hartke Theatre, and then at Moscow's Mxat Filial and Leningrad's Pushkin Theatre. The play then opened at Arena Stage on its return to the United States the same year. The subject of *Inherit the Wind*, a play about the trial of John Scopes for teaching evolution in a public school, was a good showcase for exploring Fichandler's ideas. She elaborates, "We used the notion that people gain immortality through their children and, therefore, they want their children to believe what they believe. . . . We also wanted to show the social furor that this kind of individual and group passion can cause. . . . In my research I found out that the courtroom floor actually collapsed because there were so many people, and that one afternoon session had to be held outdoors. I enlarged on that idea and set the whole play outdoors. It was really medieval, primitive, and this conceptual basis gave it a surround that was very interesting to the Soviet Union when we took the production there in 1973. It really showed them a lot about our life and how thought can be transformed into personal action and passion" (Interview, 1988, 118–19).

Fichandler directed several plays by Arthur Miller at Arena Stage, including *Death of a Salesman* in 1974 and 1976, and *After the Fall* in 1979. In 1988 Fichandler won the Helen Hayes Award as Outstanding Director for the 1987 Arena Stage production of Miller's *The Crucible*. David Richards of the *Washington Post* found the play contemporary, writing, "[I]t is now remarkably descriptive of the panic engendered by the AIDS crisis and the fanatical need to some to ascribe blame for the scourge, root out scapegoats and cleanse society." He wrote of the production, "Fichandler and a superb cast delineate all the petty and conflicting forces that come together to make an inquisition. . . . There really isn't an unsure performance in the large cast— even the supernumeraries suggest they have ongoing lives of their own. The actors sit dutifully on pews surrounding the stage, only to hurtle themselves into the fray with breathless—not to say demonic—urgency, when the time comes. Douglas Stein has covered the acting area with thick wooden planking (notice how it amplifies the forbidding sound of footsteps). . . . At first you may wonder why he has also suspended thick windows between the audience and the actors. Doesn't Fichandler know they partially block our view? Of course she does. . . . [W]e are outsiders looking in" (1987, D01).

Fichandler discusses how the idea of using windows came about. She explains, "[T]he audience in the Arena saw the first act through windows and, therefore, sometimes couldn't see much of anything. . . . We did the whole bedroom scene from behind windows and then in the next scene the windows flew up and we suddenly blended that world with the audience's because they could see clearly into it. . . . That came out of all sorts of long talks about the regimented world of the Puritans, that community that gave each person license to peer into and be responsible for the world of their neighbor. . . . It became windows because you can see in, because they are oppressive and because they reveal the secret life in the bedroom from outside" (Interview, 1988, 123). *The Crucible* was also directed by Fichandler at the Israel Festival in Jerusalem in 1987.

Fichandler's interest in Russian literature influenced her selection of plays to direct, which included works by eastern European writers during the time of the Iron Curtain. Fichandler directed several American premieres of plays from the former Soviet Union at Arena Stage, such as Chingiz Aitmotov and Kaltai Mukhamedzhanov's *The Ascent of Mt. Fuji* in 1975 and Alexander Vampilov's *Duck Hunting* in 1978.

Discussing her direction of *The Ascent of Mt. Fuji*, Fichandler recalls that the play "begins with people climbing up a mountain and having a picnic[.] I just had a box of stuff: Picnic baskets, jars, hard-boiled eggs, cucumbers, tomatoes, bread. . . . So the actors made up their own business and before you knew it, the picnic looked as if it had been worked on for six months. . . . Then we started 'scoring' it for focus, what I call shifting the 'ball of attention,' to make sure no one was hacking the cucumber while somebody else was supposed to have focus" (Interview, 1988, 119). Critics noticed the detail, with Clive Barnes of the *New York Times* writing, "The director, Zelda Fichandler, has paid the play the tribute of staging it is [sic] if it actually were Chekhov. . . . [T]he Arena cast goes about the play's business with intermeshing skill" (1975, 53).

In addition to producing many plays by Anton Chekhov at Arena Stage, Fichandler directed some Chekhov plays herself, including *The Three Sisters* in 1966 and in 1984. Of the 1984 production, Mel Gussow of the *New York Times* wrote, "Zelda Fichandler has achieved a Chekhovian balance between lingering hope and fearful despair. . . . Viewed as a whole, however, this is a well-orchestrated production that puts itself in the service of the author. There are no directorial embellishments to distract us from the play's sagacity and lyricism. It is very much a company show, drawing upon the Arena's extended family of actors, casting each with precision and not allowing any individual character or performer to outweigh the others" (1984, A83). When Fichandler directed Chekhov's *Uncle Vanya* in 1997, it was the first time she had directed at Arena Stage without being its producing director. She called the experience "[a] delirious time for me. I've always wondered what it would feel like to be an artist-in-residence" (Horwitz 1997, D07).

In 1984 Fichandler began teaching at New York University, while continuing work at the Arena Stage. In 1991 she left Arena Stage after forty years of service and became artistic director of The Acting Company, a New York City-based group that toured classical and new plays performed by a company of young performers. She remained the company's artistic director until 1994, when she directed Henrik Ibsen's *A Doll's House,* a production she had directed earlier at Arena Stage in 1990. The company provided a venue for Fichandler to focus on classical and new works.

Fichandler explains her interest in the classics, stating, "[E]very artist stands on the shoulders of other artists working in other forms in other times. Classics in new adaptations and translations are new works, and, representing profound excavations of the human spirit, belong in any theatre that claims to be contemporary" ("Whither," 2003). Whether directing a classical or modern play, Fichandler says that "theatre must reflect its times, its population, the concerns of its audience and the concerns of the people who are making the art" (Transcript, 2003, 11). When choosing a play to direct, Fichandler believes that one must "get in touch with what's on their own mind, heart, psyche, soul, spirit" (12).

Before beginning rehearsals, Fichandler spends much time researching. She says, "I always do about six months of advance research because knowledge releases my imagination. Imagination is there after you know everything; without knowledge, one's imagination may be too thin—lacking in strength and too fragile to build on. I need to know exactly how the characters in the play lead their daily lives. . . . I may never use it, but it gives me a sense of reality. That's the basis of my process. Along with that, I have to know what it is I want to find out" (Interview, 1988, 111).

Fichandler's 2006 direction at Arena Stage of Clifford Odets's *Awake and Sing!,* a story of a Depression era Jewish family living in the Bronx, provides insight into her research process. Fichandler identified with the play because it touched on her own heritage. She used a 1905 photograph of her mother as a young child, who had just immigrated to the United States from Lithuania, then Russia, to prepare for the play. She explains, "Gazing at this photograph has been part of my research for directing *Awake and Sing!,* helping me to recall very early memories of my own life in the Depression years of the thirties, the period of the play . . . and giving me a deeper awareness of how people who were to me daddy and mommy, aunt and uncle, cousin . . . and friend, were also figures of history in the Third Wave of Jewish immigrants to the United States . . . figures who as time went by became an integral part of the American culture in all its aspects" (2006).

When preparing for a play, Fichandler looks for what she calls the *zamissel,* a Russian word that she says means "the pervading sense" and is "the thought that binds together all elements or the idea" (Interview, 1988, 116). She explains, "In theatre it's that connecting tissue of that central conflict that if you find [it] will explode the meanings of the play, the reverberations of the play" (Transcript, 2003, 13). Fichandler prefers to find the central idea of the play before rehearsals begin. She states, "I feel that if you don't start with that central clue, that the designers have nothing to begin with. . . . You can't gather in a team that responds to each other all looking for the same way of embodying this thing. The actors don't have the thread upon which to string the moment-to-moment life of their character or, indeed, their relationships with each other" (13). Fichandler also believes that it is important for a director to have "a strong social and political perspective" and "to want to put their imaginative ability into the service of ideas" (Interview, 1988, 109).

Fichandler's directing is actor-based. She believes strongly in a repertoire company and sees actors as central to the production, with the other elements revolving around them. She states, "[T]he way to create the most developed, important actors is the acting company" (Transcript, 2003, 6). Fichandler looks for certain qualities in actors. She states that an actor who can play repertory needs, "not just realism, but a reality-based technique that could encompass all of the repertory . . . a physically-based technique" (15). She prefers actors from diverse backgrounds, explaining, "The more you know, the wider the arc of your imagination and the longer its trajectory. I like to train actors who come from political science, anthropology, engineering—actors who have some purchase on the world, some way to grab hold of it" (Interview, 1999, 23–24).

In an effort to create an interracial company at Arena Stage in the late 1960s, Fichandler hired about fifteen African American actors. To her surprise, the casting of African Americans in classic plays at that time was not particularly successful. Fichandler explains, "They were not really interested, nor was their audience, in the classics of Western literature. . . . What we learned from that experiment was that, if we wanted the African-American population of Washington to come, we needed to stage plays that were of immediate interest to them, that reflected and refracted their own lives. I don't know why I thought just changing the casting would make things different" (2001, 36).

Fichandler begins rehearsals by talking about the *zamissel,* or core of the play, with the performers. Then they read the play together and share what they have discovered through research. Fichandler explains, "The actors will have begun their research a month or two previous to the first rehearsal . . . to explore particular topics that interest them. . . . These aspects of that world will be shared, either verbally or using slides, photographs, tapes, etc. as the reading takes place. The documentation provides a depth and resonance to the text and a density and reality to the moment-to-moment life of the characters. Then I move from reading, which can go on for a week or ten days, to improvisations, and then back to reading" (Interview, 1988, 118).

At the beginning of her career, Fichandler blocked her plays, but now she lets the blocking emerge through rehearsals. Although she may have images of how she would like to stage key moments in the play, she observes, "You'd be surprised how bodies fall into beautiful patterns if they know just what they are doing and who they want to be near or not near, how they're relating" (1988, interview, 115). Fichandler also encourages her performers to take risks, reasoning, "I put myself at risk along with them, in the exploration of what's going on. I do it consciously because I know what I'm looking for, in general—I know what I think that moment or that scene contains. But I want the actors to find out how they want to embody it—what their bodies want to do—so that it seems to be occurring naturally" (Interview, 1999, 22). She embraces Stanislavski's psycho-physical approach to acting and says of performers, "I intervene very delicately, through sharing with them what I know and through releasing their imaginations so they can share what they know. . . . [T]he process is a living exploration" (Interview, 1988, 114). Fichandler tries to keep rehearsal open for creativity, saying, "The theatre director must also have a deep reservoir of patience and allow time for subconscious thought and feelings to arise in the bodies and minds of his/her collaborative artists. In this way, the work becomes dense and deeply revelatory, truly a collective statement about the world of the play" (110).

Fichandler prefers to spread her rehearsals out over a period of time to get the best performances from her actors. She explains, "It's not the number of hours. Rather than rehearse twelve hours a day in one week, it's better to do it four hours a day over three weeks. That has to do with the material getting into the muscle and nervous system from the subconscious. One needs enough time to acquire instinctive knowledge and to embody that knowledge in a series of creative images. Of course, the more complex the work, the more time one needs. . . . I think the way to work in a short period of rehearsal is to inform the actors and designers more fully so that they can fully be co-contributors. Because if everyone is improvising toward truth, you can get there faster" (Interview, 1988, 112–13).

Although Fichandler allows productions to evolve during rehearsals, she is prepared to discuss technical issues with collaborators. She says, "I may not come in with the blocking of a scene, but I'm very prepared for the designers, for the people doing the logo of the art, the people doing the press release, the people doing the lobby display, the marketing and all that" (Interview, 1999, 22).

Fichandler describes the end product of her work, saying, "I'm very rational. My work eventually looks very carefully selected, not haphazard. It's organized rhythmically, architecturally, thematically, as well as psychologically. . . . What one aims for, in the end, is improvisation within set form" (Interview, 1988, 113). Whether directing a classical or modern play, Fichandler aims to create a contemporary performance. She explains, "All theatre is contemporary. All theatre is about the audience via the make believe of the actors" (Transcript, 2003, 14).

In addition to directing and producing, Fichandler has lectured and taught at numerous colleges and universities. She has received numerous honorary doctorates and many awards including the Margo Jones Award for the production of new plays in 1971, the Acting Company's John Houseman Award for the commitment to the development of young American actors in 1985, the Commonwealth Award for Distinguished Service in Dramatic Arts in 1985, and the National Medal of Arts in 1997. She has also received The Brandeis University Creative Arts Award, the Washingtonian of the Year Award, and the Ortho 21st Century Women Trailblazer Award. In addition, she has received citations from the National Theatre Conference, the Southeastern Theatre Conference, and The United States Institute of Theatre Technology. In 1999 Fichandler was inducted into the Theatre Hall of Fame.

Under Fichandler's direction, Arena Stage became the first winner of the Tony Award for regional theatres in 1976. Although she is known primarily for her work as a co-founder and a longtime producing director of Arena Stage, Fichandler acknowledges, "[M]y work as a director is my private joy" (Interview, 1999, 23).

Sources

Barnes, Clive. 1975. "Theater: Soviet 'Ascent.'" *New York Times,* 8 June, 53.

Chapel, Robert. 1994. "Zelda Diamond Fichandler." In *Theatrical Directors: A Biographical Dictionary,* ed. John W. Frick and Stephen M. Vallillo, 134–37. Westport, Conn.: Greenwood.

Chinoy, Helen Krich and Linda Walsh Jenkins, eds. 1987. *Women in American Theatre.* New York: Theatre Communications Group.

Daniels, Rebecca. 1996. *Women Stage Directors Speak: Exploring the Influence of Gender on Their Work.* Jefferson, N.C.: McFarland.

Fichandler, Zelda. 1988. Interview with Arthur Bartow. In *The Director's Voice: Twenty-One Interviews,* by Arthur Bartow, 105–27. New York: Theatre Communications Group.

———. 1999. Interview with Des McAnuff. "Zelda Fichandler: The Arc of Imagination." *Journal for Stage Directors and Choreographers* 13 (2) (Fall/Winter): 20–25.

———. 2001. "Forty Years of Passion." *American Theatre* 18 (6) (July/Aug.): 36–37.

———. 2003. Transcript from *Preserving the Legacy.* TCG Oral History Project: Voices of the American Theatre. New York: Theatre Communications Group.

———. 2003. "Whither (or Wither) Art?" *American Theatre* 20 (May/June). http://www.tcg.org/am_theatre/at_articles/AT_Volume_20?MayJune03/at_web5603_zelda.html (accessed 14 May 2004).

———. 2006. "From the Director: One Hand Any Way." *Awake and Sing! Program Notes.* http://www.arenastage.org/season/2005/awake-and-sing/director.shtml (accessed 18 May 2006).

Gussow, Mel. 1984. "'Three Sisters' in Translation by Jarrell." Rev. of *The Three Sisters,* by Anton Chekhov. *New York Times,* 19 Feb., A83.

Hennigan, Shirlee. 1983. "The Woman Director in the Contemporary, Professional Theatre." Ph.D. diss., Washington State University.

Horwitz, Jane. 1997. "Fichandler's Homecoming; Arena Stage's Founder Savors Her Return Engagement in 'Uncle Vanya.'" *Washington Post,* 23 Dec., D07.

Richards, David. 1987. "The Mighty 'Crucible'; Arena Does Justice to a Timeless Parable." *Washington Post,* 12 June, D01.

———. 1990. "Arena Memories." *Washington Post,* 5 Aug., W21.

———. 1990. "Shuttered Souls in a 'Doll House'; At Arena, the Dark Insight of Ibsen." *Washington Post,* 9 March, D01.

Stanley, N. J. 1989. "Fichandler, Zelda Diamond." In *Notable Women in the American Theatre: A Biographical Dictionary,* ed. Alice M. Robinson, Vera Mowry Roberts, and Milly S. Barranger, 273–76. Westport, Conn.: Greenwood.

"Zelda Fichandler Looks for 'Main Event' in Each Play She Directs." 1990. *Christian Science Monitor,* 4 Apr., 15.

Representative Directing Credits

Regional Theatre:

> *The Firebrand* (1950), *Pygmalion* (1950), *The Playboy of the Western World* (1950), *Ladder to the Moon* (1951), *The Importance of Being Earnest* (1951, 1952), *Twelfth Night* (1951, 1952), *The Inspector General* (1951), *The Adding Machine* (1951), *The Country Wife* (1952), *Tonight at 8:30—Fumed Oak, Ways and Means, Still Life* (1952), *A Phoenix Too Frequent* (1953), *Boy Meets Girl* (1953), *Golden Boy* (1954), *Room Service* (1954), *Blithe Spirit* (1954), *The Mousetrap* (1955), *The World of Sholom Aleichem, A Tale of Chelm, Bontche Schweig, The High School* (1955), *Dream Girl* (1956), *Answered the Flute* (1957), *Witness for the Prosecution* (1957), *The Hollow* (1958), *Romeo and Juliet* (1958), *The Browning Version* (1958), *The Lady's Not for Burning* (1959), *Silent Night, Lonely Night* (1961), *Six Characters in Search of an Author* (1961, 1968), *Once in a Lifetime* (1962), *The Devils* (1963), *Twelve Angry Men* (1963), *The Skin of Our Teeth* (1965), *The Three Sisters* (1966, 1984), *Edith Stein* (1969), *A Public Prosecutor Is Sick of It All* (1973), *Inherit the Wind* (1973), *Death of a Salesman* (1974, 1976), *An Enemy of the People* (1975), *The Ascent of Mount Fuji* (1975), *Duck Hunting* (1978), *After the Fall* (1979), *A Delicate Balance* (1982), *Screenplay* (1983), *The Crucible* (1987), *Enrico IV* (1964, co-directed with Mel Shapiro—1988), *A Doll's House* (1990), *Born Guilty* (1990, 1991), *Mrs. Klein* (1992), *Uncle Vanya* (1997), *Awake and Sing!* (2006)

Tours:

> *A Doll's House* (1994, 1995)

International Theatre:

> *Inherit the Wind* (1973), *After the Fall* (1980), *The Crucible* (1987)

Fiske, Minnie Maddern

Born Marie Augusta Davey on December 19, 1865, in New Orleans, Louisiana, Minnie Maddern Fiske was the only child of a theatrical family. Performing since the age of three under the name Little Minnie Maddern, Fiske first took her mother's maiden name for the stage. She went on to become a director, producer, playwright, and performer known for her naturalistic acting style, which resembled conversation rather than theatrical declamation. A proponent of ensemble acting, she also helped to promote Ibsen in the United States and presented the works of many new playwrights, including women writers.

As a child, Fiske toured with the company managed by her father and began her career singing and dancing between theatrical acts. While on tour in Little Rock, Arkansas, she made her official acting debut in 1868 as the Duke of York in another company's production of Shakespeare's *Richard III*. Abandoned by her father at the age of six, Fiske followed her mother, a touring performer, to New York City and around the country. Soon Fiske began to tour as an actor on her own, obtaining an education at convents in Cincinnati, New Orleans, St. Louis, and Montreal, Canada. By the time she was fourteen, both of her parents were dead. Fiske continued touring, with intermittent visits to her aunt in Larchmont, New York. Fiske made her critically acclaimed adult acting debut on Broadway in 1882 as Chip in Charles Collaban's *Fogg's Ferry*. In 1890 she married Harrison Grey Fiske, editor of the *New York Dramatic Mirror*, and retired from acting to focus on marriage and playwriting.

Because programs of the period do not always list directing credits, it is difficult to mark the beginning of Fiske's directing career. It seems that it may have begun in 1893, with the direction of *Hester Crew*, written by her husband. Fiske also starred in the play, which was presented at Boston's Tremont Theatre to poor reviews. She appeared the next year in a hospital benefit as Nora in Henrik Ibsen's *A Doll's House* at New York City's Empire Theatre. This was the second time Ibsen had been performed in English in New York City, and Ibsen sent Fiske a laurel wreath and a letter of good wishes. The production received rave reviews, and Fiske resumed her career, now under the name of Mrs. Fiske. She also became a promoter of Ibsen, admiring his depth and realism. Discussing Ibsen's work, she explained, "Many a play is like a painted back-drop, something to be looked at from the front. An Ibsen play is like a black forest, something you can *enter*, something you can walk about in" (Fiske 1917, 61). She believed that Ibsen plays were more difficult to direct because of their psychological overtones ("An Actress," 1906, X2).

Devoting himself to his wife's career, Fiske's husband took on the role of co-manager. Fiske and her husband were independent managers, and beginning in 1897 they opposed the Theatrical Syndicate, also known as the Trust. The Theatrical Syndicate controlled the literary agents of many writers and numerous theatres across the United States and abroad. Therefore, the Fiskes were not able to obtain the rights of many plays and were limited to presenting their productions in independent theatres. While touring, Fiske often had to bypass cities controlled by the Theatrical Syndicate or choose to play in lesser venues, such as gymnasiums.

In 1897 Fiske starred in and directed the Broadway hit *Tess of the D'Urbervilles,* a play by Lorimer Stoddard adapted from the novel by Thomas Hardy. James Huneker of the *New York Advertiser* described the end of play, writing, "The scene is Wagnerian; it is superb, and is a final stroke of genius, for it sums up Tess's character, her love of nature, of light, of love. It gives us in a breathless moment what the rest of the play does not, the atmosphere of that half wild, unsullied sweethearted creature, Tess of the D'Urbervilles" (Binns 1955, 69). As was her pattern, Fiske toured her Broadway production around the country to make money and also to bring theatre to others. The *New York Times* review of Fiske's revival of the play in 1902 on Broadway noted, "The production as a whole was of the excellence one has learned to expect of Mrs. Fiske's management" ("Mrs. Fiske's Return," 1902, 8).

In 1899 Fiske starred in Langdon Mitchell's *Becky Sharp,* adapted from William Makepeace Thackeray's novel *Vanity Fair.* She and Fred Williams co-directed the production, which was first presented at Canada's Montreal Academy of Music to mixed reviews. However, the *New York Times* noted that the play was "well received" and that Fiske's portrayal of Becky "will be accounted her best work" ("Mrs. Fiske as Becky," 1899, 6). The play's Broadway opening at the Fifth Avenue Theatre also received mixed reviews, but audiences were enthusiastic, with the *New York Times* noting, "There can be no doubt of the popular success of this production" ("Mrs. Fiske as Rebecca," 1899, 7). The production became a national phenomenon and was featured in numerous magazines and newspapers. With other productions scheduled to open at the theatre, *Becky Sharp* was forced to close because the Theatrical Syndicate controlled all other available theatres in New York City. The production played briefly at the Brooklyn Academy of Music and then went on a critically acclaimed tour. In addition to closing Fiske out of theatres on her tour, the Theatrical Syndicate produced its own *Becky Sharp* to compete with the Fiskes's production. The Fiskes fought for their rights in court, and the Syndicate's version was judged as plagiarism and forced to close.

In 1901 Fiske and her husband leased New York City's Manhattan Theatre as a venue in which to present their productions. That year, the Fiskes opened their theatre with Anne Crawford Flexner's *Miranda of the Balcony,* which Fiske co-directed with actor Max Figman. The play, in which Fiske performed, centered on a woman of fashion who mistakenly thinks the husband she despises is dead. The *New York Times* noted the ensemble acting, stating, "It is a play which demands for its interpretation a good company, and this—wonderful to say—has been provided. More than that, Mrs. Fiske has put the play on the stage as no other play has been mounted here in many moons" ("Manhattan," 1901, 8). That same year Fiske starred in and co-directed with Figman a play by Mrs. Burton Harrison, *The Unwelcome Mrs. Hatch,* at the Manhattan Theatre. The play was based on Mrs. Henry Wood's *East Lynne,* an extremely popular novel of the Victorian era with many plot twists, in which a refined wife leaves her husband and children for another man and later returns to them as a governess.

Tackling the controversial subject of religion, Fiske performed in and directed Paul Heyse's *Mary of Magdala,* adapted by William Winter. Before the play opened at the Manhattan Theatre in 1902, it was examined by New York clergy members—including ministers, priests, and rabbis—to avoid any religious objections. Archie Binns discussed the development of *Mary of Magdala* in his book *Mrs. Fiske and the American Theatre,* writing, "The production as Minnie saw it would be in the manner of a Wagnerian opera, combining the arts of acting, poetry, music and lighting with the magnificent stage mounting introduced by Wagner. . . . Minnie assigned parts to members of the cast and studied the role of Mary of Magdala. On day coaches between one-night stands, she was usually poring over the Gospel according to John or Matthew, or Renan's weighty *Life of Jesus*" (1955, 129).

During this period, realistic sets and costumes were in vogue, and *Mary of Magdala* included these items. Describing the production's detail, Binns wrote, "By the summer of 1902 archaeologists had reconstructed the most probable architecture for the interiors and street scenes; a photographer in Jerusalem had taken pictures of a ravine through which a trail from the city led to Calvary, and scenic artists had produced five massive sets. Percy Anderson, London costume designer, had searched the museums of Europe for clues before sending a buyer to the Orient for fabrics" (1955, 129).

Fiske focused on ensemble acting and paid particular attention to minor cast members. In an article about crowds on stage, the *New York Times* discussed Fiske's work on *Mary of Magdala* as containing "probably one of the best street scenes ever shown on the American stage." The article noted that each performer "has an entity—distinct, peculiar in himself or herself—that he or she must live up to. . . . [S]he [Mrs. Fiske] has surpassed all her former efforts" ("Training," 1902, 28).

Mary of Magdala opened to excellent reviews. Binns described the production, writing, "At the beginning of the third act the curtain rose on one of the most perfect stage illusions ever seen in New York: a sun-drenched square in Jerusalem and the streets opening from it thronged with people. . . . In that magic square Mrs. Fiske made her appearance as the penitent Magdalene" (1955, 131–32). The production was discussed enthusiastically by the American and foreign press. The *New York Times* review noted, "Perhaps the most novel and striking feature of the performance was the stage management, which showed everywhere the traces of Mrs. Fiske's master intelligence. . . . To duplicate such scenic effects as these either on their mechanical or their artistic side, it would be necessary to go to Antoine's Paris or to the German repertory theatres" ("Mrs. Fiske in 'Mary,'" 1902, 9).

In 1904 Fiske and her husband formed the Manhattan Theatre Company, a permanent acting company, which continued until 1914, when Mr. Fiske declared bankruptcy. In 1906 the Fiskes stopped renting the Manhattan Theatre as other theatres became available under the management of the Shubert Brothers and David Belasco, who opposed the Theatrical Syndicate. That year Fiske appeared in and co-directed with her husband *The New York Idea*, by Langdon Mitchell. The elaborate production, which was a comedy about divorce, included Louis XV furniture and was staged with the invisible fourth wall. After successful tryouts in Chicago and St. Louis, the production opened on Broadway, where it became an instant success with critics and audiences. Acton Davies of the *Evening Sun* wrote, "It was almost a new Mrs. Fiske who, with her new play, swept into the Lyric [Theatre] last night and struck the target of success right in the bull's eye" (Binns 1955, 176).

After studying Ibsen's *Rosmersholm* for five years, Fiske performed in the play, which she co-directed with her husband in 1907. After a tryout in New Haven, Connecticut, the production was presented on Broadway to excellent reviews. The *New York Herald* noted, "If Ibsen had been interpreted in the past as Mrs. Fiske and her company interpreted him last evening there would be less discussion and more appreciation of the Norwegian's writings" (Binns 1955, 194). The *New York Times* complimented the ensemble acting and stated, "It is a magnificent ensemble[,] a worthy representation of a play that calls for the most intelligent skill in acting and stage management" ("Ibsen," 1908, 9).

The next year, Fiske performed in and co-directed with her husband *Salvation Nell,* by Edward Sheldon. The play, which focused on life in the slums, had its tryout in Providence, Rhode Island, before moving to Broadway. Although the critics were divided about the play and its unpleasant realism, which featured a minutely detailed set and people living in poverty who turned to religion as a solution, the play was a success with audiences. In a mixed review, the *New York Times* noted that the ensemble acting and attention to detail saved the production. The critic noted, "The occasion would be of little enough moment but for the brilliant acting of the principals, and the elaboration of detail with which the story is carried out. The third act set . . . showing a street on Cherry Hill, with tall tenements reaching into the flies, an extensive view of overladen fire escapes, and the varied street life of the section, excels anything that has been seen here since the remarkable street scene in Belasco's 'Du Barry'" ("Acting," 1908, 5). The production also brought public awareness about slum conditions and propelled some people to acts of charity, such as donating money to the poor (Binns 1955, 208–9). This may have pleased Fiske, who in a lecture to Harvard students in 1905 stated, "Art has a function beyond that of affording pleasure for the moment. It should be an inspiration, and it should be potent. . . . In some forms its influence works toward the alleviation of the world's misery" ("Mrs. Fiske Lectures," 1905, 9). When *Salvation Nell* toured in 1909, Fiske received a telegram from the Theatrical Syndicate offering the use of its theatres independently, ending her long struggle with the organization.

In 1910 Fiske performed in and co-directed with her husband *Pillars of Society,* by Ibsen. First presented in Rochester, New York, the play focused on the dealings of capitalists. Receiving positive reviews after opening on Broadway, Fiske's attempt to create an ensemble performance was noted in the *New York Times* review, which stated, "In producing the play, Mrs. Fiske cannot be charged with having chosen a work which would enable her to shine above her surroundings, and she is entitled to consideration for a self-repression which is very rare" ("Welcome," 1910, 9).

The next year Fiske was back on Broadway, where she performed in and co-directed with her husband *Mrs. Bumpstead-Leigh,* by Harry James Smith. Although the farce received mixed critical reviews, it was a hit with audiences.

Examining the subject of women's rights, *The High Road* by Edward Sheldon, premiered in Montreal in 1912 before moving to Chicago and Broadway in the same year. The play, which Fiske acted in and co-directed with her husband, was a critical success. In a letter to her husband that she wrote while on tour with the play, Fiske spoke of a trend away from expensive naturalistic settings. On January 22, 1914, she wrote, "I am beginning to feel certain that we are getting to the end of the day when scenery and properties will be so important as we have thought them in the past—and that will be a good thing . . . twice this season we have had to practically cut out the scenery and properties in our present play. . . . The absence of scenery and properties gave an added spur to the acting and they were never missed" (Binns 1955, 275).

After Harrison Fiske declared bankruptcy in 1914, Fiske worked under different theatrical management companies. Toward the end of her career, Fiske toured in revivals of her hits and appeared in other plays. She related her views on the theatre to critic Alexander Woollcott in a series of conversations, which were first published in *Century* magazine in 1917 and then collected into the book *Mrs. Fiske: Her Views on the Stage*. The book provides valuable insights into Fiske's acting and directing techniques.

Although a star performer throughout her career, Fiske was an accomplished director as well. Mr. Fiske explained how he and his wife divided the task of directing, saying, "Mrs. Fiske, so far as I know, is the only noted American actress who may truly be said to direct and supervise the plays in which she appears. . . . But my own work . . . has always been mainly concerned with the practical duties of preparing a play for the stage—with the arrangement of the scenery, the preparation of the prompt-book, the obtaining of the 'effects,' and similar details. Mrs. Fiske's work, on the contrary, has been essentially the psychological analysis and the rehearsal of the actors" ("An Actress," 1906, X2).

However, Fiske did not focus entirely on rehearsal of the performers. Letters to her husband show that she was very concerned with all details of the performance. In letters about *Pillars of Society,* she described in detail her vision for the set and the use of a cyclorama for special effects (Binns 1955, 223–24).

When selecting plays, Fiske was open to directing the work of unknown playwrights. She received many plays through agents and friends but also read unsolicited manuscripts. For example, *Salvation Nell* was written by a student of Professor George Piece Baker's Workshop at Harvard, and *Mrs. Bumpstead-Leigh* was written by an unknown playwright, also from Harvard. Part of the reason for Fiske's support of American writers was that the Theatrical Syndicate controlled much of the work of European authors. Fiske also avoided plays that she was not able to cast well, such as Arnold Bennett's *The Honeymoon.* Although she very much wanted to do the play, she was not able to find the right actor to play the part of the aviator (Fiske 1917, 31).

Fiske considered audiences when selecting her plays. She praised the New York City audience for its intelligence. She noted, "But let us remember that the greater the play, the more carefully must it be directed and acted, and that for every production in the theatre there is a psychologically *right* moment. Move wisely in these things, and the public will not fail" (Fiske 1917, 48). Although the audience was a consideration in her selection of plays, Fiske believed that performers should not acknowledge the audience, with the exception of technical adjustments, such as vocal projection. She said, "The actor must not admit the existence of the audience. At once this non-admission sets the actor free, and no man can work unless he is free. In refusing to admit the existence of the audience a great burden is lifted from the actor's shoulders. He is relieved of that awful and ignoble necessity of playing for effect" ("Mrs. Minnie," 1898, 14).

Fiske believed that the work of playwrights was to be treated as a work-in-progress, citing that scripts of established writers—including Shakespeare—were developed in rehearsal, with the final version appearing in the prompt-book. Although she believed that some writers, such as Ibsen, did not need alterations, she admitted to transposing two speeches in Ibsen's *Hedda Gabler* (Fiske 1917, 136). She also worked with living writers to modify scripts before and during rehearsal. For example, the Fiskes hired Stoddard to write *Tess of the D'Urbervilles,* and Fiske reviewed each act during the writing process, providing suggestions. In her work with foreign material, Fiske believed that a good director should know works from other lands but reinterpret them (Fiske 1917, 123).

Although the Fiskes had their own company for a time, they also cast independent performers in their productions. Fiske believed that it was impossible to cast perfectly with repertory. She also thought that using repertory to train actors was not fair to audiences or dramatic literature, explaining, "I do not know who started the precious notion that an actor needs half a dozen parts a season in order to develop his art. . . . If he has *one* rôle that amounts to anything, that has some substance and inspiration, he simply cannot exhaust its possibilities in less than a year. . . . Then suppose the director is incompetent. Directors usually are you know. And, under incompetent direction, is not your actor in the making better off if he need play only one part badly rather than six parts badly?" (1917, 37). Fiske also worried that performers in repertory learned tricks in order to juggle numerous roles. She said, "In all the theatre . . . there is nothing quite so deadly as this firmer and firmer touch on the wrong note" (38).

Casting for *Salvation Nell,* Fiske told Woollcott, "I cannot *begin* to tell you how many times Mr. Fiske and I virtually dismissed an entire company; how over and over again members of the cast were weeded out and others engaged; how over and over again we would start with an almost entirely new company, until every part . . . down to the very tiniest, was perfectly realized; how much there was of private rehearsal" (1917, 21–22). However, although Fiske easily replaced performers, she also cautioned against letting actors go too soon.

Fiske spent time understanding the play before rehearsing with the performers. She believed the director should try to find the spiritual essence of a scene and the meaning of the play, as well as having complete familiarity with the characters and their relationships to each other. She thought directors should convey this meaning to the actors at the first reading and that action should spring from the meaning (1917, 128). Fiske described the importance of meaning, noting, "[W]e do not stand up to rehearse at all until we have thoroughly understood and digested the play under discussion. We talk the play over and discuss the various characters. Each one of us helps the other. When we feel that we have grasped the various characters we begin to rehearse" ("Mrs. Minnie," 1898, 14).

The rehearsal process was the most interesting part of the production process to Fiske. She began rehearsals with an idea of what she wanted to do and rehearsed "eternally" ("Mrs. Fiske's Ambitions," 1901, SM4).

Fiske believed that performers needed technique for consistency in performance (1917, 79). She thought that with technique, a performer did not need to go through the tumultuous emotions of a character each night (100). An advocate of voice training as an important base for all aspects of performing, Fiske suggested that performers have three registers and practice at least one hour a day off season and three hours a day during the season (95–96). She proposed that actors create a history for their characters and research their parts by going into the streets (87). In her quest for realism, she warned actors, directors, producers, and writers to avoid becoming "theatricalized" (88).

Although she was a director, Fiske advised actors to ignore most directors because she thought most directors were unskilled. She believed that performers should be able to give their best performance no matter what the audience's size or temperament (1917, 90). Stating that audiences were not a good monitor of truth, Fiske looked down on directors who gauged their work on curtain calls or audience laughs (90, 93). She also noted that a director needed to make sure that the play took precedence over stars and an actor's vanity (137).

During rehearsals, Fiske directed performers not to rush and to have a motivation for everything that they did. While watching a rehearsal, one onlooker wrote, "Nothing is too small for the eye and the attention of Mrs. Fiske—whether it be a gesture of an actor, a detail in stage setting or lighting, a tone of voice, or a strain of music—and it is her watchful care and artistic sense that have made her company a model one to see" (Wilson 1966, 235). Fiske worked especially hard on parts of productions that she feared might be dull so that the audience would not be bored (Ormsbee 1938, 199).

An accomplished actress, Fiske helped each performer convey truth on stage (Fiske 1917, 158–59). She also thought that a director should be able to teach young performers, stating, "The principal function of the stage director is developing the actor. It would seem unduly autocratic to speak of training an actor, but one can at least remove obstacles and give him a fair chance for self-development" ("An Actress," 1906, X2). Woollcott described an incident in which Fiske worked with a performer, writing, "I remembered, too, how one onlooker at her apparently chaotic rehearsals had marveled at the results when Mrs. Fiske would lead a player off into the corner, sit down with him, talk to him for a while in phrases that he alone heard, but with indescribably eloquent gestures that fairly intrigued all eyes, and then send him back to the stage equipped, apparently, as he had never been before" (Fiske 1917, 125). In order for performers to be truthful, Fiske promoted the use of the invisible fourth wall. In 1898 she noted, "[O]ur company has been rehearsing between the four walls of a room instead of upon the stage of a theatre, and the good effect upon the actors is marked. Having rehearsed for a long time within these four walls, they almost forget when they come upon the stage that they are not there still" ("Mrs. Minnie," 1898, 14).

Although Fiske worked tirelessly on the other actors' performances, she didn't dwell very long on her own. She noted of her own parts, "I leave that until the last moment; I am so busy with the stage management" ("Mrs. Minnie," 1898, 14). A perfectionist, Fiske believed that her only flawless performance was the first production of *Salvation Nell* (Fiske 1917, 21).

Among Fiske's many awards are the League of Women Voters Award for one of the twelve greatest living American women in 1923, the Good Housekeeping Award for one of the twelve greatest living women in 1931, and honorary degrees from Smith College and the University of Wisconsin. She was also elected into the Theater Hall of Fame.

Fiske died in Hollis, New York, on February 15, 1932. Although Fiske has been remembered primarily for her naturalistic acting style, she was also a competent director. In the early 1900s, Walter Prichard Eaton of *Century* magazine wrote of Fiske, "[H]er combined talents of intellectual judgment in selecting plays, imaginative skill in stage management, and nervous intensity and spiritual insight in acting, make her, though she be a woman, the leader of the American stage to-day" (Binns 1955, 239).

Sources

"Acting Redeems Play of Sordid Life." 1908. Rev. of *Salvation Nell*, by Edward Sheldon. *New York Times*, 18 Nov., 5.

"An Actress Manager and her Ideas of Play Producing." 1906. *New York Times*, 25 Nov., X2.

Binns, Archie. 1955. In Collaboration with Olive Kooken. *Mrs. Fiske and the American Theatre*. New York: Crown.

Burns, Morris U. 1989. "Fiske, Minnie Maddern." In *Notable Women in the Ameri-*

can Theatre: A Biographical Dictionary, ed. Alice M. Robinson, Vera Mowry Roberts, and Milly S. Barranger, 282–86. Westport, Conn.: Greenwood.

Fiske, Minnie Maddern. 1917. *Mrs. Fiske: Her Views on the Stage*. Recorded by Alexander Woollcott. Rpt. New York: B. Blom, 1968.

"Ibsen Played by a Company of Artists." 1908. Rev. of *Rosmersholm*, by Henrik Ibsen. *New York Times*, 2 Jan., 9.

Knapp, Margaret M. 1996. "Fiske, Minnie Maddern." In *International Dictionary of Theatre—3: Actors, Directors and Designers*, ed. David Pickering, 280–83. New York: St. James.

"The Manhattan Theatre." 1901. Rev. of *Miranda of the Balcony*, by Anne Crawford Flexner. *New York Times*, 25 Sept., 8.

"Mrs. Fiske as Becky Sharp." 1899. Rev. of *Becky Sharp*, by Langdon Mitchell based on *Vanity Fair*, by William Makepeace Thackeray. *New York Times*, 5 Sept., 6.

"Mrs. Fiske as Rebecca Sharp at the Fifth Avenue Theatre." 1899. Rev. of *Becky Sharp*, by Langdon Mitchell based on *Vanity Fair*, by William Makepeace Thackeray. *New York Times*, 13 Sept., 7.

"Mrs. Fiske in 'Mary of Magdala.'" 1902. Rev. of *Mary of Magdala*, by Paul Heyse. *New York Times*, 20 Nov., 9.

"Mrs. Fiske Lectures for Harvard Students." 1905. *New York Times*, 13 Dec., 9.

"Mrs. Fiske's Ambitions." 1901. *New York Times*, Oct. 13, SM4.

"Mrs. Fiske's Return." 1902. Rev. of *Tess of the D'Urbervilles*, by Lorimer Stoddard, based on the book by Thomas Hardy. *New York Times*, 7 May, 8.

"Mrs. Minnie Maddern-Fiske." 1898. *New York Times*, 1 May, 14.

Ormsbee, Helen. 1938. *Backstage with Actors*. New York: Thomas Y. Crowell.

"Training Stage Mobs." 1902. *New York Times*, 14 Dec., 28.

Turner, Mary M. 1990. *Forgotten Leading Ladies of the American Theatre*. Jefferson, N.C.: McFarland.

"Welcome Mrs. Fiske at Lyceum Theatre." 1910. Rev. of *Pillars of Society*, by Henrik Ibsen. *New York Times*, 29 Mar., 9.

Wilson, Gariff B. 1966. *A History of American Acting*. Bloomington: Indiana University Press.

Representative Directing Credits[1]

Broadway:[2]

Tess of the D'Urbervilles (1897), *Becky Sharp* (co-directed with Fred Williams—1899, co-directed with Mr. Fiske—1911), *Miranda of the Balcony* (co-directed with Max Figman—1901), *The Unwelcome Mrs. Hatch* (co-directed with Max Figman—1901), *Mary of Magdala* (1902), *The New York Idea* (co-directed with Mr. Fiske—1906), *Rosmersholm* (co-directed with Mr. Fiske—1907), *Salvation Nell* (co-directed with Mr. Fiske—1908), *Pillars of So-*

ciety (co-directed with Mr. Fiske—1910), *Mrs. Bumpstead-Leigh* (co-directed with Mr. Fiske—1911), *The High Road* (co-directed with Mr. Fiske—1912)

Off and Off-Off Broadway:
Becky Sharp (co-directed with Fred Williams—1899, co-directed with Mr. Fiske?—1906), *Mrs. Bumpstead-Leigh* (co-directed with Mr. Fiske—1911)

Regional Theatre:
Hester Crewe (1893), *Becky Sharp* (co-directed with Fred Williams—1899, co-directed with Mr. Fiske—1910), *Mary of Magdala* (1902), *The New York Idea* (co-directed with Mr. Fiske—1906), *Rosmersholm* (co-directed with Mr. Fiske—1907), *Salvation Nell* (co-directed with Mr. Fiske—1908), *Pillars of Society* (co-directed with Mr. Fiske—1910), *Mrs. Bumpstead-Leigh* (co-directed with Mr. Fiske—1911 and 1914), *The High Road* (co-directed with Mr. Fiske—1912)

Tours:
Tess of the D'Urbervilles (1898), *Becky Sharp* (co-directed with Fred Williams—1900 and 1901), *Miranda of the Balcony* (co-directed with Max Figman—1902), *Mary of Magdala* (1903), *The New York Idea* (co-directed with Mr. Fiske—1907), *Rosmersholm* (co-directed with Mr. Fiske—1907), *Salvation Nell* (co-directed with Mr. Fiske—1909), *Pillars of Society* (co-directed with Mr. Fiske—1910), *Mrs. Bumpstead-Leigh* (co-directed with Mr. Fiske—1911), *The High Road* (co-directed with Mr. Fiske—1913 and 1914)

International Theatre:
Becky Sharp (co-directed with Fred Williams—1899), *Miranda of the Balcony* (1901?), *Rosmersholm* (co-directed with Mr. Fiske—1907), *Mrs. Bumpstead-Leigh* (co-directed with Mr. Fiske—1912), *The High Road* (co-directed with Mr. Fiske—1912)

Notes

1. Theatre programs of the period did not always list the directors of productions, so the listings here are most definitely an abbreviated listing of Fiske's directing credits. In some productions, Mr. Fiske received a directing credit at the beginning of the program, but additional credits at the end of the program listed Mr. and Mrs. Fiske as the directors. In these cases we have included both Mr. and Mrs. Fiske.

2. Many theatres that were designated as Broadway theatres at the turn of the twentieth century are not considered Broadway theatres today. Fiske's productions that occurred in those theatres are listed here under Broadway, as per the era.

Fornes, Maria Irene

Born on May 14, 1930, in Havana, Cuba, Maria Irene Fornes is an award-winning playwright and director, who has been presented with nine Obie Awards and numerous other grants and acclamations. She is one of the founders of the Off-Off Broadway movement and is known for her cinematic style and feminist sensibilities.

Fornes was educated mainly at home by her father. She discusses her education, explaining, "Both my parents had Bohemian inclinations—at a time when there was no such thing as Bohemian life in Havana. . . . They were never concerned about ordinary, everyday, normal things. My father was a bureaucrat, but he had no education. My mother had a degree in teaching. . . . My father was very much a thinker, philosophical. He kept a notebook in which he wrote maxims and his observations on life, on nature, on living, on the world. I learned very much from him. My whole education came from my mother and father" (Kelly 1990, A1).

In 1945, after her father's death, Fornes and part of her family moved to New York City. She began her career as a painter at the age of nineteen, studying with artist Hans Hoffmann in both New York City and Provincetown, Massachusetts. In 1954 she went to Europe to live and paint. In Paris, Fornes was greatly impressed by a production that she saw of Samuel Beckett's *Waiting for Godot*. She explains, "I didn't know a word of French. I had not read the play in English. But what was happening in front of me had a profound impact without my even understanding a word. Imagine a writer whose theatricality is so amazing that I could see a play of his, not understand one word, and be shook up. When I left that theater, I felt that my life was changed, that I was seeing everything with a different clarity" (Crespy 2003, 107).

Fornes returned to New York City in 1957 and roomed with writer Susan Sontag. The two encouraged each other to write, and Fornes wrote her first play in 1960—*Tango Palace*, an absurdist two-character play about a man who needs to make a decision. The play was first produced as *There! You Died* with San Francisco's Actor's Workshop at the Encore Theatre in 1963. The revised play, *Tango Palace*, was produced the following year at New York City's Actors Studio.

In 1964 Fornes joined the Actors Studio Playwrights Unit. She continued to write plays that were directed by others. Fornes also took acting and directing classes in New York City at the Gene Frankel Theatre Workshop, where she learned Lee Strasberg's Method technique. The Method influenced Fornes's writing and directing. She found that the Method equipped performers to work with both realistic and absurdist material (Interview, 1985, 236).

Dissatisfied with the way directors were staging her plays, Fornes began to direct her own productions. She explains, "I didn't know I had to direct my own work right away, but I did find out immediately that the position of the playwright is unbearable. . . . I learned as a playwright you 'behave.' You learn how to give up your play to people who 'know better.' . . . It is true that there is a technique to directing actors, but a playwright can learn to deal with that. In fact, I have always felt a liaison with the actors, because the lines have to go *through* the actor. . . . I have watched directors make wrong choices in rehearsal, and often the actors begin, instinctually, to say things as I thought I had written them" (Interview, 1987, 158–59).

Despite the usual approbation that playwrights shouldn't direct their own material, Fornes discusses her commitment to directing her own plays. She says, "People who say playwrights can't be objective about their own scripts seem to think playwrights have some sort of mental defect. . . . Who says directors are objective? Directors bring their own biases and beliefs to the work. I don't want to be objective. I want to be as blind as my passion would have me be" (Morrow and Pike 1986, 59–60). Fornes also insists on directing the first production of her plays. She explains, "I very seldom see productions of my work done by other people. I'm usually disappointed. I am a single creator. I'm not saying that every playwright should direct their plays, or that every play is ready for production" (Women's Project 1997, 45).

The first play that Fornes wrote and directed was *The Successful Life of 3,* which she also designed. Presented at the Firehouse Theatre in Minneapolis in 1965, Fornes was at first nervous with her role of telling others what to do. She continued to learn about directing by watching others, including Lawrence Kornfeld, who directed her play *Promenade* at the Judson Church in New York City the same year. A musical with songs by Al Carmines, the play told about two escaped convicts. Fornes explains how she learned from the experience, saying, "Watching people direct, I didn't know that I was learning how to direct. . . . The first time I directed after that I paid attention to the things that really make life on the stage interesting. I realized the importance of physical movement, changes in rhythm, tempo and time and allowing for things to happen even accidentally" (Interview, 1999, 263). Both *Promenade* and the Open Theatre's 1965 Off-Off Broadway production of *The Successful Life of 3* won Fornes two Obie Awards for Distinguished Play.

Fornes spent much time at the Open Theatre in addition to the Judson Church, a location of many avant-garde events during the 1960s. She says, "I became a Judson addict. I helped in whatever way I could. I made costumes or props for other works. . . . I was still a frequent visitor at the Open Theatre sessions and saw wonderful people who were working with techniques that involved them physically and mentally as well as emotionally. . . . The move to directing happened naturally" (Interview, 1999, 263).

In 1966 Fornes's play *The Office* was produced on Broadway with music by Robert Prince and direction by Jerome Robbins, but it closed after previews. This was the only time that one of her plays appeared on Broadway. Fornes discusses her commitment to non-commercial theatre, explaining, "I belong to the Off-Off-Broadway movement, which was the idea of doing art. And doing something that we loved doing. . . . We did theater because we needed to do it" (Interview, 1996, 113). She explains, "I don't miss popular success. I think popular success puts a kind of obligation on the artist. I think the longevity of an artist depends on always being willing, able, and unafraid to step into unknown territory. Success tends to make people afraid to try. Something inside you shrinks at the thought of doing bad work. When you are not famous and no one really cares much what you do, you are not afraid to fail" (Morrow and Pike 1986, 78).

In the late 1960s, Fornes began to direct her plays steadily in New York City, including *A Vietnamese Wedding* at Washington Square Methodist Church in 1967, *The Annunciation* at Judson Church in 1967, *Molly's Dream* at New Dramatists Committee in 1968, and *The Red Burning Light* at New Dramatists Committee in 1969.

Early on, Fornes developed a pattern of restaging her plays many times. For example, she directed her bilingual play *Cap-a-pie* first at New York City's INTAR (International Arts Relations) in 1975, and then again through INTAR at Lincoln Center Plaza in 1975, and once more at The Cloisters in 1976. Fornes explains, "The first time I direct a play, even a play I wrote, I'm just putting my feet in the water. The second time I direct it, the play begins to take shape, and the third time is when I feel that I know the play directorially" (Interview, 1996, 104). Each new space and cast provides different challenges for Fornes. She elaborates, "With a new cast, you have to find ways of working that are different because *they* are different. Then, of course, what I love is when there are moments in a play where I can do a little rewrite and improve something" (265).

Fornes first directed her play, *Fefu and Her Friends,* at the Relativity Media Lab in 1977. Presented by the New York Theater Strategy, the cinematic play—which Fornes calls a "fugue,"—revolved around the reunion of eight women planning a fundraiser. After the first scene, the audience split into four groups to witness the play's action in four different rooms—a new technique at the time. Fornes explains, "I chose to do it that way because we were looking for a place to do the play and we answered an ad for a performance place that was a loft with some partitions and a little office and a kitchen. And I had just finished the first scene, so I said, I'm going to do it here and use all these rooms. Because I thought it would be interesting" (Interview, 1996, 110).

The choice of space also affected how Fornes directed the play's performers. She explains, "[B]ecause of the closeness to the actors, the scenes had to take on a more filmlike quality, not a climax to the scenes, not an end. . . . I waited until I had sat there with them in the rooms to bring in the scenes, to adjust them to the intimacy of the place. The acting had to be brought down a lot. At that distance if the actors would act the way they acted on the stage, it would just seem histrionic" (Interview, 1996, 111). Fornes won an Obie Award for playwriting in 1977 for *Fefu and Her Friends*. The play was directed by Fornes again the next year at New York City's American Place Theatre. In his review of the 1978 production, Richard Eder of the *New York Times* wrote, "There are many . . . fine things in 'Fefu,' which Miss Fornes directs, generally well. . . . [A]lthough much of Miss Fornes's direction is skillful, it is uneven. . . . It is an imperfect evening, but there are moments of such splendor in it that it is like the imperfection of a friend" (1978, 10).

Fornes won her next Obie Award in 1979 for the direction of her play *Eyes on the Harem* at INTAR. The play was presented as a comedic vaudeville collage and examined the degeneration of the Turkish Ottomans. In his review of the production, Eder noted that Fornes directed the performers with "skill and imagination." He described the production, writing, "There is a kind of gallery, up beneath the flies, that is an elaborate red and gilt frieze of Turkish history and mythology. The players appear there from time to time, robed and sometimes fezzed, to read out chronicles about the Ottomans, or to sing, or for other mock-grandiloquent purposes. . . . The main stage below is Balkan modern" (1979, C17).

Fornes continued on her award-winning streak in 1984, when she won Obie Awards in both Playwriting and Direction for three of her plays: *The Danube, Sarita*, and *Mud*. Focusing on love and nuclear fallout, *The Danube* was first directed by Fornes in 1981 at New York City's Theater for the New City, and was restaged by Fornes in 1982 and 1983, and again in 1984 in the Obie Award-winning production at the American Place Theatre. *Sarita*, with music by Leon Odenz, focused on a single Hispanic mother and was presented in 1984 at INTAR.

The Obie Award-winning production of *Mud* was directed by Fornes at The Theater for the New City in 1983. First directed by Fornes earlier that year at Los Angeles's Padua Hills Festival, *Mud* revolved around the wife of a farmer and included staging with photographic freezes. Fornes explains her direction, saying, "I did the play in Padua Hills, outdoors, and I could not have blackouts because I had scheduled myself in daylight time. The freezes were a way to change scenes. I kept them in the New York production because there was something about the freezes that I liked. . . . The drab color also had to do with the original daylight production, which started when the sun was about to set and ended when the light became gray. The light changed during the performance, and the audiences always felt that it was deliberate because later in the play, everything becomes gray" (Interview, 1987, 161).

Fornes won another Obie Award for Best New American play with *The Conduct of Life*, which she directed at The Theater for the New City in 1985. Fornes's play, which examined dictatorship at home and in the government, grew out of her play, *No Time*, which Fornes had directed in 1984 at the Padua Hills Festival. In his review of *The Conduct of Life*, Herbert Mitgang of the *New York Times* wrote, "The drama is presented in a dozen or so vignettes, some lasting only a moment or two, that are punctuated by lighting that fades slowly and repetitively. . . . While the onstage proceedings in 'The Conduct of Life' are numbing, what Miss Fornes finally has to say does have a certain cumulative power as a feminist statement" (1985, C16).

In 1987 Fornes won yet another Obie Award for Best New American Play with *Abingdon Square*, which she directed at New York City's American Place Theatre in a production by the Women's Project. The play centered on a child bride in New York City during the time of World War I. In his review, Mel Gussow of the *New York Times* wrote, "Miss Fornes has directed the play in her signature impressionistic style. Episodes, some silent and as brief as blackouts, divided by bursts of music, are designed to accumulate into a group portrait of time, place and sensibility. Thematically and atmospherically, the work is intriguing, but even as Ms. Fornes's directorial attentiveness continues, the play itself becomes languid. . . . It is in her role as a director that Ms. Fornes has come closest to realizing her intention as a playwright" (1987, 16).

Fornes was a Pulitzer Prize finalist for her play *And What of the Night?*, an epic play that she directed at Milwaukee Repertory Theater in 1988. Early studies for this play—which was later called *What of the Night?*—included *The Mothers* and *Hunger*, which she directed at New York City's En Garde Arts Productions the same year.

After a productive decade in the 1990s, writing and directing plays, Fornes won a Special Citation Obie Award for her play *Letters from Cuba*, which she directed at New York City's Signature Theatre in 2000. The play included real letters that Fornes received throughout her life from Cuba. Bruce Weber of the *New York Times* wrote of Fornes's direction, "The play yields a rare organic sense that the production was conceived along with the script. . . . [W]ords may not be the playwright's most potent tool here. . . . [T]he eloquence of sheer movement provides the play's most moving scene, a dance, passed sequentially from character to character, to a slow 1940s swing tune" (2000, E1).

Fornes has translated and adapted plays, including Frederico García Lorca's *Blood Wedding*. With the exception of *Blood Wedding*, Fornes directs the plays that she translates. These include the INTAR productions of Pedro Calderon de la Barca's *Life Is a Dream* in 1981 and Virgilio Piñera's *Cold Air* in 1985. Fornes has also revised and directed translations of plays by other writers, including the 1987 productions of Ibsen's *Hedda Gabler* at the Milwaukee Repertory Theater and Anton Chekhov's *Uncle Vanya* at New York City's Classic Stage Company.

In addition to directing her own plays and translations, Fornes has directed plays by others. In 1990 she directed two plays at INTAR—Ana María Simo's *Exile* and Simo's *Going to New England*. That year she also directed Leo García's *Dogs* at Los Angeles's Ensemble Theatre and Cherríe Moraga's *Shadow of a Man* at San Francisco's Eureka Theatre Company. Additional plays directed by Fornes include Theater for the New City productions of Manuel Pereiras García's *It Is It Is Not* in 1993 and Caridad Svich's *Any Place But Here* in 1995.

Fornes writes her plays from a desire to investigate an issue. They are known for being nonlinear and abstract. Fornes believes her experience as a writer is helpful in directing the plays of others. In choosing plays by other writers to direct she looks for "something that is subtle, something that is usually missed" (Interview, 1994, 101). She does not want to add anything to the play, but rather, "not miss anything that is in the play. . . . The director should not manufacture something around the play" (102). She goes on to discuss how being a writer and director differ, explaining, "The writer has to concentrate inside himself, the director outside: on the actors, on the space, dealing with all the people" (103).

Rebecca Schull, who won an Obie Award for playing Fefu in Fornes's production of *Fefu and Her Friends,* notes that Fornes is a director who pays great attention to detail and enjoys stillness. She says, "She's not going to cast people who happen to be fussy" (Interview, 1997, 157). Schull also notes that Fornes will replace performers who do not seem right for the role, and states that she herself was hired to replace a previous actor (160).

Fornes recalls the process of auditioning performers for *Fefu and Her Friends,* stating, "When I was casting it was very clear to me when an actress entered the room whether she belonged in the world of Fefu. In the process of auditioning there were people who read for me who were extremely talented but I thought they would shatter the play" (1978, 222).

Casting sometimes affects the text of Fornes's plays. While writing *Mud,* an actor who had agreed to play the role of a father backed out. A younger actor agreed to do the role, and Fornes found herself changing the character of the father to that of a younger man to match the performer (Interview, 1996, 106–7).

Fornes often revises her plays during rehearsals, and may even revise them during previews and after a show opens (Interview, 2004). She says, "When I direct a play, the first time is usually a workshop, so I do a lot of revisions. And then if the play is going to be done again, or if the play is going to be published, I do more revisions. . . . No matter how much you plan it, when it's on its feet, you discover all sorts of new things. . . . When you write a play, you have the recipe, but you don't have the performance. And in rehearsal you notice how many details were left inconclusive" (Interview, 1996, 103). Fornes notes, "I am inspired by everything the actors do. I like the deadline pressure of four weeks of rehearsal. After the rehearsal I go home and write" (Morrow and Pike 1986, 53).

When directing a play written by another, Fornes may alter lines that she believes do not work. She explains, "[I]f the playwright is not around I'm convinced that they will be delighted that I changed it. If the playwright is around, I ask them if I can do it. Sometimes they explain why the line is there. In that case I will put the line back and suggest something to avoid the confusion that I myself felt. . . . I do take possession of a play when I direct it. I find it difficult not to feel as if I wrote the play" (Interview, 1999, 265).

To prepare for rehearsal, Fornes reads a play many times. She explains,

> The director . . . should read the play just to receive it, just to see what comes from the play to them. They should not start by saying, "I'm the director. I'm the boss. I'm going to do this. . . . How am I going to make this interesting?" They need to keep reading the play and if you do that, if the play is any good, the characters will pop out. . . . [T]hen you continue the process when rehearsals start with the actors. You select the acts, you read the play and when an actor reads a part you already begin to have a different sense of what the part is. . . . Then you can see what comes up from the actors and you can see how the lines activate the actor. Then you mould it or you change it if it's unacceptable. But don't start from the beginning with fixed ideas. That is even how I direct my own work. It's not that I have actors do improvisations, and I say "I'm going to use this and that." What I am choosing is something that's more subtle and less conscious on the part of the actor than what would come out in an improvisation, maybe things that are more personal. It could be something I see in the way the actor walks, or the way the actor sits and listens . . . All the time I'm taking from what the actors are providing. And I am also taking from the space. I would direct a play very differently if the space is different. . . ." (Interview, 1994, 103–4)

Fornes avoids imprinting a style on a play to create an artistic identity. She says, "I think an artist should not work on an artistic signature any more than a person would work on a personal style. If a style results from your effort, that's fine, but the moment you concern yourself with creating an image, you cease to concentrate on your work" (Interview, 1996, 100).

Open communication with the performers is important to Fornes in order to build cohesion with the cast. She explains, "When I direct, I never talk secretly to an actor. I feel that whatever I say to one actor has to be of benefit to the others. . . . [S]ecrecy is divisive. Not just divisive between one actor and another, but also in relation to the character. . . . The aim is to do a good product, to have a good show and if you have to do some sneaky tricky things then it's actually detrimental" (Interview, 1994, 98–99). Although she likes to keep things out in the open, Fornes will work with performers individually if she believes it may take up too much time for the other actors (101). She adds, "[T]heatre is an art and what is important is not that people have fun but that the final result is an art" (102).

Fornes can spend hours on small movement details. She states, "I'm very strict about blocking, but it has nothing to do with any preconceived idea. It's just that as I see the particular person moving as they do, I begin to get ideas from who they are and what they are doing" (Daniels 1996, 111). In addition to precise movement, Fornes values stillness. She explains, "I think directors and actors are afraid to be quiet on the stage, afraid to be boring, but to be quiet on the stage is as beautiful as it is in life" (Cole 1992, 36).

Fornes has collaborated often with specific artists including set designer Donald Eastman, lighting designer Anne Millitello, and costume designer Gabriel Berry. Fornes also believes her experience as a painter has helped her with stage composition and blocking. She notes, "The stage for me is a very beautiful place, nice to look at. And the space is very important. I'm very picky with actors. I will keep on positioning them—a little to the left, no, three inches more . . .—because for me, it's as important as focusing a camera" (Interview, 1987, 161).

Among Fornes's numerous grants and awards are an Obie Award for Sustained Achievement in 1982, an award from the American Academy and Institute of Arts and Letters in 1985, and a New York State Governor's Arts Award in 1990. She was also presented with a Distinguished Director's Award from the San Diego Critics Circle, an Award for Distinguished Achievement as an Artist and Educator from the Association for Theatre in Higher Education, and a Distinguished Artists Award from the National Endowment for the Arts. In 2005 she received the Theatre Communications Group Award for a theatre practitioner for extraordinary contributions to the field.

Fornes's plays have been published in periodicals, anthologies, and two volumes of her own plays. In addition to her awards, Fornes helped to found New York Theatre Strategy, a writer's cooperative in New York City, in 1972.

From 1973 to 1979 Fornes was managing director of the cooperative, which later became the Women's Theatre Council. Fornes also began teaching in 1978 at the Playwrights Workshop at INTAR, where she wrote and staged several plays.

Reflecting on her work, Fornes states, "What is beautiful about my art is the adventure of the work, not success, money, and people recognizing me on the street. When I enter the work, by myself or in a room with my colleagues, that is the supreme adventure—the adventure of putting the play on the stage and seeing if it works. That is the greatest riches one could want" (Morrow and Pike 1986, 78).

Sources[1]

Alvarez, Maria Elena. 1999. "Audience Drawn to 'Fefu.'" Rev. of *Fefu and Her Friends,* by Maria Irene Fornes. *Albuquerque Journal,* 23 June, B4.

Carter, David Payne. 1994. "Maria Irene Fornes." In *Theatrical Directors: A Biographical Dictionary,* ed. John W. Frick and Stephen M. Vallillo, 145–47. Westport, Conn.: Greenwood.

Chinoy, Helen Krich and Linda Walsh Jenkins, eds. 1987. *Women in American Theatre.* New York: Theatre Communications Group.

Cole, Susan Letzler. 1992. "Maria Irene Fornes Directs *Uncle Vanya* and *Abingdon Square.*" In *Directors in Rehearsal: A Hidden World,* 35–54. New York: Routledge.

Crespy, David A. 2003. *Off-Off Broadway Explosion: How Provocative Playwrights of the 1960s Ignited a New American Theater.* New York: Back Stage Books.

Daniels, Rebecca. 1996. *Women Stage Directors Speak: Exploring the Influence of Gender on Their Work.* Jefferson, N.C.: MacFarland.

Delgado, Maria M. and Caridad Svich, eds. 1999. *Conducting a Life: Reflections on the Theatre of Maria Irene Fornes.* Lyme, N.H.: Smith and Kraus.

Eder, Richard. 1978. "Fefu Takes Friends to American Place." Rev. of *Fefu and Her Friends,* by Maria Irene Fornes. *New York Times,* 14 Jan., 10.

———. 1979. "Stage: Intar Presents 'Eyes on the Harem'." Rev. of *Eyes on the Harem,* by Maria Irene Fornes. *New York Times,* 25 Apr., C17.

Fornes, Maria Irene. 1978. "Notes on Fefu." *SoHo Weekly News,* 12 Jan. In *The Theatre of Maria Irene Fornes,* ed. Marc Robinson, 221–23. Baltimore: Johns Hopkins University Press, 1999.

———. 1985. Interview with Scott Cummings. "Seeing with Clarity: The Visions of Maria Irene Fornes." *Theater* 17 (1). In *The Theatre of Maria Irene Fornes,* ed. Marc Robinson, 234–41. Baltimore: Johns Hopkins University Press, 1999.

———. 1986. Interview with David Savran. "Maria Irene Fornes." In *In Their Own Words: Contemporary American Playwrights,* by David Savran, 51–69. New York: Theatre Communications Group, 1988.

———. 1987. Interview with Kathleen Betsko and Rachel Koenig. "Maria Irene Fornes." In *Interviews with Contemporary Women Playwrights*, 154–67. New York: Beech Tree Books.

———. 1994. Interview with Rod Wooden. In *Contact With the Gods?: Directors Talk Theatre*, ed. Maria M. Delgado and Paul Heritage, 97–105. New York: Manchester University Press, 1996.

———. 1996. Interview with Una Chaudhuri. In *Speaking on Stage: Interviews with Contemporary American Playwrights*, ed. Philip Kolin and Colby H. Kullman, 98–114. Tuscollusa: University of Alabama Press.

———. 1999. Interview with Maria M. Delgado with Ron Wooden. In *Conducting a Life: Reflections on the Theatre of Maria Irene Fornes*, ed. Maria M. Delgado and Caridad Svich, 248–77. Lyme, N.H.: Smith and Kraus.

———. 2004. Interview with Leslie Katz. 2, Dec. University of Toronto, http://mariairenefornes.com/Academia/fornesinerview.html (accessed 17 Mar. 2006).

Gussow, Mel. 1987. "Stage: Fornes's 'Abingdon Square.'" Rev. of *Abingdon Square*, by Maria Irene Fornes. *New York Times*, 17 Oct., 16.

Karis, Carolyn. 1989. "Fornés, Maria Irene." In *Notable Women in American Theatre: A Biographical Dictionary*, ed. Alice M. Robinson, Vera Mowry Roberts, and Milly S. Barranger, 309–14. Westport, Conn.: Greenwood.

Kelly, Kevin. 1990. "Fornes Impresses, but . . ." *Boston Globe*, 7 Jan., A1.

Kent, Assunta Bartolomucci. 1996. *Maria Irene Fornes and Her Critics*. Westport, Conn.: Greenwood.

Maria Irene Fornes. http://www.mariairenefornes.com (accessed 22 Mar. 2004).

Mitgang, Herbert. 1985. "Stage: 'Conduct of Life.'" Rev. of *The Conduct of Life*, by Maria Irene Fornes. *New York Times*, 20 Mar., C16.

Morrow, Lee Ann and Frank Pike. 1986. "Playwrights." In *Creating Theater: The Professionals' Approach to New Plays*, 9–83. New York: Vintage Books.

Robinson, Marc, ed. 1999. *The Theatre of Maria Irene Fornes*. Baltimore: Johns Hopkins University Press.

Schull, Rebecca. 1997. Interview with Robert Coe. In *The Theatre of Maria Irene Fornes*, ed. Marc Robinson, 156–60. Baltimore: Johns Hopkins University Press, 1999.

Steele, Mike. 1986. "'Fefu' Given Insightful Production." Rev. of *Fefu and Her Friends*, by Maria Irene Fornes. *Minneapolis Star and Tribune*, 24 June, 01C.

Weber, Bruce. 2000. "Dancing in New York, Dreaming Still of Home." Rev. of *Letters from Cuba*, by Maria Irene Fornes. *New York Times*, 21 Feb., E1.

Women's Project & Productions. In Conjunction with the New School for Social Research. 1997. *Women in Theatre: Mapping the Sources of Power*. Conference journal, New York City, 7–8 Nov.

Representative Directing Credits

Off and Off-Off Broadway:

> *The Annunciation* (1967), *A Vietnamese Wedding* (1967), *Molly's Dream* (1968, 1973), *The Red Burning Light* (1969), *Dr Kheal* (co-directed with Michael Smith—1973, directed by Fornes—1974), *Tango Palace* (1973), *Aurora* (1974), *Cap-a-pie* (1975, 1976), *Washing* (1976), *Fefu and Her Friends* (1977, 1978), *Lolita in the Garden* (1977), *Eyes on the Harem* (1979), *Evelyn Brown (A Diary)* (1980), *Life Is a Dream* (1981), *A Visit* (1981), *The Danube* (1981, 1983, 1984), *Exile* (1982), *Mud* (1983), *Sarita* (1984), *Cold Air* (1985), *The Conduct of Life* (1985), *Lovers and Keepers* (1986), *A Matter of Faith* (1986), *Abingdon Square* (1987), *Uncle Vanya* (1987), *Hunger* (1988), *Going to New England* (1990), *Terra Incognita* (1991), *It Is It Is Not* (1993), *Any Place But Here* (1995), *The Summer in Gossensass* (1997, 1998), *Springtime* (from *What of the Night?*) (1997), *The Audition* (1998), *Letters from Cuba* (2000)

Regional Theatre:

> *The Successful Life of 3* (1965), *The Curse of Langston House* (1972), *In Service* (1978), *Fefu and Her Friends* (1979, 1986, 1987, 1990, 1999), *A Visit* (1981), *The Danube* (1982, 1984), *Mud* (1983, 1991), *No Time* (1984), *The Mothers* (1986), *Hedda Gabler* (1987), *Abingdon Square* (1988), *And What of the Night? (What of the Night?)* (1988, 1989), *Dogs* (1990), *Shadow of a Man* (1990), *Oscar and Bertha* (1991, 1992), *Drowning* (1992), *La plaza chica* (1992), *Enter the Night* (1993, 1994), *Ibsen and the Actress (A Study for The Summer in Gossensass)* (1995), *Letters from Cuba* (2000)

International Theatre:

> *Terra Incognita* (1992, 1997)

Notes

1. See Fornes's Web site for a comprehensive list of sources at http://www.mariaireinefornes.com.

Galban, Margarita

Born on October 27, 1936, in Havana, Cuba, Margarita Galban was knighted by King Juan Carlos of Spain for her contributions to Hispanic American theatre in the United States. Galban's multifaceted career includes work as a director, writer, and artistic director of Los Angeles's Bilingual Foundation of the Arts (BFA), where she has directed more than fifty productions in Spanish and English.

Galban first studied theatre and began her career as an actor in Cuba, where she performed on stage and in radio. In 1959 she moved to Mexico and became a member of El Teatro Popular de Mexico, winning awards for her acting. During this time, she also adapted plays for television. While in Mexico, Galban studied acting with a German director whom she remembered as Maestro Wagner (Interview, 2004). His ability to direct scenes that contained up to forty people onstage, while maintaining a focal point, impressed her.

In 1968 El Teatro Popular de Mexico traveled to the United States on tour. Attracted to Los Angeles, Galban decided to move there to "try something new" (Interview, 2004). Once settled in the United States, she pursued a career as a director in the United States because she felt that her Spanish accent prevented her from getting acting roles (Galban, interview, 2004). Galban was awarded a directing scholarship at Lee Strasberg Actors' Studio West, where she studied for six months. In 1969 she founded a Hollywood Spanish-language theatre company called Seis Actores, which included six actors. During this time, Galban directed pieces that she adapted from poems and stories of Frederico García Lorca, whom she cites as a great influence on her. Galban found Lorca's poetic style perfect for the kind of visual directing that she liked to do (Interview, 2004).

When Seis Actores disbanded after three years due to financial hardship, Galban was determined to continue her work in theatre. She convinced Carmen Zapata, an acclaimed actor who had appeared on Broadway, to begin another theatre group in Los Angeles with her. Joined by designer Estela Scarlata, the three women founded BFA in 1973. Galban took on the demanding role of artistic director, in addition to adapting and directing productions for BFA. At BFA, the three women aimed "to serve communities by presenting classic Spanish language drama and contemporary plays on Hispanic themes to English and Spanish speaking audiences, thereby bringing awareness of the Hispanic culture" (Bilingual 2004).

In its early years, BFA presented its productions in different Los Angeles theatres before establishing its permanent home in 1980. During the 1970s Galban directed numerous works by Hispanic and Hispanic American writers. Among these works were several plays by Lorca that Galban directed at Los Angeles's Inner City Cultural Center, including *La Casa de Bernarda Alba/The House of Bernarda Alba* in 1976, *Bodas de Sangre/Blood Wedding* in 1977 and 1979, and *Doña Rosita La Soltera/Doña Rosita the Spinster* in 1979.

Although most of Galban's work is based in Los Angeles because of the demands that she must fulfill as artistic director, she occasionally tours her productions or directs at other venues. According to Galban, her production of Rene Marquez's *Fanlights* at New York City's Lincoln Center in 1980 received excellent critical reviews (Interview, 2004). Most often Galban's productions tour to theatres in California.

Galban has received praise from critics for her visually rich productions, such as her direction at BFA in 1986 of Emilio Carballido's *Orinoco*. The play featured two Las Vegas showgirls, who find themselves on an abandoned steamer cruising through the jungle. Although *Los Angeles Times* critic Ray Loynd said Galban gave the play's two performers "too much rope," he called the play "a welcome West Coast premiere" and praised the play's ambience of "vague netherworld lighting, garish dresses, and a musical touch that winsomely underscores the mingling of illusion and reality" (1986, 16).

In 1988 Galban directed *Rosa de Dos Aromas/A Rose with Two Aromas*, another West Coast premiere with two women. Emilio Carballido's comedy, which had a long run in Mexico, focused on two women who find that the man they are visiting in jail is the husband of one and the lover of the other. In his positive review of the BFA production, Loynd wrote that the play was "tartly directed" by Galban (1988, 28).

Many of the productions that Galban directs feature women characters. In 1992 she directed Margaret Stocker's translation of Miguel Sabido's *La Falsa Cronica de Juana La Loca/Juana, Mad Queen of Spain: A False Chronicle* at BFA. The play focuses on Queen Isabel's daughter, who was declared mad by her father and son to further their own ambitions. T.H. McCulloh of the *Los Angeles Times* wrote that the play provided only a "glimpse" of Juana, but that it was "lovely to look at, and staged with imagination and fire by Margarita Galban" (1992, 23).

In addition to Lorca, another inspiration to Galban is the seventeenth-century Mexican nun, Sor Juana Inés de la Cruz. Galban admires Cruz's knowledge and perseverance in the arts during a time when women had few rights. In 1997 Galban directed the BFA production of Cruz's *Los Empeños de una Casa/Misfortunes of a Household*. The romantic farce, written in 1683, revolved around a brother, sister, and four others in a love entanglement.

Among the productions that Galban directed in 1998 for BFA's twenty-fifth anniversary season was Jose Zorrilla's 1844 verse drama *Don Juan Tenorío*, translated by Margarita Stocker. The play, which enjoys popularity in many Spanish-speaking countries, portrays Don Juan being saved by a woman, Doña Inés, and God. In his mixed review, Daryl H. Miller of the *Los Angeles Times* praised Galban's direction for "moments of lyrical beauty." He described Galban's direction, writing, "In a scene as beautiful as it is horrifying, he [Don Juan] caresses and sweet talks a dazzled Dona Ines while removing her white novice's wimple—arrogantly stealing her from God." Miller also described the memorable ending, in which Don Juan "baptized himself in tears during his salvation scene, bringing the story to an emotional resolution" (1998, 23).

Galban incorporates dance and music into many of her BFA productions. A good example of this is one of Galban's most frequently staged productions, Lorca's *Bodas de Sangre/Blood Wedding*, which she directed at BFA in 1977, 1979, 1984, and 1999. The play is based on the story of a bride who leaves her groom on her wedding day for a former lover. In addition to music and flamenco dance, Galban included a climactic knife fight between the groom and his rival, which originally occurred offstage in Lorca's play. In his review of the 1999 production, Michael Phillips of the *Los Angeles Times* wrote that a friend of Lorca described his work as a "sort of flamenco dramatism" and noted that Galban's staging "dives straight into that world" (1999, 28).

In 2002 Galban directed Pedro Calderon de la Barca's *El Alcade de Zalamea/The Mayor of Zalamea*, a story about a woman whose life is left in ruins by an army captain. The BFA production, adapted by Galban and Lina Montalvo, included live folk music and street vendors who greeted the arriving audience. Kathleen Foley of the *Los Angeles Times* wrote that the heroine's "subsequent rape and its aftermath are portrayed with brutal veracity in Galban's flawed but passionate staging" (2002, F20). Galban discussed portraying violence on stage, explaining that she shows it "with a certain elegance" because of the close proximity of the audience (Interview, 2004).

In addition to plays, Galban has staged musical productions. In 2003 Galban directed a revue of works by the Mexican composer Augustin Lara, who wrote about 600 songs and combined Mexican folk music with other Western musical genres. *Solamente una vez/You Belong to My Heart*, which Galban created with Montalvo, presented songs in Spanish in both the BFA Spanish and English productions. Miller described the revue, writing, "Gorgeously staged and thrillingly sung, this Bilingual Foundation of the Arts presentation is playing to packed, enthusiastic houses. . . . Here, the much-married songwriter-singer is surrounded by the women who inspired songs that sometimes soared with rapture, sometimes plunged into melancholy. . . . But these songs transcend words, and in Galban's artful staging . . . there is always something to delight the eye" (2003, E35).

In 2005 Galban staged the work of another one of her favorite authors, Miguel de Cervantes. An adaptation of *Don Quijote de la Mancha* by Galban and Montalvo was staged at BFA for the four-hundredth anniversary of the book's publication. First presented at the Los Angeles Theater Center in 2000, the production, called *Don Quijote: La Ultima Aventura/Don Quijote: The Last Adventure,* included a spectacular duel.

A huge achievement for Galban was the world premiere of her opera *Lorca, Child of the Moon,* which she directed at the University of California at Los Angeles in 2005. The opera, which included music by Ian Krouse and libretto by Galban, traced Lorca's life through four of his major works: *Blood Wedding, The Shoemaker's Prodigious Wife, Yerma,* and *Romancero Gitano (Gypsy Ballads).* Combining opera and flamenco singers, the production integrated different genres of music, dance, and theatre in its non-narrative presentation.

As a director Galban tries to remain faithful to the writer's vision, although she says that she must take certain liberties in order to adapt a work to the stage. She explains, "For example, if [the writer] describes the color of the leaves and the beautiful color of a flower, you can't do that. You need to say it if it's so important. If it's not important, forget it. It's out. Because in theater, you need to go ahead. You need to continue the action. You can't stop it to achieve the point that you want to say" (Interview, 2004).

A challenge for Galban is cutting the works down to size for the audience. For the 1992 BFA production of *La Celestina/The Spanish Bard,* Galban cut Fernando de Rojas's seven-hour romantic tragedy with comic elements down to two hours (Doherty 1992, 24). Galban says that if the first act is too long, "people don't come back to the second act" (Interview, 2004). Galban considers the audience when she adapts and directs a production. She explains, "You can't do anything if you don't entertain the audience. You don't make your point if people begin to look at the ceiling or another place" (Interview, 2004).

Because most performances at BFA alternate weekly in Spanish and English, Galban tries to cast performers who can speak both languages. At times different performers must be hired to play the same part in different languages. Galban discusses the difficulty of finding bilingual performers, noting, "When a person speaks very good English, they don't speak very good Spanish, and vice versa. . . . A few actresses can speak both languages without an accent . . . but the majority have an accent in one language or the other, or sometimes in both! It's not easy!" (Interview, 2004).

Rehearsals usually last for three weeks in Spanish and three weeks in English. Before beginning rehearsals, Galban likes to make sure that her adaptations are very close to complete. It takes her anywhere from four weeks to a year to create an adaptation for the stage, although she is willing to change the script during rehearsals if something is not working. About two weeks before rehearsals begin, she sends the script to the performers. At rehearsals the performers read the script, and when they are ready to begin moving, Galban encourages them to combine their characters' mental processes with the physical. From there she provides specific direction to the actors, taking into consideration each performer's suggestions.

One problem that Galban has as a director is communicating with performers who speak only English, since her native language is Spanish. Sometimes she uses a translator, but usually she is able to communicate with her performers through words and gestures. Galban believes that her experience as a performer has helped her as a director. She says, "I have a very profound respect for the actors. And I go with the actors—whatever they need or they feel. Of course, if they go the wrong way, I stop. . . . Sometimes I forget the production because my focus is the actors; it's on the acting. And sometimes [I think], 'My God, what happened with the production!'" (Interview, 2004).

Galban describes her stage direction as cinematic. She explains that in order to capture the audience's attention, "We need to adjust sometimes in theatre. . . . The audience is oriented to TV and movies" (Interview, 2004). Instead of allowing characters to discuss action that is occurring off stage, Galban prefers to show the action on stage, making her productions visually exciting. She states, "You don't narrate it. You see it. . . . You see the violence. You see everything. Because people in the audience . . . want to see it. They don't want to hear anymore" (Interview, 2004).

In addition to being knighted by King Juan Carlos of Spain, Galban received the Cross of Isabel La Catolica for her contribution to the promotion and development of Hispanic American theatre in the United States. She has also received many Back Stage West/Drama-Logue awards for direction, and has been honored by the California Hispanic Recognition Council for her contribution to the performing arts in California. She was presented with the Vesta Award from the *L.A. Weekly* for her contributions to Hispanic theatre in the United States, and has been awarded grants from the National Endowment for the Arts. In addition to her work in theatre, Galban has written and directed for television.

Galban says that her last production is always her most significant. She explains, "I try to be better every time—to go one step past it. . . . Be a little better, discover more important moments in theatre, and of course, entertain the audience" (Interview, 2004).

Sources

Bilingual Foundation of the Arts. 2004. "Mission of BFA." http://www.bfatheatre
.org/newsite/mission.htm (accessed 13 July 2004).

Burke, Anne. 2005. "UCLA to Stage World Premiere Opera." *UCLA Today,* 23
Feb. http://www.today.ucla.edu/2005/050223campus_uclatostage.html (accessed 17 Mar. 2006).

Curiel, Tony. 1994. "Margarita Galban." In *Theatrical Directors: A Biographical Dictionary,* ed. John W. Frick and Stephen M. Vallillo, 150–51. Westport,
Conn.: Greenwood.

Doherty, Jake. 1992. "It's a Classic Spanish Play—As You Like It." Preview of
La Celestina/The Spanish Bard, by Fernando de Rojas. *Los Angeles Times,*
20 Sept., 24.

Foley, Kathleen F. 2002. "Changing Mores on View in a Spanish Classic." Rev.
of *El Alcalde de Zalamea/The Mayor of Zalamea,* by Pedreo Calderon de la
Barca. *Los Angeles Times,* 4 Oct., F20.

Galban, Margarita. 2004. Telephone interview with Wendy Vierow. 13 July.

Loynd, Ray. 1986. "'Orinoco': Mysterious Journey Down a River." Rev. of *Orinoco,* by Emilio Carballido, and other plays. *Los Angeles Times,* 17 Oct.,
16.

———. 1988. "'Rose With Two Aromas' at Bilingual Foundation/'Lemming' at
Powerhouse/'Much Ado' at 21st St./'Two Over Easy' at Off Ramp." Rev. of
Rosa de Dos Aromas/Rose with Two Aromas, by Emilio Carballido, and other
plays. *Los Angeles Times,* 4 Mar., 28.

McCulloh, T.H. 1992. "'At Home' Argument Is Highlight of 'Three Acts.'" Rev.
of *La Falsa Cronica de Juana La Loca/Juana, Mad Queen of Spain: A False
Chronicle,* by Miguel Sabido, and other plays. *Los Angeles Times,* 28 Feb.,
23.

Miller, Daryl H. 1998. "Don Juan Thrives on Bilingual Compassion." Rev. of *Don
Juan, Tenorío,* by Jose Zorrill. *Los Angeles Times,* 9 Oct., 23.

———. 2003. "With a Song in His Heart: the Lara Sage." Rev. of *Solamente una
vez/You Belong to My Heart,* by Margarita Galban and Lina Montalvo. *Los
Angeles Times,* 24 Oct., E35.

Phillips, Michael. 1999. "Emotions Course Through Bilingual's 'Blood Wedding.'"
Rev. of *Bodas de Sangre/Blood Wedding,* by Frederico Garciá Lorca. *Los
Angeles Times,* 7 Oct., 28.

Representative Directing Credits

Off and Off-Off Broadway:
Fanlights (1980), *La Zapatera Prodigiosa/The Shoemaker's Prodigious Wife*
(1986)

Regional Theater:
Los Signos del Zodiaco (1973), *El Quelite* (1974), *Cada Quien Su Vida* (1975),

La Palangana (1975), *Aqui Tambien Moja La Lluvia* (1975), *Monserrat* (1975), *Rosalba y Los Llaveros/Rosalba and the Llaveros Family* (1976, 1983, 2000), *Uprooted* (1976, 1977, 1978), *La Casa de Bernarda Alba/The House of Bernarda Alba* (1976, 1982, 1997), *La Factoria* (1977), *Bodas de Sangre/Blood Wedding* (1977, 1979, 1984, 1999), *Wanted: Experienced Operators* (1978), *Doña Rosita La Soltera/Doña Rosita the Spinster* (1979, 1980, 1990), *Fanlights* (1980), *Las Many Muertes of Danny Rosales* (1980), *El Lugar Donde Mueren los Mamiferos/The Place Where Mammals Die* (1980), *Martinez* (1981), *Yerma* (1981, 1994, 2006), *Fuenteovejuna* (1982), *I Gave You a Calendar* (1983), *Okapi* (1983), *The Company Forgives a Moment of Madness* (1983), *El Cepillo de Dientes* (1983), *Do Not Negotiate Mr. President* (1983), *Maria Cristina Me Quiere Gobernar* (1983, 1984), *Equinox* (1984), *El Juego/The Game* (1984), *The M.C.* (1985), *La Zapatera Prodigiosa/The Shoemaker's Prodigious Wife* (1986), *La Muerte de Rosendo/The Death of Rosendo* (1986), *Orinoco* (1986), *Lorca, Child of the Moon* (1985, 1987, 1991, 2005), *Rosa de Dos Aromas/Rose with Two Aromas* (1988), *Mariana Pineda* (1988), *Nuestra Señora de la Tortilla/Our Lady of the Tortilla* (1989, 1998), *Dicen que la Distancia es el Olvido/A Cry of the Distance* (1989), *Cupo Limitado/Limited Capacity* (1990), *La Nona/The Granny* (1990), *Made in Lanus* (1991), *Los de Abajo/The Underdogs* (1991), *La Falsa Cronica de Juana La Loca/Juana, Mad Queen of Spain: A False Chronicle* (1992), *Contrabando* (1993), *Fuenteovejuna* (1993), *La Cruz en el Espejo/The Cross in the Mirror* (1994), *Entre Villa y Una Mujer Desnuda/Panco Villa and the Naked Lady* (1994), *Comenzando al Final/Beginning at the End* (1995), *Pedro Paramos y El Llano en Llamas/Journey to Comala* (1995), *El Huevo del Gallo/The Rooster and the Egg* (1996), *La Casa de Los Espiritus/The House of the Spirits* (1996), *Los Empeños de una Casa/Misfortunes of a Household* (1997, 2005), adaptation of *Too Many Tamales* (1997), *Desfile de Extrañas Figuras/Parade of Strange Images* (1998), *Lorca* (1998), *Don Juan Tenorío* (1998), *Guantanamera* (1999), *Don Quijote: La Ultima Aventura/Don Quixote: The Last Adventure* (2000, 2005), *Las Papas Papales/Praying with the Enemy* (2001), *Salón México* (2001), *Lorca y las Mujeres/Lorcas' Women* (2002), *El Alcalde de Zalamea/The Mayor of Zalamea* (2002), *Mar Nuestro* (2003), *Los Clásicos . . . Enredos/The Comedy of Intrigue* (2003), *En Concierto Introducción a La Zarzuela* (2003), *Solamente una vez/You Belong to My Heart* (2003), *Un Dia en la Alameda/A Day in the Alameda* (2006), *Maria La O* (2007)

Tours:
Uprooted (1979, 1980, 1983), *Wanted Experienced Operators* (1979), *Bodas de Sangre/Blood Wedding* (1985), *Orinoco* (1987)

International Theatre:
El Juego/The Game (1984), *La Falsa Cronica de Juana La Loca/Juana, Mad Queen of Spain: A False Chronicle* (1992)

Hunter, Mary

Born December 4, 1904, in Bakersfield, California, Mary Charlotte Hunter became one of the few women to direct multiple productions on Broadway in the first half of the twentieth century. In addition, she was critical in establishing the Society of Stage Directors and Choreographers (SSDC), in part due to her own battles in the courts with contract disputes.

Hunter spent her childhood in Hollywood, where she met lifelong friend Agnes de Mille at the Hollywood School for Girls. After graduating high school and working for William de Mille at Lasky Studios, she enrolled at Wellesley College in 1922 to study art history and anthropology. Due to poor health, she quit her studies at Wellesley and moved to be with an aunt in New Mexico, where she directed *Los Moros y Los Cristianos* for the Santa Fe fiesta in 1927. When she enrolled at the University of Chicago in 1928, her interest in theatre and radio flourished, and she pursued her extracurricular interests rather than finish her degree. While in Chicago she directed for a small poet's theatre, called the Cube Theatre, and later worked for radio station WGN, which in turn lead to her performance on the radio show "Easy Aces." When the show moved to New York City in 1933 to broadcast with CBS, Hunter relocated and studied acting with several former members of the Moscow Art Theatre: Maria Ouspenskaya, Tamara Daykarhanova, Vera Soloviova, and Andrius Jilinsky. Hunter studied both Stanislavski's and Michael Chekhov's methods of acting, eventually teaching at Daykahanova's School for the Stage from 1936 to 1939 while maintaining her radio career.

When Hunter moved to New York City she intended to improve her directing skills. Scholar Tamara Compton wrote, "She knew what she wanted from her performers, but not how to achieve it" (1992, 113). Hunter's immersion in Daykahanova's school strengthened her ability to coach actors and eventually led to opportunities to direct. Hunter and Jilinsky both helped teach the Daykahanova School's summer workshops for the third-year class, which they morphed into the American Actors Company (A.A.C.) in 1938. Hunter's first solo directing credit for A.A.C. in 1938, *The Trojan Women,* met with fairly poor reviews, but her primary focus at that time was on helping the company grow as a collective, experimental theatre group.

Hunter's subsequent productions were received with mixed appraisals from critics. In 1941 she directed both *Texas Town* and *American Legend* for A.A.C. *Texas Town,* company member Horton Foote's first full-length play, was a character study in which the inhabitants of a small town tell their life stories in the town drugstore. Reviews were mainly favorable. *New York Times* critic Brooks Atkinson was pleased with the progress the company made in three years, writing that they had performed the "feat of magic" of making a New York City audience feel it was in a small Texas town. *Billboard's* Eugene Burr was less enthusiastic, declaring the directing "strangely uneven" (Compton 1992, 132). For her second production that year, Hunter integrated several one-acts from A.A.C.'s workshops with dances from de Mille's company to form a musical theatre pastiche called *American Legend*. Reviews were mixed, but the project ignited Hunter's desire to work across disciplines, integrating dance into theatre and American folklore, a format to which she would return in a few years.

In 1942 Hunter directed Foote's next play, *Out of My House,* but it was his subsequent piece, *Only the Heart,* which eventually led to her Broadway debut in 1944. *Only the Heart* was set in a small Texas town and revolved around Mamie, the matriarch of a dysfunctional family. The reviewers of the 1942 production found the tragic downfall of Mamie and her family over-emotional and tedious, and Hunter's direction of the actors received mixed reviews. The play only ran one week at the Provincetown Playhouse in New York City. When it opened two years later on Broadway in 1944, it was with a reworked script. Despite the rewrites, the Broadway production earned mixed to poor reviews, although the critic for the *New York World Telegraph* called Hunter's directing "flawless" (Compton 1992, 143). Due to financial losses, A.A.C. closed its doors in 1944, but Hunter's opportunities to direct were beginning rather than ending.

Her second attempt to direct on Broadway gave Hunter the opportunity to work with Katherine Dunham, who choreographed and starred in *Carib Song* in 1945. Billed as a musical play of the West Indies, William Archibald's script revolved around the story of a newlywed woman who was seduced and impregnated by the village fisherman. The script was written in a heavy dialect, and critics found it difficult to understand, pointing to Hunter's problem of directing dancers with little or no actor training.

Hunter's early work on Broadway lead to her most contentious job: directing a new musical, which became the acclaimed hit *High Button Shoes* under a different director. Despite a contrived, sentimental script, *High Button Shoes* proved that charm, slapstick, and solid performances could win audiences in the Broadway season of 1947–48. It ran for 727 performances and garnered the producers a substantial profit (Laufe 1977, 106–10). But the same producers who hired Hunter as a director replaced her without notice. *Theatre Arts* magazine reported, "For some weeks she conferred with the authors, composer, and choreographer, till suddenly, two weeks before rehearsals were to start, she was dismissed by the producers and replaced by George Abbott; they told her they needed money, and, with Abbott's name, could get it" (Moor 1949, 54).

Hunter promptly filed a grievance against producers Monty Proser and Joseph Kipnis for breach of contract, and the producers argued that they fired Hunter for incompetence. To combat the charge, the American Arbitration Association heard testimony in Hunter's favor from theatre artists such as director John O'Shaughnessy, playwright Lynn Riggs, and choreographer Jerome Robbins. Jo Mielziner, scenic and lighting designer for *Carib Song*, testified that Hunter was "one of three or four people in the profession who understood all the elements that go into a musical show" (Moor 1949, 54). In a wry twist of fate, Hunter's production of Jean-Paul Sartre's *The Respectful Prostitute* opened during the arbitration and earned Hunter enthusiastic reviews. Atkinson enthused, "Under Mary Hunter's incisive direction, it played with the cutting stroke of a knife. . . . [T]hey [the actors] play it with style and precision" (Zolotow 1948, 27). The arbiters awarded Hunter the money she requested, but the producers took the ruling to higher courts, all of which upheld Hunter's claim. Finally, in June of 1949, the New York Supreme Court ruled in Hunter's favor, awarding her $40,000, an unprecedented win for a director at a time when no union was in existence.

Hunter's reputation as a director and her critical acclaim were boosted by her next production, *Ballet Ballads*. Returning to her love of blending American folklore, music, and dance, Hunter directed the production for the Experimental Theatre in New York City in 1948. An instant success, it transferred to the Music Box Theatre on Broadway. *Ballet Ballads*, by John Latouche and Jerome Moross, presented three separate stories in three distinct musical styles: revival hymns, jazz-blues, and folk. Hunter worked with three choreographers to stage each section of the piece. Critics were especially thrilled with the flawless integration of song, dance, and American folklore. Several compared it to *Oklahoma!*, with Walter Terry of the *New York Herald Tribune* asserting that Hunter's production of *Ballet Ballads* surpassed *Oklahoma!* in terms of "arriving at the desired integration of drama, song, and dance" (1948, 14).

Hunter continued directing musicals, both on Broadway and in Dallas, where she spent two summer seasons as the first woman director at the State Fair Casino, directing musicals and operettas. She left the State Fair Casino after two seasons "because she found the routine and the long planning time tedious" (Compton 1992, 182). The critic from the *Dallas Morning News* lamented her departure, writing, "Mary Hunter's stages were never static. . . . This is to thank Miss Hunter again and again for her contribution" (Rosenfield 1952, sec. 3, 4).

Returning to New York City, Hunter revisited her interest in combining folklore, Americana, and musical theatre. Utilizing material from *American Legend,* she co-created and directed a folk-musical entitled *Musical Americana,* which opened in New York City in 1953. The musical did well in a post-war era that cherished American sentiment. It toured for two years, with additional performances the third year. In 1954 she served as assistant director to Jerome Robbins for Broadway's *Peter Pan.* The following year she married Herman Wolf, who had three children, and Hunter retired from directing to help raise a family.

Hunter's collaborators remember her ability to work with young or inexperienced actors, for she often cast from a limited pool. At A.A.C. she cast from a group of actors still honing their skills. In other situations, such as the Broadway production of *Only the Heart,* she was forced to work with a lead that the producers and financial backers chose, an actress Hunter felt "would be unable to portray the subtleties of the role" (Compton 1992, 141). In her productions of folktale-dance pieces, such as *American Legend* and *Carib Song,* Hunter had to cast from the dance companies with whom she collaborated, teaching dancers to act and use unfamiliar dialects. In addition, Hunter sometimes chose inexperienced actors of her own accord, as she did in *The Respectful Prostitute.* Rather than casting a seasoned actor in the lead, Hunter chose a *Vogue* model whose look and demeanor she deemed right for the role. Judging from her reviews, her instincts were correct.

Those who worked with Hunter describe her leadership style as openly collaborative. She is remembered as a nurturing director with an acute ability to spot and encourage latent talent (Compton 1992, 129–30). Actors recall her relaxed atmosphere in the rehearsal hall as well: "She never tells you how to read a line, unless it's a last resort. She's always quiet, always kind, and her sort of direction gets you to loosen up and bring into play any creative imagination of your own that would make the character real. It's *in*direction, really" (Moor 1949, 53). Collaborators, including the many new playwrights she worked with, applauded her understanding of their goals. Hunter's comments about her own work confirm this: "I don't try for any 'style' or trademark of my own. I think that ought to be in accord with the script," she stated (54).

Part of Hunter's legacy is her contribution to the evolving state of musical theatre. As a director, she was proactive in coaxing performers to work across disciplines. As one journalist commented, "She has always been persuading singers and dancers to learn acting and actors to learn to sing and dance" (Pollock 1950, 22). Katherine Dunham recalls her unusual approach to rehearsals for *Carib Song,* asking all performers to meet together daily in order to incorporate music, dance, and acting rather than holding separate rehearsals, as was common at the time (Compton 1992, 163). Her passion and achievement as a director of musical theatre is evident in the publication of an article she wrote for *Theatre Arts* magazine in 1950, in which she discusses needed reforms, including the decentralization of production, encouraging theatre outside of New York City. Her goal to reach a wider audience was clear in her argument for lower prices and in her closing lines of the article: "The audience is there. It is up to us to reach it" (1950, 52).

In addition to her stage work, Hunter is one of the few women directors of this period to work across several types of media: radio, stage, and the newest innovation of the time, television. In a 1949 article for *Theatre Arts* she shared her views on how stage directing aided television directing. Hunter chastised television directors for focusing their attention on camera work rather than the actor's motivations, writing, "His [the director's] basic job in the theatre is to plan and evoke in the actor a sustained, truthful flow of actions with their resultant feelings that express the author's intention. He adjusts the production elements to support and emphasize that end" (1949, 47).

In addition to her contributions to stage and early television, Hunter was a noted educator. She co-founded the American Theatre Wing Professional Training Program, which trained students across all the performing arts. After her marriage to Wolf, she helped her local community of Hartford, Connecticut, by instituting The Center for Theatre Techniques in Education in 1970. She applied her Stanislavski-based training to help prepare schoolteachers in the areas of concentration, teamwork, imagination, and sensory awareness ("Profiles," 1987, 60). She also served as the Center's president.

No doubt her high-profile struggle of a Broadway contract dispute, without the help of a union, supported Hunter's belief in the need for union representation. At friend and collaborator Agnes de Mille's request, Hunter helped found the Society for Stage Directors and Choreographers and took early leadership roles. She served as the union's executive vice president from 1967 to 1976, during which time she "oversaw membership changes and by-law modifications, participated in arbitration hearings, developed guidelines for various projects, and led picket lines" (Compton 1992, 246). Hunter became a member of the executive board in 1976 and was elected to the honorary advisory committee in 1980.

Mary Hunter died Nov. 3, 2000, in Hamden, Connecticut.

Sources

Atkinson, Brooks. 1948. Rev. of *The Respectful Prostitute,* by Jean-Paul Sartre. *New York Times,* 10 Feb., 27.

Compton, Tamara L. 1992. "Mary Hunter Wolf—Director, Producer, Educator." Ph.D. diss., University of Nebraska.

Hunter, Mary. 1949. "The Stage Director in Television." *Theatre Arts* 33 (May): 46–47.

———. 1950. "Backtalk from a Director." *Theatre Arts* 34 (Nov.): 50–52.

Laufe, Abe. 1977. *Broadway's Greatest Musicals*. New York: Funk & Wagnalls.

Moor, Paul. 1949. "Lady on Her Way." *Theatre Arts* 33 (Jan.): 53–54.

Pollock, Arthur. 1950. "Theatre Time: Mary Hunter Stages Musical, and About Time." *Daily Compass,* 13 Feb., 22.

"Profiles and Perspectives: Mary Hunter Wolf." 1987. *Roper Review* 10 (Sept.): 60–61.

Rosenfield, John. 1950. "The Passing Show: Casino Gets a Mama." *Dallas Morning News,* 11 Jan., sec. 2, 6.

———. 1952. "The Passing Show: Stage Directing the Musicals." *Dallas Morning News,* 21 Feb., sec. 3, 4.

Saft, Marcia. 1986. "Skills Used in Theatre Are Brought to Schools." *New York Times,* 30 Nov., 11CN, 24.

Terry, Walter. 1948. Rev. of *Ballet Ballads,* by John Latouche and Jerome Moross. *New York Herald Tribune,* 10 May, 14.

Who's Who of American Women, 1999–2000. 1999. New Providence, N.J.: Marquis Who's Who, 1131.

Zolotow, Sam. 1948. "Two Disputes to Arbitration." *New York Times,* 4 Feb., 27.

Representative Directing Credits

Broadway:
> *Only the Heart* (1944), *Carib Song* (1945), *Ballet Ballads* (1948), *Great to Be Alive!* (1950), *Peter Pan* (assistant director—1954)

Off and Off-Off Broadway:
> *The Trojan Women* (1938), *Texas Town* (1941), *American Legend* (1941), *Out of My House* (1942), *Only the Heart* (1942, 1944), *The Respectful Prostitute* (1948), *The Happy Journey to Trenton and Camden* (1948), *The Victors* (1948), *Ballet Ballads* (1948)

Regional and Stock Theatre:
> *No Exit* (1946), *High Button Shoes* (1950), *Maytime* (1950), *Brigadoon* (1950), *Roberta* (1950), *Desert Song* (1950), *Annie Get Your Gun* (1950), *Where's Charley* (1951), *Song of Norway* (1951), *Texas Li'l Darling* (1951), *I Married an Angel* (1951), *Miss Liberty* (1951), *The Merry Widow* (1951)

Tours:
> *Musical Americana* (1953–55)

Josephine Abady.
Photographer unknown.
Courtesy of Cleveland Play House.

JoAnne Akalaitis.
Photo by Enrico Ferorelli.
Courtesy of Bard College.

Libby Appel.
Photo by Terrence McCarthy.
Courtesy of Libby Appel.

Pamela Berlin.
Photo by John Hart.
Courtesy of Pamela Berlin.

Martha Boesing.
Photo by Polly Pagenhart.
Courtesy of Martha Boesing.

Anne Bogart.
Photo by Dixie Sheridan.
Courtesy of SITI Company.

Jessie Bonstelle.
Photographer unknown.
Courtesy of the Burton Historical Collection,
Detroit Public Library.

Julianne Boyd.
Photo by Dana Harrel.
Courtesy of Julianne Boyd.

Tisa Chang.
Photo by James Kriegsman.
Courtesy of Tisa Chang.

Martha Clark and her horse,
Mr. Grey.
Photographer unknown.
Courtesy of Martha Clarke.

Graciella Daniele.
Photographer unknown.
Courtesy of Graciela Daniele.

Liz Diamond.
Photo by Donna Grau.
Courtesy of Liz Diamond.

Glenda Dickerson.
Photo by Nina Murano.
Courtesy of Glenda Dickerson.

Zela Fichandler.
Photographer unknown.
Courtesy of Arena Stage.

Maria Irene Fornes.
Photo by Kim Zumwal.
Courtesy of Maria Irene Fornes.

Margarita Galban.
Photo by Estela Scarlata.
Courtesy of Margarita Galban.

Mary Hunter.
Photographer unknown.
Courtesy of Bill Wolf.

Tina Landau.
Photographer unknown.
Courtesy of Tina Landau.

Sue Lawless.
Photo by Ann Carnaby.
Courtesy of Sue Lawless.

Roberta Levitow.
Photo by Chris Bennion.
Courtesy of Roberta Levitow.

Judith Malina.
Photo by Kim Nora.
Courtesy of The Living Theatre.

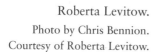

Emily Mann.
Photo by Joan Marcus.
Courtesy of McCarter Theatre.

Lynne Meadow.
Photo by Nora Feller.
Courtesy of Manhattan
Theatre Club.

Muriel Miguel.
Photo by Monica McKenna.
Courtesy of Muriel Miguel.

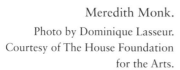

Meredith Monk.
Photo by Dominique Lasseur.
Courtesy of The House Foundation
for the Arts.

Agnes Morgan.
Photographer unknown.
Courtesy of Paper Mill Playhouse.

Sharon Ott.
Photo by Jennifer M. Tucker.
Courtesy of Seattle Repertory Theatre.

Tina Packer.
Photo by Kevin Sprague.
Courtesy of Shakespeare & Co.

Carey Perloff
Photo by Terry McCarthy
Courtesy of American
Conservatory Theatre

Shauneille Perry.
Photo by Bert Andrews.
Courtesy of Shauneille Perry.

Dorothy Raedler in Monmouth,
Maine, 1957.
Photographer unknown.
Courtesy of Arden Anderson Broecking.

Mary B. Robinson.
Photographer unknown.
Courtesy of Mary B. Robinson.

Carole Rothman.
Photographer unknown.
Courtesy of Second Stage Theatre.

Susan H. Schulman.
Photo by Bob Newey.
Courtesy of Susan H. Schulman.

Ellen Stewart.
Photographer unknown.
Courtesy of La MaMa Experimental
Theatre Club.

Susan Stroman.
Photo by Carl Rosegg.
Courtesy of Susan Stroman.

Julie Taymor.
Photo by Brigitte LaCombe.
Courtesy of Julie Taymor.

Barbara Ann Teer.
Photo by Bernard Fairdough.
Courtesy of National Black Theatre.

Mary Zimmerman.
Photo by Lisa Ebright.
Courtesy the Goodman Theatre.

Jones, Margo

Born on December 12, 1911, in Livingston, Texas, Margo Jones was a pioneer of regional theatre in the United States. Her theatre in Dallas was the United States's first permanent professional nonprofit resident theatre as well as the first professional theatre-in-the-round. During her career, Jones directed more than one hundred plays.

As a young girl, Jones had theatrical tendencies and liked to play "dress-up." At the age of four, she played a ring bearer in a reenactment of General Tom Thumb's wedding. Although professional theatre was discouraged in her hometown, which implemented heavy taxes on traveling troupes, Jones was able to see circuses that passed through. At first Jones wanted to be a lawyer like her father and worked in his office. While watching her father in court, Jones had a realization, explaining, "[O]ne day it occurred to me that the reason I enjoyed the courtroom sessions was that they were so much like plays. But at eleven I knew what I wanted to do—to put on plays—and up went a sheet in the barn where my sister and my brothers joined me in my first producing-directing venture" (1951, 40).

Jones saw her first professional production of a play when she was fourteen years old. In high school she developed her public speaking skills through winning debate and declamation contests, giving readings, and acting in her senior class play. Jones then attended the Girl's Industrial College (now Texas Woman's University) in Denton, Texas, where she was a member of the Dramatic Club, and directed theatre productions. She recalls, "I was the only student interested in directing. This was fortunate because I had a chance to direct more than the average directing student in a drama department" (1951, 41). Jones also acted in productions as a way to understand the actor's point of view. While at college, she attended the Dallas Little Theatre and began to read at least one play a day, which she continued to do throughout her life.

After attending a lecture by Dallas playwright and critic John William Rogers, Jones spoke to him about her intentions to become a director. Rogers encouraged Jones and gave her a pamphlet of George Bernard Shaw's advice to directors, which stated that "women directors are at no disadvantage in comparison with men" (Sheehy 1989, 16). In addition to Rogers, Jones was also encouraged by the *Dallas Morning News*'s John Rosenfield, to whom she gave publicity for her college productions. Jones graduated with a B.A. in speech in 1932, and a M.S. in psychology the next year, writing a thesis titled

"The Abnormal Ways out of Emotional Conflict as Reflected in the Dramas of Henrik Ibsen."

Jones next received a scholarship to Dallas's Southwestern School of the Theatre, where Rogers taught, and studied a variety of subjects, including acting and makeup. In 1934 she continued her studies at California's Pasadena Playhouse Summer School. There, Jones and another student co-directed the Chinese epic *The Chalk Circle*. Her first directing job arrived the same year at California's Ojai Community Theatre, where she directed Henrik Ibsen's *Hedda Gabler* among other plays.

In 1935 Jones had an opportunity to travel around the world by boat with friends. During the trip, she attended theatre performances in many of the world's largest cities, including New York City. She wrote, "New York made me feel that I had to go to work for the present and plan the future. The theatrical air was exhilarating, and it filled my lungs" (1951, 44). After the trip, Jones returned to Texas, where she became assistant director at the Houston Federal Theatre—part of the Works Projects Administration's Federal Theatre Project. After six months, Jones was let go when funding was cut.

The next year, Jones returned to Europe to revisit London and Paris. During her trip, she also attended the Moscow Art Theatre Festival, which she covered for the *Houston Chronicle*. In Moscow she met *New York Times* critic Brooks Atkinson, who would encourage and support Jones throughout her career. When Jones returned to Houston, she worked for the Houston Recreation Department and taught how to direct children's plays. Intent on starting her own theatre, Jones persuaded the Houston Recreation Department to let her use one of their buildings that had a stage. With a theatre at her disposal, Jones was set to direct all of the productions for her new group, the Houston Community Players. The first production was Oscar Wilde's *The Importance of Being Earnest*, which one reporter described, writing, "[F]or each smart saying of Wilde's, the actors have a smart stage movement; for each epigram they have hilarious gestures" (Sheehy 1989, 32). Jones helped to build audiences by greeting them upon their arrival and thanking them for their attendance when they left. She continued to direct successful productions, including her site-specific production in 1937 of Elmer Rice's *Judgment Day*, a play about a trial that she staged in a courtroom. That year, she directed *Hedda Gabler* again and Valentin Petrovich Katayev's *Squaring the Circle*, a Russian farce. Jones described the stylized production, which "employed ladders, ropes, sawhorses and barrels, all painted a violent red and skeletonized against a black backdrop" (1951, 46). With her theatre a success, Jones convinced the Houston Recreation Department to allow her to work full-time with her group and abandon her teaching job. In addition to her role as a director and producer, Jones frequently acted as a technician.

While attending a theatre conference in Washington, D.C., in the spring of 1939, Jones saw a theatre-in-the-round production staged in a hotel ballroom. When she returned to Houston, she convinced the City Council to allow the Houston Players to use the Lamar Hotel's Grand Ballroom for the summer, and Jones's directing in the round began. Jones discovered that she enjoyed directing in the round, which had the added bonus of eliminating costly sets. Over the next three years, Jones directed more than sixty plays. She resigned from the Community Players in 1942 and accepted a teaching position at the University of Texas in Austin. Her first production there was Maxwell Anderson's *The Eve of St. Mark,* which she directed in the University's Experimental Theatre.

On a trip to New York City in 1942 in search of new scripts, Jones met with an agent, who gave her Tennessee Williams's first full-length play *Battle of Angels.* She met with Williams later that year and established a relationship with the playwright that would last throughout her career. Unable to get the University of Texas to present a play by Williams—who was not yet famous—Jones took a job in 1943 as director at the Summer School at the Pasadena Playhouse in California, where she intended to stage *You Touched Me* by Williams and Donald Windham. After working with Williams on revisions, Jones ended up directing the world premiere of the play at the Cleveland Playhouse that year. However, her direction was cut short by the Cleveland Playhouse's artistic director, Frederick McConnell, who disapproved of Jones's collaborative directing style. McConnell took over direction of the play in its final week, implementing his own authoritarian style. Jones returned to Pasadena Playhouse to direct the play in a production that excluded critics from attending due to legal stipulations. Later that year, Jones decided to create a professional resident theatre devoted to both classics and new plays.

In 1944 Jones was still unable to convince the University of Texas to stage a play by Williams. That summer she returned to the Pasadena Playhouse, where she directed Williams's *The Purification,* a one-act play in verse. Unhappy with academic life, she applied for and received a Rockefeller grant, which she used to study the organization of other theatres and to begin the foundations for her own theatre in Dallas.

Meanwhile, Williams's new play, *The Glass Menagerie,* had been optioned for a Broadway production by producer, director, and actor Eddie Dowling. At the suggestion of Williams, Dowling invited Jones to be his assistant director. As the demands of work increased, Jones became a co-director of the play, which told the story of a young Southern woman and her dominating mother. Jones believed Williams was an extraordinary writer and defended his writing, as she did for other writers. At one point, Jones fought to keep the original ending of the play, which a producer wanted to change to a happy ending. She told the producer, "[I]f you make Tennessee change the play the way you want it, so help me I'll go around to every critic in town and tell them about the kind of wire-pulling that's going on here" (Schumach 1948, SM59). *The Glass Menagerie* made its world premiere in 1944 in Chicago to good reviews before opening successfully on Broadway the next year. Wilella Waldorf of the *New York Post* called the play "a smooth collaborative effort that fuses all of the elements of a stagecraft into an almost perfect symphonic interpretation of the author's original conception" (1945, 92).

In 1945 Jones received an offer from Dallas investors, and the Dallas Civic Theatre was established. In order to make her theatre appear current, Jones decided that the theatre's name would change each year based on the date and christened its first year as Theatre '45. Despite the ambitious starting date, Jones's theatre company had no building and did not open until a few years later.

Returning to Broadway, Jones directed Maxine Wood's *On Whitman Avenue* in 1946. The play was co-produced by and starred Canada Lee, one of the few African American actors to appear on Broadway in that era. Jones helped Wood, who was white, to rework her play about an African American family's struggle with racism. After previewing in Buffalo and Detroit, the play opened to negative reviews but maintained a run on Broadway of one hundred and fifty performances. The same year Jones directed Maxwell Anderson's *Joan of Lorraine,* which revolved around performers rehearsing the Joan of Arc tale. Jones was fired shortly after tryouts in Washington, D.C., and before the play opened on Broadway, but received full credit for the direction. Anderson believed the play needed a more authoritarian director and named his son, a stage manager, along with actor Sam Wanamaker, who also performed in the play, as co-directors—although neither one had professional experience in directing (Sheehy 1989, 120).

In 1947 Jones found a building for her Dallas theatre, which she remodeled into a 198–seat theatre-in-the-round. By staging productions in the round, Jones kept down production costs for scenery and also provided an intimate space between performers and audience. She hired technicians and a company of eight performers, which would expand in the years to come. She rehearsed a repertory of plays while running the theatre, which was still under construction in the first year. The theatre opened with a summer season of productions directed by Jones, including the world premieres of William Inge's *Farther Off from Heaven* (later revised as *The Dark at the Top of the Stairs*), Martyn Coleman's *How Now, Hecate,* Williams's *Summer and Smoke,* and Vera Mathews's *Third Cousin.* The first performance of *Farther off from Heaven* sold out, and the theatre was off to a good start. The season also included one revival, *Hedda Gabler,* which critic Rosenfield found benefited from the arena staging. He wrote, "Theatre-'47-in-the-round may be just the milieu *Hedda Gabler* has needed for half a century. . . . Never before had we found Hedda so natural and so human" (Jones 1951, 140).

Jones's direction of *Summer and Smoke* was also a success in Dallas. Rosenfield's review for the *New York Times* described how Jones staged the play, explaining, "Williams' manuscript calls for rapid changes of thirteen scenes between four ever-ready settings. . . . Two corners of the playing square, the center and a stepped-entrance, sufficed. The settings, each with its symbols, were handled effectively by a blackout technique" (1947, 18).

Jones's successful production of Williams's play presented her with another opportunity on Broadway. After previews in Buffalo, New York, Detroit, Michigan, and Cleveland, Jones directed *Summer and Smoke* on Broadway in 1948. The play received mostly negative reviews, but Atkinson of the *New York Times* wrote, "Margo Jones, who directed the original performance in Dallas, has brought it to the stage with infinite respect for its delicate qualities. On a large stage it loses some of the moving intimacy that it had in the cramped quarters of the Dallas theatre" (1948, 33). The failure of *Summer and Smoke* on Broadway temporarily cooled the friendly relationship between Jones and Williams. Despite the play's failure on Broadway, Jones directed the 1949–50 tour of *Summer and Smoke*.

Jones continued to direct almost all of the productions at her Dallas theatre. In 1949 she directed the world premiere of Dorothy Parker and Ross Evan's *The Coast of Illyria,* a drama that revolved around a shipwrecked brother and sister. Reviews were positive, although a reviewer from the *New York Times* noted, "With the authors and director still laboring over the script, the first act moved hectically and in too many directions. The other two were compact and powerful" ("'Coast,'" 1949, 37).

In 1950 Jones directed the first professional American production of Sean O'Casey's fantasy *Cock-a-Doodle Dandy.* The play "closed with universal response and loud applause" ("O'Casey's," 1950, 26). She also directed the world premiere of Owen Crump's *Southern Exposure* that year. A success with the Dallas audience, *Southern Exposure* opened on Broadway in 1950 with Jones directing. A satire about the South with inside jokes that escaped many New York City audience members, *Southern Exposure* failed on Broadway and closed after only twenty-three performances.

In 1951 Jones directed her theatre's first musical—Frank Duane and Richard Shannon's *Walls Rise Up,* based on the novel by George Sessions Perry. This world premiere, which revolved around three hobos, got excellent reviews and was popular with audiences. During the 1951–52 season, Jones split the direction of productions with Ramsey Burch, whom she had hired as associate director and actor. Jones directed only two plays the following season and worked with an African American community theatre group, called the Round-up Theatre, on their successful production of *Walls Rise Up* in 1953.

Returning to a Williams play the following year, Jones directed *The Purification* with the first professional production of Jean Girandeaux's *The Apollo of Bellac* together on the same bill. Atkinson wrote that *The Purification* "has been staged as if it were a religious ritual by Margo Jones in her best form and it is acted with grace and devoutness by a company inspired by what they are playing." He added that Jones directed "a superb performance" of *The Apollo of Bellac*. Of both plays he wrote, "Two plays as beautifully imagined as these give the theatre an aura of joy and enlightenment. Having been lucky enough to acquire them, Theatre '54 has produced them with skill and devotion" (1954, 12).

In 1955 Jones staged the world premiere of *Inherit the Wind*, a play about the trial of John Scopes for teaching evolution in a public school. Despite warnings from others about an inevitable negative reception in the South, Jones forged ahead, inviting playwrights Jerome Lawrence and Robert E. Lee to attend rehearsals. Lawrence recalls, "I'll never forget how Margo whooped up the prayer-meeting. . . . The minister was dead center—and all the participants were in the sloping aisles, so suddenly during a performance, if you were sitting in the audience, an actor right alongside you would leap to his feet and join in their fervor, so that the entire audience got caught up in it" (Sheehy 1989, 254). Virgil Miers of the *Dallas Times Herald* wrote, "It is simply one of the best plays Miss Jones has staged at her theatre, and one of the best productions she has given to a play" (1955, 255). Jones pushed to get the play produced on Broadway, but did not intend to direct it there, due to her previous failures in commercial theatre and a lack of time. However, *Inherit the Wind* opened to positive reviews and enthusiastic audiences that year on Broadway. It was directed by Herman Shumlin and produced in association with Margo Jones.

Jones died on July 24, 1955, in Dallas, Texas, poisoned from a carpet-cleaning chemical used in her apartment. Her theatre continued as the Margo Jones Theatre for four more years, shifting its repertoire from original to previously produced plays. While Jones was alive, her theatre had presented about 70 percent of its productions as world premieres and new scripts by such authors as Joseph Hayes, William Inge, Jerome Lawrence and Robert E. Lee, Sean O'Casey, and Tennessee Williams. In 1961 Lawrence and Lee began the Margo Jones Award, given to those who encourage the production of new works. The award now honors those who are committed to theatre and have had an impact on playwriting.

During her life, Jones maintained a strong work ethic. Typically, she read three or more scripts a day (Schumach 1948, SM19, 59). When selecting new scripts, she was careful to read them more than once and write each playwright an encouraging letter that included a critique of the play (Sheehy 1989, 95). Jones believed that a good play needed to have one or more of the following elements: an interesting story, fascinating characters, a strong mood, or excellent dialogue (128). She also wrote that a director "must love the play and want very much to do it" (1951, 117).

When directing premieres, Jones worked intensely with playwrights before rehearsal in order to reach a consensual interpretation of the play and to doctor the script. Although Jones preferred to have playwrights at rehearsals as well as during the run of the play, she preferred that the playwright not interact directly with the performers, but rather through her.

When casting for her own theatre, Jones selected actors who could perform in a variety of plays. Jones also broke new ground in Dallas professional theatre by casting African American actors. She discussed what she looked for in performers when casting, writing, "They must have talent, of course, but their talent must be matched by character. . . . When you search for a company, you have to look for a perfect chemical combination: people who will work together, all of them feeling that they can express themselves well in this theatre and having mutual respect for each other. . . . [T]heatre flexibility is also essential. For this reason it is advisable to select actors with experience, yet not forgetting that there is new talent continuously arriving on the theatrical scene. You must believe enough in new talent to give it a chance" (1951, 80–81). When searching for performers, Jones used a variety of methods. She hired actors with whom she had worked previously, attended plays to find new talent, took recommendations by others, or held auditions. Jones preferred to cast parts right before each play went into rehearsal.

Blocking for a proscenium stage was difficult for Jones, and she often used props, such as toy figures or kitchen matches, to help her accomplish the task. In her mind, the proscenium stage revealed a two-dimensional painting, while theatre-in-the-round revealed a sculpture.

With her charismatic personality, Jones encouraged the cast with enthusiastic talks. Williams said of her, "She is the most enthusiastic person I've ever known—and the most inexorable" (Schumach 1948, SM19, 59). Jones's rehearsal procedures varied according to each play. She wrote, "Certain scripts should be read by actors a number of times before being blocked out; others should be placed on their feet as soon as humanly possible. With a short rehearsal schedule, it is wise to start blocking the play early, memorizing the lines and working out the fine points of characterization and stage business later" (1951, 121).

During rehearsals, Jones was flexible and allowed blocking to change, incorporating actors' ideas or trying out new ideas. She wrote, "While I believe that the director should have a thorough knowledge of the play and a definite interpretation, everything cannot be taken care of in advance planning. There is a need for more experimentation in directing if we are to get away from the obvious, and the preparation of a detailed blueprint has a tendency to enslave you with its limitations. A director has to remain flexible" (1951, 122). Jones preferred to focus on the overall flow of the play rather than on details of the performances, which she left to the actors. She encouraged performers to create details for their characters and did not believe in showing performers specific business or telling them how to say their lines, unless absolutely necessary.

For arena staging, Jones asked performers to find motivations for their movements so that they could face different sections of the house. She wrote, "An actor's back can be as effective and dramatic as his face; it is only a matter of using the whole body" (1951, 123). With the close proximity of the audience, performers were compelled to provide honest performances. Jones also liked to use choreographic or stylized movement and believed productions should not be staged too literally, but rather that audiences should use their imaginations.

Jones gave designers great freedom and often approved their ideas. Staging plays in the round required creative thinking because the conventional settings specified in scripts were not always possible. Furniture, props, and platforms were often used instead of typical sets. The success that Jones had with staging arena productions is demonstrated by Joseph Hayes's *Leaf and Bough,* which she directed at her theatre in 1948. Although the play was a success at her theatre, it was unsuccessful when it was directed in 1949 by Rouboe Mamoulian on Broadway. Hayes explained, "Mamoulian had a heavy touch and he didn't get any of the emotion out of it that Margo got. On Broadway the play was overburdened by sets and furniture. In Dallas we got more reality by just the suggestion of sets on that bare stage" (Sheehy 1989, 161).

Jones worked to find ways to create smooth and cinematic scene changes. She wrote, "In most of our productions the lights go up and down at the beginning and end of a scene with the accompaniment of music. . . . Music can also be played during a scene for atmospheric effect if the tone of the play permits it" (1951, 126–27). In addition to music, Jones also used lighting to emphasize focus and mood.

While one play was running at Jones's theatre, another was in rehearsal. Rehearsals in repertory were brief, however. For Jones's first season of Theatre '47, rehearsals lasted about two weeks per play. Later, rehearsals were extended to three weeks, although she preferred to have four weeks. Jones also preferred to have one week of dress rehearsals.

Jones's awards and honors include being named one of twelve outstanding little-theatre directors outside of New York City by *Stage* magazine in 1939,

Director of the South in 1939, Pasadena Playhouse's Gilmor Brown Medal for outstanding creative and artistic achievement in 1947, Man of the Year by the *Dallas Morning News* in 1947, and a plaque honoring her from the mayor of Dallas in 1954.

Jones devoted her life to theatre. She said, "The theatre has given me a chance not only to live my own life but a million others. In every play there is a chance for one great moment, experience, or understanding" (Schumach 1948, SM60).

Sources

Atkinson, Brooks. 1948. "Summer and Smoke." Rev. of *Summer and Smoke*, by Tennessee Williams. *New York Times*, 7 Oct., 33.

———. 1954. "Theatre: Williams and Giraudoux." Rev. of *The Purification*, by Tennessee Williams, and *The Apollo of Bellac*, by Jean Giraudoux. *New York Times*, 29 May, 12.

Chinoy, Helen Krich and Linda Walsh Jenkins, eds. 1987. *Women in American Theatre*. New York: Theatre Communications Group.

"'Coast of Illyria' Offered in Dallas." 1949. Rev. of *The Coast of Illyria*, by Dorothy Parker and Ross Evans. *New York Times*, 5 Apr., 37.

Housely, Helen Marie. 1991. "To Inherit the Wind: Margo Jones as Director." Ph.D. diss., University of Maryland, College Park.

Jones, Margo. 1951. *Theatre-in-the-Round*. New York: Rinehart.

Larsen, June Bennett. 1982. "Margo Jones: A Life in the Theatre." Ph.D. diss., City University of New York.

Lea, Florence M. 1989. "Jones, Margo." In *Notable Women in the American Theatre: A Biographical Dictionary*, ed. Alice M. Robinson, Vera Mowry Roberts, and Milly S. Barranger, 477–81. Westport, Conn.: Greenwood.

Leiter, Samuel L. 1994. "Margo Jones." In *The Great Stage Directors: 100 Distinguished Careers of the Theater*, 152–55. New York: Facts on File.

"Margo Jones, 42, Producer, Dies." 1955. *New York Times*, 25 July, 19.

Miers, Virgil. 1955. "An Idea on Trial in Brilliant Play." Rev. of *Inherit the Wind*, by Jerome Lawrence and Robert E. Lee. *Dallas Times Herald*, 11 Jan. In *Margo: The Life and Theatre of Margo Jones*, by Helen Sheehy. Dallas: Southern Methodist University Press, 1989, 212.

"O'Casey's New Play Unveiled in Dallas." 1950. Rev. of *Cock-a-Doodle Dandy*, by Sean O'Casey. *New York Times*, 1 Feb., 26.

Rathkamp, Lesley. 1996. "Jones, Margo." In *International Dictionary of Theatre—3: Actors, Directors and Designers*, ed. David Pickering, 392–95. New York: St. James.

Rosenfield, John. 1947. "Play by Williams Unveiled in Dallas." Rev. of *Summer and Smoke*, by Tennessee Williams. *New York Times*, 9 July, 18.

Schumach, Murray. 1948. "A Texas Tornado Hits Broadway." *New York Times*, 17 Oct., SM19, SM59–60.

Sheehy, Helen. 1989. *Margo: The Life and Theatre of Margo Jones*. Dallas: Southern Methodist University Press.

———. 1994. "Margaret Virginia (Margo) Jones." In *Theatrical Directors: A Biographical Dictionary*, ed. John W. Frick and Stephen M. Vallillo, 206–8. Westport, Conn.: Greenwood.

Waldorf, Wilella. 1945. "High Point of the Season So Far." Rev. of *The Glass Menagerie*, by Tennessee Williams. *New York Post*, 2 Apr. In *Margo: The Life and Theatre of Margo Jones*, by Helen Sheehy. Dallas: Southern Methodist University Press, 1989, 92.

Wilmeth, Don Burton. 1964. "A History of the Margo Jones Theatre." Ph.D. diss., University of Illinois at Urbana-Champaign.

Representative Directing Credits[1]

Broadway:

> *The Glass Menagerie* (co-directed with Eddie Dowling—1945), *Joan of Lorraine* (1946), *On Whitman Avenue* (1946), *Summer and Smoke* (1948), *Southern Exposure* (1950)

Regional Theatre:

> *Hedda Gabler* (1934, 1937, 1947), *The Importance of Being Earnest* (1936, 1948), *Bury the Dead* (1937), *Judgment Day* (1937), *The Lay Figure* (1937), *The Long Christmas Dinner* (1937), *Merrily We Roll Along* (1937), *Nude with Pineapple* (1937), *Squaring the Circle* (1937), *Blind Alley* (1938), *Candlelight* (1938), *The Front Page* (1938), *High Tor* (1938), *The Learned Ladies* (1938, 1948), *Macbeth* (1938), *Special Edition* (1938), *As You Like It*[2] (1938–42?), *Johnny Johnson*[2] (1938–1942?), *Our Town*[2] (1938–1942?), *Uncle Vanya*[2] (1938–1942?), *The Circle* (1939), *Louder Please* (1939), *Room Service* (1939), *The Second Man* (1939), *Springtime for Henry* (1939), *The Taming of the Shrew* (1939, 1947), *There's Always Juliet* (1939), *A Comedy of Errors* (1939 or 1940), *Family Portrait* (1939 or 1940), *Howdy, Stranger* (1941), *Sunrise in My Pocket* (1941), *Candida* (1942, 1951), *Design for Living* (1942), *Going Up!* (1942), *A Quiet Wedding* (1942), *Rope's End* (1942), *The Shining Hour* (1942), *Personal Appearance* (1943), *Sporting Pink* (1943), *Ten Nights in a Barroom* (1943), *The Velvet Tower* (1943), *You Touched Me* (1943), *The Glass Menagerie* (1944), *Is Life Worth Living?* (1944), *The Purification* (1944, 1954), *Women in Service* (1944), *How Now, Hecate* (1947), *Farther Off from Heaven* (1947), *Lemple's Old Man* (1947, 1948), *The Master Builder* (1947), *Summer and Smoke* (1947), *Third Cousin* (1947), *This Property Is Condemned; The Last of My Solid Gold Watches; Portrait of a Madonna* (1947), *Throng O'Scarlet* (1947), *Black John* (1948), *Here's to Us* (1948), *Leaf and Bough* (1948), *The Learned Ladies* (1948), *Twelfth Night* (1948), *The Coast of Illyria* (1949), *Heartbreak House* (1949), *An Old Beat Up Woman* (1949, 1950), *The Sea Gull* (1949), *She Stoops to Conquer* (1949), *Skaal* (1949), *Sting in the Tail* (1949), *Cock-a-Doodle Dandy* (1950), *Ghosts* (1950), *An Innocent Time*

(1950), *Lady Windermere's Fan* (1950), *The Merchant of Venice* (1950), *My Granny Van* (1950), *The Golden Porcupine* (1950), *A Play for Mary* (1950), *Southern Exposure,* (1950), *A Midsummer Night's Dream* (1951), *One Bright Day* (1951), *The Sainted Sisters* (1951), *Walls Rise Up* (1951, 1953), *A Willow Tree* (1951), *The Blind Spot* (1952), *I Am Laughing* (1952), *The Day's Mischief* (1953), *The Footpath Way* (1953), *The Guilty* (1953), *The Apollo of Bellac* (1954), *As You Like It* (1954), *A Dash of Bitters* (1954), *The Heel* (1954), *The Lost Child's Fireflies* (1954), *Inherit the Wind* (1955)

Tours:
Summer and Smoke (1949, 1950)

Notes

1. Except for *Hedda Gabler,* plays that Jones directed at the Ojai Community Theatre could not be found.
2. Dates for these plays could not be found. In her dissertation "To Inherit the Wind: Margo Jones as Director," Helen Marie Housley estimates that they were probably produced between 1938 and 1942 in Houston.

 # Landau, Tina

Born on May 21, 1962, in New York City to film producers, Tina Landau is both a playwright and director. She is known for her ability to stage difficult texts with a painter's eye, employing a strong use of light, space, movement, and an intricate use of sound and music.

As a child, Landau lived in Riverdale, New York. When she was six years old, Landau decided that she would either be a director or an oceanographer. During the 1960s and 1970s, Landau's parents took her to see many Broadway plays and musicals. Productions of director and choreographer Michael Bennett and director Hal Prince helped Landau to "learn a kind of fluidity and develop a leaning towards working with music" (Landau, interview, 2004). During her childhood, Landau played piano, put on her own shows, and watched rehearsals of high school productions. At one high school rehearsal, she became fascinated watching Roberta Wallach, the daughter of Eli Wallach and Anne Jackson, portraying the role of Reno Sweeney in Cole Porter's *Anything Goes.* At about the age of seven, Landau wrote Wallach a fan letter listing one hundred things that she loved about her. In the sixth grade, Landau adapted an O'Henry story, "The Last Leaf," into a play and also wrote a one-act play based on a painting in her home. Landau recalls that she began to direct her own work "having no idea what I was doing" (Interview, 2004). Landau's only acting credits are from Stagedoor Manor, a theatre summer camp where she was a chorus member in *Once Upon a Mattress* and played the Wicked Witch in *The Wizard of Oz*. She explains, "My experience around acting—a lot of which is projection—involves terror and embarrassment. I think that's part of the reason why I love actors so much and work well with them. I know the common wisdom says in order to really understand and work well with actors, you have to have acted yourself. I never have, but what I have done is sat in awe and amazement at what they do and thought long and hard on *how* they do it" (Interview, 2004).

At the age of fourteen, Landau and her family moved to California. There she attended the famous Beverly Hills High School and wrote and directed her own musical, *Faces on the Wall,* which she later directed at Los Angeles's Coronet Theatre. Afterward, she went to Yale University, majored in theatre studies, and developed her directing skills. She graduated with a B.A. in 1984 and maintains professional contact with many people that she met at Yale. That year at Los Angeles's Olympic Arts Festival, Landau saw director Giorgio Strehler's production of *The Tempest,* which influenced her concept of directing. Landau describes his direction as "minimal and transformational" with "very pared down but metaphoric and natural theatrical elements" (Interview, 2004).

After graduating, Landau spent two years in New York City, but was frustrated because she was doing work that she did not care deeply about, such as screenwriting for horror films. Landau decided that she did not want to enter the New York City theatre scene at that exact moment and chose to leave after a friend told her, "You either have to feed your soul or you have to feed your mouth, but you can't try to do both at the same time" (Landau, interview, 2004). From 1987 through 1989 Landau attended the Institute for Advanced Theatre Training at Harvard's American Repertory Theatre (A.R.T.). Among the many prestigious artists present at A.R.T. was Anne Bogart, with whom Landau developed a professional and personal relationship. Before witnessing Bogart's collaborative directing style, Landau's directing was more autocratic. Landau adds, "And of course a lot of my ability to turn it over to actors came with confidence. The truth is, you can only do that when you're sure enough of yourself. So it took age, too" (Rhodda 2000, 308). In addition to influencing her collaborative directing style with actors, Bogart introduced Landau to the Viewpoints, a method that focuses on a physical approach to training performers and staging. During rehearsal, Landau uses the Viewpoints, which include Tempo, Duration, Kinesthetic Response, Repetition, Shape, Gesture,

Architecture, Spatial Relationship, and Topography. Landau and Bogart discuss the Viewpoints in their book *The Viewpoints Book: A Practical Guide to Viewpoints and Composition,* published in 2005.

In the 1990s Landau directed a number of works for New York City's En Garde Arts, which specialized in site-specific productions. There, she directed her own work and the works of one of her favorite playwrights, Charles L. Mee. At the Penn Yards, Landau directed a 1993 production of Mee's *Orestes,* which she had originally directed at A.R.T. in 1992. Following the direction of her own play, *Stonewall,* at Pier 25 in 1994, Landau directed Mee's *The Trojan Women: A Love Story* in 1996 at the East River Amphitheater. Landau describes the productions, saying, "It was theatre as event. And because of them being in nontraditional theatre spaces, this kind of work asked the audience from the get-go to experience everything as if for the first time. Nothing was taken for granted. It's the opposite of a dead theatre experience" (Interview, 2004).

In addition to *Orestes* and *The Trojan Women: A Love Story,* Landau directed two other plays by Mee at Chicago's Steppenwolf Theatre. First came *A Time to Burn,* based on Maxim Gorky's *The Lower Depths* in 1997, and then *The Berlin Circle,* based on the same Chinese folk tale of Bertolt Brecht's *The Caucasian Chalk Circle* in 1998. In addition to Mee's plays, Landau admires the work of José Rivera. She directed two plays by Rivera at California's La Jolla Playhouse, including *Cloud Tectonics* in 1995 and *Marisol* in 1992, for which Landau won a Drama-Logue award for Best Direction.

In 1994 Landau created *1969, or Howie Takes a Trip* in collaboration with her performers during rehearsals. The play with music examined a high school student's sexual and political journey during the late 1960s and was presented at the Humana Festival of New American Plays at Actors Theatre of Louisville in Kentucky. Landau describes the four-week creative process of the play, saying, "Everyone in the room—from the actors to the production assistants—contributed ideas, images, staging. We would spend each day either working on a section that was already on paper or we would generate raw material for a section I hadn't yet written" (1994, 180).

The same year, Landau directed *Floyd Collins,* a musical that she wrote with Adam Guettel that was commissioned by Philadelphia's American Musical Theater Festival (later called the Prince Music Theater) and premiered at Plays and Players Theater. The production was based on a true story about Floyd Collins, who was trapped in a cave in Kentucky in 1925 and whose unsuccessful rescue became one of the biggest news stories of the time. When creating the production, Landau and Guettel went to Kentucky and conducted interviews with people whose ancestors had seen the event. Using the book *Trapped! The Story of Floyd Collins* by Robert K. Murray and Roger W. Brucker as an inspiration, Landau and Guettel developed the script with performers in a series of workshops, and then worked alone on the script and music during the evenings. Landau and Guettel revised the musical, taking historical liberties to make it work. The revised production opened at New York City's Playwrights Horizon under Landau's direction in 1996 to mixed reviews, although John Simon of *New York* magazine called it "*the* original and daring musical of our day" (1996, 52). Ben Brantley of the *New York Times* felt that the show was solid, but needed more work. He praised Landau's staging, however, saying she "arranges her performers into lovely, haunting tableaux" (1996, C14).

In 1999 Landau directed *Floyd Collins* at San Diego's Old Globe Theatre and at the Prince Music Theater, where she won the Barrymore Award for Best Direction of a Musical. With additional script and music changes, *Floyd Collins* played at Chicago's Goodman Theatre to excellent reviews. Of the Goodman production Julie York of the *South Bend Tribune* wrote, "Every trickle of sand, every popping flashbulb, every cricket chirp sounds absolutely authentic, and as Floyd's exhilarated yodels reverberate from all corners of the theatre, the audience feels as if we, too, have tumbled into the vast underground cavern" (1999, C4).

Originally called *The Great Attractor*, Landau's *Space* was inspired by Arthur Clarke's *2001* and Dr. John E. Mack's *Abduction: Human Encounters with Aliens*. Created and directed by Landau, the play—originally presented as a workshop at A.R.T.—was produced at Steppenwolf Theatre in 1997. It tells the story of a research psychiatrist who begins to believe stories about alien abductions. Landau explains, "This is the story of someone who initially believes only in an exterior world, but who gradually awakens to the possibility of the existence of an internal and spiritual consciousness" (Jones 1998, 6). Landau discussed the influence of scholar Joseph Campbell's research about metamorphic stories on the work that "take us from darkness to light, ignorance to knowledge, death to rebirth. I keep returning to this in my work . . . and I think the audiences for 'Space' will pick up on my homage to four of these stories, including Alice in Wonderland, The Wizard of Oz, Dante's Divine Comedy and Dickens' A Christmas Carol" (Weiss 1997, 7). During the rehearsal for *Space*, performers brought their own resources, such as texts and photos, which Landau then edited and incorporated into the text. Landau also read about and interviewed people who claimed to have been abducted by aliens.

According to Richard Christiansen of the *Chicago Tribune,* the first half of *Space* was directed with a pace "almost faster than the speed of light," while the second half "deliberately slows down the razzle-dazzle and lets us watch" (1997, 2). The set was "a kind of conservatory with many doors, windows and other places for people, planets and stars to appear" (Henning 1997, 1). The stage also contained a projection screen for fantasy sequences and astral-patterned floor lights. Jack Helbig of the *Daily Herald* describes

Landau's production, saying, "Heavy on special effects—mysterious music, smoke machines, blinding light cues, even a slide show in the second act signifying a journey through space and time—the play never gets lost in all the razzle-dazzle. It is a measure of Landau's strengths as a writer and director . . . the play is as compelling in its quieter moments as it is during its moments of incredible spectacle" (1997, 31). The Steppenwolf Theatre production received excellent reviews and was mentioned in the 1997 Top Ten list of the *Chicago Tribune* and the Top Five of *Time* magazine.

In 1999 Landau directed *Dream True,* a musical that she wrote with composer Ricky Ian Gordon at Off Broadway's Vineyard Theater. Inspired by the novel *Peter Ibbetson* by George du Maurier, the musical follows the relationship of two boys who communicate with each other through dreams. The production received mixed reviews, however. Peter Marks of the *New York Times* called the musical, "exotic, flawed and strangely moving" and "the most intriguing" of the season's serious musicals (1999, E5).

Landau made her directorial debut on Broadway in 2001 with a revival of the musical *Bells Are Ringing* by Betty Comden, Adolf Green, and Jule Styne. The story centers on a telephone answering service operator who falls in love with one of her clients. Landau used a sparse stage that included a 1950s-style television screen and opened the show with film clips of the era and a commercial for the answering service. The reception of the musical was mixed, and Michael Feingold of the *Village Voice* wrote, "Landau handles it with more respect and delicacy than her downtown work would have led me to expect" (2001, 77).

Landau confessed that since she was a child, it has been her dream to direct on Broadway. She discusses what she learned from the experience, explaining, "I can't work with the goal of wanting to direct on Broadway. I have to keep the focus on the work only. And if it takes me there, great. . . . I enjoy knowing that there is work that is being spoken to a larger audience. . . . And if and when I end up on Broadway again, I hope it's kind of through the back door with a project that perhaps I start elsewhere and that I can stand behind one thousand percent" (Interview, 2004).

In the summer of 2002 Landau developed and directed a piece for Disney called *When You Wish* for an invited audience of about two hundred people. For the piece, she had access to the entire Disney catalog of music to create something new. Although the project was shelved, she considers the work significant because she was able to create a synthesis of traditional and experimental elements (Interview, 2004).

Returning to Chicago that fall, Landau directed William Saroyan's *The Time of Your Life* at Steppenwolf Theatre. When she first read the script, she could "barely get through it," but a few years later "it was like a totally different script." Landau explains what changed her perspective: "I turned 40, I had a big directing project with Disney fall through. And like many people in the aftermath of Sept. 11, 2001, I was in a period of questioning, asking, 'What really matters to me now?'" (Berson 2004, L1). Landau later expanded on the subject, saying, "What I had seen as a weakness, a kind of rambling non-narrative form, suddenly became a strength to me when I read it the second time. It was free form and associative, like a giant jazz improvisation with voices and instruments. . . . With that in my head, 'Time of Your Life' became a wonderful collage of moments that worked in and of themselves" ("Landau," 2004, 1). Landau also used Saroyan's words, which hung above the stage: "In the time of your life, live—so that in that wondrous time you shall not add to the misery and sorrow of the world, but shall smile to the infinite delight and mystery of it" (Hurwitt 2004, E1). She says, "I went into rehearsal for *Time of Your Life*. . . . I walked in on the first day and I knew I was supposed to talk about Saroyan, and the thirties, but all that came out of my mouth was, 'we need to make something that will be genuinely authentically *alive*, where something *happens* in the theatre each night we do this, or I'd rather go home right now'" (Interview, 2004).

The Steppenwolf Theatre production received excellent reviews, and the play was produced again in 2004 with Landau directing at both the Seattle Repertory Theatre and San Francisco's American Conservatory Theater to critical acclaim. Robert Hurwitt of the *San Francisco Chronicle* wrote, "It's a vision right out of a 1930s Thomas Hart Benton mural—with all its intercut shards of scenes vying for attention—but alive with song, dance, drinking and chatter. . . . There's action everywhere, starting a half hour before curtain time and running throughout the play and the intermission. . . . There's even a mural in progress, a little more to be filled in at each performance during the run" (2004, E1).

Between her two productions of *The Time of Your Life*, Landau directed *Beauty* at La Jolla Playhouse in 2003. The play, written by Landau, focused on the concept of beauty through a retelling of the tale of Sleeping Beauty. The production, which won the San Diego Critic's Award for Best New Play, wove back and forth between reality and fantasy and examined ideas about consciousness. Pat Launer of San Diego's KPBS-FM reviewed the play, stating, "The production is gorgeous to behold—simple, symbolic, stylized, enigmatic, musical and irresistible. . . . There is something so primal here—so deep within our collective consciousness that you cannot walk away unmoved, unprovoked undazzled" (2003).

In 2004 Landau wrote and directed the experimental *Theatrical Essays* at Steppenwolf Theatre. A collage of many different moods and stories, Landau took the form of written prose essays and translated it for the stage. She explains, "I gravitate toward things because they are not immediately and easily stage ready, or stage-able. The material invites me to think and create in more adventurous and theatrical ways. And to create a sort of poetry of theatre through visual metaphor, which ultimately is, I think, what theatre is about, where it lives most passionately" (Welsh 1999, E4). The production was praised by critics including Helbig, who wrote, "[F]ew directors have Tina Landau's commitment to do something new every time at bat" (2004, 34). Hedy Weiss of the *Chicago Sun-Times* described the production, observing, "The show begins from the moment you enter the theater and follow a pathway. . . . Scattered all around the playing area are little shrine-like environments in which each actor is performing an 'essay,' most of them by famous writers. . . . You stroll this sideshow before taking your seat for the main event" ("'Essays,'" 2004, 45). Describing the first part of the production, Michael Phillips of the *Chicago Tribune* wrote, "After a full-ensemble dance introduction, the first lengthy section begins. It's a befuddled, increasingly panicky tour of Venice. . . . [S]treets are suggested, wittily, by ever-snaking black panels on wheels, propelled by the cast. A rainy day is created by drops of water on an old-fashioned overhead projector" (2004, 4).

From the experimental *Theatrical Essays* to the Broadway musical *Bells Are Ringing*, Landau's choice of material to direct is varied. She explains, "I've always had this kind of split artistic personality. On the one hand, I've done work which lives in a more experimental imagistic nonlinear theatrical world, and on the other hand, I've done very classic American musicals. . . . I love both equally, and I've always wished in my life that somehow there would be a synthesis of the two. I feel like the work I've done that I'm most proud of is creeping toward that synthesis" (Interview, 2004). Landau further elaborates on her choice of material, stating, "I'm really interested in telling stories and entering human hearts. Combined with a canvas that is epic—somehow either large scale, or historical. Or mythological or political. I'm not that interested or versed in domestic drama or comedy. I'd say I function best at work in large scale fantasy or historical worlds" (Interview, 2004).

Landau notes that her selection of what she wants to direct has changed over time. At first she chose to do productions because the material intrigued her, or because she thought the production would be "a good exercise" in some regard. But she now has different criteria. She explains:

> This question of what to do and why has become the burning question for me. And that has to do with getting older, and it has to do with the way the world is changing. I did turn forty, and there was 9/11. . . . My sense of necessity about really being clear about what I'm doing and why has

increased. I feel like every time I do a show, I have to be accountable to the point where I would be willing to stand up on the lip of the stage in front of 500, or 800, or 30 people and tell them why it's worth spending their two or three hours and their twenty or fifty dollars to be there. . . . Life is too short, and the world is too messed up to do anything that doesn't matter to me personally on the deepest level in a way that I feel is connected to me being a citizen of this world. So, it simply means that I ask, "Why does this need to be done now? What is the 'raison d'être' for this material, this piece, in the world at this moment?" And I have to be able to deeply stand behind it. . . . There's the literal cost. . . . When you think of, "Oh, what could that million dollars be used for in the world?" I better be able to say this is worth it for a five-week run. (Interview, 2004)

When casting a production, Landau enjoys working with performers she knows, but also chooses new ones. She tries to determine which performers will best fit in the "play-world" of the production. For each person audition-ing, she writes the following words: "OF" or "NOT OF." Landau explains,

Every time I do a piece, I imagine a play-world that is it's own complete universe and has a kind of creature that inhabits it. And those beings have certain qualities that are specific only to that play-world. . . . When someone is in front of me, not only am I experiencing their talent, and their chops, and their look, and all that, but they're like a texture of being that, to me, either is "OF" the show or "NOT OF" the show. And I would say that's almost the primary thing. The second thing that is critical for me is a sense that I get of their openness, and generosity of spirit, and willingness to col-laborate. I am very collaborative, and I love actors. . . . I love experiencing the rehearsal room as a giant playground, where everyone is working on the edge of their own possibility. I love performers who do too much in a way, who offer me millions of options. I feel like I'm working best when I'm editing, so I love working with actors who generate and are empowered to generate on their own rather than people who are waiting for me to tell them what to do. (Interview, 2004)

The performers that Landau casts are important to the development of her pieces. She explains, "Most often, what I've done is I've cast a show and then developed it through workshops with those performers. Often those are things that I'm writing or creating from scratch. So, that some of my pieces, like *Floyd Collins* or *States of Independence* or *Beauty*, . . . are all things that I cast before the piece was actually done, and I built the characters and the story with certain performers in mind and eventually in the room" (Interview, 2004). Sometimes other criteria, such as life experience, are important in casting. Landau says that she cast performers for *Theatrical Essays* "not just for their ability to interpret and act a text, but because they were well-rounded people who brought a great deal into the rehearsal room from their life outside the theatre. They all had a wide range of interests and special skills" (Weiss, "Tina," 2004, 11).

Landau approaches rehearsals with advice that she heard from director Udon Slovaski while at A.R.T. She explains, "He said, 'When you work on a play, as a director, you develop an obsession, a fever, a kind of disease like something that's in your body. And your job at the beginning of rehearsal is to spread the contagion.' It's a little odd analogy, but it really made sense to me in that I spend time living in some imaginary world before I begin rehearsal. And I'd like to think of the beginning of any rehearsal process as being a time to invite everyone in the room to enter that world in their own way. So, I spend a lot of time at the beginning of rehearsal doing things that aren't specifically around text work, or table work, or blocking. Instead, they are simply about spreading the contagion. About getting everyone in the company on the same page, in the same boat, in the same play-world" (Interview, 2004).

Landau believes that performers need to approach their work in an integrated fashion. She explains, "I'm a strong believer in approaching the work from both the right and left hemispheres of the brain simultaneously. I will very often design the first week of rehearsal so we spend half the day playing in a purely spontaneous, chaotic, creative way around the material, and then spend the other half of the day either learning music if it's a musical, or sitting at the table and doing text work, or doing dramaturgical background work, so that the performers are entering the work both through their heads but also through their intuition and their dreams" (Interview, 2004).

During rehearsals, Landau sometimes starts with a single, significant word. In the case of *1969* for "1969"; for *Modern Fears,* it was "fears"; and for *Space,* it was "space." She says, "It's more about providing sources for the actors to spin off of, and to create their own materials, which I steal, edit, revise, shape" (Rhodda 2000, 299). Landau develops the script with performers and is open to changes in the script as they work together. She says, "I'm just not attached to my work" (Russo 1999, 79).

Landau's rehearsals last from three to four weeks, but she prefers working with more time. She says, "I seem to feel that when I started working in the American theatre, we rehearsed more like five or six weeks. And it seems like, if I wait another couple years, we'll be down to two or three days. It shrinks. It shrinks yearly. I will not rehearse two weeks, which some people do these days" (Interview, 2004).

In addition to working collaboratively with performers, Landau collaborates with authors, musicians, designers, and technicians. Of collaboration, Landau says, "The bottom line is that it's unquestionably true that what those twenty people come up with in a room is far more intricate and complex and detailed than anything I can imagine, sitting alone, in my little brain" (Rhodda 2000, 4).

For *Space*, Landau worked together with designers, explaining, "I gave everyone as much freedom as possible. This is a very three-dimensional epic, and we all felt that the design work was essential to the telling of the story (Jones 1998, 6). Also important to the story were the elements of sound and music. She states, "I always considered sound to be a character in the play" (6). She adds that music "is one of the most powerful tools we have to work with, and of course, one of the most manipulative" (Interview, 1998, 69).

Landau finds freelancing to be a dual-edged sword. It provides her not only with a flexible schedule, but also with an uncertainty about when her next job will appear. Her status as an ensemble member of Steppenwolf Theatre Company since 1997 gives her a stable place where she can pitch projects and a home to which she can return.

Landau has also directed opera and taught workshops at New York's SITI Company, Connecticut's Yale University, Massachusetts' Harvard University, Playwrights Horizons, New York University, and New York City's Columbia University. In addition to her previously mentioned awards, Landau was awarded a Princess Grace Award in 1988 and a Theatre Communications Group/National Endowment for the Arts (TCG/NEA) Directing Fellowship in 1991. She has also been the recipient of Pew, J. Alton Jones, and Rockefeller Awards.

Landau describes the kind of work she would like to do in the years to come as "fully expressive stagework [that is] human, detailed, and complex, but also highly theatrical, imagistic, musical, historical, and political. . . . [T]hat's the direction I would like my future work to continue in. But only if it is authentically *alive*, if it exploits the 'liveness' that can only happen in the theatre" (Interview, 2004).

Sources

Berson, Misha. 2004. "Breathing Vitality into 'Time of Your Life.'" *Seattle Times*, 8 Feb., L1.

Bogart, Anne and Tina Landau. 2005. *The Viewpoints Book: A Practical Guide to Viewpoints and Composition.* New York: Theatre Communications Group.

Brantley, Ben. 1996. "Carnival Above Ground, Tragedy Below." Rev. of *Floyd Collins,* by Tina Landau, music and lyrics by Adam Guettel, additional lyrics by Tina Landau. *New York Times,* 4 Mar., C14.

———. 1999. "In Search of the Voices Hidden in the Vastness." Rev. of *Space,* by Tina Landau. *New York Times,* 5 Dec., E5.

Christiansen, Richard. 1997. "A Galaxy of Talent Steppenwolf Whirls into Breathless Orbit in 'Space.'" Rev. of *Space*, by Tina Landau. *Chicago Tribune*, 8 Dec., 2.

Feingold, Michael. 2001. "Love Machinery." *Village Voice*, 24 Apr., 77.

Haagensen, Erik. 2001. "At the Helm: Directors on Style and Approach." *Back Stage*, 20 Apr., 28–32.

Helbig, Jack. 1997. "A Provoking Journey: Aliens, Love and Other Frontiers Are Explored in 'Space.'" Rev. of *Space*, by Tina Landau. *(Chicago) Daily Herald*, 12 Dec., 31.

———. 2004. "Director Tina Landau Remains on the Edge in 'Essays.'" Rev. of *Theatrical Essays*, by Tina Landau. *(Chicago) Daily Herald*, 11 June, 34.

Henning, Joel. 1997. "Theater: Season's Greetings From Outer Space." Rev. of *Space*, by Tina Landau. *Wall Street Journal*, 18 Dec., 1.

Hurwitt, Robert. 2004. "ACT/Seattle Rep Find the Lyrical Heart of Saroyan's Epochal 'Time of Your Life.'" Rev. of *The Time of Your Life*, by William Saroyan. *San Francisco Chronicle*, 30 Mar., E1.

Jones, Chris. 1998. "Into 'Space': Why Are Plays About the Nature, and Limits, of Science So Uncommon?" *Chicago Tribune*, 4 Jan., 6.

"Landau Adds Life to Saroyan's 'Time of Your Life.'" 2004. *Oakland (Calif.) Tribune*, 26 Mar., 1.

Landau, Tina. 1994. *1969*. In *Humana Festival '94: The Complete Plays*, ed. Marisa Smith, 177–219. Lyme, N.H.: Smith and Krause.

———. 1998. Interview with Sarah Schulman. "Tina Landau: The Rest is Metaphor." *American Theatre* 15 (7) (Sept.): 68–69, 85.

———. 2004. Telephone interview with Wendy Vierow. 4 Aug.

Launer, Pat. 2003. Rev. of *Beauty*, by Tina Landau. KPBS-FM, 26. Sept.

Marks, Peter. 1999. "Oh, to Be Back Home in Wyoming." Rev. of *Dream True*, by Tina Landau. *New York Times*, 19 Apr., E5.

Phillips, Michael. 2004. "'Essays' Rarely Dull or Provocative." Rev. of *Theatrical Essays*, by Tina Landau. *Chicago Tribune*, 7 June, 4.

Rhodda, Katherine Ellen. 2000. "Collaborative Creation: The Directing Aesthetics of Anne Bogart and Tina Landau." Ph.D. diss., University of California, Santa Barbara.

Russo, Francine. 1999. "The Outer Limits." *Village Voice*, 30 Nov., 79.

Simon, John. 1996. "Buried Treasure." Rev. of *Floyd Collins*, book by Tina Landau, music and lyrics by Adam Guettel, additional lyrics by Tina Landau. *New York*, 18 Mar., 52.

Weiss, Hedy. 1997. "Traveling in 'Space': Playwright Challenges Perceptions." *Chicago Sun-Times*, 7 Dec., 7.

———. 2004. "'Essays' Weaves a Dazzling Tapestry of Moods and Epiphanies." Rev. of *Theatrical Essays*, by Tina Landau. *Chicago Sun-Times*, 7 June, 45.

———. 2004. "Tina Landau Essays a New Approach to Drama." *Chicago Sun-Times*, 6 June, 11.

Welsh, Anne-Marie. 1999. "Notes from the Underground." *San Diego Union-Tribune,* 14 Feb., E1, E4.

York, Julie. 1999. "Underground Theater Engrossing 'Floyd Collins' Unearths Tale from America's Past." Rev. of *Floyd Collins,* book by Tina Landau, music and lyrics by Adam Guettel, additional lyrics by Tina Landau. *South Bend Tribune,* 7 May, C4.

Representative Directing Credits

Broadway:
   Bells Are Ringing (2001)

Off and Off-Off Broadway:
   Orestes (1993), *Stonewall: Night Variations* (1994), *Floyd Collins* (1996, 2003), *Trojan Women: A Love Story* (1996), *Cloud Tectonics* (1997), *Saturn Returns* (1998), *Dream True* (1999), *Space* (1999), *Miracle Brothers* (2005)

Regional Theatre:
   Marisol (1992), *Orestes* (1992), *Floyd Collins* (1994, 1999), *1969* (1994), *Cloud Tectonics* (1995), *Space* (1997, 1999), *Time to Burn* (1997), *The Berlin Circle* (1998), *The Ballad of Little Jo* (2000), *Maria Arndt* (2002), *States of Independence* (2002), *The Time of Your Life* (2002, 2004), *Beauty* (2003), *Theatrical Essays* (2004), *Cherry Orchard* (2005), *Of Thee I Sing* (2005), *Rag and Bone* (2005), *A Midsummer Night's Dream* (2006), *Iphigenia 2.0* (2007)

 # Lawless, Sue

Born September 26, 1935, in Freeport, Illinois, Sue Lawless has directed such stars as Helen Hayes, Mary Martin, James Whitmore, Larry Kert, and many others. She was among the first women to direct at many of the nation's stock and regional theatres, has directed extensively Off Broadway and Off-Off Broadway, and has served as a visiting faculty and director for several prestigious colleges and universities. Yet, with the exception of one ill-fated production on Broadway in 1981, Lawless has never had much luck breaking the glass ceiling and directing on the Broadway stage.

Growing up a strict Roman Catholic in Chicago, theatre was forbidden to Lawless as a child, thanks to the influence of the church's League of Decency. However, when Lawless reached high school and became involved with a school play, her infatuation with acting was instantaneous, and she resolved to become an actor. After earning a B.S. in physical education in 1957 from DePaul University in Chicago, Lawless moved to New York City with only two hundred dollars and forged a letter of recommendation to get into the training program at the American Theatre Wing, where she completed her program in 1959. She studied a version of Stanislavski's Method acting, an approach she adhered to both as an actor and a director. Despite her mother's discouragement, Lawless succeeded in her quest and became an actor, working steadily by the age of twenty-four.

Although she never intended to become a director, Lawless got an opportunity when George Wojatsik, managing director at the Equity Library Theatre (ELT), offered her a revival of Charles Gaynor's revue *Lend an Ear* because she "knew all the best comics in New York" (Lawless, interview, 2000). Her production at ELT was well received, and her network of theatre contacts soon offered her directing positions in New York City and across the country. When her first child was born, Lawless did not slow down, but took her daughter to rehearsal, breast-feeding her at work when necessary. Her daughter took her first steps at the Actors Theatre of Louisville.

In 1976 Lawless earned a Drama Desk nomination as Best Director of a Musical for Fred Silver's *In Gay Company*. Originally entitled *Gay Company*, the production, described in the program as "A Try-Sexual Musical Revue," played 244 performances at the Little Hippodrome in New York City before moving to Upstairs at Jimmy's. The sixteen-song revue was deemed "tasteful," "stylish," and "witty" by *New York Times* critic Howard Thompson, who wrote, "The direction of Sue Lawless has much to do with the unified brightness and breezy pacing" (1974, 57).

Lawless continued to both act and direct for the stage up to the late 1970s, with her last television appearance as an actor in 1981. By that time, Lawless had a significant directing resume and was working in regional, stock, and Off Broadway theatres.

In 1981 Lawless got an opportunity to direct a musical on Broadway, *The Five O'Clock Girl*, by Guy Bolton and Fred Thompson, with music and lyrics by Bert Kalmar and Harry Ruby. Originally on Broadway in 1927, it was a Cinderella story about a working girl who made an anonymous phone call to her would-be sweetheart at five o'clock every day. Lawless directed the production at the Goodspeed Opera House in East Haddam, Connecticut, in 1979 and again in 1980, then at the Walnut Street Theatre in Philadelphia in 1981, before opening on Broadway at the Helen Hayes Theatre. Both the production and the book and lyrics garnered mixed reviews. Several reviewers found the book and music were not worth reviving. The 1927 production of the musical only played a few months and was "not built for the ages," according to *New York Times* critic Frank Rich (1981, 372). Joel Siegel of ABC television quipped,

"Beowulf has better jokes" (1981, 375). The difficulty for Lawless was not only in directing an antique and making it entertaining, but in gathering good reviews for a musical deemed to be of limited quality. She explained, "The title there might have been *A Disaster on Its Way to the Making*. Still, it was not an unpleasant experience, just an ill-fated one" (Correspondence, 2003).

Reviews of Lawless's direction of *The Five O'Clock Girl* were mainly positive and some glowed with praise. Although Frank Rich suggested the playing style could use an infusion of camp, Clive Barnes of the *New York Post* had the exact opposite judgment, specifically praising the fact that it did not succumb to camp (1981, 374). John Beaufort of the *Christian Science Monitor* embraced the frivolous fun and rated Lawless's direction as "flawless," finding the performance style engaging, with "just the right blend of make-believe sincerity and gentle kidding" (1981, 15). Overall, the critics found the production was well executed, although the decision to resurrect the musical on Broadway was misguided.

Lawless continued to direct steadily in regional, stock, and New York City theatres through the 1980s and 1990s. She proved her success with the musical *The Rise of David Levinsky,* book and lyrics by Isaiah Sheffer with music by Bobby Paul, based on the novel by Abraham Cahan. She directed three productions of the show, first for New York City's American Jewish Theatre in 1983, then again in 1986 and also in 1987, when it moved from New Jersey's George Street Playhouse to the John Houseman Theatre, Off Broadway. The plot revolved around an immigrant who came to the United States as a Talmudic scholar but became a meteoric entrepreneur as a garment manufacturer. The *New York Times* called the George Street production a mixed bag, but admitted, "The audience really roots for Levinsky—and for the show—and much of that credit belongs to Sue Lawless' fluid staging, which has the actors coming up the aisles at crucial moments" (Klein 1986, 11NJ, 24). When the Off Broadway opening of the musical was postponed for reworking, star Larry Kert proved his confidence in Lawless by stating, "The show's opening needs tightening, but we have the luxury and guidance of a secure and strong director and a concentrated story about one man's dream" (Klein 1987, 11NJ, 22). Once the production opened Off Broadway, Beaufort praised Kert and his co-stars for their acting and singing. Although Lawless's contributions were not singled out, Beaufort praised the production for its "well chosen company" and detail to relationships, both of which reflect well on her efforts (1987, 28).

Lawless holds a fondness for *Body Shop,* Walter Marks's musical about strippers in a burlesque club who bare not only their bodies but their souls. Lawless directed the production Off Broadway at the Westbeth Theatre Center in 1994, where it reopened in 1995 for a total of fifty-six performances and nine previews. *New York Times* critic Ben Brantley praised the production, writing, "[T]his evening of song, confession and striptease is as smooth as polyester" (1995, C14).

From 1985 to 1998, Lawless made twelve trips with the Theatre Guild's "Sailing with the Stars," program, allowing her to travel the world while directing some of the biggest stars in the business in some one hundred productions. She recalls, "There was always stuff like working with Richard Kiley, Larry Kert, Mary Martin, Helen Hayes, Patricia Neal, Juliette Prowse, James Whitmore, and Barry Nelson, all together on one trip on the QE2. We traveled with eight stars and each was featured in one evening of entertainment, with everyone participating in one glorious final night. We had rehearsed in New York City and a little in Sydney, Australia, before we sailed. We did *Guys and Dolls, A Thurber Carnival, An Evening with Patricia Neal and Richard Kiley*, I think it was James Whitmore's *Will Rogers, An Evening with Mary Martin,* and a couple of put together evenings with various combinations" (Correspondence, 2003).

In an eclectic career that spans some four hundred productions, Lawless has directed Shakespeare, cabaret, and a wide variety of styles and genres in between. The range of material she has directed suggests her need to constantly adapt her auditions to the situation. She had no formal training in directing, but learned her audition and rehearsal techniques through both experience and instinct. She explains, "I think that an audition technique can only be developed after sitting through a countless number of them. You begin to unconsciously recognize behavior patterns, work habits. I find that I have no standard approach to any audition. They all require something different. . . . After awhile you just get a feel of it. It doesn't mean you aren't any good at the beginning. In fact, overzealous, perhaps. Just that it comes with experience so you just begin to find your own needs and standards" (Correspondence, 2003).

When casting a play, Lawless first looks for talent and "potential for embracing the character," then for technique, training, experience, a sense of humor, intelligence, and finally, attractiveness. She also pays attention to attitude, looking for a company player with a generous spirit. She explains, "I am interested in their behavior out of the room with helping personnel or when they don't think they are being observed. When it's a musical audition, I tend to be turned off by actors who choose to sing negative songs like "If There's A Wrong Way To Do It." . . . [Also,] I am very aware of how they treat the accompanist" (Correspondence, 2003).

Of foremost importance in rehearsal for Lawless is trust between the actor and director. Elaborating about her approach to rehearsals, she states,

> I know my work has always been organic. I was an actor and worked in the Stanislavski Method. I was also a comic, but always tried to base it organi-

cally, realizing that a comic energy is extreme and intuitive. Not always by the rules so to speak. I try never to lead an actor to a space they cannot achieve. . . . I think character evolution can be a long process and once again only experience teaches you how to speed it up. Generally in a company there are many different ways of approaching work, depending as always on talent and training. A calm safe work place is necessary. A director must be nurturing, firm without controlling but in control, supportive, encouraging, and emotionally stable. In other words, just be there fully.

Sometimes I am prone to think of directing as lion taming. It takes amazing organizational skills particularly in musical theatre, Shakespeare, pageants, operas, and works of large size. It takes inordinate patience. You need communication skills, managerial skills, sensitivity skills, a great sense of time and rhythm. . . . I also think you must have ego without being egocentric. You must be without fear. What other people think must never get in the way. Above all there is artistry and commitment in the work. (Correspondence, 2003)

She also talks about the joy of working with designers, one of her favorite parts of pre-production. "When [I was] a neophyte doing opera in Montreal, I was overwhelmed when the three designers assigned to me were the crème de la crème of their community but spoke very little English where I, on the other hand, spoke NO French. We plunged in and within minutes we absolutely understood each other. They were endlessly helpful and the production was beautiful" (Correspondence, 2003).

Reminiscing about her career, Lawless admits her initial naïveté about being a woman in a man's world. "I didn't know there was a glass ceiling. I didn't know I wouldn't get to direct [more] on Broadway because I wasn't a guy. At one point [in the 1970s] I was optioned to direct three Broadway shows, but they couldn't raise money on one. . . . I was very blessed that the people that were producing thought that they could [raise money], but they couldn't" (Interview, 2000). She notes that at the start of her career, many of her fellow directors were men who have since become successful Broadway directors. As new directors, they all began on even ground and all worked in similar theatres, earning positive reviews and excellent reputations in the field, yet she saw their opportunities on Broadway and wondered about her own station in retrospect. It never entered her mind at the time that sexism could factor into the equation, but later she reconsidered that judgment.

Although sexism may have been an obstacle in Lawless's career path, several other obstacles came into play as well. For example, she did not ruthlessly pursue fame as an end in itself. In addition, she chose productions in which she found "a moral quality or reason" which should not imply that she shied away from such issues as nudity on stage or homosexuality, as she did with such Off Broadway productions as *Body Shop* and *In Gay Company* (Lawless, interview, 2000). Because she believes that the material should have some intrinsic value, she has turned down productions with potential. For example, Cy Coleman was working on a new musical at the Coconut Grove, and Lawless was invited to direct. The musical was then entitled *Let 'Em Rot,* and the plot revolved around alimony jail. She turned it down, finding it "so obviously chauvinistic" (Interview, 2000).

In the current century, Lawless has taken leadership in the profession by serving as secretary for the Board of Directors for the Society of Stage Directors and Choreographers (SSDC), the vice president of the Stage Directors and Choreographers Foundation, and the Board of Trustees for the Broadway League/SSDC Pension and Health Funds.

Looking back over her career, Lawless realizes she has a lot for which to be thankful in terms of her successful acting and directing careers. In addition to directing opera, she has directed a variety of cabaret acts—in New York City, Las Vegas, Chicago, Cincinnati, and Toronto. She proudly states, "There is no area of the legitimate theatre that I have not been a part" (Interview, 2000). Her goal is just to continue to work steadily, finding the greatest reward in the work itself and in the knowledge that she has paved the way for those women who follow in her footsteps.

Sources

Barnes, Clive. 1981. "'5 O'Clock Girl' a Full-Time Charmer." Rev. of *The Five O'Clock Girl,* book by Guy Bolton and Fred Thompson, music and lyrics by Bert Kalmar and Harry Ruby. *New York Post,* 29 Jan. Rpt. *New York Theatre Critics' Reviews* 42 (2) (26 Jan.): 373–74.

Beaufort, John. 1981. "Broadway Harks Back to the Golden Age of Musicals." Rev. of *The Five O'Clock Girl,* book by Guy Bolton and Fred Thompson, music and lyrics by Bert Kalmar and Harry Ruby. *Christian Science Monitor,* 4 Feb., 15.

———. 1987. Rev. of *The Rise of David Levinsky,* book and lyrics by Isaiah Sheffer, music by Bobby Paul, based on the novel by Abraham Cahan. *Christian Science Monitor,* 21 Jan., 28.

Brantley, Ben. 1995. "A Musical about Strippers that Bares the Soul." Rev. of *Body Shop,* book, music, and lyrics by Walter Marks. *New York Times,* 30 Jan., C14.

Klein, Alvin. 1986. "Immigrant's Tale at George St." Rev. of *The Rise of David Levinsky,* book and lyrics by Isaiah Sheffer, music by Bobby Paul, based on the novel by Abraham Cahan. *New York Times,* 4 May, late city final edition, 11NJ, 24.

———. 1987. "'David Levinsky' Materializes Again." Rev. of *The Rise of David*

Levinsky, book and lyrics by Isaiah Sheffer, music by Bobby Paul, based on the novel by Abraham Cahan. *New York Times,* 10 Nov., late city final edition, 11NJ, 22.

Lawless, Sue. 2000. Interview with Anne Fliotsos. 16 Mar. New York City.

———. 2000. Correspondence with Anne Fliotsos. 20 Sept.

———. 2003. Correspondence with Anne Fliotsos. 18 Oct.

Rich, Frank. 1981. "Nostalgic 'Five O'Clock Girl.'" Rev. of *The Five O'Clock Girl,* book by Guy Bolton and Fred Thompson, music and lyrics by Bert Kalmar and Harry Ruby. *New York Times,* 29 Jan. In *New York Theatre Critics' Reviews* 42 (2) (26 Jan.): 372.

Siegel, Joel. 1981. "The Five O'Clock Girl." Rev. of *The Five O'Clock Girl,* book by Guy Bolton and Fred Thompson, music and lyrics by Bert Kalmar and Harry Ruby. WABC-TV 7. 28 Jan. In *New York Theatre Critics' Reviews,* 42 (2) (26 Jan.): 375.

Thompson, Howard. 1974. Rev. of *In Gay Company,* music and lyrics by Fred Silver. *New York Times,* 7 Nov., 57.

Representative Directing Credits

Broadway:
> *The Five O'Clock Girl* (1981)

Off and Off-Off Broadway:
> *Lend an Ear* (1969), *Big Charlotte* (1970), *Gay Company* (1974; *In Gay Company* 1975), *A Mark Twain Medley* (1977), *Potholes* (1979), *Sterling Silver* (1979), *Tip-Toes* (1979), *Chase a Rainbow* (1980), *The Rise of David Levinsky* (1983, 1987), *What's a Nice Country Like You . . . Doing in a State Like This?* (1986), *A Rendezvous with God* (1991), *Cut the Ribbons* (1992), *Body Shop* (1994, 1995), *The Window* (1996), *Mother, Father, Gay Son* (1996), *Toupee, or Not to Pay* (1997)

Regional and Stock Theatre:
> *A Thurber Carnival* (1971), *Spread Eagle Papers* (1972), *Rendezvous!* (1973), *As You Like It* (1977), *The Comedy of Errors* (1980), *A Midsummer Night's Dream* (1982), *Nurse Jane Goes to Hawaii* (1982), *Children of a Lesser God* (1983), *The Price* (1985), *Dames at Sea* (1986), *Taking Steps* (1987), *Funny Girl* (1987), *Mike* (1988), *The Mystery of Irma Vepp* (1989), *Bells Are Ringing* (1990), *The Stone Carver* (1990), *Hey Ma, I'm Working Hollywood Boulevard at Last* (1991)

Tours:
> Sailing with the Stars (1985–98), *The Jeweler's Shop* (1995–98)

Other:
> *Bamboo and Bone* (1997)

LeCompte, Elizabeth

Born on April 28, 1944, in Summit, New Jersey, Elizabeth LeCompte is the artistic director of New York City's experimental theatre group, The Wooster Group, whose productions she directs. Under LeCompte's direction, The Wooster Group presents multimedia performances that include a collage of dance, movement, music, theatre, and technology.

As a New Jersey high school student, LeCompte saw a variety of performances in New York City, including the ballets of George Balanchine and works by the Metropolitan Opera. With a desire to study art, LeCompte attended Skidmore College in Saratoga Springs, New York. While working as a waitress at Caffé Lena during her college years, she also became involved in theatre. The venue staged both music and theatre, and LeCompte appeared in her first plays there, including Albert Camus's *Caligula* and St. John Hankin's *The Constant Lover*. LeCompte recalls, "The acting was terrible," and added that director John Wynn Evans "always kept working on a play, and would let things go as far as they could" (Champagne 1981, 19–20).

LeCompte graduated from Skidmore College in 1967 with a B.S. in fine arts. She explains how she made the transition from art to theatre, saying, "I studied painting for four years, did some photography for a while, then gravitated to theater because there was not as much happening in painting as there was in theater. I mean happening in the broadest political sense. At the time painting was very separate from real issues. . . . I think of what I do in the theater as painting on a very large scale" (Kelly 1984, 1).

In 1970 LeCompte joined director Richard Schechner's Performance Group, a collective environmental theatre group based in New York City's The Performing Garage on Wooster Street. At first, LeCompte did graphic design and painting for the company. In 1971 she worked as Schechner's assistant director in addition to acting in The Performance Group's piece, *Commune*. When Schechner left for a six-month trip to India that year, LeCompte took over as director of the production and temporary manager of The Performance Group until his return. LeCompte continued to act in The Performance Group's productions but discovered that she did not enjoy performing. She learned about directing by watching Schechner, who created performances through a combination of different texts, improvisation in rehearsals, and a variety of acting styles. In addition to Schechner, LeCompte cites directors Richard Foreman, Meredith Monk, and Robert Wilson as influences.

In 1975 LeCompte and other Performance Group members, including Spalding Gray, began to create what would become a trilogy entitled *Three Places in Rhode Island*. The trilogy was based on Gray's life and consisted of productions named for places in Gray's past. LeCompte and Gray co-directed the trilogy's first play, *Sakonnet Point,* which focused on Gray's childhood. Opening in 1975 at The Performing Garage, *Sakonnet Point* was unlike The Performance Group's ritualistic and narrative productions because it allowed audiences to create their own meanings from a collage of images and sounds. LeCompte rejected Schechner's idea that performers should feel emotions, explaining, "I believed that an actor didn't have to feel an emotion in order to express it" (Champagne 1981, 20).

The next piece in the trilogy, *Rumstick Road,* was created and first directed by LeCompte and Gray at The Performing Garage in 1977. The production focused on the real-life suicide of Gray's mother and included family letters, photographs, and taped conversations that Gray made with his family about the suicide. It also used a taped conversation with the psychiatrist of Gray's mother. The public presentation of the tape caused a controversy because the psychiatrist had not known that he was being taped. This controversy would be the first of many for LeCompte. The production also incorporated elements of the set from the group's previous production, *Sakonnet Point,* a technique to be employed frequently by LeCompte and her collaborators in years to come.

The third piece in the trilogy, *Nayatt School,* was also created by LeCompte and Gray, but was directed by LeCompte alone in 1978 at The Performing Garage. The piece continued to examine Gray's life and the idea of madness. It included text from T.S. Elliot's *The Cocktail Party,* in which Gray had once performed, and began LeCompte's practice of deconstructing text from established works.

In 1980 LeCompte won an Obie Award for her direction of *Point Judith,* the trilogy's epilogue. Created by Jim Clayburgh, Willem Defoe, Gray, Libby Howes, LeCompte, Ron Vawter, Mathew Hansell, and Michael Rivkin, the production opened at New York City's The Envelope in 1980. Modeled around Eugene O'Neill's *Long Day's Journey into Night, Point Judith* examined the disintegration of the American family. It contained a segment about men on an oil rig and the silent movie *By the Sea,* which featured nuns played by men in drag. Mel Gussow of the *New York Times* wrote, "In common with the Rhode Island trilogy, 'Point Judith' is an abstract, kinetic collage of slapstick, farce, personal tragedy, light, sound and movement. Although each of the plays has moments of striking imagery and knockabout comedy, they seem random and do not readily lend themselves to exegesis. However, the more we learn about Mr. Gray's own life through his work, the easier it is to penetrate his creations. With understanding comes a certain degree of appreciation" (1980, C4).

That year, Schechner left The Performance Group, and some of its members reformed as The Wooster Group, maintaining their base at The Performing Garage. Along with LeCompte, the founding members of The Wooster Group included Clayburgh, Dafoe, Gray, Peyton Smith, Kate Valk, and Vawter. LeCompte became the group's director and artistic director. The next year at The Performing Garage, she directed The Wooster Group's *Route 1 & 9*, the first part in the group's next trilogy titled *The Road to Immortality*. The production included a deconstruction of Thorton Wilder's *Our Town*, a play that looked at everyday life in a white American community. For *Route 1 & 9*, scenes from a taped version of *Our Town* played like a soap opera on television monitors, while the all-white company enacted Pigmeat Markham's *The Party*, a vaudeville routine performed in blackface. In addition to this, the production included a pornographic film that portrayed a truck driver and two women hitchhikers from New Jersey's Route 1 and 9. Live telephone calls by the performers to bars, chicken stores, and other places were also amplified into the theatre.

Controversy struck the production. The Wilder estate refused to give The Wooster Group performing rights. In addition, the use of blackface resulted in accusations of racism by audience members and critics and culminated in the withdrawal of funding for the piece from the New York State Council on the Arts. LeCompte says that her intent was not to offend African American audience members and that by using blackface "we were saying, 'This is ugly, unacceptable, demoralizing, inhuman.' But the voice behind it just wasn't loud enough, clear enough" (Kelly 1984, 1). Despite these problems, there was no controversy about the pornographic film during production.

After *Route 1 & 9*, LeCompte directed two dance theatre pieces, *Hula* and *For the Good Times*. *Hula* was first presented at The Performing Garage in 1982, and then again the same year along with *For the Good Times* at Danspace in New York City. Following these pieces, LeCompte and The Wooster Group set off another wave of controversy with the second part of *The Road to Immortality*. First directed by LeCompte as a work-in-progress in 1983, *L.S.D. (. . . Just the High Points)* opened in Boston, Massachusetts, in 1984. The combination of texts in this production included a recording about LSD by Timothy Leary and Arthur Miller's *The Crucible*, which paralleled Senator Joseph McCarthy's witch hunt for communists through a story about the Salem witch trials. From a technical standpoint, the production marked the first time the group used microphones. LeCompte states, "I got the idea from the McCarthy hearings. It was the image of the politicians in front of the microphones that made me think of using them" (Zinoman 2005). During part of the piece, performers sat at a long table outfitted with microphones and monitors. As they read text from beatnik writers and other figures, they were interrupted by buzzers signaling them to stop reading. Performers at the table also recited at high-speed a section of *The Crucible*. In addition, the production included a tape of The Wooster Group rehearsing *The Crucible* on LSD that performers tried to replicate during the production. Angry about the use of his text, Miller filed a cease-and-desist order and demanded that The Wooster Group withdraw *The Crucible* from the production. As a result, performer and writer Michael Kirby rewrote the second part of *L.S.D.* to include the original Salem witch trial testimony instead, and the production reopened in 1985. However, Miller was not entirely eliminated from the revised production. Whenever performers made a reference to Miller's text, they were stopped by a buzzer. LeCompte directed a subsequent production in 1987 at the Los Angeles Festival, where it won an LA Drama Critics Award for Distinguished Achievement. A section of *L.S.D. (. . . Just the High Points)* evolved into a separate piece outside of the trilogy called *North Atlantic*, which was first directed by LeCompte in Eindhoven, Holland, in 1983.

Frank Dell's The Temptation of St. Antony, which incorporated information about Dafoe's film career and Vawter's illness with AIDS, completed the trilogy. First directed by LeCompte as a work-in-progress in 1986, the final version opened at The Performing Garage in 1988. The piece was based in part on Gustave Flaubert's *The Temptation of St. Antony* and included recordings and films of Lenny Bruce (who once used the name Frank Dell), the plot and text from Ingmar Bergman's film *The Magician*, a video of a nude cable television talk show, and Geraldine Cummins's book *The Road to Immortality: Being a Description of the Life Hereafter, With Evidence of the Survival of Human Personality*. The production was a play within a play, with Frank Dell/Lenny Bruce/Ron Vawter and his performers rehearsing *The Temptation of St. Antony* in a hotel room. LeCompte described the piece saying, "Of all the pieces we've done, this is the most polarized in its cultural references. I've set two systems against one another: Hollywood image-making, television, pop culture, where what you see is what you get; and high culture of Europe, the examination of the spiritual idea. . . . You have Hiarion the devil played on video by Willem Dafoe floating around working as an actor, and Flaubert's St. Anthony, a spiritual man questing in a cave someplace in Egypt" (Shewey 1990, 2).

With two trilogies completed, LeCompte and The Wooster Group next turned to playwright Anton Chekhov for inspiration. First directed by LeCompte in 1990 as a work-in-progress, *Brace Up!* opened at The Performing Garage in 1991. Based on Paul Schmidt's modern translation of Chekhov's *The Three Sisters*, the production also included Noh, Kabuki, Japanese films, and American soap operas. In *Brace Up!*, The Wooster Group employed a new technique that featured live performers on stage, whose images also appeared live on video. In addition to acting with each other, performers on stage interacted with performers on the monitors. For example, the part of the nurse, played by a ninety-five-year-old woman, was shown on video when she was unable to appear in person. The fourth act of *The Three Sisters* was not included in *Brace Up!* and was developed into another piece. Called *Fish Story*, LeCompte first directed it as a work-in-progress in Vienna, Austria, in 1993. It was presented again at the end of the year at The Performing Garage.

The work of Eugene O'Neill was part of The Wooster Group's next two works. O'Neill's *The Emperor Jones* was an expressionistic play that revolved around an African American running from racism and prison to a Caribbean Island, where he takes the throne. First directed by LeCompte as a work-in-progress in 1992, the play opened in Frankfurt, Germany, the same year. The production featured The Wooster Group member Kate Valk as the Emperor in blackface wearing a samurai outfit. Michael Feingold of the *Village Voice* reviewed a 1998 production at The Performing Garage, stating, "Elizabeth LeCompte's staging of The Emperor Jones is both great and outrageous. . . . Valk is the centerpiece of the staging, her presence an ultimate distancing gesture toward a work with no female roles. . . . Not only is Valk in blackface, she and Willem Dafoe, who plays the cockney trader Smithers, are costumed as samurai. They talk through mikes, Valk wielding hers like a judge's gavel while Dafoe, lurking in the upstage shadows, supplies his own soundtrack of sinister ducks and gurgles. In the first scene, while 'Emperor' Jones is ensconced in his palace, Valk whizzes about in a cushioned office chair on casters. Periodically, Dafoe joins her onstage for an inexplicable bout of what looks like archaic TV versions of disco dancing, carried out with the solemnity of a high mass" (1998, 137).

LeCompte next directed O'Neill's expressionistic play, *The Hairy Ape*, which examined class differences through the story of a stoker on a ship. First presented at The Performing Garage as a work-in-progress in 1995, the play opened there the next year. Because the steel-frame set took up most of the space in The Performing Garage, the production moved uptown to Broadway's Selwyn Theatre in 1997. The audience sat on bleachers to watch the production, which featured videos of a prizefight, microphones, contemporary music, and O'Neill's actual text—performed quickly but unaltered. Robert Burnstein of the *New Republic* reviewed the fast-paced Broadway production, writing, "The night I saw it there were so many outraged walkouts. . . . In this production, *The Hairy Ape* at last belongs to the rank of playable plays, having found its apotheosis in a dazzling experimental production that uncovers its secret heart. . . . But gifted directors such as Elizabeth LeCompte, and creative companies such as the Wooster Group, manage to show us how the spirit of a work can sometimes best be realized by ignoring the letter—or in this case of *The Hairy Ape,* the unletter—of the text" (1997, 28, 30).

Turning from O'Neill to Gertrude Stein, LeCompte directed The Wooster Group's *House/Lights,* based on Stein's *Dr. Faustus Lights the Lights,* at the Wexner Center for the Arts in Columbus, Ohio, in 1997. Stein's work was only one part of LeCompte's collage, which also included Joseph Mawra's 1964 cult bondage film *Olga's House of Shame.* In the production, performers appeared on stage, live on video, and in prerecorded video. In his review of the 1999 production at The Performing Garage, Ben Brantley of the *New York Times* wrote, "Through the use of the latest tools of . . . technology, the Wooster Group has assembled a portrait, both fractured and fluid, of a world in which any set sense of chronology, culture or identity can no longer be taken for granted. . . . That's the Faustian bargain that Stein deals with, in her typically elliptical way, in her original text, in which the Faust figure is the inventor of artificial light. Under the incisive, spectacularly resourceful direction of Elizabeth LeCompte, that text acquires at least another 60 years worth of levels of displacement. . . . The ways in which 'House/Lights' carries out the confusion of flesh and technology, of self and the projected image, are often breathtaking" (1999, E1). The play won an Obie Award in 1999 for Best Production.

LeCompte's next directing project garnered more awards. First presented as a work-in-progress in 2001 at The Performing Garage, The Wooster Group's production of *To You, The Birdie! (Phèdre)* opened at The Festival D'Automne in Paris the same year. The production was based on Paul Schmidt's translation of Jean Racine's *Phèdre,* which centers on a queen, Phèdre, who lusts for her stepson, Hippolytos. In The Wooster Group version, Phèdre is a fashion victim addicted to enemas. Her lines are mostly spoken into a microphone by a male actor, who also plays the part of a confidant of Hippolytos named Theramenes. The production included an industrial metal set, video and medical equipment, and musical recordings. In his review of the 2003 production at St. Ann's Warehouse in Brooklyn, Brantley wrote that Phèdre "is no good at all at the games she has to play: politics, love, badminton (yes, badminton.) . . . Ms. LeCompte and the company . . . make you think about a stately classic in entirely new and surprisingly logical ways. . . . The game [badminton] here becomes a multifaceted metaphor: for the formality of the play, the ritualized nature of courtly society and that big, nobody-wins sport called love" (2002, E1). In 2002 *To You, The Birdie! (Phèdre)* won an Obie Special Citation, a Back Stage West Garland, and a New York Dance and Performance (Bessie) Award for Best Production. That year LeCompte also won the Back Stage West Garland for Direction.

The Wooster Group's next production focused on Polish director Jerzy Grotowski, author of *Towards a Poor Theatre* and proponent of ritualistic, stripped-down theatre. First directed by LeCompte as a work-in-progress in 2003, The Wooster Group's production of *Poor Theatre* opened the following year at The Performing Garage. The Wooster Group brushed with controversy once again when it included a videotape of journalist Margaret Croyden in the piece. Croyden claimed that she was unaware of being videotaped during rehearsal and demanded that the segment be removed. LeCompte agreed to remove the image, but at first substituted a video of herself, lip-synching to Croyden's voice before searching for another performer to say the words. Other identities were also blurred throughout the production. Brantley described the production, stating, "Ms. LeCompte . . . is a character here, acted by Sheena See. Ari Fliakos, in turn plays Ms. See. Kate Valk . . . portrays a Polish tour guide in the show's opening segment, while Joby Emmons plays Ms. Valk. . . . On the raised monitors behind them, there hover what appear to be live transmissions of the faces of the men operating the sound and light boards. (Notice that I say appear.) Other characters, including a Polish theater critic (the real thing, as far as I can tell) and the lighting designer, Jennifer Tipton, make their appearance in only two dimensions, on flat screens, yet are very much part of the conversation" (2005, E1).

LeCompte's bold directorial choices are discovered through collaborative rehearsals. Works may take years to develop and are created from found materials, such as texts and video, as well as original images and texts. LeCompte states, "I really can't say what attracts me to a text. . . . It might just be a line [of dialogue] or an image, and I just see where that takes me" (Sterrit 1997, 14). She explains, "I gravitate toward things that are confusing, alien, or a mystery to me. . . . Most people try to illustrate some feeling they have about the world. . . . I'm illustrating—or demonstrating—my confusions and questions" (Sterritt 1985, 23).

Sometimes LeCompte places elements next to each other in time and space that may potentially result in meaning, although the meaning is not predetermined. LeCompte also juxtaposes high art and low art, which results in new perspectives for audiences. She says, "There is no question that my work has been influenced by MTV, and specifically before MTV by ads on TV—the cutting, editing, distancing, storytelling, the combination of live characters and animation in commercials, the quick pacing. Telling a sometimes disjointed story in a very rapid way is definitely a great influence" (1984, interview, 13).

LeCompte casts available company members and interns, as well as actors from outside the company. Extensive acting experience is not necessarily a priority, but a performer's personality is crucial in matching parts with performers.

LeCompte explains what she values in a performer, saying, "The thing that seems to be very important is an interest in the whole piece, being able to see the piece as a dialogue with the audience, rather than their individual part as a dialogue with the audience. So it has to be people who can come forward very strongly with a strong ego sense and at the same time step back and not feel lessened by that" (1984, interview, 13). Casting often occurs well into in the development of a piece. Sometimes a company member's wish to play a particular part, such as Valk's desire to play Phèdre, will drive the creation of a piece. The reversal of gender, race, and age as well as the playing of multiple parts may affect casting decisions. In addition, the individual experiences of performers may make their way into performances. LeCompte explains the advantage of working with a company, saying, "[B]ecause we know each other so well and we've been working together for so long, the performers in the company pick up right away and I can pick up from them right away and (we can) take an idea to its natural conclusion or its unnatural conclusion" (Isenberg 1987, 47).

Before rehearsals, LeCompte and The Wooster Group may read or examine materials relevant to the production for ideas. LeCompte often begins with a visual image for the company to explore and gives tasks to performers. She explains, "I usually begin with game structures. These slowly trick me into seeing things I might not have noticed otherwise, and I make aesthetic judgments. Also in rehearsal, I try to deal mostly with tasks. I say to the actors, 'You have information to present to the audience, and you are responsible for a clear imparting of this information.' That's giving them a mental task, so they can get through the persona thing without coloring it emotionally" (Mee 1992, 147). LeCompte tapes rehearsals and is very detail-oriented, creating her staging during rehearsals and culling from the creative work of the performers. Productions may be presented as works-in-progress for years before she sets a final version. Audience reaction is considered with each revision of a work.

LeCompte discusses her directing style, stating, "I don't think the way I work is autocratic. I like to run a tight ship. I like to have the final say, not so much because I want the power of it, but because otherwise, I lose my way. These workers bring this material to me, and I sift and siphon through it. It isn't that some material is 'better' than other material. I use it when it links up to something very particular with me, when it extends my vision slightly. Then I can encompass the material. It's a slow process and it's not democratic in any way. But autocratic is the wrong word for it" (Savran 1988, 115–16).

LeCompte and The Wooster Group are not bothered by performance or technical problems that occur during a show. Typically, performers stop the action, acknowledge the problem, and then either resume performing or wait until the technical problems are fixed. LeCompte says, "Most theatre is about tricks . . . and if the trick fails—the door doesn't close or a bit of the set falls off—it breaks the trust with the audience and leaves the performer in a place of humiliation. We never use tricks; everything is laid bare. If something goes wrong, it goes wrong and maybe the wrong will end up being a right, something interesting" (Gardner 2002, 10). LeCompte believes that theatre, which uses the fourth wall, competes unsuccessfully with television. She says, "The truth is that television does it better than Broadway ever has. . . . What has to happen to make theater work again—commercially or experimentally—is an acceptance of the audience as present and capable of interacting with the work it's watching" (Kelly 1984, 1).

Among her many awards and honors, LeCompte has won a National Endowment for the Arts Distinguished Artists Fellowship in 1991, a MacArthur Fellowship in 1995, and the Skowhegan Medal for Performance in 2005. With The Wooster Group, she has received an Obie Award for Sustained Excellence in 1991 and The Edwin Booth Award for Significant Contributions to the New York City Theater in 1993. LeCompte was also hired as associate director of the Kennedy Center of the Performing Arts in Washington, D.C. She has lectured and taught at numerous colleges and universities and has directed videos and films in addition to theatre.

Known for being an innovator in technique and content, LeCompte continues to explore new theatrical frontiers. She explains, "I want to create a world where I've never been before, one that surprises me, one that I can enter only in the theatre space" (Dolce 1990, 76).

Sources

Aronson, Arnold. 1985. "The Wooster Group's *L.S.D. (. . . Just the High Points . . .).*" *TDR/The Drama Review* 20 (2) (T106) (Summer): 65–77.

Brantley, Ben. 1999. "A Case for Cubism and Deals With Devils." Rev. of *House/Lights*, by The Wooster Group, based on *Doctor Faustus Lights the Lights*, by Gertrude Stein. *New York Times*, 3 Feb., E1.

———. 2002. "Racine's Pale Queen, Struggling With Racket Sports." Rev. of *To You, The Birdie! (Phèdre)*, by The Wooster Group, based on Paul Schmidt's trans. of *Phèdre*, by Jean Racine. *New York Times*, 19 Feb., E1.

———. 2005. "Dissecting Two Rebels of the Arts." Rev. of *Poor Theater*, by The Wooster Group. *New York Times*, 29 Sept., E1.

Burnstein, Robert. 1997. "The Descent of Man." Rev. of *The Hairy Ape*, by Eugene O'Neill. *New Republic* 216 (19) (12 May): 27–30.

Champagne, Lenora. 1981. "Always Starting New: Elizabeth LeCompte." *TDR/The Drama Review* 25 (3) (T91) Fall: 19–28.

Chinoy, Helen Krich and Linda Walsh Jenkins, eds. 1987. *Women in American Theatre*. New York: Theatre Communications Group.

Cole, Susan Letzler. 1992. "Elizabeth LeCompte Directs Frank Dell's *The Temptation of Saint Anthony.*" In *Directors in Rehearsal: A Hidden World,* 91–124. New York: Routledge.

Conlin, Kathleen. 1989. "LeCompte, Elizabeth Alice." In *Notable Women in the American Theatre: A Biographical Dictionary,* ed Alice M. Robinson, Vera Mowry Roberts, and Milly S. Barranger, 528–31. Westport, Conn.: Greenwood.

Dolce, Joe. 1990. "Liz LeCompte." *Interview* 20 (6) (June): 76.

Feingold, Michael. 1998. "Rites and Wrongs." Rev. of *The Emperor Jones,* by Eugene O'Neill; *Macbeth,* by William Shakespeare; and *Mystery School,* by Paul Selig. *Village Voice,* 24 Mar., 137.

Gardner, Lyn. 2002. "Absolutely Potty: There Aren't Many Theatre Companies That Would Turn One of Racine's Great Heroines Into an Enema Addict— and Then Expect Us to Take the Play Seriously." *The Guardian* (London), 9 May, 10.

Gussow, Mel. 1980. "Spalding Gray's 'Point Judith.'" Rev. of *Point Judith,* by Jim Clayburgh, Willem Dafoe, Spalding Gray, Libby Howes, Elizabeth LeCompte, Ron Vawter, Matthew Hansell, and Michael Rivkin; and *A Personal History of the American Theater,* by Spalding Gray. *New York Times,* 30 Dec., C4.

Isenberg, Barbara. 1987. "Los Angeles Festival 'High Points' Saucy Brew from Wooster Group." *Los Angeles Times,* 30 Aug., 47.

Kelly, Kevin. 1984. "Experimental Wooster Group Survived; The Wooster Group Performs Elizabeth LeCompte's 'L.S.D.'" *Boston Globe,* 15 Apr., 1.

LeCompte, Elizabeth. 1984. Interview with Mindy Levine. "An Interview with Elizabeth LeCompte." *Theatre Times* 3 (Aug.): 13–14.

Leiter, Samuel L. 1994. "Elizabeth LeCompte." In *The Great Stage Directors: 100 Distinguished Careers of the Theater,* 174–77. New York: Facts on File.

Mee, Susie. 1992. "Chekhov's *Three Sisters* and the Wooster Group's *Brace Up!*" *TDR/The Drama Review* 36 (4) (T136) (Winter): 143–53.

Savran, David. 1988. *Breaking the Rules: The Wooster Group.* New York: Theatre Communications Group.

Schmidt, Paul. 1992. "The Sounds of *Brace Up!*: Translating the Music of Chekhov." *TDR/The Drama Review* 36 (4) (T136) (Winter): 154–57.

Shewey, Don. 1990. "Wooster Group Not Tempted by Conventionality Stage: The Experimental-Theater Troupe Had Jumbled-Up Flaubert for Its 'Frank Dell's The Temptation of St. Antony.'" *Los Angeles Times,* 27 Aug., 2.

Smither, Nancy Putnam. 2002. "Directing the Acting Ensemble: Meredith Monk, Elizabeth LeCompte, and Anne Bogart." Ph.D. diss., New York University.

Sterritt, David. 1985. "Going Against the Grain." *Christian Science Monitor,* 24 June, 23.

———. 1997. "Barring Critics, Inventive Theater Group Still Thrives." *Christian Science Monitor,* 9 Apr., 14.

Wolff-Wilkinson, Lila. 1994. "Elizabeth Alice LeCompte." In *Theatrical Directors:*

A Biographical Dictionary, ed. John W. Frick and Stephen M. Vallillo, 233–35. Westport, Conn.: Greenwood.

Zinoman, Jason. 2005. "The Wooster Group: An Oral History." *Time Out New York*, 27 Jan., http://www.timeout.com/newyork/DetailsAr.do?file=/features/487/487.thewoostergroup.html (accessed 18 March 2006).

Representative Directing Credits[1]

Broadway:
> *The Hairy Ape* (1997)

Off and Off-Off Broadway:
> *Sakonnet Point (Three Places in Rhode Island)* (co-directed with Spalding Gray—1975, 1976), *Rumstick Road (Three Places in Rhode Island)* (co-directed with Spalding Gray—1977, 1980), *Nayatt School (Three Places in Rhode Island)* (1978, 1982), *Three Places in Rhode Island (Sakonnet Point* and *Rumstick Road* (co-directed with Spalding Gray—1978, 1979), *Point Judith (an epilogue) (Three Places in Rhode Island)* (1980, 1981, 1982), *Hula* (1981, 1982, 1984), *Route 1 & 9 (The Road to Immortality)* (1981, 1982, 1986, 1987), *For the Good Times* (1982), *L.S.D. (. . . Just the High Points . . .) (The Road to Immortality)* (1984, 1985, 1987), *North Atlantic* (1984, 1988, 1999, 2000), *Frank Dell's The Temptation of St. Antony (The Road to Immortality)* (1987, 1988, 1989, 1990, 1992), *Brace Up!* (1990, 1991, 1992, 1994, 2003), *The Emperor Jones* (1992, 1993, 1994, 1995, 1998, 2006), *Fish Story* (1993, 1994), *The Hairy Ape* (1995, 1996), *House/Lights* (1998, 1999, 2005), *To You, The Birdie! (Phèdre)* (2001, 2002), *Poor Theater* (2004, 2005), *Who's Your Dada?* (2006), *Hamlet* (2007)

Regional Theatre:
> *Rumstick Road (Three Places in Rhode Island)* (co-directed with Spalding Gray—1978, 1979), *L.S.D. (. . . Just the High Points . . .) (The Road to Immortality)* (1985, 1986, 1987), *North Atlantic* (1985, 2000), *Frank Dell's The Temptation of St. Antony (The Road to Immortality)* (1987, 1990), *Brace Up!* (1991), *House/Lights* (1997), *To You, The Birdie! (Phèdre)* (2002), *Poor Theater* (2004), *The Emperor Jones* (2007)

International Theatre:
> *Three Places in Rhode Island (Sakonnet Point, Rumstick Road, Nayatt School) (Sakonnet Point* and *Rumstick Road* co-directed with Spalding Gray—1978), *Point Judith (an epilogue) (Three Places in Rhode Island)* (1981), *For the Good Times* (1982), *Hula* (1982), *Route 1 & 9 (The Road to Immortality)* (1982, 1983, 1985), *North Atlantic* (1983, 2000, 2001), *L.S.D. (. . . Just the High Points . . .) (The Road to Immortality)* (1986, 1987, 1988, 1989, 1990), *Frank Dell's The Temptation of St. Antony (The Road to Immortality)* (1989, 1990, 1994, 1995), *Brace Up!* (1990, 1991, 1992, 1994), *The Emperor Jones*

(1992, 1994, 1996, 1998), *Fish Story* (1993, 1994, 1996), *The Hairy Ape* (1996, 1997, 1998, 2001), *House/Lights* (1997, 1998, 1999, 2000, 2001), *To You, The Birdie! (Phèdre)* (2001, 2002, 2003, 2004, 2006), *Poor Theater* (2004, 2005), *Hamlet* (2006)

Notes

1. Because The Wooster Group's pieces evolve over time, these credits include works-in-progress.

 # Le Gallienne, Eva

Born on January 11, 1899, in London, England, Eva Le Gallienne was a director, producer, performer, translator, and writer. Her dedication to repertory theatre in the United States helped to pave the way for the Off Broadway and regional theatre movements.

Drawn to theatre as a young child, Le Gallienne saw her first play in 1902 and idolized the actor Sarah Bernhardt. Wanting her own copy of Bernhardt's out-of-print memoirs, *Ma Double Vie*, Le Gallienne borrowed the book and copied it by hand. In 1909 Le Gallienne attended the College de Sevigny in Paris, transferring to the English boarding school Courtfield in 1913. The following year, she attended the Academy of Dramatic Art (also known as Tree's Academy) in London, which was later named the Royal Academy of Dramatic Art.

Beginning her career as an actor, Le Gallienne made her professional stage debut in 1914 as the Page in Maurice Maeterlinck's *Monna Vanna* at the Queens Theatre in London. The next year she moved to the United States and made her New York City debut as Rose in *Mrs. Boltay's Daughter* at the Comedy Theatre. It wasn't long before she became a Broadway star in 1921 while performing the role of Julie in Ferenc Molnár's *Liliom*. The same year, Le Gallienne directed *Casualties* at New York City's Garrick Theatre. The play was presented in a production of one-act plays by a group that she formed called Actor Friends. She described the event as "pretty ghastly" (Sheeney 1996, 95).

When the Moscow Art Theatre came to New York City in 1923, Le Gallienne attended many of their performances. She was greatly interested in Stanislavski's technique and the ensemble playing of the group. The same year she saw the actor Eleonora Duse perform in London. Duse fascinated and influenced her to the extent that Le Gallienne later wrote a biography of the performer titled *The Mystic in the Theatre: Eleonora Duse,* published in 1966. Duse's acting technique, in which she would use a natural voice, appear to listen, and use moments of stillness rather than constant movement, influenced Le Gallienne's own technique as a performer and a director.

Le Gallienne had a chance to direct again while rehearsing for a Broadway production of Gerhart Hauptmann's *The Assumption of Hannele* in 1924. During rehearsals, the director became ill and Le Gallienne took over the direction of the play. She discovered that she loved the control that directing gave her. She also enjoyed directing herself as a performer and not having to answer to another director's orders.

The next year, after the Actors Theatre rejected her proposal to play Hilda in Henrik Ibsen's *The Master Builder,* Le Gallienne decided to take her career into her own hands and to produce, direct, and perform in the play on Broadway herself. The play was a critical success, with the *New York Times* stating, "The current performance of 'The Master Builder' vibrates with the overtones of this symbolic play and by ignoring the tedious paraphernalia of producing reveals a clean shaft of acting. . . . As Hilda, Eva Le Gallienne gives . . . a daring performance. Miss Le Gallienne strips it of every embellishment. . . . The acting of the other parts is no less according to design. . . . The minor parts come off proportionately well" ("Ibsen's," 1925, XI).

After the success of *The Master Builder,* Le Gallienne decided to produce another Ibsen play on Broadway, *John Gabriel Borkman.* She successfully alternated performances of the two plays. Brooks Atkinson of the *New York Times* complimented the production's direction for achieving "dramatic contrast" and wrote, "[T]he acting . . . expresses the play perfectly. . . . [T]he dominant impression is of a well-joined group exposition, instinct with understanding. Even the subordinate part of the maid . . . bends into the general illusion" (1926, 13).

After touring the two plays for three months to promote the idea for a repertory theatre, Le Gallienne received enough donations from rich patrons and subscribers for the first season of her theatre, the Civic Repertory Theatre. On October 26, 1926, the Civic opened its doors on unfashionable Fourteenth Street, west of 6th Avenue in New York City. The theatre's founder, producer, director, and star performer was twenty-six-year-old Le Gallienne. Dedicated to presenting primarily classical plays in repertory, Le Gallienne insisted upon keeping ticket prices low so that most people could attend. As a result, most of the Civic's audience consisted of working-class people and students who could not afford to see plays on Broadway.

Le Gallienne employed a company of paid performers who were not stars but instead solid performers who agreed with her ideals about repertory theatre. She also selected a professional managerial staff that was comprised entirely of women. Le Gallienne received much criticism for selecting a staff of women, and critic George Jean Nathan referred to the management as "the Le Gallienne sorority" (1928, 122).

Le Gallienne's first critical recognition as an excellent director came with the Civic's production of Anton Chekhov's *The Three Sisters* in 1926. Critics praised the production for its ensemble acting. At the end of the year, her innovative direction of Shakespeare's *Twelfth Night* was described by a *New York Times* critic as "a 'Twelfth Night' pitched in a different key from any which has gone before—any, at least, that has been viewed by this commentator. In settings, in costumes and sometimes in playing it is definitely fantastic. The Calthrop settings are the sort that [m]ight be contributed to an 'Americana'; the wigs and facial make-up carry out the idea of puppets. . . . The same set pieces are made to do duty for Olivia's garden and Orino's palace—only the painted backdrop is varied. When Malvolio pompously struts his hour, the three conspirators are hidden behind bushes palpably fashioned by the carpenter; in fact, they are picked up and carried here and there for concealment purposes" ("Eva Le Gallienne Acts," 1926, 21).

At the Civic, Le Gallienne produced three to five plays a week, comprised mostly of classics but including some new plays and American premieres of European works. She directed thirty-two of the thirty-four plays during the Civic's history, starring in most of them. Occasionally Le Gallienne would receive offers from Broadway producers to move her shows uptown. However, she refused these offers since they went against her principles of keeping ticket prices low for the audience. Le Gallienne also disliked long runs and believed that plays in repertory were more alive than productions with traditional runs.

In addition to her acting and directing experience, Le Gallienne had an excellent knowledge of lighting, set design, props, and other technical areas of the theatre. At the Civic, Le Gallienne cast, lighted, and laid out the playing spaces for the shows. She created models of the set from which the set designer worked. Le Gallienne also opened a free school, called The Apprentice Group, which consisted of twenty to thirty acting students selected from about three hundred applicants. Of the final group, four were hired for the next season, and some were eventually asked to join the company. Because of her role in all areas of production, Le Gallienne was known as "the General," "Top Sergeant," "the Colonel," and "the Abbess of Fourteenth Street." With so many duties to perform, Le Gallienne lived in an apartment above the theatre but retreated to her home in Weston, Connecticut, to translate plays and to write when her schedule permitted it.

Despite her critical success, some reviewers wrote that Le Gallienne's directing suffered because she acted in her productions. Le Gallienne explained that she appeared in the plays for economic reasons, to draw crowds to the theatre. Reviewers also criticized her acting as being too intellectual and cool, and criticized her for not being able to play women with enough emotion. An article in the *New York Times* about Le Gallienne's performance of Hilda in *The Master Builder* noted, "Her acting . . . is extremely severe; she does not soften it with a gentle flow of gestures, oozing gradually from mood to mood" ("Ibsen's," 1925, X1). Le Gallienne's interpretation of women often confused critics, who were used to seeing more stereotypical portrayals of women, as directed by men. However, when she played men, some critics were still disapproving. Atkinson criticized Le Gallienne's performance in Clemence Dane's adaptation of Edmond Rostand's *L'Aiglon,* in which Le Gallienne played a young man. He wrote, "Although the premiere audience appeared to be consumed with admiration for the performance, and gave Miss Le Gallienne and Ethel Barrymore a cannonading of cheers at the conclusion, this reporter could never rise above the fundamental pretense at the core of the performance" (1934, 22).

The Civic was also criticized by some reviewers for presenting plays that were too serious and intellectual. In response, Le Gallienne directed a 1928 production of James Barrie's *Peter Pan* and played the flying Peter herself. The play was a success, and she decided to keep it in the repertory because children enjoyed it so much. The critic for the *New York Times* wrote, "Nothing was left undone and everything was well done, from the stage settings to the wag of Nana's tail. . . . Miss Le Gallienne's production generally is her own, with many variations in detail from the New York original" ("Eva Le Gallienne a Wistful," 1928, 27).

During the Great Depression, both Le Gallienne and the Civic began to falter. In 1930 Le Gallienne's romantic relationship with performer Josephine Hutchinson was revealed, resulting in negative publicity and a hospital stay for Le Gallienne. The next year Le Gallienne survived a fiery explosion from a heater in her home, escaping with severe burns that required surgery. With the onset of the Depression, a backlash hit Le Gallienne and other working women, as men found themselves unemployed and reclaiming the jobs that women held. Whitney Bolton of the *New York Telegram* wrote of the "disturbing fact that the theater is rapidly becoming feminized" (1932, 218–19).

In 1932 Le Gallienne presented another production for adults and children—*Alice in Wonderland.* Based on Lewis Carroll's *Alice in Wonderland* and *Through the Looking Glass,* the play was created by Le Gallienne and actress Florida Friebus. Le Gallienne directed a stunningly visual production that was popular with audiences. She played the White Queen, who literally flew on and off the stage. The performance also featured more than fifty cast members, puppets, music, and dance. In his *New York Times* review, Atkinson wrote, "For Miss Le Gallienne's 'Alice in Wonderland' is quite the most interesting variation the theatre has played on its main theme in some years. It is light, colorful and politely fantastic" (1932, 18).

In need of money for the Civic, Le Gallienne compromised her principles and moved two of her productions, *Alice in Wonderland* and Chekhov's *The Cherry Orchard*, uptown. Despite critical acclaim, she was unable to raise enough money to save the Civic. After trying to keep the company together by touring, Le Gallienne officially closed the Civic in 1935.

Afterward, Le Gallienne continued to direct, produce, and perform in productions in New York, Connecticut, Massachusetts, and on tour. In an attempt to keep her dream of repertory theatre alive, Le Gallienne created the American Repertory Theatre in 1946 with her lover, actor and director Margaret Webster, and friend, producer Cheryl Crawford. Like the Civic Theatre, the American Repertory Theatre offered an ensemble cast in repertory productions, but they were directed by Webster and Le Gallienne. A revival of *Alice in Wonderland*, directed by Le Gallienne, featured herself as the White Queen and Webster as the Red Queen. Delighted, Atkinson noted the huge scope of the production, which included masks and "a living panorama of the Tenniel drawings" (1947, 19).

Despite the determination of its founders, the theatre—located at an inconvenient address on Columbus Circle—lost money. In order to stay afloat, the partners had to compromise their ideals by raising ticket prices and abandoning the idea of presenting plays in repertory. Problems with the unions, which insisted on higher wages and more jobs, also helped to break the theatre. Reviewers criticized the choice of plays as not being contemporary enough for the public's taste. The theatre closed after two years.

From 1948 to 1958 Le Gallienne did not direct but did act occasionally. Then in 1961 she tried one last time to create a repertory theatre. She helped to found the National Repertory Theatre, which toured throughout the country for much of its existence. Le Gallienne stayed with the company for six of its seven years, and directed three and performed in six of its productions. In 1964 she received a special Tony Award celebrating her work with the company and her fiftieth year as an actress. Le Gallienne's effort to create ensemble casts in repertory theatre was instrumental in helping to build both Off Broadway and regional theatre in the United States.

After she resigned from the National Repertory Company, Le Gallienne continued to perform and direct. In 1964 she directed and acted in Chekhov's *The Seagull* to critical acclaim. In his review of the production in the

New York Times, Howard Taubman noted, "Miss Le Gallienne's staging is without flourishes, and it is not afraid of the pauses that are so meaningful in Chekhov. Between the wistful, mocking, self-revealing lines, they [the cast] are allowed to speak and chuckle and sigh" (1964, 36). Le Gallienne ended her stage career at the age of eighty-three on Broadway with a 1982 production of *Alice in Wonderland,* which she directed and in which she performed once again flying across the stage as the White Queen.

In a long career that emphasized acting, Le Gallienne's role as a casting director was crucial to her success. When casting performers, she preferred people who could work well together and often hired performers that she knew or had seen before. Because of constraints on her time, Le Gallienne asked others to attend shows to find new talent for her. She believed that performers needed ten years to learn their craft and should observe live theatre as an important part of their educational experience. Quoting the English theatrical great Granville Barker, she noted, "Education and travel are the best education for a stage career. Memory, imagination, faith, will power, sense of humor and tragic sense are all requisites" ("Sees," 1925, 7).

Le Gallienne was known for her directorial ability to create ensemble acting where no stars stood out. Even though she was a star who drew crowds to the Civic, Le Gallienne felt that the play must shine foremost, and that performers should not upstage the play. To that end, Le Gallienne took the contributions of each performer and blended them into a smooth ensemble. She was known for creating thoughtful performances in which silences were laden with meaning.

Viewing direction as a separate skill, Le Gallienne noted, "In America no one will say that he will give up the fifteen years needed to learn how to direct plays. They all think they can direct any play or stage in one year" ("Sees," 1925, 7). She believed that in addition to other skills, directors needed to have acting experience. As a performer, she was sensitive to actors' needs and altered her directing technique according to the individual performer. In her autobiography, *With a Quiet Heart,* she wrote, "No two actors can be treated alike. Some need to be flattered, some cajoled; some even bullied. Some like to be told precisely how to read a line or execute a piece of business, while others must be left strictly alone" (1953, 99).

Most of Le Gallienne's rehearsals followed a set pattern. She required performers to be familiar with the script before beginning. Then, at the first rehearsal, Le Gallienne would read the script to the cast, a practice that was common at the time. After this, the cast participated in readings and discussions of the script before moving the play onstage. During rehearsals, Le Gallienne often gave notes to actors privately, although she sometimes spoke to performers in front of the ensemble as well. When directing at the Civic, Le Gallienne used a set as soon as possible—something that performers in the commercial theatre did not usually have access to until dress rehearsals (Sheehy 1996, 182).

Because many of the plays she directed were in repertory, Le Gallienne often had only a week in which to stage a play. In order to create a clear concept and to maintain the rhythm of the production, Le Gallienne believed that the director needed to have a specific vision for the play. In general, she blocked the movement and provided suggestions for business but allowed performers to create their own characters through the use of Stanislavski's character analysis. She said, "I leave my players alone. I want their minds to be free to work intelligently. We have so few real actors and actresses because the directors want to do it all" (Parkhurst 1928, 66).

Le Gallienne's directing style varied depending upon the production. For example, two plays with very different directorial needs were Jacinto Benavente's *Saturday Night* and Chekhov's *The Three Sisters,* both presented in repertory in 1926. For *Saturday Night,* Le Gallienne blocked the play with a system that used red for men and blue for women, along with numbers and diagrams that showed the position of the performers. In contrast to that, for *The Three Sisters,* she allowed the cast to develop their own movement, which she refined in final rehearsals.

Whereas *Saturday Night* was directed in a more dictatorial style, *The Three Sisters* was created in a collaborative style. Le Gallienne took the cast to Connecticut to prepare for *The Three Sisters* while the Civic was being converted from an old burlesque house to a proper theatre. She hoped that the time together would help her new ensemble to bond as a group. After improvising their characters for several weeks, the actors began to work with the text. Le Gallienne asked performers to deliver Chekhov's lines as close to natural conversation as possible.

Le Gallienne wrote about directing Chekhov in *With a Quiet Heart,* saying, "The quality of a Chekhov production depends so tremendously on what goes beneath the lines, on the almost casual interplay between the various characters, on a truth and simplicity so thoroughly understood and digested that it becomes effective in a subtle unobtrusive way in no sense dependent on the usual theatrical externals. It is a sort of flavor that permeates the whole ensemble—a mood, an aura.... Instead of doing, one must simply be" (1953, 230–31). Le Gallienne became known for directing excellent ensemble productions of Chekhov and Ibsen. To her credit, Le Gallienne often received excellent reviews for her direction of Ibsen's plays from Atkinson, the major critic at the *New York Times,* despite the fact that he was not a fan of Ibsen.

Among Le Gallienne's awards are honorary degrees from ten colleges, a *Pictorial Review* prize (sponsored by the National Woman's Party) in 1926, the honor roll of *The Nation* in 1927, the Women's National Press Club's Outstanding Woman of the Year Award in 1947, the American National Theatre and Academy (ANTA) awards in 1964 and 1977, the American Theatre Association's Citation of distinguished service to the theatre in 1973, the Achievement in Arts Award for the Connecticut Commission on the Arts in 1980, and the National Medal of Arts in 1986. In addition to her work as a director, actor, and producer, Le Gallienne wrote books, adapted literature for theatre, and translated many plays into English. Le Gallienne died on June 3, 1991, in Westport, Connecticut.

In an address to students at Yale University, Le Gallienne noted, "The theatre must be a place where all things can be found, where the dross can be separated from the gold. . . . Let us make the theatre of America stand free and high up, with no world peers" ("Sees," 1925, 7).

Sources

Atkinson, J. Brooks. 1926. "Shadows of Death." Rev. of *John Gabriel Borkman*, by Henrik Ibsen. *New York Times*, 30 Jan., 13.

———. 1932. "Eva and 'Alice in Wonderland.'" Rev. of *Alice in Wonderland*, by Eva Le Gallienne and Florida Friebus, based on *Alice in Wonderland* and *Through the Looking Glass*, by Lewis Carroll. *New York Times*, 12 Dec., 18.

———. 1934. "Eva Le Gallienne and Ethel Barrymore in Clemence Dane's Adaptation of 'L'Aigion.'" Rev. of *L'Aigion*, by Edmond Rostand, adapted by Clemence Dane. *New York Times*, 5 Nov., 22.

———. 1947. "'Alice in Wonderland.'" Rev. of *Alice in Wonderland*, by Eva Le Gallienne and Florida Friebus, based on *Alice in Wonderland* and *Through the Looking Glass*, by Lewis Carroll. *New York Times*, 7 Apr., 19.

Bolton, Whitney. 1932. *New York Telegram*, 30 Nov. In *Eva Le Gallienne*, by Helen Sheehy, 218–19. New York: Knopf, 1996.

Cooper, Roberta Krensky. 1967. "Eva Le Gallienne's Civic Repertory Theatre." Ph.D. diss., University of Illinois.

"Eva Le Gallienne A Wistful Peter Pan." 1928. Rev. of *Peter Pan, or the Boy Who Would Not Grow Up*, by J.M. Barrie. *New York Times*, 27 Nov., 27.

"Eva Le Gallienne Acts Viola With Charm." 1926. Rev. of *Twelfth Night*, by William Shakespeare. *New York Times*, 21 Dec., 21.

"Ibsen's Prose-Poetry." 1925. *New York Times*, 15 Nov., XI.

Knapp, Margaret M. 1996. "Le Gallienne, Eva." In *International Dictionary of Theatre—3: Actors, Directors and Designers*, ed. David Pickering, 451–54. New York: St. James.

Le Gallienne, Eva. 1934. *At 33*. New York: Longmans, Green and Co.

———. 1953. *With a Quiet Heart*. New York: Viking.

Leiter, Samuel L. 1994. "Eva Le Gallienne." In *The Great Stage Directors: 100 Distinguished Careers of the Theater*. New York: Facts on File, 177–80.

Malpede, Karen, ed. 1987. *Women in Theatre: Compassion and Hope*. New York: Limelight Editions.

Nathan, George Jean. 1928. "The Theatre." *American Mercury*, 14 May, 122.

Parkhurst, Genevieve. 1928. "Pictorial Review's $5000 Achievement Award." *Pictorial Review*, 29 Jan., 66.

Ridgon, Walter, ed. 1976. *Notable Names in the American Theatre*. Clifton, N.J.: James T. White, 912–13.

"Sees America Hope of Dramatic Art." 1925. *New York Times*, 14 Dec., 7.

Shafer, Yvonne. 1989. "Le Gallienne, Eva." In *Notable Women in the American Theatre: A Biographical Dictionary*, ed. Alice M. Robinson, Vera Mowry Roberts, and Milly S. Barranger, 537–43. Westport, Conn.: Greenwood.

Shanke, Robert A. 1989. *Eva Le Gallienne: A Bio-Bibliography*. Westport, Conn.: Greenwood.

———. 1992. *Shattered Applause: The Eva Le Gallienne Story*. New York: Barricade Books.

Sheehy, Helen. 1994. "Eva Le Gallienne." In *Theatrical Directors: A Biographical Dictionary*, ed. John W. Frick and Stephen M. Vallillo, 235–37. Westport, Conn.: Greenwood.

———. 1996. *Eva Le Gallienne: A Biography*. New York: Knopf.

Taubman, Howard. 1964. "Eva Le Gallienne Brings Chekhov's 'Seagull' to the Belasco." Rev. of *The Seagull*, by Anton Chekhov. *New York Times*, 6 Apr., 36.

Representative Directing Credits

Broadway:

John Gabriel Borkman (1925), *The Master Builder* (1925), *Alice in Wonderland* (1933, 1982), *The Cherry Orchard* (1933, 1944, 1968), *L'Aigion* (1934), *The Cradle Song* (1934), *Camille* (1935), *Rosmersholm* (1935), *A Sunny Morning* (1935), *The Women Have Their Way* (1935), *Ah, Wilderness!* (1941), *The Rivals* (1942), *Hedda Gabler* (1948), *The Seagull* (1963)

Off and Off-Off Broadway:

La Locandiera (1926), *The Master Builder* (1926, 1934), *Saturday Night* (1926), *The Three Sisters* (1926), *Twelfth Night* (1926), *The Cradle Song* (1927), *The Good Hope* (1927), *Inheritors* (1927), *The Cherry Orchard* (1928), *The First Stone* (1928), *Hedda Gabler* (1928, 1933), *Improvisations in June* (1928), *L'Invitation au Voyage* (1928), *The Open Door* (1928), *The Would-Be Gentleman* (1928), *Peter Pan* (1928), *Katerina* (1929), *The Lady From Albuquerque* (1929), *The Living Corpse* (1929), *Mademoiselle Bourrat* (1929), *On the High Road* (1929), *The Seagull* (1929), *A Sunny Morning* (1929), *Alison's House* (1930), *The Green Cockatoo* (1930), *The Open Door*

(1930), *Romeo and Juliet* (1930), *Siegfried* (1930), *The Women Have Their Way* (1930), *Alice in Wonderland* (1932, 1947), *Dear Jane* (1932), *Liliom* (1932), *The Cherry Orchard* (1933), *John Gabriel Borkman* (1946)

Regional Theatre:
Hamlet (1937), *Hedda Gabler* (1941), *The Three Sisters* (1950), *The Corn Is Green* (1955), *Ghosts* (1956, 1962), *A Doll's House* (1975)

Tours:
John Gabriel Borkman (1925), *The Master Builder* (1925, 1934, 1939), *The Cradle Song* (1927), *Romeo and Juliet* (1930, 1933), *Alice in Wonderland* (1932, 1933), *Hedda Gabler* (1933, 1939, 1948, 1964), *A Doll's House* (1934), *L'Aigion* (1934, 1935), *Camille* (1935, 1936), *The Mistress of the Inn* (1936), *Ah, Wilderness!* (1941), *The Rivals* (1942), *Recital Tour* (1948, 1950), *The Seagull* (1963), *Liliom* (1964)

Levitow, Roberta

Born December 1, 1950, in Los Angeles, California, to parents who were visual artists, Roberta Levitow is known for her direction of contemporary and poetic plays. Based on the West Coast, Levitow balances a career as a freelance director, a scholar, and a teacher in academia.

During her childhood, Levitow's parents took her to many productions at Los Angeles's Mark Taper Forum and at San Diego's Old Globe Shakespeare Festival. Her parents also brought her to numerous museums, where she viewed the visual arts. Levitow attended California's Stanford University in 1968 and studied theatre with the desire to be an actor. There, she directed an experimental play, *Madmen and the Nun*, by Stansilaw Ignacy Witkiewicz, but did not consider directing a viable career for a woman as she saw few role models in the field. She graduated in 1972 with a B.A. in drama and an experimental and visual approach to theatre.

In 1974 Levitow became a member of California's Pacific Conservatory of the Performing Arts (PCPA), founded by Donovan Marley and based at Allan Hancock College. She says, "It really was a kind of extraordinary place. Donovan was young and energetic, and he went around the entire state of California auditioning young people, who he thought were really talented. He pulled them into this small group . . . as kind of teacher/students—as artists-in-residence at the junior college. In the summer all the professional artists from A.C.T. [American Conservatory Theater] in San Francisco would come down and do a summer theatre festival as part of Donovan's creation" (Interview, 2004).

Levitow left PCPA in 1976 to perform at the Oregon Shakespeare Festival for a year. She found herself becoming bored with acting and discovered that she did not like the life of a performer—with two shows a day, every other day. In 1977 she returned to PCPA and directed a play called *Kaspar* by the German writer Peter Handke. The play, which like the historical figure Kaspar Hauser, who is said to have been raised in isolation as a wild child in Germany, was also non-verbal and used mime. Levitow says, "It had an intellectual and poetic aspect. Michael Feingold [chief critic of the *Village Voice*] at one point said, 'Oh, Roberta, you're the person who directs unstageable poetic theatre.' *Kaspar* is unstageable poetic theatre. It was . . . very expressive of the things I'm interested in. . . . I think of it as very significant" (Interview, 2004). Although Marley's specialty was American musical comedies, Levitow received positive encouragement from him regarding her directing of *Kaspar*.

While at PCPA, Levitow met many guest artists that Marley brought to the theatre. Among these was Marley's mentor from the University of Texas, director James Moll. Levitow performed in Moll's productions and noticed that Moll had conferences with his wife, June, in the course of rehearsals. After conferring with his wife, Moll would ask the cast to try out June's ideas. Levitow discussed a pivotal moment, explaining, "One time I was sitting with June, and she said, 'Why wouldn't you be a director?' And I said, 'Well, 'cause girls don't do that.' She said, 'Girls *do* do that! Nina Vance started her company, The Alley. I was a director . . . now I help James. There's no reason why you shouldn't do it.' And there was Donovan saying, 'You should do it.' So these people were the determining factor" (Interview, 2004).

When Marley provided Levitow with opportunities to direct, she switched her career path. After directing Sam Shepard's *Tooth of Crime* in 1977 at PCPA, Levitow accepted a job to direct Michel Tremblay's *Les Belles Soeurs* at Seattle's Bathhouse Theater. The play, which was about French Canadian women, opened in 1979 and served as a turning point in Levitow's life. She explains, "It was political and poetic. Michel Tremblay was writing about the real difficult situation of French Canadians in a social class . . . at the time. . . . That has remained in my concerned universe. A lot of the work I'm interested in is about . . . how the body politic is composed; whether it's equitable—the belonging or not belonging of subgroups within the larger group" (Interview, 2004).

In 1978 Levitow was offered a position as artistic director of Seattle's Skid Row Theater, a small theatre named for the logs that once skidded down the road to the water. As artistic director, Levitow was able to consistently direct plays. Although she had no desire to be an artistic director, she explains, "I was looking for a job, and it . . . made sense to me that if I wanted to learn how to do this [directing], I was going to have to practice. . . . I'd been practicing for ten years to be an actor. . . . I did get into graduate schools—I got into the Goodman to study directing. . . . I couldn't stand one more minute of school. So I thought . . . I just need to practice" (Interview, 2004). While at Skid Row Theatre, which specialized in musicals, Levitow directed Bertolt Brecht and Kurt Weill's *The Threepenny Opera* in 1979, Sam Shepard's *The Curse of the Starving Class* in 1980, Jim Jacobs and Warren Casey's *Grease* in 1980, and Elizabeth Swados's *Nightclub Cantata* in 1981.

In 1982 Levitow received a National Endowment for the Arts (NEA) Directing Fellowship and directed new plays at Seattle Repertory Theatre, including Hall Corley's *An Ounce of Prevention* in 1982 and Theodore Cross's *Crossfire* in 1983. In the same year, Levitow began working at the Los Angeles Theatre Center, where she held a variety of jobs. While working at Los Angeles Theatre Center's literary department in 1985, Levitow "got assigned" to Marlane Meyer's *Etta Jenks* for a playwriting festival (Mackey 1994, 8). Since then, Levitow and Meyer have developed a personal working relationship. Levitow discusses her collaboration with Meyer, saying, "The nice thing about this kind of meeting of the minds is that less is said. We don't have to talk and say, 'Why is this good?' or 'Why is this bad?' She's tremendously generous as a playwright because she enjoys the process of making theatre" (8).

Since their acquaintance, Levitow has directed four plays by Meyer. The first, *Etta Jenks*, was presented in 1988 at the Los Angeles Theatre Center. The play chronicles a woman's fall into the pornography industry. Critic Thomas O'Conner thought the play did not provide any new insights, but praised the score by Wang Chung and the "abstract, sickly green box setting . . . a stark array of doors and empty corridors, coldly lit." He described Levitow's directing as providing "a slickly cinematic sheen and a hyped-up, pulsating pace, to match the incidental music" (1988, 22). Levitow won a 1988 Drama-Logue Award for direction of *Etta Jenks*. The play, under Levitow's direction, was also picked up by New York City's Women's Project Productions the same year, introducing Levitow to the New York theatre scene.

In 1989 Levitow won a Drama-Logue Award for her direction of Meyer's *The Geography of Luck* at California's South Coast Repertory (SCR) that year. The production, which included a blackout scene structure, centered around an ex-con and former singer who killed his wife—a Vegas showgirl. Dan Sullivan of the *Los Angeles Times* wrote, "Levitow's SCR cast makes us believe in their sleaze" (1989, 1).

In addition to the work of Meyer, Levitow likes the poetic work of playwright José Rivera. She says of Meyer's and Rivera's work, "These are plays that are located in reality—a version in reality. They're . . . made mystifying by a kind of poetic language, or imagery, or inconclusiveness in the dialogue, or evasion in the action. I love that" (Interview, 2004).

In 1990 Levitow directed Rivera's *Each Day Dies With Sleep* at the Berkeley Repertory Theater and New York City's Circle Repertory Theatre. In his review of the symbolist play about a young woman who tries to escape from the barrio, Gerald Nachman of the *San Francisco Chronicle* admitted, "In a production that must mesh the real and the imagined, it's hard to know what gaps are intentional, and what simply isn't there." Nachman, who reviewed the Berkeley production, called Levitow's direction "dreamscape-laden" and claimed "the overlapping projections, ominous guitar music and fanciful set get in the way of a compelling drama about escaping one's own history" (1990, F3).

Levitow directed two more of Meyer's plays in 1994. *Why Things Burn*, presented at San Francisco's Magic Theater, examines white extremists and included "sharply drawn performances under Roberta Levitow's direction," according to Steve Winn of the *San Francisco Chronicle* (1994, E1). *Moe's Lucky Seven* at New York City's Playwrights Horizons was described by Jeremy Gerard of *Variety* as an "updated 'The Time of Your Life.'" He wrote, "All of the performances are sporting, and Roberta Levitow has staged the play with exactly the right touch, allowing Meyer's fanciful wordplay to come through while mostly protecting it from its own self-consciousness" (1994, 47).

In 2001 Levitow began to focus on international theatre. Approached by Philip Arnoult of the Center for International Theatre Development in Baltimore, she led a theatre workshop that was based in Nairobi, Kenya, and resulted in a performance at Tanzania's Bagamoyo Arts Festival. The beginnings of Theatre Without Borders (TWB), an international community of theatre artists, was planted in 2003 by Levitow, and the group's first meeting was held the following year. The organization, of which Levitow is a co-founder, provides a forum for the exchange of ideas among the world's theatre artists. The group's purpose is "Conversation," "Hospitality," and "Information Sharing" (Theatre Without Borders). Levitow discusses her decision to work internationally:

> You think when the conditions of society are changing, the art would be changing. I think, historically, that one can see that theatre often lags behind that change. I feel things have completely changed from when I started. A lot of the things that I was doing were very immediate and connected to the society that I was living in. But I don't think that those things are connected anymore . . . and they grow less connected. . . . I feel that this world is asking for a redefinition of theatre in general. . . . I am much more interested in what

is now evolving. And although there are ways to be involved in that within the United States—the evolving theatre—I find myself ... contributing ... by being part of the evolving cross-pollenization that wants to go on. It's already happened in visual arts. And it's been really slow in the theatre. I think there's tremendous impetus from everywhere. I'm more interested in that right now. (Interview, 2004)

Levitow's interest in a redefinition of theatre is reflected by her preference for poetic plays. She says, "I'm not so committed to life as it is lived. I don't really respond to comedies of manners. . . . [T]hey're actually defending the status quo. It's like, 'Oh! Aren't we funny as we are!' . . . I'm more of a provocateur. . . . I'm pleased to see poetry on stage. . . . I like poetic, ambiguous, mysterious images; and I try to locate them in realism" (Interview, 2004). From the beginning of her career, Levitow has directed a diverse array of plays. She observes, "I have given myself, in my later years, the permission to be more experimental than I was through most of my career. . . . I started out experimental, and then I tried to get a job—and these were the jobs. I just wanted to work" (Interview, 2004).

Levitow casts performers through auditions or contacts those with whom she would like to work. As a casting director at the Los Angeles Theatre Center during the mid-1980s, Levitow learned about the different formats and variations of the process. She explains, "Some will only have a lunch. Some will only have a meeting. Some will have a meeting, but they won't read from the script. Some will read from the script, but not prepared. I mean, it just goes on and on" (Interview, 2004). However, if she is working with an institution that has specific casting procedures, she goes along with its process. When casting she looks for intelligence and a sense of humor in performers. She explains, "I like intelligent actors. I was an intelligent actor. I realize that sometimes that can be a problem. There's too much in their head. But I respond to intelligence. . . . I'm drawn to work on pieces . . . that are unstageable poetic theatre. So they have an intellectual component that you have to be able to decipher and relax around. . . . I'm dependent on actors who are intelligent in the sense that they also like intellectual puzzles on stage. I prefer someone who has their own sense of truth. . . . That without me having to ask them: 'Please be truthful,' they want to be truthful" (Interview, 2004).

Performers with strong personalities do not deter Levitow during casting. She explains, "I'm not really afraid of people who are fighters. Over the years I've gotten better . . . knowing what the rules of engagement are" (Interview, 2004). However, she prefers performers with whom she can talk to directly and who will be direct with her.

Levitow likes to work collaboratively with actors, although she will help performers with specifics if they ask. She enjoys having writers at rehearsals, also. She explains, "There's an open dialogue . . . a willingness and open-mindedness to new ideas. . . . I would say that's what the rehearsal process might feel like. A little bit like controlled chaos" (Interview, 2004).

If there is a text, Levitow asks the performers to first read the text. Afterward they explore the play verbally and physically and learn the lines. Levitow draws upon her experience as a performer when directing, explaining, "I feel as an actor I wanted to know who am I? Where am I? What's going to happen? I kind of go with my actor experience, in general" (Interview, 2004).

Levitow remains open to changes in rehearsal and does not like to get attached to initial ideas. She explains, "Sometimes I joke about it and call it fussing. I don't want people to think it's a radical change—even though it is. But you know I have a restless spirit and a restless mind. So things change" (Interview, 2004).

Levitow cites Peter Brook as the director who has most influenced her style. She says, "He's looking for some kind of essential value within the narrative. I think that's what I try to do" (Interview, 2004). Levitow considers her work based in both text and visuals, explaining, "I think American writers from the '50s forward were more influenced by Beckett than anybody else. . . . Existential and minimalist language appeals to me. It's concise. I don't need language to define character. I don't really respond to jokes for the sake of jokes. . . . I'm more minimalist both in my . . . feeling about the language and feeling about the visual. They tend not to be baroque visual images, but they would be very . . . sculpted, somehow. I think of them as both very important. As years passed I began to feel that the writing, quite frankly, was not as exciting to me as it had been. I got more and more interested in executing interesting visuals" (Interview, 2004).

Levitow does not take liberties with the text, but puts "a poetic context around it" by using such elements as visuals and sound (Interview, 2004). She tries to take the production "to a more poetical, or spiritual, or metaphysical . . . context" than the playwright had originally conceived (Interview, 2004).

In addition to her work as a director, Levitow taught at the University of Southern California at Los Angeles as an adjunct assistant professor from 1990 to 1998, and as an associate professor from 1998 to 2000. She was a visiting professor at Bennington College in Vermont from 2000 to 2005. She has taught classes at numerous schools and workshops in several countries, including China, Kenya, Uganda, Tanzania, Poland, Romania, and Egypt. She has also acted as a dramaturge for plays in regional and Off Broadway theatres, and has directed for film, television, and radio. She has been an executive board member of the Society of Stage Directors and Choreographers (SSDC) and Theatre Communications Group (TCG), where she also served as vice-president. The author of many articles, Levitow has participated in numerous conferences and organizations as a panelist, project director, and moderator. She was awarded the Alan Schneider Award for Directing Excellence in 1990 and the George Schaefer Observership in 1999.

Combining a career in direction and academia, Levitow believes her teaching experience has influenced her directorial work. She explains, "I'm much more theoretical these days; partly it's because I have been teaching . . . asking existential questions. I've been asking myself a lot more of those over the past few years" (Interview, 2004).

Sources

Daniels, Rebecca. 1996. *Women Stage Directors Speak: Exploring the Influence of Gender on Their Work.* Jefferson, N.C.: McFarland.

Gerard, Jeremy. 1994. "Moe's Lucky Seven." Rev. of *Moe's Lucky Seven,* by Marlane Meyer. *Variety,* 16 May, 47.

Levitow, Roberta. 2004. Telephone interview with Wendy Vierow. 16 July.

Mackey, Heather. 1994. "Get to Know Your Demons." Rev. of *Why Things Burn,* by Marlane Meyer. *American Theatre* 11 (2) (Feb.): 8.

Nachman, Gerald. 1990. "Barrio Struggles and Dreams." Rev. of *Each Day Dies With Sleep,* by José Rivera. *San Francisco Chronicle,* 2 Apr., F3.

O'Connor, Thomas. 1988. "Etta Jenks Lacks Insight in LA Festival." Rev. of *Etta Jenks,* by Marlane Meyer. *Orange County Register,* 22 Jan., 22.

Sullivan, Dan. 1989. "SCR's Calfest Puts 'Geography' on the Map." Rev. of *The Geography of Luck,* by Marlane Meyer. *Los Angeles Times,* 22 May, 1.

Theatre Without Borders. "History." Theatre Without Borders. http://www.theatrewithoutborders.com/about.htm (accessed 17 Mar. 2006).

Winn, Steven. 1994. "The Bruised Minds of White Extremists." Rev. of *Why Things Burn,* by Marlane Meyer. *San Francisco Chronicle,* 20 Jan., E1.

Representative Directing Credits

Off and Off-Off Broadway:
Etta Jenks (1988), *Each Day Dies With Sleep* (1990), *Miriam's Flowers* (1990), *Little Egypt* (1991), *Memory Tricks* (1993), *Moe's Lucky Seven* (1994), *Everybody's Ruby* (1998)

Regional Theatre:
The Tooth of Crime (1977), *Kaspar* (1979), *Les Belles Soeurs* (1979), *The Threepenny Opera* (1979), *The Curse of the Starving Class* (1980), *Grease* (1980), *Coming of Age* (1981), *Nightclub Cantata* (1981), *And the Birds Are Singing Again* (1982), *An Ounce of Prevention* (1982), *Crossfire* (1983), Three Plays by Heiner Muller (1983), *Beyond Therapy* (1984), *On the Verge: Or the Geography of Yearning* (1984), *Candide* (1985), *Extremities* (1985), *The Two Gentlemen of Verona* (1985), *American Dreamer* (1986), *Primafacie II*

(1986), *Salonika* (1986), *Passion* (1987), *The Seagull* (1987), *The Stick Wife* (1987), *Yerma* (1987), *Briar Patch* (1988), *Etta Jenks* (1988), *In Perpetuity Throughout the Universe* (1988), *The Model Apartment* (1988), *Tales of the Lost Formicans* (1988, 1989), *The Geography of Luck* (1989), *Love Medicine* (1989), *Miriam's Flowers* (1989), *Each Day Dies With Sleep* (1990), *The Pendleton Blanket* (1990), *Back to the Blanket* (1991), *Brilliant Traces* (1991), *Moe's Lucky Seven* (1991, 1992), *Real Women Have Curves* (1992), *Hedda Gabler* (1993), *Speed-the-Plow* (1993), *Uncle Bends: A Home Cooked Negro Narrative* (1993, 1995), *Electra* (1994), *Why Things Burn* (1994), *Having Our Say* (1996, 1997), *Speak Only of Cats* (1997), *The Faraway Nearby* (1998), *St. Joan and the Dancing Sickness* (1998), *The Secret Rapture* (1998), *Collected Stories* (2000), *Waiting for Godot* (2000), *Art* (2001), *Boy Gets Girl* (2003)

International Theatre:
Tales of the Lost Formicans (1989)

 # Malina, Judith

Born on June 4, 1926, in Keil, Germany, Judith Malina is a director, writer, producer, and performer. Influential in the Off-Off Broadway movement, Malina is co-director of The Living Theatre, a political theatre group, which has performed in the United States and abroad since the 1950s.

At the age of two, Malina emigrated with her parents from Germany to New York City. Malina's parents laid the foundation for her interest in political theatre. Her father, a Rabbi, was focused on raising awareness about Nazi Germany and Jewish persecution, while her mother, a devoted Jewish wife and former actress, continued to dream about theatre. At the age of seven, Malina appeared at anti-Nazi rallies in New York City's Madison Square Garden as the Talmud's burning lamp, which produced oil for eight days. A few years later, she appeared as Tiny Tim in an elementary school production of Charles Dickens's *A Christmas Carol*, a story that revolved around the inequities of the rich and the poor. Malina saw more politics in theatre when she attended Butler Davenport's free theatre, which included Davenport's speeches at intermissions promoting the use of birth control (Tytell 1995, 8–9).

While a student at Julia Richman High School in 1943, Malina met Julian Beck, a student at Yale. At the time, Malina had aspirations of becoming a performer, while Beck wanted to be a visual artist. The two attended many theatre performances together and spoke of creating a social and political avant-garde theatre together. During this formative time, Malina worked as a singing waitress at New York City's Beggar's Bar, run by Vlaeska Gert, who performed at the bar in the German Expressionist and Dada traditions.

Malina pursued her studies in theatre in 1945, attending German director Erwin Piscator's Dramatic Workshop at New York City's New School for Social Research. Influenced by Piscator, whose interpretive directing style focused on "epic theatre," Malina decided that she wanted to be a director. She wrote in her diaries, "I entered the Dramatic Workshop fervent to be an actress and after a few days of watching Piscator's work I knew I wanted to do the more encompassing work that is called Directing. . . . Piscator . . . does not have a high regard for the staying power of women in the masculine professions. He expressed his suspicion that I would 'get married and forget about the theatre,' that for this reason I had better study acting" (1947, 201). Despite Piscator's reservations, Malina convinced him to allow her to take classes in directing, as well as lighting, stage design, and theatre management. Upon finishing her studies, she received certificates in acting and directing.

Afterward, Malina continued to perform in plays, and in 1948 she and Beck signed papers to incorporate The Living Theatre. Her explanation of the group's name is as follows: "[W]e originally called it the Living Theatre, because it tries to change with the changing times" (Nott 2003, P16). Malina was to be the company's primary director, while Beck was to design most of the productions. However, they would not present their first production for many years. Malina became pregnant that year, and they married soon afterward.

In 1951, restless to begin work, Malina made her professional directing debut and returned to performing at New York City's Cherry Lane Theatre with Richard Gerson's *The Thirteenth God*, a play based on Alexander the Great. The same year, The Living Theatre presented its first production in Malina's living room with four short plays under her direction. At first, The Living Theatre focused on poetic works written by others. Later that year, Malina directed The Living Theatre production of Gertrude Stein's *Doctor Faustus Lights the Lights* at the Cherry Lane Theater. The critic for the *New York Times* was unsure of how to review the artistic production of Stein's play and wrote, "It is difficult to describe the sensations that follow. . . . A straight dive from the high board into a dry swimming pool might produce similar effects" (J.P.S. 1951, 33).

The next year at the Cherry Lane Theatre, Malina directed a play written by her psychoanalyst, Paul Goodman, despite the fact that Goodman told Malina that "he has never known a woman who is an artist" (Malina 1984, 203). Goodman's play, *Faustina*, focused on the wife of the Roman emperor Marcus Aurelius. In addition to Goodman, Malina was influenced by psychologist Wilhelm Reich, director and theorist Antoin Artaud, and political activist Dorothy Day, who took part in many demonstrations and shared a prison cell with Malina at one point.

In 1952 Malina directed Alfred Jarry's *Ubu Roi*, the company's last production at the Cherry Lane Theatre before the theatre was closed by the fire department for violations. The Living Theatre reopened uptown in 1954 at The Loft with W.H. Auden's verse play, *The Age of Anxiety*, directed by Malina. However, the New York City Department of Buildings closed that theatre in 1955, and the group moved back downtown in 1957, naming its new location The Living Theatre.

The Living Theatre had its first major success in 1959 when Malina directed Jack Gelber's play about drug addiction, *The Connection*. The production included a documentary film crew, a live jazz band, and performers who destroyed the illusion of character by breaking the fourth wall and panhandling audience members during intermission. Malina explains, "*The Connection* represented a very important advance for us in this respect: from then on, the actors began *to play themselves*" (Biner 1972, 48). In his positive review, Brooks Atkinson of the *New York Times* wrote, "[T]he intangible form that Miss Malina has imposed on the production, and the pungent acting . . . give the drama an inescapable immediacy. . . . Everyone in the audience recognizes the improvised parts . . . as devices that have been planned. . . . But these strokes of rehearsed unpremeditation . . . make 'The Connection' look more like an experience than a play. . . . By designing the performance on an informal basis, Miss Malina has purged 'The Connection' of artificiality—using artificial means to do it. Its derisive humors and repellent crises sound and look genuine. 'The Connection' with the audience is close" (1960, X1). The production won Obie Awards for Best New Play and Best All-Around Production. The Living Theatre toured the production along with other plays from 1961 to 1962 in Europe, and won more awards there, including the Grand Prix of the Théâtre des Nations and the Paris Theatre Critics Circle award.

Back in New York City, Malina directed Kenneth H. Brown's *The Brig* at The Living Theatre in 1963. The play focused on the harsh oppression inflicted by guards in a military brig in Japan. In order to make performers understand the play, Malina required performers to read *The Guidebook for Marines* and adhere to strict rehearsal rules, such as punctual attendance and the banning of food during rehearsals. Howard Taubman of the *New York Times* found the production intense and called Malina's direction "taut," noting, "Judith Malina . . . had drilled her cast . . . to sound and move like creatures possessed" (1963, 40). The production won Obie Awards for Best Production, Best Direction, and Best Design.

During the run of *The Brig*, the Internal Revenue Service seized the theatre building for tax violations. Undeterred, the audience climbed ladders to get through the locked theatre's windows to attend the final performance of the play. After the production was shut down, performers—some of whom had lived at the theatre during rehearsals of *The Brig*—began to live with Malina and Beck. After their trial for tax evasion, Malina and Beck toured *The Brig* in Europe but returned to the United States in December of 1964 to serve their prison sentences for contempt of court—thirty days for Malina and sixty days for Beck, as well as five years of probation and a fine. While Malina and Beck were in jail, the company, now living together in Europe, continued rehearsals.

Malina and her husband were arrested many times in numerous countries throughout their careers as a result of their controversial performances and political protests. Authorities also repeatedly closed down their theatrical venues. Malina explains why they were harassed, saying, "We're anarchists and pacifists. People are afraid of peace. Everyone wants it, but they're afraid of it. They often think that if we don't have a strong puritan system, we'll run wild; that people can't have faith in each other. We tell people to disarm in an armed world; we tell them to be vulnerable in a world in which they are already scared to death. It's frightening to some people. That's what had made them harass us and make us feel we're endangering a moral structure that is based on fear and obedience" (Nott 2003, P16).

After serving time in jail, Malina and Beck returned to Europe in 1965, and remained there for many years. In Europe, The Living Theatre developed into an ensemble that lived and worked together, emphasizing theatre as a tool for social change. The group also began to develop its own works that were sometimes based on the works of others. Malina explains, "Julian and I have always had a commitment to using all our art, all our work, all our time, all our effort, and all our communication to answering the question: How can our work make it better? And what is this 'it'? The suffering. That's a very big category. And very generalized. But then when we put on a play, it's no longer so generalized. In the Living Theatre we try to combine each of our lives, every aspect of our lives—our sexual life, our domestic life, our economic life, our personal life, our artistic life, our political life—into as holistic a community as possible" (1986, 386–87).

In Europe, the company created and presented some of their most well-known pieces: *Mysteries and Smaller Pieces, Frankenstein, Antigone,* and *Paradise Now.* First presented in Paris in 1964, *Mysteries and Smaller Pieces* became one of The Living Theatre's most popular works in Europe. The production, which was composed of nine rituals and required audience participation, included no set or costumes and utilized performers who played themselves. Malina is credited as co-director of some productions of *Mysteries and Smaller Pieces* and as the sole director of others. In 1965 Malina and Beck directed a group adaptation of Mary Shelley's *Frankenstein,* which focused on themes of domination and human suffering. The production, first presented in Venice, stressed spectacle rather than text and evolved through subsequent productions. In 1967 in Germany, Malina directed her adaptation of *Antigone* that she had translated while in prison by combining the texts of Sophocles, Bertolt Brecht, and Friedrich Hölderlin. The following year Malina and Beck directed the company's collaborative production of *Paradise Now* in Avignon, France. The production focused on ways to improve life and encouraged audiences to act rather than observe. It began with performers confronting audience members about the social restrictions on their lives and ended with the performers and audience spilling out in various states of undress into the streets, sometimes only to be met by police.

The company toured these collaborative pieces throughout the United States, but avoided the South. At Yale University in 1968, the group was met with enthusiastic audiences but mixed critical reactions. Some critics noted contradictions, such as the group's use of aggressiveness to oppose aggression and its use of funds from the wealthy, while burning money on stage (Tytell 1995, 239). Walter Kerr of the *New York Times* attended the group's performances of *Frankenstein, Antigone,* and *Paradise Now* at Yale and at the Brooklyn Academy of Music (BAM) and noticed a clear change in the directing style, writing, "At one time . . . Miss Malina as a director, was often able to impose a clear discipline on a production. Whether one cared for the materials being produced or not, a firm, skilled, passionate hand could be felt at work. . . . Now in the new freedom, all disciplines have gone soft. . . . The majority of the performers do not seem to be actors at all. They are converts" (1968, D1).

Following the Yale performance, Malina and Beck were arrested for indecent exposure after taking the performance into the street with audience members. Malina says of the piece, "[W]e broke every rule. . . . We burned money. We tore out the seats and carried them up on the stage. We got busted in city after city because we ended the piece with, 'The theater is in the streets' and led the audience into the streets and half the people were naked" (Hurwitt 2004, C1).

The productions caused a journalistic war between *New York Times* critics. Eric Bentley first accused Clive Barnes of evaluating the group "in purely esthetic terms." Barnes responded that Bentley and Kerr "have castigated The Living Theatre with an almost infectious enthusiasm" and added that the group was "a smash hit both in New Haven and in Brooklyn." He added, "In Brooklyn they played to large, generally enthusiastic audiences, arousing marked antagonism in some, but indifference, so far as I could judge, in almost nobody" (1968b, D1).

Bentley had reacted to Barnes's review of *Frankenstein,* directed by Malina and Beck in 1968 at the Brooklyn Academy of Music. Barnes wrote of the production:

> This is essentially a non-verbal theater. With its emphasis on spectacle and movement, its concern with visual rather than intellectual images, it is a type of theater that will be most readily immediate to the dance-oriented. It is also a theater of action—political action. It is a theater of protest, as, historically, probably most good theater is. . . . It is, I presume, a very carefully rehearsed improvisation: an exercise in dramatic collage in which are to be found movement, noise (the actors may not have much to say but they sure do grunt and wheeze a lot), and the intellectual debris of Western civilization. . . . When the actors speak they speak in mufti with the flat, slightly embarrassed non-voices of nonactors. But when they move they move with the discipline and purposefulness of trained dancers. . . . [P]erhaps it is the beginning of a new type of dance-theater." (1968a, 54)

Frankenstein won an Obie Award in no particular category since no categories were designated in 1969. That year Beck and Malina also won Obie Awards for *Antigone.*

In 1969 The Living Theatre returned to Europe, where it split up into four different cells the following year. Malina and Beck headed the Paris cell, whose objective was political theatre. There, they developed a political cycle of plays called *The Legacy of Cain,* which focused on social injustices. The next year they traveled with their cell to Brazil, where they continued to work on *The Legacy of Cain,* and focused on political street theatre. They worked with poor people and encouraged them to express their views and needs through theatre.

In 1971 the group returned to the United States, where they lectured around the country, participated in anti-Vietnam War rallies, and continued work on *The Legacy of Cain.* In 1973 writer, performer, and director Hanon Reznikov joined the group and began to perform in a play that was part of *The Legacy of Cain* called *Seven Meditations on Political Sado-Masochism,* directed by Malina. The play was composed of seven themes, including Domination and Submission, Authority, Property, Money, Violence, Death, and Revolutionary Change. That year The Living Theatre also began work on another play in *The Legacy of Cain* called *The Money Tower.* The production, influenced by the work of poet Vladimir Mayakovski and director Vsevolod Emilevich Meyerhold, focused on different socioeconomic classes. Malina developed the first sketch of the set, which featured a thirty-five-foot-high pyramid with five levels that placed the rich at the top and the poor on the bottom. In 1974 the group was awarded a Mellon Foundation grant to produce theatre in Pittsburgh, where they presented *The Money Tower* and other plays in *The Legacy of Cain* cycle. At this point, the group attempted to become entirely collective in its decisions and eliminate the director, who represented an authority figure. In 1975 the company returned to Europe and remained primarily stationed in Italy. There they created and produced more plays in *The Legacy of Cain* cycle as well as other productions, such as 1978's *Prometheus in the Winter Palace,* which focused on the constrictions of society.

In 1983 Beck was diagnosed with cancer and underwent surgery in France. Later that year, the company returned to the United States. They presented four plays at New York City's Joyce Theatre the following year. Poor reviews cut short an American tour, and part of the company returned to Europe while Beck and Malina remained in New York.

After Beck's death in 1985, Malina resumed directing the next year with *Living Theatre Retrospectacle* at New York City's Great Hall at Cooper Union. The production featured performers who had worked with The Living Theatre throughout its history and scenes from the company's repertoire. Malina explained, "It's the first time we've ever taken a sort of final look backward. . . . We're always very forward-looking and continue to be" (Fraser 1986, 70). Malina won a Special Citation Obie Award for the production.

In 1988 Malina and Reznikov married, having been lovers since 1973. The two worked together as co-directors to continue the work of The Living Theatre. As a writer, Reznikov has written plays and text for The Living Theatre. Among Reznikov's plays, Malina directed New York City productions of *Capital Changes* in 1998 and *A Dream of Water* in 2003. Malina also directed and performed in The Living Theatre's 2001 production of *Resistance,* with text by Reznikov. Produced at New York City's Chashama Theatre, the production focused on the resistance of northern Italians to the Nazis and Mussolini during World War II. *New York Times* reviewer D. J. R. Bruckner wrote of Malina, "[T]he performance shows that the theatrical insights she has given her young associates here are far from commonplace. Harrowing violence and death during the war are powerfully evoked, and the cast moves and speaks with that suggestion of shared trance that this company has always let one feel" (2001, B16).

Malina's methods of working have evolved along with The Living Theatre. She explains, "We try to remain cognizant of the stream of history so as to stay valid within it. This means a constant change of vocabulary, form, and vision" (Shank 2002, 34). When preparing for a production, Malina researches, translates, adapts sources, and works with writers on changes. She clarifies her ideas visually through sketches of scenes and detailed charts. During the early years of the company, Malina pre-blocked scenes, but later she let the staging emerge through rehearsals.

Malina recorded her early ideas about casting in her diary, writing, "Casting a play is cruel work. Friends feel cheated and scorned. The worst part is saying no. . . . I am disturbed by the authoritarian position, which, like all power, corrupts. I try to overcome it with a friendliness which I tremble to think unconvincing" (1984, 146).

Most rehearsals are collaborative and inventive, although with *The Brig*, Malina imposed strict rules that contrasted with her usual rehearsal procedures. Collaboration on projects may be lengthy as a group consensus often takes a long time to achieve. Although Malina and Beck eventually encouraged the group to direct themselves, they often guided rehearsals and provided a final eye. Beck discussed the problem between collaboration and direction, explaining, "The problem was that during the last five or six weeks [of *Frankenstein*] . . . it was no longer possible to have twenty-five directors on the stage. The pieces of the puzzle had to be assembled. Judith and I were holed up in a hotel room. Then the same thing happened the following year . . . for *Paradise Now* in 1968" (Biner 1972, 160).

Beck discussed how he co-directed productions with Malina, explaining, "The actors make all sorts of contributions. Judith understands them very well. She utilizes whatever technique may be best suited to each, because they come from different backgrounds. . . . [S]he tells them just the right things to set their imaginations working and give them, I believe, a feeling of freedom. She inspires them. She senses what will make an actor arrive at useful discoveries. She doesn't tell them anything that will trouble them or add to the confusion, if there is confusion. With me, it's very different. I offer the actor poetry and theory. I propose improvements in visual arrangements. . . . Judith is always very practical; she'll find a reason why a group should be in a given place at a given time. She doesn't give orders" (Biner 1972, 162). He added, "I do not have Judith's eye for focusing right on the heart of the matter. That's what makes all the difference!" (34).

Malina considers the audience as part of her collaborative effort when directing, explaining, "What The Living Theatre is trying to say to them is to be hopeful that they can participate in changing the structures of things, that they can make changes. Our whole effort toward audience participation has always been with the hope that we can make people feel less helpless, that they can be participants in the social structure, and that we're not just helpless sheep going to the slaughter" (Nott 2003, P16).

In addition to her previously mentioned awards, Malina's many honors include numerous fellowships as well as the Lola D'Annunzio Award by the *Village Voice* to Malina and Beck for their contribution to the Off-Broadway movement in 1958, the 1960–61 Brandeis University Creative Arts Award to Beck and Malina, an Obie Award for lifetime achievement in the theatre to Malina and Beck in 1975, the Peace Award to The Living Theatre from the War Resisters League in 1996, and the Otto René Castillo Award for Political

Theatre in 1999 to Malina, Reznikov, and The Living Theatre. In 2004 Malina and Beck were inducted into the Theatre Hall of Fame. In addition Malina and The Living Theatre ensemble were awarded a special Obie citation for the 2007 revival of *The Brig,* which Malina directed.

Malina has appeared in numerous films and television productions and has directed opera as well. Of her ongoing work with The Living Theatre, she states, "We're asking: How do we make peace? In a way, the Living Theatre has been doing research on that for 50–something years. . . . That's what all of our work is about." Although she believes it is important to learn from the past, Malina adds, "I want to know about the future. Because that's where I'm going" (Hurwitt 2004, C1).

Sources

Aronson, Arnold. 2003. *American Avant-Garde Theatre: A History.* New York: Routledge.

Atkinson, Brooks. 1960. "'The Connection' Jack Gelber's Harrowing Drama About Social Life Among the Junkies." Rev. of *The Connection,* by Jack Gelber. *New York Times,* 7 Feb., X1.

Barnes, Clive. 1968a. "The Living Theatre Gives 'Frankenstein' at Brooklyn Academy." Rev. of *Frankenstein,* by The Living Theatre. *New York Times,* 2 Oct., 54.

———. 1968b. "Clive Barnes vs. Eric Bentley." *New York Times,* 27 Oct., D1.

Beck, Julian. 1986. *The Life of the Theatre.* New York: Limelight Editions.

Biner, Pierre. 1972. *The Living Theatre.* New York: Horizon.

Bruckner, D. J. R. 2001. "Into a Trance, to Relive Wartime Defiance." Rev. of *Resistance,* created by The Living Theatre, text by Hanon Reznikov. *New York Times,* 10 Mar., B16.

Fraser, Gerald C. 1986. "The Living Theatre Looks Back Before Resuming Its Avant-Garde Ways." *New York Times,* 12 Oct., sec. 1, 2, 70.

Gussow, Mel. 1984. "The Living Theatre Returns to Its Birthplace." *New York Times,* 15 Jan., H6, H24.

Hurwitt, Robert. 2004. "The Living Theatre Takes Its Act of Protest Everywhere It Goes." *San Francisco Chronicle,* 26 July, C1.

J.P.S. 1951. "From the High Board." Rev. of *Doctor Faustus Lights the Lights,* by Gertrude Stein. *New York Times,* 3 Dec., 33.

Kerr, Walter. 1968. "You Will Not Be Lonely." Rev. of *Antigone,* by Sophocles and Bertolt Brecht; *Frankenstein,* by The Living Theatre; and *Paradise Now,* by The Living Theatre. *New York Times,* 6 Oct., D1.

The Living Theatre. http://www.livingtheatre.org (accessed 27 Nov. 2004).

Living Theatre Collective. 1974. "Money Tower." *TDR/The Drama Review* 18 (2) (T62) (June): 20–25.

MacAdams, Lewis. 2001. *Birth of the Cool: Beat, Bebop and the American Avant Garde.* New York: The Free Press.

Malina, Judith. 1947–51. "Judith Malina: Selections: From the Diaries, 1947–51." In *Women in Theatre: Compassion and Hope,* ed. Karen Malpede, 199–213. New York: Limelight Editions, 1983.

———. 1965. "Directing the Brig." In *The Brig,* by Kenneth H. Brown. New York: Hill and Wang.

———. 1972. *The Enormous Despair.* New York: Random House.

———. 1984. *Diaries of Judith Malina, 1947–1957.* New York: Grove.

———. 1986. Interview with Joanie Fritz. "About the Future." In *Women in American Theater,* eds. Helen Krich Chinoy and Linda Walsh Jenkins, 386–88. New York: Theatre Communications Group, 1987.

Maschio, Geraldine and Sullivan White. 1994. "Julian Beck." In *Theatrical Directors: A Biographical Dictionary,* ed. John W. Frick and Stephen M. Vallillo, 24–26. Westport, Conn.: Greenwood.

Neff, Renfreu. 1970. *The Living Theatre: USA.* New York: Bobbs-Merrill.

Nott, Robert. 2003. "Love Politics and Hope." *Santa Fe New Mexican,* 16 May, P16.

Reinelt, Janelle. 1989. "Malina, Judith." In *Notable Women in the American Theatre: A Biographical Dictionary,* ed. Alice M. Robinson, Vera Mowry Roberts, and Milly S. Barranger, 577–81. Westport, Conn.: Greenwood.

Rosenthal, Cindy. 2000. "Antigone's Example: A View of the Living Theatre's Production, Process, and Praxis." *Theatre Survey* 41 (1) (May): 68–87.

Ryan, Paul Ryder. 1974. "The Living Theatre's 'Money Tower.'" *TDR/The Drama Review* 18 (2) (T62) (June): 9–19.

Shank, Theodore. 2002. *Beyond the Boundaries: American Alternative Theatre.* Ann Arbor: University of Michigan Press.

Solomon, Alisa. 2001. "The Living Theatre Meets the Legacy of Civil War and Israeli Occupation on the Road in Lebanon." *Village Voice,* 18–24 July. http://www.villagevoice.com/issues/0129/solomon.php (accessed 3 Dec. 2004).

Taubman, Howard. 1963. "Theater: Marines in Jail." Rev. of *The Brig,* by Kenneth H. Brown. *New York Times,* 16 May, 40.

Tytell, John. 1995. *The Living Theatre: Art, Exile, and Outrage.* New York: Grove.

Representative Directing Credits[1]

Off and Off-Off Broadway:
  Childish Jokes (1951), *The Dialogue of the Mannequin and the Young Man* (1951), *Doctor Faustus Lights the Lights* (1951), *He Who Says Yes and He Who Says No* (1951), *Ladies' Voices* (1951, 1952), *The Thirteenth God* (1951), *Desire Trapped by the Tail* (1952), *Faustina* (1952), *The Heroes* (1952), *Sweeney Agonistes* (1952), *Ubu Roi* (1952), *The Age of Anxiety* (1954), *Spook Sonata* (1954), *The Young Disciple* (1955), *The Connection* (1959), *In the Jungle of*

Cities (1960, 1961), *The Marrying Maiden* (1960), *The Apple* (1961), *The Connection* (1961, 1963), *The Brig* (1963, 2007), *Frankenstein* (co-directed with Julian Beck—1968, 1969), *Antigone* (co-directed with Julian Beck—1968, 1969, 1984), *Paradise Now* (co-directed with Julian Beck—1968, 1969), *The One and the Many* (1984), *The Archeology of Sleep* (1984), *The Living Theatre Retrospectacle* (1986), *Us* (1987), *I and I* (1989), *German Requiem* (1990), *Mysteries and Smaller Pieces* (co-directed with Steve Ben Israel—1994), *Capital Changes* (1998), *Resistance* (2001), *A Dream of Water* (2003)

Tours:

Antigone (co-directed with Julian Beck—1968, 1969), *Frankenstein* (co-directed with Julian Beck—1968, 1969), *Paradise Now* (co-directed with Julian Beck—1968, 1969)

International Theatre:

The Connection (1961, 1962), *The Brig* (1964, 1965, 1966), *Frankenstein* (co-directed with Julian Beck—1965, 1966, 1967, 1968, 1969), *The Maids* (1965), *Antigone* (co-directed with Julian Beck—1967, 1968, 1969, 1970), *Paradise Now* (co-directed with Julian Beck—1968, 1969, 1970), *Seven Meditations on Political Sado-Masochism* (1977), *Mysteries and Smaller Pieces* (1997)

Notes

1. The complete production history of The Living Theatre has not been documented, and a comprehensive listing of Malina's directing credits is spotty. Sources state that she directed most of the group's productions, but that Beck and other group members directed productions as well. In addition to this, performers were often encouraged to direct themselves, making a definitive list of credits difficult to compile.

 # Mann, Emily

Born in Boston, Massachusetts, on April 12, 1952, Emily Mann has a multifaceted theatrical career as a director, playwright, and artistic director of New Jersey's McCarter Theatre. Her work in documentary theatre, which she calls "theatre of testimony," has its roots in the social documentary theatre of the 1930s Living Newspaper productions and has influenced modern playwrights.

Mann grew up in the academic communities of Boston, Northhampton, and Chicago. She became interested in theatre while attending high school in Chicago. There, a theatre teacher told her that she had a "director's head" and that directing would allow her to put all the things she loved together (Mann, interview, 2004). At the age of 17, she directed her first play in high school. While attending Harvard University, Mann searched for a new play to direct and examined some transcripts on her father's desk from the American Jewish Committee's Oral History Project on Holocaust survivors. She thought the interviews would make a touching play, but her father suggested she do her own interviews (Women's Project 1997, 31). Graduating from Harvard in 1974 with a B.A. in English literature, Mann began her theatre career by writing a play, *Annulla Allen: Autobiography of a Survivor,* about a holocaust survivor whom she interviewed while on a trip to Europe. This was the first of her many documentary plays, which are constructed through the use of interviews, newspaper clippings, court transcripts, archival videotape, and other media. As a writer and director of her own work, Mann presents information for the viewer to evaluate. She explains, "Most of what I know about human experience comes from listening. That's why it's very natural for me to believe in direct address in the theatre. It's an extension of listening. I hear the stories, then I let *you,* the audience, have the same experience I had as a listener" (Interview, 1987a, 281).

After returning from Europe, Mann went to work at the Guthrie Theater in Minneapolis, Minnesota, on a directing fellowship. In 1976 Mann directed *Annulla* at the Guthrie 2, the same year that she received her M.F.A. in theatre arts from the University of Minnesota. She got her first big break when the artistic director of the Guthrie Theater asked her to direct Tennessee Williams's *The Glass Menagerie* on the Guthrie Theater's mainstage. This made her the first woman as well as the youngest director to direct on that stage at age 27.

Mann's second "theatre of testimony" play, *Still Life,* premiered in 1980 at the Goodman Studio Theatre in Chicago and transferred the following year to Off Broadway's American Place Theatre. Mann created *Still Life,* which examined the personal and political effects of the Vietnam War, through the interviews of a Vietnam veteran, his pregnant wife, and his girlfriend. Accented by slides related to the Vietnam War, the production left the viewer "shellshocked," according to Rick Kogan of the *Chicago Sun-Times* (1980, 55). The play was also directed by Mann and received numerous awards, including an Obie Award for Best Production.

From 1981 to 1982 Mann was a resident director at New York City's Brooklyn Academy of Music (BAM), where she directed *He and She* and *Oedipus the King.* In 1983 San Francisco's Eureka Theatre Company commissioned *Execution of Justice,* another "theatre of testimony" play written by Mann. The play, a co-winner of the Actors Theatre of Louisville's 1983 Great American Play Contest, examines the trial of Dan White, who murdered San Francisco's mayor and openly gay city supervisor in 1978. Created from newspaper clippings, courtroom transcripts, and interviews, its scenes skipped around chronologically and used music and video. The play was produced at regional theatres, including the Guthrie Theater and the Arena Stage in Washington, D.C., before transferring to Broadway in 1986 under Mann's direction. There, it closed after only a few performances to mixed reviews. However, critic Ron Cohen of *Women's Wear Daily* wrote, "It's a big, horrific story, but Mann, as both playwright and director, moves with sureness and balance through much of it" (1986, 350). Although the play was a financial failure on Broadway, it received numerous awards, including a nomination for Drama Desk Award for Outstanding New Play, co-winner of the Great American Plays Contest, the Helen Hayes Award, the Bay Area Theatre Critics Circle Award, the HBO New Plays USA award, and inclusion in *The Burns Mantle Theater Yearbook: The Best Plays of 1985–1986*.

Wanting to settle down and raise her son, Mann accepted the position of artistic director at the McCarter Theatre in Princeton, New Jersey, in 1990. Her goal was to produce different kinds of plays than the previous management, which had produced mostly British and European revivals as well as contemporary new British plays. Shortly after accepting the position, she stated, "There are invisible racial and economic barriers that I want to break down with this theater. I want to create a theater of different American voices" (De Vries 1991, 5).

During her first season at the McCarter Theatre, Mann directed a rhythm-and-blues musical about an African American girl's coming-of-age called *Betsey Brown*. She co-wrote the musical with Ntozake Shange, and Baikida Carroll composed the music. *Betsey Brown* was the first time in the McCarter Theatre's history that a work by an African American artist had been presented on its stage.

While acting as the artistic director of the McCarter Theatre, Mann occasionally directed in other regional theatres as well. In the spring of 1993, she directed the world premiere of Anna Deavere Smith's documentary drama *Twilight: Los Angeles, 1992* at Los Angeles's Mark Taper Forum. She won the Greater Los Angeles NAACP Best Director Award and The Beverly Hills/Hollywood Area NAACP Theatre Award for Best Director. The play, which focuses on the 1992 Los Angeles riots, received its East Coast premiere under Mann's direction in 1993 at the McCarter Theatre. A 1994 production of the play, directed by George C. Wolfe at Off Broadway's Public Theater, transferred to Broadway. That same year, Mann was honored when the McCarter Theatre received a Tony Award for Outstanding Regional Theater.

In 1995 Mann directed her next "theatre of testimony" play, *Having Our Say*, at the McCarter Theatre and later that year on Broadway. The production was based on the book of the same name by Sarah and Bessie Delaney with Amy Hill Hearth, as well as Mann's own interviews with the Delaney sisters—two elderly African American women whose memories spanned back to the beginning of the twentieth century. Mann cut the script as she directed the play, partly to deal with the slower rhythm of the two actresses. In the play, the sisters address serious issues, such as Jim Crow laws and lynching, while preparing dinner. Throughout, the sisters speak to the audience, as guests in their home. The set included projected photographs showing historical and personal events from the sisters' lives that *New York Times* critic Vincent Canby said "compliment," rather than "upstage" the performance (1995, C1).

Having Our Say was nominated for Tony Awards, Drama Desk Awards, and Outer Critics Circle Awards in the Best Play and Best Director categories. It won the Dramatist Guild's Hull Warriner Award for Best Play and the Jefferson Award for Best Play and Best Direction. The play was also well received by reviewers and audiences. *Variety* critic Jeremy Gerard wrote, "Mann has staged the three relatively brief acts with a keen eye for the jigsaw fit that a hundred years of living together would bring" (1995, 53). Canby commented, "[T]he performance takes on the excitement of a revival meeting" (1995, C1). *Having Our Say* was one of the few plays on Broadway about women that was written, directed, produced, and performed solely by women.

Mann continued to present culturally diverse productions at the McCarter Theatre. In 1997, she adapted and directed García Lorca's *The House of Bernarda Alba* creating, according to Alvin Klein of the *New York Times*, a production "so specific in its allusions and images, and so precise in its rhythm, that it would appear to set a standard for García Lorca in English" (1997, NJ14).

In 2002 Mann won an Obie Award for her direction of Edward Albee's *All Over*. First presented at the McCarter Theatre and then Off Broadway, the play focused on the struggles within a family of a dying man. For the blocking of the production, Mann used stillness with actor Rosemary Harris, who made only two crosses during the entire play. One *New York Times* critic commented, "Every time Ms. Harris crosses her legs with such commanding crispness, it feels like a tiny victory against the cosmic terrors always waiting on the edges of Mr. Albee's world" ("Souls," 2002, E3). Mann explains her constriction of movement, saying, "The power of stillness—to me, it's the most powerful thing on the stage" (Interview, 2004).

In 2003 Mann directed Anton Chekhov's *Uncle Vanya,* in which the lives of those on a Russian estate are cast into chaos upon the arrival of the head

272 American Women Stage Directors

of the family's new wife. The production, presented at McCarter Theatre, received an excellent review from Klein in the *New York Times*. He wrote, "Emily Mann's adaptation and staging of 'Uncle Vanya' . . . gets it sublimely right. You are teary one moment, then realize that the play is farce, funny indeed. . . . Ms. Mann and her lovely cast capture the essence of performing Chekhov. The purity that arises from deep exploration of character and language illuminate this production. . . . The theme of eternity shines through Ms. Mann's production" (2003, NJ9–10).

In the same year Mann directed Nilo Cruz's Pulitzer Prize–winning *Anna in the Tropics* at the McCarter Theatre and on Broadway. The play concerns a lector reading Tolstoy's *Anna Karenina* in 1929 to Floridian Cuban cigar workers, who are affected by the book in different ways. Although Charles Isherwood of *Variety* thought the Broadway production would be better served by "an embracing, intimate space" (2003, 42), Terry Teachout of the *Wall Street Journal* wrote that the play "touched me as much as anything I've seen since I started writing this column" and that Mann's "simple, transparent direction leaves the superior ensemble cast plenty of room in which to make theatrical magic" (2003, W13).

Traveling from the setting of the tropics to the tundra, Mann directed Theresa Rebeck's *The Bells,* a reworking of a nineteenth-century theatre piece. Naomi Siegel of the *New York Times* wrote that the play, which was presented in 2005 at the McCarter Theatre, examined the question "What does it mean to be human in the wilderness?" and received "a bone-chilling, visually splendid world premiere production" with Mann's "superb job of directing" (2005, NJ14).

In 2007 Mann directed her new play, *Mrs. Packard,* at the McCarter Theatre. Like other plays by Mann, it was based on a true story. However, unlike her documentary plays, Mann created scenes and characters rather than using found text. Set in the mid-1800s, *Mrs. Packard* tells the story of a mother of six who was sent to an insane asylum by her minister husband for questioning his religious beliefs. The play touches upon women's rights, religion, and the conditions of asylums for the mentally ill. In her *New York Times* review, Siegel praised the acting of "a cast that injects dramatic nuance at every turn" and noted that "'Mrs. Packard' closes the McCarter season with distinction while introducing audiences to a fascinating historical footnote" (2005, NJ14).

Mann approaches directing and writing by choosing subjects that interest her. She prefers plays that are political, yet personal to her, and that have a spiritual and emotional center. Mann is drawn to work of social significance and believes it is often women and people of color who write this work. She thinks that theatre can have a strong influence on people, explaining, "I think anything you put on a stage is a great responsibility because you have the power to move and change. . . . You've got to take complete responsibility for both the statements you make and the effect you have on a crowd" (Interview, 1987, 158).

When Mann took over the McCarter Theatre, it had a repertory company. She disbanded it, however, because she prefers to choose plays freely, rather than select ones that fit a company. She explains, "I do plays that are very varied ethnically and racially. I want the writer, especially of the new plays, to have the right people for the roles. . . . Then there's also the fact that it's very hard to keep the best actors in America employed ten months a year through what you can pay them" (Interview, 2004). At the McCarter Theatre, she has also staged or adapted works by some writers that have influenced her. Among her influences are Chekhov, Lorca, William Shakespeare, and Issac Singer. She also admires Tennessee Williams as a writer and a director. In addition, Peter Brook's and Bertolt Brecht's techniques have influenced her directing.

When casting a play, Mann may telephone a performer that she thinks is right for the part or hold auditions. She also goes into New York City to scout for new talent. She says that, in callbacks, "I really work people hard. I want to see that they work the way that I work. I work very emotionally and ask people to make huge emotional risks. . . . I want to see if they'll go there, even in an audition situation. So I work with them and see how well they take direction. And then, if it becomes clear who the best people are, you cast them" (Interview, 2004).

Mann finds the most difficult actors to cast are leading white men between the ages of forty and sixty because many of them have turned to television or film to make more money. She also notes that many performers of her generation and younger will agree to do a role, but leave if something better comes along. In contrast, she says that older performers have a different work ethic and will turn down films when they have previously committed to doing a play (Interview, 2004).

Mann tries to cast without regard to race whenever possible, although she also uses race-specific casting. In her production of Chekhov's *The Cherry Orchard*, which tells the story of a family in the Russian land-owning class who must sell their cherry orchard in order to pay off debts, Mann specifically cast African Americans as Russian serfs to create parallels to American race relations. Critics commented on the casting of the production, directed by Mann at the McCarter Theatre in 2000. In his *New York Times* review, Klein wrote, "Among Ms. Mann's idea-laden directorial strokes, the old-hat concept of non-traditional casting is deliberately turned around to be actually traditional. How Chekovian! For Ms. Mann, purposefully aware of and attentive to color, casts black actors as Lopaknin, Varya and Firs, the 87–year-old valet is left behind. . . . All at once, parallels between the emancipation of the serfs in Russia and the freeing of the slaves in America, four years later, resonate, in your consciousness, not in your face" (2000, NJ12).

Mann may also change the gender of roles. In Shakespeare's *The Tempest,* which she directed at the McCarter Theatre in 2003, Mann changed the name of the magician Prospero to Prospera, and the name of the king Alonso to Alonsa. She also altered the script of Shakespeare's romance, explaining, "I changed any word in a line that didn't make it clear. I wanted to make it as accessible as possible so that you could understand it on first hearing. There are 500-year-old jokes, and if they're not funny you either change them or you cut them. . . . And I cut and trimmed a lot. It was sort of like a screenplay because it had so much physical, visual stuff going on" (Interview, 2004).

Mann prefers to go into rehearsals with a finished play, but she reworks her own scripts throughout the rehearsal process. When working with a living playwright, she discusses possible changes with the writer. Since the new millennium, Mann usually begins rehearsals with a breathing/yoga warm-up as she attempts to "hook up the mind and the body . . . to clear the head and get the body moving" (Interview, 2004). Afterward she may add a vocal exercise to warm up the voice. Mann finds that working around a table is valuable for new plays, especially if the writer is there to answer questions. For some plays she likes to begin moving immediately. She says, "Some plays I think you intellectualize too much and need to get people up immediately. When I did *The Tempest,* I did a four-day workshop. But we never sat down and read the play. I said we're all getting up now. You can do no wrong. . . . And in four days the whole play had come alive" (Interview, 2004).

Mann believes that one of the best ways to prepare for a rehearsal is "to know exactly how you want to stage it and be willing to throw it out" (Interview, 2004). She stopped telling performers where to move on stage about the time she came to the McCarter Theatre. In working with performers and others, Mann prefers collaboration, explaining, "I believe very strongly in being a partner of the people I work with rather than a dictator. I honestly believe that's the difference between a good director and a bad director" (Daniels 1996, 78–79).

Mann has received numerous awards, including the Rosamund Gilder Award for Outstanding Creative Achievement in the Theater in 1983, The Brandeis University Woman of Achievement Award in 1995, The YWCA of Trenton Celebration of Women Award in 1995, the Douglas College of New Jersey Woman of Achievement Award in 1996, *New Jersey Monthly*'s New Jersey Pride Award for outstanding contribution in the arts in New Jersey in 1999, and the Barbara Boggs Sigmund Award in 2004. In addition, she has been honored with the Edward Albee Last Frontier Directing Award. She has also received many awards for her work as a playwright, as well as awards for her work in other media, including the Christopher Award in 2000 and the Peabody Award in 1999 for the CBS production of *Having Our Say*. Mann has taught courses in Princeton University's Theater and Dance Program as well as master classes.

With many talents in the theatre, Mann approaches her three jobs as one. She says, "I write, and I direct, and I run a theatre. It's all one to me. I know I wear all these different hats, but really what I do is I make theatre. It's all in the mix" (Interview, 2004).

Sources

Brustein, Robert. 2000. "Women in the Theater." Rev. of *The Cherry Orchard*, by Anton Chekhov and *The Green Bird*, by Carlo Gozzi. *New Republic*, 222 (20) (15 May): 32–34.

Canby, Vincent. 1995. "A Visit With 2 Indomitable Sisters." Rev. of *Having Our Say*, adapted by Emily Mann from the book by Sarah L. Delany and A. Elizabeth Delany with Amy Hill Hearth. *New York Times*, 7 Apr., C1.

Cohen, Ron. 1986. "Execution of Justice." Rev. of *Execution of Justice*, by Emily Mann. *Women's Wear Daily*, 14 Mar. Rpt. *New York Theatre Critics' Reviews* 47 (3 Mar.): 350.

Cole, Susan Letzler. 1992. "Emily Mann Directs *Execution of Justice*." In *Directors in Rehearsal: A Hidden World*, 56–74. New York: Routledge.

Daniels, Rebecca. 1996. *Women Stage Directors Speak: Exploring the Influence of Gender on Their Work*. Jefferson, N.C.: McFarland.

De Vries, Hillary. 1991. "Creating a Theater of Different American Voices." *New York Times*, 13 Jan., 5.

Gerard, Jeremy. 1995. "Having Our Say." Rev. of *Having Our Say*, adapted by Emily Mann from the book by Sarah L. Delany and A. Elizabeth Delany with Amy Hill Hearth. *Variety*, 10 Apr., 53.

Isherwood, Charles. 2003. "Anna in the Tropics." Rev. of *Anna in the Tropics*, by Nilo Cruz. *Variety*, 24 Nov., 42.

Kilkelly, Ann Gavere. 1989. "Mann, Emily." In *Notable Women in the American Theatre: A Biographical Dictionary*, ed. Alice M. Robinson, Vera Mowry Roberts, and Milly S. Barranger, 584–87. Westport, Conn.: Greenwood.

Klein, Alvin. 1997. "A Woman as Oppressing as Her Creator's Killer." Rev. of *The House of Bernarda Alba*, by Garcia Lorca, adapted by Emily Mann. *New York Times*, 2 Nov., NJ14.

———. 2000. "Casting Keeps Chekhov Relevant: Jane Alexander in 'Cherry Orchard.'" Rev. of *The Cherry Orchard*, by Anton Chekhov. *New York Times*, 9 Apr., NJ14.

———. 2003. "Life in the Country With Uncle Vanya: It's Farce and Drama." Rev. of *Uncle Vanya*, by Anton Chekhov. *New York Times*, 11 May, NJ9–10.

Kogan, Rick. 1980. "'Still Life' Probes Pain of Three Lives." *Chicago Sun-Times*, 27 Oct., 55.

LoBiondo, Maria. 1995. "Profile: Emily Mann: Artistic Director of McCarter Theatre." *Princeton Patron Magazine.* http://princetonol.com/patron/emann/ (accessed 26 Nov. 2000).

Mann, Emily. 1987a. Interview with Kathleen Besko and Rachel Koenig. "Emily Mann." In *Interviews with Contemporary Women Playwrights,* by Kathleen Bosko and Rachel Koenig, 274–87. New York: Beech Tree.

———. 1987b. Interview with David Savran. "Emily Mann." In *In Their Own Words: Contemporary American Playwrights,* by David Savran, 145–60. New York: Theatre Communications Group, 1988.

———. 1993. Interview with Leigh Buchanan Bienen. In *Speaking on Stage: Interviews with Contemporary American Playwrights,* ed. Philip C. Kolin and Colby H. Kullman, 206–15. Tuscaloosa: University of Alabama Press, 1996.

———. 1995. Interview with Melissa Salz-Bernstein. "Emily Mann: Having Her Say." University of Cincinnati. http://blues.fd1.uc.edu/www/amdrama/mannint.html (accessed 29 Jan. 2001).

———. 2000. "In Conversation." *Theatre Topics* 10 (1): 1–6.

———. 2004. Interview with Wendy Vierow. 24 May. Princeton, N.J.

Miyasaki, June. 1994. "Emily Mann." In *Theatrical Directors: A Biographical Dictionary,* ed. John W. Frick and Stephen M. Vallillo, 259–60. Westport, Conn.: Greenwood.

Morrow, Lee Ann and Frank Pike. 1986. *Creating Theater: The Professionals' Approach to New Plays.* New York: Vintage Books.

Siegel, Naomi. 2005. "Melodrama in the Land of the Noonday Moon." Rev. of *The Bells,* by Theresa Rebeck. *New York Times,* 3 Apr., NJ14.

———. 2007. "Daring to Disagree, and Sent to an Asylum. Rev. of Mrs. Packard, by Emily Mann. *New York Times,* 27 May, NJ14.

"Souls Alone in the Universe, Connected by a Dying Man." 2002. Rev. of *All Over,* by Edward Albee. *New York Times,* 28 June, E3.

Teachout, Terry. 2003. "Theatre—View: Read 'Em and Weep." Rev. of *Anna in the Tropics,* by Nilo Cruz and *Henry IV,* by William Shakespeare. *Wall Street Journal,* 21 Nov., W13.

Women's Project & Productions. In Conjunction with the New School for Social Research. 1997. *Women in Theatre: Mapping the Sources of Power.* Conference journal, New York City, 7–8 Nov.

Representative Directing Credits

Broadway:
Execution of Justice (1986), *Having Our Say* (1995), *Anna in the Tropics* (2003)

Off and Off-Off Broadway:
Still Life (1981), *A Weekend Near Madison* (1983), *Annulla* (1989), *All Over* (2002), *Miss Witherspoon* (2005)

Regional Theatre:
> *The Birthday Party* (1975, 2006), *Matrix* (1975), *Cold* (1976), *Annulla Allen: Autobiography of a Survivor* (1977), *Ashes* (1977, 1980), *Dark Pony & Reunion* (1978), *The Farm* (1978), *On Mount Chimborazo* (1978), *The Roads in Germany* (1978), *Surprise, Surprise* (1978), *The Glass Menagerie* (1979, 1990), *He and She* (1980), *Still Life* (1980), *Dwarfman: Master of a Million Shapes* (1981), *A Doll's House* (1982, 1986, 1995), *Execution of Justice* (1982, 1983), *A Tantalizing* (1983), *Through the Leaves* (1983), *The Value of Names* (1983, 1984), *A Weekend Near Madison* (1983), *Execution of Justice* (1985), *Hedda Gabler* (1987, 1988), *Betsey Brown* (1989, 1991), *Cat on a Hot Tin Roof* (1992), *Miss Julie* (1992), *Three Sisters* (1992), *The Perfectionist* (1993), *Twilight: Los Angeles, 1992* (1993), *The Matchmaker* (1994), *Having Our Say* (1995), *The Mai* (1996), *Betrayal* (1997), *The House of Bernarda Alba* (1997), *Meshugah* (1998), *Safe as Houses* (1998), *Fool for Love* (1999), *The Cherry Orchard* (2000), *Because He Can* (2001), *Romeo and Juliet* (2001), *All Over* (2002), *Anna in the Tropics* (2003), *The Tempest* (2003), *Uncle Vanya* (2003), *Last of the Boys* (2004), *The Bells* (2005), *Miss Witherspoon* (2005), *Mrs. Packard* (2007)

 # Meadow, Lynne

Born on November 12, 1946, in New Haven, Connecticut, Lynne Meadow is artistic director of New York City's Manhattan Theatre Club, where she has directed more than thirty productions. Meadow's directing has taken her to regional theatres to Broadway, and to such Off Broadway theatres as the Phoenix Theatre and the Public Theater. Her career has been devoted to staging works by new and contemporary playwrights.

Both of Meadow's parents had theatrical backgrounds. Meadow's father worked in film, and her mother worked at Yale University, where she also acted in plays. Meadow's mother, who wrote plays and music, encouraged her daughter to critique her work. Meadow acted in her mother's plays at the local temple and accompanied her to auditions at Yale. Because Yale did not admit women at the time, local women and girls appeared in Yale productions, providing Meadow with opportunities to act.

Meadow became fascinated with directing in 1958 while acting in a Yale musical by Richard Maltby and David Shire called *Grand Tour*. She recalls watching the director, Bill Francisco, at work, explaining, "[H]e was such an important figure to me and what he did was so interesting. So I guess somewhere an idea was planted. I remember very distinctly a moment: they were doing a sort of musical interlude and there was no dialogue—and I remember watching him go up on stage and talk to a few people, organize a few things and sit down. The whole thing transformed! And I was enchanted, enraptured" (Pereira 1996, 19). Meadow was inspired by her experience performing at Yale and decided that one day she would enter the graduate program at Yale School of Drama.

In eighth grade, Meadow asked her teacher if she could help to direct the school play and ended up directing the play herself. She pursued her interest in theatre, acting in many high school plays. Later, she attended Pennsylvania's Bryn Mawr College, an all-woman's school, which helped Meadow to believe that she could achieve virtually anything. At Bryn Mawr, Meadow directed plays in both English and French and spent her junior year abroad in France. Upon graduating with a B.A. in French in 1968, Meadow turned her attention to Yale School of Drama, certain that she would be accepted. When Yale rejected her application, she was devastated and sought out Gordon Rogoff, the head of the Directing Department. Meadow asked Rogoff if she was rejected because of her gender. She recalls, "He certainly didn't say, 'yes, that's what we thought, and that's why we turned you down,' but I will never forget him saying these words. He said, 'Well, I must tell you that we haven't had much luck with the women here'" (Pereira 1996, 21). Meadow wrote Yale a passionate letter explaining why, as a woman, she would be able to direct and should be accepted at the school. While waiting for Yale's response, she directed and acted at the Exit Coffee House Theatre, which was run by Yale students. Meadow was finally accepted into Yale, where she was the only woman in her class.

At Yale, Meadow was exposed to new types of theatre. When the avant-garde group The Living Theatre visited the school during her first year in 1968, Meadow remembers, "It was very upheaving. . . . [S]uddenly I was confronted with why are you doing theatre? what is the value of theatre in society? what is the value to anyone's life? It was very provocative. . . . I'd grown up with a very provincial view of the theatre . . . and suddenly to see Judith Malina and Julian Beck stomping around naked and saying . . . 'I'm not allowed to travel without a passport,' calling *that* theatre—my horizons were tremendously opened up" (Pereira 1996, 26).

Other guest artists at Yale who influenced Meadow include actor, director, and producer Jean-Louis Barrault and his company and director Paul Sills—who taught an improvisation workshop that Meadow attended. Speaking of Sills, who was co-founder of Chicago's Compass Players and The Second City, Meadow reflected, "[H]e talked about breaking down our idea of what the theatre was. He was a very, very inspiring teacher, working with a lot of exercises and improvisations for the theatre. I was very intrigued by his work" (Pereira 1996, 28).

Meadow was also influenced by her classmates and teachers, from whom she learned much about theatre. She discusses the impact of director Andre Gregory, who replaced Rogoff as head of directing, saying, "[H]e made me think about what the different possibilities of doing theatre were, he made me aware of different forms. . . . For a while I remember saying, 'I'm not interested in text anymore'" (Pereira 1996, 26–27). From director Nikos Psacharopoulos, one of Meadow's teachers who was also artistic director of the Williamstown Theatre Festival in Massachusetts, Meadow says that she learned about directing, including "not pushing for results and allowing scenes to happen, allowing things to evolve . . . trying to learn an actor's language" (Masson 1987, 12–13).

In addition to directing plays at Yale, Meadow gained additional experience at the Williamstown Theatre Festival, where she assisted Psacharopoulos on the direction of Bertolt Brecht's *The Caucasian Chalk Circle* when she was an instructor there in 1969. The next summer, she was the director of the Apprentice School, and directed a production of Dylan Thomas's *Under Milkwood*.

On the advice of Psacharopoulos, Meadow took a year off from Yale in 1970 to go to France. There she attended rehearsals of Barrault and taught and directed productions at the American Center in Paris. While in Paris, Meadow resolved to be a director. Upon returning to Yale, Meadow lost the desire to finish her last year of school. Psacharopoulos encouraged Meadow to go to New York City and direct plays. Meadow recalls, "Because I was a young woman who wanted to direct—and there weren't women directors back then—he was concerned that I would get into an assistant position. He felt that I should get into a leadership position" (Gener 2003, 22).

The time that Meadow spent at Yale provided her with many contacts in the theatre world and opened doors for her. Meadow admits, "Yale introduced me to people. I made acquaintances there, and I definitely learned something. . . . So it was a very positive experience for me, and it also allowed me to begin to think of myself as a director, and to call myself a director. I wouldn't have been able to come to New York and begin directing plays without it" (Pereira 1996, 28–29).

Although Meadow arrived in New York City at a time when there were scores of small theatres and lots of theatrical activity, she was unable to obtain work. She explains, "I was offered a staged reading here, something there, not too much while a lot of my [male] colleagues coming out of Yale at the time were given productions to do. I wasn't" (Masson 1987, 18). Taking matters into her own hands, she directed her own production of Alfred Jarry's *Ubu Roi* at St. Clement's Church in New York City in 1971. The performance did not go well, and Meadow set out to direct another project. The next year she rented a space at the multistage Manhattan Theatre Club, which had been newly incorporated in 1970. There, she produced and directed Anthony Scully's *All Through the House,* a play about a family's confrontational Christmas reunion. The production caught the attention of the theatre's board, whose members offered her a tentative three-month contract as executive artistic director. Although Meadow had not planned to run a theatre, she realized that the opportunity offered her a place to direct plays, as well as a source of income. With youthful enthusiasm, twenty-five-year-old Meadow accepted the position and inherited a theatre with substantial debt. As a producer, she was able to select which plays she wanted to direct, and the theatre became known for producing primarily new plays and providing a place for developing new talent.

As artistic director, Meadow occasionally needed to help or take over the work of other directors. The first production that she directed as artistic director at the Manhattan Theatre Club was Amos Kenan's *Jesus as Seen by His Friends* in 1973. Meadow is credited with co-directing because she took over the direction of the play after the actors had difficulty working with the original director.

The next year, Meadow faced a turning point in her career when she directed Mark Medoff's *The Wager* at the Manhattan Theatre Club. The play revolved around a wager involving the seduction of a professor's wife. When the play was ready to open, Medoff refused to allow the press to review it, although Meadow thought the production was ready for critics. Unfortunately, Meadow had used producers to help her obtain the rights and to provide financing, and they moved the show to the Eastside Playhouse and then to Broadway, with Tony Perkins as director. Meadow says, "I was not hired to go on . . . after doing an incredible amount of work on that production. . . . I think that that production, and my work as a director and producer on that production, was seminal in the development of the Manhattan Theatre Club. I think if I could name one of the largest turning points that we ever had, that was it. Suddenly, there was a commercial interest present at the Manhattan Theatre Club, so the issue wasn't simply about my skills as a director, or the value of the play; it was about people who were there on not-for-profit territory who had commercial interests, and who had approvals. . . . After that experience, I limited what an outside producer's role could be at the Manhattan Theatre Club" (Pereira 1996, 66–67).

Meadow found that her production duties as artistic director took away from time that she would rather spend directing plays. In 1975 Barry Grove was hired as managing director, and this gave Meadow more time to direct. From that point on, Meadow began to direct an average of one or two productions each year at the Manhattan Theatre Club.

In 1976 Meadow received critical acclaim with her direction of David Rudkin's *Ashes,* which was co-produced by the Manhattan Theatre Club and Joseph Papp of New York City's New York Shakespeare Festival. The story focused on a couple's unsuccessful attempts to have a child and chronicled their journey to doctors' offices and through the adoption process. The production, first performed at the Manhattan Theatre Club, was set on a sparse set with numerous curtains that could be moved to indicate changes of locale. Mel Gussow of the *New York Times* praised the play, the acting, and the direction when he wrote, "[T]here is a suitable starkness and coolness about Lynne Meadow's staging" (1976, 64). Erika Munk of the *Village Voice* noted that the "spareness of the technique forces us to make connections. . . . [T]his minimalism focuses each object and action sharply and the smallest details of daily life radiate significance—structure rather than spectacle creates their impact" (1976, 165). With good reviews, *Ashes* moved to the New York Shakespeare Festival's Public Theater in 1977. Meadow reworked the staging for a thrust stage, and the play continued to receive excellent reviews and praise for her direction. *New York Times* critic Clive Barnes wrote, "The play is beautifully given. It has been directed by Lynne Meadow. . . . It has style and understanding. I personally preferred this staging to the London staging a couple of years back. It has more compassion and more of that archetypal oxymoronic quality of bitter-sweetness. It works" (1977, 43). *Ashes* appeared in many top ten lists of the year, including one in *Time* magazine. It was also selected for Otis Guernsey's *The Best Plays of 1976–1977,* which described the Public Theater's production as "the peak of the Off-Broadway season and the spear point of the theatre of shock. . . . It is hard to imagine how the acting . . . and the brutally direct staging of Lynne Meadow could have been bettered" (1977, 23).

In 1982 Meadow directed her first professional classical play—Anton Chekhov's *Three Sisters,* translated by Jean-Claude Van Itallie. The play was not well received by most New York City critics, however. Meadow says, "The biggest lesson I learned was that for me it was lunacy to try to mount such a vast, massive play in a four-week rehearsal period without a permanent company of people used to working together" (Masson 1987, 267).

In 1984 the Manhattan Theatre Club moved its theatre to New York City's City Center, and Meadow took two years off for maternity leave. Upon her return to the Manhattan Theatre Club, she directed two productions before directing the 1988 American premiere of Alan Ayckbourn's *Woman in Mind,* for which she received a Drama Desk nomination for Best Director. The play focused on an affection-starved woman who fantasizes about an ideal family. Frank Rich of the *New York Times* wrote that Meadow's direction was generally "sharper than Mr. Ayckbourn's own West End staging in 1986" (1988, C21).

An admirer of Ayckbourn, who had achieved more success in Great Britain than the United States, Meadow directed a successful production of his play *Absent Friends* in 1991 at the Manhattan Theatre Club. The following year, she made her directorial debut on Broadway with Ayckbourn's *A Small Family Business*, a satire about middle-class business. Co-produced with Weissman Productions, the play opened directly on Broadway in part because it required enough space to construct a two-story set (Pereira 1996, 336). The play received mixed reviews and ran for only forty-eight performances. Rich, who gave the production a mixed review, wrote, "Ms. Meadow, following the rough blueprint of Mr. Ayckbourn's original staging, does an expert job of keeping the action bouncing from room to room as the actors and such props as a cash-stuffed briefcase ricochet between four different households that sometimes occupy the stage simultaneously" (1992, C13). John Beaufort of the *Christian Science Monitor* described the play, stating, "If I counted correctly, this is a 10–door comedy with plenty of closet space for concealment. The between-scenes intervals are enlivened by flashing lights and jazzy breaks—technical equivalents of the verbal snippets that add up to Ayckbourn dialogue" (1992, 12).

Meadow gained another Drama Desk nomination for Best Director with Lesley Ayvazian's *Nine Armenians* in 1996. Presented at the Manhattan Theatre Club, the play spans three generations of Armenians and focuses on an Armenian American girl in search of her cultural roots. The play also addresses Armenian genocide by the Turks during World War I. Ben Brantley of the *New York Times* wrote, " [U]nder Lynne Meadow's assured, gentle direction, the evening is bathed in a warmth that is enriched by the sense of a fearful, unacknowledged chill behind it. . . . [T]he smooth-running 90–minute production casts its own tender spell. The sound of snuffling in the audience throughout the evening isn't just a result of the flu" (1996, C15).

In 2000 the Manhattan Theatre Club joined forces with outside producers to stage a Broadway production of Charles Busch's *The Tale of the Allergist's Wife*, directed by Meadow. The comedy, which focused on an unhappy, middle-aged woman living in uptown New York City, ran for 777 performances. Brantley wrote, "[U]nder Ms. Meadow's direction, the actors provide a balancing quality of restraint that both enhances comic impact and disguises cliches" (2000, E5). Meadow was nominated for a Tony Award for her direction of the play. In 2003 the Manhattan Theatre Club opened its own Broadway stage at the Biltmore—a 650–seat theatre—adding to their two stages at City Center.

Over the years, the bulk of Meadow's work has involved the direction of new plays. She explains, "[N]ew work has been my passion. I think, the part of my spirit that is creative and intrepid loves the idea of cutting a new path through the jungle. I like the idea of creating something that has never been seen, as opposed to reinterpreting works. Some of the reasons for that has to do with the era I came from—I was a child of the '60s and early '70s, and we wanted to break the mold and invent new things" (Gener 2003, 21).

At first, Meadow did not like to direct a play more than once, but now she finds the experience challenging, explaining, "As I've grown older, I've had more patience to re-look at things and go deeper. I think I've mellowed as a person and an artist, and I probably have a greater attention span and more ease. I think I could re-look at something today and say, 'Well, I did it and got a certain amount out of it this time. And now I could do it again and be able to go deeper and learn something else'" (Gener 2003, 21).

Meadow prefers to direct linear plays with a fairly traditional format. She also likes life-affirming plays that involve families or close relationships. She observes, "Ultimately the plays I love the most are the things where you really can laugh and then really feel something deeper" (Gener 2003, 22). She adds, "If you look at the body of my work, it's very eclectic. I am an interpreter, not an auteur. Probably my best work has been the work that is closest to me emotionally. *Ashes* by David Rudkin, *Tale of the Allergist's Wife* by Charles Busch, or some of the Alan Ayckbourn plays—all those plays spoke to me" (21).

Meadow views directing as a collaborative process. She discusses how she has evolved as a director, stating, "The very thing that made me want to be a director was to want to control what reality was. As I've grown more and I try to better understand my craft, it seems that I am trying to learn how not to control and let things happen, to control in a different way, to control in a looser way, to guide with an easier hand" (Masson 1987, 109–10).

When working with playwrights, Meadow makes suggestions for rewrites and helps writers to clarify and trim their scripts before handing them to the actors. Although she considers playwrights' suggestions about casting and technical matters, Meadow makes the final decision herself. One exception, however, was with *The Wager;* she had to concede to the producers' wishes to fire an actress because they thought she was not attractive enough (Pereira 1996, 65).

Casting a play may take a month for Meadow because she believes that casting is important and determines the shape of a play. She casts both unknown and well-known performers, and roles may be cast without or with an audition. In 2004, the Manhattan Theatre Club provided *Back Stage* with their casting preferences, which included a truthful performance, good training, and experience ("Manhattan," 2004, A3–A4).

Playwrights are usually invited to attend early and late rehearsals, although a few are allowed to attend most of them. During rehearsals, Meadow prefers that writers do not address performers without her permission. At the start of rehearsals, Meadow has performers read the play several times. Before getting the play on its feet, she works with performers by clarifying the setting and discussing character and other issues. Rather than tell them what to do, Meadow prefers to ask actors questions to help them define their parts.

Although Meadow pre-blocked scenes early in her career, she now encourages performers to explore the space instead. Beyond a few specific movement ideas, she allows actors to fill in the rest. Meadow encourages performers to express their views about scenes and to create full-bodied characters. However, she may ask actors to discard some physical manifestations of what they have created, keeping certain details invisible. Meadow says, "I'm very demanding. I'm a perfectionist. I have definite ideas about what I work on, but I try to create an atmosphere in rehearsal where actors don't feel they are being judged" (Gener 2003, 22).

During rehearsals Meadow takes notes and often lets scenes run through without interruption. She later talks to performers as a group or individually, in private. Meadow notes that performers are all different, and says, "[S]ome people want to deal more with their minds intellectually and want to talk through things. Other actors have other nerve centers that need to be touched" (Masson 1987, 151). When communicating with performers, Meadow says that she helps them to create the best performances possible by acting as a mirror to "let them know what they were doing wasn't what they thought or wasn't what you'd like" (89). Rehearsals usually last four weeks, with the first week devoted to exploration of the play. Meadow continues to give notes during previews, treating them as a dress rehearsal.

Known for her excellent editing ability, Meadow tries to make sure her productions are clear and simple. She directs with a light touch, remaining true to the spirit of the text and the playwright, rather than imposing a certain style. Meadow feels that any style should come from the text and that performers should be natural and not appear to be acting.

Although Meadow also spends much time with designers for each production, she is not interested in creating spectacles. She discusses how she works with set designer John Lee Beatty, with whom she has collaborated often, explaining that she tries "not to impose what I see but to try to talk as generally as I can about the play, try to get him to see something, and then combine what it is I see with what he sees" (Masson 1987, 133).

As an artistic director and a stage director, Meadow plays a dual role in the theatre. She discusses the challenge of both jobs, explaining, "My soul is nourished by being in rehearsal and by working with playwrights. There's no question that directing is the most intense and time consuming. . . . The wonderful thing about going back to the office after you've done a play is that somehow your life in the theatre continues. . . . I'm not going to be unemployed the next day" (Gener 2003, 20).

In addition to the awards already mentioned, Meadow's honors include an Outer Critics Circle Award for Perceptive and Supportive Contribution to the American Theatre in 1977, the Margo Jones Award for Continued Encouragement of New Playwrights (with Manhattan Theatre Club) in 1981, the Special Theatre World Award for Discovering, Developing, and Encouraging New Talent (with Barry Grove and Manhattan Theatre Club) in 1982, the Torch of Hope Award in 1989, the Person of the Year from the National Theatre Conference in 1992, and the Stage Directors and Choreographers Foundation's (SDCF) "Mr. Abbott" Award for lifetime achievement in 2003. Other awards include the Lee Reynolds Award from the League of Professional Theatre Women, the Drama Desk Award with Barry Grove for Outstanding Contribution to the Theatre, and a Special Citation Obie Award in 1977 for Sustained Excellence to the Manhattan Theatre Club. Meadow has served on the board of the Theatre Communications Group and numerous panels, including the advisory panels for the National Endowment for the Arts, the New York State Council on the Arts, and the Fund for New American Plays. She has also taught at New York City's Circle in the Square Theatre School, Yale University, and New York University.

Meadow discusses her future as a director, saying, "For many years, I was a mom with a child at home, and that influenced my choices about how much directing work I would do. I'm entering a different phase now; I have an opportunity to nurture my directing work more than I have in the past. I'm an artist at heart. Directing is what I treasure most" (Gener 2003, 20).

Sources

Barnes, Clive. 1977. "Theater: Truths Captured by 'Ashes.'" Rev. of *Ashes,* by David Rudkin. *New York Times,* 9 Feb., 43.

Beaufort, John. 1992. "A Small Family Business." Rev. of *A Small Family Business,* by Alan Ayckbourn. *Christian Science Monitor,* 7 May, 12.

Brantley, Ben. 1996. "When a Legacy of Massacre Rises Up to Haunt a Family." Rev. of *Nine Armenians,* by Leslie Ayvazian. *New York Times,* 13 Nov., C15.

———. 2000. "A Woman on the Verge of Another Breakdown." Rev. of *The Tale of the Allergist's Wife,* by Charles Busch. *New York Times,* 1 Mar., E5.

Chinoy, Helen Krich and Linda Walsh Jenkins, eds. 1987. *Women in American Theatre.* New York: Theatre Communications Group.

Fleischer, Yolanda. 1989. "Meadow, Lynne." In *Notable Women in American Theatre: A Biographical Dictionary,* by Alice M. Robinson, Vera Mowry Roberts, and Milly S. Barranger, 622–26. Westport, Conn.: Greenwood.

Gener, Randy. 2003. "Lynne Meadow's Next Stage." *American Theatre* 20 (10) (Dec.): 18–22.

Guernsey, Otis, ed. 1977. *The Best Plays of 1976–1977 (The Burns Mantle Yearbook)*. New York: Dodd, Mead.

Gussow, Mel. 1976. "Searing 'Ashes'—Unflinching Drama." *New York Times,* 15 Dec., 64.

Manhattan Theatre Club. http://www.mtc-nyc.org (accessed 23 Apr. 2004).

"Manhattan Theatre Club." 2004. *Back Stage,* 10 Sept., A3–A4.

Masson, Linda Joyce Krasnow. 1987. "Lynne Meadow, Director." Ph.D. diss., New York University.

———. 1994. "Lynne (Carolyn) Meadow." In *Theatrical Directors: A Biographical Dictionary,* ed. John W. Frick and Stephen M. Vallillo, 265. Westport, Conn.: Greenwood.

Munk, Erika. 1976. "Resurrection from the Ashes." Rev. of *Ashes,* by David Rudkin. *Village Voice,* 3 Jan. In "Lynne Meadow, Director," by Linda Joyce Krasnow Masson. Ph.D. diss., New York University, 1987, 165.

Pereira, John W. 1996. *Opening Nights: 25 Years of the Manhattan Theatre Club.* New York: Peter Lang.

Rich, Frank. 1988. "The Stage: 'Woman in Mind.'" Rev. of *Woman in Mind,* by Alan Ayckbourn. *New York Times,* 18 Feb., C21.

———. 1992. "From Alan Ayckbourn, A Family of Thieves." Rev. of *A Small Family Business,* by Alan Ayckbourn. *New York Times,* 28 Apr., C13.

Representative Directing Credits

Broadway:
A Small Family Business (1992), *The Tale of the Allergist's Wife* (2000)

Off and Off-Off Broadway:
Ubu Roi (1971), *All Through the House* (1972), *Jesus As Seen by his Friends* (co-directed with Sergei Retitov—1973), *The Shooting Gallery* (1973), *Hopscotch; Spared* (1974), *The Wager* (1974), *Bits and Pieces* (1974), *Golden Boy* (1975), *Marco Polo* (1976), *The Pokey* (1976), *Ashes* (1976, 1977), *Chez Nous* (1977), *Catsplay* (1978), *Artichoke* (1979), *Jail Diary of Abie Sachs* (1979), *Biography* (1980), *Vikings* (1980), *Close of Play* (1981), *Sally and Marsha* (1982), *Three Sisters* (1982), *Park Your Car in Harvard Yard* (1984), *Principia Scriptoriae* (1986), *Bloody Poetry* (1986), *Woman in Mind* (1988), *Eleemosynary* (1989), *The Loman Family Picnic* (1989, 1993), *Absent Friends* (1991), *Pretty Fire* (1993), *Nine Armenians* (1996), *Captain Courageous: The Musical* (1999), *The Tale of the Allergist's Wife* (2000, 2002), *Blur* (2001), *Boy Gets Girl*[1] (2001), *Last Dance* (2003), *Rose's Dilemma* (2003), *Moonlight & Magnolias* (2005)

Regional Theatre:
Caucasian Chalk Circle (1969), *Under Milkwood* (1970), *Hollinrake's Gambit* (1975), *Marco Polo* (1975), *Benefit of a Doubt* (1976), *Secrets of the Rich*

(1976), *Eminent Domain* (1977), *Two Small Bodies* (1977), *Sally and Marsha* (1981)

Tours:
   The Tale of the Allergist's Wife (2003)

International Theatre:
   Wandering (1970), *Climb* (1971), *Forensic and the Navigators* (1971)

Notes

1. Meadow is often credited with directing *Boy Gets Girl,* but some sources credit her as supervising the production. Meadow restaged *Boy Gets Girl* at the Manhattan Theatre Club after it transferred from the Goodman Theatre because its original director died.

 Miguel, Muriel

Muriel Miguel is a director, choreographer, writer, actress, and the artistic director of Spiderwoman Theater, the longest-running women's theatre company in North America. She is known for directing productions that often combine storytelling, song, movement, humor, and important issues concerning Native Americans and women.

Born on August 14, 1937, in Brooklyn, New York, to a Rappahannock mother and Kuna father, Miguel grew up in an environment in which storytelling, singing, and dancing were an integral part of her life. At the age of nine, she was a founding member of Thunderbird American Indian Dancers, which continues to perform today. At this early age, Miguel began to direct and learn "how to cooperate and how to think in a collective way. And how to pull things up from people that they could do" (Miguel, interview, 2004).

Miguel took dance classes at a local theatre and at the Henry Street Playhouse in 1960 with Alwin Nickolais and Murray Louis. She also studied dance with Jean Erdman, Erick Hawkins, and Lynn Laredo—a teacher who was knowledgeable in Rudolf Laban's modern dance theories. In 1962 Joseph Chaikin asked Laredo to bring dancers to his Open Theater in New York City, which was just beginning. Chaikin's method of working appealed to Miguel. She felt at home in the Open Theatre, where she could experiment with dance. Miguel's choreography was expressive and she often choreographed to pop music, which she says was looked down upon by others as being crude. She enthusiastically embraced the exercises of the Open Theater and appeared in productions throughout the 1960s, including Jean-Claude van Italie's *The Serpent,* Alfred Jarry's *Ubu Roi,* and Megan Terry's *Viet Rock.* At the Open Theatre, Chaikin worked on storytelling, and Miguel came away from the group "fascinated with everybody's stories. All kinds of stories" (Miguel, interview, 2004).

Miguel left the Open Theatre to pursue a career as a performer, but became dissatisfied by a lack of good roles. She was often asked to do Indian princess roles, with lines that required her to say "such ungodly things." She explains, "I mean, how could you possibly say that if you had any kind of a political conscience?" (Interview, 2004). In addition to this, Native American parts were usually given to non-Native Americans. When she told her agent that she did not want to do stereotyped roles anymore, she stopped getting offers for parts.

In 1972 Miguel became a founding member of the Native American Theatre Ensemble at La MaMa, an experimental theatre in New York City, and stayed involved for a year. Miguel loved working with groups, and decided to form another group with a woman who had been part of the Bread and Puppet Theatre and another woman who was a former member of the political group, The Weathermen. In 1972 they formed Womanspace Feminist Theater, which employed consciousness raising (CR) in their development process. They created a piece called *Cycles,* and in the course of the process Miguel realized that she was directing. She explains, "It just kind of happened" (Interview, 2004). The group had a falling out, however, and this caused Miguel to cast more carefully the next time. Miguel explains, "I started to realize that if I really wanted to do this kind of work, I had to have people that were actors. They couldn't be people I just met on the street. . . . I started to really look for an avenue into this. Now I was a committed feminist. I wanted to work with women. So I started to look for other women" (Interview, 2004).

After finding new collaborators, Miguel began to work on a piece that included avant-garde musicians, a childhood friend, and performer Lois Weaver—who would later form the feminist theatre group Split Britches. The piece focused on spiritual stories and included Miguel's childhood friends' telling of the story of Spiderwoman, in which a Hopi goddess teaches people how to weave. Miguel recalls, "I started to get a feeling about what I wanted to do with this because there were three stories. They were similar, but they weren't similar. They all went someplace. So I started to chop it up and work on it. I made this huge tapestry of all these sounds, and we had these musicians . . . and so my vision was to take . . . these stories, and we would go in and out, and weave in and out of each other. And sometimes we were together, and sometimes we were separate. But they were all creation stories. And it was the first time that I ever thought of weaving stories or doing that type of story weaving" (Interview, 2004).

After the first workshop, her childhood friend passed away. Miguel decided to continue the group and asked other women to join, including her two sisters, Gloria Miguel and Lisa Mayo. Miguel explains, "I was absolutely determined to do this. I was still very involved in the women's movement. And I was also walking around in great rage and could not understand the rage. So I started to investigate . . . just what is rage? What does it come from? How come I have so much of it?" (Interview, 2004).

While the group worked on their first piece, which would eventually become *Women in Violence,* Miguel invited members of the Open Theatre to their rehearsal. During the rehearsal, the Open Theatre members began to laugh, thinking the group was both funny and shocking. This response surprised Miguel and the group because they considered their work as very serious. Miguel thought about the reaction and realized that they were funny because they had told stories that were not didactic, unlike most performances by women's groups at the time (Interview, 2004).

Miguel liked the idea of a simple and portable production for *Women in Violence.* She and the group began by piecing together Native American quilts and cloth with the other pieces of cloth to create a backdrop that the group still uses today. In addition to the quilted backdrop, Miguel used simple lighting in her early productions, citing "Grotowski and his one light" as an influence (Interview, 2004).

Founded in 1976 by Miguel, Spiderwoman Theater took its name from the group's story-weaving techniques. In the first year, Miguel directed *Women in Violence* at the Washington Square Methodist Church, combining a slapstick performance style with serious subject matter. The text was an interweaving of the group members' own stories about violence with that of "a well-known revolutionary leader in the 1970s American Indian movement who saw no discrepancy between his fight for native rights and his own brutality toward women" (Schneider 1993, 241).

After their New York City premiere, Spiderwoman Theater toured the United States and Europe. While *Women in Violence* shocked many people, the group was equally shocked by how they were treated by some theatre professionals. In 1977 when Spiderwoman Theater arrived at Le Festival Mondiale du Théâtre in Nancy, France, the group's members were given brooms and told to sweep the performance space before the show. The group refused and word got out that Spiderwoman Theater had forced a male producer to sweep the floor. Because of the news, male hecklers arrived at the packed performance, only to find themselves heckled by the women in the audience. There were fights at the door. In Bologna, Italy, where the women's movement was just beginning, organizers cancelled Spiderwoman Theater's performance, afraid that riots would occur.

Spiderwoman Theater's next creation, *The Lysistrata Numbah!*, was based on Aristophanes' *Lysistrata* and incorporated stories of Spiderwoman Theater's members. The production, directed by Miguel in 1977 at La MaMa, attacked stereotyping of women. Miguel explains, "You know I can play a princess. I can play a prostitute. I can play a mother. But no one thinks of me as the girl next door or . . . Juliet. That was part of *Lysistrata* . . . the sky's the limit. You can be anything and anybody you want to be" (Interview, 2004). The play's ending was also changed to make a statement about lesbianism. Miguel explains, "Well, maybe I don't want to go home with my husband! Maybe I want to go home with her [another woman]!" (Interview, 2004).

In 1981 Spiderwoman Theater split into two groups—Spiderwoman Theater and Split Britches—due to a schism in the group that divided members over lesbian/heterosexual issues and white/native ways. Spiderwoman Theater, which had been a multicultural ensemble up to that point, now became a group featuring three Native American sisters. That same year Miguel directed Spiderwoman Theater's *Sun, Moon and Feather,* which marked the beginning of its focus on Native American issues. Miguel explains, "Before we told stories with many different people, but now we were telling the stories of three sisters growing up—three Native women growing up in Brooklyn" (Interview, 2004).

In 1987 Miguel and Spiderwoman Theater began to develop *Winnetou's Snake Oil Show from Wigwam City,* which explored stereotypes of Native Americans and attacked the idea of the appropriation of one culture by another. The production was inspired by German Carl May's fictional book called *The Legend of Winnetou,* which presented a romanticized and stereotyped portrayal of Native Americans. The show first toured the United States in 1989 under Miguel's direction and caused controversy among Native Americans and whites. Miguel states that when they presented the production at reservations, people laughed hysterically. However, in venues in San Francisco and Seattle, it was not well received by non-Native audiences. Spiderwoman Theater received hate mail accusing them of making money off of Native American culture and the women's movement. Despite the controversy, Miguel explains that the positive reaction from young Native Americans who saw the show "is why we work" (Interview, 2004).

Miguel comments about the public's reaction to her pieces, saying, "My feeling, all the time, is that . . . I don't want the magic of theatre, I want it to go [She twists up her face.]!" (Interview, 2004). The Spiderwoman Theater performance of *Winnetou* in 1990 at San Francisco's Life on the Water Theater drew a similar response from the critics. Steven Winn of the *San Francisco*

Chronicle wrote, "[T]he performers offer a kind of collective raspberry to the dominant culture's reductive notion of Native American culture. They launch into opera when they feel like it, talk dirty or bark like dogs" (1990, E12).

In 1990 Miguel directed Spiderwoman Theater's *Reverb-ber-ber-rations* at New York City's Theatre for the New City. While *Winnetou* focused on fake shamanism, *Reverb-ber-ber-rations* focused on spiritual development. In a review of the production at Dance Place in Washington, D.C., in 1993, Sarah Kaufman of the *Washington Post* noted how the group's "brash, boisterous humor . . . brought their testimonials to otherworldliness down to earth." Kaufman also thought the direction ambitious, writing, "It seems that in burrowing so deeply into their own histories they discovered more anecdotal threads than they could spin into a coherent whole. Still the value of their journey is undeniable" (1993, F04). Miguel says that viewers often call her projects "ambitious." She says of her work, "I don't care how ambitious it is, as long as you think" (Interview, 2004).

Miguel says that she never planned to be a director. She explains, "Collectives can go on forever. You never make a decision on anything. I was going crazy. . . . Not another meeting! . . . So in the beginning I was called the 'final eye' . . . which was OK with me. But . . . call it 'final eye,' call it 'director,' . . . people still treat you the same. . . . It came to that point where I had to say 'I'm the director.' And if I had to go to bat, I went to bat" (Interview, 2004).

As a director, Miguel does not hold auditions. For Spiderwoman Theater, the three sisters are always in each piece. If the production requires additional actors, Miguel invites performers to join them. For her own projects, Miguel invites people whom she would like to work with to be in her productions.

Rehearsals in Spiderwoman Theater are an intuitive collaborative process. Miguel explains the process of story weaving, saying, "Basically we tell stories. We sometimes start in the middle; sometimes start at the end; sometimes start at the beginning. And sometimes there's all three of us telling from different points of view at the same time . . . and that is what I call story weaving. We get this real thick tapestry" (Interview, 2004).

When directing other people's productions Miguel's approach is still collaborative, but less so than when working with Spiderwoman Theater. She says, "When I'm working with people that have commissioned me, I spend at least the first two rehearsals talking to them about what they want, what they see, and what they think" (Interview, 2004). Although Miguel rarely starts with a written script, she helps those with scripts to develop ideas through discussion and exercises. She explains, "I'll . . . see what comes out of the premise" (Interview, 2004).

During rehearsals, Miguel develops the pieces as a director and acts as dramaturg. She selects things she sees in rehearsal and may ask performers,

"'Where were you going? What were you doing? What were you thinking? Can that be enlarged? Can I see more of it? Can we use it in five places?'" (Interview, 2004). Although she deals with serious subjects, Miguel often creates humor by pushing an idea into the realm of the absurd. She explains, "You go until it becomes so absurd you can't go any further with it" (Interview, 2004). In addition to humor, she also incorporates movement into her productions, stemming from her interest in dance.

The amount of time needed for rehearsals varies because it includes the development of a piece. Miguel explains that a piece is not done "until you say it's done in your own words. So we open a piece, and sometimes it's not where we want it to be. Really it's never done. . . . It takes us a year sometimes to get where we want to" (Interview, 2004).

Because Miguel performs in Spiderwoman Theater productions and also directs her own one-woman shows (*Hot 'N' Stuff, Trail of the Otter, Red Mother*), she is conscious of directing herself. She says, "I go in, and I come out. . . . Sometimes I can hear it. Sometimes I know it's not working. Sometimes I stop and talk to people. . . . What they say a lot of times makes me go back into it. I know where I am in the piece as the person that has directed it" (Interview, 2004).

Miguel also performs in plays by others, and she sometimes develops performance pieces from her experiences. In 2003 her one-woman show, *Red Mother,* was created after Miguel was part of the Aboriginal Brecht Project at the Aboriginal Arts Program at The Banff Centre in Alberta, Canada. The project was directed by a German Brecht expert and focused on Brecht's concept of justice as interpreted through the experience of Native people. Miguel felt "like an Indian playing a German" and began to create *Red Mother* in 2003 as a response to the experience (Interview, 2004).

Miguel did not realize that she was a role model to others until after a performance in Toronto when three Objiway Cree girls came up to her and introduced themselves as Lisa, Gloria, and Muriel—pretending that they were the three sisters of Spiderwoman Theater. Miguel recalls, "The mother came up and said, 'This was the first time they'd ever seen women of their color doing things that they want to do on stage. You are really important to them. They want to be you. You are their role models.' And DONG! I mean, we never thought about that! I mean, we really didn't. We didn't think of ourselves as role models. We thought of ourselves as actresses writing and touring. You know, all the stuff that goes with that. And teaching. But not as role models. It was the first time it really clicked" (Interview, 2004). As a conscious role model, Miguel conducts workshops with Native American Youth and directs the work of other Native Americans. She says, "I think it's important, as a director, to [help] . . . Native people get their work out there. . . . No matter how" (Interview, 2004).

Miguel's many awards and honors include the Indian of the Year (New York City) awarded by The Thunderbird American Indian Dancers in 1987, the Mayor's Office and Law Department Civic Award in 1992, selection for the Bread and Rose's International Union Native and Hawaiian Women of Hope poster in 1997, an honorary Doctorate of Fine Arts in 1997 from Ohio's Miami University in recognition of life's work in theatre, honors as an elder and role model for two spirit women of color by the Brothers of the Sisters of Astraea in 2000, and the Paul D. Fleck Fellowship in the Arts from the Banff Centre for the Arts in 2002. Miguel and the members of Spiderwoman Theater were also honored at the Smithsonian's National Museum of the American Indian in New York City in 2005.

Miguel has taught at Bard College in New York, the Centre for Indigenous Theatre in Toronto, and the Aboriginal Arts Program at the Banff Centre for the Arts, and has conducted workshops and developed shows with inner-city youth on HIV/AIDS for The Minnesota Native American AIDS Task Force in Minneapolis. Miguel also founded and was director of the Italian Women's Theatre Company in 1979, Off The Beaten Path Theater Company in 1986, and Shy Woman Singers and Dancers in 1996.

In spite of Miguel's innovative contributions to theatre, her work begins and ends with storytelling because it is universal to all cultures. She states, "I listen, and listen, and listen. Then I try to give back to you what you have given to me. I try to start someplace within your stories" (Interview, 2004).

Sources

Canning, Charlotte. 1996. *Feminist Theaters in the U.S.A.: Staging Women's Experience.* London: Routledge.

Dace, Trish. 2001. "Making Their Own Opportunities. Women's Theatres in New York." *Back Stage,* 9 Mar., 28–31.

Jenkins, Linda Walsh. 1987. "Spiderwoman." In *Women in American Theatre,* ed. Helen Krich Chinoy and Linda Walsh Jenkins, 303–5. New York: Theatre Communications Group.

Kaufman, Sarah. 1993. "Spiderwoman Theater." Rev. of *Reverb-ber-ber-rations,* by Spiderwoman Theater. *Washington Post,* 19 Mar., F04.

Mayo, Lisa, Gloria Miguel, and Muriel Miguel. 1996. Interview with Larry Abbott. "Spiderwoman Theater and the Tapestry of Story." *Canadian Journal of Native Studies* 16 (1): 165–60.

Miguel, Muriel. 2004. Interview with Wendy Vierow. 9 June. New York City.

Schneider, Rebecca. 1993. "See the Big Show: Spiderwoman Theater Doubling

Back." In *Acting Out: Feminist Performances,* ed. Lynda Hart and Peggy Phelan, 227–56. Ann Arbor, Mich.: University of Michigan Press.

"Spiderwoman Theater: Lisa Mayo, Gloria Miguel, Muriel Miguel." Online exhibit of Spiderwoman papers, photos, posters, and manuscripts. Native American Women Playwrights Archive, Miami University, Oxford, Ohio. http://staff.lib .muohio.edu/nawpa/Spiderwoman.html (accessed 13 May 2004).

Winn, Steven. 1990. "Spiderwoman Troupe Hustles 'Snake Oil.'" Rev. of *Winnetou's Snake Oil Show From Wigwam City,* by Spiderwoman Theater. *San Francisco Chronicle,* 26 Oct., E12.

"Women's Theatre Companies." 1996. *Back Stage,* 26 April, 29–30.

Representative Directing Credits[1]

Off and Off-Off Broadway:
> *Women in Violence* (1975, 1976, 1985), *Lysistrata Numbah!* (1977), *Trilogy: Friday Night, Jealousy, My Sister Ate Dirt* (1978), *Cabaret: An Evening of Disgusting Songs and Pukey Images* (1979), *Sun, Moon and Feather* (1981, 1982, 1997), *The Three Sisters from Here to There* (1982), *Banana Bunch* (1983), *I'll Be Right Back* (1984), *Coyolxauhtui* (1989), *Reverb-ber-ber-rations* (1990, 1993), *Sky Woman Falling* (1991), *Blood Speaks* (1992), *The Pause That Refreshes* (1992), *Power Pipes* (1992), *Indian Givers* (co-director—1993), *The Rez Sisters* (co-directed with Linda Chapman—1994), *Hot 'N' Soft I and II* (1994), *Trail of the Otter* (1996), *Conversations with the Dead* (2004), *Red Mother* (2004)

Regional Theatre:
> *Power Pipes* (1991), *Your Grandmother's Love* (1991), *Returning the Gift* (1992), *More Than Feathers and Beads* (1994), *Fear Into Sacred* (1999)

Tours:
> *Women in Violence* (1976), *The Fittin' Room* (1981), *Sun, Moon and Feather* (1981, 1982, 1983, 1984, 1986, 1989, 1995, 1996, 1997, 2001?), *Winnetou's Snake Oil Show from Wigwam City* (1989, 1990, 1993, 1994, 1996, 1999, 2001), *Power Pipes* (1992), *Hot 'N' Soft* (1993, 1996), *Reverb-ber-ber-rations* (1993, 1994, 1999, 2000), *Persistence of Memory* (2002, 2003, 2004), *The Scrubbing Project* (2005)

International Theatre:
> *Lysistrata Numbah!* (1977, 1981, 1982), *Women in Violence* (1977, 1978), *Cabaret: An Evening of Disgusting Songs and Pukey Images* (1980), *The Fittin' Room* (1980, 1981), *Sun, Moon and Feather* (1981, 1982, 1989, 1995, 1997), *Give 'Em a Carrot (For as Long as the Sun is Green)* (1985), *Double Take a Second Look* (1986), *Winnetou's Snake Oil Show from Wigwam City* (1987), *Princess Pocahontas and the Blue Spots* (1990), *Hot 'N' Soft* (1991, 1992, 1993), *Hot 'N' Soft II* (1993), *Reverb-ber-ber-rations* (1994, 1998, 1999), *Trail of the Otter* (1996), *Throw Away Kids* (1999), *The Scrubbing*

Project (2000, 2001, 2002, 2005), *Persistence of Memory* (2002), *Red Mother* (2003), *She Knew Who She Was* (2003), *Evening in Paris* (2006)

Notes

1. In early productions, Miguel was called the "final eye" rather than the "director" (Miguel, interview, 2004).

 # Monk, Meredith

Born on Nov. 20, 1942, in New York City,[1] Meredith Monk is a composer, singer, director, choreographer, filmmaker, installation artist, and creator of musical theatre works. A forerunner of performance art, her work involves an interdisciplinary approach to performance that includes images, light, movement, music, and sound that results in new perspectives for viewers.

Monk spent her early childhood in New York City's borough of Queens. At an early age, she sang, played piano, and studied Eurythmics, a method created by composer Emile Jaques-Dalcroze that integrates movement and sound. Monk explains, "I have a visual impairment, where I see two images when I look out of both eyes. I can't fuse images. I think because of that I was really quite uncoordinated as a child. My mother, knowing I had a very natural musical and rhythmic talent, sent me to Dalcroze Eurythmics as my first movement experience. . . . I was lucky, in a sense, because then music and movement became so integrated for me that I don't think of them as two separate things" (Highwater 1997, 88). Monk describes the musical tradition in her family, stating, "My great-grandfather was a cantor; my grandfather was a bass-baritone from Russia who, along with my concert pianist grandmother, opened a music conservatory in Harlem and performed at places like the Brooklyn Academy of Music and Carnegie Hall. My mother was a professional pop singer. Much of my early childhood was spent in radio control rooms, watching and listening to my mother sing jingles for soap operas and swing tunes for radio variety shows" (1999, sec. 2, 36).

Monk moved with her family to Connecticut when she was eight. In junior high and high school she sang folk music. While in high school at Bucks County, Pennsylvania, Monk acted in plays and choreographed dances and musicals. Afterward, she attended Sarah Lawrence College in Bronxville, New York, where she studied dance, music, acting, and other subjects. Monk's attitude toward art was influenced by her college dance teacher, Bessie Schoenberg. She notes, "The first thing Bessie taught me was not to take myself so seriously—that everything that I came up with was not perfect by any means; it could be thrown away (and mostly should be thrown away) in order to start again. She also taught all of us to be respectful of each other, to appreciate each person's talents, styles, rates of growth for what they were. In other words, not to have a preconceived idea of what a body is, a dance is, a song is, a play is. This basic attitude . . . has given me the courage to try to find new ways of putting art forms together by working between the cracks; it has taught me never to assume anything; it has made the process of discovery one of the joys of my life and it has kept me curious" (1985, 127).

While at college, Monk began to create and choreograph pieces that blurred the boundaries among art forms. She explains, "I began to glimpse how I could combine my interests in music, movement, visual images, and theater into one unified form. I made pieces in which I sang and moved at the same time; I composed a vocal piece, which I recorded on tape, and made movement as a counterpoint to that; I made disjunctive visual events with objects, and put music in between" (1999, sec. 2, 36). At Sarah Lawrence, Monk also created a vocabulary of movement and developed a choreographic style (Interview, 1997, 74). Monk graduated in 1964 with a B.A. in combined performing arts. In addition to her studies at Sarah Lawrence, Monk studied dance in New York City with Merce Cunningham, Robert Dunn, Martha Graham, Mia Slavenska, and at the Joffrey School and the Ruth Mata/Eugene Hari studio.

After graduation, Monk arrived in New York City with a desire to combine dance, music, theatre, and visual art. She marks the beginning of her career with her piece *Break*, which she directed at New York City's Washington Square Galleries in 1964. During the performance, she wore a raincoat and moved to the sound of car noises. Monk gravitated to the Judson Dance Theatre, where artists were experimenting with new forms of dance and theatre and breaking boundaries. There, Monk choreographed and directed many of her early compositions, which crossed genres. Monk comments about her role as an interdisciplinary artist saying, "European culture is the only culture in the world that separated these functions into storytelling, dance and music. In most cultures, there's no concern about specialization. It's always interconnected" (Breslauer 1993, 1).

At first Monk worked primarily with text and movement, but in 1965 she had a realization about her voice. She explains, "One day, I started vocalizing, and I guess I had a kind of 'Eureka!' flash, the idea that the voice could have the kind of range that movement has—that there could be a vocabulary for voice as individual as movement. . . . When you're working with the voice, one of the most powerful and universal instruments, you come upon archetypal sounds that exist from many cultures" (Pareles 1985, C3). With a range of three octaves, Monk created a method called "extended vocal technique." This technique focuses on the expressiveness of the voice using any means possible—from clicking noises to whispers. Monk notes, "Within the voice there are limitless colors and textures and landscapes" (Smith 1996, 1).

Beginning with *16 Millimeter Earrings* at Judson Memorial Church in 1966, Monk began to focus more on combining dance, film, music, sound, and theatre. In the piece, which Monk created and directed, images were projected onto a screen, Monk's body, and a paper globe that she wore over her head. Monk describes her creative evolution as follows: "I saw that I could make a performance form that had a sense of poetry, nonverbal poetry—a theatre of images, sounds, and textures—and by weaving the various elements together, a very powerful and multidimensional experience could occur. I started seeing how you could work with images and sound in a painterly way to create or reflect another level of reality. . . . [I]t was also the first time I composed a full score of music from beginning to end. Before that time I had done taped sound and some vocal work in my pieces, but there was a lot of silence in them" (Interview, 1997, 72).

In 1968 Monk founded her company called The House, which focuses on an interdisciplinary approach to performance. Her performance group changes in size according to the needs of each production. The multicultural members of the company include people of different backgrounds and body types who study a variety of disciplines ranging from science to art.

In 1969 Monk created and directed a site-specific performance called *Juice: A Theater Cantata in 3 Installments,* which examined the idea of a quest. *Juice* featured eighty-five performers and required the audience to move from site to site. Monk states, "Different kinds of audience/performer relationships have always interested me in one way or another" (Interview, 1997, 69). Monk had begun to create and direct site-specific performances two years earlier with *Blueprint,* which required the audience to follow the action in both the upstate New York town of Woodstock and New York City. In the first installment of *Juice,* the audience viewed the production from different parts of New York City's Guggenheim Museum. The second part of the piece was performed three weeks later at New York City's Barnard College, while the third part was performed one week after that at The House Loft in New York City.

Beginning with *Juice,* Monk began to include subtitles in her works. She explains that they "are working titles for me to clarify the forms I was trying to work in. I'm always interested in making a crossover form. That's been difficult for people though. Grants organizations pass my applications around and around from one department to another. And audience members watching my pieces spend three-quarters of the time worrying about trying to figure out what it is. I've spent most of my life trying to break that down" (Solomon 1986, 366).

Monk's *Vessel: An Opera Epic* was also a site-specific performance, but had Joan of Arc as its central figure. First directed by Monk in 1971, the action began at The House Loft, moved to New York City's Performing Garage, and ended in a parking lot near a church. The production included a cast of eighty performers, twenty-seven motorcycles, a Volkswagen bus, and a welder's torch to stage Joan's death. Monk explains her unconventional use of design elements, stating, "The piece was like a tapestry of images that sometimes had a lot of humor within them. Joan of Arc wore sneakers. Her armor was made of paper bags painted silver, shields were made of egg crates. Joan's fire was the sparks of an arc welder. *Vessel* presented a very contemporary way of working with ordinary materials, then transforming them. . . . I like to play with that by taking ordinary things and doing something different with them. The bricollage idea" (Highwater 1997, 85). Writing for the *Boston Herald Traveller,* critic Marsha Siegel described her experience as a viewer noting, "Meredith Monk's imagination is so clever, so far-reaching, yet so careful. With a sacrificial purity, an unaggressive assurance, she drags us down into the city's viscera, only to transport us out of the grit and garbage in an elaborate, watertight fantasy" (1971, 39). The New York City production of *Vessel* won a Special Citation Obie Award.

Monk called *Vessel* an opera, and thereafter, called many of her pieces operas. She defines them broadly as "a multi-perceptual form combining music, movement, theater and visual images. I'm a fan of the idea of opera but not the way it has been done" (Albright 1991, 53).

In 1973 Monk directed the final version of her piece, *Education of the Girlchild: An Opera,* at The House Loft and at New York City's Cathedral of St. John the Divine. She had begun work on it years earlier and had staged different versions of the production around the world. The piece explores the life of a woman played by Monk, who begins as an old woman and ends as a young girl. Monk explains, "I was excited about the idea that you could show the change of time through gesture and through sound, vocal sound. . . . By actually seeing how age changed the gestures—subtle variations of the same gesture performed by the old woman, the middle-aged woman, and the young woman—you could see the whole process of aging, but backwards" (Jowitt 1997, 78). Don McDonagh of the *New York Times* wrote, "Meredith Monk's canny assemblage of biographical incidents from the past and present . . . reveals her imagination operating at a high creative pitch" (1973, 14). *Education of the Girlchild* won the Venice Biennale First Prize in 1975.

Monk's *Quarry: An Opera* had three acts titled "Lullaby," "March," and "Requiem." The piece was first directed by Monk at New York City's La MaMa Experimental Theatre Club (e.t.c.) in 1976 and included dialogue, movement, music, and film. The audience looked down on the action from two sides of the stage as Monk portrayed a sick child with the action occurring around her. Monk comments on her choice of staging, saying, "I was thinking of a mandala when I was working on it, one of those Tibetan mandala filled with detail. . . . It was a different way of using space, not frontally organized" (Pareles 1985, C3).

Monk created *Quarry: An Opera* after visiting Europe and becoming interested in the two World Wars, as well as her own Jewish/Eastern European heritage. However, she avoided a literal portrayal of her subject, stating, "I felt the most honest way of dealing with the theme was to do it through the eyes of a child from far away, so it was more like an American child who was sick and the sickness became metaphoric of the society, which became more and more sinister" (Highwater 1997, 84). Monk found *Quarry* to be a turning point in her career, noting, "'Quarry' was the end of a cycle, the ultimate statement of a certain way of thinking about things—building something by little increments of detail adding up. It's put together in such a complex way. In the music, there's a sense of building little strands and having them woven together; there's a sense of time moving forward and backward, and a feeling that you're indoors and outdoors at the same time" (Pareles 1985, C3).

Quarry won a Special Citation Obie Award. As with many of Monk's pieces, *Quarry* was reviewed by both theatre and dance critics. While the dance critics had a vocabulary for discussing movement, the theatre critics often lacked this faculty and had difficulty with Monk's pieces. In his review of the La MaMa production, theatre critic Clive Barnes of the *New York Times* was at a loss as how to evaluate the production. Although he noted that Monk "deploys her forces of movement with consummate skill," Barnes was confused by the structure and wrote, "There seems to be a certain dramatic aimlessness to it" (1976, 24). By contrast, the piece was accessible to dance critic McDonagh of the *New York Times*. In his review of the Brooklyn Academy of Music production in 1976, McDonagh wrote, "It is one of Miss Monk's most effective searches through the past" (1976, 22).

In 1979 Monk directed her work *Recent Ruins* at La MaMa. The piece involved a group of archaeologists piecing together a broken pot. She states, "I think *Recent Ruins* was an unusual investigation because in that piece I actually took the elements apart. Usually my large composite pieces are mosaics or weavings of many means of perception: music, movement, objects, and light put together into a complex whole. . . . *Recent Ruins* . . . wasn't like taking small tiles and placing them in a mosaic, or taking little strands and weaving them together into a larger whole. The structure itself had a more monolithic, hewn continuity. It dealt with isolating and intensifying the various elements" (Jowitt 1997, 71–72). In his review of *Recent Ruins,* which won a Villager Award for Outstanding Production, John Rockwell of the *New York Times* wrote, "[F]or sheer literalness in interpreting the idea of an artwork by one person that extends through all mediums, Meredith Monk must surely take the prize. . . . Miss Monk works with endless bits of personal reference, weaving them into a tapestry of imagery, gesture, movement and sound that can appear deliberately obscure. . . . But what is clear is that 'Recent Ruins' should be seen by anyone interested in the future of theater, dance or music" (1979, 65).

Written and directed by Monk, *Turtle Dreams (Cabaret)* opened in 1983 at Plexus in New York City and won a Villager Award for Outstanding Composition. Later presented in 1986 at La MaMa, the production included two films of a turtle making its way across a map and then through empty city streets to signify the apocalypse. Jack Anderson of the *New York Times* described the La MaMa production, writing, "[I]t was a sort of abstract cabaret. Like conventional cabarets, revues or floor shows, it offered a string of musical and choreographic 'routines.' . . . [I]t was as if Miss Monk were celebrating the energy—as well as the magic and absurdity—of all types of performance without bothering to cite or depict any specific sort of show" (1986, H22).

During the 1980s Monk focused more on musical concerts. Earlier, in 1978, Monk had founded a group called Meredith Monk and Vocal Ensemble, made up of professional singers who sometimes dance and act, in order to explore musical forms. She describes her shift to music, stating, "I became interested in the real-time, immediate situation of beginning as myself and letting each song become a transformation rather than creating an overall world in which performers had to stay throughout the evening" (1999, sec. 2, 36). Returning to her operas, Monk first directed her work *Atlas: An Opera in Three Parts* at Houston's Wortham Theater Center in 1991. In *Atlas,* a girl explores the world in three acts titled "Personal Climate," "Night Travel," and "Invisible Light." Based on the life of Belgian explorer Alexandra Daniels, the opera contains few words and is communicated through movement, voice tones, and nonsense syllables. Monk explains the pieces, stating, "Travel is a metaphor for spiritual quest. . . . [T]he quest for meaning and transcendence during a time in which the notion of an uncorrupted society has been steadily eroded and the survival of the earth is in question" (Ward 1991a, 21). In his review of the Houston performance, Charles Ward of the *Houston Chronicle* noted that many audience members left early—probably because of Monk's unconventional music. However, he added, "[E]veryone who left missed a striking experience. . . . A black and white film of a horse gamboling in a field was shown in reverse, as if the audience were looking at the negative. Miniature models of a plane, ship and car carried across the stage suggested Alexandra's journey. . . . Sometimes, there was no point in thinking about the precise meaning of the images. The overall 'message' was clear: that many people take quests of discovery" (1991b, 1).

The Politics of Quiet was the first piece that Monk created in which she did not perform. In 1996 Monk directed the piece at New York City's Performance Space (PS) 122. She explains how the piece differed from her previous creations, stating, "I was trying to create a democratic form where everybody had the same amount of material. . . . I was also trying to eliminate visual and theatrical tricks. I was just going for the essentialized performer—the performer unadorned, no mask of any kind" (Interview, 1997, 76). In his favorable review of the performance directed by Monk at the Brooklyn Academy of Music in 1996, Neil Strauss of the *New York Times* describes the piece, writing, "Miss Monk looks at the psychological and technological detritus of this century, examines the communal dynamic of past centuries and prepares a rite of passage into the next. Yet . . . all there was on the bare white stage were 10 performers in exaggeratedly plain street clothes and several black microphones hanging from the ceiling. Occasionally, two children scampered out onto the stage or a cultural artifact like a croquet mallet or a toilet plunger was displayed, and several slides or a few minutes of a video were shown. But for the most part 'The Politics of Quiet' . . . was a thesis made of brief movements and monosyllabic utterances, with almost no dialogue or narrative" (1996, C15).

Although Monk usually creates the visual design for her pieces, she collaborated on her work *mercy* with visual artist Ann Hamilton, who did the installations. The production premiered at North Carolina's American Dance Festival in 2001 and was shown at the Brooklyn Academy of Music and other venues across the country in 2002. Monk defines the piece as "a kind of meditation on mercy and the lack thereof" (Connors 2002, 15). The piece explored human vulnerability with the use of tiny cameras to project live images in extreme close-up on a huge screen. The cameras focused primarily on Hamilton's pencil as she wrote and on the inside of Monk's mouth as she sang. The production received excellent reviews, with Mark Swed of the *Los Angeles Times* writing of the Los Angeles production, "[W]hat this intensely moving, drop-dead gorgeous, can't-be-categorized fluid piece of meditative music, movement and milieu presents is an immersion into the process of transcendence" (2002, F1).

Monk's *Impermanence*, a multimedia work that included music, film, and movement, premiered in 2004 at the Riverside Studios in London, England. A meditation on mortality, the work went on tour in the United States to excellent reviews in 2006. Joshua Kosman of the *San Francisco Chronicle* described the San Francisco production, writing, "Melodies come and go, dancers move in and out of the spotlight, physical gestures flutter and vanish. Nothing lingers much longer than it requires to make a quick and sometimes haunting impression" (2006, E2). In his review of the same production, Dennis Harvey of *Variety* wrote, "At 63, after more than four decades in the U.S. avant garde, Monk's work remains as difficult to encapsulate as ever, its mix of compassion, lyricism and delight just as invigorating" (2006, 46).

Monk's interdisciplinary and multimedia works involve a long creative process that begins with the composition of her pieces. Different stimuli may inspire her to begin work on a piece. For *Impermanence*, Monk was influenced by the death of her partner from cancer in 2002 and by her work with an English hospice organization (Harvey 2006, 46). For *Atlas* and *The Politics of Quiet*, she was inspired in part by Willa Cather's writings, which provided a skeptical view of technology. Monk's pieces avoid linearity and, instead, present information that viewers need to assemble for themselves. She explains her reason for working this way, stating, "Linear thinking is not the way the human mind works" (Stearns 1991, 5D).

When creating a piece, Monk says, "I try to start each piece from zero. . . . Trying to see if I can come to that level of purity, to let the next world of the new piece come through without any kind of assumptions" (Highwater 1997, 85, 88). Monk may spend years developing a piece before she even goes into rehearsal. Of content she says, "Many people think my work is autobiographical, but in fact I work from the belief that we have universal images, which can be read, and if you work with your own vocal instrument you come upon sounds that have existed throughout all time. I believe the more personal you are, the more universal you become" (80).

Because her pieces are interdisciplinary, Monk must consider each artistic element in terms of how it will affect the whole work. She explains, "I begin by generating different layers or materials such as musical materials, images, costume and lighting ideas, spatial concepts, movement material. At a certain point, I'll chart out these layers and try different ways of putting them together. This usually happens after I have been in rehearsal trying out the material. . . . The joy and challenge of working this way is that the unknown is very much part of the process" (Monk n.d.).

Music plays an important part in all of Monk's works. She notes, "The directness of musical communication creates a heart-to-heart relationship" (Solomon 1986, 367). Although full of music and sound, Monk's pieces often do not contain much text. Instead, she uses sounds or nonsense words, rather than language. She elucidates, "[T]ext points to something particular and I want to be very nonmanipulative of an audience. . . . The images, hopefully, have enough layers of sensory and emotional compression that everybody can find their own way in there, and in a sense, come back to themselves" (Highwater 1997, 82). Monk acknowledges sensory overload in today's world and notes that her pieces focus on the spiritual, attempt to break down barriers, and try "to cleanse the senses and offer emotional riches to make people more aware" (Goff 1995, 1F).

Monk also likes to include humor in her pieces. She states, "I don't think I would ever feel comfortable about doing a piece that didn't have humor in it. . . . It's just something that I feel is part of human nature. It's odd the way we're taught in this culture that there is either tragedy or comedy. Within one piece I like to work with a full palette" (Highwater 1997, 85).

Performers in Monk's pieces usually need to be able to act, dance, and sing. Monk says, "I've always been interested in working with people of all shapes, sizes, and body types and the authenticity of people who move well but have not been trained" (Highwater 1997, 82). When casting, Monk often works with performers that she has used before. However, casting may go beyond the known group if the piece requires it. Sometimes, such as in the case of *Quarry*, she casts herself in a part because others are unable to meet the vocal requirements of the part. In other cases, Monk adjusts roles according to the abilities of the cast. She may even develop characters based on the performers. For example, Monk explained that the characters in *Quarry* were created from the performers in a "combination of the way I see them, and the way they see themselves" (Interview, 1976, 91).

The way Monk runs rehearsals varies depending upon the piece. For her 1966 production of *16 Millimeter Earrings*, Monk worked through ideas first, explaining, "Every element was totally controlled, carefully constructed" (Interview, 1997, 73). Over time, Monk's approach to directing has changed from one of control to one of experimentation. She explains her later working method, saying, "I usually come in with ideas rather than material that's actually been realized yet. . . . We improvise and work with some of these theatrical ideas and try different solutions" (Cunningham 2001, 49). Although performers improvise in rehearsals, Monk rarely uses the improvisations for the final piece. She states, "I like to stay open to suggestions and try different possibilities, but I always go back to my own overview" (Interview, 1997, 76). Because Monk often works with members of The House, she is able to curtail part of the rehearsal process that might involve teaching her vocal and movement vocabularies. She explains, "I can't just use a pickup company. People learn my language so I can go in and talk in shorthand" (Cunningham 2001, 49).

Monk often uses the proscenium stage unconventionally in order to explore the idea of space. She discusses her use of time and space, stating, "I've done pieces that started at 11 A.M. and pieces that were performed in three different places; I never wanted to make the kind of piece where you walk in at 8:30, sit down in front of a proscenium stage knowing what to expect, and forget about it the next morning" (Pareles 1985, C3).

Over the years, Monk perceives a shift in what her work seeks to communicate, explaining, "I'm more interested in trying to see life in a fresh way. With *Recent Ruins, Specimen Days,* and *Turtle Dreams* I felt it was important to do warning pieces, to state what's wrong. Now it's more important to offer an alternative—not in the sense of '60's alternative lifestyles, but in terms of ways of seeing things" (Solomon 1986, 367).

In addition to the awards already mentioned, Monk's honors include a Brandeis Creative Arts Award in 1974, the Creative Artist Program Service Award in 1977 and 1982, a Bessie Award for Sustained Creative Achievement in 1985, an Obie Award for Sustained Achievement in 1985, the National Music Theater Award in 1986, the Rockefeller Foundation Distinguished Choreographer Award in 1987, a Dance Magazine Award in 1992, the MacArthur Foundation Fellowship in 1995, and the Sarah Lawrence College Distinguished Alumnae Award in 1996. She has also received numerous honorary doctorates, fellowships, and many music and dance awards. In addition to founding the Meredith Monk and Vocal Ensemble in 1978, she has created recordings, films, and art installations. In 2005 more than one hundred musicians paid tribute to Monk by performing her compositions in a four-hour concert in New York City.

Monk continues to create innovative interdisciplinary theatre pieces. She reflects, "It's fascinating to be in a position where you're always learning . . . those moments of discovery are worth everything. And then you share them" (Campbell 1999, 19).

Sources

Albright, William. 1991. "Opera the Wordless Libretto: There's an Absence of Text in Avant-Garde Meredith Monk's 'Atlas,' But No Absence of Adventure." *Los Angeles Times,* 3 Mar., 53.

Anderson, Jack. 1986. "Meredith Monk Salutes the Familiar." Rev. of *Acts From Under and Above* and *Turtle Dreams (Cabaret),* by Meredith Monk. *New York Times,* 18 May, H22.

Banes, Sally. 1987. "Meredith Monk: Homemade Metaphors." In *Terpsichore in Sneakers: Post-Modern Dance,* 149–55. Middletown, Conn.: Wesleyan University Press.

Barnes, Clive. 1976. "Is It a Play? Is It a Dance?" Rev. of *Quarry,* by Meredith Monk. *New York Times,* 7 Apr., 24.

Breslauer, Jan. 1993. "Meredith Monk: Faith in the Mixed Message Dance: The

Genre-Crossing Choreographer Sees New Horizons for Multidisciplinary Art."
Los Angeles Times, 12 Mar., 1.

Campbell, Karen. 1999. "Innovator Asks Art's 'What If' Questions." *Christian Science Monitor,* 14 May, 19.

Chinoy, Helen Krich and Linda Walsh Jenkins, eds. 1987. *Women in American Theatre.* New York: Theatre Communications Group.

Connors, Thomas. 2002. "Monk Meditates on Risky 'Mercy.'" *Chicago Tribune,* 24 Mar., 15.

Cunningham, Carl. 2001. "Weaving Movement and Music." *Dance Spirit* 5 (7) (Sept.): 49.

Dorris, George. 1999. "Meredith Monk." In *Fifty Contemporary Choreographers,* ed. Martha Bremser, 159–64. New York: Routledge.

Goff, Nadine. 1995. "Artist Uses Song to Break Down Barriers." *Wisconsin State Journal* 5 (Nov.): 1F.

Harvey, Dennis. 2006. "Impermanence." Rev. of *Impermanence,* by Meredith Monk. *Variety,* 27 Feb., 46.

Hendrix, Erlene. 1989. "Monk, Meredith." In *Notable Women in the American Theatre: A Biographical Dictionary,* ed. John W. Frick and Stephen M. Vallillo, 660–63. Westport, Conn.: Greenwood.

Highwater, Jamake. 1997. Interview with Jamake Highwater. "Meredith Monk in Conversation with Jamake Highwater." In *Art Performs Life: Merce Cunningham/Meredith Monk/Bill T. Jones,* 80–92. Minneapolis, Minn.: Walker Art Center, 1998.

Jowitt, Deborah, ed. 1997. *Meredith Monk.* Baltimore: Johns Hopkins University Press.

Kosman, Joshua. 2006. "Monk's Newest Work An Ode to Loss." Rev. of *Impermanence,* by Meredith Monk. *San Francisco Chronicle,* 17 Feb., E2.

Martin, Kathryn Sarell. 1993. "The Performance Works of Meredith Monk and Martha Clarke: A Postmodern Feminist Perspective." Ph.D. diss., University of Colorado at Boulder.

McDonagh, Don. 1973. "Meredith Monk Work Full of Imagination." Rev. of *Education of the Girlchild,* by Meredith Monk. *New York Times,* 16 June, 14.

———. 1976. "The Dance: Meredith Monk Thinks Big." Rev. of *Quarry,* by Meredith Monk. *New York Times,* 25 Dec., 22.

Monk, Meredith. n.d. "Frequently Asked Questions." Meredith Monk. http://meredithmonk.org/monk/faq.html (accessed 11 Dec. 2004).

———. 1976. Interview with Liza Bear. "Meredith Monk: Invocation/Evocation: A Dialogue with Liza Bear." *Avalanche* 13 (Summer). In *Meredith Monk,* ed. Deborah Jowitt, 79–93. Baltimore: Johns Hopkins University Press, 1997.

———. 1985. "Excerpts from Sarah Lawrence Commencement Address, May 24, 1985." In *Meredith Monk,* ed. Deborah Jowitt, 127–28. Baltimore: Johns Hopkins University Press, 1997.

———. 1997. Interview with Deborah Jowitt. "Meredith Monk in Conversation with Deborah Jowitt." In *Art Performs Life: Merce Cunningham/Meredith Monk/Bill T. Jones,* 66–79. Minneapolis, Minn.: Walker Art Center, 1998.

———. 1999. "Still the Place to Take a Chance." *New York Times*, 31 Oct., sec. 2, 36.

Pareles, John. 1985. "Meredith Monk: Two Decades Later." *New York Times*, 17 May, C3.

Rockwell, John. 1979. "'Recent Ruins,' A Meredith Monk Work." Rev. of *Recent Ruins*, by Meredith Monk. *New York Times*, 18 Nov., 65.

Siegel, Marsha. 1971. Rev. of *Vessel*, by Meredith Monk. *Boston Herald Traveler*, 14. Nov. In *Meredith Monk*, ed. Deborah Jowitt, 36–39. Baltimore: Johns Hopkins University Press, 1998.

Smith, Sid. 1996. "After 3 Decades, Her Performance Is Still Art." *Chicago Tribune*, 21 Feb., 1.

Smitherner, Nancy Putnam. 2002. "Directing the Acting Ensemble: Meredith Monk, Elizabeth LeCompte, and Anne Bogart." Ph.D. diss., New York University.

Solomon, Alisa. 1986. "Doubly Marginalized: Women in the Avant-Garde." In *Women in American Theatre*, ed. Helen Krich Chinoy and Linda Walsh Jenkins, 363–71. New York: Theatre Communications Group, 1987.

Stearns, Patrick David. 1991. "Monk Creates a Majestic 'Atlas.'" *USA Today*, 28 Feb., 5D.

Steinman, Louise. 1986. *The Knowing Body: Elements of Contemporary Performance and Dance*. Boston: Shambhala.

Strauss, Neil. 1996. "A New Look At 'Less Is More.'" Rev. of *Politics of Quiet*, by Meredith Monk. *New York Times*, 14 Oct., C15.

Swed, Mark. 2002. "In 'mercy,' Looking for Truths in Human Nature; Meredith Monk and Ann Hamilton Join Forces to Create a Moving Forum for Big-Picture Questions." Rev. of *mercy*, by Meredith Monk. *Los Angeles Times*, 16 Feb., F1.

Ward, Charles. 1991a. "'Atlas' Explores World of New Opera." *Houston Chronicle*, 17 Feb., 21.

———. 1991b. "Don't Leave Early: Challenging 'Atlas' Is Worth the Wait When Monk Enters Stage." Rev. of *Atlas*, by Meredith Monk. *Houston Chronicle*, 25 Feb., 1.

Walker Art Center. 1998. *Art Performs Life: Merce Cunningham/Meredith Monk/Bill T. Jones*. Minneapolis, Minn.: Walker Art Center.

Representative Directing Credits[2]

Broadway:
  Title: Title (1969), *Untidal: Movement Period* (1969)

Off and Off-Off Broadway:
  Break (1964), *Beach* (1965), *Blackboard* (1965), *Cartoon* (1965), *Radar* (1965), *Relâche* (collaboration with Dick Higgins—1965), *Duet With Cat's Scream and Locomotive* (1966), *Portable* (1966), *16 Millimeter Earrings* (1966), *Excerpt from a Work in Progress* (1967), *Goodbye/St. Mark's Win-*

dow (1967), *Overload (Blueprint 2)* (1967), *Blueprint (4)* (1968), *Blueprint (5)* (1968), *Coop* (1968), *Juice: A Theatre Cantata in 3 Installments* (1969), *A Raw Recital* (1970), *Vessel: An Opera Epic* (1971), *Education of the Girlchild* (solo—1972), *Paris* (collaboration with Ping Chong—1972), *Education of the Girlchild: An Opera* (1973), *Roots* (collaboration with Donald Ashwander—1974), *Anthology and Small Scroll* (1975), *Quarry: An Opera* (1976), *The Travelogue Series (Paris, Chacon, Venice/Milan)* (collaboration with Ping Chong—1977), *The Plateau Series* (1978), *Recent Ruins* (1979), *Specimen Days: A Civil War Opera* (1981), *Turtle Dreams (Cabaret)* (in collaboration with Lanny Harrison—1983), *The Games* (American version collaboration with Ping Chong—1984), *Acts from Under and Above* (in collaboration with Lanny Harrison—1986), *Facing North* (collaboration with Robert Een—1990), *American Archeology #1* (1994), *Volcano Songs* (1994), *A Celebration Service* (1996)

Regional Theatre:

Blueprint (1967), *Blueprint (3)* (1968), *Tour: Dedicated to Dinosaurs* (1969), *Tour 2: Barbershop* (1969), *Tour 3: Lounge* (1969), *Needlebrain Lloyd and the Systems Kid: A Live Movie* (1970), *Tour 4: Organ* (1970), *Tour 5: Glass* (1970), *Tour 6: Gym* (1970), *Tour 7: Factory* (1970), *Tour 8: Castle* (1971), *Chacon* (collaboration with Ping Chong—1974), *Plateau #2* (1976), *Venice-Milan* (collaboration with Ping Chong—1976), *Plateau Series: Plateau #3* (1977), *Tablet (House of Stills)* (1977), *Atlas: An Opera in Three Parts* (1991), *Magic Frequencies* (1998), *mercy* (2001), *Impermanence* (2006)

International Theatre:

Dying Swan With Sunglasses (1967), *Overload* (1967), *The Games* (collaboration with Ping Chong—1983), *The Politics of Quiet: A Music Theater Oratorio* (1996), *The Impermanence Project* (2004)

Notes

1. Sources cite different places as Monk's birthplace, but Deborah Jowitt states that Monk was born in New York City.

2. These credits include premiere performances only. Many of these productions toured the United States and abroad. For a comprehensive list of performances, see "Chronology" on the Meredith Monk Web site at http://www.meredithmonk .org/monk/chronology.html.

Morgan, Agnes

Born on Oct. 31, 1879, in Le Roy, New York, Agnes Bangs Morgan was a woman of theatre who directed, wrote plays and lyrics, produced, worked as a theatre technician, and occasionally acted for her art. Although her career is chronicled in only a handful of books or articles, she was a true pioneer, directing for the innovative Neighborhood Playhouse, on Broadway, and at the Paper Mill Playhouse in Milburn, New Jersey. Her directing career spanned an impressive forty-six years—from 1915 to 1961.

Unlike most women of her era, Morgan was very well educated, earning a B.A. in 1901 and a M.A. in 1903, both from Radcliffe College in Cambridge, Massachusetts. She had the good fortune of studying under one of the forefathers of theatre education, George Pierce Baker, who encouraged her both to write plays and to study overseas. After studying theatre in London and Berlin for a year, Morgan joined Baker's infamous Harvard playwriting class, 47 Workshop, and wrote a play entitled *The Professor's Assistant,* which was subsequently produced at Radcliffe (Eisenberg [1929], n. p.).

After college she worked in publicity for the Shubert Organization and also launched her artistic career by translating and writing scripts. In 1910 she both wrote and directed *When We Two Write History,* which opened to favorable reviews in Chicago. Her sustained work as a director began at New York City's Neighborhood Playhouse, an integral part of the Little Theatre movement. Run on a voluntary basis by amateurs, the goal of the Neighborhood Playhouse was to produce high-quality, artistic plays not ordinarily seen in commercial theatres. According to Playhouse co-founder Alice Lewisohn Crowley, when staging the first production at the Neighborhood Playhouse on the Lower East Side in 1915, their director had little experience with "the technical side of production" (1959, 31). The management invited her friends Helen Arthur and Agnes Morgan to help, and the result was a lasting collaboration. Crowley writes, "[N]ever had five people [the production team] cast in such different molds joined forces with more congeniality" (31). Looking back at the variety of roles Morgan ultimately filled for the Playhouse, Crowley recalls, "[S]he developed the technical side of lighting, and had an instinctive gift for stage direction, as [also] for the function of stage manager. As an amateur she responded to any production need while pursuing her professional career as playwright" (84). Though she wore many hats as full-time staff, Morgan directed over thirty productions at the Playhouse, some of which transferred to Broadway, solidifying her status as a stage director of repute. Through her Playhouse contacts, she gained additional opportunities to direct or co-direct, as she did with Lewisohn Crowley[1] in 1922 for the Theatre Guild's production of George Bernard Shaw's *Back to Methuselah,* Parts I and II.

While at the Neighborhood Playhouse, Morgan directed a wide variety of theatricals, many of which were original works and little-produced plays. For example, the 1924 production of King Shudraka's *The Little Clay Cart* proved to be a "1500–year-old Hindu drama that Morgan adapted and staged with a swirl of color and movement" (Knapp 1989, 667). Stark Young, critic for the *New York Times,* called the production "one of the most admirable entertainments in town," writing, "Everywhere the sentiment and the action is gracious, noble and delicate at the same time. The flavor is one of grace and lyricism and wit" (1924, 13).

In stark contrast, Morgan directed the satirical, silly, and irreverent *Grand Street Follies,* for which she also created the book and lyrics. Originally written as birthday party entertainment, Morgan's *Follies* satirized the Playhouse productions of the past season. The burlesque became an annual, although private, event until the management found themselves in need of a "special invitation" production for subscribers in 1922 (Crowley 1959, 117). Morgan and Arthur expanded the material to include parodies of events elsewhere on New York City stages, and the response was tremendous. According to Crowley, word-of-mouth exploded, creating "almost a panic of excitement. I had never before heard the walls echo with such robust applause" (117). Crowley claims that some patrons stormed the doors and pretended to be subscribers in order to gain admittance. Ultimately, *Grand Street Follies* grew so popular that it transferred to Broadway theatres from 1927 to 1929, with Morgan continuing to write and direct each production.

In an article about creating and staging the *Follies,* Morgan wrote that she limited herself to lampooning "the conspicuous hits, the experimental ventures, the oddities and the very ambitious productions" (Eisenberg [1929], n.p.). She often attended Broadway plays several times in order to find the most memorable scenes, then worked to maintain the proper style of the production while portraying broad caricatures of the leading actors. At times Playhouse actors were assigned specific stars to imitate and at other times the actors requested to imitate particular celebrities. Two of the players best known for their impressions were Albert Carroll and Dorothy Sands, who spoofed such stars as John and Ethel Barrymore, Anna Pavlova, Irene Castle, Harpo Marx, Fanny Brice, and Gertrude Lawrence (Knapp 1975, 357). According to historian Margaret Knapp, "[I]t became fashionable for Broadway stars such as Fanny Brice and John Barrymore to visit the *Grand Street Follies* and pose for photographs with their imitators," much to the credit of the show's creator–director as well as the actors (362).

Reviews of the *Grand Street Follies* often remarked on the exuberance of the performers and the joyful, romping quality of the productions, although Brooks Atkinson of the *New York Times* revealed the unevenness between the quality of the acting and the script in the 1928 production. "The uninspired numbers are merely dull. But several of the good ones are incomparably fine. . . . Shrewd as the impersonations may be, they become monotonous without lines and business to make them independently amusing" (1928, 16). His review of the 1926 production was also mixed, although he was amused by the material in the second half of the bill, which satirized the modernist European influences of the time. For example, Atkinson admired a scene from *Uncle Tom's Cabin,* performed "in a Constructivist Setting—an Example of The Sympathetic Elastic Theatre" (1926, 23). His description of this sketch, which made "excellent sport of the radical theatre," gives us a further indication of the type of buffoonery staged in the *Follies:* "While choruses on platforms catch the motives of the melodrama and broaden them into absurdity, Little Eva, Topsy, Uncle Tom, and Simon Legree enact their sentimentalities and villainies across a stage cluttered with meaningless junk in the modernistic spirit" (23). Despite the mixed reviews of critics like Atkinson, audiences continued to flock to the *Follies* until their end in 1929.

In 1927 Morgan and Arthur formed a new professional company, The Actor-Managers, which drew on many of the designers and actors from the dissolving Neighborhood Playhouse (temporarily known as the Grand Street Follies Company while producing the Follies on Broadway). According to historian Shirlee Hennigan, one newspaper labeled their cooperatively-run company as "part of the feminist movement in drama" (1987, 205). With her new professional home uptown, Morgan had the opportunity to increase her Broadway directing credits. The same year that her *Follies* transferred to Broadway, 1927, she directed three plays in Broadway theatres: Robert E. Sherwood's *The Love Nest,* Lord Dunsany's *If,* and Boris Artzybasheff's *Lovers and Enemies.* Her most controversial production, Simon Gantillon's *Maya,* followed in 1928 on Broadway. The French play, set in a house of prostitution, followed the life of Bella as she tried to be all things to all men. Unfortunately for The Actor-Managers, the police found the play morally offensive and invoked the Wales Padlock Law for the first time in New York, threatening to close the theatre if the production did not shut down (32). Rather than take that risk, the Shuberts closed the production amidst a flurry of sensationalistic press, and eleven plays on Broadway were subsequently closed. Despite the controversy, Morgan continued to direct professionally on a steady basis. Her credits in the 1930s included three productions for the Federal Theatre Project, *Behind the Verdict, Class of '29,* and *American Holiday,* as well as summer productions at the Westchester County Playhouse in Mt. Kisco, New York, from 1930 to 1933 and summer productions for the Casino Theatre in Newport, Rhode Island, from 1935 to 1939.

From the genesis of her directing career, Morgan found herself working collaboratively. Although it is uncommon to employ co-directors in the commercial theatre, the Neighborhood Playhouse often used directing teams. She continued this pattern when working at one of the first regional theatres in the country, the Paper Mill Playhouse in Milburn, New Jersey, where she directed alongside the theatre's co-founder, Frank Carrington, from 1940 to 1961. Together, they directed over 150 productions, with several popular productions restaged from season to season, such as Sigmund Romberg's musical *The Desert Song,* which they co-directed in 1944, 1945, 1947, 1949, 1951, and 1958. From 1941 to 1959 the duo directed anywhere from five to nine productions each season, at times directing the entire season of eight or nine shows, most of which were musicals. Several of their productions received attention from top New York critics. In 1940 *Jeannie,* a sentimental Cinderella story by Aimee Stuart imported from the London stage, received acclaim from Atkinson. He found it to be "an excellent production of a innocuous British comedy.... Frank Carrington and Agnes Morgan as directors are putting on a thoroughly professional performance with good actors." Atkinson concluded, "Broadway has no monopoly on good theatre work" (1940, 29). A few Paper Mill productions transferred to Broadway, including Patterson Greene's *Papa Is All,* which toured the Eastern United States before opening at the Guild Theatre in 1942. Atkinson found the performance "conspicuously well oiled" with "considerable humor," writing, "*Papa Is All* has been well staged by Frank Carrington and Agnes Morgan" (1942, 22).

A newspaper article from 1941 highlights Morgan and Carrington's unusual collaboration. No one director appeared to have the upper hand in rehearsal, but instead they directed as if by one voice. "By their own admission, Agnes Morgan and Frank Carrington get along 'like birdies in the spring'—which, by all laws known to mankind, they certainly shouldn't.... The secret of their success, perhaps, is that they ydyo [sic.] all their arguing in conferences before rehearsals, so that when they actually start putting the actors through their paces they present a solid and united front.... During rehearsal they direct the players individually, as though the thought occurs to them. Sometimes they both speak at once and, when they do, they usually say the same thing. The actors direct their questions to either of them and frequently are answered by the other" ("Codirectors," 1941, n. p.). The article goes on to credit both of their backgrounds in the Little Theatre movement, attesting to their willingness to direct as collaborators. Although her last directing credit appears in 1961, Morgan remained on staff at the Paper Mill until her retirement in 1968, and greatly aided "the Paper Mill's advancement as a major regional theatre" ("Paper," n.d.).

Unfortunately, there are few additional accounts of Morgan's work in the rehearsal hall, nor is much written about her direction in reviews from the period. What little more can be gleaned of her direction and demeanor comes from Crowley's book about the Neighborhood Playhouse, in which she introduces the young Agnes Morgan as "quiet, serious, watchful" (1959, 31). Crowley recalls that Morgan had a talent for working with crowd scenes, as evidenced in her work on a British drama, John Galsworthy's *The Mob*. She writes, "Agnes was as skillful as indefatigable in dealing with *The Mob*. Although no attempt was made to impersonate a British crowd, the temper of the scenes was so sincere that the British flavor was not missed" (106). *The Mob* marked the Playhouse's first production to introduce a professional company in the midst of their amateur and student players. Crowley and Morgan co-directed, straddling the gap between the two classes of actors and trying to ease tensions. Recalls Crowley, "The rehearsals for *The Mob* were launched amid 'Sturm und Drang' [storm and stress], for the student players were still suffering from the invasion of the professionals" (105). Despite their uncertainty about the outcome of the production, the two factions of the company became united as one during the four-week rehearsal process, the performances sold out, and the critics were impressed. When the playwright attended, he complemented the cast, saying their production surpassed the London version, under his own direction (107–8). All of these factors contribute to the idea that Morgan was a wholly capable director in the face of challenging circumstances. Wade Miller, the former General Manager of the Paper Mill Playhouse, supports this supposition, recalling, "She was a beautiful person and a real theatre person. She came to rehearsal completely prepared. She knew exactly what every person from the lead to the lowliest chorus person should do, and exactly where they should be. She had a great feel for the theatre . . . remarkable . . . a fantastic person" (Hennigan 1987, 206).

Morgan began her career as a playwright, but left her legacy as one of the pioneering women to make a career of stage directing in the early and mid-twentieth century. She directed or co-directed nearly two hundred productions over the course of her impressive career, which extended into her eighties. Morgan died May 25, 1976, in California.

Sources

Atkinson, Brooks. 1926. "Frivolity in Grand Street." Rev. of the *Grand Street Follies*, book and lyrics by Agnes Morgan. *New York Times*, 16 June, 23.

———. 1928. "Grand Street Moves Uptown." *New York Times,* 29 May, 16.

———. 1940. "Out Where the West Begins." Rev. of *Jeannie,* by Aimee Stuart. *New York Times,* 13 Nov., 29.

———. 1942. Rev. of *Papa Is All,* by Patterson Greene. *New York Times,* 7 Jan., 22.

"Codirectors of Theatre Guild Play Here." 1941. *Sun-Baltimore,* 18 Nov., n.p. Billy Rose Theatre Collection, clippings. New York Public Library for the Performing Arts.

Crowley, Alice Lewisohn. 1959. *The Neighborhood Playhouse.* New York: Theatre Arts Books.

Eisenberg, Emanuel. [1929]. "And Who Are the Actor-Managers?" *New York Sun,* n.p. Billy Rose Theatre Collection, Agnes Morgan—scrapbooks. New York Public Library for the Performing Arts.

Hansen, Harry. 1928. "Society Women Fail . . ." *New York Telegraph,* 28 Feb. n.p. Billy Rose Theatre Collection, clippings. New York Public Library for the Performing Arts.

Hennigan, Shirlee. 1987. "Women Directors—The Early Years." In *Women in American Theatre,* ed. by Helen Krich Chinoy and Linda Walsh Jenkins, 203–6. New York: Theatre Communications Group.

"How the Victims Are Selected." n.d. *New York Post,* n.p. Billy Rose Theatre Collection, Agnes Morgan—scrapbooks. New York Public Library for the Performing Arts.

Knapp, Margaret M. 1975. "Theatrical Parody in the Twentieth-Century American Theatre: *The Grand Street Follies.*" *Educational Theatre Journal* 27 (Oct.): 356–63.

———. 1989. "Morgan, Agnes." In *Notable Women in the American Theatre,* ed. Alice M. Robinson, Vera Mowry Roberts, and Milly S. Barranger, 666–67. Westport, Conn.: Greenwood.

League of American Theatres and Producers. Internet Broadway Database. http://www.ibdb.com (accessed 20 Apr. 2004).

"The Librettist of Grand Street." 1927. *New York Times,* 7 Aug. Billy Rose Theatre Collection, clippings. New York Public Library for the Performing Arts.

"Paper Mill Life of the Theatre." n.d. Unpublished manuscript. Paper Mill Playhouse: Milburn, N.J.

Rigdon, Walter, ed. 1976. *Notable Names in The American Theatre.* Clifton, N.J.: J. T. White.

Young, Stark. 1924. "Grand Street Delights." Rev. of *The Little Clay Cart,* by King Shudraka, translated from the Sanskrit by Arthur William Ryder. *New York Times,* 6 Dec., 13.

Representative Directing Credits (including co-directing)

Broadway:[2]
Back to Methuselah (1922), *Grand Street Follies* (1927–29), *The Love Nest*

(1927), *If* (1927), *Lovers and Enemies* (1927), *Maya* (1928), *If Love Were All* (1931), *Class of '29* (1936), *American Holiday* (1936), *I Killed the Count* (1942), *Papa Is All* (1942)

Off and Off-Off Broadway:

Tethered Sheep (1915), *The Maker of Dreams* (1915), *The Glittering Gate* (1915), *The Waldies* (1915), *Captain Brassbound's Conversion* (1915), *The Subjection of Kezia* (1916), *The Inca of Jerusalem* (1916), *Great Catherine* (1916), *The Queen's Enemies* (1916), *Black 'Ell* (1917), *A Sunny Morning* (1917), *The People* (1917), *Pippa Passes* (1917), *Tamara* (1918), *Fortunado* (1918), *Guibour* (1918), *Free* (1918), *The Eternal Megalosaurus* (1918), *The Noose* (1918), *Everybody's Husband* (1919), *The Beautiful Sabine Women* (1920), *Innocent and Annabel* (1920), *The Madras House* (1921), *Grand Street Follies* (1922, 1924–27), *The Little Legend of the Dance* (1923), *This Fine Pretty World* (1923), *The Little Clay Cart* (1924), *Exiles* (1925), *The Legend of the Dance* (1925), *The Critic* (1925), *The Romantic Young Lady* (1926), *The Lion Tamer* (1926)

Regional and Stock Theatre:

The Critic (1936), *Inconstant Moon* (1937), *Grandpa* (1938). Over one hundred and fifty productions co-directed with Frank Carrington at the Paper Mill Playhouse, Milburn, N.J., including the following: *The Chocolate Soldier* (1941, 1948, 1952), *The Merry Widow* (1941, 1944, 1949, 1953), *Naughty Marietta* (1942, 1943, 1947, 1950), *Blossom Time* (1943, 1944, 1945, 1948, 1953), *Rio Rita* (1943, 1947), *The Desert Song* (1944, 1945, 1947, 1949, 1951, 1958), *The Student Prince* (1944, 1945, 1947, 1949, 1952, 1958), *Roberta* (1945, 1946, 1950), *The Mikado* (1946, 1948, 1953), *Song of Norway* (1949, 1951), *Show Boat* (1950, 1952), *Brigadoon* (1950, 1953, 1959), *Annie Get Your Gun* (1951, 1959), *Finian's Rainbow* (1951), *Kiss Me Kate* (1952, 1956), *High Button Shoes* (1952), *Carousel* (1952), *Call Me Madam* (1953), *Paint Your Wagon* (1954), *Oklahoma!* (1954, 1957), *Carmen* (1954), *South Pacific* (1955, 1957), *Guys & Dolls* (1955), *The King and I* (1956), *Can-Can* (1957), *Damn Yankees* (1958), *Pal Joey* (1959), *Redhead* (1960), *Destry Rides Again* (1961)

Notes

1. Alice Lewisohn Crowley went by her maiden name, Lewisohn, during her years at the Neighborhood Playhouse and later published under her married name, Crowley.

2. The Internet Broadway Database (www.ibdb.com), sponsored by the League of American Theaters and Producers. in association with Theatre Development Fund and New York State, lists other Broadway credits which could not be verified, including *R.U.R.* (1922), *The Critic* (1925), *The Little Clay Cart* (1926), *The*

Lion Tamer (1926), *Ruth Draper* (1929), and *A Hero Is Born* (1937). Several of these productions from the 1920s were known to be performed at the Neighborhood Playhouse, but may have received limited special engagements in Broadway houses.

 # Muzio, Gloria

Born in North Haven, Connecticut, Gloria Muzio has directed on Broadway, Off Broadway, in regional theatres, and abroad. Focusing primarily on new plays, Muzio has directed the works of new and established playwrights, including many premieres at Kentucky's Actors Theatre of Louisville that later transferred to Off Broadway.

As a child Muzio loved the theatre and attended many theatre productions at the Yale Repertory Theatre, the Long Wharf Theatre in New Haven, and on Broadway. From this extensive exposure, she knew she wanted a career in the theatre by the time she went to college. While attending Mount Holyoke in Massachusetts as a theatre major, Muzio took a directing class and discovered that directing was what she wanted to do. She says, "I realized that's the area where I would have the most influence in a production" (Interview, 2004). At Mount Holyoke, Muzio was encouraged by teachers, who told students that they were capable of accomplishing anything they set out to do. After graduating from Mount Holyoke, Muzio attended Florida State in Tallahassee and received an M.F.A. in directing. She then taught theatre for four years before arriving in New York City (Cole 1996).

Muzio discusses her influences as a director, explaining, "I was highly influenced by film. . . . I was always interested in visually how stories were told and . . . found myself more influenced by and attracted to film directors than I was by theatre directors. . . . I was very influenced by Jon Jory. . . . He became a real mentor for me—his specific kind of attention to detail and character development and overall creation of the world of a play. . . . Mike Nichols was always an inspiration to me" (Interview, 2004).

As a director who prefers to work with living playwrights, Muzio developed a professional relationship with playwright Richard Dresser. In 1988 she directed Dresser's *Splitsville* at Primary Stages's 45th Street Theater in New York City. Stephen Holden of the *New York Times* called the play a "nightmarish satire of American junk culture" and added "Gloria Muzio has directed the action in a genial comic style that treats the absurd goings-on as the perfectly natural behavior of Americans on the move" (1988, 15). Between 1995 and 1998, Muzio also directed Dresser's *Below the Belt* and *Gun Shy* Off Broadway as well as in regional theatres. She says of Dresser, "We had a period of time when we did a lot of work together. . . . You understand his sense of humor. You understand . . . what's on his mind. It's a great asset" (Interview, 2004).

Muzio's first big break in the New York City theatre scene came with her direction of Jerry Sterner's *Other People's Money*, which opened Off Broadway in 1989. The play originally opened at Harvard Stage the previous year, under Muzio's direction. Muzio discusses the significance of the play in relation to her career, explaining,

> It was a play with a slightly different form. . . . It was about a take-over of a company, and there were front page stories about similar cases almost every day in the paper. It was the right play at the right time. I was able to combine a very topical subject and a very current staging style. . . . It also was very important for me, in that it was kind of a man's play, in that it was about money and about business. It had a very strong male leading character. Although it sounds ridiculous, up until that point . . . any new plays that were coming my way were mainly about mothers and their children or sisters. Or [producers] were looking for a woman director—and it would be some pasty play about some sentimental [subject]. . . . I knew that if I could make a success with that play [*Other People's Money*], it would put me in a different circle—only because it would seem like a play that was traditionally directed by a man. (Interview, 2004)

Muzio's sense that the play's content was not associated with women was confirmed in an article written by Mel Gussow of the *New York Times*. In the article, Gussow discussed women directors and mentioned Muzio's unlikely fit for *Other People's Money*. Muzio recalls, "It stunned me because, although he meant it as quite a compliment, he said there was no way you would know or guess the play was directed by a woman. And his point was, 'Don't think that because a woman is a director, it means it's going to be a sweet family play.' . . . So that was the climate. . . . I had to direct a play that people wouldn't think was traditionally a woman's play. And that was my play. And that's why it was significant. And it was successful and also made money. . . . I thought, 'Notice here that this is a commercial effort directed by a woman that made a lot of money'" (Interview, 2004).

The success of *Other People's Money* helped to open doors for Muzio in New York City. In his review of the long-running production, Gussow wrote, "The actors are allied under Gloria Muzio's fluid direction" (1989, C3). For her direction of the play, Muzio won the Joe A. Callaway Award and was nominated for an Outer Critics Circle Award.

Although Gussow gave Muzio a backhanded compliment, he clearly admired her directing ability. In 1991 Gussow reviewed Muzio's direction of the Women's Project's production of Kathleen Tolan's *Approximating Mother* at the Judith Anderson Theater in New York City. Gussow noted that he was uncomfortable watching the play, which examined relationships between women and men, and wrote, "[A] man may feel he is eavesdropping on an intimate conversation among women. That effect is somewhat akin to what might be a female response to plays by David Mamet. . . . The dialogue is pungent and not flattering to the men in the play. They are bystanders . . . and they deserve the implied criticism" (1991, C21). Gussow went on to praise the direction, observing that "Muzio's production has an understated ease" and that two of the main characters "speak like real people rather than fictional characters, breaking up their sentences with distinctive turns of phrase" (C21). The following year, Gussow called Muzio's direction of Ellen Gould's one-woman musical *Bubbe Meises, Bubbe Stories* at the Cherry Lane Theater "impeccable" (1992, C15).

Muzio continued to direct Off Broadway, including productions of New York City's non-profit Roundabout Theater Company, which operates both Off Broadway and Broadway stages. In 1992 she directed her first Broadway production of the Roundabout Theater with Tom Stoppard's *The Real Inspector Hound*, a mystery play-within-a-play, and *The Fifteen Minute Hamlet*, a comedic and condensed version of Shakespeare's Hamlet. The two one-act plays received mixed reviews as some critics felt the pace was slow. However, other critics praised Muzio's direction, with Edwin Wilson of the *Wall Street Journal* writing, "Guiding her performers with a shrewd comic touch and a sure hand, she provides an evening of first-rate theater" (1992, A8). Muzio also directed two other plays on the Roundabout's Broadway stage: George Bernard Shaw's *Candida* in 1993 and P. G. Wodehouse's *The Play's the Thing*, an adaptation of Ferenc Molnár's comedy *The Play at the Castle*, in 1995.

Like Stoppard's *Fifteen Minute Hamlet*, Paula Vogel's *Desdemona: A Play About a Handkerchief*, took an abbreviated and intellectual look at Shakespeare. Directed by Muzio in 1993 at New York City's Circle Repertory Company, the play featured three of Shakespeare's characters from *Othello*: Desdemona, Bianca, and Emilia. Critic Ben Brantley of the *New York Times* found problems with the play, but praised Muzio's direction, writing, "'Desdemona' has been briskly and stylishly directed by Gloria Muzio, who uses camera-like flashes of light and character-freezing tableaux to divide its many scenes. These are usually used to underscore telling comic and dramatic moments and are the visual equivalent of the clash of cymbals that follows a punch line in a vaudeville show" (1993, C20).

In 1997 Muzio directed the popular Off-Broadway production of Ted

Dykstra and Richard Greenblatt's 2 *Pianos, 4 Hands,* which had been previously produced in Canada. The comedy featured the two authors and was based on their autobiographical journey to become concert pianists. Except for a negative review from the *New York Times,* the production received excellent reviews. Clive Barnes of the *New York Post* wrote, "These funny, funny actors, fine natural comedians, unobtrusively helped by Gloria Muzio's staging, are clever, deft and dazzlingly amusing" (1997). He also included the production in his yearly top-ten list. The production moved to Washington, D.C.'s, Kennedy Center, where it also received excellent reviews. William Triplett of the *Washington Post* described the production, writing, "Gloria Muzio hasn't directed the show so much as she has—appropriately, to be sure—conducted it. The dialogue has the rhythm and nuance of a musical score, which she alternately highlights or counterpoints with either gesture or movement. Visually as well as aurally the production evokes a simple lyricism" (1998, BO2). The production then moved, still under Muzio's direction, to several Canadian theatres, including Toronto's Royal Alexandra Theatre and the Vancouver Playhouse.

Muzio usually prepares for a play for three months before hiring performers. She approaches the material from the text and likes to find out as much as possible about the playwright to understand the playwright's world. Muzio explains, "That's where you're going to find the secret. That's where you're going to find the specific work or philosophy or world that's going to make that play unique or that playwright unique. I always felt that . . . the playwright was the star of the production. You need to find what makes that playwright tick, or why they wrote the play, and to make sure that you understand intrinsically before you even get to the structure and the craft of it" (Interview, 2004).

Although a star may sometimes be pre-cast for a play, Muzio prefers to do her own casting. She looks for the best match between the performer and the material. She says, "Sometimes an actor walks in, and you can see that the language sits well in their mouth. . . . It's a tough thing because some actors don't audition as well. If I see one moment in the audition that it just all comes together, that's all I need" (Interview, 2004). Although not the deciding factor, personality is also important when choosing an actor. Muzio explains, "You just have to know that you're going to be able to get along creatively for four weeks, and that you want the same thing. You want to tell the same story" (Interview, 2004).

Muzio likes to begin rehearsals with table work. During this time she encourages playwrights to participate. However, once the actors begin to move, she prefers that playwrights do not talk directly to the performers, although she still values their presence and participation. In some instances, she will make an exception and let the playwrights speak to performers. For example, she welcomes Dresser's contributions during rehearsals because she knows him and trusts him to work well with the actors. Muzio believes that playwrights are an asset to rehearsals, saying, "I want them [playwrights] to see when the scenes are working or when there's a particular problem—for them to really be an organic part of the process rather than a visitor. I think the more the playwright's around, the more the actors feel comfortable and relaxed" (Interview, 2004).

Muzio likes to approach projects as if she's "peeling an onion." She explains, "I don't like to start too deep, too soon. I like to take it easy, work on the text, then . . . guide the actors to the areas where I want them to do the exploration. . . . I'll do my work, and you do your work. I'm not one of those directors who wants to get inside the actor. . . . I do the outline and the subtopic, and let the actors fill in the space—and then make sure that we're telling the same story. I work with a lot of respect for the actors" (Interview, 2004). Although she directs with respect for performers, she adds, "I'm also very clear about what I want. There's no need to be authoritarian" (Cole 1996).

Muzio prefers to interpret the playwright's work in a way that moves the audience or makes them think. Her goal is to communicate the playwright's world as accurately as possible to the audience without making her own statement. She notes, "What I've always believed is that the play dictates the style of your work. . . . The director's work should feel invisible. . . . I shouldn't have a stamp or a trademark. My work should be sort of sublimated, so that it looks as though it all just happened that way." She adds, "My strength always has been . . . in the creative interpretation of the play—not in the creation of a theatrical event about what I wanted. About a story I want to tell. And I think there is a difference. And I think that comes from doing more new plays than doing classics. I think classics are more open to interpretation. They're open to sort of a creative slant that isn't necessarily what the playwright had in mind. But I found great satisfaction in working with the playwright—bringing that playwright's world to the stage" (Interview, 2004).

While directing, Muzio pays attention to detail—both in the play's emotional content and its visual presentation. She discusses the visual aspect of her productions, saying, "I always wanted to try to tell the story visually as though . . . there were no words. You should still be able to tell what the story was. And I think that's a lot of the film influence" (Interview, 2004).

Critics often describe Muzio's style as clean and sharp. John Simon of *New York* magazine wrote of Muzio's "razor-sharp direction" in *Gun Shy* (1998, 128); Barnes noted that David Bottrell and Jessie Jones's *Dearly Departed* was "sharply directed" (Second Stage 1991); and Michael Sommers of New Jersey's *Star-Ledger* wrote that *2 Pianos, 4 Hands* was "crisply directed" (Second Stage 1997).

In addition to her previously mentioned awards, Muzio's Canadian production of Arthur Miller's *Death of a Salesman* received three Dora nominations. She has also directed and developed plays at Sundance Institute's Playwright's Lab and directed at several Young Playwrights Festivals. Among other achievements in theatre, she was an artistic associate at the Roundabout Theatre Company and a member of Circle Repertory Company. Her directing credits also include numerous television shows.

At the end of the twentieth century, Muzio shifted her career toward directing for television. However, as one of the few women in the 1990s to direct on Broadway, Muzio provides advice for her success, stating, "[I]f you come to your assignment prepared, respectful and knowing how to collaborate, you can earn respect for your authority" (Cole 1996).

Sources

Barnes, Clive. 1997. "'Two Pianos' a Grand Success." Rev. of *2 Pianos, 4 Hands,* by Ted Dykstra and Richard Greenblatt. *New York Post,* 31 Oct. Rpt. "Reviews: New York." *2 Pianos, 4 Hands.* http://www.2pianos4hands.com/pages/r_nyc .html (accessed 19 Aug. 2004).

Brantley, Ben. 1993. "Iago's Subterfuge Is Made the Truth." Rev. of *Desdemona: A Play About a Handkerchief,* by Paula Vogel. *New York Times,* 12 Nov., C20.

Cole, Gloria. 1996. "Women Theatre Directors Still Scarce." United Press International (UPI). 1 Mar. In LexisNexis Academic Database, http://web.lexis-nexis .com (accessed 20 Apr. 2004).

Daniels, Rebecca. 1996. *Women Stage Directors Speak: Exploring the Influence of Gender on Their Work.* Jefferson, N.C.: McFarland.

Gussow, Mel. 1989. "Straightforward Corporate Raider." Rev. of *Other People's Money,* by Jerry Sterner. *New York Times,* 17 Feb., C3.

———. 1991. "Of Childbearing and Ticking Clocks." Rev. of *Approximating Mother,* by Kathleen Tolan. *New York Times,* 7 Nov., C21.

———. 1992. "Tribute to Grandmothers." Rev. of *Bubbe Meises, Bubbe Stories,* by Ellen Gould. *New York Times,* 30 Oct., C15.

Holden, Stephen. 1988. "Laughter Amid the Ruins of Kitsch and Junk Food." Rev. of *Splitsville,* by Richard Dresser. *New York Times,* 28 May, 15.

Muzio, Gloria. 2004. Interview with Wendy Vierow. 19 July.

Second Stage Theatre. 1991. "Season 13." http://www.secondstagetheatre.com/ season13.html (accessed 30 Dec. 2004).

———. 1997. "Season 19." http://www.scondstagetheatre.com/season19.htm (accessed 30 Dec. 2004).

Simon, John. 1998. "Rapid-Fire and Ice." Rev. of *Gun Shy,* by Richard Dresser. *New York,* 23 Feb., 128.

Triplett, William. 1998. "'2 Pianos, 4 Hands': A Crescendo of Pleasure." Rev. of 2

Pianos, 4 Hands, by Ted Dykstra and Richard Greenblatt. *Washington Post,* 10 Apr., BO2.

Wilson, Edwin. 1992. "Stoppard's Gold-Medal Gymnastics." Rev. of *The Real Inspector Hound* and *The Fifteen Minute Hamlet,* by Tom Stoppard. *Wall Street Journal,* 14 Aug., A8.

Representative Directing Credits

Broadway:
> *The Real Inspector Hound* and *The Fifteen Minute Hamlet* (1992), *Candida* (1993), *The Play's the Thing* (1995)

Off and Off-Off Broadway:
> *Alice and Fred* (1985), *Splitsville* (1988), *Feast Here Tonight* (1989), *Other People's Money* (1989), *The Value of Names* (1989), *Price of Fame* (1990), *Approximating Mother* (1991), *Dearly Departed* (1991), *Bubbe Meises, Bubbe Stories* (1992), *Desdemona, A Play About a Handkerchief* (1993), *The Truth-Teller* (1995), *Below the Belt* (1996), *Grace and Glorie* (1996), *2 Pianos, 4 Hands* (1997), *Gun Shy* (1998)

Regional Theatre:
> *They Dance to the Sun* (1983), *Other People's Money* (1988), *Autumn Elegy* (1989), *Hazelle!* (1994), *D. Boone* (1992), *Below the Belt* (1995), *Gun Shy* (1997), *2 Pianos, 4 Hands* (1998)

Tours:
> *Bubbe Meises, Bubbe Stories* (1993)

International Theatre:
> *Death of a Salesman* (1997), *2 Pianos, 4 Hands* (1998)

 # Ott, Sharon

Born February 27, 1950, in Corry, Pennsylvania, Sharon Ott has become a celebrated stage director and has served as artistic director for two regional theatres: the Berkeley Repertory Theatre in California and the Seattle Repertory Theatre in Washington. She also served as an associate director for Theatre X in Milwaukee, Wisconsin, and as resident director at Milwaukee Repertory Theatre, where she directed over twenty productions. In addition to her demanding directing schedule at her resident theatres, she has been an active freelance director in regional theatres across the United States, winning a string of awards in the process.

Ott grew up in western Pennsylvania and enjoyed the arts from a young age. Her knowledge of theatre was broadened through her liberal arts education at Bennington College in Bennington, Vermont, where she earned a B.A. degree with a major in anthropology, theatre, and music in 1972. She shifted her attention to theatre rather than graduate school almost on a whim. "After Bennington, I went—briefly—to California Institute for the Arts," she explains. "I had always acted in plays, and suddenly I just decided to take acting seriously" (Kelly 1992, Arts 31). Ott won a spot with experimentalist Herbert Blau's advanced acting class while at California Institute for the Arts, and then acted with his ensemble, Kraken. It was an influential time for the director-to-be, who recalled, "Julie Taymor, Bill Irwin and David Chambers were part of the group. The funny thing is that Herb was a brilliant teacher, but essentially he taught us a lot about everything else except about acting! He's a thoroughly analytic kind of man. He gave us a Renaissance feel for the arts" (Arts 31). After two years with Kraken, Ott joined Camera Obscura, an ensemble with residence at New York City's La MaMa e.t.c. and the Mickery Theatre in Amsterdam, Holland. When the company took up residence in Amsterdam, Ott was privileged to see the work of several master European companies and directors. "It just seemed that every single great European and American director came through. I was exposed to so many of them that I started to make the transition [from] acting to directing," she explained (Arts 31). While with Camera Obscura she performed in Holland, Germany, France, Belgium, and in the United States.

Ott's foray into directing began in the mid-1970s at the Odyssey Theater in Los Angeles, where she formed her own theatre company, Aleph, and staged Witold Gombrowicz's *The Marriage*. The company was subsequently hired as artists-in-residence at the University of Wisconsin, Milwaukee, which brought her new opportunities. Ott first directed productions at Milwaukee's Theatre X from 1975 to 1979 and eventually served as associate director there. Her reputation as a director grew with productions such as Amlin Gray's *The Fantod* in 1978 and the direction of two company-created works: *The Wreck: A Romance* in 1977, based on a poem by Adrianne Rich, and *A Fierce Longing* in 1978, based on the writing of Yukio Mishima. *A Fierce Longing* was produced on the east coast as well, winning further praise for Ott as director. The Maryland Public Broadcasting System named it best production of 1978–79 for its run at the Theatre Project in Baltimore. The *Soho Weekly News* also nominated the play as best production of the year, stating, "This unpretentious, graceful, artistically integrated ensemble and their visionary director have created a work as controversial and haunting and corrosive as Mishima himself." The *Village Voice* critic concurred, writing, "Sharon Ott's direction shows a creative sensibility that one does not often see" ("Blurbs," n.d.).

Ott served as resident director from 1979 to 1983 at the Milwaukee Repertory Theatre, where she honed her skills in American realism, with which she had little previous experience. She also directed non-realistic productions. The wide variety of plays she staged there included Tom Cole's *Medal of Honor Rag,* the premiere of Gray's *How I Got That Story,* Cole's adaptation of Gogol's *Dead Souls,* and such classics as Steinbeck's *Of Mice and Men,* Dickens's *A Christmas Carol,* Brecht's *Mother Courage,* and Williams's *A Streetcar Named Desire,* which toured to Japan in 1981 to critical acclaim. While in Japan on two separate tours, Ott furthered her study of Asian theatre, to which she remains strongly drawn.

In 1984 Ott signed on as artistic director of the Berkeley Repertory Theatre, where she spent a successful thirteen years. She surprised audiences with controversial approaches to plays and forged ties with other Bay area theatres, creating many co-sponsored productions. When she arrived at Berkeley Repertory, her aggressive leadership style first gained her a reputation of being mercurial. At the same time, she gained the respect and artistic admiration of her co-workers and audiences, in part through cultivating a younger, hipper audience than the aging subscriber base she inherited. Before she left in 1997, she accepted a special Tony Award for Outstanding Regional Theatre, a reflection of her artistic success, which brought the theatre to national prominence.

Despite her many managerial duties, Ott directed consistently during her tenure at Berkeley Repertory Theatre, including productions of Sam Shepard's *The Tooth of Crime,* Shakespeare's *Twelfth Night* and *The Winter's Tale,* Brecht's *Good Person of Szechuan,* de Vega's *Fuente Ovejuna,* Congreve's *The Way of the World,* Ibsen's *The Lady from the Sea,* and Shaw's *Heartbreak House,* which the *San Francisco Examiner* declared "a stunningly well-acted, masterfully-paced production that tempered Shaw's verbal brilliance with the musical riches of his great drama" (Hurwitt 1996). Ott is particularly proud of promoting Asian American theatre to the Berkeley community, primarily through the works of Philip Kan Gotanda. She premiered three of his plays at Berkeley Repertory: *Yankee Dawg You Die,* which transferred to the Los Angeles Theatre Center then to Playwrights Horizons in New York City; *Fish Head Soup;* and *Ballad of Yachiyo,* which she subsequently directed at South Coast Repertory Theatre in Costa Mesa, California, and later at the Public Theater in New York City.

In addition to her work at Berkeley Repertory Theatre, Ott directed at other theatres, either through joint productions, through transferred productions, or as a freelance director. In 1990 she staged Gotanda's *The Wash* at New York City's Manhattan Theatre Club, where the play received a Drama Desk nomination for Outstanding New Play. The plot revolves around a Japanese American couple who separate after forty years of marriage. Despite the new estrangement, the wife returns to her ex-husband's home to visit with him and do his laundry, symbolizing her continued subservience to him. *New York Times* critic Mel Gussow was taken with the delicate, realistic scenes, writing, "There is a quietude and even a fragility about many of the scenes that makes the few emotional outbursts by the husband carry even more weight. . . . [T]he play embraces understatement and avoids sentimentality." He praised Ott for the fluidity of the production, concluding, "As appealingly performed under Ms. Ott's direction, it remains a touching slice of life" (1990, C28).

In addition to directing a wide range of styles, one of Ott's talents is her ability to breathe new life into a play from the past. It is a talent that has also caused controversy, whether from older subscribers used to traditional fare or from critics. For example, in 1985 Ott stunned traditionalists with her directorial debut (co-directed with Richard E. T. White) at Berkeley Repertory Theatre: Sam Shepard's *Tooth of Crime*. Ott claims the audience was in "shock and denial" when confronted with her hard-rocking, profane production that had more in common with fringe theatre productions in the area (Berson 1993, 17). Her 1990 direction of Lope de Vega's fifteenth-century play *Fuente Ovejuna* at Berkeley Repertory Theatre stirred controversy as well. The tale of the Spanish town that takes revenge upon its tyrannical overlord struck a chord with Ott, who found a contemporary link to the atrocities committed by Romanian President Nicolae Ceausescu. She inserted visual references to newsreel events in Bucharest in her production, "as much for the actors as it is for the audience . . . a way of priming the company to the play's emotional universe" (Winn 1990, 41). In an unusual reaction, critic Gerald Nachman of the *San Francisco Chronicle* responded with an angry review of the rarely-produced play and a follow-up column asking patrons to protest against staging such "obscurities" (Berson 1993, 18).

In 1993 at Berkeley Repertory, Ott brought her artistic perception to Ibsen's *The Lady and the Sea*, a play with a thick plot and a sea of poetic and paranormal pitfalls into which the production could drown. The play centers on a married woman who is haunted by the memory of a previous lover, a Finnish sailor. In a dreamlike state, she envisions herself as a mermaid and he as a merman who impregnates her. *Boston Globe* critic Kevin Kelly praised Ott's joint production between Berkeley Repertory and Boston's Huntington Theatre, writing, "Ott's direction does all it can with the static nature of Ibsen's text and, as indicated, it pays off. The performances are well played" (1993, 48). He was particularly impressed with her ability to cut to the quick of Ibsen's intent, evident through the performance of the leading actor, Norwegian guest artist Juni Dahr. He wrote, "[S]he's the perfect goddesslike/cello-voiced woman for the role, a figurehead riding the fjord, an image director Sharon Ott plays for all its dramatic worth. What happens from all this is a kind of fake conviction that has us believing while shaking our heads. Ibsen's psychological feinting and sea chantey poesy fall away; 'Lady from the Sea' becomes an impressive statement about the freedom of will" (1993, Arts 49).

One of the productions Ott is most proud of is the premiere of *The Woman Warrior,* Deborah Rogin's adaptation of Maxine Hong Kingston's novel. Ott had Broadway ambitions for the play, which she premiered at Berkeley Repertory Theatre and then played at Boston's Huntington Theatre in 1994, and at Los Angeles's Doolittle Theater in 1995. The play is set in the 1950s in Stockton, California, and the plot follows a troubled Chinese American girl who refuses to speak. In the face of the racist and sexist world in which she lives, the protagonist finds she must transform herself into a woman warrior in order to survive. *USA Today* named *The Woman Warrior* the Best Play of 1994, with critic David Patrick Stearns writing, "Nearly every aspect of the production is at the highest level, from Sharon Ott's direction to Ming Cho Lee's set design and Jon Jang's incidental music" (1994, Life 4D). According to Ott, it was one of the most difficult plays to develop, requiring three workshop productions to make it producible. The hard effort paid off. Ott considers the entire process and outcome "a seminal event as a director" (Interview, 2004).

In 1997 Ott became the artistic director at the Seattle Repertory Theatre, at first shuttling back and forth between Seattle and the San Francisco Bay area, where she was finishing her term at Berkeley Repertory Theatre. She replaced artistic director Daniel Sullivan, who had built the Seattle Rep an excellent reputation and a strong subscriber base twenty thousand strong. Ott went back to her anthropology training as she tried to match the demographics of the community to the offerings of the season. According to the *Seattle Times,* "Ott wanted to create a new Seattle Rep for a new Seattle[,] a city in the midst of a high-tech boom, a population explosion and a transition into a more cosmopolitan metropolis" (Berson 2004b, D1). She set to work by creating an eclectic mix of plays for her theatre by showcasing new, ethnically diverse playwrights, focusing on non-traditional interpretations of classics, and importing prominent guest directors.

Ott made her directorial debut at the Seattle Repertory Theatre in 1997 by restaging a successful production she had directed in the past: Philip Kan Gotanda's *Ballad of Yachiyo.* The story, based on a true incident of one of Gotanda's relatives, is about a young Japanese Hawaiian girl, Yachiyo, who apprentices to a master potter and has an affair with him. Ott comments, "He's writing what could almost be a classical Kabuki play. But his perspective is subtle and contemporary, and he has wonderful empathy with Yachiyo and the choices she makes" (Berson 1997, M1). Ott approached the piece visually, with large puppets, gliding Japanese screens, and lighting effects that added a cinematic effect. Gotanda approved, stating, "Sharon understands this material and how to make it work. She's text-oriented and a visualist, and very good at taking things off the page, to give them visual life on stage" (M1). The play moved to the Public Theater in New York City that fall, where *Daily News* critic Fintan O'Toole wrote, "In Sharon Ott's brilliant, visually gorgeous production, Yachiyo[,] beautifully played by Sala Iwamatsu[,] is like a butterfly caught in a delicate net of dying traditions. This idea is given life on the stage through the use of traditional Japanese dramatic techniques. By giving these old techniques new meanings, the production makes its own poignant comment on its main character" (1997, 51).

As she did at Berkeley, Ott continued directing a mix of classics, such as Shakespeare's *As You Like It, Twelfth Night,* and *Romeo and Juliet* along with new works. Ott enjoys play development and is particularly proud of her work with playwright Amy Freed in 2001 on Freed's second production of *The Beard of Avon.* The play presents a farcical account of Shakespeare's early days as a ghostwriter of sorts for Edward De Vere, Earl of Oxford. Ott and Freed worked diligently to improve the play and finally cut three scenes at the end, rewriting and restaging several scenes immediately before opening. Misha Berson of the *Seattle Times* approved, writing, "Directed stylishly by Sharon Ott and performed by an adroit ensemble on Kent Dorsey's playhouse set, *The Beard of Avon* manages the neat trick of balancing antic, Monty Python-esque satire with sincere inquiry into why the works ascribed to Shakespeare are so remarkable" (2001, E8).

One of the last plays she directed at Seattle Repertory was the West Coast premiere of Nilo Cruz's *Beauty and the Father* in 2004. A poetic, lyrical play set in a small town in Spain, it tells the story of unrequited love of a sculptor. Working in both the real and spiritual realms, Cruz includes the ghost of playwright Frederico Garcia Lorca, who advises the love-torn sculptor. Berson gave a favorable review, writing, "It's a compliment to Sharon Ott's graceful staging of the play (which debuted at Florida's New Theater) that some script indulgences and missteps don't overburden this chimerical tale of love and angelic intervention" (2004a, C1).

Ott states that she has been happy to work in Seattle, where there is a strong resident pool of actors from which to cast. She knows their work well and has cast some of the same actors numerous times. Ott explains, "It's the best of both worlds—the benefits of ensemble without the perils" (Interview, 2004). When casting, she is very actor-centered, to the point of letting the actors help her understand the play. Watching the different interpretations of various actors gives her a better idea of "what's right, what's wrong, and the voice of the playwright," which she can hear musically, rhythmically (Ott, interview, 2004). Ott finds the same philosophy carries into rehearsal, where she prides herself in leaving the process open to discovery. On average, her actors spend three to four days doing table work with the script before they start staging the play. But even after blocking, she often returns to the text with actors to hear it again, as if for the first time, often unlocking new and better ideas. In addition, she goes back to the rehearsal hall with actors during technical rehearsals, an uncommon practice among directors. She explains that she does not want to force the actors to dwell on the technical aspects and also wants to provide one last opportunity to affect change, even starting from scratch if necessary.

Scholar Rebecca Daniels observed Ott's collaborative style at rehearsals, writing, "I could definitely see the openness to input as well as her position at the center of the work. The playwright and actors were constantly asked for their opinions and impressions. Ott often used the phrases 'Your ideas are my ideas,' 'Let's see how this feels,' 'Let's explore that idea for awhile,' or 'Feel free to move if an impulse happens,' when experimenting with staging or interpretation in the early rehearsals. Playwright Heather McDonald voiced her appreciation of Ott's openness . . . noting that she had worked with some directors who had never asked for her opinion" (1996, 104). Daniels was quick to observe that Ott remained the leader, in control of the production. "On one occasion, when too many ideas were flying fast and furiously, she cut off the input and tried to simplify what was happening in order to clear the air and, perhaps, to bring the process back around to something closer to her own emerging vision" (104).

Ott sees her productions as having a strong narrative as well as a strong sense of style, which encompasses not just the visual, but all sensory elements of performance. She chooses to celebrate the eclectic mix of styles available in twenty-first century theatre. As an artist who recognizes growth and change, she sees her early direction as very visual, usually with a non-realistic bent. Gradually, as she has worked with new plays and an increasing variety of plays, she has come to embrace narrative and to emphasize the text, though she sees herself moving back, pendulum-like, to her previous appeal to the senses. In all, her style is changing, not static. Thinking of her own career and how she has been pigeonholed in the past, Ott comments, "In this country, we don't really know how to celebrate the continuing growth of artists" (Interview, 2004).

Over the years Ott has gained an outstanding critical reputation for her directing and has received a number of awards and honors, including five Hollywood Drama-Logue Awards, two citations from the San Diego Theatre Critic's Association, and several Bay Area Theatre Critics awards. She has served her profession as a panel member and observer for the National Endowment for the Arts and is a past vice-president of the Theatre Communications Group.

Ott has earned a reputation as an ever-evolving, eclectic director who is not afraid to take risks. She declares, "We, of all the arts, should be doing the new and controversial and sparking criticism" (Berson 2004b, D1).

Sources

Berson, Misha. 1993. "What Makes Sharon Ott Run?" *American Theatre* 10 (7–8) (Jul./Aug.): 14–19.

———. 1997. "All Eyes Are on Director Sharon Ott in Her First Production for Seattle Rep." *Seattle Times*, 26 Jan., M1.

———. 2001. "*Beard of Avon* an Entertaining, Literate Fantasy." Rev. of *The Beard of Avon*, by Amy Freed. *Seattle Times*, 14 Nov., E8.

———. 2004a. "The Beauty of Nilo Cruz: *Father* Casts Complex Spell." Rev. of *Beauty of the Father*, by Nilo Cruz. *Seattle Times*, 30 Apr., C1.

———. 2004b. "Will Flagship Stay on Edgy Course or Change?" *Seattle Times*, 22 Jun., D1.

"Blurbs." n.d. Typed manuscript. Billy Rose Theatre Collection, clippings. New York Public Library for the Performing Arts.

Carrell, Jennifer Lee. 2000. "Building a Believable Fantasia." *Arizona Daily Star*, 11 Feb., C1, C4.

Daniels, Rebecca. 1996. *Women Stage Directors Speak: Exploring the Influence of Gender on Their Work*. Jefferson, N.C.: McFarland.

Gussow, Mel. 1990. Rev. of *The Wash*, by Philip Kan Gotanda. *New York Times*, 8 Nov., C28.

Hurwitt, Robert. 1996. "Berkeley Rep's Ott Heading for Seattle." *San Francisco Chronicle*, 7 Nov. In Newsbank Review of the Arts, Performing Arts, fiche 9, grid B9.

Kelly, Kevin. 1992. "Sharon Ott: From Fossils to Floodlights." *Boston Globe*, 22 May, Arts 31.

———. 1993. "Ibsen's Gift from the Sea." Rev. of *The Lady from the Sea*, by Henrik Ibsen. *Boston Globe*, 22 Oct., Arts 49.

Marx, Bill. 1987. "Ott for Art's Sake." *Boston Phoenix*, n.p. Billy Rose Theatre Collection, clippings. New York Public Library for the Performing Arts.

O'Toole, Fintan. 1997. "East and West Collide in 'Yachiyo.'" Rev. of *Ballad of Yachiyo*, by Philip Kan Gotanda. *(New York) Daily News*, 13 Nov., 51.

Ott, Sharon. 2004. Telephone interview with Anne Fliotsos. 21 Jul.

Stearns, David Patrick. 1994. "Eloquent Emotions Elevate *The Woman Warrior*." Rev. of *The Woman Warrior*, adapted by Deborah Rogin, based on the novel of Maxine Hong Kingston. *USA Today*, 4 Oct., Life 4D.

Winn, Steven. 1990. "15th Century Spain Alive on Berkeley Stage." *San Francisco Chronicle,* 9 Sept., 41.

Representative Directing Credits

Off and Off-Off Broadway:
  Yankee Dawg You Die (1989), *The Wash* (1990), *Alligator Tales* (1997), *Ballad of Yachiyo* (1997)

Regional Theatre:
  The Wreck: A Romance (1977), *The Fantod* (1978), *A Fierce Longing* (1978), *The Tooth of Crime* (co-directed with Richard E. T. White—1985), *Twelfth Night* (1986), *The Good Person of Szechuan* (1987), *The Winter's Tale* (1987), *Fuente Ovejuna* (1990), *The Way of the World* (1992), *The Lady from the Sea* (1993), *The Woman Warrior* (1994, 1995), *Ballad of Yachiyo* (1995, 1996, 1997), *Heartbreak House* (1996), *Twilight, Los Angeles: 1992* (1996), *An Almost Holy Picture* (1997), *Alligator Tales* (1998), *Pygmalion* (1998), *Golden Child* (1999), *Sisters Matsumoto* (2000), *As You Like It* (2000), *New Patagonia* (2000), *A Midsummer Night's Dream* (2001), *The Beard of Avon* (2001), *When Grace Comes In* (2002), *Romeo and Juliet* (2003), *Misalliance* (2003), *Beauty of the Father* (2004), *Anna in the Tropics* (2004), *Restoration Comedy* (2005, 2006)

Packer, Tina

Born Christina Packer on September 28, 1938, in Wolverhampton, England, and raised in Nottingham, Tina Packer has become one of the foremost directors of Shakespeare in the United States. As the founder and artistic director of Shakespeare & Company, she has directed over forty productions in the Berkshires of Massachusetts. In addition, she is the former artistic director of the Boston Shakespeare Company and has directed in several regional and many university theatres. Over the course of her impressive career as an actor, director, artistic director, and teacher, Packer has won numerous awards and honors, including two honorary doctorates.

Packer was raised by liberal, permissive parents who sent her to a Quaker boarding school, where tolerance of differences was the norm. She memorized passages from Shakespeare for school and participated in theatrical productions as a student. While still in high school, she attended performances at the Royal Shakespeare Company (RSC) in Stratford-upon-Avon. With the intent to enter college and become a writer, Packer passed her qualifying examinations then departed for Paris in 1956, but she never returned to England for college. Instead, she fell in love with a much older man and enjoyed a bohemian lifestyle in Paris while the relationship lasted. Two years later she returned to England, heartbroken and disillusioned. Packer moved to London, where she worked a day job and saw all the theatre she could. She wrote briefly for a women's magazine, then auditioned for theatre schools. After six months of auditioning, she was accepted into the prestigious Royal Academy of Dramatic Arts (RADA), one of twenty students accepted from a pool of over five hundred applicants (Epstein 1985, 19). Packer found she did not like the regimentation of the program, nor did she care for RADA's approach to Shakespeare, an external approach that emphasized deportment and elocution. Despite her disagreements with their pedagogical methods and artistic approaches, Packer excelled and received the Ronson Award for Most Promising Actress upon her graduation in 1964.

Within a year Packer joined the ranks of the RSC as an associate artist and met her future husband there. She left the RSC to take the part of Dora in the British Broadcasting Company's (BBC's) adaptation of Dickens's classic, *David Copperfield*. After the birth of her son, she went back to working in repertory theatre and even acted in the BBC's production of *Dr. Who*, but found herself increasingly dissatisfied, in part because she had very little power as a performer. Packer recalls, "I wanted power because I couldn't bear not having a voice. As a mere actor in the theater world, you have no voice. You're cast based only on what you look like, and you begin to lose all sense of who you really are. . . . Even though at the time I was with some of the best theatre directors in the English-speaking world, I still felt as if I was of no consequence. . . . I had to step out and start saying what I thought; otherwise I would remain voiceless" (Whitney and Packer 2000, 36).

While working on a television adaptation of Henry James's *The Heiress*, she found her character on the cutting room floor and took that opportunity to walk away from both acting and her increasingly dysfunctional marriage. "It took me time to focus and get courage," Packer recalled. "I know what I *really* wanted to do was develop my own style of doing Shakespeare. I realized I couldn't do that at the Royal Shakespeare—because there I was known as an actress and a junior person" (Epstein 1985, 30). Instead, she found work as a director at the London Academy of Music and Dramatic Arts (LAMDA), directing *Measure for Measure* in 1971, followed by one of her favorites, *The Winter's Tale*. In addition to Shakespeare, Packer directed plays by Chekhov, Orton, Ostrovsky, Strindberg, and Sheridan while at LAMDA.

Once she became a director, Packer began to solidify her quest: to bring her own brand of acting and directing Shakespeare to the United States, where a fresh approach to the Bard was welcome. Through sheer tenacity and some naïveté, in 1974 she applied for and won a CBS Foundation Grant for $11,000 plus a $132,000 Ford Foundation Grant to fund an experimental company that would train in Shakespeare and perform his plays. Packer gathered an impressive group of master teachers, including renowned voice teacher Kristin Linklater, and began her company under the title Shakespeare & Company, after her favorite bookstore in Paris. By April of 1973, her group was performing, first in England, where they received enthusiastic press, then in the United States, where their reviews were mixed to poor. In running the company, Packer took a democratic approach, shunning the authoritarianism she hated, but she soon found that the company was increasingly dysfunctional and unhappy. Her funding ran out, her experiment with her first company ended poorly, and she returned to England.

After a fallow period of soul-searching, world travel, and est training (Erhard Seminar Training, which presents a psychological approach to life), Packer again found the courage to return to directing, first through universities, then in London and elsewhere. She directed Moliere's *The Learned Ladies* at Smith College in Northampton, Massachusetts, in 1977, and the following year directed it at the Kennedy Center in Washington, D.C. Gradually, Packer's passion for theatre rekindled, and she decided once more to start her own company, calling upon the group of master teachers who aided her in 1973. She returned to the United States and began a systematic approach to finding a community that could support a Shakespeare theatre. After searching for traditional theatre spaces, Packer fell in love with a dilapidated mansion in the Berkshire mountains of Massachusetts, not far from Boston. It was the former home of novelist Edith Wharton, who named her house and its grounds "the Mount."

Packer directed the first company performance there in 1978, *A Midsummer Night's Dream*, which played outdoors for lack of a theatre facility. The local newspapers were delighted to find "nothing high and mighty and classical about it," calling Packer's production "down to earth and yet, very, very classy." Another newspaper printed, "Sheer, roistering energy is the hallmark of Shakespeare & Company's production. . . . There is not a pallid, pedantic moment during the entire evening" (Epstein 1985, 76). The company extended the run and was reviewed in the *Village Voice,* bolstering its name recognition and credibility in New York City. "Packer's production is . . . astonishingly forthrightly 19th century. Packer has chosen the play not for its modern, passionately arbitrary sexuality, but further for its bucolic splendor. She has played the play as pastoral—lines are basically declaimed, Bottom's transfiguration is a model of ass-head beauty, and Kiki Smith's quite wonderful costumes blend the characters into the setting rather than pushing them out of it" (77).

With a heady new beginning, Packer put herself to work finding money for the fledgling company to remain in residence. Their summer season in 1979 drew excellent reviews, with critics repeatedly commenting on the marvelous vocal quality of the actors, who could always be understood and who conveyed an enlightened sense of meaning through the language. The following summer, Terry Curtis Fox, critic for the *Village Voice*, raved about the performances, writing, "For the past three summers, the best theater I have seen has been at the Mount in Lenox, Massachusetts. . . . Packer's production is a model of insight, clarity, vision—well, magic" (Epstein 1985, 95). Again, comments were centered on vocal abilities, thanking Linklater's techniques for making the actor's speech "truly idiomatic. . . . There is no pompous breaking of meter; no pausing for Art. There are simply actors who are at home in the language, using its subtle shifts of rhythmic intensity to make the essential textual points clear." He continued by complimenting the quality of the productions as a whole, noting that the connection between training and performance created "such deep and textured work" (95).

Despite the glowing reviews of the *Village Voice*, Packer could not get the *New York Times* to come to the Berkshires and take notice of the group. Instead, she decided to bring the company to New York City. She routinely wrote to producer Joseph Papp until he agreed to help her find an outlet in the city. In 1982 Packer directed her company in *Twelfth Night*, and they performed not only at their home at the Mount, but also in Brooklyn at Prospect Park and at the American Shakespeare Theatre in Stratford, Connecticut. With the addition of Packer's touring educational program, Shakespeare in the Schools, she was finally reaching a wider audience than her Berkshire regulars.

When Artistic Director Peter Sellars left the Boston Shakespeare Company (BSC), Packer found yet another outlet for her administrative and directing talents. Despite its financial woes, Packer took over the company as interim artistic director in 1984, and as artistic director thereafter. For two years she tried to make the company work, but her deficit was overwhelming in the face of high Boston prices. She announced a merger of the BSC with Shakespeare & Company in 1986. While running BSC, Packer directed Athol Fugard's *Master Harold and the Boys*, Ron Hutchinson's *Rat in the Skull*, and Frank McGuinness's *Observe the Sons of Ulster Marching Towards the Somme*. Of the latter, Kevin Kelly of the *Boston Globe* wrote of McGuinness's diatribe against war: "Let me make it clear that it's impeccably acted, with a standard of performance the rest of the season (resident or commercial) may find hard to beat. Packer has created a poeticized reality that somehow captures the specific eloquence and reach of Yeats, Lady Gregory, Edward Martyn, Synge and O'Casey" (1988, Arts and Film 24).

Over the decades, Packer has directed an average of two plays a year for

Shakespeare & Company and occasionally she has found opportunities to direct elsewhere. In addition to her guest direction at colleges and universities, Packer directed a production of *Hamlet* at the North Shore Music Theatre in Beverly, Massachusetts, in 1991. Specifically geared toward a high-school audience, Packer cut one-third of the text, doubled and tripled the roles played by each actor, and set the play in West Africa with an African American cast, with the exception of the actor playing Polonius. Packer explained, "I think the [Shakespearean] plays should be acts of the imagination. But when I began thinking about *Hamlet,* I became aware of the political turmoil going on behind the action. . . . The band of soldiers isn't just wandering around, they're about to take over. Fortinbras, the man strong in arms, is waiting to come in. And some of this—most of this—began to suggest to me the turmoil in Africa. I wanted to find a state where new ideas were coming in, a state itself not steady, not safe. It became Africa, my act of the imagination. Polonius—he's really my Uncle John, who was head of adult education in Nigeria—is a leftover white man, the old high commissioner from another regime" (Kelly 1991a, Arts 43). Kelly approved of her results, writing, "Packer's attempt is bold and well-reasoned." Although he found the production missed a few opportunities, he noted, "Packer keeps her young audience alert to the excitement of the narrative, hoping, I guess, that other matters will be mulled over later" (1991b, Arts 78).

Although she continues to direct a steady roster of Shakespeare, Packer breaks with the Bard from time to time. In reverence to Wharton, whose home Shakespeare & Company occupies, Packer has directed several adaptations of Wharton's novellas, producing *Roman Fever* in 1989 and 1990, and *Summer* in 1999. In 1993 she directed two plays for the Boston Center for the Arts: Tom Kempinski's *Duet for One* and J. L. Balderston's *Berkeley Square.* The same year she directed a production at the Canadian Stage Company in Toronto, a rape drama entitled *Scheherazade,* by Marisa Chamberlain. In the 1990s and into the new century she has continued to act from time to time as well, taking a break from directing. "Directing is such a sedentary occupation," Packer observed. "You sit there with all your emotions and tensions and have no way of letting them out, where as an actor gets to go through the cathartic experience night after night. That's the one thing I miss about acting" (Epstein 1985, 113).

One of Packer's struggles as a beginning director and artistic director in 1973 was taking on the authority of a leader, but she learned from her mistakes. Packer discovered that democratic company meetings could escalate emotionally, with no decisive outcome, becoming negative and divisive in the process. With the advice of Peter Hall, then director of the National Theatre of London, she came to the understanding that actors want to be led. Hall put it bluntly: "[I]f she was running a group, she was a leader. She couldn't start something and then not take responsibility for it. Leaders must be checked and abused but they are certainly necessary" (Epstein 1985, 88). Packer no longer shuns the leadership role, though she strives to be inclusive, empowering her actors.

From the beginning, Packer has been a proponent of color-blind casting, giving opportunities to gifted actors of color who rarely were cast in Shakespeare's major roles, particularly in the 1970s and early 1980s. Company member Gregory Cole explained, "What really fascinated me was that this was a company interested in transcending stereotypes, crossing barriers, being international and multi-cultural without any fuss. I like being a black actor and getting to play major roles without much ado. That just doesn't exist elsewhere. And I like the philosophy of the company, that striving for a larger experience that characterizes us" (Epstein 1985, 94). Natsuko Ohama, a founding company member, agreed, stating that she would never have the opportunities to play roles traditionally cast as Caucasian roles in other Shakespeare companies. She portrayed Titania in Packer's acclaimed production of *A Midsummer Night's Dream* in 1984.

Although Packer occasionally directs guest artists, most of the actors she casts are company members, trained in the methods developed at Shakespeare & Company over the decades. In keeping with her non-authoritarian approach, Packer gives her casts ample room to experiment and grow, even in performance. Ohama commented, "Tina is my favorite director because she is not as form-directed as other directors. There are many actors for whom this is a problem. They want more of a structure than she provides. But for me, her way of working is incredible. I have a real sense of creation in every performance. Most shows you see are geared toward opening night. They're set. And then, gradually, the performances die. Our productions always seem to get better, so that, by the end, we are doing our best shows instead of being glad it's over" (Epstein 1985, 92).

Packer demands much of her actors in rehearsal, for Shakespeare also demands much. "To do Shakespeare you need not only voice and text, but training in fighting and tumbling, dance, mask work, clown work and the structure of verse," she explains (Nemy 1984, C3). Her rehearsal techniques are somewhat unusual. She goes in without preconceived notions, and her actors almost never hold scripts. Instead they are fed lines when necessary, allowing them to establish eye contact and a personal connection as they rehearse.

Packer believes that actors hold the emotional truthfulness of each character within them. Her job as director is to facilitate its release. "Our bodies hold all the good and bad things that have ever happened to us. The good things tend to pass through the body—we let them out with a laugh, for example—while the bad things stay," she states (Siegel 1996, N1). Her actors practice "dropping in," or tapping into their personal traumas, as needed. "I don't think it's possible to get to that same place [without it]. The blocks in the body have to do with suppressed feeling, and I think people tend to avoid them because they think they're bad and nasty. I don't think of them as bad and nasty or good or anything else. I think of deeper connection; that's what we're looking for" (N1). Although she's aware of the criticism that says this method turns the director into a therapist, Packer sticks with it because it produces exciting, emotionally truthful results.

Observers of Packer's classes and workshops see the moment-by-moment coaching so essential to her actors' performances. Biographer Helen Epstein observed Packer's Winter Workshop for actors, reporting: "Packer held on to her actors, with her hands, arms, legs, sometimes with her entire body, even wrestling one of the actresses to the floor in pursuit of characterization. Emotionally and intellectually, too, Packer was relentless, as hard on the pairs of trainees working on their scenes as Linklater" (1985, 113). Packer led her students through individual character work, posing probing questions. To an actor playing Friar Lawrence in *Romeo and Juliet* she asks, "What's Friar Lawrence's life been like before Romeo and Juliet came along with their problems? . . . There's somewhere in you a great desire to be committed and because you know you never will, you allow yourself to get involved vicariously. . . . Have you ever muscled in on anyone's life yourself? How far do you think he gets involved? He's been a celibate for a long time and who knows which of those weeds he's been chewing on. Have you ever been vicariously involved in someone else's love affair yourself? How did it make you feel? Now, say the lines" (115).

In a workshop at the Massachusetts Institute of Technology (MIT), Packer took a word-by-word approach to helping performers make sense of the lines. Student actors were asked to speak their lines, paying particular attention to their breathing and their emotional connection. Ed Siegel of the *Boston Globe* observed the workshop and reported on one student in particular:

> He recites his lines—"Lovers and madmen have such seething brains," from *Midsummer Night's Dream*—well enough to get an A in just about any English class, but it's not what Packer wants. She works on his voice by loosening his facial muscles and trying to get him to speak from his abdomen rather than his chest—to drop his breath into his lower belly. As she's working on his voice she asks him to draw upon a story he told earlier—about how he never got a message that his girlfriend was going to be late, so that he ended up stewing over her no-show for a couple of hours.
>
> The two then practice a variation of "dropping in," in which they work on one word of Shakespeare at a time by drawing on the actor's associations. ("The word itself," Packer had said earlier, "holds a hundred images. We teach how an actor taps into those resonances.")

Packer will give the student an association and then he'll recite the word in question. It goes something like this:
"Who is it that you love most? Lovers."
The student says, "Lovers."
"Can you imagine making love to the most beautiful woman you've ever seen? Lovers."
"Lovers."
"Did you ever see your parents making love? Lovers."
"Lovers."
They do the same thing with "madmen," and then he recites the lines again. The result is amazing. . . . The singsong delivery that most of us use when reciting poetry is gone. Instead the words are round where they should be round and sharp where they should be sharp. He recites the passage as if he means every word of it. Another student says, "His words have music and shape." Or as Packer says, it's now more "connected." (1996, N1)

Epstein sees the same transformation in actors working with Packer. "To watch Packer work with the actors is nothing short of amazing," she writes. "Bodies which have been wooden suddenly become supple. Readings which have been superficial become charged with meaning. It is as though Packer lights a fire within each actor and it is like watching creation" (1985, 116).

Packer's legacy as a director has been to bring audiences accessible Shakespeare, clearly spoken and connected to meaningful emotional expression. Her main focus is on the actor and the text. In fact, she produces a "Bare Bard" production annually, with a small cast doubling and tripling roles and utilizing bare-bones production elements. Her no-nonsense approach has demystified Shakespeare for her American audiences. In response, Packer has won a plethora of awards, including two honorary doctorates, prestigious grants, and two awards for directing: the Henry Hewitt Prize for Outstanding Direction in 1992, as part of the Elliot Norton Awards, and the L.A. Critics Award for Best Direction of *Measure for Measure* in 1997. In addition to Epstein's 1985 biography, *The Companies She Keeps,* Packer is the subject of a PBS documentary from 1984, "Sex, Violence, and Poetry: A Portrait of Tina Packer." She has lectured extensively at colleges and universities across the United States, sending out her message: that the transformative power of theatre is "based on humanity's ever-present need to tell their own personal stories of survival and enlightenment" (Packer 2004).

Sources

Cummings, Scott T. 1995. "At the Mount with Tina Packer." *American Theatre* 12 (1): 26–28.

Eckert, Thor Jr. 1980. "The Bard and Carpentry Make a Well-Rounded Company."
    Christian Science Monitor, 8 Sept., 11.

Engstrom, John. 1985. "Documentary on Packer Lacks Depth She Deserves."
    Boston Globe, 24 Sept., 79.

Epstein, Helen. 1985. *The Companies She Keeps: Tina Packer Builds a Theater.*
    Cambridge, Mass.: Plunkett Lake.

Gaines, Judith. 2001. "Re-creating the Rose." *Boston Globe Magazine,* 12 Aug.,
    12–22.

Kelly, Kevin. 1988. "*Sons of Ulster:* Long Lyrical Assault on War." Rev. of *Observe
    the Sons of Ulster Marching Towards the Somme,* by Frank McGuinness.
    Boston Globe, 24 Sept., Arts and Film 24.

———. 1991a. "Packer Sets *Hamlet* a Continent Apart." *Boston Globe,* 19 Apr.,
    Arts 43.

———. 1991b. "Packer's High-Energy *Hamlet.*" Rev. of *Hamlet,* by William
    Shakespeare. *Boston Globe,* 8 May, Arts 78.

Nemy, Enid. 1984. "A Company that Gets the Stiff Upper Lip Out of Shakespeare."
    New York Times, 7 Sept., C3.

Nesbitt, Caroline. 1989. "In the Woods with Shakespeare & Company." *American
    Theatre* 16 (1): 30–33, 92–97.

Packer, Tina. 2004. "Tina Packer: Artistic Director of Shakespeare & Company."
    Unpublished manuscript. Lenox, Mass.: Shakespeare & Company.

Siegel, Ed. 1996. "Shakespeare in Good Company; Dropping in on Packer's
    Method." *Boston Globe,* 22 Sept., N1.

Whitney, John O. and Tina Packer. 2000. *Power Plays: Shakespeare's Lessons in
    Leadership and Management.* New York: Simon & Schuster.

Representative Directing Credits

Off and Off-Off Broadway:
The Taming of the Shrew (1974), *Twelfth Night* (1982)

Regional Theatre:
A Winter's Tale (1974, 1979), *A Midsummer Night's Dream* (1978, 1984, 1993, 2001), *The Learned Ladies* (1978), *The Tempest* (1980, 1989), *As You Like It* (1981, 1988, 1990), *Twelfth Night* (1981, 1982), *Macbeth* (1982, 2002), *Romeo and Juliet* (1983), *The Comedy of Errors* (1983, 1985), *Master Harold and the Boys* (1986), *Rat in the Skull* (1986), *Antony and Cleopatra* (1986), *Observe the Sons of Ulster Marching Towards the Somme* (1987), *Roman Fever* (1989, 1990), *Hamlet* (1991), *A Life in the Theatre* (1992), *Duet for One* (1992, 1993), *Julius Caesar* (1992, 1993), *Berkeley Square* (1993), *Mrs. Klein* (1994), *Much Ado About Nothing* (1995), *The Merry Wives of Windsor* (1996), *Measure for Measure* (1996, 1997), *Henry IV Part 1* (1997), *The Death of the Father of Psychoanalysis (& Anna)* (1997), *The Merchant of Venice* (1998), *The Millionairess* (1998), *Richard III* (1999), *Summer* (1999),

Coriolanus (2000, 2001), *The Scarlet Letter* (2002), *King Lear* (2003), *The Fly-Bottle* (2003), *King John* (2005)

International Theatre:
   King Lear (1975), *Scheherazade* (1993)

 # Perloff, Carey

Born in Washington, D.C., on February 9, 1959, Carey Perloff is a playwright, director, and artistic director. She is known for directing innovative productions of both contemporary and classic plays and for making historical plays come alive for modern audiences.

Growing up in Washington, D.C., Perloff had dreams of becoming an archaeologist. As a child she enjoyed reading, in addition to writing poetry and fiction. Although she attended performances at prominent Washington, D.C., theatres, such as Arena Stage and Folger Theatre, Perloff spent more time going to the vast array of museums in the nation's capital. In 1976 she entered Stanford University in California to study Greek and Latin. While there, she read and staged Greek tragedy in Greek. She found this a wonderful way to learn about directing, saying, "You have to really learn how to tell a story without anybody knowing what the language is" (Interview, 2004). Perloff became involved with Stanford's drama department and discovered that she enjoyed directing. She says, "It drew upon so many different things that I loved and things that I studied. I had danced all my life. I'd done a lot of choreography. I had done a lot of art history. I'd done an enormous amount of literary analysis, so I knew my way around the text. I knew how to take a text apart" (Interview, 2004). Perloff graduated from Stanford University in 1980 with a B.A. in classics and comparative literature and a minor in theatre and dramatic literature. Awarded a Fulbright Fellowship, she then went to England to study at St. Anne's College at Oxford University, where she received an M.A. in English Literature in 1981. While there, Perloff directed many plays. In addition to her academic studies, Perloff has also studied dance at American University in Washington, D.C.; directing with British director Frank Hauser in London; and Kabuki at Theater Der Welt in Stuttgart, Germany.

After graduation from Oxford, Perloff went to New York City to begin a theatre career and supported herself with theatrical day jobs. In 1981 she became program manager for New York's International Theater Institute, where she met theatre luminaries from around the world, including Peter Brook and Meredith Monk. The next year Perloff became a casting assistant for New York City's New York Shakespeare Festival. There, she met scores of performers and discovered that "the best training you could ever have as a director is to work in casting" (Interview, 2004). Perloff knocked on many doors of New York City's theatres, seeking directing jobs. At first she directed many readings and worked with new playwrights. Wanting to direct classical plays, she visited theatres and presented them with a list of plays that she wanted to direct. With youthful energy, she worked during the day and directed plays at night.

While in New York City, Perloff was encouraged to pursue directing by JoAnne Akalaitis. She explains, "I just really admired what she'd done and her taste in material. . . . And her courage in going after exciting, interesting stuff. She was great. She was really helpful to me" (Interview, 2004). Although she was not influenced by Akalaitis's directing style, Perloff says she was influenced stylistically by the work of directors Giorgio Strehler and Lev Dodin (Interview, 2004).

Perloff's first big break occurred when she directed Thorton Wilder's *The Skin of Our Teeth* in 1986 at New York City's Classic Stage Company (CSC). That year, the theatre asked her to become its artistic director, and she agreed— even though she had little desire to run a theatre. She explains, "I wanted to do certain plays, and it was going to be very hard to be handed those plays. Nobody was going to easily give me Greek tragedy to direct, or Shakespeare, or big classical plays. . . . Women just didn't get those plays. . . . And suddenly I was running this fantastic Off Broadway theatre. It was utterly bankrupt" (Interview, 2004).

At CSC, Perloff learned how to raise money and to run a theatre. The first play that she directed there was the 1987 world premiere of Ezra Pound's version of Sophocles's *Electra*. The production was a success, and Perloff continued to present new translations of classic plays at CSC, as well as modern plays by Pinter and Beckett.

In 1992 Perloff accepted an offer to become artistic director of San Francisco's American Conservatory Theater (A.C.T.). Perloff talks about her decision to leave CSC, saying, "I had a fantastic time at CSC. I never thought I would leave. I mean, I could do all the plays I wanted to do. . . . I remember thinking at the time, 'These days are over in New York.' . . . The recession was coming. New York was getting much more conservative. There was less and less classical theatre. Whatever classical there was ended up being British" (Interview, 2004).

With her move to A.C.T., Perloff set about rebuilding another bankrupt theatre. Perloff acknowledges that as artistic director, she can provide herself with steady work as a director and stay in one location to raise a family. She hoped to present productions at A.C.T. that were "highly theatrical, very challenging, very culturally diverse and very actor-oriented. . . . I don't believe classics are plays you do in English accents for upper-middle-class people who went to college. Forty thousand people at a pop went to see Sophocles' 'Ajax' or 'Electra.' How do we recapture that now, when we don't share a common mythology? That's the great challenge and the great excitement of doing classics" (Winn 1991, E1). At A.C.T. Perloff brought in living writers and presented the work of others, such as Schiller, Euripides, and Strindberg in a theatre that had previously focused on such playwrights as Shakespeare and Ibsen. Because of the paucity of roles for women in Shakespeare's plays, Perloff prefers to stage other classic plays that include strong women's roles (Interview, 2004).

In 1991 Perloff directed her first production at A.C.T., Strindberg's *The Creditors,* which she had directed earlier that year at CSC. The new production, which revolved around a man, his ex-wife, and her new husband, featured a new cast. In his review of the play, Steve Winn of the *San Francisco Chronicle* called the production "crisply staged" (1993, 25).

Perloff began to work closely with British playwright Tom Stoppard at A.C.T. She first directed the West Coast premiere of his play *Arcadia* in 1995. Other Stoppard plays directed by Perloff at A.C.T. include the American premiere of *Indian Ink* in 1999, the American premiere of *Invention of Love* in 2000, and *Night and Day* in 2002. Perloff says of working with Stoppard, "It was really a defining moment for me as a director to start collaborating with him" (Interview, 2004). Stoppard encouraged Perloff to direct his plays differently than previous directors. She explains, "He always encouraged me to just start clean. . . . Directing is a completely intuitive art form. You read a script, and you meet it half way. Something in that script speaks to you, and you start to create. You start to see images. You start to see actors. You start to see patterns" (Interview, 2004).

In 2004 Perloff directed the A.C.T. production of Stoppard's *The Real Thing,* a play about love and reality. Robert Hurwitt of the *San Francisco Chronicle* described how Perloff reframed the play, writing, "Perloff and her design team confront and confound expectations from the beginning. In place of the anticipated drawing-room-comedy realism of the opening scene, the curtain rises on a vast abstract canvas. J.B. Wilson's stunning set is a Mark Rothko-influenced wall of rough-edged burnt purple and orange with deep black holes for doorway and windows. A second, interior, gilded proscenium, mirroring the one that frames the Geary stage, signals the blurred lines between reality and fiction. A long, solid deep purple couch serves as the scene's domestic focus. . . . The couch—moved from place to place, altered to become railway seats—anchors each successive scene as Stoppard moves through layers of theatrical and real infidelities" (2004c, E6).

Perloff has also directed American premieres of plays by British playwright Harold Pinter. At CSC Perloff directed two plays by him: *The Birthday Party* in 1988 and 1989, and the American premiere of *Mountain Language* in 1989. The following year at the Mark Taper Forum, Perloff directed Pinter's *The Collection,* for which she won a Drama-Logue Award for Outstanding Direction. The play involved two households and accusations of adultery. Sylvie Drake of the *Los Angeles Times* described the production, writing, "The pace is deliberate, the action pregnant with those notorious Pinter pauses, the air fraught with confrontation and repressed violence, the language laconic" (1990, 1). Plays by Pinter that Perloff directed at A.C.T. include *Old Times* in 1998 and the American premieres of *Celebration* and *The Room* in 2001.

In addition to premieres of productions by Pinter and Stoppard, Perloff has directed several world premieres at A.C.T., including Leslie Ayvanzian's *Singer's Boy* in 1997, Marc Blitzstein's *No for an Answer* in 2001, and David Lang and Mac Wellman's *The Difficulty of Crossing a Field* in 2002, originally performed in a workshop at A.C.T. in 1998. She has directed the world premieres of adaptations including Constance Congdon's *A Mother,* adapted from the 1910 Gorky play *Vassa Zheleznova,* and David Mamet's *The Voysey Inheritance,* an adaptation of the 1905 Harvey Granville-Barker play. *A Mother* featured an acclaimed performance by Olympia Dukakis as a ruthless mother. Hurwitt described Perloff's direction, writing, "Perloff's production is masterfully paced and beautifully developed. Capitalism clashes and dances with broad caricatures in performances that fill out the effect of Beaver Bauer's brightly conceived, slyly exaggerated peasant/petty bourgeois costumes. Intimate scenes collide with boisterous eruptions of full-family mayhem, with Perloff making delightful use of a doorway as an inner stage. Performances bounce off and enhance each other" (2004b, E1).

Perloff has directed many new translations of plays, including an adaptation and translation of Euripides's *Hecuba,* by Timberlake Wertenbaker. Presented in 1995 and 1998 at A.C.T. and in 1998 at the Williamstown Theatre Festival in Massachusetts, the production focused on the Trojan queen Hecuba after the Greeks conquered Troy. Perloff's production included a vocal ensemble of women called Kitka, who sang traditional Baltic and Slavic songs as the Greek Chorus. She explains her choice for the production, stating, "It's a very haunting, slightly nasal, a cappella sound that's quite dissonant and ancient. It feels somehow connected and not decorative; it's very organic to the world of this play" (Hartigan 1998, C1). Patti Hartigan of the *Boston Globe* found that Williamstown audiences were able to make connections between the play's depiction of post-war Troy and war-torn Bosnia. She wrote that the production did not "impose a high-minded concept of the play. The resonance is built in" (C1).

In 1998 Perloff directed Michael Feingold's new verse translation of Friedrich Schiller's *Mary Stuart* at A.C.T. The play, which focused on the relationship between Mary Queen of Scots and Elizabeth I of England, was directed by Perloff again in 2000 at Boston's Huntington Theatre. As with *Hecuba,* Perloff used music, this time by a Renaissance group called Chanticleer that performs both songs and instrumental music. Jon Lehman of the *Patriot Ledger* wrote of the Boston production, "[T]his production dissolves the boundary between Elizabethan England and the 21st century." He went on to say, "One of the small marvels of this play is the freshness with which Schiller, Feingold, and Perloff invest it. Although tragedy is often said to carry the air of inevitability, here there is a constant sense that nothing is foreordained, that anything may still happen at any moment, that no deed is final until it is done" (2000, 39). Ed Seigel of the *Boston Globe* agreed, writing, "Perloff and translator Michael Feingold have fashioned a knockout of a production, that, like the best of classical drama, feels rooted in its original while resonating with the political and personal issues of the day" (2000, C1). *Mary Stuart* won the Elliot Norton Prize for Best Production in a Regional Theater in 2000.

Perloff discusses how her production of *Mary Stuart* differs from others, explaining, "The trap with this play is that people might mistakenly think that it's an Elizabethan play. It's a postrevolutionary play. American Revolution. French Revolution. It has nothing to do with the questions Shakespeare was asking. This is set in a time of incredible excess and asking questions about personal liberty. Personal liberty wasn't even a question when Shakespeare was writing. In Schiller's time, it's the individual versus the state, religion versus the state, individual sexual freedom versus the state. Schiller doesn't allow you to decide whose side you're on. He was a lawyer and a historian who created this deliberately dialectical play where both arguments are strong" (Blowen 2000, N1).

Other new translations of plays directed by Perloff at A.C.T. include Moliere's *The Misanthrope* in 2000, Luigi Pirandello's *Enrico IV* in 2001, and Henrik Ibsen's *A Doll's House* in 2004. Written in 1879, *A Doll's House* examined women's oppression through the marriage of a housewife, Nora, and her husband. Although Perloff had never wanted to stage Ibsen before because she thought his plays predictable, she found her experience of directing *A Doll's House* humbling. She explains, "It is such a radical play. . . . The audiences were shocked by it. . . . Sometimes it's very humbling what material starts to speak to you. . . . [D]irecting is . . . such a benchmark of your own development as a person because different material speaks to you at different times of your life" (Interview, 2004). Hurwitt praised Perloff's direction and Paul Walsh's translation, writing, "Clarity—emotional, thematic and metaphoric— is one of Perloff's primary strengths as a director and sometimes one of her principal weaknesses. Here, for the most part, she resists the temptation to overexplain the emotional subtext or social significance. Ibsen's text is clear enough. . . . Paul Walsh's crisp, clear, plain-spoken new translation is a decided asset" (2004a, D2).

Whether she is directing a new translation of a play or an established script, Perloff follows a process of exploration with each play. When Perloff selects a play, she prepares by reading and researching her project. She also works with a dramaturg. Although Perloff is not interested in deconstructing plays or setting classics in different time periods, she says, "I love plays that are sort of richly ambiguous and open to interpretation" (Interview, 2004). She discusses what attracts her to certain plays in the selection process, saying, "I love rich, complex, exciting theatrical language. I love complexity. I love plays about ideas. I don't do social issue plays. I don't do living room drama, particularly. American realism doesn't interest me very much. You know I love ambiguity. I love plays with great roles for women; I look for that a lot. Those are the people who need the work and are willing to do it. I'm very, very actor-based" (Interview, 2004).

Perloff carefully examines each play before directing it. She explains, "I'm interested in the historical moment in which it was created. I don't tend to do very faithful kinds of literal productions. . . . The fascinating thing about classical theatre is its otherness—the fact that it's so different—that also makes us realize how close it is. . . . Maybe because I was an archaeologist, that's what really interests me. I never see the point of saying, 'It's Hedda Gabler, but it's really an American housewife.' It isn't an American housewife. . . . You have to figure out what's the key. . . . How do you look at the heartbeat of what that period is? . . . That affects the music, and the visual world, and the playing style, and everything else" (Interview, 2004).

Because A.C.T. is a repertory company, Perloff often selects plays with certain performers from the core company in mind. She explains, "I think the best way to work is to have really deep consistent relationships with ac- tors. It doesn't mean you always have to work with the same actors, but the shorthand that happens is absolutely unbelievable. It's really knowing what your palette is, and who you're painting with. It's not a coincidence that great choreographers always work with the same dancers. You have a sense of how far you can push them, of what they'll bring to the table. . . . You save two weeks of the process, basically" (Interview, 2004). Some A.C.T. company members are also consulted about which plays and roles they would like to do (Guthmann 2004, D1).

Sometimes, Perloff also hires performers outside the company. When casting, Perloff looks for certain characteristics in actors that will challenge her as a director. She states,

> I look for actors who really love language and really know how to handle language. I always find that if you find an actor who's funny—who has a great sense of humor—they can almost always do anything else. I think that's the hardest thing, really. And I love actors who are excited about process. You know I'm a very, very process-oriented director. I really love the rehearsal process. I love walking in every day and not knowing exactly what's going to happen next. I do best with actors who are game for that, who really enjoy the process of exploration, who are willing to rethink and start over every day and not know everything right up front. That really appeals to me. I love very . . . fierce, strong-minded people. I tend to work with actors that other people think are difficult . . . very demanding, very passionate, very committed people for whom it's more than just a job. I sort of do best with actors like that. (Interview, 2004)

Rehearsals usually last from four to five weeks. Perloff describes the process as a give-and-take between her and the actors, saying, "I always walk in knowing the landscape of the play. . . . I expect actors to bring a lot to the table. Ultimately, it's not a democracy, and I have to shape it the way that I want to shape it. But really good actors can surprise you all the time. So I really love to stay open to that. . . . I expect people to make strong choices, and then I expect them to be willing to go and try something else. In that sense, it's very process-oriented. I don't come in with a game plan and say, 'This is the way it's going to look.' If it's a very complicated play, I may have physically sculpted it out in my mind, so that I know where it's going to live. But sometimes, things really change and surprise you" (Interview, 2004).

Perloff likes to use music early in rehearsals. She also likes to involve designers and writers in rehearsals to hear their ideas. She describes the process of working with designer Annie Smart on *A Doll's House*:

> I had said to her, "I want the whole space to be Nora's space. I want it to be absolutely luscious. . . . I don't want you to know that it's going to be a prison." It's usually done very mahogany and very dark. I said, "I don't want it to be like that at all. I want it to be absolutely delicious. The first act, I want it to be pink and beautiful. I want you to just feel like you want to move in there. And then slowly Nora wakes up to it." And Annie came back and said, "You know I sort of see Nora as being like the chocolate in the little Godiva chocolate . . . wrapping paper." And that's what it ended up looking like! It was absolutely fantastic! But it just came from one idea. And that's when directing is such a joy and such a pleasure. . . . I see things

in my own mind. . . . But, what's really great is handing it to somebody else, and they'll say, "This is what I see." (Interview, 2004)

Because she is also a writer, Perloff honors the playwright and does not change words without collaborating with the writer. She reasons, "You have to assume that they have thought with enormous care about every word in the play, and that it's up to you to make those words really sing and not to change them just to change them" (Interview, 2004). Perloff, however, works with writers in rehearsal to improve the script. She says, "Tom Stoppard has rewritten a lot of stuff for us. As he always says, 'It's an experiential art form. If it doesn't work, fix it.' To me that's the greatest thing about theatre. It's just endless problem solving. Nothing's ever written in stone" (Interview, 2004).

In the case of Stoppard's *The Invention of Love*, Perloff, Stoppard, and the performers spent ten days at a table going over the play line by line. However, the amount of table work that Perloff does on a play varies. She explains, "When you've worked with really good actors, then you know what they're capable of. They can do a lot of that table work themselves. So, sometimes I spend . . . a lot of time at a table if it's really difficult material that needs it. And sometimes I just try to dive in and start to really let the relationship pop sooner, because it's so much of how to find a play. It's how it lives in the bodies of a group of people. There are things that you simply can't tell sitting at a table" (Interview, 2004). Once the performers are up on their feet, Perloff works with a movement specialist and may use games and improvisations during rehearsals to make the process fun.

Perloff believes that the audience is the final collaborator in theatre. She states, "I love audiences. I never denigrate our audience. . . . They tell you so much, and so that's also a big part of the collaboration" (Interview, 2004).

Because she loves collaboration so much, Perloff does not like to direct her own plays. She explains, "I love being in the room with other exciting people and seeing what's going to happen. So to me, if you direct your own material, you're minus one collaborator really. And I love seeing what other people will do with something that I've written" (Interview, 2004).

Perloff has also directed opera, including the 1993 world premiere of *The Cave* by Steve Reich and Beryl Korot at the Vienna Festival and at New York City's Brooklyn Academy of Music. In addition to directing, Perloff taught at New York City's Lincoln Center Institute from 1983 until 1986, was an adjunct professor at New York University for the Dramatic Writing Program from 1987 until 1992, and has taught at A.C.T. She has delivered lectures at universities and organizations, served on advisory committees for numerous organizations, published many articles, and has authored six plays. In addition to the awards already mentioned, Perloff's many honors include the Theater

Conference Award in 1987, the Obie Award for Artistic Excellence/CSC Repertory in 1988, the Koret Israel Prize in 1994, and the Jujamcyn Award to A.C.T. for Creative Contribution to the Field in 1997. She was also awarded the Citation of Honor from the League of Professional Theater Women in New York.

With a career that encompasses management, writing, and directing, Perloff's opportunities for creativity are numerous. Reflecting on her position as a director in the theatre, Perloff says, "In the end the only thing that counts is the truthfulness of what you put onstage" (Winn 1994, 19).

Sources

Blowen, Michael. 2000. "There's Still Something About 'Mary Stuart' One Detail at a Time: The Huntington Takes on the Rich History of a Classic Story." *Boston Globe*, 12 Mar., N1.

Choate, Emily Teresa. "The Harridan, the Whore, and the Hausfrau: The Changing Faces of the Female in Stagings of Sophocles' 'Electra' in Twentieth-Century America." Ph.D. diss., University of California, Los Angeles.

Drake, Sylvie. 1990. "Taper's Visions Makes Connections." *Los Angeles Times*, 15 Mar., 1.

Guthmann, Edward. 2004. "Augesen is Foundation of 'A Doll's House.'" *San Francisco Chronicle*, 20 Jan., D1.

Hartigan, Patti. 1998. "Greek Tragedy as Current as Today's News." *Boston Globe*, 14 Aug., C1.

Hurwitt, Robert. 2004a. "ACT Draws Out Sexual Politics in 'Doll's House.'" Rev. of *A Doll's House*, by Henrik Ibsen. *San Francisco Chronicle*, 16 Jan., D2.

———. 2004b. "Dukakis Portrays Courageous 'Mother.'" Rev. of *A Mother*, by Constance Congdon; based on the play *Vassa Zheleznova*, by Maxim Gorky. *San Francisco Chronicle*, 21 May, E1.

———. 2004c. "Sharp Staging Keeps Stoppard Play 'Real.'" Rev. of *The Real Thing*, by Tom Stoppard. *San Francisco Chronicle*, 29 Oct., E6.

Lehman, Jon. 2000. "Finding the Passion in a Conflict of Queens." Rev. of *Mary Stewart*, by Friedrich Schiller. *(Boston) Patriot Ledger*, 18 Mar., 39.

Perloff, Carey. 2004. Telephone interview with Wendy Vierow. 4 Aug.

Seigel, Ed. 2000. "A Vigorous Modernist Take on 'Mary Stuart.'" Rev. of *Mary Stuart*, by Friedrich Schiller. *Boston Globe*, 17 Mar., C1.

Winn, Steven. 1991. "New Artistic Director at ACT." *San Francisco Chronicle*, 20 Nov., E1.

———. 1993. "Stage Candidate: Win Some, Lose Some." *San Francisco Chronicle*, 3 Jan., 25.

———. 1994. "Perloff's Midseason Balancing Act: ACT Director Juggles Budget Crisis, Ponders a Yerba Buena Cent." *San Francisco Chronicle*, 13 Feb., 19.

Representative Directing Credits

Off and Off-Off Broadway:

> *The Silver Tassie* (1982), *Candy and Shelley Go to the Desert* (1984), *Hearts on Fire* (1984), Young Playwrights Festival (three short plays, 1985), *Leverage* (1985), *Cheapside* (1986), *Skin of Our Teeth* (1986), *St. Joan of the Stockyards* (1986), *E & O Line* (1987), *Electra* (1987), *The Birthday Party* (1988, 1989), *Phaedra Britannica* (1988), *Yesterday's People* (1988), *Mountain Language* (1989), *Don Juan of Seville* (1989), *Happy Days* (1990), *The Tower of Evil* (1990), *Bon Appetit!* (1991), *The Resistible Rise of Arturo Ui* (1991), *Swadosized* (1991), *Candide* (1992), *Creditors* (1992), *Shakuntala* (1992), *Hilda* (2005)

Regional Theatre:

> *Greek* (Associate Director—1982), *Gunplay* (1983), *The Man Who Could See Through Time* (1984), *Cheapside* (1985), *The Collection* (1990), *Happy Days* (1990), *Creditors* (1992), *Bon Appetit!* (1993), *Antigone* (1993), *Uncle Vanya* (1994), *Home* (1994), *Arcadia* (1995), *Hecuba* (1995, 1998), *The Rose Tattoo* (1996), *The Tempest* (1996), *Singer's Boy* (1997), *Iphegenie en Tauride* (1998), *Mary Stuart* (1998, 2000), *Old Times* (1998), *Threepenny Opera* (1998, 1999), *The Difficulty of Crossing a Field* (1999), *Indian Ink* (1999), *Invention of Love* (2000), *The Misanthrope* (2000), *Celebration* (2001), *Enrico IV* (2001), *No for an Answer* (2001), *The Room* (2001), *The Difficulty of Crossing a Field* (2002), *For the Pleasure of Seeing Her Again* (2002), *Night and Day* (2002), *The Colossus of Rhodes* (2003), *Happy End* (2003), *The Three Sisters* (2003), *Waiting for Godot* (2003), *A Doll's House* (2004), *A Mother* (2004), *The Real Thing* (2004), *A Christmas Carol* (2005), *Hilda* (2005), *The Voysey Inheritance* (2005), *Happy End* (2006)

International Theatre:

> *The Bed Bug* (1981), *Satyricon: A Grotesque Farce in Seven Courses* (1981), *Second Lady* (1983)

Perry, Antoinette

Born to a wealthy family on June 27, 1888, in Denver, Colorado, Antoinette Perry was a performer, producer, and director of Broadway plays. Known as Tony to her theatre friends, she was the person for whom the Tony Awards were named in 1947.

Perry attended Miss Wolcott's School in Denver and Miss Ely's School in New York City. During the summers she often traveled with her aunt and uncle, who were performers. She first performed at the age of four for her mother, and by the age of six considered herself an actor. At age nine, she had a theatre in her backyard. There, she wrote, produced, and directed her own productions, making sure friends memorized their lines. At the age of fifteen, Perry acted during the summer in a stock company, which also employed her aunt, at Lake Minnequa Theater in Pueblo, Colorado. In the fall she went on tour with her uncle's theatre company.

In 1905 Perry made her professional acting debut in Frank Wyatt's *Mrs. Temple's Telegram* at Chicago's Powers Theatre. She soon became a successful performer on Broadway, but retired in 1909 to lead the life of a socialite and to raise a family after marrying Frank Frueauff, who discouraged her life in theatre. During this time Perry participated in at least one charity production ("Theater," 1935, n.p.). According to *Playbill,* she was also an "angel" for producer and director Brock Pemberton's 1920 production of the Pulitzer Prize-winning *Miss Lulu Bett,* by Zona Gale (Nassour 1998). However, most sources, including Pemberton, claim that Perry first met Pemberton in 1921 at a concert in Carnegie Hall, after which she took him home to meet her husband. Their meeting led to a long friendship and productive business relationship in the theatre.

Two years after her husband's death in 1922, Perry returned to the theatre using her maiden name. She performed in the 1924 Pemberton production of Gale's *Mr. Pitt* on Broadway. She continued to act in plays produced by Pemberton and others before turning to directing. Her last acting role was as Clytemnestra in Margaret Anglin's Broadway production of Sophocles's *Electra* in 1927. Perry's daughter, Margaret, explained Perry's decision to stop performing, saying, "Mother came to a decision to leave acting. The effects of a stroke [in 1918] had taken a toll. Mother was no longer the beauty . . . at the prime of her acting career and her interests had changed" (Nassour 1997).

Inspired by playwright and director Rachel Crothers, Perry decided to direct (Nassour 2000). She began her directing career by co-directing numerous productions with Pemberton, who also produced them. In 1928 Perry made her directing debut with the Broadway production of *Goin' Home,* which she co-directed with Pemberton. The play, by Ranson Ridenout, was about interracial marriage. The same year Perry and Pemberton co-directed Paul Osborn's *Hotbed* on Broadway.

The next year Perry co-directed Preston Sturges's *Strictly Dishonorable* with Pemberton, this time creating a Broadway hit. When rehearsing the play, pace was important to Perry. *Variety* recounts, "[A] small green lamp was placed in the footlight trough, Miss Perry telling the actors that if the light was turned on they would know the pace was wrong. She sat in the balcony with an electric light button in her hand at the premiere, but never did flash the lamp" ("Antoinette Perry Dies," 1946, n.p.). Produced by Pemberton, *Strictly Dishonorable* featured Perry's daughter, Margaret, who replaced the star when she came down with measles. The play, which focused on prohibition and virtue, received favorable reviews and brought Perry into the spotlight as a director. J. Brooks Atkinson of the *New York Times* wrote, "Imaginative direction by Brock Pemberton and Antoinette Perry keeps the performance as spontaneous as the play" (1929, X1). One critic praised Perry "for doing a man's job" (Nassour 1998).

In 1931 Perry was the sole director of Katherine Roberts's comedy *Divorce Me Dear,* which was not produced by Pemberton. As the title indicates, the play concerned a woman contemplating divorce. The *New York Times* review was not positive about the play, but noted that the producer, Mr. Biddle, did a good casting job and "he has obtained Antoinette Perry to perform what miracles of direction she is able to accomplish" (J.B. 1931, 29).

Perry and Pemberton continued to co-direct Broadway plays, which he produced, including Valentine Davies's *Three Times the Hour* in 1931 and Hawthorne Hursts's *Christopher Comes Across* in 1932. The last play that they co-directed together proved to be a Broadway hit. In 1934, they co-directed Pemberton's production of Lawrence Riley's *Personal Appearance.* The comedy, which focused on a movie star who shakes things up in a small town, was later made into a film by Mae West called *Go West Young Man.* In his review of the play, Atkinson wrote, "Mr. Riley, Mr. Pemberton, Antoinette Perry and a jaunty band of actors have conspired to make the current cartoon the first of the knockout satires of the season" (1934, 26).

In 1935 Perry began directing without Pemberton. She achieved moderate success with her direction of Frank Wead's *Ceiling Zero,* produced on Broadway by Pemberton and featuring her daughter, Margaret. The play was an adventure story set during World War I. In his mixed review, Atkinson wrote, "The pace is swift. The tone is hearty. The suspense and horror are artfully overwhelming" (1935, 26). An article in the *New York Sun* noted, "One minor point in the acting of 'Ceiling Zero' had been pilloried by several critics on the grounds that it had been done by a woman director, and Miss Perry was so gleeful when she found the same bit of action in another Broadway play which was done entirely by a man" ("Theatre," 1935, n.p.).

Perry staged three Pemberton productions on Broadway in 1937: Mary Chase's *Now You've Done It,* Warren Lewis E. Lawes and Jonathan Finn's *Chalked Out,* and Walter Charles Roberts's *Red Harvest.* To accomplish this daunting task, Perry alternated rehearsals of all three casts. The plays, however, all had short runs in the end.

In 1938 Perry directed Maxwell Selser's comedy *Eye on the Sparrow,* which was produced by Giruan Higginson. Later that year, she directed Pemberton's Broadway production of Clare Boothe Luce's *Kiss the Boys Goodbye,* which had a long and successful run. The comedy was a spoof of the movie industry's search for a leading actress to play Scarlett O'Hara in the film version of Margaret Mitchell's novel *Gone with the Wind.* Performer Benay Venuta appeared in *Kiss the Boys Goodbye* and said she learned about acting technique from Perry, who discouraged broad performances. Venuta said, "She told me, 'Don't go for every laugh. It's better to ride over the little laughs and go for the big laugh'" (Nassour 1997). In his review of the play, Atkinson wrote, "Brock Pemberton, as producer, and Antoinette Perry, as director, have hired some good actors and set them talking fast. The pace is terrific; If you close your eyes for a split second, you will miss the seduction scene and the shooting" (1938, 30).

Although Perry's lively pace helped many productions to become successful, they also caused others to falter. In 1940 Perry again directed three Pemberton productions on Broadway—perhaps winding up the pace too much. *Glamour Preferred,* by Florence Ryerson and Colin Clement, was one of many plays about Hollywood presented that season. Atkinson wrote, "Antoinette Perry's direction is frantic, too. The actors can hardly get on and off the stage swiftly enough and they hardly have time enough to speak their lines. It would take a sorcerer's apprentice to define a part in circumstances like that" (1940a, 19). Like *Glamour Preferred,* John Walter Kelly's *Out from Under* was presented at top speed. Richard Lockridge of the *New York Sun* noted, "Miss Antoinette Perry's direction keeps everybody hurrying, and there does not seem to be a single good reason why" (1940, 315). Both *Glamour Preferred* and *Out from Under* closed in less than two weeks. Perry's direction that year of the comedy *Lady in Waiting,* based on Margery Sharp's novel *The Nutmeg Tree,* fared slightly better, closing after eighty-seven performances.

Perry had a better year in 1941 with her direction of Parker W. Fennelly's madcap mystery, *Cuckoos on the Hearth.* Pemberton's Broadway production received good reviews. John Mason Brown of the *New York World-Telegram* wrote, "Antoinette Perry has directed this deliberate potpourri with unction" (1941, 305).

The following year, Perry directed another Pemberton production, which went on to become a Broadway hit. Josephine Bentham and Herschel Williams's *Janie* was a comedy about a teenager whose life is changed during war years. This time, Perry's use of quick pace aided the production. Wilella Waldorf of the *New York Post* wrote, "Antoinette Perry's smooth direction keeps it flowing along just the proper pace" (1942, 244). Howard Barnes of the *New*

York Herald Tribune also noted the pace, stating, "Antoinette Perry has used all her guile to keep the comedy spinning at top speed" (1942, 245). In addition, John Anderson of the *New York Journal-American* observed, "With her usual talent for comic detail Miss Perry had directed it to get the most out of the rattlepated scenes of confusion and running around" (1942, 245).

In 1943 Perry directed the Pemberton production of Rose Simon Kohn's *Pillar to Post* with less success, closing after thirty-one performances on Broadway. However, the following year, Perry directed her longest running Broadway hit, Mary Chase's *Harvey*. Produced by Pemberton, the play centered on a drinking man who saw a large rabbit that was invisible to others. In his review of the production, Barnes wrote, "Miss Perry has staged the show for laughter, and she should have, but she has not failed to underline it with considerable profundity. Harvey is a Pooka, a large animal spirit, originating in Celtic folklore. 'Harvey' is a full-bodied and irresistible comedy, which no theater-lover can afford to miss" (1944, 95). Harvey ran for 1,775 performances on Broadway—an extremely long run for a straight play.

Perry's success as a director for more than sixteen years on Broadway was partly due to her ability to apply her craft to any play she was assigned to direct. To select a play, Perry first read through piles of original scripts. She then gave the ones she liked best to Pemberton, who made the final decision as to which one she should direct. If the script needed improvement, Perry usually worked with the writer, as she did with Mary Chase on *Harvey* (Gustaitis 1997, 19). In some cases, Perry would even receive a writing credit. For example, the *New York Times* listed writing credits to Margery Sharp, Brock Pemberton, and Antoinette Perry for 1940's Broadway production of *Lady in Waiting* (Atkinson 1940b, 27). Sometimes, the critics suspected rewriting even if Perry and Pemberton were not credited. In one such case, Atkinson suspected that the two touched up the script of *Personal Appearance* because of its quick-paced dialogue (1934, 26).

Plays were cast primarily by Pemberton, although Perry helped with casting in difficult situations. Once the plays were cast, Perry directed them with little interference. Pemberton indicated why he let Perry take over the direction of his productions. He explained, "I was a lazy director. I'd let the actors do what they pleased. . . . It never seemed to work right. She does in direction what I'd like to do if I were smart enough. Trouble is she wants perfection before we start. I overlook many things—hoping they will come out all right. I don't have a mind for detail at all. I can't possibly do the things she attempts—and succeeds at" (Arnold 1938, n.p.).

Perry prepared in detail for rehearsals. First, she analyzed scripts to find the author's intent. She noted, "I see the whole thing from the beginning. . . .

I don't read words. I see scenes as I go through a script. I see every actor on the stage—and I see every gesture made by every actor. I know how I want a play done before I start rehearsals" (Arnold 1938, n.p.). Pemberton believed that Perry's perfectionism lead to procrastination at times. He said, "She'll try to stall off the beginning of rehearsals. She'll say, 'I'm not ready to start. Let's wait another week.' If I left it to her we'd never get going. . . . But once she starts, she's the finest director I've ever known" (n.p.).

Elliot Arnold of the *New York World-Telegram* described Perry in rehearsal, writing, "[W]hen the rehearsals start, Miss Perry is on the stage, everywhere. She darts from actor to actor, directing the smallest gesture, demanding the exact inflections. Every line and movement is detailed." He quoted Pemberton who said that once Perry began to direct, "I daren't open my mouth. . . . I might make a small suggestion . . . that a chair ought to be here instead of there. But nothing else" (1938, n.p.).

Perry sometimes cut scripts during rehearsal. Venuta discussed working with Perry on *Kiss the Boys Goodbye*. She says, "She'd have us learn pages and pages of dialogue, then say, 'I'm cutting this, this, and this.' We asked why. 'Now you know what's essential,' she replied" (Nassour 2000).

Perry said that her goal in directing was to realize each play to its fullest extent. She stated, "To my way of thinking, the important thing is to make each play that you do as beautiful as possible—and let each play take care of itself. . . . After all, each play that one does is a unit in itself. The director has to form the whole thing with no other thought than that of the completed job. He has to think in terms of architecture, which is movement—of ballet, of music, of emphasis" (Crowther 1937, XI-2). Perry explained further, noting, "A good director should work so smoothly; should do the job of producing so well; that the audience doesn't realize there has been any coordinator between the author and the actors" ("Theatre," 1935, n.p.).

Perry believed that diction was of primary importance for performers. She said, "What disqualifies young aspirants for the stage most often is their inability to speak with as fine a diction and pronunciation as the theatre requires" (Gustaitis 1997, 18). A performer in the beginning of her career, Perry had much respect for actors. Helen Hayes said of her, "She was an easy director to work with; she didn't impose her will on actors" (Morehouse 1991, 36). Perry explained her thoughts about working with performers, saying, "There is nothing in the world so damaging for a director to do as bawl an actor out. . . . [T]hey are people, after all, whose self-esteem is most sensitive to criticism. . . . I don't think anybody outside the theatre realizes how carefully actors analyze their lines. They may not be right everytime—but they try with intense sincerity" (Crowther 1937, X2).

After her plays opened, Perry attended three performances a week to check the tempo. Perry's productions were known for their quick pace and attention to detail, even in minor roles.

In addition to her work as a director, Perry was also known for her work in theatrical organizations. Pemberton wrote of Perry, "Probably a third of her life was given to our work, the other two-thirds to helping people individually or through organizations she headed" (1946, 39). Among the organizations that she assisted were American Theatre Council's Apprentice Theatre, Actors' Equity's Experimental Theatre, Actors' Fund of America, the Stage Relief Fund, and the Actors' Thrift Shop. Perry helped to found the American Theatre Wing (ATW) in 1940 and staged Rudolf Besier's *The Barretts of Wimpole Street* for ATW in a European production for Allied military audiences. She received a gold cross from producer, composer, writer, and director John Golden for her work of auditioning some one thousand theatre applicants for the Apprentice Theatre in 1939.

Perry died on June 28, 1946, in New York City. One year after her death, the Antoinette Perry Awards, or Tony Awards, were established by ATW for excellence in theatre. In 2004 she was inducted into the Colorado Women's Hall of Fame.

After her death, Pemberton wrote of Perry, "She could sing, she could play the piano, she was a beautiful actress, she was one of the finest directors the American theatre has produced, she could write, she could give" (1946, 39). The critic Burns Mantle called her theatre's "most active and most admired worker" (Morehouse 1991, 38).

Sources

Anderson, John. 1942. "'Janie' New Comedy at the Henry Miller." Rev. of *Janie*, by Herschel Williams and Josephine Betham. *New York Journal-American*, 11 Sept. Rpt. *Critics' Theatre Reviews* 3 (20) (14 Sept.): 245.

"Antoinette Perry Dies at 58 of Heart Attack; Star Stage Director." 1946. *Variety*, 3 July, n.p. Billy Rose Theatre Collection, clippings. New York Public Library for the Performing Arts.

"Antoinette Perry Directed Hit Plays." 1946. *New York Times*, 29 June, 19.

Arnold, Elliot. 1938. "Two Heads Are Better." *New York World-Telegram*, 11 Nov., n.p. Billy Rose Theatre Collection, clippings. New York Public Library for the Performing Arts.

Atkinson, J. Brooks. 1929. "Considerably Better Than Life." Rev. of *Strictly Dishonorable*, by Preston Sturges. *New York Times*, 29 Sept., XI.

———. 1934. "Satire of the Hollywood Dementia in 'Personal Appearance' by Lawrence Riley." Rev. of *Personal Appearance*, by Lawrence Riley. *New York Times*, 18 Oct, 26.

———. 1935. "'Ceiling Zero,' Being Frank Wead's Melodrama About Aviation." Rev. of *Ceiling Zero*, by Frank Wead. *New York Times*, 11 Apr., 26.

———. 1938. "Opening of 'Kiss the Boys Goodbye' by the Author of "'The Women.'" Rev. of *Kiss the Boys Goodbye*, by Clare Boothe. *New York Times*, 29 Sept., 30.

———. 1940a. "Hollywood Is Selected as the Topic of a Satirical Comedy Entitled 'Glamour Preferred.'" Rev. of *Glamour Preferred*, by Florence Ryerson and Colin Clements. *New York Times*, 16 Nov., 19.

———. 1940b. "Gladys George Returns in Margery Sharp's First Theatre Work, 'Lady in Waiting.'" Rev. of *Lady in Waiting*, by Margery Sharp, Brock Pemberton, and Antoinette Perry, derived from Miss Sharp's novel. *New York Times*, 28 Mar., 27.

Barnes, Howard. 1942. "Juniors Meet the Army." *New York Herald Tribune*, 11 Sept. Rev. of *Janie*, by Herschel Williams and Josephine Bentham. Rpt. *Critics' Theatre Reviews* 3 (20) (14 Sept.): 245.

———. 1944. "Fay in Wonderland." Rev. of *Harvey*, by Mary Chase. *New York Herald Tribune*, 2 Nov. Rpt. *Theatre Critics' Reviews* 5 (19) (13 Nov.): 95.

Brown, John Mason. 1941. "Killers Are on the Loose in Cuckoos on the Hearth." Rev. of *Cuckoos on the Hearth*, by Parker W. Fennelly. *New York World-Telegram*, 17 Sept. Rpt. *Critics' Theatre Reviews* 2 (13) (22 Sept.): 305.

Crowther, Bosley. 1937. "The Lady in the Case." *New York Times*, 14 Mar., X1–2.

Gustaitis, Joseph. 1997. "The Woman Behind the Tony." *American History* 32 (1) (Mar./Apr.): 16–21.

J. B. 1931. "Matrimonial Difficulty." Rev. of *Divorce Me Dear*, by Katherine Roberts. *New York Times*, 7 Oct., 29.

Keller, Allan. n.d. "Miss Perry Feels Real Only in World of Make-Believe." n.p. Billy Rose Theatre Collection, clippings. New York Public Library for the Performing Arts.

Lockridge, Richard. 1940. "'Out from Under,' a Small Spring Farce, Opens at the Biltmore." Rev. of *Out from Under*, by John Walter Kelly. *New York Sun*, 6 May. Rpt. *Critics' Theatre Reviews* 1 (1) (27 May): 315.

Morehouse, Rebecca. 1991. "Tony's Namesake: Antoinette ('Tony') Perry . . . As They Remember Her." *Playbill* 91 (5) (May): 36–38.

Nassour, Ellis. 1997. "Friend and Daughter Recall 'Tony' Perry, the Woman." *Playbill*, 27 May. http://www.playbill.com/news/article/34089.html (accessed 23 Apr. 2004).

———. 1998. "Remembering Tony Namesake Antoinette Perry." *Playbill*, 4 June. http://www.playbill.com/news/article/39338.html (accessed 23 Apr. 2004).

———. 2000. "Antoinette Perry Makes a Name: The Tony Awards Memorialize Tony." http://www.theatermania.com/news/feature/index.cfm?story=752&cid=1 (accessed 1 Feb. 2003).

Pemberton, Brock. 1929. "This Business of Getting a Hit." *New York Times,* 19 Sept., X2.

———. 1946. "Memories of Antoinette Perry." *New York Times,* 7 July, 39.

"Theater Credo of Miss Perry." 1935. *New York Sun,* 1 May, n.p. Billy Rose Theatre Collection, clippings. New York Public Library for the Performing Arts.

Trauth, Suzanne. 1989. "Perry, Antoinette." In *Notable Women in the American Theatre: A Biographical Dictionary,* ed. Alice M. Robinson, Vera Mowry Roberts, and Milly S. Barranger, 724–26. Westport, Conn.: Greenwood.

Waldorf, Wilella. 1942. "'Janie' a Merry Comedy of Flaming Youth, 1942 Brand." Rev. of *Janie,* by Herschell Williams and Josephine Bentham. *New York Post,* 11 Sept. Rpt. *Critics' Theatre Reviews* 3 (20) (14 Sept.): 244.

Watt, Eva Hodges. 1996. "In Search of Antoinette Perry." *Theater Week* (3 June): 42–52.

Representative Directing Credits[1]

Broadway:

Goin' Home (co-directed with Brock Pemberton—1928), *Hotbed* (co-directed with Brock Pemberton—1928), *Strictly Dishonorable* (co-directed with Brock Pemberton—1929), *Divorce Me Dear* (1931), *Three Times the Hour* (co-directed with Brock Pemberton—1931), *Christopher Columbus Comes Across* (co-directed with Brock Pemberton—1932), *Personal Appearance* (co-directed with Brock Pemberton—1934), *Ceiling Zero* (1935), *Chalked Out* (1937), *Now You've Done It* (1937), *Red Harvest* (1937), *Eye on the Sparrow* (1938), *Kiss the Boys Goodbye* (1938), *Lady in Waiting* (1940), *Out from Under* (1940), *Glamour Preferred* (1940), *Cuckoos on the Hearth* (1942), *Janie* (1942), *Pillar to Post* (1943), *Harvey* (1944)

Regional Theatre:

Kiss the Boys Goodbye (?), *The Noble Prize* (1933)

Tours:[2]

Strictly Dishonorable (?)

International Theatre:

The Barretts of Wimpole Street (1944, 1945), *Strictly Dishonorable* (?)

Notes

1. There are a number of Pemberton productions, which Perry probably directed, that have no directing credits. We have only included the shows in which she receives a credit.

2. Although Broadway tours of Perry's shows occurred, dates could not be located.

Perry, Shauneille

Born July 26, 1929, in Chicago, Shauneille Perry is the first cousin to playwright Lorraine Hansberry and, like her cousin, chose a life in the theatre. Perry—a performer, director, playwright, and educator—became one of the first major African American women directors in New York City in the 1960s. During her four decades in the theatre she has directed more than one hundred plays, including many for the New Federal Theatre at the Henry Street Settlement on Manhattan's Lower East Side. She has won numerous awards, including The Lloyd Richards Award for Directing.

Growing up in Chicago, Perry discovered she had an innate need to imitate people as well as an impulse to write. She went to Howard University in Washington, D.C., to become a journalist, but ended up studying drama instead. Perry became a member of the Howard Players, performing with them on tour in Scandinavia and Germany. After earning her B.A. in drama at Howard in 1950 and working in African American summer stock theatres, Perry earned her M.F.A. in directing at the Goodman School of Drama at the Art Institute of Chicago in 1952. She continued her studies on a Fulbright scholarship to the Royal Academy of Dramatic Arts (RADA) in London, but was disenchanted with their curriculum, which included elementary work she had already mastered. She transferred to the London Academy of Music and Dramatic Arts (LAMDA), where she was pleased with their attention to foreign students who had classical training.

When Perry returned from England, she moved to Chicago to be with her ailing mother, and she taught and directed at the Goodman School in addition to writing for the *Chicago Defender*, an African American newspaper. This was just the beginning of her long career as an educator, for eventually Perry taught theatre, speech, and black studies at numerous colleges and universities.

In the late 1950s, Perry won a trip to Paris through an essay contest. While overseas she performed in Richard Wright's adaptation of a French play, *Papa Bon Homme* (translated to *Daddy Goodness*) for the American Theatre in Paris. In 1960 Perry moved to New York City to become an actor. She worked fairly steadily in the early 1960s, but was cast in demeaning roles such as slaves and servants. Unwilling to continue as a performer, she resumed her teaching career which included directing. Her first opportunity to direct a professional company arose when Douglas Turner Ward of New York City's Negro Ensemble Company called her to direct a workshop production in 1969. At that point she was in the midst of raising a family, but accepted the position. The workshop production, *The Mau Mau Room,* was by J. E. Franklin, a woman whose plays she would go on to direct many times in her career.

The year 1971 became Perry's turning point as a professional director. Ward invited her back to direct Carlton and Barbara Molette's *Rosalee Pritchett,* and subsequently Franklin suggested Perry direct her play, *Black Girl,* that same year at the New Federal Theatre. *Black Girl* was well received and transferred Off Broadway to the Theatre De Lys, where it exceeded 230 performances. The episodic story told of a black girl's struggles growing up in a matriarchal family in Texas. Clive Barnes of the *New York Times* wrote that the coming of age story had an "air of honesty." He praised the acting, and added, "Shauneille Perry's direction stressed the play's episodic nature and domestic tone" (1971a, 49). Later that year Perry added a third production on her directing resume, *The Sty of the Blind Pig,* produced by the Negro Ensemble Company at St. Marks Playhouse in Greenwich Village. Set in Chicago in the 1950s, Phillip Hayes Dean's play revolves around a blind street singer from the south who comes to Chicago to look for a woman named Grace. The symbolism and the tone of the play are more important than the literal story, however. Barnes interpreted, "Here is a picture of America at a time of enormous change and the way those changes affected black America." He congratulated the set designer on evoking the right air of sadness into the environment and wrote, "Shauneille Perry's staging had the same subdued feeling to it that completely characterized the pain. Lines and feelings faded away as in Chekhov" (1971b, 21).

Perry continued to collect positive reviews and build her directing resume throughout the 1970s. In 1972 she directed *Jamimma* at the New Federal Theatre. Critic Howard Thompson of the *New York Times* described Martie Evans-Charles's play as "a mousehole look at life in a Harlem apartment house." He praised the cast and characterization, adding, "Individually and collectively, under Shauneille Perry's direction, a trim cast vivifies and deepens the characters" (1972, 17). Perry directed a gospel-based bible musical in 1974 called *Prodigal Sister.* Book and lyrics were by Franklin, with music and lyrics by Micki Grant, who was already known for her successful collaboration with director Vinnette Carroll on *Don't Bother Me, I Can't Cope.* Barnes applauded the simplicity of the staging and of the piece itself, writing, "Its [sic] good nature and fervor seems to stand somewhere between a black block party and a revival meeting. There is a simple joyousness here that is thoroughly engaging" (1974, 30).

In 1976 Perry directed another production for the New Federal Theatre: Don Evan's *Showdown,* an adaptation of Shakespeare's *The Taming of the Shrew* set in a black neighborhood in Philadelphia. Stylistically, the playwright and director stressed broad, stereotypical humor and were rewarded with laughter. Critic Mel Gussow of the *New York Times* was at first annoyed by the style of humor, then realized, "There is an exuberance about the writing, direction and performance that is catching . . . high-spirited, glad-hearted entertainment" (1976, 44).

In the 1980s and 1990s Perry's attention turned toward playwriting, but she often directed what she wrote, and she continued to teach as well. In 1984 she conceived and directed "Celebration" as a black history program in New Rochelle, New York, and in 1985 it became a part of *Jubilee! A Black Theatre Festival*, an annual event sponsored by the American Place Theater in New York City. Critic D. J. R. Bruckner of the *New York Times* wrote, "Shauneille Perry, who has been working in New York theater for 20 years, has woven together all or parts of 17 musical numbers from gospel to 'Purple Rain,' poetry and stories by seven black writers and dialogue of her own into a spirited lesson in history that has the whole theatre jumping" (1985, C22).

In 1999 Perry directed a historic production for the New Federal Theatre: *In Dahomey*, the first musical written and performed by African Americans that originally premiered on Broadway in 1903. Perry herself rewrote the book, deleting what modern audiences would perceive as racial slurs. In the process, she streamlined the plot and added some feminist overtones, but retained the essence of Jesse A. Shipp's characters. The story tells of Dahomian Prince Akanji and his quest to return a royal necklace from his cousin. He hires two detectives in Florida and takes them back to his village, Dahomey, where they are amazed to find people who remind them of friends at home (played by the same actors). Despite the updated plot, the original ragtime music by Will Marion Cook remained intact, and in deference to the historical musical, Perry had the cast sing without amplification. According to one reviewer, "A near-capacity audience enthusiastically greeted the cast at the end of the show" (Lipfert 1999).

At the turn of the twenty-first century, Perry was teaching both theatre and black studies at Lehman College, City University of New York. Her continuing work as a director included a 2002 production of Rudolph Fisher's *The Conjure Man Dies* at Kuntu Repertory Theatre in Pittsburgh. She also continued writing, including her screenplay for *The Old Settler*, broadcast by the Public Broadcasting System in 2002, and *Black Beauties*, performed as a Broadway Cares/Equity Fights AIDS presentation Off Broadway in 2003.

Despite her fairly high profile as an actor, writer, director, and educator, Perry's work in the rehearsal hall is not well-chronicled. In a 1983 interview, Perry reveals her most basic approach to rehearsals: "I believe firmly in rehearsal, rehearsal is what we're doing, not other things. Not improvisation stuff. . . . I don't read very long, around the table. I encourage discussion, but much more work. I believe that discussion can be a means to more discussion and sometimes what we discuss . . . has nothing to do with the work. So I believe in rehearsal" (Hennigan 1983, 152). Perry believes it is the playwright, not the director, who determines the statement of a play, so she is loyal to the author's intent. Her very definition of directing is "being as honest as you can to the playwright." She hastens to add, "If you want absolutes about a play's meaning, see the playwright" (Boehm 1972, 76).

Perry comes into rehearsal with blocking already diagramed, but not in detail. She lets the action of the play dictate the movement, then works with the actor to determine whether the blocking she has envisioned will work. She explains, "When I'm in harmony and I know when I am, then the actor wants to go there. . . . I can sense when an actor is uncomfortable. And I can just say, . . . 'Well, we'll work that out or we'll come back to it, but we don't have to debate it'" (Hennigan 1983, 152–53). Perry works with actors as individuals, taking them aside when needed, and expending the energy to help them find harmony in the role. She also allows the actors to put down the script in their own time, when they are comfortable, out of a concern that they find the rhythm of the play before memorizing their lines.

Perry admits that she will not direct what she finds offensive or antithetical to her political stance. "If I'm responsible for certain imagery for both women and for black people, I'm going to be very careful what comes out," she reasons. Longtime friend and producer Woodie King Jr. comments, "Race pride born out of Africa's contributions to civilization is/was a part of Shauneille Perry's life" (2003, 145). Although much of what Perry has directed professionally has been about the African American experience, she was ready and willing to take on other productions as well. She notes that in educational institutions she directed "everything from Shakespeare to G & S [Gilbert and Sullivan]" and states that she would have accepted similar professional offers, if only they had been made (Tallmer 1971, 15).

Perry's work as a writer and director has earned her four AUDELCO Awards, two Ceba Awards, The Lloyd Richards Award for Directing at the North Carolina Black Theatre Festival, the Black Rose of Excellence from *Encore* Magazine, Distinguished Howard Player and Alumni Awards, and a Lehman Scholar Achievement Award. She has been a pioneering figure in African American theatre and serves as an early role model for those women who have followed.

Sources

Barnes, Clive. 1971a. Rev. of *Black Girl,* by J.E. Franklin. *New York Times,* 17 June, 49.

———. 1971b. Rev. of *The Sty of the Blind Pig,* by Phillip Hayes Dean. *New York Times,* 24 Nov., 21.

———. 1974. Rev. of *Prodigal Sister,* book and lyrics by J.E. Franklin, music and lyrics by Micki Grant. *New York Times,* 26 Nov., 30.

Boehm, Arthur. 1972. "To Shaunee, with Love," *Village Voice,* 27 Apr., 75–76.

Bruckner, D.J.R. 1985. Rev. of *Celebration,* conceived by Shauneille Perry. *New York Times,* 30 May, C22.

Gussow, Mel. 1976. Rev. of *Showdown,* by Don Evans. *New York Times,* 19 Feb., 44.

Hennigan, Shirley. 1983. "The Woman Director in the Contemporary, Professional Theatre." Ph.D. diss. Washington State University.

King, Woodie Jr. 2003. *The Impact of Race: Theatre and Culture.* New York: Applause Books.

Lipfert, David. 1999. Rev. of *In Dahomey,* by Shauneille Perry, inspired by the characters of Jesse A. Shipp, music by Will Marion Cook. CurtainUp. http://www.curtainup.com/indahomey.html (accessed 21 June 2004).

Mapp, Edward. 1990. *Directory of Blacks in the Performing Arts.* 2nd ed. New York: Scarecrow Press.

Public Broadcasting Service (PBS). 2002. *The Old Settler.* http://www.pbs.org/hollywoodpresents/ theoldsettler/prodroles/pr_screenw.html (accessed 16 June 2004).

Tallmer, Jerry. 1971. "Director Shauneille Perry: What We Don't Know Hurts Us." *New York Post,* 4 Dec., 15.

Thompson, Howard. 1972. Rev. of *Jamimma,* by Martie Evans-Charles. *New York Times,* 18 Mar., 17.

Thompson, Kathleen. 1997. "Perry, Shauneille." In *Facts on File: Encyclopedia of Black Women in America,* ed. by Darlene Clark Hines, 174–75. New York: Facts on File.

Representative Directing Credits

Off and Off-Off Broadway:
Rosalee Pritchett (1971), *Black Girl* (1971), *Sty of the Pig* (1971), *Jamimma* (1972), *Ladies in Waiting* (1973), *Prodigal Sister* (1974), *Bayou Legend* (1976), *Gilbeau* (1976), *Showdown* (1976), *Things of the Heart: Marian Anderson's Story* (1981), *Keyboard* (1982), *Who Loves the Dancer* (1982), *On Stiver's Row* (1984), *Celebration* (1985), *Williams and Walker* (1986), *The Balm Yard* (1991), *Looking Back* (1994), *In Dahomey* (1999), *The Conjure Man Dies* (2002), *Paul Robeson* (2005)

Tours:
Black Girl (1972?), *Williams and Walker* (1986?)

International Theatre:
Sty of the Pig (1971?), *On Stiver's Row* (1984?)

Raedler, Dorothy

Born February 24, 1917, in New York City, Dorothy Raedler directed and produced over sixty productions of Gilbert and Sullivan operettas in repertory during the 1950s and '60s, a time when very few women directors were working professionally. Audiences had a hunger for Gilbert and Sullivan, perhaps brought on in part by recent Broadway tours of the famous D'Oyly Carte company, which produced Gilbert and Sullivan's original works in Great Britain. Notably, two British women took the helm of directing the D'Oyly Carte troupe during those tours: Anna Bethnell in the 1947–48 season and Eleanor Evans in the 1950–51 season.

Raedler's interest in theatre was apparent in high school, where she served as the secretary of a playwriting club and participated in the glee club and operettas. It was in high school that she wrote and produced her first musical comedy. While studying biology at Hunter College in New York City, she formed an amateur Gilbert and Sullivan company called the Masque and Lyre Light Opera. Raedler finished her bachelor's degree in 1942 and discovered that the Masque and Lyre, which she had founded on a lark, was becoming a career. Thanks to the growing popularity of Raedler's group, she hired a semi-professional cast and established a permanent repertoire in 1948. Raedler directed and produced their first New York season in the basement of the Jan Hus House on East 74th Street in 1949, performing a repertory of *The Mikado*, *H.M.S. Pinafore*, *The Pirates of Penzance*, *Iolanthe*, and *The Gondoliers*. The Masque and Lyre's new space, repertoire, and cast brought praise from New York critics, boosting the company's reputation further. According to one report, "They became the first 'Off-Broadway' theatrical troupe to operate on a year-around basis in the same theatre for more than three and a half years, with a record run of 575 performances" (*Current* 1954, 526).

With the success of her New York City performances, Raedler traveled to England in 1952 to conduct research on Gilbert and Sullivan and the staging of their operettas. She consulted their original promptbooks, paying careful attention to staging, with the intent of blocking her operettas in a manner similar to the originals. A press release clarifies her intent, stating, "Miss Raedler devised her own staging—guided, of course, by Gilbert's intentions but with a sparkle, gaiety, and spontaneity which is typically American" (Dorfman n.d.). Her idea was to create productions similar to those of the British D'Oyly Carte company, but with a younger company and standard American stage diction.

Upon her return to the United States, Raedler renamed her troupe the American Savoyards in honor of the British home of Gilbert and Sullivan productions: The Savoy. This newly formed company was comprised of young Equity actors. They retained their home base, the Jan Hus House, and established a summer home in Monmouth, Maine, in 1953. Under Raedler's leadership, the American Savoyards prospered. The core group, from the Masque and Lyre days, showed their dedication and talent not only through performance, but also through teaching classes to apprentices and helping out where needed, with costumes, sets, or other needs. "Without the dedication of this close-knit group of people," former company member Elizabeth Johnson wrote, "I doubt very much . . . the American Savoyards could ever have got off the ground" (Correspondence, 2002).

Raedler's group performed at several New York City theatres, including Shakespearwright's Theatre, the New York City Center, the President Theatre, and the Jan Hus House. Between 1952 and 1959 they spent much of their season touring the United States and Canada, with summers remaining at their home base in Maine. When the American Savoyards returned to the Jan Hus House in the winter of 1960, *New York Times* critic Brooks Atkinson welcomed them back in his column, lavishing praise on the company. He noted that when the group first began performing, they had nothing to go on "except enthusiasm, ingenuity and taste." He continued, "The enterprise was good when she (Raedler) began. Now it is about as close to perfection as circumstances permit" (1960b, 14). Raedler's production of *H.M.S. Pinafore* was presented "with humor and respect," and Atkinson singled out Raedler's direction as "impeccable," commenting that although the D'Oyly Carte touring productions had a full orchestra and expensive sets and costumes, "Miss Raedler's band-box company is better than the D'Oyly Carte company has been during one or two invasions when morale was not at its peak. . . . It is always pleasant to have Miss Raedler's modest and enlightened troupe in town. It preserves a dry, humorous decorum that no longer exists in the theatre" (1960a, sec. 2, 1). That season, Raedler announced that their four-week engagement had been extended to twenty-five weeks by popular demand.

Time and time again, critics remarked on Raedler's success as a director. William Bender of the *New York Herald Tribune* wrote of *The Gondoliers,* "[T]here is an abundance of style and energy on the part of all hands which at times even threatens to burst the confines of the theatre. And for all of this credit must go to Miss Raedler" (1963). Several years later, Alan Rich, also of the *Herald Tribune,* wrote, "[A] performance unfolded that for wit, precision and musical quality can challenge any work being done in the Savoy Operas anywhere today. . . . Miss Raedler's ideas on stage direction are a seamless crazy-quilt" (1967).

Although most of Raedler's directing career was spent with the American Savoyards, she occasionally directed elsewhere. In 1958 she directed Off Broadway at the Sullivan Street Playhouse. Three one-act musicals were put into an evening's entertainment called *From Here to There*. The *New York Times* review was unenthusiastic, panning the material. Noting that Raedler's direction of the American Savoyards had made audiences happy in the past, the critic continued, "Miss Raedler does well enough with her present undertaking, but it is not likely that she will make too many happy this time" (Funke 1958, 37). She was a guest director at several theatres, including the Coconut Grove Playhouse in Miami, Carter-Barron Amphitheatre in Washington, D.C., the National Theatre in Washington, D.C., and the Goodspeed Opera House in East Haddam, Connecticut. Raedler also directed a number of operas, including *Cavalleria Rusticana* and *I Pagliacci* at the Lyric in Baltimore, *Carmen* at the Baltimore Civic Opera, and *Madama Butterfly* at the New York City Opera.

In the early days of her troupe, Raedler worked with actors in their twenties. At auditions, she sought singers who could "coordinate the Gilbertian gestures with Sullivan's music" (*Current* 1954, 527). The performers who worked with Raedler remember her as extremely detail-oriented and as tough, but fair with her cast. Performer Arden Anderson-Broecking recalls, "She gave me my first professional job, and she was an excellent director. She was extremely precise in what she wanted, and our chorus work was the cleanest and most precise anyone could ask for. She trained people, actually, and insisted on our having a professional attitude towards our work" (Correspondence, 2002). Simon Sargon, Raedler's music director for one season, and his wife Bonnie Glasgow, a company member for many years, agreed that discipline was one of Raedler's key elements as a director. They described her as "a director of taste and restraint, who would not allow the Savoy style to be hammed up, to become 'campy' or distorted" (Sargon, correspondence, 2002).

Johnson performed with Raedler from 1953 to 1963 and disclosed that Raedler was a micromanager during the design and rehearsal process. Johnson explains, "In her directing she was a purist, a perfectionist, and, I would have to say, a martinet. Although she had highly competent people in charge of the various departments, such as Properties, Costumes, etc. she was never content to relinquish her authority in these areas, but maintained absolute control over all aspects of production. No detail was too trivial to escape her eagle eye" (Correspondence, 2002). Johnson also commented on Raedler's "directorial genius," writing that she had the "uncanny ability to design choreography which not only looked as if it had been created by the composer of the music, but which, although spirited and attractive, was extremely easy for singers to perform" (Correspondence, 2002). Part of her "uncanny ability" with movement may be explained by a colleague who wrote, "Dorothy had learned all of the original Gilbert staging for all of the operettas, and knew the movements for both the actors and singers inside out. She was a superb mime, who could easily demonstrate what she was after in the way of characterization, attitude, movement or line reading" (Sargon, correspondence, 2002).

Johnson noted former cast members state that Raedler was tough on her performers, and that she polished the chorus "with a vengeance." Johnson recalls, "I have seen strong men in tears after some ineptitude they'd committed incurred the sharp edge of Dorothy's tongue. But these militaristic techniques worked—even neophytes to the genre learned to execute the synchronized moves and to speak with a reasonably convincing British accent with the remarkably short rehearsal time available" (Correspondence, 2002). Despite her tough approach, Raedler earned their respect and admiration. Anderson-Broecking wrote that she was difficult and subjective at times, but "absolutely even-handed and fair" (Correspondence, 2002). Johnson described her as an imposing, impressive presence with a keen business acumen. "Though strident to the point of grimness at times," she writes, "she could also display abundant charm and social grace." She goes on to write that Raedler did not exhibit "'theatrical' behaviors, but conducted herself rather more like a CEO of General Motors" (Correspondence, 2002).

Raedler's business sense extended to her mastery of public relations. While still at the Masque and Lyre, Raedler had the company members meet with the audience in the green room of the Jan Hus House after every performance. Theme-oriented refreshments and artwork depicting Gilbert and Sullivan's characters were for sale, adding to the sense of event. When the company spent summers at Monmouth, Maine, at the Gilbert and Sullivan Festival Theatre, Raedler gave strict instructions to the members about their behavior. As "theatre people" from the big city, their decorum was to be beyond reproach. For example, she did not allow them to wear shorts in town. Ingratiating herself and her company one step further, Raedler arranged for company members to perform as soloists at local churches on Sunday mornings, thereby gaining a trusting audience of church-goers who in turn welcomed the company to church suppers and other community events (Johnson, correspondence, 2002).

Raedler also ensured profits by cutting costs where possible and playing small venues. Small choruses and minimal sets were the rule, and musical accompaniment was by organ and piano rather than orchestra. When asked how she could keep the top ticket price under four dollars, Raedler commented, "By cutting costs, and because of a healthy following. We have a 6,000 name mailing list; we get theatre parties and other group business, and many of our customers buy several tickets at a time. When our box office opened this season, the first person on line bought $100 worth of tickets" (Harris n.d.).

The cost cutting helped ensure that attention was paid to the performers and staging, and not to the technical aspects. The reviewers took note.

A promotional flyer for the American Savoyards in 1967 boasts the following quotation from Atkinson: "Simple but cheerful scenery—refined costumes—and impeccable direction by Miss Raedler—these are the chief assets that the American Savoyards bring to the light operas. And the greatest of these is the direction. . . . Miss Raedler has easy access to the genius of the operas. She presents them with humor and respect" (Johnson, correspondence, 2002). Johnson's collection of reviews, pamphlets, and clippings provide material which supports Atkinson's praise. Critics called Raedler's productions "fresh, lively, tasteful, enthusiastic," full of "wit, precision, and musical quality," and said her work stood up to the quality of "Savoy Operas anywhere today" (Johnson, correspondence, 2002).

The combination of Raedler's business acumen, dedicated company, and painstakingly precise direction produced a professional Gilbert and Sullivan company that lasted sixteen years, including regular New York City seasons, tours, and summers in Maine, where reportedly the American Savoyards turned away four hundred audience members at one matinee (*Current* 1954, 527). Anderson-Broecking laments, "So few people remember and appreciate Dorothy, and they have forgotten that the American Savoyards was the only professional Gilbert and Sullivan company in the world except for the D'Oyly Carte" (Correspondence, 2002).

Before her death, Raedler helped establish the St. Croix School of the Arts in the U.S. Virgin Islands, where she spent the last twenty-five years of her life. She served as the associate director of the Virgin Island Council on the Arts and as both director and president of the St. Croix School of the Arts. Over the course of her career she was distinguished with two directing awards: the *Show Business* Award for Best Off-Broadway Director in 1951 and the *Show Business* Award for Best Musical Director in 1954. She was also made an honorary member of the Gilbert and Sullivan Society.

Raedler died of cancer in St. Croix on Dec. 11, 1993, at the age of seventy-six. Although Raedler's work was not limited to Gilbert and Sullivan, her direction of those masterpieces has become her legacy, and rightfully so.

Sources

Anderson-Broecking, Arden. 2002. Correspondence with Anne Fliotsos. 5 Apr.

Atkinson, J. Brooks. 1960a. "American Savoyards." *New York Times,* 7 Feb., sec. 2, 1.

———. 1960b. "American Savoyards at Jan Hus House." *New York Times,* 29 Jan., 14.

Bender, William. 1963. Rev. of *The Gondoliers*, lyrics by William S. Gilbert, music by Arthur S. Sullivan. *New York Herald Tribune*. Quoted in correspondence from Elizabeth Johnson, 8 Apr. 2002.

The Biographical Encyclopedia and Who's Who of the American Theatre. 1966. New York: Heineman, 757.

Cohn, Al. 1967. "If You're a G and S Buff Why She Can't Do Enough." *Newsday*, 1 Feb., n.p. Billy Rose Theatre Collection, clippings. New York Public Library for the Performing Arts.

Current Biography. 1954. New York: H. W. Wilson, 525–27.

Dorfman, Irvin. n.d. "Dorothy Raedler and the American Savoyards." Unpublished press release. Billy Rose Theatre Collection, clippings. New York Public Library for the Performing Arts.

Funke, Lewis. 1958. Rev. of *From Here to There*. *New York Times*, 24 Apr., 37.

Harris, Leonard. n.d. "Miss Raedler's Lot Is Happy with G & S." *New York-World Telegraph and Sun*, n.p. Billy Rose Theatre Collection, clippings. New York Public Library for the Performing Arts.

Johnson, Elizabeth. 2002. Correspondence with Anne Fliotsos. 8 Apr.

Morgenstern, Joe. 1960. "G & S Score Success at the Jan Hus." *New York Herald Tribune*, 3 Apr., n.p. Billy Rose Theatre Collection, clippings. New York Public Library for the Performing Arts.

Raedler, Dorothy. 1959. "A Training School for Singers." *Music Journal* 17 (2): 14, 52, 53.

Rich, Alan. 1967. *New York Herald Tribune*. Quoted in correspondence from Elizabeth Johnson, 8 Apr. 2002.

Sargon, Simon. 2002. Correspondence with Anne Fliotsos. 8 Apr.

Shepard, Richard F. 1964. "R & F Have Another Go at G & S." *New York Times*, 15 Mar., n.p. Billy Rose Theatre Collection, clippings. New York Public Library for the Performing Arts.

Who's Who in the Theatre. 1981. vol. 1. Detroit: Gale, 559.

Representative Directing Credits

Off and Off-Off Broadway:[1]

The Mikado (1949, 1954, 1957, 1960, 1964), *H.M.S. Pinafore* (1949, 1954, 1957, 1960), *The Pirates of Penzance* (1949, 1954, 1957, 1960, 1964), *The Gondoliers* (1949, 1954, 1957, 1960, 1964), *Iolanthe* (1949, 1954, 1960, 1964), *Yeomen of the Guard* (1954, 1957, 1960), *Ruddigore* (1954), *The Sorcerer* (1954), *Utopia, Limited* (1957, 1960), *From Here to There* (1958), *The Grand Duke* (1960), *Princess Ida* (1960), *Patience* (1964)

Tours:

Gilbert and Sullivan repertory (1952–60s) (Tours were in the United States and Canada, with summers spent at Monmouth, Maine; specific dates, titles, and places are unavailable.)

Notes

1. Although the American Savoyards presented a repertory season each year from 1952 to 1968, the information given here reflects only those seasons posted in *Theatre World* or *The Biographical Encyclopedia and Who's Who of American Theatre*.

 # Robinson, Mary B.

Born November 17, 1953, in Schenectady, New York, Mary B. Robinson has become a freelance director of national repute and is the former artistic director at the Philadelphia Drama Guild as well as the former associate artistic director for Hartford Stage in Connecticut. In addition to her career as an award-winning professional director, Robinson has taught and directed at several universities and is the head of directing at Playwrights Horizons Theatre School in New York City.

Raised near Philadelphia, Robinson recalls going to touring productions as a child. She acted in high school plays and was inspired by her high school drama teacher, who became her role model. Robinson considered becoming a teacher, but when barely out of her teens she decided she wanted to run a theatre instead. She directed plays while an undergraduate at Smith College, in Northampton, Massachusetts, where she earned a B.A. in theatre and history in 1975.

After graduation, she started working toward her goal of running a theatre. She interned and assisted at several regional theatres before turning her attention to New York City. As an inroad, Robinson became a script reader for several New York City theatres, at first for no pay. Eventually, she earned her living at it, reading some thirty-five scripts a week. In addition, she started to direct for theatre festivals in order to gain experience and build her resume. She was able to use her contacts with New York literary managers, who were often doubling as casting directors, to help her cast productions and to come see her work. In 1978 she became a member of the Ensemble Studio Theatre in New York City, where she directed. The following year Robinson was hired as the associate literary manager at Circle Repertory Company Off Broadway and also directed at the Hudson Guild in New York City.

Robinson says she was at the right place at the right time when she wrote to Mark Lamos, the artistic director at the Hartford Stage in Connecticut, to inquire about opportunities. Lamos hired her as the company's literary manager and let her direct the lunchtime one-act series and the children's theatre program. In 1982 she co-directed *The Greeks* with Lamos. Based on Greek tragedy, mythology, and history, the set of plays was adapted by John Barton and Kenneth Cavander and performed as a trilogy in a seven-hour performance schedule. Eventually, she was appointed as associate artistic director and had opportunities to direct some challenging plays, including Eugene O'Neill's *Desire Under the Elms* and Constance Congdon's *No Mercy*, as well as a premiere of Mary Gallager's *Dog Eat Dog*. In 1984 she had an opportunity to apply her degree in theatre and history when directing John Russell Brown's version of *The Mystery Plays*. Drawing from six medieval pageant plays, mainly in the York and Wakefield cycles, Brown's plays tell stories from the Bible, including the creation and the nativity. *New York Times* critic Mel Gussow found the production "marked by simplicity and bucolic charm," commenting, ". . . Robinson skillfully brings a country square indoors. Surrounding a rough-hewn platform is a field of straw and wood shavings. The six actors are dressed in homespun garments. The effect is that of an animated primitive painting" (1984, 98).

During her last year at Hartford Stage, Robinson guest directed for South Coast Repertory Theatre in Costa Mesa, California. She soon realized that it was time for her to begin a freelance directing career, and upon leaving Hartford in 1985, Robinson immediately found work at both the Cincinnati Playhouse and the Actors Theatre of Louisville. During this fertile period in her directing career she earned recognition with a Drama Desk nomination in 1986 for her direction of Lanford Wilson's *Lemon Sky* Off Broadway at the Second Stage Theatre. *Lemon Sky* is a memory play about an adult son coming to terms with his parents and their past as a family. Robinson created a delicate environment for these memories and stressed the protagonist's changing perceptions of the family's relationships. Frank Rich of the *New York Times* was complimentary, writing that the play was "fluidly choreographed by the director" and "up to the high standards" of the Second Stage Theatre. Rich applauded the lighting and set design choices, which presented "a shimmering stage environment that is as much a part of the landscape of memory as of California" (1985, sec. 3, 17).

With the success of *Lemon Sky*, Robinson began getting more offers for directing jobs. Just as her career was picking up, she became the first recipient of the $10,000 Alan Schneider Award in 1987. Sponsored by the Theatre Communications Group, the award was "designed to assist mid-career freelance directors who have exhibited exceptional talent and established local or regional reputations" (Theatre 2004). As part of the award, Robinson was appointed to direct for two prominent regional theatres, the Seattle Repertory Theatre and the Milwaukee Repertory Theater. Also in 1987, Robinson directed *Copperhead* at the WPA Theater in New York City, written by her husband-to-be, Erik Brogger.

Robinson solidified her growing reputation by directing the Off-Broadway premiere of Barbara Lebow's *A Shayna Maidel,* a production that ran for over five hundred performances at the Westside Arts Theater in 1987. Gussow praised the "beautifully matched performances" by Gordana Rashovich and Melissa Gilbert as two sisters reunited after twenty years, one a Holocaust survivor, the other raised as an American. He commented, "Under Mary B. Robinson's assured direction, both actresses are mutually responsive. Each watches the other with a kind of compulsive concern—as Ms. Rashovich is unable to rid herself of the pain of memory and as Ms. Gilbert is repeatedly demeaned by their rigid and demanding father" (1987, C16).

In 1990 Robinson directed David Mamet's *Speed the Plow* at the South Coast Repertory Theatre. The *Los Angeles Times* published an article on her work, focusing attention on the fact that a woman was directing Mamet's male-dominated play about the gritty life of the film industry. Robinson responded to the reporter by stating that Mamet's plays "express a human condition, not solely a male condition. . . . The question of what a woman director brings to a play that might be different than what a male director brings is a question I don't know the answer to and have always somewhat resented. . . . But, after directing this particular play, I find some of those questions make more sense" (Isenberg 1990, 41). She found Mamet's male characters were more fleshed out than his supporting (sole) female character, but welcomed the chance to make the female character an enigma, forcing the audience to put the pieces of her psychological puzzle into place.

Having established her reputation as a prominent freelance director, Robinson secured the title of artistic director when she took the reigns of the Philadelphia Drama Guild from 1990 to 1995. She brought a mixture of classics and new works by playwrights of color to the theatre. At the time she accepted the appointment, she reflected, "I've done a lot of naturalistic plays the past ten years, which I love, but now I'm particularly excited by new things which can stretch me. I feel quite comfortable in naturalistic plays, and I want to do more projects that keep me a little more off-balance and scare me a little more" (Isenberg 1990, 44). The result was an eclectic mix of productions she directed at the Philadelphia Drama Guild, including Daniel Sullivan's *Inspecting Carol,* Brian Friel's *Dancing at Lughnasa,* Ingmar Bergman's *Nora,* Moliere's *The Misanthrope,* Eugene O'Neill's *A Moon for the Misbegotten,* Shakespeare's *Macbeth,* Milcha Sanchez-Scott's *Dog Lady and the Cuban Swimmer,* Athol Fugard's *Boseman and Lena,* and Erik Brogger's *A Normal Life.*

One of Robinson's seminal productions at the Drama Guild was *A Midsummer Night's Dream* in 1991, for which critics lauded her directorial concept. As previous directors had done in past productions, Robinson double cast one pair of actors in the roles of Theseus/Hippolyta and Oberon/Titania, highlighting the "power games beneath their sexual relationships" (Mazer 1991, 14). Part of Robinson's scheme was not only to draw relationships clearly between the actors on stage, but also to make the audience a part of the dream through the use of tall, portable mirrors that reflected the audiences' presence. Cary M. Mazer, critic for Philadelphia's *City Paper,* concluded, "Robinson's production is fresh, clear, direct, inventive, amusing, human, soulful and intelligent. This *Dream* definitely puts the Drama Guild back on the national map of American regional theatres as a company to pay attention to" (14).

Robinson's last year directing at the Philadelphia Drama Guild, 1995, coincided with the closing of the theatre. Despite her best efforts, the theatre succumbed to the financial losses that had been building before her arrival. Before she left, Robinson directed John Steinbeck's *Of Mice and Men* and won a Barrymore Award for directing. Clifford A. Ridley of the *Philadelphia Inquirer* wrote, "If you haven't seen it for awhile, you may remember it as dated, or melodramatic, or even preachy. But it is none of those things, a fact that Mary B. Robinson's Drama Guild Production makes thrillingly clear. . . . Robinson has invested the play with a steadily escalating tension, a sense of inevitability waiting to happen" (1995, E1, E6). Ridley praised Robinson not for an innovative concept, but for finding the heart of the play through the relationships of the characters.

After leaving the Drama Guild, Robinson returned to freelance work and eventually settled with her family in the New York City area, where her husband had a teaching job. Despite slowing her directing career down in order to raise her son, Robinson's string of positive reviews continued. In 1995 she staged Jeffery Hatcher's *Three Viewings* for the Manhattan Theatre Club Stage II. Composed of three monologues recited by visitors to a funeral parlor, Hatcher had a unique approach to creating a play. Howard Kissel of the *Daily News* was intrigued and proclaimed the production "elegantly mounted and directed" (1995, Now 59). In 2003 she directed *String Fever,* Jaquelyn Reingold's romantic comedy about a middle-aged woman, Lily, and the problems with her physicist boyfriend. Robert Dominguez of the *Daily News* praised the performances at the Ensemble Studio Theatre, writing, "Under Mary B. Robinson's brisk direction, *String* unspools as an appealing romantic comedy populated by oddball characters whose eccentricities never seem forced. Evan Handler, as Lily's goofy actor friend from Iceland, is a standout. A seasoned stage actress, [Cynthia] Nixon gives a layered performance that's a pleasure to watch" (2003, Now 36).

Although Robinson relied on the help of her network of casting directors in New York City when she was a novice director, she has since become incisive in casting her own plays. Robinson likes to see surprises from actors and tries to keep an open mind at auditions. "I sometimes have very specific ideas about the roles, but I'm also willing to be and interested in being surprised. I certainly look for actors who will fit into an ensemble and be collaborative with each other," she states (Daniels 1996, 158). As with most directors, Robinson follows her instincts about which performers are right for the role. She says finding the right person to stir her is "a little bit like falling in love," though chemistry is only half of the equation (Interview, 2004). Her actors must also be of a generous and open spirit to work in an ensemble atmosphere. She took part in a non-traditional casting symposium in 1986 and looks for opportunities to cast across boundaries, particularly in Shakespeare's plays.

On the first day of rehearsal Robinson likes to think of herself as a host at a party, trying not to be too eager or get in anybody's way. She wants to observe actors' impulses and alert herself to the "vibes in the room" (Interview, 2004). Robinson clarifies that she is not "laid back," but rather "engaged and involved" during this process, explaining, "[E]arly on, as we explore the play on its feet for the first time, I'm frankly more interested in what the actors have to offer than what I do. I can introduce my own ideas at any time: I want to see what *their* impulses are first. And of course, my own ideas evolve as they intersect with the actors' work, as they do in all collaborative work" (Interview, 2004). She sees her work as actor-driven, declaring, "I'm an actor's director as opposed to a conceptual director" (Daniels 1996, 105).

Considering her actor-centered approach, it is not surprising that Robinson has earned a reputation among actors for being open-minded in rehearsal. One actor observed, "I think she is less embarrassed than most directors about talking about ideas." Another performer stated, "She gives you rein to try and experiment, which is so imperative" (Isenberg 1990, 41). Robinson's ultimate goal is to get each performer to establish a connection with the audience, even with a character like Iago in *Othello*. Elaborating about Iago, she explains, "What we're both [actor and director] looking for here is where the audience will connect with him. Not because we're trying to make him sympathetic or loveable, but because I think the really disturbing thing about Iago is that there's an Iago in all of us" (Daniels 1996, 165). Having critiqued her productions for several seasons, Ridley observed that Robinson is known for directing plays with deep characterization and strong relationships (1995, E6).

Like many other directors, the director's collaboration with actors, designers, and other production staff is a key for Robinson—so key that she is writing a book on collaboration. Robinson clarifies that she is not indecisive, but she prefers making consensual choices with actors and designers rather than making decisions on her own. "I sometimes find it actually rather hard to arrive at a choice when I have to make it on my own," she explains (Daniels 1996, 105). Her open, collaborative attitude dovetails with her approach to actors in rehearsal. She seeks to draw the character from the performer rather than telling the actor what she is looking for. Robinson comments, "Even if I know exactly what I want, I think it's much better if it can be arrived at by the actor because then it is the actor's choice and it is much more organic and informed and personal. . . . I want to know if the actor will arrive at the same choice in a different way and bring different colors to it and maybe show me something I didn't know" (105).

Robinson's excellence as a director has been recognized with her Drama Desk Nomination for *Lemon Sky* in 1986, her Alan Schneider Award in 1997, and her Barrymore Award for directing *Of Mice and Men* in 1995. In addition to serving as head of directing at the Playwrights Horizons Theatre School, Robinson has taught directing at New York University and Brooklyn College. Through all of these educational venues Robinson has taught her students what has become her mantra: direct the plays that you love.

Sources

Daniels, Rebecca. 1996. *Women Stage Directors Speak.* Jefferson, N.C.: McFarland.

Dominguez, Robert. 2003. "Trying to Untangle Her Knotty Love Life." Rev. of *String Fever,* by Jaquelyn Reingold. *(New York) Daily News,* 5 Mar., Now 36.

Gussow, Mel. 1982. Rev. of *The Greeks,* adapted by John Barton-Kenneth Cavander, based on the plays of Euripides and Sophocles. *New York Times,* 28 Feb., sec. 1, 50.

———. 1984. Rev. of *The Mystery Plays,* by John Russell Brown. *New York Times,* 9 Dec., 98.

———. 1987. Rev. of *A Shayna Maidel,* by Barbara Lebow. *New York Times,* 30 Oct., Weekend Desk, C16.

Isenberg, Barbara. 1990. "Mamet Can't Buffalo Her." *Los Angeles Times,* 3 June, Calendar, 41, 44.

Kissel, Howard. 1995. Rev. of *Three Viewings,* by Jeffery Hatcher. *(New York) Daily News,* 21 Apr., Now 59.

Mazer, Cary M. 1991. "*Dream* Fulfilled." Rev. of *A Midsummer Night's Dream,* by William Shakespeare. *(Philadelphia) City Paper,* 15–22 Mar., 14.

Rich, Frank. 1985. Rev. of *Lemon Sky,* by Lanford Wilson. *New York Times,* 12 Dec., sec. 3, 17.

Ridley, Clifford A. 1995. "Dreaming of Dignity in 'Of Mice and Men.'" Rev. of *Of Mice and Men,* by John Steinbeck. *Philadelphia Inquirer,* 1 Jan., E1, E6.

Robinson, Mary B. 2004. Telephone interview with Anne Fliotsos. 9 Sept.

Siegel, Fern. 1990. "Letting Audiences in on the Process: A Profile of Mary Robinson." Billy Rose Theatre Collection, clippings. New York Public Library for the Performing Arts.

Theatre Communications Group. 2004. Theatre Communications Group (TCG). http://www.tcg.org/about/press/071803_schn.htm (accessed 12 Aug. 2004).

Representative Directing Credits

Off and Off-Off Broadway:

Buddies (1982), *Lemon Sky* (1985), *Twelfth Night* (1987), *Copperhead* (1987), *A Shayna Maidel* (1987), *Moonchildren* (1987), *Three Viewings* (1995), *String Fever* (2003), *Women on Fire* (2003)

Regional Theatre:

The Greeks (1982), *Dog Eat Dog* (1983), *Of Mice and Men* (1983, 1995), *Medieval Mystery Plays* (1984), *No Mercy* (1985), *Desire Under the Elms* (1985), *Painting Churches* (1985), *How to Say Goodbye* (1986), *Serenading Louie* (1988), *Loot* (1988), *The Jeremiah* (1990), *Speed the Plow* (1990), *Boseman and Lena* (1990), *A Normal Life* (1991), *A Midsummer Night's Dream* (1991), *Macbeth* (1991), *Dog Lady and the Cuban Swimmer* (1991), *A Moon for the Misbegotten* (1992), *The Misanthrope* (1992), *Nora* (1993), *Dancing at Lughnasa* (1993), *Othello* (1994), *Holiday Memories* (1994), *Molly Sweeney* (1997), *Full Bloom* (2000), *This Is Our Youth* (2001), *Dinner with Friends* (2001), *Copenhagen* (2005)

 # Rothman, Carole

Born in St. Louis, Missouri, Carole Rothman is a director and the artistic director of Second Stage Theatre in New York City. Rothman knew that she wanted to be a director by the time she got to high school. There, Rothman's theatre teachers were women and also directed school productions, giving her the idea that directing was a possible career choice. Later, she realized that there were few professional women directors, but was still determined to direct.

Rothman went to Northwestern University in Evanston, Illinois, and majored in theatre, graduating in 1970. In 1973 she graduated from New York University with an M.F.A. in directing. In addition to graduate school, she studied at Circle Repertory Theatre with Marshall Mason for two years. Rothman learned about directing from her teachers and by watching productions of directors such as Peter Brook and Richard Schechner. Rothman says, "I don't think that I had any one particular style or one particular person that was more important than the other. Marshall [Mason] had a very specific way of working which was helpful to me just in terms of structure. But I think I'm one of those people that really learned on the job because I was so young. I was able to assimilate a lot of different techniques, learn from a lot of different people, and use my own instincts" (Interview, 2004).

Rothman was a freelance director until founding Second Stage Theatre in 1979 with actress Robyn Goodman. One reason that Rothman started the company was her desire to work on a consistent basis. She explains, "I wanted to be able to hire myself. . . . There weren't a lot of women directing in New York. I wasn't going to get a lot of chances. If I wanted to do things a certain way, I was going to have to do it myself" (Interview, 2004).

The original mission of Second Stage Theatre was "to give 'second stagings' to contemporary American plays that originally failed to find an audience due to scheduling problems, inappropriate venues or limited performance runs" (Second Stage n.d.). Later the theatre expanded its mission to include the production of new plays and to provide a place where artists could develop. During Second Stage Theatre's first season, Rothman directed Michael Weller's *Split,* which consisted of two one-act plays: *At Home* and *Abroad.* However, it was during the theatre's second season that Rothman had a breakthrough with her direction of Amlin Gray's *How I Got That Story,* which focused on the unraveling of a reporter during the Vietnam War. Rothman described her process of working on the play in an interview with Lee Alan Morrow and Frank Pike, authors of *Creating Theater: The Professionals' Approach to New Plays.* In the book, Rothman notes, "To have a really good concept of how to do a play, you have to know what it's going to look like, how it's going to move, how it's going to affect an audience. When I did *How I Got That Story,* I did a lot of reading about Vietnam, but I also read *Gulliver's Travels* and other satire" (Morrow and Pike 1986, 106). The play succeeded on many levels, with Frank Rich of the *New York Times* calling it, "an explosion of young talent—in writing, directing and acting—and a bracing demonstration of what such talent can do when everything goes right" (1980, C9). The play transferred to Off Broadway as well as to Washington, D.C.'s, Kennedy Center in 1981.

While at Second Stage Theatre, Rothman developed a directorial relationship with playwright Tina Howe. In 1983 Rothman directed Howe's *Painting Churches,* which examined the relationship between a painter and her aging parents. Rothman described the process of directing the play, noting, "We did a significant amount of cutting in *Painting Churches.* There were scenes we'd rehearsed for weeks that we cut out. The actors were very flexible, though after the first week of previews they didn't want any more changes. We have to beat our heads against a scene a lot of times before we begin to talk of cutting. You must let the playwright see the scene as well as it can be played for them to realize that it doesn't work" (Morrow and Pike 1986, 120). Rothman describes the importance of developing a visual concept of the play. She explains, "I like to work with the designers really early. Since *Painting Churches* was about an artist dealing with light, designers and I looked at a lot of Impressionist paintings. The paintings gave us a feel for the play, a common ground out of which the set, the lighting, and the costumes developed" (125).

In 1986 Rothman directed Howe's *Coastal Disturbances,* which explored different kinds of love. Rich wrote that Rothman's direction of the Second Stage Theatre production was, "unfailingly sensitive to Ms. Howe's airy technique. . . . [T]he director begins or ends most scenes with a theatrical equivalent of candid Polaroid snapshots: a glimpse of private behavior is fixed and emblazoned on memory, then fades quickly" (1986, C25). Rothman's focus on the visual was evident once again as she transformed the stage into a beach setting with designer Tony Straiges. In his review, Rich wrote, "In league with Mr. Straiges, the director creates the illusion that a small stage is a vast stretch of coast, seen from an ever-rotating vantage point and rippling with overlapping waves, action and conversation" (C25). The play transferred to Broadway the following year, earning Rothman a Tony nomination for Best Director.

Rothman went on to direct other Second Stage Theatre productions of plays by Howe, including 1989's *Approaching Zanzibar,* which followed a family's cross-country journey to visit an aunt. A review in New York's *East Side Express* noted, "The ensemble acting is magnificent. Carole Rothman's direction makes this spiritual journey from A to Z a memorable and provocative experience" (Second Stage 1989). Rothman's ability to direct ensembles well was also noted by Alexis Greene of *Theater Week* in her review of Howe's *One Shoe Off,* which centered on an eccentric middle-aged couple who act inappropriately in front of their guests. The Second Stage production was directed by Rothman at Manhattan's larger Public Theater in 1993. In her review of the play, Greene wrote, "Supported by Carole Rothman's sure, precise directing . . . and by the ensemble acting on [sic] a superb cast, the play's highly fantastical nature is realized" (Second Stage 1993).

In 1991 Rothman's husband died unexpectedly, leaving her with two very young children to parent alone. The following year her founding partner, Robyn Goodman, left to pursue other interests. Rothman found that she needed to make hard choices in her life and decided to stop directing. The last play that she directed at Second Stage Theatre was a revival of Wendy Wasserstein's *Uncommon Women and Others* in 1994. She explains how the three elements of being a single mother, running a theatre company, and directing plays affected her, stating, "It wasn't that I lost the urge to direct, or that I didn't want to be creative, or was disappointed or disillusioned. . . . It was pure fate that stepped in, and said, 'You just don't have time to do all three of these things'" (Interview, 2004).

During the years that she directed, Rothman cast productions by holding auditions, by calling performers she thought were right for roles, and also by going to theatre productions to check out talent. She says, "I do happen to agree with that standard wisdom that casting is ninety percent of the production. You get the right cast and your life is much easier. I know actors hate to hear this, but there are certain plays where you can't act the character, you have to be it" (Morrow and Pike 1986, 122). Rothman says that she prefers performers who "bring their own ideas, their own business, to their roles. The kind of actor I like to work with experiments constantly. The work of such actors inspires me and inspires the other actors" (118).

Rothman prefers to begin rehearsals with finished plays, saying, "The script must be in the best shape you think it can possibly be, until you find out it's not" (Morrow and Pike 1986, 120). She reads the play several times and uses visual works for inspiration. Rothman explains, "Directors want to work with tangible things, which is why you go to books, painting, photographs, and so forth for stimulation" (125). As a text-based director, Rothman says her goal is "[t]o serve the play in the most creative way you know" (134). Preparation for rehearsals begins with a thorough breakdown of the script. Rothman explains, "I break plays down into big beats first. That helps me to get a feeling for the structure, the pacing, and the music of the play—how the rhythms rush over you. I'll say what happens in each scene, name each scene. . . . I fill the margins of my scripts with notes, anything that comes into my head. I jot down questions to ask the playwright. I may not refer to my notes until well into rehearsal, but they can remind me of things I've forgotten" (106).

Rothman prefers to work with writers before rehearsals begin. She explains, "A lot of times playwrights think they're making a certain point which their play doesn't actually do. If you know where the playwright thinks she's going, you can help get her there. You point out where the focus is off. You question every line. This questioning process also helps you make sure you're on the right track" (Morrow and Pike 1986, 107).

Howe described her working relationship with Rothman, explaining,

> You have to have one director, or it helps to have a director who is sympathetic to your work, because you have this shorthand, you understand each other, and for me it's been crucial to have Carole. And it's not just having the same person, but it's also having her, because she's really a unique

person in many respects. It's this combination of her being tremendously fair and steady and yet creative at the same time. There's very little ego and game playing and conspiracy, which is the way so many directors work—through conspiracy and suspicion and innuendo. Carole is very forthright and honest. But at the same time she's really inspired as a director. She has a vision, and she's daring, she understands about the dramatic gesture. And that combination of being rather earthbound in terms of the way she works and air bound in terms of her vision is really unusual. So I feel very fortunate in having been able to work with her. . . . I know that Carole is game for just about anything. And she loves the impossible, and that's sort of my tendency anyway, to try to take on the impossible, and knowing that she's responsive to that is a goad. (Interview, 1989, 264)

At the first rehearsal, Rothman conducts a read-through with the performers and playwright. She says, "At the first read-through the play shifts from the playwright's to the director's hands. It's no longer how the playwright sees the play but how the director is interpreting the play" (Morrow and Pike 1986, 109). Rothman believes that playwrights are not objective in rehearsals and encourages them to view the play as if they were an audience member, rather than the writer.

Rothman blocks the entire play in about a week or a week and a half. She says, "I have the actors come in with their parts memorized. Since the actors don't have their scripts in their hands, they're on their feet from the first moment. I don't believe in sitting around a table reading a play" (Morrow and Pike 1986, 110). During the rehearsals, Rothman encourages performers to be creative. She explains, "I allow a tremendous amount of freedom. I know what I want from the beginning and try to shape the performance. But I want the actors to bring their own ideas, their own business, to their roles. The kind of actor I like to work with experiments constantly. The work of such actors inspires me and inspires the other actors" (118).

Rothman's work as an artistic director has won her many awards, such as the honoring of Second Stage Theatre in 2002 with the Lucille Lortel Award for Outstanding Body of Work. However, Rothman has also won numerous awards for her work as a director, including an Obie for Sustained Excellence in Directing in 1987 and the Rosamund Gilder Award for Outstanding Creative Achievement.

Although she has put her directing career on hold, Rothman hopes to return to directing one day. She explains, "I have thought often as the theatre [Second Stage Theatre] gets more on an even keel, and as my children are grown and don't need me anymore—yes. I'd like to go back to doing it again" (Interview, 2004).

Sources

Howe, Tina. 1989. Interview with Judith E. Barlow. In *Speaking on Stage: Interviews with Contemporary American Playwrights,* ed. Philip C. Kolin and Colby H. Kullman, 260–76. Tuscaloosa: University of Alabama Press, 1996.

Morrow, Lee Ann and Frank Pike. 1986. "Directors." In *Creating Theater: The Professionals' Approach to New Plays,* 89–136. New York: Vintage Books.

Rich, Frank. 1980. "Stage: Echo of Vietnam, 'How I Got That Story'; Two with Many Faces." Rev. of *How I Got That Story,* by Amlin Gray. *New York Times,* 9 Dec., C9.

———. 1986. "From Tina Howe, 'Coastal Disturbances.'" Rev. of *Coastal Disturbances,* by Tina Howe. *New York Times,* 20 Nov., C25.

Rothman, Carole. 2004. Interview with Wendy Vierow. 14 July.

Second Stage Theatre. n.d. "What's 2ST?" http://www.secondstagetheatre.com/into_mission.html (accessed 14 Jan. 2003).

———. 1989. "Season 10." http://www.secondstagetheatre.com/season10.html (accessed 14 Jan. 2005).

———. 1993. "Season 14." http://www.secondstagetheatre.com/season14.html (accessed 14 Jan. 2005).

Representative Directing Credits

Broadway:
> *Coastal Disturbances* (1987)

Off and Off-Off Broadway:
> *Death Story* (1975), *Abroad* (1978), *Minnesota Moon* (1979), *Split* (1980), *How I Got That Story* (1980), *My Sister in This House* (co-directed with Inverna Lockpez—1981), *Pastorale* (1982), *Painting Churches* (1983), *Linda Her and the Fairy Garden* (1984), *The Vienna Notes* (1985), *Coastal Disturbances* (1986), *Approaching Zanzibar* (1989), *What a Man Weighs* (1990), *Lake No Bottom* (1990), *One Shoe Off* (1993), *Uncommon Women and Others* (1994)

Regional Theatre:
> *How I Got That Story* (1981), *Painting Churches* (1983), *Kathy and Mo: Parallel Lives* (1987)

Schulman, Susan H.

Born July 6, 1947, in New York City, Susan H. Schulman was one of the few women on Broadway entrusted to direct musicals in the 1980s and 1990s, including *Sweeney Todd, The Secret Garden, The Sound of Music,* and several staged readings in the City Center's *Encores!* series. She took the helm of Pittsburgh Civic Light Opera from 1981 to 1989 before pursuing her successful career as a professional director in New York City.

Unlike many women directors, Schulman always knew she wanted to direct. She credits the start of her theatre education to her early exposure to theatre, for she had the benefit of growing up in New York City and seeing performances from the age of six. In addition, Schulman attended New York City's High School for the Performing Arts where Vinnette Carroll, a woman director, was her teacher and role model. After earning her B.A. in 1968 from Hofstra University in Hempstead, New York, she applied to the M.F.A. program in directing at Yale University, but they rejected her. "They didn't want to invest the time and money training a woman who, in their view, would get married, ultimately have a family, and drop out of the profession," Schulman explained (Horowitz 1992, 22). Having already written and published a play at the age of sixteen, she applied for a scholarship through Yale's playwriting program, got the scholarship, and as a playwriting student proceeded to take courses in directing and acting before graduating. By the 1980s, Schulman had proven Yale wrong in their initial rejection of her application, for she had forged a career as a professional director.

Schulman's road to Broadway was not an easy one. After finishing graduate school she sought out every opportunity to direct, often without pay. Eventually, she found venues for her work; first directing for the Studio Arena Theatre in Buffalo, New York, then directing elsewhere, including several productions for the Equity Library Theatre in New York City. Although many of the jobs paid only little or no money, she managed to build her resume and subsequently landed a job at the helm of the Pittsburgh Civic Light Opera, where she directed thirty-five productions from 1981 to 1989.

Despite her growing experience, a professional directing career in New York City eluded Schulman for some time. After almost two decades of struggling, she nearly quit. She explains, "I would arrive at a producer's office with clips of wonderful reviews I had received and nobody was impressed. I was seen as a *stock* director and not taken seriously. Stock was '*commercial*,' and in New York, it was implied, 'we do *art*' [emphasis Horowitz's]" (Horowitz 1992, 25). The crisis in her career forced Schulman to reevaluate her priorities and accomplishments, ultimately leading to a new perspective about her work as a director. "I had to come to terms with the fact that I might never direct a Broadway play. At that point, I wasn't even sure I'd direct a commercial Off-Broadway play. But then after a lot of soul searching, I decided that even if I never made it commercially in New York, I could still make a living elsewhere at what I loved to do. . . . Once I accepted the fact that I might not work on Broadway a big weight was lifted from me. I suddenly felt freer to take theatrical risks" (25).

In retrospect, Schulman sees the connections that can lead from unpaid, small-scale jobs all the way to Broadway. She traces her unlikely path from a production of Hugh Wheeler's *Look We've Come Through*, which she and a group of friends self-produced in a rented theatre in New York City, to her opportunity to direct a revival of the Stephen Sondheim and Hugh Wheeler musical *Sweeney Todd* at the York Theatre Company in New York City in 1989. Wheeler was impressed with her production of *Look We've Come Through*, and when Schulman was hired to direct Sondheim's *Company* at the York Theatre Company in 1987, Wheeler mentioned to Sondheim, "Oh, I know her. She's great" (Schulman, interview, 2000). *Company* in turn led to her direction of *Sweeney Todd*, which transferred to Broadway. "And had I not made that happen, that little production, nothing would have happened after that," Schulman mused (Interview, 2000).

When she was approached to direct *Sweeney Todd* in the York Theatre Company's tiny one-hundred-seat theatre, Schulman's initial reaction was to laugh because the original Broadway production, directed by Hal Prince in 1979, was of enormous proportions. However, when she re-read the script, Schulman decided that intimacy could be a key to the production's success rather than a stumbling block, for with intimacy came renewed attention to the characters and their relationships. "I think that feeling Sweeney's passion and obsession, really being able to totally empathize with it, rather than being overwhelmed by it . . . makes a big difference," she explains. "My choice was to tell a more personal story" (Rothstein 1989, sec. 2, 1). Part of that personal story was a fresh interpretation of Mrs. Lovett, who was depicted as a crazed, desperate woman in Harold Prince's original Broadway production. Schulman explains her more compassionate view of Mrs. Lovett: "She held onto these razors for 15 years. . . . She was obsessed with this man. And I think there's a tremendous physical obsession with him as well. She's very passionate about him. . . . I think that sometimes when women get obsessed with a man they wreak havoc on their souls. And I think that's what Mrs. Lovett is doing" (1).

The result was a portrayal of Mrs. Lovett that was more heartbreaking than reprehensible, more human than caricature.

Lavishing praise on Schulman's production of *Sweeney Todd,* which transferred to Broadway, critic Frank Rich of the *New York Times* revealed, "I have usually been moved by *Sweeney Todd,* but never in the way Ms. Schulman's rendering moved me" (1989, C15). He described the audience at the York Theatre Company as "spellbound" by her intimate production, which focused less on the politics and the industrial revolution and more on the human themes and characters of *Sweeney Todd.* Rich wrote, "[I]t is from the human point of view rather than the theatrical perspective that Ms. Schulman most radically rethinks the tale of the Demon Barber of Fleet Street" (C15).

Two years later, Schulman was back on Broadway with a new musical, Lucy Simon and Marsha Norman's *The Secret Garden,* in which emotion and intimacy played heavily as well. The plot revolved around Mary Lennox, an orphan who is forced to live at her uncle's manor house. While there, she meets her sickly cousin Colin and explores the secrets of the massive house and its mysterious garden. In doing so, Mary discovers some of life's secrets as well. Schulman rescued the musical *The Secret Garden* when it was in a workshop phase under the original (male) director. According to book writer Marsha Norman, the original director kept rewriting the script on paper rather than working with the production on stage. "The director's job is not to revise the script," Norman complained (*Dialogue* 1992). The all-female creative team of the musical never felt they were in synchronization with the director. Something was missing, both in the musical and in the collaborative effort. Schulman's impulse was to start with a simple question, posed to the creative team: "How do you see this?" (*Dialogue* 1992). She explained her own response to the question, which led to a framing device of seeing the world through a child's eyes: "[T]he first thing [impulse] was very emotional, which I think it always is. And my emotional feel was that we were seeing it through Mary Lennox's emotions, her perceptions, and that things would be out of scale" (Interview, 2000). She elaborated, "It is basically Mary's journey, and she brings the household back to life. And the garden, which she discovers and thinks dead, is symbolic of that" (Wolf 1991, 6). Happily, the collaborators' ideas meshed with Schulman's. The lack of communication with the previous director dissolved, and the production team finally found themselves working in the same world of the play—a child's world haunted by ghosts. Although the story revolved around two children, Schulman did not want to make the musical a children's tale, but instead found an overarching theme that struck a nerve with her own background, "that women [in this case, Mary] need independence and the ability to make choices, that you're not just predestined to do what other people tell you to do" (McGee 1991, 71).

The Secret Garden made headlines, especially as the musical found success on Broadway and garnered awards. Frequently, the female collaborative team had to respond to the inevitable yet ridiculous question about it being a "women's show." "No more than *Oklahoma!* is a men's show," came the reply (Bilowit 1991, 7). Questions over construction and pacing of the production rippled through the reviews, although the reviews were mainly positive. John Beaufort of the *Christian Science Monitor* wrote, "*The Secret Garden* revels in theatrical imagination and stylishly traditional showmanship. . . . Under Miss Schulman's guidance, the singing actors prove themselves dedicated storytellers" (1991, 14). When the musical went on tour, Hedy Weiss of the *Chicago Sun-Times* deemed it a tighter, stronger production, noting that the "imaginatively and fluidly restaged" production had not solved all its problems, but "nonetheless, there is much to cherish" (1992, sec. 2, 39). Although the production received a Tony nomination, Schulman did not. Heidi Landesman, one of the producers, called the omission outrageous and said it "communicates a vast misunderstanding of how a musical is put together" (Witchel 1991, C2). Schulman could take comfort in the fact that the musical was a hit with audiences, however. It played for nearly two years, totaling over 700 performances.

Schulman tackled her second Broadway revival when *The Sound of Music* was revived in 1998, after nearly forty years. Schulman's staging of the Rodgers and Hammerstein classic featured swastikas throughout the production, which stirred some controversy. Schulman received reams of letters and answered every one of them, assuring the audience that the use of swastikas was historically accurate (Litson 1999, R16). She decided the tale of the dysfunctional Von Trapp family and the novice nun who becomes their nanny needed to have a new political point of reference. "[P]eople come to *The Sound of Music* with an expectation—but also to present new things. It is the 1990s, soon to be beyond that, and we have a different perspective on that period of time [the late 1930s]. We went to Salzburg and we did a lot of research, and I think that helped us make it an edgier production, with more of a 90s take on it" (R16). Not all of the critics embraced the revival, in part because they felt the script and score were overly sentimental. Ben Brantley of the *New York Times* wrote that in spite of it being "a perfectly respectable production, it remains the same old cup of treacle" (1998, E1). Despite the critics, the production did well with audiences, playing thirty-eight previews and 533 performances before touring nationally. Schulman also staged the Australian tour in 1999.

Schulman acknowledges that commercial productions such as *The Sound of Music* make it financially possible for her to take on lesser-known works, such as her subsequent direction of Jeannie Tesori and Brian Crawley's new musical, *Violet*. Based on the Doris Betts story, "The Ugliest Pilgrim," Crawley's book for *Violet* follows a woman's cross-country bus trip in 1964 and her search for a televangelist who can pray away the disfiguring scar on her face. As Violet discovers a world much larger than her backwoods North Carolina home, flashbacks of her upbringing reveal the unhappy accident that scarred her. After extensive workshops and development at the Eugene O'Neill Theater Center in Waterford, Connecticut, and Lincoln Center in New York City, *Violet* opened Off Broadway at Playwrights Horizons in 1997. Schulman also directed the first regional production at A Contemporary Theatre (ACT) in Seattle in 1998. Critics focused mainly on Tesori's gospel-inspired score, giving only slight notice to Schulman's staging. Howard Kissel of the *Daily News* noted, "The large cast moves fluidly under Susan Schulman's knowing direction. . . . *Violet* made me more hopeful about the American musical than anything I've seen in ages" (1997, 44).

Around the turn of the twenty-first century, Schulman was busy directing musicals for the Stratford Festival in Ontario, Canada. She directed *Man of La Mancha* in 1998, *Fiddler on the Roof* in 2000, and *The King and I* in 2003. Once again, the direction of revivals helped support her direction of new musicals: *Time and Again* in 2001 at New York City's Manhattan Theatre Club, *Heartland* in 2003 at the Madison Repertory Theatre in Wisconsin, and *The Little Princess* in 2004 at the Mountain View Center for the Performing Arts near San Francisco. Schulman will likely continue to direct a combination of old and new works. "I love doing revivals and I love doing new works, and it's a totally different experience," she observes (Interview, 2000).

By her own admission, instinct and emotion have been crucial components of Schulman's work, and they play strongly into Schulman's casting process as well. She admits that casting is very subjective. She explains, "I find that I almost know immediately when someone comes in the door whether I find them interesting or not, and it's very, very personal. . . . I try to find a person who's interesting, who I'm attracted to, who there's more to find out about. It has very little to do with whether someone thinks a person is handsome or pretty. It's the entire package to me. I love people who make strong choices, I love people who have lots of ideas, and I find that very attractive as a director." Schulman seeks risk takers, maintaining, "[I]f I sense there's potential, I really push them into making strong choices and going with it one hundred percent. That kind of risk taking, that kind of courage is very inspiring for a director" (Interview, 2000).

She seeks a similar connection with designers and collaborators, stating, "I'm a very close collaborator. I count very much on my designers, my choreographer, my musical director for input. I love working with people who have opinions. I love set designers who will come up to me at a certain point in previews and say, 'You know, watch that scene. I think maybe there could be a cut from here to here. I've been thinking about it for a few days.' I mean, I love that—that a set designer is that involved. I try to surround myself with those kind of people" (Interview, 2000).

Perhaps it was the freedom to take risks that helped Schulman trust her instincts and follow her emotional impulses. Words relating to emotion repeatedly surface in Schulman's discussion of her directing, particularly about her conceptualization of the script. Although she does not intentionally apply a feminist agenda in her work, she cannot help viewing the world from a female perspective. When she searches for a lens through which to view the story, that lens is often through a woman's eyes—a world to which she can relate. For example, when asked to direct the national tour of *Sunset Boulevard,* she had to admit that she did not originally connect to the story. But on rereading the book and listening to the music, Schulman discovered, "I had a very strong emotional response to it. I was actually crying. I was crying because I felt the loss this woman was suffering. I felt she had put herself in such an unreal world. . . . She knew nothing else. . . . So it very much has to do with emotional feeling first" (Interview, 2000). As she had with *Sweeney Todd,* Schulman found the intimate story more compelling than the theatrical trappings of the original Broadway production. "I told them I wanted to make it very personal," she explains (Rawson 1998). In viewing the musical from the protagonist's perspective, Schulman chose to stage it on a Hollywood sound stage, highlighting Norma's blurred vision of fiction and reality.

Schulman comes into rehearsals communicating her concept, which may have a political underpinning. She is an open communicator and likes to think outside the box, with the aid of contributions from creators, actors, and designers. Tapping into her own intuition as a director, as well as those of her performers, she works to highlight the emotional connection between the actor and the audience through the script. As a risk taker, she elicits big choices from her actors as well. Like her former teacher, actor and director Vinnette Carroll, Schulman finds that it is difficult to end the rehearsal process, because the work is never done. She sees theatre as a "living, breathing thing" that continues to evolve. "I keep in touch with productions, even on tour, and every time I go back I think, 'Gee, I want to go back into rehearsal now!' And sometimes I'm lucky enough to get a chance to do it" (Interview, 2000). When she directed an Australian production of *The Secret Garden* six years after the Broadway premiere, she was amazed at how different the experience was. "I approached it with much more perspective," Schulman recalls. While she was proud of her initial work in the Broadway production, she realized that "you grow older, [and] you hopefully get wiser and smarter" (Interview, 2000).

Schulman's artistic achievements as a director have been recognized many times. She was nominated for a Tony Award for Best Director of a Musical for *Sweeney Todd* in 1990, followed by an Obie Award for directing *Merrily We Roll Along* in 1995. In addition, she received Drama Desk nominations as Outstanding Director of a Musical for *Sweeney Todd*, *The Secret Garden*, and *Violet*. The South Florida Critic's Association chose *The Secret Garden* as best road show for 1991–92 and Schulman as Best Director. Her alma mater, Hofstra University, also awarded her an Honorary Doctorate for her career achievement.

Schulman is happy to find more women directors in the field in the early twenty-first century, but is also surprised that she is still singled out as one of the "women directors." She explains, "I've always said, 'Either you can do it, or you can't.' And sex doesn't make a bit of difference. You either know what you're doing, or you don't" (Interview, 2000).

Sources

Beaufort, John. 1991. "*The Secret Garden* Grows into a Musical." Rev. of *The Secret Garden*, book and lyrics by Marsha Norman, music by Lucy Simon. *Christian Science Monitor*, 3 May, Arts 14.

Bilowit, Ira J. 1991. "It Blooms for Everyone." *Back Stage*, 26 Apr., 7, 37.

Brantley, Ben. 1998. "Sweetness, Light, and Lederhosen." Rev. of *The Sound of Music*, book by Howard Lindsay and Russel Crowse, music by Richard Rodgers, lyrics by Oscar Hammerstein II, based on *The Trapp Family Singers*, by Maria Augusta Trapp. *New York Times*, 13 Mar., E1–18.

Dialogue with Marsha Norman, Susan Schulman, and Heidi Landesman. 1992. Videocassette. Produced by the New York Public Library's Theatre on Film and Tape Archive.

Horowitz, Simi. 1992. "Inside the Secret Garden." *Theatre Week*, 10–16 Feb., 22–27.

Kissel, Howard. 1997. "*Violet* is a Rosey New Musical." Rev. of *Violet*, book and lyrics by Brian Crawley, music by Jeannie Tesori. *(New York) Daily News*, 12 Mar., 44.

Litson, Jo. 1999. "The Other Side of the Mountain." *Weekend Australian*, 2 Oct., R16.

McGee, Celia. 1991. "Gambling on a 'Garden.'" *New York*, 22 April, 65–71.

Rawson, Christopher. 1998. "The Women behind *Sunset Boulevard*." *(Pittsburgh) Post-Gazette*, 29 Nov. http://www.petulaclark.net/theatre/pgsunset29.html (accessed 18 June 2002).

Rich, Frank. 1989. "On Stage, the Feminist Message Takes on a Sly and Subtle Tone." Rev. of *Sweeney Todd*, book by Hugh Wheeler, music and lyrics by Stephen Sondheim, based on *The String of Pearls* by Christopher Bond. *New York Times*, 19 Apr., C15.

Rothstein, Mervyn. 1989. "Does the Demon Barber Have a Human Face?" *New York Times*, 10 Sept., sec. 2, 1.

Schulman, Susan. 2000. Telephone interview with Anne Fliotsos. 23 Mar.

Simpson, Janice C. 1991. "The Women of the *Secret Garden*." *TheatreWeek,* 6 May, 16–21.

Weiss, Hedy. 1992. "*Secret Garden* Grows Stronger As Touring Show." *Chicago Sun-Times,* 11 June, sec. 2, 39.

Witchel, Alex. 1991. "On Stage, and Off." *New York Times,* 10 May, C2.

Wolf, William. 1991. "Tending Her Garden." *Playbill,* 91 (Apr.): 6–10.

Representative Directing Credits

Broadway:

> *Sweeney Todd* (1989), *The Secret Garden* (1991), *Allegro*[1] (1994), *The Boys from Syracuse* (1997), *The Sound of Music* (1998), *A Connecticut Yankee in King Arthur's Court* (2001), *Little Women* (2005)

Off and Off-Off Broadway:

> *Carnival* (1977), *Angel Face* (1978), *Annie Get Your Gun* (1979), *Feathertop* (1984), *A Little Night Music* (1985), *Company* (1987), *Sweeney Todd* (1989), *Merrily We Roll Along* (1994), *Decline of the (Middle) West* (1995), *Jack's Holiday* (1995), *Violet* (1997), *Time and Again* (2001)

Regional and Stock Theatre:

> *Follies* (1983), *110 in the Shade* (1984), *West Side Story* (1984), *1776* (1987), *Funny Girl* (1988), *Royal Family* (1996), *Violet* (1998), *Heartland* (2003), *The Little Princess* (2004)

Tours:

> *The Secret Garden* (1991, 1992), *Annie Get Your Gun* (1992), *The Sound of Music* (1998), *Sunset Boulevard* (1999)

International Theatre:

> *The Secret Garden* (1997), *Man of La Mancha* (1998, 2002), *Fiddler on the Roof* (2000), *The King and I* (2003)

Notes

1. *Allegro* was part of New York City Center *Encores!* series of staged readings.

Stewart, Ellen[1]

Arriving in New York City in 1950 to study fashion design, Ellen Stewart became one of the pioneers of the Off-Off Broadway theatre movement in the United States and an acclaimed director of classical plays, which she adapts for international audiences. She is also a proponent of international exchange and collaboration among theatre artists.

Although she had no aspirations to be in theatre as a child, Stewart says, "I was always interested in theatre, but I didn't know what theatre was. Some of my people were in vaudeville and burlesque. And I had a brother who aspired to be a playwright. When we were still children, we'd convert shoe boxes into theatres and make up stories for the stage" (Greenfeld 1967, 10).

After building a successful fashion career in New York City, Stewart began to search for another challenge in her life. She decided to create a theatre for her brother and his friend, both of whom were playwrights. Although she had no experience in theatre, Stewart had confidence, and states, "I never had self-doubt. I was always taught by my mama that I'm on an island and there's not a soul on the island but me. And so whatever gets done, I have to do it. That's the way I was brought up. So I never thought about self-doubt. But anything that I've wanted to do, I always believed that somehow—I believe in the somehow—that I could find a way to do it" (70 Up).

In 1961 Stewart signed a lease for a basement on Manhattan's East Side, thinking that it might be a good place for a boutique for her fashion designs (Greenfeld 1967, 10). At first, the basement became a boutique by day and a theatre, named Café La MaMa, by night. Opening in 1962, the theatre was renamed La MaMa Experimental Theater Club (e.t.c.) in 1964 and became a nonprofit organization. Over its history, it has changed locations a number of times and has opened branches around the world.

Stewart soon arrived at an experimental visual aesthetic, which combined music, dance, and drama that audiences of any culture would be able to understand. She explains that La MaMa was "experimental in the sense that it often departs from what is thought of as traditional theater. When I took some of our productions to Europe, starting in 1965, the plays that worked best were the ones that were primarily visual and not so dependent on English, which many in the audiences didn't understand. The ones that didn't work at all were the traditional sort with people sitting around on the stage doing a lot of talking. That was a message to me, that the traditional kind of theater was not what I wanted to do. I wanted theater that would communicate. . . . I started encouraging people to try to find ways to communicate through means that went beyond language. . . . That's our goal" (Anderson 1997, 29).

Stewart directed her first production in 1970, while touring Europe with *Arden of Faversham,* a play published in 1592 by an anonymous author and directed by Andrei Serban. As a refugee from Romania, it was dangerous for Serban to travel to communist countries. When *Arden of Faversham* was scheduled to be performed in the former Yugoslavia, Stewart took over the direction of the play, staging it inside of a Roman burial cave lit by candles. At first, Stewart did not intend to continue directing and only staged plays, originally directed by Serban, out of necessity. She explains, "It was like a choice—if we got invited to go someplace and Andrei couldn't go, because it was dangerous to go into a communist country for him, either the troupe had to stay at home or I would have to do it. That's the way it was. . . . I was very proud that we got invited to go, and that fact that he couldn't—I didn't want the work to stop. And he didn't want it to stop either, so he trusted me" (Interview, 2004).

In 1970 Stewart brought Serban to La MaMa, where he worked with composer Elizabeth Swados and Stewart's La MaMa Repertory Company, renamed the Great Jones Repertory Company in 1974. As Serban became busy with outside projects, Stewart began creating and directing more productions for the Great Jones Repertory. Focusing on epic works, the company's productions often contained ancient languages, such as Latin and ancient Greek, to convey "primal emotions that are seldom experienced by modern audiences" (La MaMa, "Seven," n.d.). The company's productions, many of which are directed by Stewart, are known for their use of theatre, dance, pageantry, and eclectic music. They typically present ancient tales and have inspired awe in audiences around the world.

Stewart's concept of theatre changed while visiting friends in Lebanon. On the trip she visited the Roman ruins of Baalbeck and says, "I was just struck with awe. And I wanted to do theatre in those ruins" (Interview, 2004). She convinced Serban to direct a 1972 production of *Medea* at the Palace of Dionysus and its surrounding ruins. The experience caused Stewart to think in terms of creating work in a particular space. She explains, "Since then, whatever I do, I look for a space to do it" (Interview, 2004).

Back in New York City, Stewart searched for a large space where she could present plays—and in 1974 she found La MaMa's Annex Theater, which is a block long and two stories high. She explains, "The Annex was as close as I could come to having an environment. . . . It's a very flexible space. You can make it into a proscenium or whatever you want" (Interview, 2004).

At the Annex, Stewart created and directed a revue called *The Cotton Club*

Gala, which recreated the atmosphere of the famous New York City nightclub that operated from the 1920s to the 1940s. Originally presented in 1975, the production was revived in 1985 and presented the diverse entertainment of the original club with music, dance, and other acts. The La MaMa audience became the nightclub's audience during the performance.

Invited to participate in a seminar in Salzburg in 1982, Stewart decided to forego lecturing and opted to create and direct a version of Shakespeare's *Romeo and Juliet* with eighteen students from different countries who spoke different languages. Stewart's critically acclaimed multilingual production was presented on the estate of Max Reinhart's castle, where audience members followed the performers around the grounds. Stewart created music by using pots, pans, and garden tools and made costumes from sheets and curtains. Although Stewart says the production was not intended to be political, it took on contemporary significance because Romeo was an Arab performer speaking Arabic and Juliet was a performer from Jerusalem speaking Hebrew.

Mythos Oedipus, conceived and directed by Stewart, premiered in Delphi, Greece, in 1985. Like *Romeo and Juliet,* the audience followed the performers around the ruins of Delphi. Stewart discusses the text, explaining, "When we do the Greek classics, we do them using our way of employing language, with a mixture of words from Greek, Latin, Hebrew and other languages, all combined with music" (Anderson 1997, 29–30). The play was also directed by Stewart at La MaMa the same year, and again in 1988, 1989, and 1996.

To celebrate the 750th anniversary of the birth of Yunus Emre, a mystical poet, Stewart created *Yunus,* which she directed in Istanbul in 1991. Beginning as a workshop with Turkish actors, the visual production included Emre's poetry, as well as music and lyrics. It was also directed by Stewart the next year at La MaMa with the original Turkish cast along with an American multiethnic cast.

Seven Against Thebes, created and directed by Stewart, premiered in 2001 at La MaMa and was later staged in Italy, Austria, Poland, and Croatia. An adaptation of Aeschylus's *Seven Against Thebes* and a sequel to *Mythos Oedipus,* the play contained more than twenty actors, dancers, and musicians. In his review, David Finkle of the *Village Voice* wrote, "By striking a kind of awe in today's audiences, she [Stewart] wants to suggest how early theatergoers might have been previously awestruck" (2001, 76). D. J. R. Bruckner of the *New York Times* describes the spectacular production:

> In a vast space at La MaMa, blind Oedipus rises to Olympus on a slender ladder of light that disappears into the 40–foot ceiling before his two sons fall into their fated lethal battle over his throne at Thebes. . . . From courts of gleaming gold facing each other atop enormous staircases, 14 warriors

leap into combat, two at a time (one drops out of the ceiling onto his terrified victim), whipped into frenzy by reedy seers or . . . monsters materializing out of the walls. . . . One combatant sizzles to a cinder when Zeus hurls a thunderbolt, another dies shooting fire from his fingers. Pairs hanging onto nets high above the floor tear at one another with daggers; others joust on clattering horses formed by trios of dancers. One man jogging inside a great wheel crushes his rival; another is swallowed by the earth, watched from above by a hero on winged Pegasus gliding over the audience. Finally the Oedipal sons, each whirling pairs of lead balls on the ends of silk ropes, circle in a hair-raising dance of whizzing death that end with each strangling the other. . . . In her long history of making classic myths her own, Ms. Stewart has occasionally produced more coherent work, but none more exciting. (Bruckner 2001, E5)

In 2004 La MaMa produced *Seven,* which consisted of seven Greek plays in repertory spanning from 1972's *Medea* to 2004's world premiere of *Antigone.* In addition to *Antigone,* Stewart directed her previous productions of *Mythos Oedipus, Seven Against Thebes,* and *Dionysus Filius Dei,* and restaged Serban's original direction of *Medea, Electra,* and *The Trojan Women.* The seven plays were performed by the thirty-six multicultural and international members of the Great Jones Repertory Company. The music was also multicultural, with African, American, Asian, and Middle Eastern influences created by Alan Bezozi, Genji Ito, Bob Morffi, Heather Paauwe, Michael Sirotta, Stewart, Swados, and Yukio Tsuji. Stewart said of the venture, "There's nobody really doing repertory in America, to speak of, and to do this is like a dream to me. I've always, always wanted to do these plays in repertory. We've done the MEDEA, ELECTRA, TROJAN WOMEN trilogy in rep before, and the other four plays one at a time. But to do all seven together, well, I wanted to see if we could meet the challenge, and on a very limited budget, I might add. It's an enormous task logistically, and for the actors, of course" (La MaMa, "True," n.d.).

Antigone, created by Stewart, was the third play in the Oedipus sequence. Margo Jefferson of the *New York Times* praised Stewart's direction, saying, "We read Greek plays before we see them. We analyze structure and theme; we don't experience them as spectacles full of music and ritual. This primal whole is what Ellen Stewart creates with a vibrantly staged 'Antigone,'" Jefferson goes on to describe what she calls Stewart's "most dazzling theatrical coup," explaining, "She stages a taut, compact version of the ancient Olympic games. Eight muscular men run along the balcony of the theater holding torches. Music salutes their entrance into what is now a stadium. . . . [T]he suspense is acute. It's wonderful to see theater joined with sports again, and I say "again" because in ancient Greece the tragedies were part of a spring festival (the Dionysia) that included athletic games" (2004, E3).

The next year, Stewart directed another spectacle at La MaMa with *Perseus,* which she adapted from the works of Apollodorus, Hesoid, and Ovid, augmented with additional text by herself. The production tells the story of Perseus, a son of Zeus, who kills Medusa and marries a woman whom he saves from a sea monster. Jason Zinoman of the *New York Times* described the production, which featured more than twenty-five performers, writing, "This is a show about spectacle. . . . An ensemble of athletic performers . . . descend from a hole in the ceiling, float above the audience suspended by cables and perform gymnastics climbing up a velvety rope. . . . Expect to see billowing smoke, giant puppets and tightrope walking" (2005, E5).

When selecting plays to stage, Stewart usually chooses Greek myths that will fit the members of the Great Jones Repertory Company. While researching, she picks which versions of the play to use, always basing her productions on solid sources. Stewart says that her interest in classical plays originally stemmed from a desire to find decent roles for African Americans, who often were cast in stereotypical roles during the 1960s and 1970s.

Stewart casts from the company of multicultural performers in The Great Jones Repertory Company, some of whom have been with the company from its beginning. She usually knows who she will cast in individual roles from the company and includes performers of different cultures in each performance.

Because of the number of performers involved, it is challenging to organize rehearsals, which are arranged around the schedules, jobs, and commitments of company members. Rehearsals, which may begin with an hour here and there, eventually culminate in a two-week intensive rehearsal period. Performers may choose to read the play before rehearsal, but Stewart says, "They know mine [my version] is going to be different" (Interview, 2004). Stewart does not begin with a prearranged idea, but develops the production and music during rehearsal. Stewart generally begins working on the script when she starts rehearsals with the ensemble. She adapts myths and plays "into a form resembling a film treatment" (La MaMa, "Seven," n.d.).

Music plays a great part in Stewart's productions, and she works with different musicians to create sound and music for each production. Stewart explains, "I love music. . . . I don't really know how to do anything without music. So all of the things that I've done are music-based" (Interview, 2004).

The music of each production adds to the power of the performances. In 1986 Jennifer Dunning of the *New York Times* wrote about the music in *Orfei,* an adaptation of the Greek myth of Orpheus that was directed by Stewart. Dunning noted, "[T]he production owes much of its power to its rich score, composed by Genji Ito for an extraordinary variety of traditional folk and modern electronic instruments" (Anderson 2001, C13). Stewart's incorporation of music in her work *Dionysus Filius Dei,* which she also directed, led critic Allan Kozinn of the *New York Times* to write of a production with "otherworldly hues" that is "heavily percussive but also uses sharp-edged violin figures and exotic and electronic sounds. The vocal writing—Ms. Swados's contribution—is mostly for chorus. Its gestures are ritualistic and rhythmic with a Minimalist accent" (2002, B14).

Stewart has received many awards and honors, including numerous honorary doctorates. She has been honored with a Special 20-Year Obie citation, France's Ordre des Arts et Lettres in 1979, the MacArthur Fellowship Award in 1985, the National Endowment for the Arts Award for Art and Culture in 1990, the Kurbas Award for Distinguished Service to Art and Culture of the Ukraine in 1991, an induction into the Theatre Hall of Fame in 1993, and the "Order of the Sacred Treasure, Gold Rays with Rosette" from the Emperor of Japan in 1994. Stewart also founded an artist residency in Spoleto, Italy, is a member of the Seoul International Theatre Institute (SITI), and has taught and lectured at many institutions. She has also won numerous grants and awards for La MaMa and its resident companies. Her legacy includes giving a start to many well-known performers, directors, and writers—all of whom call her "Mama."

Summarizing her philosophy, Stewart underscores the importance of connections. She explains, "I believe that we are one big world and that all of us are connected. It's as if there were some kind of genetic residue in each of us that binds us all together. If we could find a way to communicate through the part of our common geneticism, so to speak, there'd be an almost umbilical understanding among people. To find a way to do that—to strike a chord inside you that makes you respond to me, is what should be happening" (Anderson 1997, 30). She adds, "I love to see and be a part of what comes out. Now that's what I like" (Interview, 2004).

Sources

Anderson, George W. 1997. "Visiting La MaMa's Founder: An Interview with Ellen Stewart." *America* 176 (4) (8 Feb.): 28–32.

Anderson, Jack. 2001. "Genji Ito, 54, Theater Composer Known for Stylistic Diversity." *New York Times,* 27 Apr., C13.

Bruckner, D. J. R. 2001. "'Oedipus' Sons Battle It Out in a Spectacle of Fiery Rage." Rev. of *Seven Against Thebes,* by Ellen Stewart based on the play by Aeschylus; music by Elizabeth Swados, Michael Sirotta, and Genji Ito. *New York Times,* 7 May, E5.

Finkle, David. 2001. "Even Theban." Rev. of *Seven Against Thebes,* by Ellen Stewart based on the play by Aeschylus; music by Elizabeth Swados, Michael Sirotta, and Genji Ito. *Village Voice,* 15 May, 76.

Greenfeld, Josh. 1967. "Their Hearts Belong to Mama." *New York Times Magazine,* 9 July, 10.

Horn, Barbara Lee. 1993. *Ellen Stewart and La Mama: A Bio-Bibliography.* Westport, Conn.: Greenwood.

Jefferson, Margo. 2004. "Look Out, Antigone, Creon Still Means What He Says." Rev. of *Antigone,* by Ellen Stewart based on the plays of Sophocles and Euripides; music by Elizabeth Swados; additional music by Michael Sirotta, Heather Paauwe, Bill Ruyle, Yukio Tsuji, and Ellen Stewart. *New York Times,* 27 May, E3.

Kozinn, Allan. 2002. "Distilling Dionysus from the Ancient Greeks and Bringing His Power to Life." Rev. of *Dionysus Filius Dei,* by Ellen Stewart; vocal score by Elizabeth Swados; music and orchestrations by Shelia Dabney, Genji Ito, and Michael Sirotta. *New York Times,* 29 June, B14.

La MaMa Experimental Theatre Club (e.t.c.). n.d. "Seven Against Thebes." http://www.lamama.org/AchievesFolder/20012002/SEVENAGAINSTTHEBES.htm (accessed 23 Sept. 2004).

———. n.d. "True Repertory Theatre Returns to Our Shores for One Month May 19 to June 13: La MaMa ETC Presents SEVEN." http://www.lamama.org/ArchivesFolder/2004/GREATJONESINREPERTORY.htm (accessed 23 Sept. 2004).

Schillinger, Liesl. 2005. "Drama Queen: An Interview With Ellen Stewart." *Words Without Borders: The Online Magazine for International Literature.* http://www.lamama.org/nowplaying_frame.htm (accessed 16 Mar. 2006).

70 Up. "Ellen Stewart." http://www.70up.org/stewart.htm (accessed 23 July 2004).

Stewart, Ellen. 2004. Telephone interview with Wendy Vierow, 23 Sept.

Zinoman, Jason. 2005. "Keeping the Ancient in an Ancient Greek Saga." Rev. of *Perseus,* by Ellen Stewart, based on the works of Ovid, Hesiod, and Apollodorus with additional text by Ellen Stewart; music by Elizabeth Swados, Michael Sirotta, Heather Paauwe, Yukio Tsuji, and Carlos Valdez. *New York Times,* 4 May, E5.

Representative Directing Credits

Off and Off-Off Broadway:

Cotton Club (1975, 1976, 1985), *Orfei* (1975, 1985, 1986), *Mythos Oedipus* (1985, 1988, 1989, 1996), *Another Phaedra Via Hercules* (1988), *Dionysus Filius Dei* (1989, 2002), *Yunus* (1992), *Tancredi and Erminia* (1993), *Seven Against Thebes* (2001), *Draupadi* (2002), *Carmilla* (2003), *Seven*[2] (2004), *Antigone* (2004), *Perseus* (2005), *Herakles Via Phaedra* (2006), *Romeo and Juliet* (2007)

Regional Theatre:

The Monk and the Hangman's Daughter (1986), *Romeo and Juliet* (1991)

International Theatre:

> *Arden of Faversham* (1970), *Romeo and Juliet* (1981, 1988), *Bamba* (1984),
> *Mythos Oedipus* (1985, 1988), *Phaedra* or *(Fedra)* (1986), *Cordilera* (1988),
> *Jerusalem Liberata (or Gerusalemme Liberata)* (1990, 1992), *Precepio Vivente*
> (1990), *Ciacinta* (1991), *Yunus* (1991), *Sacred Music of the World (or Ecu-
> menical Music of the World)* (1992), *The Monk and the Hangman's Daughter*
> (2000), *Seven Against Thebes* (2001)

Notes

1. Sources indicate that Stewart was born around 1920 in Alexandria, Louisiana; Chicago, Illinois; or New York City. According to scholar Cindy Rosenthal in a 2006 article entitled "Ellen Stewart: La MaMa of Us All" in *TDR: The Drama Review* (volume 50, issue 2, T190) Stewart was born on November 17, 1919, in Alexandria, Louisiana. Rosenthal states that Stewart was raised by her mother in Chicago and Detroit and had an aunt and uncle in show business, both of whom worked in a Detroit nightclub.

2. *Seven* included seven plays directed by Stewart: *Antigone, Mythos Oedipus, Seven Against Thebes, Dionysus Filius Dei, Medea, Trojan Women,* and *Electra.*

Stroman, Susan

Born October 17, 1954, in Wilmington, Delaware, Susan Stroman became the first woman director/choreographer to have four Broadway productions running simultaneously in the new millennium: *Contact, The Music Man, The Producers,* and *Thou Shalt Not.* Although her first critical recognition was for her Tony Award-winning choreography, Stroman gained acclaim as a director for both *Contact* and *The Music Man* in 2000 and subsequently won Tony Awards for her direction and choreography of *The Producers.*

Stroman, known in the industry as "Stro," credits her father with instilling a love of music in her when she was young. She grew up listening to him play Kern, Gershwin, and Rodgers and Hammerstein on their grand piano, explaining, "[S]inging and dancing was very much a part of the household. To choreograph and direct is what I wanted to do" (CNN 2001). When she saw a touring production of *Seesaw,* starring Tommy Tune, it solidified her drive to make theatre a part of her life. Stroman earned a B.A. in English from the University of Delaware in 1976, then headed to New York City, where she found work touring as a dancer in *Chicago* and *Sugar Babies.* Her first significant break as a choreographer was with John Kander and Fred Ebb's *Flora, the Red Menace* at New York City's Vineyard Theatre in 1987. Soon after, Hal Prince and others discovered her talent, and her career as a Broadway choreographer began in earnest. One notable success was *Crazy for You* in 1992, for which she won a Tony Award for her choreography and met her future husband, British director Mike Ockrent.

Despite her award-winning, high-profile career as a choreographer, Stroman's break into directing was not immediate. By 1987 she had choreographed and directed several productions around New York City, including *Living Color* at a cabaret club, the Off Broadway revue entitled *Broadway Babylon*, a show called *The Music is Kern*, and several productions of Fats Waller's *Ain't Misbehavin'*, as well as industrial shows and club acts ("Stroman," n.d.). However, it was not until her conception, direction, and choreography of the Broadway hit *Contact* that her career as a director became prominent.

Of her directorial debut on Broadway, Stroman recalls: "It all began when André Bishop [artistic director of Lincoln Center Theatre] came to see *Steel Pier*," a musical by John Kander and Fred Ebb that she had choreographed. "[Bishop] called me in—I'd never met him—said he'd loved the show, loved the poetry in it, and if I ever had an idea. . . . I went home and called [book writer] John Weidman, with whom I've been dear friends ever since we did *Big* together. I told him about André Bishop and he said: 'Get right over here because I have a *lot* of ideas.' So John came right over, and from there we proceeded until we'd worked up *Contact*" (Tallmer 1999, 50). More dance-theatre than traditional musical theatre, *Contact* tells three distinct stories through music and dance, all linked by the theme of isolation. Overall, they are "all about people connecting or their inability to connect," she explains (50). Originally, the production opened at The Mitzi E. Newhouse Theater at Lincoln Center in October of 1999, then transferred to Lincoln Center's Vivian Beaumont Theater in April of 2000. Calling Stroman the alchemist of a new anti-depressant, Ben Brantley of the *New York Times* raved, "*Contact* is a sustained endorphin rush of an evening, that rare entertainment that has you floating all the way home" (1999, E1). He gave Stroman credit for defining character within the dances, a trait for which she is proud to be known. Audiences agreed with the critics' enthusiasm for *Contact*, for Stroman's creation ran for over one thousand performances and went on a national tour.

Stroman opened her revival of Meredith Wilson's *The Music Man* in 2000 as well. She was nominated for two Tony Awards for direction that year, a first for any woman director. The well-known musical about a con-man named Harold Hill and his love for the bookish Marian the librarian won the Tony Award for Best Musical in 1958. As with any revival, one of Stroman's biggest challenges was to give the musical a fresh, new feel while honoring it as a traditional part of the heritage of American musical theatre. Critic Tony Brown of the *Plain Dealer* lauded the balance of the two in her production, writing, "*The Music Man* is pure American corn. Rather than try to overcome that, director and choreographer Susan Stroman capitalizes on it, injecting swirling energy into every number in the revival that opened last night at the Neil Simon Theatre. . . . Stroman doesn't deconstruct, she innovates, from putting the orchestra on stage for a few minutes for the opening overture to a raucous, closing second encore (do not dare leave early) that literally brings out the trombones (maybe not 76, but a lot)" (2000, 5B). Brantley praised the dances, but not the scenes, writing, "When the show is singing or especially dancing, it often seems to have winged feet; when it's just talking or clowning around, those feet are decidedly flat. What Ms. Stroman gets right, she gets wonderfully right, and that goes back to the idea of what the Gershwins called "fascinatin' rhythm" (2000, E1). Brown's closing remark seems prophetic in light of Stroman's next production: "*The Music Man* establishes Stroman as Broadway's newest master of the Great American Musical. With corn or without" (2000, 5B).

"With corn" may be the best way to describe the farcical humor in Mel Brooks's masterful stage version of his movie *The Producers*. Stroman, originally collaborating as a choreographer, took over the direction when her husband, the director, was stricken with leukemia and passed away in 1999.

The plot revolves around Max Bialystock, a failing Broadway producer who lassos his accountant, Leo Bloom, into some creative mathematics. By raising too much money on a surefire flop, they hope to skip town and live off of the investors' money. Part of the fun is watching the flop become a hit. Critics and audiences guffawed at Brooks's outrageous slapstick humor, but Stroman got credit as well for keeping pace with her divinely silly staging and choreography. Of their collaboration, Brooks wrote:

> What an imagination she has! I would write a song, and then she would take over. It was her imagination that made the show the monster hit it is. Take the scene where Leo Bloom has just met Max Bialystock and Max asks him to join his world of show business. Leo is scared to death because Max has touched upon his dream, so he flees back to his accounting office. I wrote a simple, touching song for Leo to sing all by himself, "I Wanna Be a Producer." Stro took the song and multiplied it by a million pink gels. She created a drab, soul-crushing accounting office where Leo secretly ruminates about his fantasy. The dream sequence was entirely her idea—beautiful chorus girls in golden costumes stepping out of filing cabinets, the water cooler becoming an enormous Dom Pérignon champagne bottle. She knows the human heart so well, she knew what Leo would be fantasizing about, and she put it right there on the stage. (2001)

A *Playbill* feature on Stroman also gave credit to her whimsy and inventiveness. "Susan Stroman is not exactly God, but it's tiny picture-perfect details, like capping a hilarious black-cat/broken-mirror/'good luck' gag sequence with (her touch) Max Bialystock deliberately walking under a ladder to jinx his own show—not to mention such brilliant numbers as (1) a bunch of little old ladies . . . tap-dancing with their walkers or (2) a Busby Berkeley overhead shot that turns into a giant pinwheeling swastika—that make *The Producers* what it is" (Tallmer 2001, 58).

Critics and audiences responded to the pure joy and silliness of the high-energy production. Steve Winn of the *San Francisco Chronicle* wrote, "Director-choreographer hotshot Susan Stroman (*Contact, The Music Man*) supplies the Teutonic shtick (wurst-topped showgirls, swastika dance spirals) for the 'Hitler' show-within-the-show and plenty of fizz for the musical's other production numbers" (2001, C2). Fred Kaplan of the *Boston Globe* agreed, writing, "Susan Stroman's direction and choreography are seamless when they need to be seamless and wildly over-the-top when they need to be that." He added kudos for the risky job of handling parody as well: "Everything about the enterprise is so expertly crafted, and exudes such palpable verve and joy, that it hardly seems risky at all" (2001, C9). *The Producers* broke all previous Tony Award records, winning twelve Tonys, including awards for Stroman's directing and choreography. It played for 2,502 performances before closing in 2007. In addition, Stroman won the 2004 National Broadway Theatre Award for her direction of the tour of *The Producers*.

Stroman had less critical success with *Thou Shalt Not,* a dramatic musical based on Emile Zola's novel *Therese Raquin*. Opening only a month after the terrorist attacks of September 11, 2001, the production received poor reviews and closed quickly. Transported from its original Parisian setting in the 19th century, this tale took place in 1940s New Orleans. Critics expected sparks from the partnership of Stroman and composer Harry Connick Jr. Brantley reported, "Ms. Stroman, with her upbeat kinetic playfulness, and Mr. Connick, with his wistful minor-key melodies, are like Siamese twins unhappily pulling in different directions." He continues, "Ms. Stroman . . . has a restlessly inventive intelligence, and she no doubt wanted to take the book-musical form, of which she has established herself as a first-rate interpreter, into new, darker frontiers. You can see glimpses of what she was trying for, especially in the second-act choreography. But intention and ambition merge only rarely here" (2001, 10E). Despite bad reviews and poor attendance, Stroman looked on the project not as a failure, but as an opportunity to grow as an artist. "I always try to reach out for something challenging, even *Thou Shalt Not* . . . gave me a chance to stretch. It wasn't a popular success; the timing was off. Nobody wanted to see anyone doing anything wrong, like murder, two weeks after the (twin) towers went down. But I like to reach out and expand because I always take a little bit from that last show and apply it to the next" (Ostlere 2004, 36).

In 2004 Stroman directed another original Broadway musical, Lincoln Center's production of *The Frogs*. Based on Aristophanes's Greek comedy, Bert Shevelove and Stephen Sondheim adapted the play into a one-act musical, originally performed at the Yale University swimming pool in 1974. In Stroman's production, comic actor Nathan Lane freely adapted the script further, adding current political jokes and new songs by Sondheim, and stretching the production to over two hours. The tale follows the journey of Dionysos, portrayed by Lane, to Hades, where he seeks a genius playwright to bring back to the living world in hopes of saving a corrupt society. Despite a stellar team of collaborators, the production faltered. Critic Brantley commented, "Even the creme de la creme can curdle every now and then" (2004, E1). He placed blame on the mismatch of style, writing, "Much of the score of *The Frogs* exhales . . . musical complexity. Even many of the choral numbers, with their use of dissonant counterpoint and lonely solo lines, convey somber, barbed introspection. . . . This inwardness unfortunately clashes like cymbals with the flashy outwardness of Ms. Stroman's floor-show staging and of the gag-driven book" (E1).

As a director and choreographer, Stroman admits to being a workaholic. At one point in 2001 she was tweaking details on *The Producers* in the evenings, rehearsing the national touring company of *Contact* in the mornings, and auditioning for *The Music Man* in the afternoon. At the same time, she was preparing for *Thou Shalt Not*. Soon after the death of her husband, she reported that her work in theatre had been her salvation. She explains, "My nighttimes and my mornings are simply unbearable. I find great solace in being in a studio with music and being with actors. Theatre is such a life force. It brings me great comfort" (Simonson 2000, 28).

Stroman's approach to choreography supports her work as a director, for she starts with clarity of plot and character, even in dance. "It was quite a natural transition for me, from choreographer to director," Stroman said. "As a choreographer, I have always been a storyteller. There is always a beginning, a middle and an end. I love to work on stories of human nature" (Brown 2001, 32). She explained further, "I feel that I am a writer of dance. . . . When I am dancing and choreographing, I am telling a story. So therefore, every dance step I do is plot-oriented, and it's always about pushing the plot forward" (CNN 2001). She uses a similar approach for both comedy and drama, explaining that regardless of the genre, the movement is tied to a particular characterization (Wood 2001, 5). She also ties characterization closely to her own experiences and personal philosophies, admitting that there is a part of her in all female characters, whom she describes as "vulnerable and human, but never victims" (Brooke 2001, 22). If casting dancers, she looks for dancers who can act and take direction. "I'll take a combination and then I'll toss out emotions to them. I'll say, 'Now dance this like you're aggressive,' or 'Dance this like you're flirtatious,' or 'Dance this same combination like you've had six margaritas'" (Wartofsky 2002, G01).

In both *Contact* and *The Music Man*, Stroman gained a reputation for casting little-known performers in leading roles, with great success. She is credited with the discovery of Deborah Yates, the lady in the yellow dress in part three of *Contact* who not only danced superbly, but "can act, too, projecting the requisite fire of wistfulness beneath the icy exterior" (Pogrebin 2000, sec. 2, 6). At auditions, Stroman immediately recognized a special quality in the former Rockette: "emotional depth as well as physical technique" plus "that certain something that made the choreographer and her colleagues feel as if they had just made a significant discovery" (sec. 2, 6). She has a sixth sense when actors are extremely likeable, explaining, "When they walk in, there's a special aura about them, even before they open their mouths" (sec. 2, 6).

Her sixth sense was employed when she stood up for Craig Bierko to fill Robert Preston's shoes as the original Harold Hill of *The Music Man*. Although the producers wanted a television or movie star for the role of Hill, Stroman recognized the crucial talents required for the role and stuck with Bierko through three auditions. She notes, "The one thing Craig Bierko has is a complete command for the language—he has a beautiful speaking voice and perfect diction. In *The Music Man,* part of the show's success is the rhythm of the pitch of the traveling salesman. Craig has it. When he does "Trouble," it's almost Shakespearean how he can wrap his mouth around the lyrics" (Simonson 2000, 26, 28). After seeing his third audition, the producers agreed, and Bierko went on to win a Tony Award for his polished portrayal. When casting for *The Producers,* she looked for a sense of comedy throughout the audition. "Every person had to sing, dance, and tell a joke. They had to be funny the minute they walked into the room," she explained (Fanger 2001, 20).

In the rehearsal hall, Stroman brings her joy for theatre, her inventiveness as a director–choreographer, and her sense of rhythm, a trademark of her work. Brooks credits Stroman with bringing comic genius as well: "She loves pratfalls and pranks, and she encourages comic anarchy. What's not to love?" (Brooke 2001, 24). *The Music Man* also proved to be a good match for Stroman's talents. She concluded, "The whole show is based on pitch and the rhythm and sound of the traveling salesmen and the people of Iowa. ... And my signature—whether it's choreographing for the Martha Graham Company or the New York City Ballet or doing a Broadway musical—is always rhythmic" (Pacheco 2000, D11). When coaching actors who are not dancers, she returns to rhythm as grounding, explaining, "They have to have great rhythm. All the actors that I work with have to have rhythm. And once I have that, then I can do wonders with any of them" (CNN 2001).

Stroman tends to respect tradition when reviving a musical, but looks to freshen it rather than revise it. On the first day of rehearsals for *The Music Man* she told the actors, "Get rid of any images of *The Music Man* you've ever had. This is a real town with real people with individual background stories and real relationships to each other. The comedy will come out of a real place, not out of parody" (Pacheco 2000, D11). She focused on Hill's ability to unblock locked emotions through music, a philosophy she applies herself. "I have such a passion for music that I visualize music," she said. "Ever since I was a little girl, I would imagine hordes of people dancing through my head" (CNN 2001).

As with any good director, Stroman watches for the rhythm and flow of the entire production as well, aware that modern audiences are used to the seamless scene changes in television and film. During previews for *The Producers*, she would give notes to actors at 7:30 P.M., then "watch from every seat in the house, including the highest row of the balcony. . . . I'm not just looking at the acting and the dancing, but the set as well. We have to be sure that the audience has an unobstructed view" (Fanger 2001, 20). Producer Rocco Landesman was impressed by her directing style, stating, "Watching Susan Stroman direct 'The Producers' was a revelation; talk about velvet glove, iron fist!" ("Why," 2005, sec. 2, 9).

Stroman has gained national recognition for her work through a number of prestigious awards. From 1992 to 2002 she won four Tony Awards and four Drama Desk Awards for choreography and a Tony Award and Drama Desk Award for her direction of *The Producers*. In 2000 Stroman received the Lucille Lortel Award for Outstanding Direction of *Contact*, and in 2001 she won the Drama League's Distinguished Achievement in Musical Theatre Award.

The rewards of the job are what drive Stroman in her career. "I'm not a material person, so it's not about the money," she states. "It's about the art. But I do feel responsibility that my shows are successful so people who write the checks to produce them also consider women [to direct them]" (Brooke 2001, 24). Stroman continues to vary her artistic endeavors as well, choreographing for the New York City Ballet or the opera when not on Broadway. If the first few years of the twenty-first century are any indication, Stroman will have many opportunities for art and much success ahead of her.

Sources

Brantley, Ben. 1999. "Musical Elixer Afoot." Rev. of *Contact,* book by John Weidman, conceived by Susan Stroman and John Weidman. *New York Times,* 8 Oct., E1.

———. 2000. "Rogue Sells Horns; Hope is Free." Rev. of *The Music Man,* book, music, and lyrics by Meredith Wilson. *New York Times,* 28 Apr., E1.

———. 2001. "*Thou Shalt Not* Not without Flaws." Rev. of *Thou Shalt Not,* by Harry Connick Jr., based on the novel *Therese Raquin,* by Emile Zola. *New York Times,* 26 Oct., 10E.

———. 2004. "Gods, Greeks and Ancient Shtick." Rev. of *The Frogs,* freely adapted by Nathan Lane, based on book by Burt Shevelove, music and lyrics by Stephen Sondheim. *New York Times,* 23 July, E1, 20.

Brooke, Jill. 2001. "Art of the Matter." *Avenue,* 1 Dec., 22–24.

Brooks, Mel. 2001. "Broadway Director: Susan Stroman." CNN.com. http://www .cnn.com/SPECIALS/2001/americasbest/stroman.sidebar.html (accessed 10 May 2004).

Brown, Tony. 2000. "Strike Up Band for 'Music Man' Revival." Rev. of *The Music Man,* book, music, and lyrics by Meredith Wilson. 28 Apr., Metro, 5B.

———. 2001. "Director's Broadway Bonanza Began with *Contact.*" *(Cleveland) Plain Dealer,* 2 Nov., 32.

CNN. 2001. "All the Right Moves." CNN.com. http://www.cnn.com/ SPECIALS/2001/americasbest/ppro.sstroman.html (accessed 20 Jan. 2003).

Fanger, Iris. 2001. "'Stro' Is Once Again at Center Stage." *Christian Science Monitor,* 13 Apr., 20.

Kaplan, Fred. 2001. Rev. of *The Producers,* book, music, and lyrics by Mel Brooks. *Boston Globe,* 27 Apr., C9.

Ostlere, Hilary. 2004. "Kissing Frogs Choreographer Susan Stroman Veers from Ballet to Buster Keaton to Aristophanes." *(London) Financial Times,* 17 Jan., 36.

Pacheco, Patrick. 2000. "The Music Woman." *(New York) Newsday,* 23 Apr., D11, D21.

Pogrebin, Robin. 2000. "For Those Who Dance and Those Who Dream About It." *New York Times,* 5 Mar., sec. 2, 6.

Simonson, Robert. 2000. "The Idol Maker." *Playbill* 18 (May): 26, 28.

"Stroman, Susan." n.d. Billy Rose Theatre Collection, clippings. New York Public Library for the Performing Arts.

Tallmer, Jerry. 1999. "Making Contact." *Playbill* 17 (Sept.): 50.

———. 2001. "The Hit Maker." *Playbill* 20 (Oct.): 56, 58.

Wartofsky, Alona. 2002. "Stroman Candle; Despite Loss and Heartache, the Choreographer-Director of 'Contact' Is Burning Bright." *Washington Post,* 17 Feb., G01.

"Why Female Directors Are Broadway's Smallest Club." 2005. *New York Times,* 11 Dec., sec. 2, 9.

Winn, Steven. 2001. "Producers Is Star-Crossed." Rev. of *The Producers*, book, music, and lyrics by Mel Brooks. *San Francisco Chronicle*, 20 Apr., C2.

Wood, Mark Dundas. 2001. "Susan Stroman: Reflections from a Golden Talent." *Back Stage*, 6 July, 5.

Representative Directing Credits

Broadway:
> *Contact* (2000), *The Music Man* (2000), *The Producers* (2001), *Thou Shalt Not* (2001), *The Frogs* (2004), *Young Frankenstein* (2007)

Off and Off-Off Broadway:
> *Contact* (1999)

Tours:
> *Contact* (2001), *The Music Man* (2001)

 # Taymor, Julie

Born December 15, 1952, in Newton, Massachusetts, a suburb of Boston, Julie Taymor became the first woman to win a Tony Award for directing a musical, *The Lion King*, which also won her the Drama Desk Award, Outer Critics Circle Award, and Drama League Award for direction in 1998. Taymor has directed and designed numerous acclaimed theatre pieces, and her artistry extends to opera, television, and film.

Taymor credits her parents for nurturing her creativity, and she particularly thanks her mother for being a role model and inspiring her to become a director. Taymor's exposure to puppetry came early, when she received a marionette theatre as a child. At age seven, she was inspired by her first play, *A Midsummer Night's Dream*, and she performed the role of Hermia in *Midsummer* at the Children's Theatre of Boston by age nine. Consumed by theatre she started directing productions in her backyard. While in her last year of high school Taymor became the youngest member of an experimental theatre group, Julie Portman's Theatre Workshop of Boston. "It was the Grotowski era, and we created theatre from scratch," she recalled. "Being part of a company like that gave me a very early understanding of how to be a creative theatremaker—a theatremaker as opposed to a playwright or an actor" (Gold 1998, 22). A bright and driven student, Taymor finished high school at sixteen and went to

Paris, where she studied mime with Jacque LeCoq and began her influential training with masks.

Upon return from Europe, Taymor enrolled at Oberlin College in Ohio, but rather than studying theatre, she pursued her interest in folklore and mythology, a choice which served her well as a director. As a budding entrepreneur during her undergraduate years, Taymor offset her lack of curricular theatre at Oberlin by arranging to train in New York City, where she was in residence with the Open Theatre, the Chelsea Theatre Company, and the Bread and Puppet Theatre (Blumenthal and Taymor 1999, 11). When she learned that Oberlin had hired experimental director Herbert Blau to form a theatre company, called Kraken, Taymor headed back to Ohio and won a place in the company. Taymor recalled, "That was probably the most formidable, exciting, creative time for me. Seven incredible people [one of them was Bill Irwin] locked in a gymnasium in Ohio, where you could really concentrate. . . . And the work was exceptional, though probably more interesting as process than as product" (123). Blau focused his group on conceptualizing new works in a collaborative, experimental setting.

After graduating Phi Beta Kappa in 1974, Taymor performed with Blau's theatre group in Chicago and New York City. When the group dissolved at the end of the summer, she won a Watson Fellowship and later a Ford Foundation Grant. She traveled to Eastern Europe, Japan, and Indonesia, a trip that lasted four years, to study visual theatre. While in Indonesia she started her own theatre company, Teatr Loh, and created her first major theatre work, *Way of Snow,* a trilogy that employed Balinese-style masks and Javanese shadow puppets as well as rod puppets, which she constructed herself (*Current* 1998, 563). "It wasn't like I was just starting," she clarified. "It was a sort of seminal work that put together ten years of theatre experience" (Gold 1998, 23).

Back in the United States, Taymor struggled at first to find work as an artist in New York City, though design work came more readily than directing or acting jobs. Between design projects she restaged *Way of Snow* at New York City's Ark Theatre in 1980 with an American cast. At Manhattan's La MaMa Experimental Theatre Club (e.t.c.) in 1981 Taymor restaged *Tirai,* another production she had created with Teatr Loh. Having seen both productions, critic Eileen Blumenthal wrote in the *Village Voice* that Taymor "was not merely a collector of exotic traditions but a first-rate director" (1981, 85).

Although Taymor continued to design some high-profile productions, including Andrei Serban's production of *The King Stag,* it was not until 1984 that Taymor directed again professionally. The Ark Theatre produced *The Transposed Heads,* adapted by Taymor and Sydney Goldfarb and based on a Thomas Mann novella. With a goal to explore the play visually and not just through language, Taymor told the story of two friends in love with the same woman. The men decapitate themselves, but magically come back to life with each other's head attached. Mel Gussow of the *New York Times* was impressed with the visual imagery, but thought that the production did not illicit the dramatic or lyrical quality of the original novella (1984, C24).

The following year Taymor co-created and directed a musical work titled *Liberty's Taken,* described as a bawdy "tragicomic romance about the American Revolution and the men and women who fought it" (Blumenthal and Taymor 1999, 95). Taymor designed 150 masks and puppets for the visual production, which she described as "extremely earthy, with talking ships' figureheads, hobbyhorses that fall apart and get eaten, Punch and Judy, and a brothel that's a 30–foot-tall woman who has copulating shadow puppets in her torso" (*Current* 1998, 563). The musical play was produced outdoors at the Castle Hill Festival in Ipswich, Massachusetts.

In 1986 Taymor directed her first Shakespeare play, *The Tempest,* for the Manhattan-based troupe, Theatre for a New Audience, at the Classic Stage Company. Taymor's imagination was well-suited to this magical play. She stripped down the visual detail, yet produced striking effects through her minimalist depictions and incorporated her signature mask and puppetry work. *New York Times* critic Alvin Klein was duly impressed, writing,

> In concept and in design, Julie Taymor's ingenious production, in an abridged, intermissionless 90–minute version, is an object lesson to anyone concerned with how to put young people in touch with Shakespeare. . . . True to Shakespeare's dictates, this is a *Tempest* of "wonder and amazement"—for everyone. Ms. Taymor's interpretation is influenced by the miraculous Piccolo Teatro di Milano staging of *The Tempest* (*La Tempesta*) by Giorgio Strehler, which was seen at the 1984 Olympics in Los Angeles and at the Summerfare Festival in Purchase, N.Y. Strehler's vision was an awesome celebration of theater; in his words, the play's fantastical elements are "not an imitation of life, but a metaphor for life." Ms. Taymor's *Tempest,* too, highlights theatricality and the supernatural, so that, ultimately, illusion can be stripped away. With that, the characters—and the audience—face the real world. For example, when the androgynous, delicate spirit Ariel, who symbolizes the magician's control over air and fire, is finally freed, a puppet is discarded and a puppeteer revealed. (1987, CN35)

The Tempest was subsequently produced at the Shakespeare Festival Theatre in Stratford, Connecticut, in 1987 and aired on PBS Television's "Behind the Scenes" in the 1993–94 season. She directed another Shakespeare play in 1988, *The Taming of the Shrew,* produced for Theatre for a New Audience at the Triplex Theatre in New York City and in Beverly, Massachusetts.

Having gained critical acclaim as a director, Taymor went on to direct her next project, a second music-theatre piece co-created with her partner Elliot

Goldenthal: *Juan Darien: A Carnival Mass*. Produced by the Music-Theatre Group in New York City in 1988 and 1990, the production subsequently traveled to festivals in Edinburgh, Lille, Montreal, Jerusalem, and San Francisco. Imagery and music were the prime means of communicating the tale, as the spoken text was in Spanish and Latin. Part passion play, part folktale, the piece is based on a short story by Uruguayan writer Horacio Quiroga. The plot revolves around an orphaned jaguar cub that is transformed into a boy until the fear and cruelty of the neighbors force him to transform back into a wild beast. Much more than a story, the play served as an allegory for a larger conflict. "It's showing the conflict between religion—specifically in South America the Catholic church—and the jungle, the natural state of man," Taymor explained. "You have the theme of the beast, the jaguar, against the human. From the human point of view, the jaguar is constantly devouring the human. And the human fights back against the primitiveness and the baseness with religion" (Blumenthal 1988, sec. 2, 5).

As a vehicle for folklore and magic, the project was ripe for Taymor's artistry. "*Juan Darien* incorporates and adapts ideas from all over," Blumenthal writes. "Its techniques include a Punch-and-Judy style schoolhouse with little glove-puppet urchins; a life-size Bunraku-type doll manipulated by three handlers; masks that recall the Bread and Puppet Theater; a version of Indonesian shadow puppets, and 'black theater' effects, in which handlers, shrouded in black, disappear behind walls of light" (1988, sec. 2, 5). Critics took notice of the magical transformations and stunning theatricality. Writing of a subsequent production of *Juan Darien* in 1989, Gussow called it one of the year's best. Of Taymor, he wrote, "She has grown from being an imaginative scenic designer and puppeteer into a conceptual director with a fabulist's view of the mythic possibilities of theater" (1989, sec. 2, 3). The imaginative production won Taymor an Obie Award for directing in 1988, gaining her further status as a director and theatremaker. Taymor staged the production again at Lincoln Center in 1996, and it earned five Tony Award nominations, including one for Best Musical.

In 1992 Taymor took a brief hiatus from theatre to direct her own adaptation of an Edgar Allen Poe story for the PBS Television production of *Fool's Fire* and to direct operatic productions of Stravinsky's *Oedipus Rex* and Mozart's *The Magic Flute*. Her return to the realm of theatre was a short-lived production of Shakespeare's *Titus Andronicus* for Theatre for a New Audience in New York City in 1994. Considered one of Shakespeare's most gruesome tales, the play is rarely staged, in part because of its overt violence. Taymor herself was shocked at the violence in the script and sought a way to "reawaken spectators to the visceral horror of violence" in a culture that is regularly flooded with realistic portrayals of violence in television and film (McCandless 2002, 487). She studied depictions of violence through the ages, in sculpture, photography, and painting, including romanticized depictions of the Rape of the Sabine Women. In an attempt to break away from purely realistic depictions, Taymor mixed realistic portrayals of violence with highly stylized presentations. The result was a Brechtian Verfremdungseffekt, alternately pulling the audience in and out of the theatrical and the real (488). One theatrical device was her use of "Penny Arcade Nightmares": strange tableaux revealed upstage of the action, harkening back to carnival and vaudeville spectacles (494). By flying in a large gilded frame draped with a red velvet curtain and revealing a surrealistic image, Taymor created meta-theatrical moments, with the spectators as voyeurs. Scholar David McCandless describes one example of the tableaux in production: "[A]s Titus pleads feverishly but futilely for the release of Martius and Quintus, the curtain unfurls to reveal the grotesque figure of a lamb-man, a creature with the head and arms of a man and the body of a lamb, upside down and seemingly floating within the frame" (495). *New York Times* critic David Richards gave a mixed review to Taymor's efforts at the St. Clement's Church Theatre, writing, "Evincing no squeamishness but considerable imagination, Julie Taymor stages the work as galloping Grand Guignol: nothing less, nothing more" (1994, C14). She reached a much larger audience with her film version, *Titus,* released five years later.

Taymor directed two operas, Strauss's *Salome* and Wagner's *The Flying Dutchman,* before returning to theatre in 1996 to direct Carlo Gozzi's *The Green Bird* for both Theatre for a New Audience Off Broadway and at La Jolla Playhouse in California. Gozzi's tale is of two royal orphans, found and adopted by a sausage-seller and his wife. More important than the fairy-tale plot, however, is the biting satire applied to eighteenth-century culture. Taymor used a quote from the play as a focal point: "You've got to examine the human heart in all its conditions." A beating heart inside a skeletal chest became a key image in her production. She explains, "This production is conceived around the interplay between the body's warring parts: the heart, the brain, and the stomach; love, the intellect, and the sexual and digestive desire" (Blumenthal and Taymor 1999, 206). *New York Times* critic Ben Brantley was amazed by the spectacle, writing, "Mixing melting dream logic with scholarly precision, Ms. Taymor has turned Gozzi's philosophical parable into a dizzying pageant of images out of Velazquez and de Chirico, Fellini and Bunuel" (1996, C3). Taymor took *The Green Bird* to Broadway in 2000.

Taymor's most famous success was her masterful production of Disney's *The Lion King,* which opened in 1998. She admits to being an unlikely partner for the Walt Disney Company. It was crucial that Disney permitted her to work on script development and to continue her experimental techniques while trying to create a commercial hit. The combination intrigued her, as did the challenge to stage such filmic events as the wildebeest stampede and the chase scenes, complete with herds of wild animals. She states, "I found the combination of a dramatic and moving story, the possibility of creating original music, and the enormous size of the project totally seductive" (Blumenthal and Taymor 1999, 210). Taymor sought first to shape the script and to provide a cohesive aesthetic, including the placement of new songs and choreography. The story of young Simba and his journey to become king begins with the central image of a circle as the cast sings "The Circle of Life." Taymor was attracted to the rituals of birth, death, and rebirth in the story—themes common in folklore. In keeping with her style, Taymor emphasized the magical, theatrical elements of performance, in part by revealing the actors who manipulated the puppets and animal masks. She wanted to foreground the live theatrical event, not duplicate the film on stage. "For me, it all goes back to the earliest form of theater, which is the shaman," she explains. "You watch the shaman put on a mask and transform himself. And the audience is allowed to participate in that simple power of transformation. That's all I'm doing. I'm saying, 'Come join in'" (Richards 1997, G01). Scalpers reportedly asked for $1,000 per ticket, such was the popularity and demand to see Taymor's intelligent, imaginative staging. Critics raved of her "triumphant" production at the New Amsterdam Theatre, and were duly impressed that she designed the costumes, a portion of the masks, and helped write some lyrics as well. *Newsweek* hailed the musical as "a landmark event in American entertainment" (G01). In addition to her Tony for directing, Taymor received a Tony for Costume Design and the production won a Tony as Best Musical. By 2004, *The Lion King* had been produced around the world in fifteen countries.

After her stellar success with *The Lion King* and staging of *The Green Bird* on Broadway, Taymor turned her attention toward film, directing both *Titus Andronicus* and *Frida*. Taymor explains her shift of medium by explaining that she had "done puppets up the wazoo" and wanted to explore other options. "What about Franco Zeffirelli or Mike Nichols or Orson Welles?" she reasoned. "What if people had said, 'Stay with the Mercury Theater, Mr. Welles'? Come on! When you're an artist, you're always looking for different ways of telling your story" (Richards 1997, G01).

Taymor's need to explore new horizons extends to challenging her performers. When casting, she may look for physical dexterity, mask work, and puppetry skills as well as acting. In addition, Taymor's actors must be able to swing between a naturalistic style to abstract and even absurdist techniques. She makes demands of actors' creative forces and their willingness to take risks. When auditioning, Taymor looks not solely for puppeteers, but for "inventive actors who move well. A strong actor gives an idiosyncratic performance, because he infuses the puppet character with his own personality instead of relying on generic puppet technique" (Taymor 1997, 136).

Taymor perceives a shift in her leadership style over the years, revealing, "I enjoy collaboration, and I enjoy telling people what to do. I like both equally. I like having people be able to carry forward my ideas and have them work and having people get excited about them. It's a very thrilling experience, like weaving. I'm beginning to recognize the way that I work, how I look at material and open it up. So, I have a self-confidence that's nice now. That comes with experience and age. I welcome challenge" (Daniels 1996, 133).

Taymor draws creative impulses from the actors by employing "ideograph," a tool for character development that she learned from Blau in her Oberlin days. She explains: "In the visual arts, an example of an ideograph would be a Japanese brush painting of a bamboo forest: just three or four quick brush strokes capture the whole. In the theatre, an ideograph is also a pared down form—a kinetic, abstract essence of an emotion, and action, or a character" (Taymor 1997, 139). Blau described the ideograph as a vortex; in action, the actor expresses "the kernel of each action without the distracting details" (Blumenthal and Taymor 1999, 12).

In rehearsals, Taymor gets actors on their feet early, experimenting with movement and characterization, but not to the detriment of exploring the text. Her rehearsals for *Titus Andronicus* began with a read-through of the script on the first day, then several days either exploring the text or the themes of the play in what she calls "a freewheeling, improvisatory" manner (Daniels 1996, 190). She was eager to establish a safe place where actors could feel free to investigate the violent acts of the play. Both together and individually, the cast explored ideographs, which she recalled "summoned up a huge amount of potential material." As rehearsals progressed, certain speeches or moments demanded "that the actors continue to explore in an abstract, physical manner while discovering their characters" (109). Taymor continually worked with the juxtaposition of naturalistic and stylized acting, reflected in her similarly diverse choices in design elements. In scenes where gestalt was important, she invoked metaphor by asking the actors to consider themselves as "instrumentalists in a symphonic work rather than as soloists" (191).

Another example of her rehearsal techniques is from her 1996 production of *The Green Bird*, based in commedia dell'arte. Taymor writes: "Rehearsals began with the exploration of the masks—telling the story without words, finding the dance, the individual physical vocabulary of each character. Then, in the true commedia tradition, the actors improvised each scene. In many cases, the improvs lasted for up to an hour, and much of the verbal as well as the physical explorations were recorded and subsequently worked into the play. Although I was fascinated with the possibility of fresh improvisation for each performance, not all of the actors were comfortable with that kind of freedom. Once the rehearsal period was over, the script was set" (Daniels 1996, 206).

Taymor has earned a reputation of blending theatrical traditions of various cultures in productions that are particularly magical, symbolic, and often ritualistic. Her settings often transcend time, seeming at once both ancient and timeless, both primitive and contemporary. She works in the physical and spiritual spheres of the theatrical event, but not to the detriment of intellectual meaning. She is as well-known for the design style of her puppets and masks as she is for the physical transformations that actors make into animals, spirits, or caricatures. Despite these common threads, Taymor insists, "Every piece I do demands a different approach. I respond to the original material, whether it is a book, a play, an opera. Or an idea. I like doing a project that comes out of a concept or thought" (Munro 2000, 510). According to biographer Eileen Blumenthal, "She prefers to start out *not* knowing how things are supposed to be done—and what supposedly cannot be done. She immerses herself in research, formulates a plan, and jumps in" (Blumenthal and Taymor 1999, 9). Looking back over her work of twenty years, Taymor sees a through-line in her artistry, which she describes as "a way of perceiving. Of finding. Of going through multiple layers to get to the ideograph. . . . To the core image. The emblematic symbol" (Munro 2000, 512).

Other artists have marveled at Taymor's productions and have tried to describe the magic she creates on stage. Robert Brustein, founding director of the Yale Repertory and American Repertory Theatres, comments that she has "a great capacity to turn a fairy story into reality and reality into a fairy story" (2000, sec. 2, 18). Thomas Schumacher, the Walt Disney executive who chose Taymor to direct *The Lion King*, states, "When you look at Julie's work, she deals with mythic material, legends, stories that have something deeper at their roots, and then she finds literally fantastic ways of telling them" (*Current* 1998, 564). Others simply describe Taymor's work as "genius," apropos in light of her five-year MacArthur Foundation "genius" Fellowship, which she was awarded in 1991. In addition to her numerous awards for *The Lion King* and her Obie Award for directing *Juan Darien*, Taymor received a Special Citation Obie Award in 1985 and is the recipient of the 1990 Dorothy Chandler Performing Arts Award and the 1996 Joe A. Callaway Award for excellence in directing for *The Green Bird*.

Sources

Blumenthal, Eileen. 1981. "Short Takes: Tirai." *Village Voice*, 26 Nov., 85.
———. 1988. "Theater: An Eerie Tale of Civilization and the Jungle." *New York Times*, 6 Mar., sec. 2, 5.
Blumenthal, Eileen and Julie Taymor. 1999. *Julie Taymor: Playing with Fire*. 2nd ed. New York: Harry N. Abrams.

Brantley, Ben. 1996. Rev. of *The Green Bird,* by Carlo Gozzi. *New York Times,* 8 Mar., C3.

Brustein, Robert. 2000. "Recapturing the Fantasy in Our Lives." *New York Times,* 16 Apr., sec. 2, 5, 18.

Current Biography Yearbook. 1998. New York: H. S. Wilson, 562–65.

Daniels, Rebecca. 1996. *Women Stage Directors Speak: Exploring the Influence of Gender on Their Work.* Jefferson, N.C.: McFarland.

DeVries, Hilary. 1986. "Julie Taymor: Giving Theater a Touch of Cross-Cultural Whimsy." *Christian Science Monitor,* 31 Oct., 26.

Gold, Sylviane. 1998. "The Possession of Julie Taymor." *American Theatre* 15 (Sept.): 20–25.

Gussow, Mel. 1984. Rev. of *Transposed Heads,* adapted by Julie Taymor and Sydney Golfarb, based on a novella by Thomas Mann. *New York Times,* 23 May, C24.

———. 1989. "Stage View: Civilization and Savagery Collide in Metaphor." Rev. of *Juan Darien,* by Julie Taymor and Elliot Goldenthal, based on a short story by Horacio Quiroga. *New York Times,* 24 Dec., sec. 2, 3.

Klein, Alvin. 1987. "'The Tempest' Staged in Stratford." Rev. of *The Tempest,* by William Shakespeare. *New York Times,* 10 May, CN35.

McCandless, David. 2002. "A Tale of Two Tituses: Julie Taymor's Vision on Stage and Screen." *Shakespeare Quarterly* 53 (Winter): 487–511.

Munro, Eleanor. 2000. *Originals: American Women Artists.* Cambridge, Mass: Da Capo.

Richards, David. 1994. Rev. of *Titus Andronicus,* by William Shakespeare. *New York Times,* 16 Mar., C14.

———. 1997. "The Pride of Broadway; Julie Taymor Turns *The Lion King* into Brilliant Theater." *New York Times,* 28 Dec., G01.

Taymor, Julie. 1997. *The Lion King: Pride Rock on Broadway.* With Alexis Greene. New York: Hyperion.

Representative Directing Credits

Broadway:
> *Juan Darien: A Carnival Mass* (1996), *The Lion King* (1998), *The Green Bird* (2000)

Off and Off-Off Broadway:
> *Way of Snow* (1980), *Tirai* (1981), *Transposed Heads* (1984), *The Tempest* (1986), *The Taming of the Shrew* (1988), *Juan Darien: A Carnival Mass* (1988, 1989, 1996), *Titus Andronicus* (1994)

Tours:
> *The Lion King* (1999)

International Theatre:
  Juan Darien (1990–91)
Other:
  Liberty's Taken (1985), *Juan Darien: A Carnival Mass* (1990–91)

 Teer, Barbara Ann

Born June 18, 1937, in East St. Louis, Missouri, Barbara Ann Teer has put her passion for theatre into many venues, as a dancer, actor, director, writer, educator, and producer. She has dedicated the majority of her professional career to the advancement of the black theatre movement, primarily through her founding and development of the National Black Theatre (NBT) in Harlem as a cultural and educational venue. Since that time she has won over sixty awards commending her excellence as a leader, artist, visionary, and contributor to the community.

Teer learned the value of education and the desire to serve the African American community from her parents. Her father was an assistant mayor of East St. Louis and an educator; her mother worked in educational administration, and both parents worked toward improving life for African Americans in East St. Louis. She and her sister took dance classes from their aunt growing up, and Teer subsequently pursued a degree in dance in college. She attended four different universities, graduating in 1957 with high honors from the University of Illinois with a B.A. in dance education. After college Teer continued studying dance in Germany, Switzerland, and Paris. She returned and started a masters program at Sarah Lawrence College, but "had just had it with education," and returned to professional dance (Teer, interview, 1985, 220). Teer was working with Alwin Nikolais in New York City when a knee injury stopped her career as a dancer and turned her attention toward theatre. The consummate student, she began to study acting with several master teachers: Lloyd Richards, Paul Mann, Philip Burtain, and Sanford Meisner.

As an actor, Teer found work on and Off Broadway, winning a Vernon Rice Award as Best Actress for her role in *Home Movies* in 1964. Despite her success, she became disillusioned with the types of roles she was getting as a woman of color: stereotypical maids, prostitutes, or matriarchs. Teer reached a turning point, at which she could no longer be satisfied with her status as an actor. "By that time I had directed a couple of shows and had done a number of films and TV shows, but I wasn't getting credit for the work I was doing," she explained. "I realized I was in a profession that did not value my contribution. So, I began to walk out of shows. The press said I was in revolt of theatre" (Schoichet 1980, 2). With Robert Hooks, Teer helped found the Group Theatre Workshop in New York City, which developed into the Negro Ensemble Company in 1967. However, Teer had her own idea about what an African American theatre company should be and what it should do for its community. In traditional theatre, she explained, "[Y]ou're not free to be spontaneous and to let go because the form is more important than the feeling. . . . What the other black theatres are doing is fine, within that form, but I wanted to add to the form, transform the form, actually open it up so that we could really express our magnitude, our omnipotence, our fire" (Harris 1979, 42).

In 1968 Teer was directing an Off-Broadway production of *The Believers: The Black Experience in Song,* a musical journey through the history of African Americans, when the opportunity to form her own group arose. Eight of the cast members chose to study performance with Teer, and when they found a permanent working space in Harlem, the group blossomed to almost fifty members (Teer, interview, 1985, 223). This group became the genesis of Teer's NBT. Teer and her students worked in close collaboration to flesh out a standard for their art before they performed publicly. Many in the group were not actors, but had a desire to participate in something vital and transformative to their community. Teer reports, "I didn't attract performers—you know, I attracted people who were committed to expressing themselves in a way that was not oppressed or 'less than'—people with college degrees, people of all sorts; we called ourselves The Liberators. These people had a mission, a purpose, a commitment that went beyond day-to-day survival. For two and a half years we went behind closed doors, and we experimented. There were no books, there were not films, no models" (Interview, 1985, 223).

To understand Teer's directing at the NBT is to understand her concept of theatre and its potential power. From the beginnings of the NBT in 1968, Teer was a woman who wore many hats, serving as artistic director, writer/ creator, performer, and director of their theatre pieces. She does not believe in distinguishing these roles exclusively, which she finds limiting, but in blending creative tasks as needed. In fact, in 1971 she shunned the term "director" entirely, stating, "To direct is limiting. I don't use people, [or] tell them to move from here to there. Therefore, I'm not a director" ("Teer," 1971, n.p.). She explains her distaste for the authoritarian concept of direction, stating: "I gave up acting because I couldn't be directed. No one could tell me what had to be done, because I knew better than anyone else" (n.p.).

Teer's objectives as a creative artist are reflected in her six holistic goals for the NBT: "1) the creation and perpetuation of a black art standard, 2) eliminating the competitive aspect of most commercial theatre, 3) reeducating the audience, 4) restoring spirituality and a cultural tradition . . . stripped from blacks in America, 5) creating an alternate system of values to the Western concept, and 6) creating a black theory of acting and liberation" (Thomas 2002, 350). Biographer Lundeana M. Thomas writes of Teer's aesthetic, "The ritualistic revivals conducted by Teer were visions of spectacle aimed at enlightening and inspiring the audience. Each performance was a celebration of life, of identity, and artistic expression" (367). Teer draws the form and content of her productions from her own African American community; from West African (especially Yoruban) forms of song, dance, music, and ritual; and from the spiritual and dialectical form of celebration in Pentecostal and holy-roller churches. She seeks to liberate the spirit of her participants, both the audience and the actors, through their mutual interaction.

Despite the intensive commitment of time and concentration needed to start her new theatre, Teer continued to direct professionally while the NBT was in its formative stages. In addition to her aforementioned 1968 production of *The Believers,* she directed a 1970 production of Charles Russell's *Five on the Black Hand Side,* a middle-class comedy about an African American barber and his clashes with his militant wife. Clive Barnes of the *New York Times* praised the American Place Theatre's production for strong characterizations, writing, "Barbara Ann Teer's direction sensibly accentuates the amiable eccentricities of Mr. Russell's racy and lively Harlem, but equally manages to keep those eccentricities within certain limits, so that the acting has a grace and a pace to it and never slips into caricature" (1970, 32).

Following *Five on the Black Hand Side,* Teer and her new theatre gained visibility through the NBT's first production, *A Ritual to Regain Our Strength and Reclaim Our Power.* Teer recalls that when it was performed on New York City's Channel 13 (Public Broadcasting System) they got "a thousand phone calls, and the show was aired three times consecutively, back to back. That caused the show to go national" (1987, 43). Basing the work on ritual rather than traditional Western theatre, the NBT showcased the unique form they had been exploring since their inception. Mainstream critics did not seem to know how to write about their new creation. *New York Times* journalist Thomas Johnson described a performance of *A Ritual* at the NBT in play-by-play style, as if it were a sports event. He described the opening song, "Sometimes I Feel Like a Motherless Child," the affirmations by liberators (performers), the series of dramatic and musical scenes, and finally, the testifying. Johnson concluded, "The ritual ended with a revival like finale—with both liberators and audience members together in the performing space dancing, clapping hands, and singing together, 'We are an African people, together we can change this mixed-up land'" (1971, E44). Critics were impressed by the pure energy from the cast to the audience, fulfilling at least part of Teer's goal as a director: to celebrate self in a rousing, affirming gathering. When Teer began to tour the production to colleges, she was overcome with the enthusiastic response to the power of affirmation. "During the performances people would get so turned on they would spontaneously start running up and down the aisles just celebrating themselves—you never saw anything like it. By this time I had changed all the standard theatrical titles. I said we were not actors, we were liberators. Our theatre wasn't a theatre—it was a temple. Our techniques were in a form I called ritualistic revival—we were doing revival form, we weren't doing play form" (1987, 44).

In July 1972 Teer followed up her success by directing a work she created collaboratively with Charles Russell for the NBT: *A Revival to Change, Love Together, Organize!* In this production, liberators welcomed the audience informally, chatting and asking what the audience expected from the performance. Liberators also presented improvisations on the street life of pushers, prostitutes, and pimps in Harlem during the introductory phase. A sequence of scenes followed, in which a junkie could not pay the money he owed his pusher. As the conflict escalated, the junkie's story was juxtaposed with the descent of Oshun, the Yoruba goddess of love, who asked the community to love one another. In the second part of the performance the audience was transported to a different part of the theatre, at a temple during a revival meeting of sorts, in which liberators presented facts about failings of the black community and the need for reform and spiritual revival. The action escalated to violence with the entrance of the junkie and pusher, and an evangelistic moment of healing and reformation concluded the storyline. Critics were again impressed by the energy transferred between the cast (liberators) and the audience (participants). Reviewer Albert DeLeon of the *Black American* wrote, "When the first act is over, one is raised to such an intense level of excitement that it seems impossible for the second act to sustain that sensation. It does. Indeed, the second act raises one's involvement with the show even higher" (1972, 11). He appreciated the improvisatory structure, particularly in the greeting of the audience, with the "tremendously inspirational atmosphere for everyone" (11). Critic Howard Thompson of the *New York Times* was impressed with the "boiling realistic simulation of Harlem street horror," writing, "The effect of watching all this is almost unnerving, with the shrewd staging and lacerating realism uncannily leavened by ethnic pride and optimism. The performers, primarily young people, are so convincing they seem to be stepping from life" (1972, 43). Clearly, Teer's techniques had a profound effect on her audience.

Teer again used improvisatory greetings between the NBT's liberators and participants in her direction of a work she created, *Soljourney into Truth*, in 1974. In this case, liberators introduced themselves as "flight captains," explaining, "We're going to hold hands, sing, and get a chance to feel good inside. Would you like that?" (Conley 1976, 53). During the introductions, the music began and the audience was transported to the Liberation Temple. Songs, scenes, and soliloquies all revolved around a common theme: relief from the oppressive belief systems of the Western world, deemed "The Land of Not" (53). An African chieftain appeared as the dancers twirled, lights flashed, and liberators chanted their ritual ceremony. Teer herself descended from a throne and asked participants to join in song and offer testimonials. Both *A Ritual* and *Soljourney into Truth* toured the United States, the Caribbean, South America, and Nigeria.

Although Teer and others have published essays about her theoretical perspectives on theatre, she has written and spoken less about topics like casting and directing—in part because these labels reflect Western conceptions of theatre, not her ritualistic, holistic approach to creating a performance event. However, she has described how she puts her theories into practice with the NBT company and how and why her ritualistic practices developed.

The NBT functions as both a training ground in Teer's techniques and a producing organization. One of Teer's main objectives was to throw out any Stanislavski-based methods of actor training and come up with organic techniques. Scholar Jessica B. Harris explains Teer's logic, writing, "As the black experience in America is quite different from the white one, black actors are frequently asked to play roles that have nothing to do with the basic reality of their lives. This may seem to be a contradiction but Stanislavsky's 'as if' theory does not always work for black actors in these times. With the theories established by the NBT, the black actor can return to himself, to his culture, to his heritage, and to his people" (1987, 285). Instead, Teer's approach to performing is to liberate the spirit in order to create from within, based on her study of Yoruba religion in West Africa. There are no rules or "rights and wrongs" in the religion, and it calls for no form to which one must adhere. Teer explains, "Nothing is sacred and holy because everything is just created, spontaneous" (Interview, 1985, 229).

From her own experience as an actor, Teer learned that she needed to give her performers room for individual interpretation, what some directors would call an organic approach to character. "I give you the space to fall on your face because that's the best way to learn," she states. "I'm there to make sure you look good. . . . If it's not gutsy and it doesn't come from the heart and it's not honest and open, then I will guide them [the performers] so that does happen. As a director that's my job, but by and large, I think you need to give performers the space to develop on their own" (Daniels 1996, 107).

During the two-and-a-half years in which the NBT searched for its own voice, Teer visited Baptist and Pentacostal churches, bringing their techniques into her theatre. "I went back to the theatre and tested some of those things myself with my own people. It worked, and basically [it worked] through trial and error," she explained (Interview, 1985, 226). She started her explorations with a drummer, allowing the performers to discover their inner rhythms and free their creative spirits. These exploration sessions were augmented with the NBT's Sunday symposiums, which featured speakers from the African American community. She noted, "We would rap and talk and exchange and try to get in touch with what this overwhelming force was that was called blackness. . . . We realized that we had a standard, but we didn't have a form to hold the standard, and that's when we began creating rituals" (227).

The "standard" she spoke of was her five cycles of evolution, based in studying essences. Performers worked to understand the characteristics of these cycles and apply them to character. Teer explained:

> We went through what I call the "nigger" cycle, "negro" cycle, and militant, nationalistic, and revolutionary cycles. We analyzed each of those cycles from a social point of view, a religious point of view, a political point of view. We found out about the colors, the foods, the lifestyle of the family, the relationships of people within each of those cycles. Each performer was required to go through each cycle. Each person had to keep a notebook of pictures and experiences when they went into each cycle. They would have to dress their cycle; they would have to live around those people. It was a total educational process. Then when we got to the revolutionary cycle we found it was all the same. That's when we decided we wanted to perform. (Interview, 1985, 226–27)

After eight years of researching approaches to performance, Teer created what she calls the Pyramid Process of Performing. She explained, "[W]e call it God-Conscious art, which means art that is conscious of life, art that is conscious of love, of energy—you know, art that comes spontaneously and fearlessly from within and allows you to be in the now and experience yourself moment to moment without having to hold onto a form" (Interview, 1985, 230). In essence, Teer's technique is unlocking what she calls the secret of soul in order to liberate creative energy. Improvisational techniques play heavily into these journeys of discovery.

Teer reflects on the changing styles of leadership and collaboration over the years, explaining that she resisted her authoritative side for years until she became comfortable with her own warrior-like strength. She explains, "It had been previously revealed to me that the acceptance of me as a woman would be lessened if I were the warrior type [i.e. 'demanding, authoritative, penetrating, and hard-line']. . . . The historical discourse in this country is that women should be more feminine and gentle and caring and loving, which meant that if I wanted to be comfortable with the opposite sex, I would have to give up my ability to be warrior[-]like because it was intimidating, and it would cause men not to like me" (Daniels 1996, 133). Her attitude changed when she started working with real estate developers and found she had to state her intentions outright. "You cut through it, and you go about your business. So I can say that I've come full circle. I do not worry about intimidating people anymore" (133). Her changes in leadership style translated to rehearsal as well. Teer relates, "In earlier years, I think I was so tolerant that very often I spoon fed them [the actors]. . . . I'd be so solicitous, and I'm not sure most directors work this way. Certainly now as all the pressures increase and we're asked to produce more on less and in less time, I'm less tolerant" (120).

The African American community in New York City has shown support of Teer's work through numerous awards and honors, including the AUDELCO Recognition Award in 1973 for her pioneering work founding the NBT and the Monarch Merit Award for outstanding contributions to the performing arts in 1983. In addition, the Harlem community showed its regard for the NBT by presenting sixteen thousand signatures to New York state in support of the theatre's restoration after a disastrous fire in 1983. Teer has two honorary doctorates for her outstanding contributions as well.

Teer sums up her life's work simply and directly, stating, "Theatre is here to support this country, not just to take some money for its tickets for an evening. It's a celebration" (Interview, 1985, 229).

Sources

Barnes, Clive. 1970. Rev. of *Five on the Black Hand,* by Charles Russell. *New York Times,* 2 Jan., 32.

Conley, Larry. 1976. "NBT: Theatre of Soul." *City Scope,* 53.

Daniels, Rebecca. 1996. *Women Stage Directors Speak: Exploring the Influence of Gender on Their Work.* Jefferson, N.C.: McFarland.

DeLeon, Albert. 1972. "Can There Be a Revival?" Rev. of *A Revival,* by Barbara Ann Teer and Charles Russell. *Black American,* 11 Sept., 11.

Fabre, Geneviève. 1983. *Drumbeats, Masks, and Metaphor: Contemporary Afro-American Theatre.* Trans. Melvin Dixon. Cambridge, Mass.: Harvard University Press.

Harris, Jessica B. 1987. "The National Black Theatre: The Sun People of 125th Street." In *The Theatre of Black Americans,* ed. Errol Hill, 283–91. New York: Applause Books.

Harris, Valerie. 1979. "Power Exchange 2: Barbara Ann Teer." In *Third World*

Women: The Politics of Being Other, vol. 2., 42. New York: Heresies Collective.

Harrison, Paul Carter. 1972. *The Drama of Nommo.* New York: Grove.

Johnson, Thomas. 1971. "On Harlem Stage." *New York Times,* 11 May, E44.

Schoichet, Gary. 1980. "Barbara Ann Teer." *Other Stages,* 17 Apr., 2.

"Teer, Barbara." 1971. Billy Rose Theatre Collection, clippings. New York Public Library for the Performing Arts.

Teer, Barbara Ann. 1985. Interview with Karen Malpede. "Barbara Ann Teer." In *Women in Theatre,* ed. Karen Malpede, 220–30. New York: Limelight Editions.

———. 1987. "Ritual and the National Black Theatre." In *Women in American Theatre,* ed. Helen Krich Chinoy and Linda Walsh Jenkins, 43–44. New York: Theatre Communications Group.

Thomas, Lundeana M. 1997. *Barbara Ann Teer and the National Black Theatre: Transformational Forces in Harlem.* New York: Garland Publishing.

———. 2002. "Barbara Ann Teer: From Holistic Training to Liberating Rituals." In *Black Theatre: Ritual Performance in the African Diaspora,* ed. Paul Carter Harrison, Victor Leo Walker II, and Gus Edwards, 345–77. Philadelphia: Temple University Press.

Thompson, Howard. 1972. "Black Theatre Stages 'Revival.'" Rev. of *A Revival,* by Barbara Ann Teer and Charles Russell. *New York Times,* 30 July, 43.

Representative Directing Credits

Off and Off-Off Broadway:
The Believers: The Black Experience in Song (1968), *Five on the Black Hand Side* (1970), *A Ritual to Regain Our Strength and Reclaim Our Power* (1970, 1971), *A Revival to Change, Love Together, Organize* (1972), *Soljourney into Truth* (1974), *Softly Comes a Whirlwind Whispering in Your Ears* (1976, 1979), *The Owl and the Pussycat* (1978), *The Trials and Tribulations of Staggerlee* (1980), *The Best of Both Worlds* (1983), *Power Play* (1996), *Testify* (1996), *Nzinga's Children* (1997, 1998), *Judgment Day and the Liberation of the Invisible Man* (1997, 1998), *Serenade the World: The Words and Music of Oscar Brown, Jr.* (2004)

Tours:
A Ritual to Regain Our Strength and Reclaim Our Power (1970, 1971), *Soljourney into Truth* (1974–79)

Vance, Nina

Born as Nina Eloise Whittington on October 22, 1914, in Yoakum, Texas, Nina Vance was a pioneer in the regional theatre movement in the United States. She was a producer and a director at the Alley Theatre in Houston, Texas, where she directed more than one hundred plays.

Vance grew up in a small town and loved the movies. Her interest in theatre grew after taking speech in the second grade. Vance made her acting debut as a buttercup in grade school and began directing plays on her aunt's porch. She continued her interest in high school by performing oral recitations and acting in plays. Vance attended her first professional theatrical production when she was an undergraduate at Texas Christian University in Fort Worth, Texas, where she was *Mary, Queen of Scots* on tour. She graduated with a B.A. in public speaking in 1935 and continued studying theatre at the University of California in Los Angeles. Vance returned to Yoakum to teach speech at a grammar school in the fall. In the spring of 1936 she studied at the American Academy of Dramatic Arts in New York City. While there, Vance attended many Broadway plays and took courses in education at Columbia University. She returned to Yoakum that same year to teach speech and drama at the high school, where she directed her first play. During this time, Vance began to read many plays and a collection of reviews by *New York Times* critic George Jean Nathan. She cites Nathan as an influence on her directing knowledge. By reading the plays that Nathan reviewed along with his critiques, Vance was able to further educate herself about theatre.

In 1939 Vance went to Houston, where new opportunities awaited her. In addition to teaching and directing at several high schools, Vance began performing technical work and acting at Margo Jones's Houston Community Players. Vance was greatly influenced by Jones, who taught her much about running a theatre and selecting new plays. Vance also learned about the Houston Little Theatre from her husband, lawyer Milton Vance, whom she married in 1941. At the Houston Little Theatre, she acted, performed technical work, and learned about directing from the company's artistic directors.

The year 1945 was a turning point in Vance's career. While attending a party, Vance met the musical conductor Efrem Kurtz, who asked her what she most wanted to do. She said, "It was a decisive question from a great man and I couldn't sleep all night. . . . So, I thought, well why am I not a DIRECTOR? I became, at that moment, a self-announced director" (Holmes 1986, 15).

That year Vance taught acting classes in her home and directed plays for the Jewish Community Center's Player's Guild, including John Van Druten and Lloyd Morris's *The Damask Cheek,* John Patrick's *The Hasty Heart,* Alfred Perceval Graves's *Out of the Frying Pan,* George S. Kaufman's *The Butter and Egg Man,* Philip Barry's *Tomorrow and Tomorrow,* and Hagar Wilde and Dale Eunson's *Guest in the House.* Locations for productions ranged from living rooms to conference rooms, and Vance tried to convert each location into a theatre-in-the-round whenever possible. Like Jones, she believed that theatre-in-the-round was more like a sculpture, while a proscenium stage was more like a painting. When directing productions, Vance began to use music—as Jones did—to open, close, and underscore scenes.

In 1947 the Player's Guild closed due to financial difficulties. The same year Bob Altfeld, who had worked at the Player's Guild, convinced Vance to start a theatre in his wife's dance studio. Vance sent out postcards inviting people to come to a meeting for the formation of a new theatre. At the meeting, people donated money and the theatre's organizational structure was determined with Vance as director. The Alley Theatre, an eighty-seven-seat theatre-in-the-round, was named for its location in an alley. Because the theatre was also a dance studio, sets had to be dismantled after each performance so that dance classes could take place during the day. Performers were not paid, and in addition to acting, they performed technical and janitorial duties. The first play, Harry Brown's war drama *A Sound of Hunting,* opened that year, directed by Vance. The play had received critical praise on Broadway in 1945, but failed commercially. Vance's version was met with a warm reception, with Hubert Roussel of the *Houston Post* writing that the production was "handled with considerable skill" (Beeson 1968, 11).

Toward the end of 1948, the Alley Theatre was declared a fire hazard and closed. It reopened early the next year in a converted fan factory with 215 seats, and later expanded to 231 seats. The new arena theatre opened with Vance directing *The Children's Hour,* a Lillian Hellman play that revolved around a student who accuses two female teachers of having an affair. It was an instant success in Houston. Publicist Vyneta Johnson recalled, "We began to see what ensemble playing meant that night. . . . The lights went down at the end and for the longest time—it seemed minutes to me—there wasn't a sound. But the lights came up and it broke. Men were standing on chairs, tears streaming down their faces. . . . Then the stomping began. People all over the arena were stomping their feet on the floor" (Beeson 1968, 29).

In 1949 Vance directed a critically acclaimed Alley Theatre production of Eugene O'Neill's *Desire Under the Elms,* a drama depicting an affair between a woman and her stepson. Vance staged her arena production on four different levels of platforms and used evocative movement. She explained, "By

. . . using simple balletic movements of seated bodies—leaning to the left or right of their chairs or forward in posture and with synchronization of these patterns between the two actors—the completely faithful preservation of the author's intent of sexuality and desire was maintained. No bed was needed. . . . Instead the audience who saw the ballet of two bodies in pinpointed light was filling in a setting in their own imagination and one was furnished with an usual stage picture of fine worth" (Stanley 1990, 45).

In 1950 Vance opened the Alley Academy, expanding the Alley Theatre into an educational institution. Two years later the theatre took on a semi-professional status, combining both paid and unpaid performers. In 1954 the Alley Theatre became an Equity theatre in order to extend its run of Arthur Miller's *Death of a Salesman,* which starred Equity actor Albert Dekker who was also the Alley Theatre's first star performer. With this performance, Vance began to hire stars in order to increase attendance and the quality of productions. In addition to directing *Death of a Salesman,* Vance directed several other Miller plays at the Alley Theatre, including *All My Sons* in 1955, *A View from the Bridge* in 1957, and *The Crucible* in 1959.

In addition to her admiration of Miller, Vance loved the work of O'Neill. In 1959 Vance directed another acclaimed production of O'Neill—*The Iceman Cometh*—at the Alley Theatre. First presented on Broadway in 1946, the play is set in a saloon, with its patrons spouting unrealistic dreams. In his review of the play, Roussel wrote, "Nina Vance has shown herself to be one of the most brilliant directorial talents in the country today" (1959, 160). Vance continued to direct O'Neill at the Alley Theatre with *Moon for the Misbegotten* the next year and the Pulitzer Prize–winning *Long Day's Journey into Night* in 1963. The autobiographical play about the tormented Tyrone family won Vance great acclaim. Howard Taubman wrote in the *New York Times* that Vance's direction "constitutes the most impressive credentials any company could offer to prove its worthiness. . . . Mrs. Vance, who has learned to handle a stage without the customary three walls, has found the means to convey the concentrated realism of that day in August in which the four Tyrones tear away from one another layer after layer of illusion" (1963, 25). Roussel also praised the production and the direction, writing, "Directed by Nina Vance with penetration and high technical ingenuity, and acted with rare passion and truth, the production is one of the finest of the Alley's history and a major theatre experience" (1963, 161). Vance co-directed her last O'Neill play, *Mourning Becomes Electra,* with Beth Sandford at the Alley Theatre in 1970.

Besides O'Neill and Miller, Vance also directed numerous productions by Jean Girandeaux and Tennessee Williams at the Alley Theatre. Of Girandeaux's works, she directed *The Enchanted* in 1951, *The Madwoman of Chaillot* in 1958, *Ondine* in 1960, *Amphitryon 38* in 1962, and *Duel of Angels* in 1966.

Vance's direction of Williams's plays included *The Rose Tattoo* in 1953, *The Glass Menagerie* in 1955, *Orpheus Descending* in 1959, *Camino Real* in 1971, and *The Purification* in 1973.

In addition to established playwrights, new playwrights were featured at the Alley Theatre. In 1965 Vance directed the world premiere of Paul Zindel's *The Effect of Gamma Rays on Man-in-the-Moon Marigolds,* a play that centers on the conflicts between a disturbed mother and her two daughters. Taubman found the play somewhat puzzling, but wrote, "Mrs. Vance's direction, which makes the most of the rectangular playing space in this arena stage, sharpens these antagonisms. . . . [I]t is to Mrs. Vance's credit that they are willing to produce a difficult and allusive play" (1965, 48). The play won a Pulitzer Prize in 1971.

During the mid-1960s Vance began to direct one or two productions per year, as she spent more time on her duties as an artistic director. In 1968 the Alley Theatre opened a newly built theatre, which contained both a thrust stage and an arena stage. For the thrust stage's first production, Vance directed Bertrolt Brecht's *Galileo,* which focused on Galileo's struggle for scientific progress, personal gain, and self-preservation in the face of intolerance. Vance's efforts continued to gain attention from New York City critics. Clive Barnes of the *New York Times* noted the fine ensemble work, writing, "The production moved well and sounded well and was essentially a team effort rather than an explosive series of virtuoso performances. . . . The company that stays together usually plays together, and these Houston actors have a nicely judged sense of ensemble acting that is depressingly rare in America" (1968, 88).

Directing for the first time in the new building's arena stage, Vance staged Albee's *All Over* in 1973. The play, which examines the topic of death, was originally produced unsuccessfully on Broadway in 1971 with only forty performances. Ann Holmes of the *Houston Chronicle* wrote that the play was "the Alley's best so far this season, and a production well within the category of the theatre's luminous, long-time successes. Nina Vance, working on the arena stage for the first time in the downtown building, directed with adeptness and broadened the gesture as if it were on a wider open stage—effective for a play of revelations" (1973, 209).

Vance preferred directing on the theatre's more intimate arena stage than on its large thrust stage. In 1975 she directed a critically acclaimed arena production of T.S. Eliot's *The Cocktail Party,* a verse drama that explores the search for meaning. The production was praised by Holmes, who wrote, "Nina Vance has made a few cuts, shaped and placed the complex but fascinating play to achieve a precise enunciation of the knotted plot and has singled out the clues to the obscure thesis Eliot suggests. . . . It is easily the best thing the new Alley Theater has housed" (1975, 212).

In 1977 Vance was one of several American directors invited by the Soviet Ministry of Culture, the Russian Copyright Agency, and the United States Department of State to observe theatre productions in Moscow and Leningrad. Later that year, she directed her last production at the Alley Theatre, Friedrich Schiller's *Mary Stuart,* a play about the strained relationship between the Scottish Queen, Mary Stuart, and the English Queen, Elizabeth I. Holmes praised Vance's interpretation of the play, writing, "Vance's direction powerfully structured the dichotomy of the play: the inner core of these women, as people, and the dangerous games they had to play as political rivals in explosive political climates" (1977, 212).

Although Vance directed primarily in Texas, she also directed some performances elsewhere, including Thornton Wilder's *The Matchmaker* at Philadelphia's Playhouse in the Park in 1960. In 1962 Vance directed Ben Johnson's *Volpone* at the Arena Stage in Washington, D.C., after having directed the production at the Alley Theatre the previous year. Preferring to focus her attention on the Alley Theatre, Vance turned down an offer to direct Jerome Lawrence and Robert E. Lee's *The Laugh Maker* Off Broadway in 1963.

When searching for new plays, Vance traveled to New York City, where she saw Broadway productions and met with literary agents, who could provide her with new scripts. Her desire to present new works was greatly influenced by Jones, her mentor. Vance selected mostly contemporary American plays, some European classics, and Broadway plays that had been critical successes but commercial failures. Vance preferred serious, realistic plays to comedies and lighter fare, which she often handed over for others to direct. However, she had a difficult time relinquishing control and often supervised and cast plays for other directors.

Vance wanted to communicate particular ideas with the plays she selected. She believed that a director should "have something to say that coincides with the author's need to communicate a special thing" (Stanley 1990, 72). She added, "A director's purpose is to interpret as deeply as he can know an author's intent, and when the author's dead it's harder" (158).

Vance's approach to casting changed over her years at the Alley Theatre. At first, she assembled a group of available performers and then selected possible plays to fit the cast. She asked performers to read potential scripts aloud, and then chose the best combination of performers and script. Because of this method, she could not announce a season of plays in advance. Later this practice changed, and a season's lineup of plays was announced beforehand at the Alley Theatre (Stanley 1990, 41). Vance also shifted her pool of performers over the years. In the beginning, she used her local repertory of actors, but later hired other performers from outside the company. To scout for talent, Vance and her staff attended productions in numerous cities and negotiated with agents. Eventually she held auditions in New York City and Los Angeles, as well as attended Chicago's Theatre Communications Group auditions.

Vance carefully studied the script before beginning rehearsals. She often asked her cast to research the setting and other aspects of the play through observation. For example, in 1962 Vance directed a successful Alley Theatre production of William Gibson's *The Miracle Worker,* a play about Helen Keller and her teacher. During rehearsals for the production, Vance brought her cast to the Center for Blind Children to observe and conduct research.

Although Vance was known for maintaining a calm and relaxed atmosphere in rehearsals, she expected a certain amount of discipline from her actors and staff. She always began rehearsals on time, regardless of whether all were present or not. Vance allowed staff members to be present at most rehearsals, although they were required to be still. Holmes described Vance in rehearsal, writing, "She [Vance] sits quietly in the dark—watching, mostly watching. There is no shrill correction, no badminton of interrupting commentary. Occasionally, she'll stop rehearsal to make suggestions, redo some blocking, discuss a large meaning or a small one. . . . She never says do it this way and never walks an actor through a part. She has met with each player earlier, talked over the whole. . . . And afterwards in her office she becomes confidante, psychiatrist and final authority" (Beeson 1968, 10).

Ensemble acting was of primary importance to Vance. With the arena staging, actors had to perform honestly and without a declamatory style. She encouraged performers to find motivations for their movements rather than move only for the sake of letting different sections of the arena audience see their faces. She would sometimes ask performers for input. For example, a week before the opening of *Long Day's Journey into Night,* Vance realized that one scene was not working. The performers told Vance that they had too much to do on the stage, and she re-blocked the scene, taking out the business that she had given to them. She valued her actors' feedback and at the end of each season, she asked performers to write down their opinions about various issues, including roles that they might want to perform.

Over a lifetime of achievement in theatre, Vance garnered a number of honors and awards for her work. Among them are the Matrix Award from Theta Sigma Phi in 1960, the Distinguished Alumni Award from Texas Christian University in 1964, the Woman of the Year by the Houston Y.M.C.A. in 1965, outstanding woman in the field of theatre by the editors of *Who's Who of American Women* in 1967, and numerous grants. She contributed to her profession through membership on the advisory group of the National Cultural Center and through service on the United States Advisory Commission of International Education and Cultural Affairs. In addition, Vance received an honorary doctorate of letters from the University of St. Thomas in Houston.

Vance died in Houston on February 18, 1980, at the age of sixty-five. She described the type of theatre to which she devoted her life as "a theater of continuity that emphasizes the ensemble actor and a repertory of merit" (Kakutani 1980, B5).

Sources

Barnes, Clive. 1968. "Theater: 'Galileo's' Challenge Is Met." Rev. of *Galileo,* by Bertolt Brecht. *New York Times,* 1 Dec., 88.

Beeson, William, ed. 1968. *Thresholds: The Story of Nina Vance's Alley Theatre.* Houston: Wall & Herndon.

Chinoy, Helen Krich and Linda Walsh Jenkins, eds. 1987. *Women in American Theatre.* New York: Theatre Communications Group.

Henahan, Donal. 1968. "Passionate Supporter of the Theater: Nina Eloise Whittington Vance." *New York Times,* 27 Nov., 34.

Holmes, Ann. 1973. "The Spotlight: 'All Over' Erratic—Splendidly Absorbing." Rev. of *All Over,* by Edward Albee. *Houston Chronicle,* 24 Jan. In "Nina Vance: Founder and Artistic Director of Houston's Alley Theatre, 1947–1980," by Nina Jane Stanley. Ph.D. diss., Indiana University, 1990, 209.

———. 1975. "The Spotlight: 'Cocktail Party' Ignites That Alley Glow of Old." Rev. of *The Cocktail Party,* by T.S. Eliot. *Houston Chronicle,* 20 Nov. In "Nina Vance: Founder and Artistic Director of Houston's Alley Theatre, 1947–1980," by Nina Jane Stanley. Ph.D. diss., Indiana University, 1990, 212.

———. 1977. "Some Magnetic Passages in 'Mary Stuart' at the Alley." Rev. of *Mary Stuart,* by Friedrich Schiller. *Houston Chronicle,* 21 Oct. In "Nina Vance: Founder and Artistic Director of Houston's Alley Theatre, 1947–1980," by Nina Jane Stanley. Ph.D. diss., Indiana University, 1990, 212.

Holmes, Ann Hitchcock. 1986. *The Alley Theatre: Four Decades in Three Acts.* Houston: Alley Theatre.

Kakutani, Michiko. 1980. "Nina Vance, Leader of Alley Theater." *New York Times,* 19 Feb., B5.

Lea, Florence M. 1989. "Vance, Nina." In *Notable Women in the American Theatre: A Biographical Dictionary,* ed. Alice M. Robinson, Vera Mowry Roberts, and Milly S. Barranger, 886–89. Westport, Conn.: Greenwood.

LoMonaco, Martha Schmoyer. 1994. "Nina Vance." In *Theatrical Directors: A Biographical Dictionary,* ed. John W. Frick and Stephen M. Vallillo, 409–10. Westport, Conn.: Greenwood.

Roussel, Hubert. 1959. "Alley Proclaims Full Artistic Maturity in O'Neill's 'The Iceman.'" Rev. of *The Iceman Cometh,* by Eugene O'Neill. *Houston Post,* 9 July. In "Nina Vance: Founder and Artistic Director of Houston's Alley Theatre, 1947–1980," by Nina Jane Stanley. Ph.D. diss., Indiana University, 1990, 160.

————. 1963. "'Long Day's Journey' in Alley Rendition a Searing Tragedy." Rev. of *Long Day's Journey into Night,* by Eugene O'Neill. *Houston Post,* 23 May. In "Nina Vance: Founder and Artistic Director of Houston's Alley Theatre, 1947–1980," by Nina Jane Stanley. Ph.D. diss., Indiana University, 1990, 161.

Stanley, Nina Jane. 1990. "Nina Vance: Founder and Artistic Director of Houston's Alley Theatre, 1947–1980." Ph.D. diss., Indiana University.

Taubman, Howard. 1961. "Theater: Alley Players." Rev. of *Six Characters in Search of an Author,* by Luigi Pirandello, and other plays. *New York Times,* 11 May, 41.

————. 1963. "Theater: O'Neill at Houston's Alley." Rev. of *Long Day's Journey into Night,* by Eugene O'Neill. *New York Times,* 27 June, 25.

————. 1965. "Theater: 'Effect of Gamma Rays.'" Rev. of *The Effect of Gamma Rays on Man-in-the-Moon Marigolds,* by Paul Zindel. *New York Times,* 7 June, 48.

Representative Directing Credits[1]

Regional Theatre:

A Sound of Hunting (1947), *Another Part of the Forest* (1948), *Caroline* (1948), *Clash by Night* (1948), *John Loves Mary* (1948), *Payment Deferred* (1948), *Another Language* (1949), *The Children's Hour* (1949), *Desire Under the Elms* (1949), *Gentle People* (1949), *No Exit* (1949), *The Warrior's Husband* (1949), *Joshua Beene and God* (1950), *Light Up the Sky* (1950), *The Magic Fallacy* (1950), *Season with Ginger* (1950), *The Wingless Victory* (1950), *The Enchanted* (1951), *Golden Boy* (1951), *Goodbye, My Fancy* (1951), *The Hasty Heart* (1951), *The Man* (1951), *Thunder Rock* (1951), *The Barretts of Wimpole Street* (1952), *Burlesque* (1952), *Home of the Brave* (1952), *Life with Mother* (1952), *Miss Julia* (1952), *The Skin of Our Teeth* (1952), *Elizabeth the Queen* (1953), *I Am a Camera* (1953), *My Dear Delinquents* (1953), *The Rose Tattoo* (1953), *Stalag 17* (1953), *Affairs of State* (1954), *Death of a Salesman* (1954), *Mrs. McThing* (1954), *My Three Angels* (1954), *Open House* (1954), *Picnic* (1954), *The Play's the Thing* (1954), *The Shrike* (1954), *All My Sons* (1955), *The Glass Menagerie* (1955), *The Lady's Not for Burning* (1955), *The Rainmaker* (1955), *The Remarkable Mr. Pennypacker* (1955), *The Tender Trap* (1955), *Anastasia* (1956), *Anniversary Waltz* (1956), *Career* (1956), *Detective Story* (1956), *Hedda Gabler* (1956), *A Roomful of Roses* (1956), *The Chalk Circle* (1957), *The Lark* (1957), *The Matchmaker* (1957, 1960), *Time Out for Ginger* (1957), *A View from the Bridge* (1957), *Wedding Breakfast* (1957), *Gigi* (1958), *The Madwoman of Chaillot* (1958), *Middle of the Night* (1958), *Three Love Affairs (A Phoenix Too Frequent, Bedtime Story, Still Life)* (1958), *The Crucible* (1959), *The Iceman Cometh* (1959), *Orpheus Descending* (1959), *Rashomon* (1959), *Waltz of the Toreadors* (1959), *Jane* (1960), *The Library Raid* (1960), *The Matchmaker* (1960), *A Moon for the*

Misbegotten (1960), *Ondine* (1960), *Mr. Roberts* (1960), *The End of the Beginning* (1961), *An Enemy of the People* (1961), *Misalliance* (1961), *Six Characters in Search of an Author* (1961), *Volpone* (1961, 1962), *Amphitryon 38* (1962), *Beckett* (1962), *Garden Spot, U.S.A.* (1962), *The Miracle Worker* (1962), *One Woman Show* (1962), *Long Day's Journey into Night* (1963), *The Queen and the Rebels* (1963), *The Three Sisters* (1964), *The Trojan Women* (1964), *The Effect of Gamma Rays on Man-in-the-Moon Marigolds* (1965), *The Tenth Man* (1965), *Duel of Angels* (1966), *Right You Are (If You Think You Are)* (1966), *The Caretaker* (1967), *The Sea Gull* (1967), *Galileo* (1968), *Mourning Becomes Electra* (co-directed with Beth Sanford—1970), *Camino Real* (1971), *Pantagleize* (1972), *All Over* (1973), *The Purification* (1973), *Wilson* (1974), *The Cocktail Party* (1975), *The Contest* (1975), *The Dock Brief* and *The Collection* (1976), *Tiny Alice* (1976), *Mary Stuart* (1977)

Notes

1. Credits listed include primarily those for the Alley Theatre.

 # Webster, Margaret

Born on March 15, 1905, in New York City to two British actors on tour, Margaret Webster's birth was announced by her father from Broadway's New Amsterdam Theatre, where he was performing. Webster would become both the first woman to direct Shakespeare's plays on Broadway and a pioneer in interracial casting on Broadway. Known to everyone as Peggy, Webster held dual citizenship in the United States and Great Britain, but lived most of her adult life in the United States.

Webster spent most of her childhood in England around theatres. She made her acting debut in 1911 as an angel in *Pageant of the Stage* in London's Albert Hall. Webster was a student at Burlington School for Girls in London and, after school, attended rehearsals with her parents, meeting many famous theatre professionals. One such person was the daughter of actress Ellen Terry, Edith Craig, who as a stage director was a theatrical role model for Webster. In 1914 to avoid World War I air raids on London, Webster's parents sent their daughter to Bradley Wood House, a boarding school in Devonshire, England. At boarding school, Webster dabbled in directing, staging scenes from *The Merchant of Venice*. In 1917 she attended Queen Anne's School in Reading,

England, where she played roles in school plays. After graduating from Queen Anne's School with a certificate in 1923, Webster enrolled at London's Etlinger Dramatic School, which was managed by her mother. In addition to her theatre training, she took economics and history at London University in 1924 and 1925, and a summer session at Oxford University in 1925.

In 1924 Webster made her professional acting debut in Euripides's *The Trojan Women* as a chorus member. Webster continued to work as a performer in British repertory companies as well as in commercial theatre. However, she usually played character roles and minor roles because her appearance was not compatible with ingenue parts.

In 1934 Webster made her professional directing debut with *Henry VIII* for the British National Federation of Women's Institutes in Kent, England, with eight hundred performers in an outdoor arena. From 1935 to 1936 Webster got minor directing assignments for tryout theatres,[1] stage societies, and other lesser venues, which was common for British women directors during this period. Because she was a woman, Webster found she had to prove herself on Broadway before directing on London's West End (Barranger 1994, 7).

Webster's life changed with an offer from British actor Maurice Evans. She had met Evans years earlier when he came to the Etlinger Dramatic School to rent the stage for an amateur production of George Bernard Shaw's *Major Barbara,* in which Webster performed. The offer came about when Evans was given an opportunity to star in a repertory of Shakespearean plays on Broadway. He telephoned Webster in London to ask if she would direct him in the first play, *Richard II.* Historian Milly Barranger believes that Evans selected Webster because he thought that "he could influence Webster's artistic choices and control the production from center stage. In the bargain, he gained an actress to play the Duchess of York, and a director that would not demand unreasonable remuneration for her services. Out of gratitude, she did not quarrel over the billing: 'Maurice Evans Presents . . .'" (2004, 66). Despite Evans's attitude, Webster would direct him in several productions in ensuing years.

Webster arrived in the United States with five weeks to cast and rehearse *Richard II.* She decided to cast someone other than herself to play the Duchess of York, thereby taking on the sole role of director. During the casting process, one actor refused to read because he would not work with a woman director (Barranger 2004, 67). In subsequent years Webster would experience problems with other performers who did not want to work with a woman director, including George M. Cohan, whom she directed in Sidney Howard's *Madam, Will You Walk* in a Baltimore tryout in 1939, and Helen Hayes, whom she directed in the Broadway production of *Twelfth Night* in 1940 (102, 106).

Webster made her Broadway directing debut with *Richard II* at St. James Theatre in 1937 with Evans in the title role. *Richard II* was a success, and

Webster received excellent reviews. Critics praised Webster's direction, with Brooks Atkinson of the *New York Times* calling it "fresh-minded;" Richard Watts Jr. of the *New York Herald-Tribune* calling it "one of the fine achievements of modern Shakespearean staging;" and John Anderson of the *New York Evening Journal* writing, "It is blinding to confront a Shakespeare play as if it had never been played, for that is how 'King Richard II' must stand" (Barranger 2004, 71). By focusing on the story, rather than the play as literature, Webster had made Shakespeare's plays come alive for American audiences. Although *Richard II* was an artistic and financial success, Webster did not reap its profits. She had made a bad business decision by agreeing to a flat fee rather than a percentage of the box office.

Because the play was a hit, Evans cancelled his plans for the repertory of Shakespearean plays, letting *Richard II* run its course on Broadway. Webster would collaborate with Evans throughout her life, directing him in principal Broadway roles in *Hamlet* in 1938, *Henry IV, Part I* in 1939, *Twelfth Night* in 1940, *Macbeth* in 1941, Michael Redgrave's adaptation of Henry James's *The Aspern Papers* in 1951, and George Bernard Shaw's *The Devil's Disciple* in 1962. Webster also directed Evans in the 1951 Off-Broadway productions of *Richard II* and *The Taming of the Shrew*.

After Webster's success on Broadway with *Richard II*, she returned to London in hopes of being offered work as an actor, but did not receive any acting jobs. Instead, she directed two tryout plays and one West End play, *Old Music*, by Keith Winter. Although the 1937 production of *Old Music* received good reviews, Webster returned that year to the United States, where more opportunities awaited her. On Broadway, she directed her father as the older Mr. Disraeli in an unsuccessful production of Elswyth Thane's *Young Mr. Disraeli*. The following year she achieved another coup when she directed Broadway's first uncut production of *Hamlet,* starring Evans. The play received excellent reviews and was performed on two tours. Webster said, "I wanted the play not to seem abstruse or obscure; to speak directly to its listeners in human terms" (1972, 28).

Webster's stagings of Shakespeare were presented to a very popular audience at the 1939 World's Fair in Flushing, New York. At a replica of the Globe Theatre, she staged forty-minute versions of *As You Like It, The Comedy of Errors, A Midsummer Night's Dream,* and *The Taming of the Shrew*. Even these edited versions received praise from both critics and the public.

Webster's clear and powerful directing style was applauded by audiences and critics alike. Like many critics, James Mason Brown of the *New York World-Telegram* mentioned her in reviews, explaining the key to her popularity. He wrote, "When it comes to Shakespeare, Miss Webster is a genius. More than any other person who has set him behind the footlights in our day . . .

she has the gift for making audiences forget the fact that the great William was ever a schoolroom assignment. . . . Miss Webster approaches Shakespeare creatively. In other words, she refuses to treat him as a classic—at least a dead one" (1941, 222).

In a decision to try something new, Webster signed a contract with Paramount Pictures in 1940, explaining, "I knew perfectly well that no woman director had ever 'made it' in Hollywood. I didn't really want to direct pictures; I'd rather have acted in them; I wasn't greedy for the money. Certainly I was keenly aware of the challenge and intrigued by it" (1972, 52). However, Webster let her option run out, realizing that her chances of succeeding in Hollywood as a director were slim, and returned to New York City.

Branching out from Shakespeare, Webster agreed to direct the Theatre Guild's production of *Battle of Angels,* the first full-length play of a new playwright named Tennessee Williams. Although she was fond of Williams and thought him talented, his inexperience and inability to rewrite the play in its Broadway tryout caused problems for the performers as well as Webster. *Battle of Angels* opened in Boston in 1940 to much controversy. In addition to poor reviews, the play—which centered on a drifter with sexual magnetism—was condemned by the conservative Boston City Council as indecent and outraged audience members, who walked out. The play was later revised and produced as *Orpheus Descending.* Webster's relationship with the Theatre Guild also deteriorated during this time because of differing working methods as well as quarrels about her fee, which the Theatre Guild wanted to reduce when the play did not transfer to Broadway. Webster discusses Theatre Guild member Lawrence Langer's attitude, explaining that he "made me conscious that I was a woman doing what is more often a man's job. He would insist on patting me on the head (metaphorically) and saying 'There, there!' A 'wise old owl' who knew us both counseled me to take advantage of this 'little woman' status by flinging myself on his manly chest and pleading for help; but I was stiff-necked and couldn't play it that way" (1972, 68).

Webster believed that experimental theatres should not be subject to the same Union rules as Broadway. A new venture called the Experimental Theatre was such a theatre, committed to providing an environment for creative productions. In 1941 Webster directed the Experimental Theatre's first production of *The Trojan Women,* starring her mother as Hecuba and herself as Andromache. However, Webster was criticized for producing an old play on Broadway and for casting her mother, a foreigner, as its star. Despite these criticisms, the play touched many theatregoers and was timely as World War II raged abroad.

Webster made Broadway history in 1943 with her production of *Othello.* The endeavor began in 1939 after the African American actor Paul Robeson asked Webster to direct him as Othello, a role he had already played in London to mixed reviews in 1930. No African American actor had ever played Othello on Broadway. Webster ran into problems casting the play with Robeson in the leading role. She recalls, "We wanted Maurice [Evans] to play Iago. . . . But Maurice shook his head and said the public "would never go for it." Everybody else said the same. Stars wouldn't play Iago, nor, of course, Desdemona. . . . In America—a white girl play love scenes with a black man . . . they were appalled. . . . Everyone gave different reasons, but they were all plain scared" (1972, 107).

Produced by Webster and Robeson, the play premiered in 1942 at the Brattle Theatre in Cambridge, Massachusetts, and then played in Princeton, New Jersey, at the McCarter Theatre to critical praise. The same year, Webster received an award from the Interracial Councils of Newark, New Jersey, for the contribution *Othello* made to interracial understanding. Webster tried to find producers to back a Broadway production, but it was difficult because of the interracial cast. The Theatre Guild finally agreed to produce the play, which opened in 1943 on Broadway with Robeson as Othello, Jose Ferrer as Iago, and Uta Hagen as Desdemona. In addition to directing, Webster played Emilia. The play received an ovation of about twenty minutes. Burton Rascoe of the *New York World Telegram* wrote, "Never in my life have I seen an audience sit so still, so tense, so under the spell of what was taking place on the stage as did the audience at the Shubert last night" (Barranger 1994, 14). *Othello* played for 296 performances—more than any other Broadway Shakespearean production. As a result, Robeson, Hagen, and Ferrer all became Broadway stars, and Webster won the 1944 Drama Club New York Award for direction. The play toured in the United States and Canada for thirty-six weeks with a new actor in Webster's role. Because of prejudices, the tour skirted cities that forbade African Americans in white theatres.

In 1944 Webster joined Eva Le Gallienne to stage a Broadway production of Chekhov's *The Cherry Orchard*, in which Le Gallienne also performed. Webster recalls of the dual direction, "The process of double direction worked well. It is one which I mistrust and had never experienced before—nor have I since. . . . Eva knew it [the play] much better than I, having done it at her Civic Theatre. . . . The basic concepts were hers and the early rehearsal period entirely in her hands. Gradually, as she became more absorbed in her own performance, it slid into mine; I could be eyes for her, a judge of balance and result. To me fell the lighting, and the orchestration of that symphony of off-stage sounds with which Chekhov plays are always filled—the distant music, the dogs that bark, the wheels-on-gravel and all those important tragic sounds which embody and end the play" (1972, 136–37).

Webster continued to cast interracially after the success of *Othello*. In

1945 she cast and directed Canada Lee, an African American performer, as Caliban in a Broadway production of *The Tempest,* which Webster produced with her friends Le Gallienne and producer Cheryl Crawford. That same year, Webster directed her mother's last Broadway appearance as Madame Raquin in *Therese,* an adaptation of Emile Zola's *Thérèse Raquin* by Thomas Job.

Also in 1945 Le Gallienne, Webster, and Crawford founded the American Repertory Theatre, dedicated to staging classic plays in repertory. They opened the next year on New York City's Columbus Circle at the International Theatre. Among the plays presented in the first year, Webster directed *Henry VIII,* James M. Barrie's *What Every Woman Knows,* and George Bernard Shaw's *Androcles and the Lion.* In 1948 Webster directed the American Repertory production of Henrik Ibsen's *Ghosts,* but it received poor reviews. The company folded the same year for a variety of reasons, including the location at Columbus Circle that drew only scattered audiences, an unpopular selection of plays, and issues with the unions.

That year, Webster founded the Margaret Webster Shakespeare Company (Marweb) to take Shakespeare to high schools across the United States and Canada. From 1948 to 1950 she directed *Hamlet, Macbeth, Julius Caesar,* and *The Taming of the Shrew.* The company of performers included two African Americans. However, as with the tour of *Othello,* they were banned from places that prohibited African Americans from appearing on the same stage as whites. Although extremely popular, Marweb disbanded in April 1950 due to financial reasons. Looking back, Webster surmised, "I have not the slightest doubt that it was the most valuable contribution I ever made to theatre in America" (1972, 173).

In 1950 Webster became the first woman to direct at New York City's Metropolitan Opera Company with her production of Giuseppe Verdi's *Don Carlos,* which received excellent reviews. From that year until 1960, Webster directed six more operas in New York City, all to good reviews.

Although the year 1950 brought Webster acclaim with her direction of *Don Carlos,* it also brought her trouble. That year, she was listed in the FBI booklet *Red Channels: The Report of Communist Influence in Radio and Television,* which included names of people and organizations suspected of sympathizing with communists. Webster's name had been mentioned in hearings as early as 1947, but it was not until publication of *Red Channels* that her persecution by the government began. Her name appeared in the booklet listing suspicious committees, meetings, organizations, and other activities with which she was associated. Additional problems arose when the Theatre Guild hired Webster to direct George Bernard Shaw's *Saint Joan,* which opened on Broadway in 1951. Protests over Webster's appointment prompted the Theatre Guild to ask Webster to defend herself. Webster refused, stating that she should be judged on her ability as a director. The play continued as planned with Webster as director, and received a glowing review from the *New York Times.*

Denied a United States passport to travel to Paris in 1953, Webster was forced to use her British passport. The same year she appeared before Joseph R. McCarthy's Senate subcommittee to answer questions. Ferrer, her former Iago in *Othello,* had named Webster to authorities in May 1951. Eventually, Webster was exonerated, but remained blacklisted in television and film, and was never again able to work on Broadway to the extent that she had before. The experience also destroyed her long love affair with Le Gallienne, although the two remained friends until Webster's death. Webster wrote, "Professionally, I have no doubt that my so-called 'career' was undermined. . . . All in all, my life did, very profoundly, change after those years, and in part as a result of them" (1972, 273). With work offers slow to come, she lectured and performed on college campuses, as well as directing Ferrer in an Off-Broadway production of *Richard III* in 1953, which was not a success.

Webster soon began a period of transatlantic crossings in search of work. In England she directed *The Merchant of Venice* at Stratford-on-Avon in 1956 and *Measure for Measure* the following year in London, both to good reviews. In 1958 she began work on the American tour of George Bernard Shaw's *Back to Methuselah,* which, while successful on tour, was not well received on Broadway. In Europe once again, she directed the 1960 production of Noel Coward's *Waiting in the Wings* in Dublin to excellent reviews and in London to moderate reviews. Overall, Webster's career in Britain was not as successful as it was in the United States. She explained, "The British do not like women directors and they do not like people who have made reputations in America" (1972, 301).

With the government putting the McCarthy hearings behind it, the United States Department of State asked Webster to travel to South Africa, where she directed Eugene O'Neill's *A Touch of the Poet* in 1961 and gave lectures, interviews, and recitals. The next year she directed Robert Bolt's *A Man for All Seasons* in Johannesburg.

The last successful play that Webster directed on Broadway was the 1962 production of Michael Redgrave's *The Aspern Papers,* a literary mystery adapted from the story by Henry James. It was also her last play with Evans. Howard Taubman of the *New York Times* wrote, "Margaret Webster's staging captures the genteel mood of the Nineties as it develops the story with tension and illuminates character" (1962, 24). Webster's final West End play was the 1964 production of Reginald Rose's *Twelve Angry Men,* which was extremely successful.

Webster's last involvement with repertory was in 1965 when she directed the National Repertory Theatre productions of Jean Giraudoux's *The Mad-*

women of Chalet and Euripides's *The Trojan Women,* which both opened outside of New York. She continued to direct other plays and published an autobiography shortly before her death from cancer at the age of sixty-seven on November 13, 1972, in London.

Webster's work in repertory and on Broadway required versatility from casting through rehearsals. In addition to making strides with interracial casting in *Othello,* Webster and Evans changed the Broadway casting system when casting *Richard II.* Instead of auditioning numerous performers at the same time, they saw each performer individually, and, if they thought the performer had potential, asked him or her to return to read later (Barranger 2004, 66–67). However, because Webster often worked on Broadway, she did not always have control of casting. She says, "In the productions I did in New York the leading actor was often a part of the initial plan. . . . The other stars and leading players were cast by mutual agreement, as and when we could obtain their services. I never could, or did, undertake a production, which I thought seriously miscast" (1972, 88). Casting in repertory theatre was challenging as well. Webster says that without performers who are capable of playing demanding leading roles, "[T]he plays won't work—or many of them won't" (88).

Webster noted her frustrations in working with producers who controlled casting, especially the Theatre Guild for *Battle of Angels.* She wrote, "Despite their desire to get the best actors they were masters of miscasting and their collective indecision made auditions a nightmare for director and actors alike" (1972, 68). She also wrote of her dislike of the Guild's tendency to replace performers, saying, "I am thrown off balance when I have to go back and redo an old scene for the sake of a new actor, with the resultant waste of time and loss of rhythm and tempo. But the Guild batted actors to and from like so many ping-pong balls" (68).

Whether directing modern or classic plays, Webster prepared thoroughly before rehearsals began. For *Battle of Angels,* she traveled to the South with Tennessee Williams to learn about the play's setting. For Shakespearean productions, Webster looked for the most authentic text among Shakespeare's folios. She believed that the Shakespearean director "should determine first the mood of the play, its material and spiritual atmosphere, its structural pattern, the wholeness of its effect. . . . Knowing his [Shakespeare's] method, we may guess at his mind; perceiving the familiar, we may divine the transcendental. With the former, we must sometimes take liberties of adaptation; the latter we may not violate except at our own peril" (1942, 419). Webster's aim was to interpret an author's text for theatre. She said, "First and foremost, I never set out to impose myself on a play, but always to reveal it" (1972, 89). Believing that there were many possible interpretations of a play, Webster thought it was important to consider the modern audience before selecting an interpretation.

In discussing which interpretation of *Hamlet* to choose, Webster elaborated, "Which of them, in effect, presents to the audience to which it is played the best theatre and the most vital illustration of the play Shakespeare wrote?" (1941, 443–44).

Webster emphasized the spoken word over stage tricks. She did not believe in updating plays to contemporary times or imposing other attention-grabbing devices on the production. She said, "I never found it desirable to 'gimmick' the plays in order to bring them up to date or make them what is hideously known as 'relevant.' . . . It is more difficult to achieve a universal 'relevance'; but it is there, if you begin at the beginning, that is to say, with the author" (1972, 89).

Webster familiarized herself with the text, sometimes to the point of memorization. She also used ground plans and tiny puppet figures to block scenes. Prompt books were invaluable to her. She explained that her prompt book for *Hamlet* included notes, "business, music cues, effects, prop lists, scene plans, light plots, everything" (1972, 29).

As she rehearsed the play, Webster tried to remain open to new ideas. She explained, "During rehearsals I have invariably gained new insights which prolonged study had never revealed. Sometimes they were provided by the actor's own vision. . . . In the theatre you have to be flexible, to adjust, to concede or sometimes to refuse. . . . Sometimes your fancy theories, to which you were so devoted, become plainly ineffective in practice" (1972, 88–89).

Webster focused on external elements, rather than internal ones. She stated, "Sometimes I sacrificed introvert detail and the lingering caress in the cause of impetus, energy, and tempo. Tempo is not the equivalent of haste. It is rhythm and variety, exactly as in a musical score" (1972, 89). During the last week of rehearsals, Webster refined the performances. Her ability to get along well with technical crews helped productions to run smoothly, too.

Influenced by the rehearsals of English director Harcourt Williams, Webster tried to create a comfortable rehearsal atmosphere for her own performers that encouraged experimentation (Barranger 2004, 69–70). Webster wrote, "The director must make his actors trust him and feel both easy and safe in his hands. He must stimulate their creative faculties, controlling and, in the most exact sense of the word, 'directing' them, but never riding rough-shod over them" (1938, 347–48).

An experienced performer, Webster understood many of the likes and dislikes of a cast. During rehearsals, Webster made general comments to the company, but gave more personal notes to performers privately. She also avoided telling performers exactly how to say their lines, explaining, "[A]s an actor, there is nothing which throws me off balance more completely than a dictated tune imposed on me for some reason that I do not understand"

(1972, 14). She also gave performers time to develop their roles. She wrote, "I hate rushing an actor; many of the best of them can't be rushed. You have to wait and coax them and have faith and pray you're right" (68).

Webster did not require her performers to be original all of the time, as long as their choices worked with the play. Of her work on *Hamlet* she said, "I did not want to reproduce other people's 'effects' or business unless they sprang naturally and inevitably from prepared soil. On the other hand I saw no reason to avoid an illuminating piece of action just because it had been done before or to think that novelty was in itself a virtue" (1972, 25).

Webster gave her full attention to performers, whether they were playing a minor or leading role. She explained that she spent much time with small roles, stating, "Even the bystanders, the 'crowd,' must be individually realized; even soldiers think" (1972, 90). Because Webster worked with many Broadway stars, she needed to understand the advantages and limitations of working with them. She explained, "[W]hen you have actors of outstanding personality and talent, you cannot negate them or plow ahead on the theory that they should be quite different" (89). Webster used various techniques to get performances that she needed. When directing *Othello,* she found Robeson had difficulty expressing certain emotions on stage and noted that she might have been able to obtain a better performance from Robeson if she had been a Method director. In order to elicit a good performance from Robeson, Webster admitted, "I learned the tricks to help him—speed above everything; if he slowed down, he was lost. I learned to mask his heaviness of movement by having him stay still, while other actors moved around him. I devised all sorts of detours round the difficult bits" (110–11).

Although Webster sometimes performed in her own productions, she did not enjoy directing herself. She explained, "I have never been much in favor of the director acting in his own show. . . . I don't really like doing it myself; especially when the play is one of depth and stature. I don't believe my work as a director suffers; with a good technical staff and a reliable understudy, the rehearsal stages can be well covered; but my acting does. I find it very difficult to close my directorial eyes and ears and to become subjective, immersed, spontaneous" (1972, 111). For *Othello,* Webster used an understudy in her stead, until late in rehearsals when she eventually played the scene herself (Barranger 2004, 134).

Webster received many awards throughout her life and was active in many theatrical organizations including the Council of American Equity, in which she pushed for rulings that helped develop Off Broadway contracts and professional resident theatres in the United States. She also received seven honorary degrees. Among her many citations and awards are the Annual Achievement Award from the Women's National Press Club in Washington, D.C., in 1945;

the Drama Teachers Association of Southern California Gold Medal Award for Services to Shakespeare in 1961; the University of Santa Clara, California, first annual Shakespeare Festival Award in 1963; and a Citation from the Yale University School of Drama in 1965. She was also named one of the Ten Outstanding Women of the Year by the Women's National Press Club in Washington, D.C., in 1946; one of the Five Key Women of the Year by the Fashion Division of the Federation of Jewish Philanthropies of New York in 1948; and a Distinguished Woman of the Theatre by the Theatre Arts Division of the Federation of Jewish Philanthropic of New York in 1953. Webster was inducted into the Theatre Hall of Fame in New York City in 1979. Webster was also a prolific writer who wrote articles as well as books, including *Shakespeare Without Tears* and *Don't Put Your Daughter on the Stage.*

In her book *Don't Put Your Daughter on the Stage,* Webster provided advice to those aspiring to a career in the theatre. She ended her book with these words: "[I]f you can make yourself a skilled artisan and an average artist, proud of your craft, and willing to use it for affirmation and not just for vanity, go ahead. Say 'yes' now and 'thank you' at the end. Good luck" (1972, 379).

Sources

Barranger, Milly S. 1994. *Margaret Webster: A Bio-Bibliography.* Westport, Conn.: Greenwood.

———. 2004. *Margaret Webster: A Life in the Theater.* Ann Arbor: University of Michigan Press.

Brown, John Mason. 1941. "The Most Successful Macbeth of Our Day Is Presented." *New York World-Telegram,* 12 Nov. Rpt. *Critics' Theatre Reviews* 2 (19) (17 Nov.): 222.

Hassencahl, Fran. 1989. "Webster, Margaret." In *Notable Women of the American Theatre: A Biographical Dictionary,* ed. Alice M. Robinson, Vera Mowry Roberts, and Milly S. Barranger, 908–13. Westport, Conn.: Greenwood.

Le Gallienne, Eva. 1953. *With a Quiet Heart.* New York: Viking.

Leiter, Samuel L. 1994. "Margaret Webster." In *The Great Stage Directors: 100 Distinguished Careers of the Theater,* by Samuel Leiter, 306–9. New York: Facts on File.

Nelson, Stephen. 1994. "Margaret Webster." In *Theatrical Directors: A Biographical Dictionary,* ed. John W. Frick and Stephen M. Vallillo, 425–26. Westport, Conn.: Greenwood.

Song, Oak. 1982. "A Promptbook Study of Margaret Webster's Production of 'Macbeth.'" Ph.D. diss., University of Oregon.

Taubman, Howard. 1962. "'The Aspern Papers' Opens at Playhouse." Rev. of *The Aspern Papers,* adapted from Henry James's story by Michael Redgrave. *New York Times,* 8 Feb., 24.

Webster, Margaret. 1938. "Credo of a Director." *Theatre Arts* 22 (May): 347–48.

———. 1941. "On Directing Shakespeare." In *Producing the Play,* ed. John Gassner, 443–44. New York: Dryden.

———. 1942. "Producing Shakespeare." *Theatre Arts Magazine* 26 (Jan.): 43–48. Rpt. *Directors on Directing,* ed. Toby Cole and Helen Krich Chinoy, 418–20. New York: Macmillan, 1963.

———. 1957. *Shakespeare Today.* London: J.M. Dent & Sons.

———. 1972. *Don't Put Your Daughter on the Stage.* New York: Alfred A. Knopf.

Weiss, Steven Marc. 1994. "The Rise of Directorial Influence in Broadway Shakespearean Production: 1920–1950 (New York City)." Ph.D. diss., Ohio State University.

Worsley, Ronald Craig. 1972. "Margaret Webster: A Study of her Contributions to the American Theatre." Ph.D. diss., Wayne State University.

Representative Directing Credits

Broadway:

> *Richard II* (1937, 1940), *Young Mr. Disraeli* (1937), *Hamlet* (1938, 1939), *Family Portrait* (1939), *Henry IV, Part 1* (1939), *Twelfth Night* (1940), *Macbeth* (1941), *The Trojan Women* (1941), *Flare Path* (1942), *Counterattack* (1943), *Othello* (1943), *The Cherry Orchard* (co-directed with Eva Le Gallienne—1944), *The Tempest* (1945), *Therese* (1945), *Androcles and the Lion* (1946), *Henry VIII* (1946), *Three to Make Ready* (sketches) (1946), *What Every Woman Knows* (1946), *Ghosts* (1948), *The Devil's Disciple* (1950), *Saint Joan* (1951), *The Strong Are Lonely* (1953), *Back to Methuselah* (1958), *The Aspern Papers* (1962)

Off and Off-Off Broadway:

> *The Old Globe Theatre* (1939), *Othello* (1945), *The Tempest* (1945), *The Devil's Disciple* (1950), *Richard II* (1951), *The Taming of the Shrew* (1951), *Richard III* (1953), *Carving a Statue* (1968)

Regional Theatre:

> *Henry IV, Part 1* (1937), *Madam, Will You Walk* (1939), *Viceroy Alice* (1939), *Battle of Angels* (1940), *Tonight at 8:30* (1940), *Twelfth Night* (1940), *Ladies in Retirement* (1941), *Macbeth* (1941), *Othello* (1942, 1943), *The Tempest* (1945), *Henry VIII* (1946), *An Evening with Will Shakespeare* (1952, 1953), *Antony and Cleopatra* (1963), *Measure for Measure* (1964), *Julius Caesar* (1966), *The Three Sisters* (1969)

Tours:

> *Richard II* (1937), *Macbeth* (1942, 1948, 1949), *The Cherry Orchard* (co-directed with Eva Le Gallienne—1944, 1945), *Othello* (1944, 1945), *The Tempest* (1945), *Ghosts* (1948), *Hamlet* (1948, 1949), *Julius Caesar* (1949,

1950), *The Taming of the Shrew* (1949, 1950), *An Evening With Will Shake-speare* (1953), *Back to Methuselah* (1958), *The Madwoman of Chaillot* (1965, 1966), *The Trojan Women* (1965, 1966)

International Theatre:

Henry VIII (1934), *Love of Women* (1935), *No Longer Mourn* (1935), *Snow in Winter* (1935), *Tarakin* (1935), *Family Hold Back* (1936), *The Four Partners* (1936), *Heads I Win* (1936), *The Lady from the Sea* (1936), *A Ship Comes Home* (1936), *The Three Set Out* (1936, 1937), *Lover's Meeting* (1937), *Old Music* (1937), *The Strong Are Lonely* (1955, 1956), *The Merchant of Venice* (1956), *Measure for Measure* (1957), *Waiting in the Wings* (1960), *A Touch of the Poet* (1961), *Ask Me No More* (1962), *A Man for All Seasons* (1962), *Twelve Angry Men* (1964), *Mrs. Warren's Profession* (1970)

Notes

1. A tryout theatre is a place where playwrights can stage their new work. Tryout also refers to a play in performance, with the aim of production on Broadway.

 # Zimmerman, Mary

Born on August 23, 1960, in Lincoln, Nebraska, Mary Zimmerman is known for her visually stunning direction and creative adaptations of old texts from many cultures. She has helped to bring performance art to the mainstream, most notably with her 2002 Broadway production of *Metamorphoses,* which she wrote and directed.

The daughter of two college professors, Zimmerman grew up in Lincoln, but traveled to London and Paris with her parents during their sabbaticals. As a child, she staged plays in her backyard and participated in community youth theatre with aspirations of becoming an actress. She discusses how she stumbled upon a rehearsal of Shakespeare's *A Midsummer Night's Dream* in the woods behind her childhood home, explaining, "I think that the combination of the enchantment of this playfulness of the grownups in my woods and the really clear-cut fun they were having was a hook to me that I haven't gotten over" (Women's Project 1997, 36).

Zimmerman grew to love myths when reading Edith Hamilton's *Mythology* as a child. When her school teacher in England read Homer's *The Odyssey* to the class, Zimmerman identified with the story, imagining herself "to be in exile from my homeland of Nebraska . . . I was just absolutely transfixed" (Interview, 2002). Later on, Zimmerman was also influenced by the works of Joseph Campbell, a writer and scholar of mythology.

With a love of literature, Zimmerman entered Northwestern University as a comparative literature major, but quickly switched to theatre. One of her theatre professors, Dr. Leland Roloff, taught her to think of herself as a performance artist. She explains, "He would say, 'Today we have Performance Artist Zimmerman. Please welcome Performance Artist Zimmerman.' Being called Performance Artist Zimmerman by a very distinguished . . . gentleman made me that" (Women's Project 1997, 37).

While taking graduate classes at Northwestern University, Zimmerman began to create performance art pieces. She explains how she segued into directing, saying of her performance pieces, "[T]hey got so elaborate that it was difficult for me to be in them and still see what they looked like. So I stepped out of them. Then I don't know how this happened, but somehow I understood that I could take this very image, non-narrative, very dream-oriented type of performance and combine it with my obsessive-compulsive reading and textual interest" (Women's Project 1997, 37). Zimmerman states, "I found out that directing is a way to be in the theater that perfectly suits me, because I love rehearsing. The director is everywhere and nowhere; she is invisible, and that suits me very well" (Dorbian 2002, 60).

In addition to Roloff, Zimmerman cites Tony Award-winning director and Northwestern University Professor Frank Galati as an influence. She relates, "[M]ostly the things I picked up from Frank are very practical. . . . Instead of staging left to right, stage upstage to downstage. How much more dynamic that is. I think he was teaching me that there is a craft to it. He's an intensely generous director" (Abarbanel 2000, 3). Zimmerman believes that Galati helped her to acquire a positive attitude about every production that she viewed as an audience member by trying to find good in each production. Zimmerman also cites as influences Peter Brook, Julie Taymor, and Pina Bausch (3).

While a master's student at Northwestern University, Zimmerman began her teaching career as an adjunct assistant. She received her M.A. in 1985, and then worked as an instructor and teaching assistant there. She received her Ph.D. in Performance Studies in 1994 and became an assistant professor the same year. Only five years later she became a full professor at Northwestern University, becoming one of a minority of people to earn all three degrees at one school and then teach there.

Zimmerman's association with Northwestern University has been important in her work. In 1988 Zimmerman and seven other Northwestern University graduates started the Lookingglass Theatre, of which Zimmerman is an ensemble member. Zimmerman often begins development of her pieces at Lookingglass Theatre or in the classes that she teaches at Northwestern University.

A turning point in Zimmerman's career was the Lookingglass Theatre's 1991 production of *The Secret in the Wings,* which Zimmerman wrote and directed. She explains, "[A] lot of important Chicago theater people saw that show, and it led to my association with the Goodman. That led to my doing *The Notebooks of Leonardo Da Vinci*—this time produced by them—and that was a big success" (Dorbian 2002, 60). *The Secret in the Wings,* which looks at the dark side of European fairy tales through words, song, and movement, was revised in 2003 for a new production in the Lookingglass's new theatre. It was also directed by Zimmerman in 2005 at the McCarter Theatre in Princeton, New Jersey, to positive reviews.

Another important event that happened after the production of *The Secret in the Wings* was Zimmerman's appointment as an artistic associate of the Goodman Theatre in 1991, making her the first woman director on the Goodman Theatre's staff. Zimmerman became a Manilow Resident Director at the Goodman Theatre in 1999.

The Goodman Theatre's production of *The Notebooks of Leonardo Da Vinci,* written and directed by Zimmerman, was presented in 1994—four years after the play's premiere at the Lookingglass Theatre. The show, which was named Best Production of the Year by the *Chicago Sun-Times* and the *Chicago Tribune,* won Zimmerman a Joseph Jefferson Award for Best Direction. In addition to stunning images, *The Notebooks of Leonardo Da Vinci* includes text from Da Vinci's notebooks regarding his personal and scientific thoughts. In her review of the Off-Broadway production in 2003, Roberta Smith of the *New York Times* described the piece, writing, "Take the writings of a leading Renaissance man. Sprinkle with Surrealist uncanniness and other entrancing visual effects. Simmer in the juices of a 1960s avant-garde dance and 70's performance art and garnish with eight talented, attractive, gymnastically inclined actors. The result is A SHOW WORTHY OF DA VINCI!" (Second Stage Theatre 2003).

One year after Zimmerman directed *The Notebooks of Leonardo Da Vinci* at the Goodman Theatre, she made her writing and directorial debut Off Broadway with *The Arabian Nights.* First produced in 1992 at the Lookingglass Theatre, the play was based on lesser-known tales from *The Book of One Thousand Nights and One Night* and featured song, narrative, and stylized movement. The original production won five 1992 Joseph Jefferson Citations including Best Direction. Although some critics of the Off-Broadway production thought it too long at two and one-half hours, the reviews were excellent. Ben Brantley of the *New York Times* wrote, "Ms. Zimmerman has orchestrated her ensemble into a seamless narrative of recital, song and carefully stylized movements in which stories endlessly beget other stories, like the boxes within boxes in a Chinese puzzle toy" (1994, C18). For the Off-Broadway production, Zimmerman was awarded the New York Drama Desk Award for Best Director. The show won additional awards after playing in 1997 at Chicago's Steppenwolf Theatre and Los Angeles's Actors Gang, including an *LA Weekly* Award for Best Production of the Year and twenty-two Drama-Logue Awards.

In 1995 Zimmerman returned to the Goodman Theatre to direct her adaptation of the Chinese epic *Journey to the West,* which chronicles a Buddhist monk's journey to India. The play, which Zimmerman condensed from a four-thousand-page story spanning sixteen years into about three hours, depicts a physical and spiritual journey using spectacular visual effects and Eastern music. Richard Christiansen of the *Chicago Tribune* described Zimmerman's imaginative staging, writing, "With cables, trapdoors and springs, pigs descend from heaven, monsters arise from the deep and cudgels pop up from the ground. A Goddess descends a staircase, her long golden robe shimmering as she moves toward the earth. A whole village slides over miles of frozen river" (1995, 22). *Journey to the West* won many awards including the 1995 Joseph Jefferson Award for Best New Work and three Gay Chicago Awards. It was also named one of the Top Ten Best Productions of the Year by *Time* magazine. The production played at Boston's Huntington Theatre in 1996 and at California's Berkeley Repertory Theatre, where it won more awards in 1997.

The Goodman Theatre's 1997 production of Zimmerman's adaptation of a Persian epic poem, *Mirror of the Invisible World,* won several Joseph Jefferson Awards. The play, which was directed by Zimmerman, used simple yet effective visual effects, such as moving black fabric to show a crow flying. In his review of the play, David Patrick Stearns of *USA Today* praised Zimmerman's development, writing, "Her work just keeps growing richer as she manipulates viewpoint and perspective in her highly atmospheric style" (1997, 8D).

The next year, Zimmerman wrote and directed *Eleven Rooms of Proust,* based on Proust's *Remembrance of Things Past,* presenting her version of the monumental work in under an hour. First developed at Northwestern University, it was staged at Chicago's Berger Mansion, and later in a Chicago warehouse. During the production, small audience groups moved through the space to view different scenes.

While audiences actually traveled through space to view *Eleven Rooms of Proust,* they remained seated to watch Zimmerman's direction of the long journey of Odysseus in her adaptation of Homer's epic *The Odyssey,* produced at the Goodman Theatre in 1999. The Goodman Theatre production won three Joseph Jefferson Awards—adding to the four Joseph Jefferson Citations, including Best Direction, for the Lookingglass Theatre's original production of the piece in 1990. In his review of the Goodman Theatre production, which incorporated dialogue, poetry, dance, film, and music, Joel Henning of the *Wall Street Journal* described Zimmerman's striking use of shadow puppetry. He wrote, "Using no more than backlighting, some shadows, the gigantic voice of actor Ed Dixon, a few dolls and a sheet, Ms. Zimmerman lets us join in the grisly feast, as the Cyclops munches on the heads of Odysseus' men as if they were canapés" (1999, A24).

In 2002 Zimmerman made her Broadway debut as a writer and director with *Metamorphoses,* a play based on Ovid's mythological poem that explores the theme of metamorphosis. The action of the play revolves around a large pool of water, which Zimmerman says "is itself transformative. It is corrosive and turbulent. It symbolizes drunkenness, lust, tears of grief and speech" (Johnson 1999). Zimmerman incorporated the use of water when staging each of the ten chosen myths. In one case, Apollo's son Phaeton wears sunglasses and lies on a raft in the water. Sitting in a chair on the pool's deck is a therapist, who takes notes and makes comments about Phaeton's issues with his father. Apollo appears upstage softly singing an Italian opera—weaving quotes that Phaeton attributes to him into his song.

The play's journey to Broadway took many years. Originally performed as *Six Myths* in 1996 at Northwestern University, the play opened as *Metamorphoses* in 1998 at Chicago's Ivanhoe Theatre. The Lookingglass Theatre's production won the Joseph Jefferson Award for Best New Work/Adaptation and moved the following year to California's Berkeley Repertory Theatre, where it won five Bay Area Critics Awards. In 2000 it played at the Seattle Repertory Theatre before moving to Los Angeles's Mark Taper Forum, where it won three Ovation Awards including Best Director. Laden with awards, the show then opened Off Broadway in 2001, shortly after the terrorist attacks of September 11. Many audience members were deeply moved by the play. Amy Gamerman of the *Wall Street Journal* noted that the production offered "the power to console" (2001, A14). Brantley later wrote, "It was less than a month after the terrorist attacks of Sept. 11, and the show's ritualistic portrayal of love, death and transformation somehow seemed to flow directly from the collective unconscious of a stunned city. 'Metamorphoses' became a sold-out hit, and every night you could hear the sounds of men and women openly crying" (2002, E1). Zimmerman states that the play was not changed after the attacks of September 11, but that its words took on new meaning. She reflects, "[T]here is something about these stories being so ancient. And they have something to say because they are so ancient that [they] help you take the long view. . . . [W]e've suffered incredible disasters and transforming events, and yet the story goes on" (Interview, 2002).

In 2001 *Metamorphoses* was named Best Production of the Year by *Time* magazine and won five Drama Critic Awards. *Metamorphoses* then transferred to Circle in the Square's Broadway theatre in 2002. Among her awards for the New York City productions of *Metamorphoses,* Zimmerman won the 2002 Tony Award for Best Director. That year she also was won awards for her directing with the Drama Desk Award, the Obie Award, the Outer Critics Circle Award, and the Lucille Lortel Award. Although Zimmerman's success on Broadway has made her one of the few women directors ever to win a Tony Award, she is committed to nonprofit theatre. She has also turned down Hollywood offers that required alterations in her text (Stein 1996, C1).

Zimmerman has collaborated with composer Philip Glass on two of his operas. She directed Glass's *Akhenaten* in 2000 at the Boston Lyric Opera and the Chicago Opera House. In 2002 Zimmerman collaborated with Glass to create the libretto and provide the direction for *Galileo Galilei,* which follows Galileo's life—traveling backward in time from his last days as a blind lonely man, through his discoveries and inventions, to his early childhood. The production played at the Goodman Theatre, the Brooklyn Academy of Music, and London's Barbicon Theatre.

In addition to directing her own work, Zimmerman sometimes directs the works of others, such as the Goodman Theatre productions of Paula Vogel's *The Baltimore Waltz* in 1993 and of Shakespeare's *All's Well That Ends Well* in 1995. Zimmerman enjoys directing Shakespeare because it is especially open to interpretation. Her 2004 direction of Shakespeare's *Pericles,* a tale of travel presented at the Shakespeare Theatre in Washington, D.C., was praised by critic Peter Marks of the *Washington Post.* He wrote, "Her imaginative fingerprints are all over this staging. . . . Ostling's superb set puts 'Pericles' in a towering room with a massive vertical window; all during the play, faces and model ships and goddesses peer in and sail by and fly through the window. Adding to the sense of a magical playroom is a wall of drawers and cabinets, out of which cast members pull props and bits of scenery, such as the fabrics used to suggest stormy ocean swells and virginal bridal beds. . . . Zimmerman's coups here are not merely cosmetic. She makes a drastic but highly effective change in the script, altogether eliminating a central character in the play— Gower, the hardbitten narrator—and apportioning his lines to the rest of the cast" (2004, C01).

When creating and directing her own pieces, Zimmerman likes to work with ancient texts from an oral tradition. She explains, "To me, they translate extremely well back into performance because they come from performance. They come from being told aloud and then are fixed in some print form or another. Also the things that novels or stories do—different than things written for the stage—are interesting. The way they move through time really quickly, or slow down time, or dwell on a moment, or go over fifteen years in two sentences. They can invoke the absolutely fantastical in a way a playwright would not because he knows he's writing for the theatre, and that this would be an impossible image. I like to confront those impossible images and try to do them" (Abarbanel 2000, 2).

Zimmerman casts productions herself and turns down offers to produce her work if she is required to recast the production with stars or other performers who she thinks may not be appropriate. She states why she often likes to work with the same performers: "[W]hen you work with people you trust, it's like starting at the third week of rehearsal. You just have an incredible shorthand" (Jones 2002, 22). Many of the performers that Zimmerman works with have been students or alumni of Northwestern University. Because performers may play more than one role in her pieces, assigning parts may be challenging. She explains, "Certain central roles are assigned at the beginning, but the ensemble isn't. So every night, when I'm getting ready to bring in a scene, I have to be casting in my head. And I'm nowhere near ruthless enough to give someone something and then take it away from them, even though I announce at the very first rehearsal that that might happen. It's a huge chess game in my head; it's really stressful" (Abarbanel 2000, 2).

Zimmerman develops the play in rehearsal, selecting text and stories that fit the cast and writing between rehearsals. In the beginning of her career, Zimmerman was faithful to the texts that she selected. However, she says, "Now I will create characters. I will rearrange the sequence of things. I've gotten confident enough to do that" (Stein 1996, C1). The longest time that Zimmerman has taken to write a piece is four weeks during rehearsal. She explains, "But I'm not really writing them because I'm cribbing them, basically, from these great, great works and just figuring out how to stage them" (Women's Project 1997, 38). Zimmerman also alters or cuts text during rehearsal if she feels it needs to be changed.

Zimmerman usually begins rehearsals with an image. For inspiration, she uses dreams and print sources, such as photographs. She explains, "I don't adapt a story unless, as I'm reading it, I have a huge idea of how to do it visually. That's what draws me to the story as much as its intrinsic meaning and value" (Smith 1998, 14).

Explaining her rehearsal process, Zimmerman says, "I will start on the first day, and there will be a scene I am thinking of doing or an episode or a story. And we'll sit in a circle and pass the book around, and everyone reads a paragraph or stanza and passes it on to the next person. And we talk about it, talk about what we like in it, what seems to be important about it. So there is always a text that's backgrounding. So it's not a total free-fall at all. . . . I'm a real stickler about saying this: I don't do verbal improvisation. I write

it. But what I will do is tons of physical and imaginistic improvisation. . . .
Usually, 80% works or doesn't, and then we ditch it or improve, and go on
to something else" (Abarbanel 2000, 2).

In addition to the awards already mentioned, Zimmerman's honors include
being named as one of the *Chicago Tribune*'s 25 Most Influential Chicagoans
in the Arts in 1993, *Chicago Magazine*'s 50 Brightest Stars of Chicago Theatre in 1993, *Crain*'s Forty Under 40 Outstanding Achievers in 1994, *Crain*'s
Chicago Business 100 Most Influential Women in Chicago in both 1995 and
2004, and the *Chicago Sun-Times* 25 Most Influential Women in Chicago Arts
in 2004. Zimmerman also won the Sarah Siddons Society Great Women of
American Theatre Award in 1997, the Loyola University Mellon Humanities
Award in 1999, the Northwestern Alumnae of the Year Award in 1999, and
the Annual Chicago Drama League Award in 2000. Among her many grants
is the coveted MacArthur Fellowship, which she was awarded in 1998.

With a new and imaginative style, Zimmerman has helped to change the
face of commercial theatre. She examines the significance of theatre, saying,
"It's obviously doing something very profound that television and movies
aren't. And . . . what the theater's always about is transcendence" (Interview,
2003).

Sources

Abarbanel, Jonathan. 2000. "Mary Zimmerman Explains It All for You: Jona-
    than Abarbanel Chats with the Director About Classic Texts in the Age of
    Image." *TheaterMania*, 12 May, 1–3. http://theatermainia.com/content/news
    .cfm?int_news_id=682&int_city_id=1&intPage=2 (accessed 24 June 2003).
Brantley, Ben. 1994. "A Classic of Storytelling as a Force of Good." Rev. of *The
    Arabian Nights*, by Mary Zimmerman, based on *The Arabian Nights: The
    Book of 1,001 Nights. New York Times*, 21 Mar., C18.
———. 2002. "Dreams of 'Metamorphoses' Echo in Larger Space." Rev. of *Meta-
    morphoses*, by Mary Zimmerman, based on the myths of Ovid. *New York
    Times*, 5 Mar., E1.
Christiansen, Richard. 1995. "Sightseeing 'Journey' Marvelous Images Border
    Chinese Tale's Occasionally Rocky Road." Rev. of *Journey to the West*, by
    Mary Zimmerman, based on the Chinese epic. *Chicago Tribune*, 9 May, 22.
Dorbian, Iris. 2002. "Mary Zimmerman" in "Women in Theatre: The Fairest Sex."
    Stage Directions 15 (3) (Mar.): 35, 60.
Gamerman, Amy. 2001. "A Timely Gift of Timeless Ovid—Ms. Zimmerman's
    'Metamorphoses' Haunts, Humors and Consoles with Deeply Human Myths."
    Rev. of *Metamorphoses*, by Mary Zimmerman, based on the myths of Ovid.
    Wall Street Journal, 10 Oct., A14.
Henning, Joel. 1999. "Mary Zimmerman Gives Homer's Epic Journey a Contem-

porary Spin." Rev. of *The Odyssey*, by Mary Zimmerman, based on the epic by Homer. *Wall Street Journal*, 14 Oct., A24.

Johnson, Kevin. 1999. "Genius at Play." *Northwestern* (Spring). http://www .northwestern.edu/magazine/northwestern/spring99/genius.htm (accessed 14 Jan. 2003).

Jones, Chris. 2002. "Zimmerman Touch." *American Theatre* 19 (3) (Mar.): 19–22.

Marks, Peter. 2004. "A 'Pericles' with the Wind in Its Sails." Rev. of *Pericles*, by William Shakespeare. *Washington Post*, 16 Nov., C01.

Second Stage Theatre. 2003. "Season 24." http://secondstagetheatre.com/season24 .html (accessed 14 Jan. 2005).

Smith, Sid. 1998. "Director, Actor, Artist Scholar Where Else But the Theatre Could Mary Zimmerman Play Out All the Roles She Lives?" *Chicago Tribune Magazine*, 22 Nov., 14.

Stearns, David Patrick. 1997. "Bright Theater Lights Beyond Broadway 'Streetcar,' 'Rage,' 'Mirror' With Bold Strokes." Rev. of *Mirror of the Invisible World*, by Mary Zimmerman, based on the Persian epic poem; and other plays. *USA Today*, 19 May, 8D.

Stein, Ruth. 1996. "Chinese Saga Takes 'Journey to the West.'" *San Francisco Chronicle*, 29 Nov., C1.

Women's Project & Productions. In Conjunction with the New School for Social Research. 1997. *Women in Theatre: Mapping the Sources of Power*. Conference journal, New York City, Nov. 7–8.

Zimmerman, Mary. 2002. Interview with Bill Moyers. "Transcript: Bill Moyers Interviews Mary Zimmerman." *NOW With Bill Moyers*, 22 May. http://www.pbs .org/now/transcript/transcript_zimmerman.html (accessed 21 Apr. 2004).

———. 2003. Interview with Bill Moyers. "Transcript: Mary Zimmerman." *NOW With Bill Moyers*, 30 May. http://www.pbs.org/now/transcript/transcript_ zimmerman2.html (accessed 24 June 2003).

Representative Directing Credits

Broadway:
Metamorphoses (2002)

Off and Off-Off Broadway:
The Arabian Nights (1994), *The Notebooks of Leonardo Da Vinci* (1994, 2003), *Henry VIII* (1997), *Measure for Measure* (2001), *Metamorphoses* (2001), *Galileo Galilei* (2002)

Regional Theatre:
The Notebooks of Leonardo Da Vinci (1989, 1993, 1997, 2003), *The Odyssey* (1990, 1999, 2000), *The Actor Retires* (1991), *Hapgood* (1991), *The Secret in the Wings* (1991, 2003, 2005), *The Arabian Nights* (1992, 1997), *Laughter in the Dark* (1992), *The Baltimore Waltz* (1993), *Frida: The Last Portrait* (1994), *All's Well That Ends Well* (1995), *Journey to the West* (1995, 1996),

The Magic Flute (1996), *S/M* (1996), *Mirror of the Invisible World* (1997, 2007), *Eleven Rooms of Proust* (1998, 2000), *Metamorphoses* (1998, 1999, 2000, 2003, 2004), *A Midsummer Night's Dream* (1999), *Akhenaten* (2000), *Galileo Galilei* (2002), *The Trojan Women* (2003), *Pericles* (2004, 2006), *Silk* (2005), *Argonautika* (2006)

International Theatre:
Galileo Galilei (2002)

Appendix A: Chronology of Women Directors by Birthdate

Minnie Maddern Fiske (1865–1932)
Jessie Bonstelle (1870?–1932)
Rachel Crothers (1870s–1958)
Agnes Morgan (1879–1976)
Antoinette Perry (1888–1946)
Osceola Archer (1890–1983)
Eva Le Gallienne (1899–1991)
Mary Hunter (1904–2000)
Margaret Webster (1905–72)
Margo Jones (1911–55)
Nina Vance (1914–80)
Dorothy Raedler (1917–93)
Ellen Stewart (1919?–)
Vinnette Carroll (1922–2002)
Zelda Fichandler (1924–)
Judith Malina (1926–)
Shauneille Perry (1929–)
Maria Irene Fornes (1930–)
Sue Lawless (1935–)
Martha Boesing (1936–)
Margarita Galban (1936–)
Libby Appel (1937–)
Barbara Ann Teer (1937–)
JoAnne Akalaitis (1937–)

Muriel Miguel (1937–)
Tina Packer (1938–)
Graciela Daniele (1939–)
Tisa Chang (1941–)
Meredith Monk (1942–)
Elizabeth LeCompte (1944–)
Martha Clarke (1944–)
Julianne Boyd (1944–)
Glenda Dickerson (1945–)
Lynne Meadow (1946–)
Susan H. Schulman (1947–)
Josephine Abady (1949–2002)
Sharon Ott (1950–)
Roberta Levitow (1950–)
Anne Bogart (1951–)
Emily Mann (1952–)
Pamela Berlin (1952–)
Julie Taymor (1952–)
Mary B. Robinson (1953–)
Liz Diamond (1954–)
Susan Stroman (1954–)
Carey Perloff (1959–)
Mary Zimmerman (1960–)
Tina Landau (1962–)

Note: The list does not include Gloria Muzio or Carole Rothman, whose birthdates are unavailable. Both of these women worked in the late twentieth century. See individual entries for specific production dates.

Appendix B: The Tony Awards: Women Nominees and Winners

The American Theatre Wing's Antoinette Perry Awards for excellence in Broadway theatre began in 1947. Before 1960 there was only one director category, for which no women were nominated. As of 2007, over the course of sixty years, only ten women have been nominated for best direction of a play, with two winners. Eighteen women have been nominated for directing musical theatre, again with only two winners.

Best Direction of a Play

1961 Joan Littlewood, *The Hostage*

1969 June Havoc, *Marathon '33*

1982 Geraldine Fitzgerald, *Mass Appeal*

1987 Carole Rothman, *Coastal Disturbances*

1995 Emily Mann, *Having Our Say*

1998 Garry Hynes (**winner**), *The Beauty Queen of Leenane*

1999 Garry Hynes, *The Lonesome West*

2002 Mary Zimmerman (**winner**), *Metamorphoses*

2003 Deborah Warner, *Medea*

2007 Melly Still, *Coram Boy*

Best Direction of a Musical

1965 Joan Littlewood, *Oh, What a Lovely War!*

1973 Vinnette Carroll, *Don't Bother Me, I Can't Cope*

1977 Vinnette Carroll, *Your Arms Too Short to Box With God*

1978 Elizabeth Swados, *Runaways*

1985 Barbara Damashek, *Quilters*

1990 Susan H. Schulman, *Sweeney Todd*

1991 Graciela Daniele, *Once on This Island*

1991 Eleanor Reissa, *Those Were the Days*

1997 Julie Taymor, *Juan Darien*

1998 Julie Taymor (**winner**), *The Lion King*

1999 Richard Maltby Jr. & Ann Reinking, *Fosse*

2000 Susan Stroman, *Contact*

2000 Susan Stroman, *The Music Man*

2000 Lynne Taylor-Corbett, *Swing*

2001 Susan Stroman (**winner**), *The Producers*

2003 Twyla Tharp, *Movin' Out*

2004 Kathleen Marshall, *Wonderful Town*

2006 Kathleen Marshall, *The Pajama Game*

Appendix C: General Bibliography on Women Directors

Adams, Rebecca Daniels. 1992. "Perceptions of Women Stage Directors Regarding the Influence of Gender in the Artistic Process." Ph.D. diss., University of Oregon.

Armistead, Claire. 1994. "Women Directors." *Women: A Cultural Review* 5 (2): 185–91.

Bartow, Arthur. 1988. *The Director's Voice: Twenty-one Interviews.* New York: Theatre Communications Group.

Bennetts, Leslie. 1984. "Women Directing More Plays but Broadway Still Elusive." *New York Times,* 16 Jan., C11.

———. 1986. "Is the Road to a Theatre Career Rockier for Women?" *New York Times,* 2 Nov., 72.

Berson, Misha. 1994. "Women at the Helm." *American Theatre* 11(5): 14–22, 66.

Bogart, Anne. 2001. *A Director Prepares: Seven Essays on Art and Theatre.* New York: Routledge.

Canning, Charlotte. 2005. "Directing History: Women, Performance and Scholarship." *Theatre Research International* 30 (1): 49–59.

Chinoy, Helen Krich and Linda Walsh Jenkins. 2006. 3rd ed. *Women in American Theatre.* New York: Theatre Communications Group.

Compton, Tamara L. 1970. "The Rise of the Woman Director on Broadway, 1920–1950." Master's thesis, University of California, Santa Barbara.

Dace, Tish. 1994. "Women's Work: Six Directors on Their Lives in the Theatre." *Back Stage,* Mar., 1, 20–24.

Daniels, Rebecca. 1996. *Women Stage Directors Speak: Exploring the Influence of Gender on Their Work.* Jefferson, N.C.: McFarland.

———. 1996. "Women Stage Directors Speak Out." *On-Stage Studies* 19: 95–100.

Donkin, Ellen and Susan Clement. 1993. *Upstaging Big Daddy: Directing Theater as if Gender and Race Matter.* Ann Arbor: University of Michigan Press.

Fichandler, Zelda, Liz Diamond, JoAnne Akalaitis, Roberta Levitow, Tisa Chang, Timothy Near, and Sharon Ott. 1998. "Gender, Creativity and Power." *American Theatre* 15 (7): 30–31, 80–81.

Fliotsos, Anne L. 2008. "Open a New Window, Open a New Door: Women Directors Take the Stage." In *Women in American Musical Theatre: Composers, Lyricists, Librettists, Arrangers, Choreographers, Designers, Directors, Produc-*

ers, and Performance Artists, ed. Bud Coleman and Judith Sebesta. Jefferson, N.C.: McFarland.

Frick, John W. and Stephen M. Vallillo, eds. 1994. *Theatrical Directors: A Biographical Dictionary.* Westport, Conn.: Greenwood.

Hendrick, Pamela. 1996. "'We Will Not from the Helm to Sit and Weep' (Margaret, Henry VI, Part 3)." *On-Stage Studies* 19: 101–4.

Hennigan, Shirlee. 1983. "The Woman Director in the Contemporary, Professional Theatre." Ph.D. diss., Washington State University.

Hoggard, Liz. 2004. "Good for a Girl: There Are Plenty of Women Directing Plays Up and Down the Country—But They Are Not Being Asked to Run Our Major Theatres." *The Observer* (London), 31 Oct., Review: 7.

Horowitz, Simi. 2002. "The Status of Women in Theatre: Improved, but Not There Yet." *Back Stage*, 2 Feb. http://www.backstage.com.

Housely, Helen M. 1993. "The Female Director's Odyssey: The Broadway Sisterhood." Paper presented at the 2nd Annual Seminar on Women, Marist College, Poughkeepsie, N.Y.

Jonas, Susan, with preparation by Celia Braxton. 1998. "Report on the Status of Women Directors and Playwrights in the New York City Theater." 21 Sept. New York: New York State Council on the Arts.

Jonas, Susan and Suzanne Bennett. 2002. "Report on the Status of Women: A Limited Engagement?" Executive Summary. New York: New York State Council on the Arts Theatre Program.

Leiter, Samuel L. 1994. *The Great Stage Directors: 100 Distinguished Careers of the Theater.* New York: Facts on File.

Lodge, Mary Jo Michelle. 2002. "Dancing Up the Broken Ladder: The Rise of the Female Director/Choreographer in the American Musical Theatre." Ph.D. diss., Bowling Green State University.

Manfull, Helen. 1997. *In Other Words: Women Directors Speak.* Lyme, N.H.: Smith and Kraus.

Mitter, Shomit and Maria Shevtsova, eds. 2005. *Fifty Key Theatre Directors.* London: Routledge.

Pogrebin, Robin. 1998. "Where Footlights Illuminate Women's Work." *New York Times*, 29 Dec., E3.

Robinson, Alice M., Vera Mowry Roberts, and Milly S. Barranger, eds. 1989. *Notable Women in the American Theatre: A Biographical Dictionary.* Westport, Conn.: Greenwood.

Schafer, Elizabeth. 2000. *Ms-directing Shakespeare: Women Direct Shakespeare.* New York: St. Martin's.

Smithner, Nancy Putnam. 2002. "Directing the Acting Ensemble: Meredith Monk, Elizabeth LeCompte, and Anne Bogart." Ph.D. diss., New York University.

Taylor, Nancy Elizabeth. 2001. "Women Directors and Shakespeare on the 1990s American Stage." Ph.D diss., Tufts University.

Tolkoff, Esther. 1999. "The League of Professional Theatre Women Showcases.

. . . Top Women Directors Interpreting Their Craft." *Back Stage*, 16 Apr. http://www.backstage.com.

Towey, Maureen. 2003. "Status of Women in Theatre." nytheatre.com, 28 Jan. http://www.nytheatre.com/nytheatre/voiceweb/v_nysca.htm.

Trussell, Robert. 1999. "Directing Women." *Kansas City Star,* 7 Oct., E1.

Venables, Claire. 1980. "The Woman Director in the Theatre." *Theatre Quarterly* 10 (Summer): 3–7.

Vierow, Wendy A. 1997. "Women on Broadway: 1980–1995." Ph.D. diss., New York University.

"Why Female Directors Are Broadway's Smallest Club." 2005. *New York Times,* 11 Dec., sec. 2, 9.

Index

ANNE FLIOTSOS is an associate professor of theatre at Purdue University. An active scholar who also directs, she is coeditor of *Teaching Theatre Today: Pedagogical Views of Theatre in Higher Education.*

WENDY VIEROW is an educator and a freelance writer and editor who holds a doctorate in performance studies. She has written and directed performance art at numerous New York City venues and has performed in works shown internationally.